Portrait of Elgar

MICHAEL KENNEDY

Portrait of Elgar

Third Edition

CLARENDON PRESS · OXFORD

Oxford University Press, Walton Street, Oxford OX2 6DP
Oxford New York Toronto
Delhi Bombay Calcutta Madras Karachi
Kuala Lumpur Singapore Hong Kong Tokyo
Nairobi Dar es Salaam Cape Town
Melbourne Auckland Madrid
and associated companies in
Berlin Ibadan

Oxford is a trade mark of Oxford University Press

Published in the United States
by Oxford University Press Inc., New York

British Library Cataloguing in Publication Data
Data available

Library of Congress Cataloging in Publication Data
Kennedy, Michael, 1926–
Portrait of Elgar.
Includes index.
1. Elgar, Edward, 1857–1934.   2. Composers—England—
Biography.   I. Title.
ML410.E41K5   1987   780'.92'4[B]   87–5502
ISBN 0–19–816365–7

1 3 5 7 9 10 8 6 4 2

Printed in Great Britain
on acid-free paper by
Biddles Ltd., Guildford and King's Lynn

Contents

Illustrations

These illustrations, with the exception of plates x, xiv, xv, and xvii, are reproduced by kind permission of Mrs Elgar Blake and the Trustees of the Elgar Will. Plate x is reproduced by kind permission of Sir Ralph Millais, and plates xiv and xv by kind permission of the Radio Times Hulton Picture Library. Plate xvii is from a private collection. Plate xi (*a*) is from a photograph by Mr Alan Webb.

The Elgar Family

William Henry Elgar, *b.* Dover, September 1821; *d.* Worcester, 30 April 1906

Ann Elgar (née Greening), *b.* Weston-under-Penyard, Herefordshire, ?December 1821; *d.* Worcester, 1 September 1902

Henry Elgar ('Uncle Henry'), *b.* Dover, 1833; *d.* Worcester, 24 February 1917

Henry John ('Harry'), *b.* Worcester, 15 October 1848; *d.* Worcester, 5 May 1864

Lucy Ann, *b.* Worcester, 29 May 1852; *d.* Worcester, 23 October 1925

?Mary, *b.* and *d.* Worcester, 1853

Susannah Mary ('Pollie'), *b.* Worcester, 28 December 1854; *d.* Bromsgrove, 18 November 1936

Edward William, *b.* Broadheath, 2 June 1857; *d.* Worcester, 23 February 1934

Frederick Joseph ('Joe' or 'Jo'), *b.* Worcester, 28 August 1859; *d.* Worcester, 7 September 1866

Francis Thomas ('Frank'), *b.* Worcester, 1 October 1861; *d.* Worcester, 7 June 1928

Ellen Agnes ('Dot' or 'Dott'), *b.* Worcester, 1 January 1864; *d.* Stroud, Gloucestershire, 10 December 1939 *for*

Neville, John, and Martin

Preface

This third edition of *Portrait of Elgar* incorporates corrections and additional information made available by the publication in 1984 of Dr Jerrold Northrop Moore's magnificently documented *Edward Elgar: a Creative Life*. No future writer on Elgar can fail to take his cue from the wealth of detailed research which Dr Northrop Moore's book represents. I have also benefited from the researches of K. E. L. and Marion Simmons in their invaluable pamphlet on the Elgar family's peregrinations around Worcester. Four other important Elgar source-books have appeared since *Portrait of Elgar* was first published on 16 May 1968. Dr Percy M. Young has given us a fully annotated edition of the Birmingham lectures in his *A Future for English Music* (London, 1968) and has written a biography of Lady Elgar, published under the title *Alice Elgar: Enigma of a Victorian Lady* (London, 1978). Controversial but revealing memories of the young Elgar were the principal interest of *Edward Elgar: the Record of a Friendship* (London, 1972) by Rosa Burley and Frank C. Carruthers. An indispensable revelation of Elgar's correspondence and relationships with the officials of the Gramophone Company from 1914 almost until the day of his death is given in *Elgar on Record: the Composer and the Gramophone*, by Dr Northrop Moore (London, 1974). Of great importance also is the correspondence, stretching from 1890 to 1933, between Elgar and his principal publishers, Novello's. This was not available in 1968, and I should like to express my gratitude to Novello's, and in particular to Miss Margaret Pace, for their readiness to give me unrestricted access to this treasure-trove and for permission to quote from it. In revising and enlarging my book, I have taken advantage of the material provided by these eminent Elgarian authors. I am also indebted to Geoffrey Hodgkins's pamphlet *Providence and Art* and to Dr Louie Eickhoff's researches into the Elgars' life at Severn House, Hampstead. Valuable material, giving many illuminating sidelights on the composer and his associates, is contained within the pages of the Elgar Society *Newsletter* and its successor, the Elgar Society's *Journal*. Many kind people have written to me over the years with Elgarian information. To them all I now offer formal thanks.

I chose the title *Portrait of Elgar* to emphasize that this is not an official biography nor an analytical study of the music. It is my attempt to paint, in words, his portrait. A portrait should be a recognizable likeness of the sitter, as I hope this is, and it also reflects the painter's own view of and approach to the subject. So although I hope this book is factually as accurate as I can make it and is therefore a true likeness in that respect, it still is the portrait I want to draw of the composer whose music has occupied a paramount place in my life.

Since 1968 also, many major and smaller works by Elgar have been recorded, enabling much closer study of and acquaintance with the music than is possible by score alone or on a piano. So I have now been able to write rather more fully about *The Starlight Express, The Sanguine Fan,* the wind quintets, and the *Coronation Ode* among others. I have revised my opinions of the chamber music and the two major oratorios, I hope sensibly. Another important development since 1968 has been the transfer to LP of all the recordings Elgar conducted, thus making generally available again what had, in many cases, become collectors' items. Strauss (to a lesser extent), Stravinsky, Britten, Copland, Walton, and many other composers have recorded their interpretations of their own music, thus providing an historic documentation for posterity. But Elgar was the pioneer in this field and it is little short of miraculous that he should have conducted for the gramophone so many of his important and several of his lesser works, in several cases more than once. The resulting performances are in all cases instructive and in some incomparable. Thus we have a self-portrait of Elgar in sound beside which words can only be of secondary value and complementary.

When the first edition of this book was in typescript, it was read by Elgar's daughter, the late Mrs Carice Elgar Blake. This was a privilege I greatly valued and it led to a friendship which I shall always remember with pleasure and pride. The late Sir Adrian Boult was extremely helpful. I would like to renew my thanks to Mr Alan Webb, former curator of the Elgar Birthplace and to Miss Pamela Willetts and Mr Hugh Cobbe, Assistant Keepers in the Department of Manuscripts, British Library. To the foregoing I would now like to add the names of Dr Jerrold Northrop Moore, most generous of colleagues; Mrs Sybil Wöhlfeld; Mr Jack McKenzie, former curator of the Elgar Birthplace, and Mrs McKenzie; Mr E. Wulstan Atkins, chairman of the Elgar Foundation; Mr Raymond Monk; Dr Louie Eickhoff; Mr John Knowles; Mr Vernon Jones; Mr Norman Lebrecht; Mr David A. Symington; Mr Noel Hilliard; Mr David Bury; Mr Fritz Spiegl; Mr Phillip Brookes; Mr T. C. Fenemore-Jones; and Mr Michael Pope.

I renew my gratitude to the Trustees of the Elgar Will for permission to reproduce extracts from Elgar's letters and writings and Lady Elgar's diaries; to Messrs. Novello, and Breitkopf and Härtel for permission to reprint music examples from Elgar's scores; to Macmillan & Co. for permission to reprint an extract from Sir Osbert Sitwell's *Laughter in the Next Room*; to the Society of Authors and the Public Trustee for the use of extracts of letters written by Bernard Shaw; to Longmans Green & Cò. for permission to quote from Bernard Shøre's *Sixteen Symphonies* and from Sir Arnold Bax's *Farewell, My Youth*; and to J. M. Dent & Sons for permission to reprint an extract from W. H. Reed's *Elgar*. I now add my thanks to Oxford University Press for permission to quote from Dr Northrop Moore's *Edward Elgar: a Creative Life* and his *Elgar on Record*, to Barrie & Jenkins for permission to quote extracts from *Edward Elgar: the Record of a Friendship* by Rosa Burley and Frank C. Carruthers, to Dennis Dobson for permission to quote from *Alice Elgar: Enigma of a Victorian Lady* by Percy M. Young, and to Hamish Hamilton for quotations from *Music and Friends: Letters to Adrian Boult*. I renew my thanks to the Editors of *The Times*, *The Daily Telegraph*, *The Guardian*, and *The Sunday Times* for allowing me to quote from articles which appeared in their newspapers. Acknowledgement is made to the Executors of the Britten Estate for permission to quote from the late Lord Britten's Aldeburgh Festival programme-note of 'For the Fallen', and to the editor of the Elgar Society *Journal* for permission to quote from articles which have appeared in its pages.

Since 1968 two of the dedicatees of this book, Sir Neville Cardus and Sir John Barbirolli, have died. They were great Elgarians and great friends of mine. I re-dedicate it to them in grateful and unfading memory. The third co-dedicatee, Martin Milner, served Elgar for many years as leader of the Hallé Orchestra – one of those musicians described by Elgar in his dedication of *Cockaigne* as 'my many friends the members of British orchestras'.

Manchester, 1987   M.K.

Part I

ASCENT
1857–1898

1 Prelude

On 13 December 1921 Elgar confided to his friend Sir Sidney Colvin:
'I am still at heart the dreamy child who used to be found in the reeds
by Severn side with a sheet of paper trying to fix the sounds and
longing for something very great. I am still looking for this . . . but as
a child and as a young man and as a mature man no single person was
ever kind to me.'

Elgar was sixty-four when he wrote this letter. He was
acknowledged to be the foremost English composer of his time;
nearly every kind of official honour had come his way; self-taught, he
had risen from provincial obscurity to international fame; he had
achieved in his music the 'something very great'. Yet he still regarded
himself as an 'outsider' and looked back on his early struggles not
with self-satisfaction but with bitterness. What did he mean when he
said that no one was 'kind' to him? Biographical facts prove that he
was offered many a helping hand. Nevertheless he spoke and wrote
often of the discouragement he received from his friends and of their
slighting attitude to his music. 'One's own friends are the people to be
most in dread of,' he wrote shortly before *Froissart* was performed, 'I
have always been wrong hitherto'. And after *The Dream of Gerontius*:
'All my best friends only made one remark: "Now a popular song or
two will make up for this."' His musical self-portrait, the last of the
Enigma Variations, has a defiant ring because it was a retort to friends
who were 'dubious and generally discouraging' about his future as a
composer. It was this that rankled: he told Colvin in the same letter
how much he admired Bernard Shaw for his friendly encouragement
of young people. He may have been thinking ruefully of his father,
William Elgar, who regarded Edward's musical skill with mixed
pride and envy. Almost up to the time of Elgar's knighthood (1904),
William would concede only that his son possessed above-average
musical competence.

From his youth onwards Elgar knew that he possessed special
gifts, and he resented the circumstances which made him work as a
'local musician' until he was nearly forty. He is often described as a
'late developer'. He himself knew better. He could have written
Caractacus (1898) ten years earlier, he said, if he had not been
compelled to earn his living by teaching, by the chores of music, by
helping behind the counter in his father's music-shop in Worcester
even after he had had a work produced at the Three Choirs Festival.
He encountered prejudice against both his Roman Catholic religion

and his lower-class social origins, and it wounded him and produced an outsize chip on his shoulder.

But ambition spurred him, as it did many nineteenth-century youths of poor birth who were determined to 'get on'. The story has often been told of an occasion when he was asked his name at school. 'Edward Elgar.' 'Say sir.' 'Sir Edward Elgar.' This sounds apocryphal. Elgar's eyes were on a much loftier target than the mere acquisition of a title – something he said he accepted only out of a sense of gratitude to his wife, to whom these outward signs of esteem meant a great deal. Compton Mackenzie[1] gives us the truth: 'Elgar once told me that when he was a young man he had declared to his mother that he should not be content until a postcard from abroad addressed "Edward Elgar, England" should find him.' But the obituary Eric Blom wrote[2] in 1934 began with words which tell the whole story of this book: 'Elgar. That is how we shall think of him now. Just Elgar. We shall say it as we say Byrd or Purcell. . .'.

[1]In *The Gramophone*, June 1957.   [2]*Birmingham Post*, 24 February 1934.

2 Wand of Youth

Edward William Elgar was born in the village of Broadheath, just outside Worcester, on 2 June 1857. He was the fourth (or perhaps the fifth) child of William and Ann Elgar. They had married in 1848, and she had become a convert to Roman Catholicism in 1852; her husband was not baptized as a Roman Catholic until he was on his deathbed in 1906. He is said to have 'detested' papism and – jocularly – to have threatened to shoot his daughters if he saw them going to confession. A Dover man born in 1821, William Elgar settled in Worcester in 1841. He had served a musical apprenticeship with Coventry and Hollier of Dean Street, Soho. This firm was approached by the Comptroller of the Household of the Queen Dowager, Adelaide (widow of William IV), to provide a piano-tuner for the instruments at Witley Court, Worcestershire, where Adelaide took up residence in 1844. They immediately selected their former apprentice, who had established a music business in Worcester, then a city of 27,000 people. Thus he naturally received similar piano-tuning commissions from the other 'county families' and was drawn into various musical activities as pianist and violinist. Though he was a Protestant he was appointed organist of St George's Roman Catholic Church in 1846 at a salary of £40 a year.[1] The picture could no doubt be multiplied from towns throughout England – lower-middle-class tradesman with musical gifts, able to display a royal warrant on his business stationery, on call to the homes of the gentry. William Elgar was fortunate in his wife, daughter of Joseph and Esther Greening, at whose home he lodged when he first went to Worcester. Ann Elgar was a remarkable woman. She was born in 1821 or 2, daughter of a Herefordshire farmworker, and spent her childhood in the Forest of Dean. Her natural bent was towards the arts. She read widely and remembered what she read. She sewed, collected wild flowers, sketched, and wrote verse. Her strength of character was such that bringing up three children did not, as would usually be the case, stifle her pursuit of learning and artistic matters. Few husbands of the Elgars' social class in the 1850s would have expected to receive, as William Elgar did, a sonnet from his wife on the birth of their first daughter. In a memoir written in 1912, which may be read at Elgar's Birthplace, their eldest daughter Lucy wrote

[1]His piety may be doubted. It was said of him that he handed round his snuff-box before Mass, 'damned' the organ-blower and, during the sermon, slipped out for a drink at Hop Market – an endearing and convincing picture.

of their mother that she was 'romantic by temperament and poetic by nature. She had the unmistakable air of good breeding. . . . She often drove out with father in the country on his business tours, and while he was occupied she would sketch the churches and little bits of pleasing scenery. . . .' Altogether, life was good to William and Ann Elgar. They had not much money – William was not very interested in the book-keeping side of his business, though he showed a marked sense of showman–salesmanship by riding to his piano-tuning engagements on a thoroughbred horse – but both were able to indulge the artistic side of their nature, and they had a certain standing in Worcester's provincial but not entirely sterile musical life. William was engaged to play in the Three Choirs Festival orchestra when it was Worcester's triennial turn and he was sufficiently influential for his advice to be sought and taken on programme-planning – he suggested the inclusion of Masses by Cherubini and Hummel. From 1848 to 1856 they lived at 2, College Precincts, a terraced row of three-storey houses near the cathedral. There Henry (Harry) (1848), Lucy (1852), and Susannah (known as Pollie) (1854) were born. In 1856 they moved to a cottage (known at that time as 'The Firs')[2] three miles north-west of Worcester at the village called Broadheath. Elgar said that his father rented the cottage 'as a weekend sort of thing', which implies that Mrs Elgar and the children probably spent most of their time there, especially in the summer, while William spent the working week in the city. Harry was baptized in the Anglican church of St Michael. It is possible that another daughter, Mary, who died before baptism, was born between Lucy and Pollie. In 1859 William was joined in business (as employee, not partner) by his twenty-seven-year-old brother Henry, who had worked for Kirkman's of London and for Hime and Anderson in Manchester where he had tuned pianos for Charles Hallé. He had lived and worked intermittently in Worcester since 1851. When another child was expected in 1859, the cottage was obviously too small and William pressed for a return to Worcester. From 1859 to 1861 the Elgars lived at 1, Edgar Street (now demolished), returned to 2, College Precincts (which still exists) from 1861 to 1863, and moved into 10, High Street[3] in 1863. Three more children were born in Worcester: Joe (1859), Frank (1861), and Ellen Agnes (known as Dot) (1864), who became a nun in 1903 and eventually Mother General of the Dominicans in

---

[2]Or it may have been known as Newbury Cottage, since it was the cottage of Newbury House. The village comprised a few houses, a clump of fir-trees near the house, and a wide stretch of heath called 'the common'. The cottage, of two storeys, had six small rooms.
[3]10, High Street has been demolished. A plaque on a wall of the Giffard Hotel complex marks its approximate site.

England. Edward was the only child to be born at Broadheath. He was baptized at St George's on 11 June 1857.

Although Edward was one of seven children (of whom two brothers, Harry and Joe, died young, in 1864 and 1866) it seems that he was always of a solitary, introspective disposition, lonely by nature.

In 1874 his mother wrote couplets about each of her surviving children. That on 'Ed' ran:

> Nervous, sensitive & kind
> Displays no vulgar frame of mind.

He was particularly responsive, as was to be shown by his music, to topography, to landscape, and to the countryside in all its moods; and as he had a remarkable memory, these early impressions made an indelible mark on his personality. He explored the historic nooks and crannies of Worcester, and when he returned to Broadheath to stay on a farm he came to know intimately rural Worcestershire: country sayings, customs, and personalities. He was encouraged by his mother to read everything he could lay hands on. He was one of those people – Vaughan Williams was another – with a lifelong habit of early rising, so that hours before the rest of the household were awake Edward was reading Voltaire or Holinshed, Drayton and Sidney, anything historical or translated from the classics. Mrs Elgar was a devotee of Longfellow and her son followed her taste. He came to know by heart *The Saga of King Olaf* and *Hyperion*. I possess a copy of *Hyperion* which belonged to Elgar. He knew it so well that he has noted in the margin all textual divergences from an earlier edition.

In a household which derived its living from the sale and tending of musical instruments, in particular the pianoforte, all the children received some degree of instruction. Joe, who died aged seven in 1866, was regarded by the family as the musical prodigy. Edward showed an early brilliance as a pianist, especially in the art of improvisation, and William Elgar liked to show off his son's talent to his clients, taking the boy with him to the gentry's houses and encouraging him to display his prowess on the newly-tuned instrument. It seems to be incontrovertible that Elgar's yearning to be 'a gentleman' derived from these expeditions with his father, who also clearly relished hobnobbing with those whom he would then have regarded as 'his betters'.

When Edward was six, in 1863, he went to a Roman Catholic 'dame school', run by Miss Caroline Walsh in Britannia Square, Worcester, and had pianoforte lessons from Pollie Tyler. At the same time, he had lessons in music theory from Miss Sarah Ricketts, a singer in the choir of St George's Church; and, like many another organist's child, Edward sat in the organ-loft at St George's to watch his father at work. It was about this time that Edward was found sitting on the river bank with a pencil and music paper. He said he was 'trying to write down what the reeds were saying'.

Years later, W. H. Reed recalls in his *Elgar As I Knew Him*, when Sir Edward Elgar was rehearsing the London Symphony Orchestra in the Trio of the second movement of the First Symphony, he told them 'Play it like . . . like something you hear down by the river.' Reed was also taken on many a tour of Elgar's boyhood haunts by the old composer in the 1930s. In his book he wrote: 'When a piano had to be tuned at Croome Court or at Madresfield the boy Edward was taken for what was practically a delightful day's outing. While the piano was being attended to, he could roam about in the grounds until he was taken into the house and refreshed. No detail or happening of those far-off times escaped him; he could tell me as we ambled about the lanes and passed those great houses, and many others too, the names of all the people who lived in them long ago. . .'

Elgar's improvising at the pianoforte impressed more than his father's customers. Dora Penny ('Dorabella' of the *Enigma Variations*) said that 'he almost seemed to play like a whole orchestra. It sounded full without being loud and he contrived to make you hear other instruments joining in.'[4] Nora Crowe, in whose house Elgar gave violin lessons in 1895, told Dr Jerrold Northrop Moore[5] that while Elgar's pupils were playing scales, he extemporised accompaniments which incorporated parts of the composition on which he was then at work, *King Olaf*. We today can hear Elgar's piano-playing: in 1929, at his own request, he recorded five improvisations. These were issued for the first time in 1975.[6]

From 1866 to 1868, young Edward attended a Roman Catholic school at Spetchley. This was under the patronage of the Lord of the Manor, Robert Berkeley. Many years later Elgar told Ernest Newman[7] that 'as a boy he used to gaze from the school windows in rapt wonder at the great trees swaying in the wind; and he pointed out to me a passage in *Gerontius* in which he had recorded in music his subconscious memories of them'. Although Newman did not enlarge upon this, it is fairly reasonable to suppose that the passage concerned is in Part II, rehearsal cue [68] at 'the summer wind among the lofty pines'. At the age of eleven he went to Littleton House, a school for about thirty boys in Powick Road, run by Francis Reeve. He it was who, as Elgar himself liked to relate, fired the young pupil's imagination, during a scripture lesson on Christ's

[4] Dora M. Powell: *Edward Elgar: Memories of a Variation*, London, Methuen and Co., 1937, p. 1.
[5] J. Northrop Moore: *Edward Elgar and the Piano*, issued with Prelude record of Elgar's complete pianoforte music.
[6] In 'Elgar on Record', H.M.V. RLS 713.
[7] *Sunday Times*, 23 October 1955.

disciples, with the remark: 'The Apostles were young men and very poor. Perhaps, before the descent of the Holy Ghost, they were no cleverer than some of you here.' This observation brought these men to life as human beings so that they fascinated Elgar, with the results to be heard in *The Apostles*.

In 1869 Elgar and his brothers and sisters devised, but never completed, *The Wand of Youth*, an allegory 'occasioned [Elgar wrote] by the imaginary despotic rule of my mother and father (The Two Old People) ... it was proposed to shew that children were not properly understood. The scene was a 'Woodland Glade', intersected by a brook; the hither side of this was our fairyland; beyond, small and distant, was the ordinary life which we forgot as soon as possible. The characters on crossing the stream entered fairyland and were transfigured. Our orchestral means were meagre: a pianoforte, two or three strings, a flute, and some improvised percussion were all we could depend upon; the double-bass was of our own manufacture and three pounds of nails went into its making ... But we had the gorgeous imagination of youth, and the ubiquitous piano became a whole battery of percussion, a whole choir of brass or an array of celestial harps as demanded by the occasion.' Elgar described how the bass part at one point 'consists wholly of three notes (A-D-G) the open strings of the (old English) double bass; the player was wanted for stage management, but the simplicity of the bass made it possible for a child who knew nothing of music on any instrument to grind out the bass.' The incidental music, according to Elgar, was begun in boyhood and 'not completed until 1906–7' when he published it as the two *Wand of Youth* orchestral suites.[8]

Edward by this time was becoming proficient on three instruments. The violin was his chief interest. In September 1869, after he had heard 'O thou that tellest' sung in Worcester Cathedral during a performance of *Messiah*, he returned home determined to master the instrument so that he could play this aria, and this he did by teaching himself and by having lessons from Frederick Spray, leader of the Worcester Glee Club ensemble. When he left school at the age of fifteen in 1872 he wanted to go to Leipzig to study music, and had been studying German for the purpose. But the family finances could not run to such a venture. A boy had to make his way, or go under. So Edward was sent to work in the office of a solicitor, William Allen, a member of St George's congregation. He had been head boy of Littleton House for his last nine months and his lifelong friend, Hubert Leicester, who was at school with him and whose

[8] From '*The Wand of Youth*: a note by the composer', accompanying HMV Album no. 80, issued in 1929, and from typewritten notes for an article on the second *Wand of Youth* suite retained at the Birthplace.

family printing business was near to the Elgars' music shop,[9]
described him at this stage of his life as 'a most miserable-looking lad
– legs like drumsticks – nothing of a boy about him. One great
characteristic, always doing *something*.' Yet the boy's looks belied his
physical prowess, for he would ride the Malvern Hills bareback,
saving himself from death on one occasion when his horse bolted.
Allen thought his new employee a 'bright lad', but the drudgery of a
lawyer's office, even though it taught Elgar some methodical ways,
was unattractive to a boy of artistic imagination and he left at some
time in 1873. During the time of his employment by Allen, two
important events occurred in Edward's musical life. On 14 July
1872, according to his sister Lucy's diary, 'Ted played the organ at
church for Mass for first time'; and in January 1873 he made his first
public appearance as a vocalist at a concert at the Union Workhouse
when, with others including his father and uncle and Frederick
Spray, he took part in works by Rossini, Weber, and Hullah. No
doubt these events stood him in good stead when he told his parents
that he had no use for the law, nor, which he contemplated at one
time, for a career in chemistry. He considered that he could be of use
to his father's business, perhaps helping to straighten the erratic
book-keeping. But we can be sure that, while he had been in the
dead end of Allen's office, he had pondered ways of achieving the
enormous ambitions he cherished and had decided that by helping
his father he could also help himself. Here are his own words on the
subject:

'When I resolved to become a musician and found that the
exigencies of life would prevent me from getting any tuition, the only
thing to do was to teach myself . . . I saw and learnt a great deal about
music from the stream of music that passed through my father's
establishment . . . I read everything, played everything, and heard
everything that I possibly could . . . I am self-taught in the matter of
harmony, counterpoint, form, and, in short, the whole of the
'mystery' of music . . . First was Catel, and that was followed by
Cherubini. The first real sort of friendly leading I had, however, was
from *Mozart's Thorough-Bass School*. There was something in that to go
upon – something human.'[10]

In his father's shop he had unrestricted access to the scores of
Mozart's masses and Beethoven's sonatas and his symphonies in
pianoforte-duet arrangements. 'In studying scores,' he said in 1904,
'the first which came into my hands were the Beethoven symphonies

---

[9]Elgar spent much time in the printing-shop and it was from these days that the
critical and knowledgeable interest he took in the printing and engraving of his
scores came.
[10]From *Interview with Dr Edward Elgar*, by Rupert de Cordova, *Strand Magazine*, May
1904, pp. 538–9.

... I remember distinctly the day I was able to buy the Pastoral Symphony. I stuffed my pockets with bread and cheese and went into the fields to study it. That was what I always did.'[11] One of his favourite places for studying a score was in Claines churchyard, to the north of Worcester, where he would sit near the gravestones of his grandparents. He told Percy Scholes[12] in 1916 that it was the scherzo of Beethoven's First Symphony which first awakened him to 'the possibilities of music'. When he first saw the score he ran from the house to a place of solitude where he could pore over this 'revelation of romance, fire, poetry.'

The textbooks to which he referred were Cherubini's *Counterpoint*, Catel's *Treatise on Harmony*, translated by Mary Cowden Clarke, Stainer's *Composition* and *Harmony*, and Sabilla Novello's translation of *Succinct Thorough Bass*, then thought to be by Mozart and which, so Shaw wrote in his Preface to *Music in London* (1935), Elgar said was 'the only document in existence of the smallest use to a student composer'. From the organ tutors of Rink and Best he learned so that he could relieve his father of some of his St. George's duties. He played the pianoforte works of C. P. E. Bach, Schobert, and Kotzeluch. He wrote a church anthem. He went to the Anglican cathedral, where William Done, a staunch conservative who abhorred Schumann as 'a modern', was in the midst of his long reign in the organ-loft (1844–95). There he heard Byrd, Tallis, Gibbons, and Purcell, music which it is probable his temperament even then rejected as being too austere, for he said in later years that, with a few exceptions in Purcell, English music of the sixteenth and seventeenth centuries interested him only as museum-pieces.

Notwithstanding his Roman Catholic upbringing, Elgar's love for Worcester Cathedral both as a building and a place in which to hear music dated from early childhood when he 'romped among the tombs'. Later, he told an interviewer in 1904,[13] 'I attended as many of the Cathedral services as I could . . . The putting of the fine organ into the Cathedral at Worcester [1874] was a great event, and brought many organists to play there at various times. I went to hear them all. The services at the Cathedral were over later on Sunday than those at the Catholic church, and as soon as the voluntary was finished at the church I used to rush over to the Cathedral to hear the concluding voluntary.' As an old man, Elgar liked to take his friends over to the Cathedral to show them where he sat when he first heard *Messiah*. Similar landmarks in his musical experience were commemorated, as

[11] *Interview with Dr Edward Elgar*, 1904, op. cit.
[12] 'Sir Edward Elgar at Home', *The Music Student*, August, 1916, pp. 343–8.
[13] *Interview with Dr Edward Elgar*, 1904, op. cit.

Sir Steuart Wilson noted,[14] 'to the exact inch and square of the pavement where he was placed. He was – consciously I think – creating his own mythology, a fascinating task.' It is only fitting, therefore, that the statue of him erected in his native city in 1981 should face the Cathedral.

If, as it is reasonable to assume he did, Elgar attended the concerts of the Worcester Festival Choral Society, of which Done was conductor, he made close acquaintance with the music of Corelli, Haydn, and Handel. But he was a performer more often than a passive listener and his most active musical education was at the concerts of the Worcester Glee Club, of which his father had long been a member. This club met at the Crown Hotel in Broad Street and its members drank and smoked at candlelit tables while music was performed. Mozart, Handel, Bellini, Auber, Rossini, and Balfe were the composers favoured by the Glee Club. Young Edward Elgar accompanied the singers at these functions, but he soon became violinist, composer, arranger, and, in 1879, conductor. It was the eighteenth-century musician's life and in its diversity, despite its parochialism, it stood Elgar in good stead. Worcester was indeed well served for music, by standards then applicable, and it was visited on occasions by the Haig-Dyer Opera Company. Elgar had first heard them before he was ten, and so came to know *Il Trovatore*, *La Traviata*, *Don Giovanni*, and *Norma*. In his father's workshop, too, he extended his literary knowledge in company with Ned Spiers, an odd-job-man, who had been a Shakespearean actor. They recited the great speeches together, and Edward went to the theatre to see Mrs Macready.

Throughout the 1870s Edward Elgar learned his craft. With his father in 1875 he was among the second violins for the Worcester Philharmonic's *Messiah*. Four years later he was the leader. In 1876 he arranged Wagner's overture to *The Flying Dutchman* for a Glee Club concert. In 1877 there was formed the 'Worcester Amateur Society for the Cultivation of Instrumental Music', and Elgar was appointed its leader. He was also giving violin lessons to help bring him in some money. His aim again was to go to Leipzig for instruction, but he could not afford it. So instead he went to London for twelve days for violin lessons from Adolphe Pollitzer, aged forty-five and leader of the New Philharmonic. Teacher and pupil got on well together, but Elgar's resources would not run to a full course. His visit cost him £7.15s. 9d. [£7.79½], of which £3.12s. 6d. [£3.62½] accounted for the rail fare and Pollitzer's five lessons. He was 'living on two bags of nuts a day', he said later. Pollitzer discerned exceptional musicianship in Elgar and pleaded with him to return for a full course of tuition, because he felt sure he had the makings of a

[14] *Some Reminiscences of Elgar*, by Sir Steuart Wilson, Elgar Society Newsletter, September 1978, pp. 7–10.

fine soloist. Elgar did return intermittently but later, after hearing Wilhelmj play, he decided he had not a full enough tone to justify cherishing ambitions of an outstanding career and gave up the idea and the lessons. Dora Powell, 'Dorabella' of the *Enigma Variations*, told Alice Stuart-Wortley's daughter, in a letter dated 15 May 1939, that her stepmother (*née* Mary Baker, eldest sister of W. M. Baker, 'W.M.B.' in the *Variations*) 'used to say that his [Elgar's] playing was very hard, and cold ... I can easily imagine that he had a fine technique'. Over fifty years later, when he was Master of the King's Musick, Elgar wrote out a list of the expenses for his general and musical education. His estimate was as follows:

1866–9 Miss Walsh at 11 Britannia Square	...	£16
1870–2 Littleton House	...	£18
Books – music, piano instruction book	...	£2 15*s*.
Piano lessons 2 yrs before 9 years old	...	£1
Violin lessons 1874	...	£3
Violin lessons from Pollitzer 1877–8	...	£15 15*s*.
	Total	£56 10*s*.

Home in Worcester he continued his private life of composing and his growing activities in public as a talented local musician. He arranged Christy Minstrel songs for 1*s*. 6*d* [7½p] apiece, and on 12 June 1878, ten days after his twenty-first birthday, at a concert by the 1st Worcestershire Artillery Volunteers' Amateur Christy Minstrels, his *Introductory Overture*, 'written expressly for this occasion', was performed. That year the Three Choirs Festival met in Worcester and Elgar was among the second violins; three years later he was in the firsts. (Elgar's father was also in the violin section and his sister Pollie was among the sopranos.) By this time, too, he was a member of a wind quintet, playing the bassoon (and later the cello) with his brother Frank (oboe), Hubert Leicester and Frank Exton (flutes), and William Leicester (clarinet). Elgar arranged and wrote music for them and, by the light of a carriage lamp, they serenaded their girl friends with 'Sweet and Low'. 'We met on Sunday afternoons', Elgar said,[15] 'and it was an understood thing that we should have a new piece every week. The sermons in our church used to take at least half an hour, and I spent the time composing the thing for the afternoon'. Also in 1877 he was among the players in the attendants' band at the County of Worcester Lunatic Asylum at Powick. The band played at dances for the staff. It comprised piccolo, flute, clarinet, two cornets, euphonium, about eight violins, and viola, cello, double bass, and

[15] *Interview with Dr Edward Elgar*, 1904, op. cit.

pianoforte. Quadrilles were much in demand as well as arrangements of the classics and when, in 1879, Elgar was appointed conductor, he not only arranged music for this unusual assembly but included some pieces of his own. His salary was £32 a year, with an additional 5s [25p] for each polka or quadrille that he composed. He went to Powick on one day of every week for five years.

The years 1877–82 were crucial to Elgar's career. Whether he resented the denial of an academic career, it is certain that his genius as an orchestrator, his absolute certainty of effect, so that he could later boast to Jaeger 'I never have to alter anything', were due to the lessons learned in the multitude of activities which he undertook as a local jack-of-all-trades musician in his early twenties.

He knew by this time the standard oratorios of Handel, Mendelssohn, Haydn, Spohr; he was soaked in Beethoven and Mozart, and in the lighter overtures (Balfe, Gounod, Rossini, Auber, Weber, etc.); he knew the keyboard works of C. P. E. Bach and Chopin; at St George's he studied and played motets and organ music by Pergolesi, Haydn, Hummel, Beethoven, and others. All this spurred his busy creative mind. For the wind quintet he gave himself the exercise of arranging the last movement of Beethoven's op. 23 violin sonata, a Corelli concerto, and various other works. For St George's he arranged the Allegro from Mozart's violin sonata in F (K.547) as a Gloria. He took themes from Beethoven's Fifth, Seventh, and Ninth Symphonies and, under the pseudonym Bernhard Pappenheim, arranged them as a Credo. For the orchestras in which he played he arranged Handel's *Ariodante* overture and *Adeste Fideles*. For friends he arranged a *Fantasia on Irish Airs* for violin and pianoforte. There is also the famous exercise which he set himself in 1878 – the Symphony in G minor, after Mozart: 'I once ruled a score for the same instruments and with the same number of bars as Mozart's G minor symphony, and in that framework I wrote a symphony, following as far as possible the same outlines for his themes and the same modulations. I did this on my own initiative as I was groping in the dark after light, but looking back after 30 years I don't know any discipline from which I learned so much.'[16]

This brings us to the original compositions of those years. In 1876–8, for St George's he wrote a *Salve Regina*, a *Tantum Ergo*, two hymn tunes, one in G major and other in F major. The latter was later published in the *Westminster Hymnal* as No. 151. It is quoted in the Aubade of the *Nursery Suite* of 1931. In 1879 there was a Credo in E minor, a *Domine Salvam fac*, an Easter anthem 'Brother, For Thee He Died', and in 1882 a bass solo *O Salutaris Hostia*. An earlier setting of *O Salutaris Hostia* is dated 1880 and was published by Cary in 1888. The setting of the Credo was begun in 1872. Unlike the conventional

16 *Interview with Dr Edward Elgar*, 1904, op. cit.

major-key declaration of faith, Elgar's begins pianissimo in E minor and stays in the minor. The harmonic influence of Beethoven's Mass in C has been discerned by some commentators, and it is not without religious significance that the phrase 'Et homo factus est' ('And was made man') is repeated four times. This early work was one of several which Elgar looked at again after his wife died in 1920; something very like the setting of 'Dei unigenitum et ex patre natum' turned up in the last movement of the *Arthur* incidental music of 1923.

For orchestra there exists a Menuetto (scherzo), dated 1 October 1878, which may have been part of a symphony. Under this heading come the compositions for Powick Asylum: five Quadrilles called *La Brunette*, five called *Die Junge Kokotte*, dated 19 May 1879 and dedicated to Miss Holloway, the asylum's staff pianist and organist, five called *L'Assommoir* (11 September 1879), five called *Paris*, also dedicated to Miss Holloway (17 October 1880), *The Valentine – 5 Lancers* (2–15 February 1880), and polkas dated 1880, 1881, 1882, 1883, and 1884. A *Minuet grazioso* was played at a concert of the Worcester Early Closing Association on 22 January 1879. At a concert of the Worcester Amateur Instrumental Society on 17 May 1881, with Elgar leading the orchestra, A. J. Caldicott conducted the first performance of Elgar's *Air de Ballet*. This was repeated 'by desire' the following season, on 20 February 1882, when Caldicott also conducted another Elgar first performance, that of the *March – Pas Redoublé*. Both works were performed again at the Society's concert on 14 March 1882. Another *Air de Ballet* was played on 16 August 1882, at a soirée held by the British Medical Association, meeting in Worcester. But it was in the field of chamber music that he was most copious, in music for himself to play at recitals or for his friends of the wind quintet and other combinations. There were, for violin and pianoforte, an incomplete *Fantasia* of 1878, two unfinished *Polonaises* (1879), a *Fugue in F sharp minor* (1881, incorporated over 50 years later into sketches for the opera *The Spanish Lady*), and, for violin, a *Study for Strengthening the Third Finger* (1877, re-copied in 1920 and dedicated to Jascha Heifetz). From 1878 date two incomplete string quartets, a string trio and a pianoforte trio, and the wind quintet pieces known as *Promenades* (including the titles 'Madame Tussaud's' and 'Hell and Tommy'). The seven *Harmony Music* works for wind quintet are dated 1878, 1879, and 1881, and also from 1879 are five *Intermezzos* which, when he looked at them again in later life, Elgar called 'mine own children', as indeed they are. An Allegretto, a Gavotte, a Sarabande (also re-copied for *The Spanish Lady*), a Gigue, an Andante con Variazioni (sub-titled 'Evesham Andante' and dedicated to Hubert Leicester), and an Adagio Cantabile are all 1878–9 wind quintet products. An Allegro for oboe, violin, viola, and cello of late 1878 was unfinished, and a Fugue in D minor for oboe and violin, written in May 1883 'for Frank Elgar and Karl Bammert', displays contrapuntal skill.

The music for wind quintet is of exceptional importance. It was restored to the repertoire in 1976 in a BBC broadcast by the Athena Ensemble whose leader, the flautist Richard McNicol, had examined the manuscript parts contained in a folio in the British Museum. Elgar's autograph scores and parts seem to have disappeared. The parts McNicol studied were in five different hands and had been copied by members of a wind quintet run by John Parr, Sheffield amateur bassoonist and collector of instruments. Some were dated 1935. It has been said that Parr performed these works at his enterprising concerts of unusual music, but McNicol thinks that this is unlikely because the parts were so full of errors and mistranspositions as to be virtually unplayable. It is clear from the music that William Leicester was only a moderate clarinettist, but both flautists must have been good and Frank Elgar was obviously a fine player. The bassoon parts Elgar wrote for himself are far from easy and he cued in double stops and chords so that they could be played by a cello. At a first hearing these works can easily be regarded as uncharacteristic, of giving little sign of the real Elgar. But further exploration, afforded by the issue of a recording in 1978, shows that Elgar's gift for composing light, witty, and melodious vignettes, which reached an apotheosis in the *Enigma Variations*, is already marked. The *Intermezzos* are polished miniatures, one of them, 'The Farm Yard', being the descriptive tone-poem its title implies! Some of the other sub-titles must refer to private jokes, though Elgar would have seen 'Mrs Winslow's Soothing Syrup' (*Adagio Cantabile*) advertised on the back of sheet-music. *Harmony Music No. 5* (the title adapted from the German *Harmoniemusik*, music for wind band) is a full-scale, four-movement Wind Quintet, impeccable in its sonata-form structure, masterfully written for each instrument, and indicative of close study of the classical masters. The *Four Dances* are accomplished, witty, and wholly endearing. Perhaps what deludes the casual listener into regarding these delightful pieces as unElgarian is the absence of his idiomatic writing for strings. But when we hear the *Menuetto* of *Harmony Music No. 5* and the fifth (*allegro molto*) of the *Six Promenades* in their 1930 guise as the minuet and scherzando sections of the Minuet of the *Severn Suite* and *Intermezzo No. 2* (*adagio solenne*) in *Cantique*, op. 3 of 1912, then their 'characteristically Elgarian' quality is apparent. It is this quality – a freshness of melody, a touching innocence, a distinctive turn of phrase which converts cliché into a visionary glimpse of truth – that gives Elgar's so-called 'salon' pieces, such as *Rosemary*, a distinction and distinctiveness which put them in a

class of their own. In *Chanson de nuit*, for example, is the embryo of the
First Symphony.

Obviously 1879 was an important year for the development of
Edward Elgar's gifts. There are not many composers whose music
written at the age of twenty-two betrays its authorship so strongly.
The *Romance* for violin and pianoforte published in 1885 by Schott
was written in 1878 or 1879. There is a breath of 'Nimrod' in the 1882
O Salutaris Hostia. The *Nursery Suite*, supposedly of 1931, opens with
a tune composed in 1878, and other parts of the suite date probably
from as far back. *Rosemary* (1915) was written at Settle, Yorkshire,
on 4 September 1882. Parts of *King Olaf* (1896) were developed from
1879 sketches. So was the opening of *The Black Knight* (1893). The
overture of the first *Wand of Youth* suite exists as sketches dated 1879,
and 'Fairies and Giants' Elgar himself dated 1867. The Minuet existed
in 1881, and 'Sun Dance' was an 1879 waltz. Of the second suite, 'Wild
Bears' was a Powick quadrille and 'Moths and Butterflies' was sketched
in 1879. But the origins of these pieces can safely be dated between
1867 and 1871, according to Elgar. And in 1901 when Edward VII
congratulated Elgar on the tune of the Trio of the first *Pomp and
Circumstance* march, the composer replied 'I've been carrying that
around in my pocket for 20 years' – which dates 'Land of Hope and
Glory' at about 1880. What is more, as W. H. Reed pointed out, the
Quadrilles for Powick contain striking examples of sudden 'crashes'
in the middle of a bar, such as can be found in the Second Symphony
finale, in the finale of the Cello Concerto and elsewhere. The style was
the man.

3 Apprentice

The 'Paris' quadrilles of 1880 were a souvenir of Elgar's first visit abroad, when he went to the French capital with Charlie Pipe, who was to marry Lucy Elgar the following year. They heard Saint-Saëns play the organ at the Madeleine and saw Molière's *Le Malade Imaginaire*. Edward evidently had another brief preoccupation for in 1933, when Elgar visited Delius in France, after he left Grez-sur-Loing the scent of the countryside 'recalled a romance of 1880 . . . I decided to go to Barbizon, but when I passed the cross-roads the longing had passed away. That belonged to the romance of 1880, now dead.'[1] He returned to Worcester, to his teaching and his work at the asylum; he took the Royal Academy of Music's local examination in violin and 'general musical knowledge', passing with honours in company with the blind musician William Wolstenholme, then aged fifteen; and he was promoted to the first violins at the Worcester Festival, where the orchestration of Mackenzie's cantata *The Bride* impressed him. This led in the following year to his engagement to play in the first violins of W. C. Stockley's orchestra in Birmingham. Stockley's Popular Concerts were a well-established Midland event and he was also chorus-master for the Birmingham Triennial Festival.

An important friendship, which was to last for fifty years, began in 1882 when the British Medical Association held their fiftieth anniversary meeting in Worcester. At a musical *soireé*, Elgar's *Air de Ballet* was played on 16 August. In the orchestra was one of the delegates to the conference, Dr Charles Buck, of Settle, Yorkshire. Buck, who was born in 1852, was a country doctor with a practice spread over a hundred square miles of Yorkshire moorland. He was also a gifted amateur musician, playing the viola and cello in chamber music and local orchestras, conducting, collecting folk-songs, and occasionally composing. He was introduced to Elgar in Worcester by John Beare (1847–1928), a London musical instrument dealer who did business with Elgar Bros. He was the son of a Settle lawyer and had known Buck as a boy. Buck later (1884) married, as his first wife, Beare's sister Emma. Buck and Elgar liked each other from the first. Music was the obvious shared interest, but it was only one of many. Both loved the countryside – Buck was a keen naturalist – and enjoyed golf, tennis, and walking. Most important of all, they shared a similar sense of humour.[2]

[1] *The Daily Telegraph*, 1 July 1933.
[2] See *A Yorkshire Friendship* by Dennis Clark, Elgar Society Journal, January 1980, pp. 14–17.

In the first fortnight of January 1883 Elgar achieved his ambition, after hard saving, to visit Leipzig, not, as he had once hoped, to study, but to hear concerts by the Gewandhaus Orchestra conducted by Carl Reinecke, and to go to the opera. Schumann's *Overture, Scherzo and Finale* seems to have made a deep impression on him – 'my ideal!' he called Schumann in a letter to Buck. 'I have heard no end of stuff,' he wrote on 13 May 1883. 'Schumann principally and Wagner no end. They have a good opera ... & we went many times.' 'We' comprised Elgar, a seventeen-year-old English girl, Edith Groveham, later Mrs Wood-Somers, of Blewbury, Berkshire, and Helen Jessie Weaver, daughter of the proprietor of a prosperous shoe shop at 84, High Street, Worcester. Helen's brother Frank played in the first violins of the Worcester Amateur Instrumental Society which Elgar conducted from autumn 1882. Helen was a violin student at the Leipzig Conservatory of Music and she was the principal reason for Elgar's visit to Germany. He looked forward eagerly to her holidays in Worcester. Writing to Dr Buck on 1 July 1883, he said: 'The vacation at Leipzig begins shortly; my "Braut" arrives here on Thursday next remaining till the first week in September; of course I shall remain in Worcester till her departure. After that 'twould be a charity if you could find a brokenhearted fiddler much trio-playing for a day or two. Please do not let me intrude on you. . . . I can only say that I should dearly love to come.'

In the summer of 1883 Elgar and Helen (he called her Nelly) were engaged. She was born in High Street on 27 December 1860 and they must have known each other from early childhood. Two of the Powick polkas and two of the wind quintet pieces were inscribed to her between 1878 and 1882. Her father, William, died in 1880, her stepmother on 13 November 1883, two days after Elgar wrote to Dr Buck: 'Well, Helen has come back!! Mrs Weaver is so ill, dying in fact, so the child thought it best to return and nurse her; so we are together a little now & consequently happy.' On 14 January 1884, in a letter to Buck in which Elgar referred to himself as 'the only person who is an utter failure in this miserable world ... I am disappointed, disheartened & sick of this world altogether', he added a postscript: 'Miss Weaver is remaining in Worcester and the little music etc. that we get together is the only enjoyment I get and more than I deserve no doubt.' The engagement was broken off in April 1884. Helen was a Unitarian and it has been surmised that family opposition to her marriage to a Roman Catholic was the reason for the break. But as her parents were both dead, this seems unlikely. Mrs Weaver died from tuberculosis and a year later Helen herself was affected. She had abandoned Leipzig and, after her stepmother's death, stayed for a time with Edith Groveham in Bradford. She caught smallpox and later developed tuberculosis.

Possibly she herself self-sacrificingly advanced religious objections as a screen for sparing Elgar the risk of infection from a disease that was still a scourge. To Buck, who had himself recently become engaged, Elgar wrote in the summer of 1884 that 'my prospects are worse than ever & to crown my miseries my engagement is broken off & I am lonely.... I have not the heart to speak to any one.... Once more accept my good wishes for your happiness, these I can give you the more sincerely since I know what it is to have lost my own for ever.' On 7 October 1885 he informed Buck that 'Miss W. is going to New Zealand this month – her lungs are affected I hear & there has been a miserable time for me since I came home'. In New Zealand Helen's health improved and in 1890 she married an Auckland banker, John Munro, and lived in the suburb of Mount Eden. Their daughter, Joyce, born in 1893, died from tuberculosis in 1921, at the age of twenty-eight. Mr Munro died in 1925 and Helen died on 23 December 1927, four days before her sixty-seventh birthday, from cancer.

A happy occasion Helen had shared with Elgar and his mother was a visit to Birmingham on 13 December 1883 for the performance by Stockley's Orchestra of Elgar's *Intermezzo: Sérénade Mauresque*. Edward played in the orchestra. 'Melodious, graceful and pleasing' was one critic's description, 'and the scoring, more particularly for the strings ... is tasteful and musicianly'. This was some encouragement, and Elgar sent the parts to Pollitzer in London who had offered to try to interest August Manns in it for a Crystal Palace concert. The first performance had been given on 4 April 1883 by the Worcestershire Musical Union, conducted by Edward Vine Hall.

Elgar's eyes were on a fame wider than that so poignantly conveyed by the phrase 'talented local composer'. Already he had experienced something of the harsh side of musical life when he had offered to re-score a church musician's anthem, after the original effort had failed disastrously, and had not received even a word of thanks when the revision was a success. He wrote to Buck in explanation of an adverse criticism of the *Intermezzo*: 'The man who wrote the slighting article is a Mus. Bac. who had sent in two pieces and they were advertised and withdrawn because the orchestration wanted so much revision as to be unplayable.' And in the same letter: 'My father was ill just before Xmas ... the younger generation at the Catholic Ch: have taken an objection to him and have got him turned out of the organist's place; this he had held for 37 years!!' Here, in these early letters, we see the Elgar so many came to know – ebullient one minute, downcast the next. 'My prospects are about as hopeless as ever,' he wrote to Buck in April 1884. 'I am not wanting in energy I think; so, sometimes, I conclude that 'tis want of ability and get in a mouldy desponding state which is really horrible.'

As he taught the young ladies of Malvern the violin – he had
extended his practice to the spa late in 1883 – and used up his earnings
on journeys to London to hear a Manns concert or to try to sell his
work to a publisher, he must have known only too well what kind of
struggle lay ahead of him. In an unpublished article which he wrote in
the last years of his life, he described his day trips to London in his
twenties: 'I lived 120 miles from London. I rose at six, walked a mile
to the railway station, the train left at seven; arrived at Paddington
about 11, underground to Victoria, on to the [Crystal] Palace arriving
in time for the last three-quarters of an hour of the rehearsal; if
fortune smiled, this piece of rehearsal included the work desired to be
heard; but fortune rarely smiled and more often than not the principal
item was over. Lunch. Concert at three. At five a rush to Victoria;
then to Paddington, on to Worcester arriving at 10-30. A strenuous
day indeed; but the new work had been heard and another treasure
added to a life's experience.' One of his own compositions was played
in Worcester on 1 May 1884, when the organist Dr Done – he who
disliked Schumann – conducted *Sevillana* at a Worcester Philharmonic
Society concert. *Sevillana*, dedicated gratefully to Stockley, also went
to Pollitzer and thence to Manns, who included it in a Crystal Palace
afternoon concert on 12 May 1884, the first music by Elgar to be performed in London. On the same evening Elgar heard the first
English performance of Brahms's Third Symphony, conducted by
Hans Richter.

Elgar went for a holiday to Scotland in August 1884. 'I got in a
very desponding state . . . (you ken what happened),' he explained to
Buck, 'and it behoved me to do something out of the common to
raise my spirits. . . . Came home "well". I have been working away
ever since.' As was always to happen, a change of scenery stimulated
his creative faculty and in 1885 he had begun a 'Lakes' overture,
souvenir of a previous Windermere holiday with Buck, and a
'Scottish' overture. In later life Buck recalled the 'extraordinary'
effect on Elgar of his first sight of Lake Windermere. 'Not a word
could be got out of him, and then suddenly he began to write
furiously. . . . He said he had never known quite the same sensation
before and that he was simply obliged to write.' Both these overtures
were abandoned. Elgar described them as 'of no account but they
serve to divert me somewhat and hide a broken heart'. He showed
the Scottish overture later in 1885 to 'old Stockley' who was 'afraid
of it. He says candidly he cannot read the score and would like to
hear it first – I am sorely disappointed.' He returned to the subject in
another letter to Buck six weeks later, this time adding that Stockley
had found it 'disconnected'. 'So I have retired into my shell and live
in hopes of writing a polka some day – failing that a single chant is
probably my fate.'

There is plenty of the jocular, facetious, and whimsical Elgar in these letters to Buck, a hearty yet curiously ill-at-ease strain which intensified as he grew older and is particularly prevalent in letters to Jaeger, Dora Powell, and Troyte Griffith. He carried writing material wherever he went so that he could use time spent in waiting for trains in keeping his correspondence up to date – 'I am busy now [1884], and have to "fake" considerably to get lessons in – not that I am full up really, but it takes so much time getting from one place to another.' His gift for friendship is always evident in his letters, with their conversational style and detail. Buck and his wife gave Elgar a collie, Scap, in 1885, and accounts of Scap's adventures punctuate the musical news in the letters sent from Worcester to Settle over the next few years.

'I took him up the road for a run before turning in. This morning I had him out at 7.30 into the river and he had his first fight with a Newfoundland brute which began it—; no harm done. . . . The Bath Road presents a perfect paradise of new smells all of which he has duly examined and *"reported"* on. . . .' 'I took him over to Stoke [Stoke Prior] for the weekend & had a vagabond day on the common after rabbits etc. . . . He has developed into a much more affectionate animal than I anticipated & loves me. . . . I shut him up at the shop this morn: while I went to give a lesson, he whined so his grandmother [Elgar's mother] let him out, he darted down the stairs, caught his leg in twenty concertinas that are piled on the staircase & rolled over with all the lot into the middle of the shop! There were some ladies there & my old father enjoyed it awfully. We live in an atmosphere of Scap. . . .' '. . . got an 'orrid cold, shouting in the rain election night. Scap & I were out 'till 12.30!! & owing to our exertion we have got a Conservative in – for this Radical hole. Scap wore his colours like a man. . . .' 'Scap is getting fat & is very well now; no news in particular of him; he stole ½ a fried sole up here & a beef steak at mother's & has caused the cat to kitten prematurely by his antics. . . .' 'He slipped his collar again; jumped a door a foot higher than my head & without a run, &, finding he was still a prisoner, *tore* a hole in the next door, bit it and clawed it 'till he got thro' and was at large again. Bless him! . . . 'I did not know Scap could fight, but I was rejoiced to see that he pulled three good lumps of wool out of the enemy [a St. Bernard], which floated gaily in the breeze. . . .' 'My only regret about leaving . . . is about my dear, dear companion, poor old Scap; he is lying at my feet now as he has ever done these 3½ years: my sister Lucy will take great care of him & he knows her as well as he does me. . . .' 'He is *an old man* now & very sedate: something dim with one eye: he still keeps his old faddy ways & rolls over to have his stomach scratched etc. but all the old fire is gone & he wd. rather not fight any more, thank you: bless him! we *were* companions once but he is made more fuss of now with Lucy than I could find time for & so he will stay there'. Scap died on 7 September 1892: there were to be no more dogs in Elgar's life until his wife died in 1920.

There is nothing in either the *Intermezzo* or *Sevillana* to suggest that Elgar was the possessor of anything but a picturesque and melodious talent for salon music. He himself knew his own possibilities better, and few events can have had a greater effect on his future development than the Three Choirs Festival at Worcester in September 1884, marking the cathedral's 800th anniversary, when Dvořák, who had visited England for the first time the previous March, conducted his *Stabat Mater* and his nowadays too rarely heard D major symphony (op. 60, formerly known as No. 1 and now as No. 6). Elgar again played in the first violins, played this gay and melodious symphony dedicated to Dr Hans Richter, and wrote of it to Buck: 'I wish you could hear Dvořák's music. It is simply ravishing, so tuneful & clever & the orchestration is wonderful; no matter how few instruments he uses it never sounds thin. I cannot describe it; it must be heard.'

Much is said of the influence of Brahms and Wagner on Elgar's music, but in neither case is their influence as strong as has sometimes been made out. For a much more powerful influence, both instrumentally and aesthetically, it is profitable to look at the works of Schumann and Dvořák, two composers whose combination of romantic lyricism and strong rhythmical contrast finds similar expression in the music of Elgar. That he learnt much from a study of their scores is obvious whenever we hear the transition passage from scherzo to finale of Schumann's D minor symphony, the overture and the introduction to Act III of *Manfred*, the first climax of the first movement of Dvořák's D minor symphony, op. 70, and a passage towards the end of the finale of the G major symphony, op. 88: they might have been scored by Elgar. Most remarkable of all is the slow movement of Dvořák's early D minor symphony, op. 13 (now known as No. 4 in D minor), which might almost be by Elgar and contains an extraordinary anticipation of the 'New Faith' theme in *The Kingdom*. Both Elgar's concertos effectively 'borrow' Dvořák's scheme in his Cello Concerto of nostalgically recalling earlier themes towards the end of the finale. In Elgar's own B minor concerto, for violin not cello, his theme from the slow movement:

is strongly reminiscent of this, from the slow movement of Dvořák's Violin Concerto:

Ex. 2

Tovey found a similar relationship between Elgar's Violin Concerto and Saint-Säens's Third Violin Concerto, also in B minor. This points to another, less obvious continental influence but one which is nearer in some ways to Elgar's musical character than are either Wagner or Brahms. At any rate, the 1884 experience of Dvořák, repeated two years later, on 21 October 1886, when Dvořák again conducted the D major symphony at Birmingham with Stockley's orchestra, seems to have spurred Elgar to further efforts on his own behalf. As soon as the Worcester Festival was over he went to London to try to interest the Covent Garden Promenade Concerts in his work, without any luck, and he told Buck he had 'a big work in tow' – no one has discovered what that may have been: perhaps a violin concerto which he eventually destroyed in 1890, or a string quartet. Charles Buck's brother-in-law, John Beare, a London musical instrument dealer and publisher, with whom Elgar sometimes stayed, helped him, as did Pollitzer, to get his music into print for the first time. *Une Idylle* (op. 4, No. 1) written in 1884 and dedicated to Miss E. E. of Inverness, another 'long-forgotten romance' of the Scottish holiday in 1884, was published by Beare – 'John was good enough to encourage me by taking the little piece for violin', Elgar wrote to Buck on 8 March 1885, still, incidentally, addressing him as 'My dear doctor' and signing himself 'Edward Elgar', nothing less formal – and Schott brought out the op. 1, a *Romance* for violin and pianoforte which was written in 1878 and played in Worcester at a concert in the Deanery on 20 October 1885. Elgar's friendly loyalties are displayed in the dedications of these early pieces – the *Romance* to the grocer Oswin Grainger, who played in local bands with Elgar; a violin *Gavotte*, published by Schott, to Dr Buck 'in memory of the old days'; *Virelai*, op. 4, No. 3, to Frank Webb, a Worcester furniture dealer and member of the W.A.I.S. (who evidently wrote to its new conductor urging more adventurous programmes and received the reply: 'The average taste in music, as you must have seen, is extremely low. . . . I fear 'tis useless asking them to devote their energies to something higher and consequently more difficult.'); the *Allegretto* for violin and pianoforte on a theme of five notes G E D G E, dedicated to the Gedge sisters of Malvern Wells to whom Elgar was tutor, and published by Schott. In November 1885, he became organist of St George's, with Hubert Leicester as choirmaster, and it must have seemed as though this put the final seal on his role for life: local musician, available for all occasions, sacred or secular.

Elgar's violin and piano pieces are worth more than a cursory mention for, trifles though they may be, they are neither unconsidered nor inconsiderable. They have a panache and craftsmanship found only in the chips from a master's workshop. The finest of them is the GEDGE *Allegretto*, ingeniously devised, tuneful, making poetic use of pizzicato, and with a brilliant, Chopinesque piano part. It is not fanciful to detect in the tender coda a foretaste of the slow movement of the Violin Concerto of 1910. *La Capricieuse* (1891, although the dates of most of Elgar's early pieces are arbitrary) was written for a male pupil, Fred Ward, who must have been above average. It is a virtuoso study, and could be mistaken for one of the pieces Fritz Kreisler was to write. This Kreislerian quality may also be found in *Bizarrerie*, with its Spanish-flavour rhythms. The early (1877) *Reminiscences*, also written for Oswin Grainger and never published, has a melody based on sequences and is proof that Elgar's melodic style was formed before most of the wind quintet pieces were written. The *Romance* is in E minor and has a quiet poetic beauty instantly recognizable, for all its Brahmsian suggestions, as Elgar's work, especially the dying fall. The *Gavotte* is conventional and rather plodding in rhythm but the central section has a lyrical touch which is found in more striking proportion in *Virelai*, one of the best of these pieces with its wide-ranging melody and exploitation of the instrument's capacity for singing tone. The *Offertoire* (*Andante religioso*) avoids mawkishness by reason of the aristocracy of its melodic line; and while there is little remarkable in *Pastourelle* apart from craftsmanship and charm (notably in the piano part), *Une Idylle* has a long and skilfully unfolded melody which in its first phrases suggests a Scottish folk-song as tribute to the Inverness romance.

. . . . .

This period of Elgar's life coincides with what is known as the English Musical Renaissance. But the more steadily one looks at those years, the less apparent does the renaissance become. It was, unquestionably, a renaissance of *atmosphere*. Music began to be taken much more seriously and to be seen as an integral part of human life rather than as mere titillation of the ear. It became entwined with romantic literature and philosophy, not always to its advantage. The opening of the Royal College of Music, the foundation of the Oxford University Musical Club, the Bach revival, the Crystal Palace concerts under Manns, the Handel festivals, visits to London of great musicians, such as Wagner and Hans Richter, and of great instrumentalists and singers – all these educational and expository happenings betoken a genuine revival of musical life which was not wholly confined to the capital. Hallé in Manchester, Stockley in Birmingham, and, later, Godfrey in Bournemouth made their contributions. The Leeds, Birmingham, and Three Choirs Festivals were regarded as the goals to which all composers should aspire – and since the public's appetite for oratorios appeared to be insatiable, they catered for this taste in a manner which now seems almost indecently callous.

Out of all this activity how much living, creative music has come down to us after nearly a hundred years? Parry's *Scenes from 'Prometheus Unbound'*, in 1880 at Gloucester, is often used as the first milestone on the road to revival, and a broadcast performance in 1980 proved of exceptional interest in allowing listeners a century later to perceive that Elgar may well have learned something from its vocal and choral writing, as well as from the grace of the scoring of its best passages. But milestones soon become covered with weeds and obscured from view. Stanford's *Veiled Prophet*, Mackenzie's *La Belle Dame Sans Merci*, Cowen's *The Water Lily* – who now knows a note of these 'milestones', and who outside a very select few knew a note of them seventy years ago? Stanford and Parry were remarkable men, as teachers, administrators, and publicists. As composers they were overshadowed, even in their own day, not only by their European counterparts, but by Arthur Sullivan – and Stainer's *Crucifixion*. Sullivan was the genuine, creative, thoroughly musical talent of English Victorian music, the creator of a *genre*, the Savoy operas – Offenbach in gaiters – which by its tunefulness and resource looks like staying the course for a long time still to come. An obituarist of Frederic Cowen wrote in 1935 that Cowen had offered his listeners and performers 'a great deal of refined enjoyment'. Compared with Cowen's kind of refinement, Sullivan seems almost crude. Yet there is no need to analyse the reasons for Sullivan's pre-eminence. Quality tells. His tunes were better, his scoring was better, his sense of rhythm was better than those of his contemporaries. Eduard Hanslick, revisiting London in 1886 after twenty-four years, remarked that Sullivan's music was 'stylistically consistent' and that the composer 'has accomplished something, if in a secondary genre, which no Englishman has ever accomplished before: to be melodious and amusing for an entire evening'. He spoke from experience, for after enduring Mackenzie's opera *The Troubadour* – 'one of the dullest and most disagreeable affairs I have ever encountered in the form of music in costume' – he concluded that opera 'requires melodic invention, strong sensuality and a fresh, consistent style – all characteristics with which the English are not notably endowed'. Strong sensuality is hardly to be found in the Savoy operas, but the melody and style are proof against change. Yet Sullivan was out of favour with the musical intelligentsia because of this lighter side of his art – the same disfavour which was eventually to be transferred to Elgar by the same people.

Parry and Stanford laboured in a different vineyard from Sullivan –

Stanford's lighter side, his genuinely beautiful Irish rhapsodies and songs, suggests that he might have enjoyed similar success had luck run his way – and no doubt they felt his artistic and financial success as an injustice. 'The English public is curious,' Parry said in 1918 to Thomas F. Dunhill. 'It can only recognise one composer at a time. Once it was Sullivan. Now it is Elgar.' Later it was Vaughan Williams, then Britten. All the four composers named, to use another of Parry's phrases which he originally applied to Elgar, 'reached the hearts of the people' without debasing their ideals and without stooping to vulgarity. The big men will always win acclaim; the smaller men make their contribution to the age which produces the big man. These contributions may be of great value and one does not make Elgar's achievement any greater, rather the reverse, by belittling his contemporaries. But facts remain; and if we really wish to set a *realistic* date to the renaissance of English musical composition, or, at any rate, to its coming-of-age, then it is 19 June 1899, when Hans Richter conducted the first performance of the *Enigma Variations*.

. . . . .

The four years from 1886 occupy hardly any space in books about Elgar, yet in them his frustration must have been greater than at any other time. Yet he did not lose heart. His organ-playing led to renewed church compositions: an *Ave verum* (composed as a *Pie Jesu* in memory of William Allen, his former solicitor-employer) in January 1887, four Litanies in 1888 and *Ecce sacerdos magnus*, dedicated to Hubert Leicester and first performed at St George's on 9 October 1888, when the Roman Catholic Bishop of Birmingham visited the church to bless a statue. 'Some special things had to be sung for which we had no music,' he told Buck 'thus I had to set to work & compose it all & copy out the parts! Had to get it in anyhow & broke my neck doing it. Anyway the leading paper says the new composition was "exquisite" so I suppose 'twas good enough.' He was determined, he told Buck, 'to do everything I can lay my hands on'.

The *Ave verum corpus* was not published until 1902. Its fluent melody in G major and the antiphonal writing in the coda contribute to its effective devotional simplicity. Even finer is the *Ecce sacerdos*: here can be recognized Elgar's innate sense of occasion. The rhythm on the organ pedal seems designed to accompany the Bishop's progress, and there is the authentic Elgarian hallmark on the main theme, the majestic four-part writing, and the meditative coda.

He gave violin recitals – his fee was two guineas – violin lessons, and played in orchestras throughout the Midlands – an experience at a Hanley Festival in the then new Victoria Hall was typical: 'The arrangements for our accommodation were "frightful" & we all

struck & eventually the committee telegraphed to all the neighbour-
ing towns to get hotels for us. I was travelling all night after & sitting
up & incessant playing has made my eye very queer.' That is the first
mention of a chronic complaint which was to plague him all his life.
He frequently mentioned his ailments to Buck; for example: 'I have
been ill for a long time off and on; got a severe cold which has, as
usual, played the plague with my b—ls. . . . I have lost ever so much
work.' He needed all the money he could get so that he was no burden
on the married sister with whom he lived.[3] In 1886 he added to his
other tasks a teaching post at Worcester College for the Blind where
he again came into contact with William Wolstenholme, accompanying him as amanuensis in the following year when he went for three
days to Oxford to sit for his Mus. Bac. degree, a typical act of
generosity. Elgar read out the questions to him and, according to F.
Bonavia,[4] noticed a mistake in one of them with the result that the
authorities agreed it must not be attempted.

His only major encouragement, in a relative sense, in these years
was the performance at Birmingham on 1 March 1888 by Stockley's
orchestra of the *Suite in D*, originally of four movements including the
March – Pas Redoublé (first played separately at Worcester on 20 February 1882) and incorporating the *Sérénade Mauresque*. When this
was revised for publication as op. 10 ten years later the March was
dropped. The suite, obviously, was not a particularly 'new' work. He
had told Buck in November 1883 that it was finished 'in my head if I
could but get time to write it down'. He had hoped for an earlier
performance (letter to Buck 12 December 1887, 'My Suite is still silent
& postponed at Birmingham: fate!'). He conducted the work and
attributed some unfavourable notices to this fact: 'The critics, save
two, are nettled. I am the only local man who has been asked to
conduct his own work – & what's a greater offence, I *did it* – and *well*
too; for this I must needs suffer.' One critic recommended 'judicious
operations with the pruning knife' and the *Musical Times* correspondent, writing of the composer as 'Mr Algar', noted 'fancy as
well as tunefulness' and also a lack of 'cohesion and artistic
development' – a fair example of fence-sitting. The revised suite
contains, in the finale 'Contrasts: the Gavotte A.D. 1700 and 1900',[5]
one of Elgar's most delightful lighter pieces, a thoroughly charming

[3] Elgar left 10, High Street, Worcester, his parents' home above the shop, in 1879. He
then lived with his sister Pollie and her husband William Grafton at Loretto Villa, 35,
Chestnut Walk (now re-numbered as no. 12). When the Graftons moved to Stoke
Works, Bromsgrove, in 1883, he moved in with his eldest sister Lucy and her
husband Charles Pipe at 4, Field Terrace, just off the Bath Road, staying there until
his marriage in 1889.
[4] In 'Elgar', *The Music Masters* (ed. A. L. Bacharach), iii, p. 138.
[5] The original order of movements was: Mazurka, Intermezzo, Fantasia gavotte,
March.

example of pastiche, ingeniously handled. This movement derives from an incident during the Leipzig visit of 1883: 'I saw two dancers once in Leipzig who came down the stage in antique dress dancing a gavotte: when they reached the footlights they suddenly turned round & appeared to be two very young & modern people & danced a gay & lively measure: they had come down the stage *backwards* & danced away with their (modern) faces towards us – when they reached the back of the stage they suddenly turned round & the old, decrepit couple danced gingerly to the old tune.'[6]

On 7 May 1888 the Rev. Edward Vine Hall conducted the Worcestershire Musical Union in Elgar's Three Pieces for String Orchestra. The manuscript of this work is lost, but there seems every reason to suppose that, in a revised form, it became the well-known *Serenade for Strings*, op. 20. The titles of the original suite are in themselves a strong clue: I Spring Song (Allegro), II Elegy (Adagio), III Finale (Presto). '*I like 'em* (the first thing I ever did),' he told Buck in July; and in later life he often referred to the *Serenade* as his favourite work. (The *Serenade* in the form we know it was completed in May 1892 and was probably played for the first time at the Ladies' Orchestral Class in Worcester which Elgar conducted and trained.) The same letter to Buck adds jubilantly, 'Also there's a terrific (!!!) song in this month's Maga. of Music'. This song, 'The Wind at Dawn', won Elgar £5 in a competition organized by Joseph Williams, the publishers. Its words were by Caroline Alice Roberts.

Miss Roberts had become one of Elgar's Malvern pianoforte pupils on 6 October 1886. He was then twenty-nine. She was thirty-seven (born at Bhuj, Kutch, Bombay on 9 October 1848[7]), an age, at that period of history, at which spinsterhood seemed confirmed. She was the daughter of Major-General Sir Henry Gee Roberts, a stalwart of the Indian Army in the Mutiny and the Sikh Wars, and his wife Julia Raikes, granddaughter of Robert Raikes, founder of Sunday Schools. The General died in 1860 when Caroline Alice, youngest of his four children, was twelve. The other three children were boys: one died young, and the other two were educated at Cheltenham and joined the Indian Army, one of them dying in 1882. Alice, therefore, like many a Victorian daughter, was left to look after her mother in Hazeldine House, the Georgian house at Redmarley d'Abitot in Gloucestershire. She had an artistic nature. She studied geology, she translated Hoffmann's *Ritter Glück*, and she wrote and had published in 1882 a two-volume novel *Marchcroft Manor* (still worth reading), and some poetry. There was a streak of mild radicalism, certainly a sense that social conditions must change, in her writings, but the circumstances

[6] Letter to A. J. Jaeger, 4 February 1899.
[7] Confirmed by her birth certificate. See *Alice Elgar, Enigma of a Victorian Lady* by P. M. Young (London, 1978), pp. 21–2.

of her life killed any chance of her becoming a 'liberated woman'. She also took part in Shakespeare readings and in village concerts. She sang in a choir which was often accompanied by a string orchestra in which Elgar played, and she attended the concerts of the Worcester Amateur Instrumental Society which he conducted.

After the piano lessons from Elgar had continued for some time, 'the old coachman who had been with [the Roberts family] for many years, and who of course had to drive [Alice] into Malvern was heard to say that he thought "there was more in it than music".'[8] Thereafter the poems she was writing were often on the twin themes of love and music, for example (1887):

> Art and music are thine own,
> And thine the soul to whom must speak
> The higher voices heard alone
> By those who long and those who seek.

It was not long before Edward was formally invited to afternoon tea at Hazeldine. On 30 May 1887 Lady Roberts died and Alice, who inherited a small private income, left Redmarley and in April took a furnished room in 'Saetermo', No. 7, The Lees, Great Malvern. Here she was able to see Edward more often. She attended the performance of the Three Pieces for String Orchestra in May 1888 and this, too, was the cause of another poem, 'On hearing some orchestral music', in which she wrote that the subtle melodies 'tell of far and flowery meads, Of rivers fringed with wavering reeds, Of hills awakening to the Spring'. Then, in the slow movement 'they seem Hushed to a finer mystic dream . . . and love and pain Now mingle in the strain again, While mystically the music swells . . . and ever tells Of joy and love, and yearnings past: Of hopes divine and longings vast.' This was an emotional response to Elgar's music of a kind which many other listeners have expressed in similar terms in the years since 1888.

At the end of August Elgar went for a holiday in Settle with Dr Buck and his wife. Before he left, Alice gave him a poem she had written on 16 August, entitled 'Love's Grace'. While at Settle Elgar returned the compliment by composing a piano piece *Liebesgruss* (*Love's Greeting*), better known as *Salut d'Amour*. He dedicated it 'à Carice', his first use of a name derived from Caroline Alice and which they later bestowed on their only daughter. Elgar sent *Liebesgruss* to the publisher Schott's, who bought it, together with an orchestral version and an arrangement for violin and pianoforte, for two guineas. The contract was dated 10 December 1888. (In June 1899 there was a further contract for more arrangements for a fee of ten

[8] Manuscript memoir of Alice Elgar, by her daughter Carice Elgar Blake, quoted in P. M. Young's *Alice Elgar*, op.cit., p. 86 and *passim*.

guineas.) On his return from Settle, Elgar proposed to Alice and they became formally engaged on 22 September. Carice Elgar Blake described the result:[9] 'This news brought cries of horror from the Roberts & Raikes (with the notable exception of Mr and Mrs W. A. Raikes and her mother who lived in Norwood and were always most helpful). They said he was an unknown musician; his family was in trade; and anyway he looked too delicate to live any length of time. One of the aunts was going to leave Alice a substantial sum, but, on hearing the news, she forthwith cast her out of her will altogether.'

But not only was Elgar a tradesman's son, he was a Roman Catholic. Another of Alice's relatives stipulated that certain family money allowed to Alice should not pass to any children of the marriage. When Alice Elgar died in 1920, Elgar wrote to Frank Schuster (17 April 1920): 'I am plunged in the midst of ancient hate and prejudice – poor dear A's settlements & her *awful aunts* who cd. allow nothing to descend to any offspring of *mine* – I had forgotten all the petty bitterness but I feel just now rather evil that . . . my Carice [his daughter] should be penalised by a wretched lot of old incompetents simply because I was – well – I.'

But Alice Roberts knew what he was, and all credit to her for it. She knew, to use a metaphor some of her family might have understood, that the colt she had picked was a Derby winner. Never in all the years that followed did she waver in her faith and belief, born of some deep instinct, that Edward Elgar was a creative genius of the highest order. She must have persuaded him during their engagement to abandon his teaching and his choir practices, his organ-playing and Stockley's orchestra, his amateur instrumentalists and his chamber music in Malvern villas, and to move to London, the centre of music-making, and to try his fortune with publishers. On 8 May 1889 they were married at Brompton Oratory. Elgar was within a month of his thirty-second birthday; Alice was forty. The ceremony was brief because the bride was not a Roman Catholic.[10] Of Elgar's relatives, only his Uncle Henry (who was passionately fond of him) and Pollie and Will Grafton were there; and Charles Buck from Settle. On Alice's side only her cousin William Raikes and his wife Veronica attended. Father Knight of St George's Church, Worcester, gave as a wedding present to his departing organist John Henry Newman's poem *The Dream of Gerontius*, into which he had copied underlinings and markings made by General Gordon in the copy sent to him at Khartoum five years earlier. But Elgar had already owned such a copy since 1885 and he had given one to Alice in 1887 when her mother died.

[9] MS memoir of Alice Elgar, by C. E. Blake, op.cit.
[10] Alice Elgar was received into the Roman Catholic faith at St George's, Worcester, on 21 July 1894.

4 Retreat from London

The years 1889 to 1899 are the most important in Elgar's life. In this decade he went from obscurity to fame, by way of cruel discouragement. These are the years which explain how the composer of *Salut d' Amour* turned into the composer of the *Enigma Variations*. He did not, as has often been implied, become a great composer overnight in one work. No artist in any art in the history of mankind has done that. The seeds and roots of greatness grow obscurely sometimes, but their progress is traceable and recognizable.

After a honeymoon in the Isle of Wight, the Elgars settled on 28 May at 3, Marloes Road, West Kensington. When their lease expired in July, they went to stay in Malvern, where Alice still had the lease of 'Saetermo' until 29 September 1889. While there, Elgar began to compose a cantata, *The Black Knight*, to a text by Longfellow. They then moved for a short while into 4, The Lees, Great Malvern, until, on 10 October, they returned to London to move into 'Oaklands', Fountain Road (now Fountain Drive), Upper Norwood, near the Crystal Palace and the Manns concerts, at one of which, on 11 November 1889, *Salut d'Amour* was performed in Elgar's orchestration. (Alice attended, but Elgar was playing in Birmingham.) During this time Elgar wrote the *Eleven Vesper Voluntaries* for organ, which he dedicated to Veronica Raikes, whose house contained a chamber organ.

There can be no doubt that Elgar was blissfully happy at this time. Marriage appears to have lifted a weight off his mind. What this was can only be a matter for speculation, but that it was psycho-sexual may be inferred from two letters Elgar wrote to Charles Buck, who was not only his closest male friend but a doctor. From his honeymoon at Ventnor, where they stayed in a guest-house, 3, Alexandra Gardens, he wrote on 25 May: 'This is a time of deep peace & happiness to me after the vain imaginings of so many years & the pessimistic views so often unfolded to you on the Settle highways have vanished! God wot!' Then, from Malvern five months later, on 6 October, came more in the same vein: 'And now (after all our talks about the mystery of living) I must tell you how happy I am in my new life & what a dear, loving companion I have & how sweet everything seems & how *understandable* existence seems to have grown: but you may forget the long discussions we used to have in your carriage when driving about but I think all the difficult problems are now solved and – well I don't worry myself about 'em now!'

Two exciting events made the turn of the year 1889–90 memorable for the Elgars. In November 1889 Elgar was invited by the Worcester Festival committee to write a short orchestral work for the 1890 meeting of the Three Choirs; and soon after New Year 1890 Alice knew that she was pregnant. This meant that they had to find a new house. In dismal weather Elgar walked from estate agent to estate agent in search of somewhere. It depressed him, but not so much that he lost his sense of humour: he wrote an amusing parody of *Hiawatha* on 19 January after a fruitless week of house-hunting:

> But I never found the Agents'
> Siren-songs one jot fulfillèd;
> Mere delusions, sad & sorry,
> Found I ever everywhere –
> . . .
> And I thought & whispered softly –
> What a lying lot they are!

Eventually, on 24 March 1890, they moved into 51 Avonmore Road, West Kensington, on a three-year lease.

Elgar entered fully into all the possibilities of hearing music which living in London presented. In addition to the Crystal Palace concerts there were Wagner and Verdi at Covent Garden; the Richter concerts; celebrity recitals. They went frequently to the London Library to read. Alice entertained on a scale rather beyond what they could probably afford (one day she sold her pearls). Visitors from Worcestershire, relatives (the Dowager Lady Thompson), Army-family friends: she was determined they should all know her Edward. When they went for a Malvern holiday for festivities with the Fitton family, they called on the Hon. Mrs Roper-Curzon – and Edward wrote in his diary, as well he might, 'Gosh!' The true business of life, in London, was on a less exalted level. Elgar, overcoming a natural shyness, swallowed his pride and visited publisher after publisher with his short pieces, not without success. Orsborn and Tuckwood accepted pieces for violin and pianoforte and the organ voluntaries ('E . . . *drew cheque*', Alice noted in her diary about these), and a setting of Tennyson, 'Queen Mary's Song'; Novello's took the un-accompanied part-song 'My Love Dwelt in a Northern Land', to words by Andrew Lang. There was a crisis over this part-song when Lang refused permission for the poem to be used. So Alice wrote words to fit the already-composed music. 'Very clever', Elgar commented. Later, Lang relented – 'with a very bad grace', according to the irritated composer. The first lines of Alice's poem were 'Afar, amidst the sunny Isles We dwelt awhile, my love and I'.

In September 1889 he had received proofs of *Liebesgruss* and wrote to Buck (by now 'My dear Charles') on 6 October: 'I sent you the *score* which may amuse you: they (Schott's) do it for p.f. solo – v. & p.f. – orch. parts & score!!! four editions!! gusto!!! I forget whether the ending of your 'cello arrngt is the same as at present.' At first few copies of *Liebesgruss* were sold. Schott's then switched to the title *Salut d'Amour* and printed the composer's name as Ed. Elgar, leaving his nationality vague. He explained in a letter to Frank Webb dated 29 November: 'About "Salut d'Amour", the arrangement for *Strings* I did not think satisfactory so it was not proceeded with; but the arrangement for small orchestra is now done.... About giving French titles to things: it is only done so that they may sell abroad: if you put an English title only, you confine yourself to the English market while a French title secures its circulation in France (if it's of *any good*), Italy, Russia, anywhere in fact. I *don't like* doing it as my own name is so "peremptorily" English ... but I can't afford to wait 'till the English is the universal language & *don't intend to* if I could. ... By the way there are several things with *Latin* names, but people never grumble at these. I would try Greek if it would sell! ....' Sell it did, making its publisher a fortune and its composer nothing beyond the purchase fee, enough to pay a bill or buy more music paper. Much superior scorn has been poured on *Salut d'Amour*. Café music, yes; but not lacking in charm, melodic distinction and period flavour. Possibly in the late twentieth century, when we are exposed daily to a ceaseless torrent of banality, *Salut d'Amour* seems less offensive to squeamish tastes than it did fifty years ago. It is a pretty trifle, especially in its original orchestration, marked by taste and restraint. Its companion-piece *Mot d'Amour* (*Liebesahnung*) has a wistful, attractive melody which rises to a passionate central climax, but it has understandably been overshadowed by the earlier work.

But selling songs and salon pieces to publishers was not Elgar's principal reason for moving to London. He hoped to have his music played and sent his *Suite*, his string pieces, and a revised *Sevillana* to various conductors. The directors of the Covent Garden Promenade Concerts were sufficiently impressed to invite him to rehearse them one morning. He went along, and it was explained to him that some songs had to be rehearsed first. While they were in progress, Sir Arthur Sullivan arrived unexpectedly wanting to run through a selection from one of his operas. He used up all the rehearsal time. Elgar went despondently home. Two similar occurrences befell him at the Crystal Palace; on one occasion the conductor had received a Royal command to give up some rehearsal time to a composition by Ethel Smyth. Not every cloud was black, however. Besides conducting *Salut d'Amour*, August Manns conducted the *Suite* on 20 February 1890 and repeated it only four days later. Of another occasion Alice's diary records that at a rehearsal 'string pieces played through roughly'. Frederic Cowen, then the conductor of the

Philharmonic Society and perhaps the most illustrious executive English musician of the day, also took an interest in the unknown young man from Worcestershire and, probably by introductions to publishers, gave a 'helping hand' which was publicly acknowledged by Elgar many years later in a speech at a banquet in honour of Cowen in 1925.

The conclusion is inescapable that, bitterly as he looked back on this first London venture, Elgar had very little at that time to offer the metropolitan concert-goer. Much no doubt was 'in his head', but he had again had no time to write it down, and the eye and throat trouble which throughout his life recurred at intervals – usually when the creative flame was low – afflicted him in the first year of marriage. If she had not known it before, Alice must by now have realized that she had married a hypochondriac. He suddenly 'took cold', or his eyes were inflamed, or his teeth ached, or his ears. His letters to friends are full of his ailments – a sudden quinsy or a 'great & giddy headache'. To all this, Alice was solicitously sympathetic; he was, after all, an artist. He was also at this point in his life a regular worshipper. In 1890 he attended church fifty times, or rather, he attended several churches: sometimes he went to St Mary's, Chelsea, or to the pro-Cathedral in Kensington, the Carmelite church, Farm Street, Brook Green, and Haverstock Hill.[1]

Six days after their first anniversary, when Alice was six months pregnant,[2] she wrote in her diary 'E. commenced a tale'. This referred to the work for Worcester, which was to be the overture *Froissart*, composed between April and July of 1890. On 29 July he wrote to Frank Webb with revealing candour about his misgivings regarding Worcester: 'My overture is finished & I do not think will be liked but that must take its chance: I find in my limited experience that one's own friends are the people to be most in dread of: I could fill a not unentertaining book with the criticisms passed on my former efforts: when I have written anything slow they say it ought to have been quick – when loud, it shd. have been quiet – when fanciful – solemn; in a word I have always been wrong hitherto – at home.' Having offered the score in June and July to Novello's and to Goodwin & Tabb, he heard on 8 August that Novello's had accepted it, although they had told him on 31 July that they doubted if they would publish it because 'there is so little demand for that class of music'. The string parts were printed in time for the first performance in the Public Hall on 9 September 1890. Elgar conducted.

[1] See *Providence and Art* by Geoffrey Hodgkins (Elgar Society, 1980).
[2] A daughter was born on 14 August 1890. She was christened Carice Irene, a 'most wonderfully lovely infant', Elgar told Buck. He also informed him that he had been 'promoted to nurse my offspring – a fearful joy & fatal to trousers . . . I wd. as soon nurse an *"automatic irrigator"*. But it's a pretty little thing'.

We shall see what effect *Froissart* had on the professional critics. But more important was its effect on one individual, for here we have an early testimony to the extraordinarily personal impact Elgar's music makes. A young musician, Ivor Atkins, later to become organist of Worcester Cathedral, attended the festival. Elgar was pointed out to him. 'There he was, fiddling among the first violins, with his fine intellectual face, his heavy moustache, his nervous eyes and his beautiful hands. The Wednesday evening came . . . I crept up the steps leading to the back of the orchestra . . . I watched Elgar's shy entry on to the platform. From that moment my eyes did not leave him, and I listened to the overture, hearing it in the exciting way one hears music when among the players . . . But there was something else I was conscious of – I knew that Elgar was the man for me, I knew that I completely understood his music, and that my heart and soul went with it.' Atkins and Elgar became good friends, Elgar bestowing the special accolade of his friendship by initiating nicknames. In 1902 Atkins introduced Elgar to a reprint of Caxton's version of *Reynart the Fox* and henceforward Elgar signed himself 'Reynart' and addressed Atkins as 'Firapeel', the Leopard.[3]

Froissart, said the critic of the *Musical Times*, was much applauded although in his view it lacked coherence of ideas and conciseness of utterance and betrayed the marks of youth and inexperience. The *Manchester Guardian* spoke of 'spirited themes' but also of 'excessive elaboration and a tendency to monotony'. Despite the poor acoustics of the Public Hall, in which Elgar's orchestration must have sounded to its disadvantage, Elgar was pleased by the way the work was received. He wrote on 28 September to Frank Webb, 'I have had very good notices in nearly all the papers especially in those most to be feared & the overture was much liked by the *musicians* present'. *Froissart* had its origin in a passage from Scott's *Old Mortality* in which John Graham of Claverhouse speaks of his enthusiasm for Froissart's historical romances with their loyalty to kingship, pure faith towards religion, hardihood to the enemy, and fidelity to woman. On the score Elgar inscribed a line from Keats, 'When chivalry lifted up her lance on high'. It would be unreasonable to expect the critics of the day to have remarked upon what now first strikes the listener guided of course by hindsight – the flashes of mature Elgar. But they ought to have noticed the polish of the scoring. This overture and what I feel sure I am correct in regarding as its predecessor, the *Serenade for Strings*, show that Elgar was already a master of the orchestra rare in English music, that he lived and breathed the orchestra as naturally as the air around him, and that, given the spur of the chance of performance in a suitable setting, this kind of music was already

[3]'Music in the provinces: the Elgar–Atkins letters', by E. Wulstan Atkins. *Proceedings of the Royal Musical Association* 1957–8, pp. 28–9.

within his power. All Elgar's characteristics are in *Froissart* and the *Serenade*; the love of sequences, the upward sweeps, the detailed use of expression marks. Anticipations of *Gerontius*, the symphonies, and the *Enigma Variations* abound. What could be more typical of Elgar than these two themes from *Froissart*:

Ex. 3 Andante

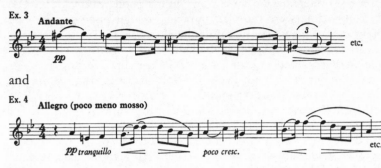

and

Ex. 4 Allegro (poco meno mosso)

or this from the *Serenade*? –

Ex. 5 Larghetto

Already in *Froissart* is the profusion of themes that is found in the symphonies and the Violin Concerto. The orchestration is clear and assured. W. H. Reed[4] points out that at the second bar the woodwind and brass are combined against the holding-note of all the strings except the double-basses, 'showing that even at this period Elgar had discovered the inherent weakness of the bass of the orchestral wind and so used his double basses to reinforce the bassoon and the bass trombone instead of wasting them to double the strings.' It is a work quite obviously conceived in terms of the orchestra: it is not a piano piece orchestrated. On the other hand, the two critics quoted above were by no means unperceptive. The work does tend to monotony because the tunes are never developed, merely repeated or inflated. Having invented a beautiful slow melody, Elgar did not seem to know what to do with it. The overture sounds to contemporary ears like a mixture of Dvořák with short but vivid bursts of the real Elgar. It is striking as an example both of how much Elgar already knew and how much he had to learn. But it survives because of its vitality and because, like Mahler in the case of his *Das klagende Lied*, Elgar could have said of it that it was the work in which he became Elgar.

[4] *Elgar* (London, 1939), p. 50.

Alice Elgar had been unable to attend the first performance because of Carice's birth, but Stockley's orchestra played it at Birmingham on 5 February 1891, where she was proud to see Edward called on the platform to acknowledge cordial applause. 'I think it is too long,' he told Frank Webb, and nine years later he was to write to Jaeger: 'It's old & not quite what I'd write now but it's good healthy stuff.' The critics this time were more favourable, though none grasped the significance of the work: that Elgar had lifted up his lance on high in his first real assault on the citadel held securely in 1890 by Cowen, Sullivan, Parry, Stanford, and Mackenzie. But one overture does not make a reputation, and back in London after the Worcester performance there was no sign that any citadel was under siege. No conductor rushed to put *Froissart* into his programmes, though Elgar took the parts to Manns at Crystal Palace. He wrote another song. He started, or re-started, a violin concerto, felt it was of no quality, and destroyed it. He had more eye trouble and a septic tooth. Alice had the baby to tend, but each day she ruled the bar lines on his manuscript paper to save him time. An advertisement for pupils was unanswered, so he resumed weekly visits to Malvern and Worcester. A German had taken over his 'practice' in the area, and to help build it up again Elgar wrote on New Year's Eve, 1890, to Manns, to the tenor Edward Lloyd, whom he had met, to William Wolstenholme seeking permission to give their names as references. The previous night Alice wrote in her diary: 'A. thought this the coldest day she ever felt (I cried with the cold)'. Their brave venture had failed and in that bleak winter they acknowledged it and prepared to retreat. 'The winter has been truly awful,' he wrote to Frank Webb, 'the fogs here are terrifying & make me very ill: yesterday [7 February 1891] all day & today until two o'clock we have been in a sort of yellow darkness. I groped my way to church this morning & returned in an hour's time a weird & blackened thing with a great & giddy headache.' The weather always seems colder when the world is indifferent to one's work, and Elgar was not the first nor the last man from the provinces to experience the chilling frost of London's complacent unconcern. So in January 1891 he sent out notices in Worcester about his teaching, and soon had such a response there and in Malvern that the Kensington house was vacated. For a few months they lodged at 4, The Lees, Malvern, and on 20 June 1891 moved into a house in Alexandra Road, Malvern Link, which they called 'Forli', after the Italian Renaissance painter of angel musicians Melozzo da Forli. (Forli is near Ravenna.)

He resumed his old activities as if the intervening two years had never been: teaching; leading the orchestra for the Hereford Philharmonic and various choral societies; giving violin recitals; forming a ladies' orchestral class. It is probably from this period that an amusing story comes which Elgar many years later told to

Vaughan Williams. He was sometimes driven from one teaching
engagement to another in a countryman's pony and trap. On their
journeys Elgar would tell his companion stories and anecdotes. One
day, feeling jaded, he said: 'Now, Joe, I'm always telling you things.
You tell me something for a change today.' A heavy and prolonged
silence prevailed while Joe thought. Then at length inspiration came.
'Charlie Peace,' he intoned, "'e feared the rope.' Elgar's composition
reverted to salon music and violin solos such as *La Capricieuse*. The
London years had undermined his health, and the inevitable reaction
set in: quinsy, influenza, headaches, from April until the following
spring. 'Edward very mouldy' was Alice's frequent description of
him at this time. This extremely sensitive and thin-skinned man felt
deeply that he had failed. The composer of *Froissart* was back
teaching the fiddle to genteel young ladies. 'I am not writing much
now, but hope to sometimes,' was the best he could manage to
Charles Buck at Christmas. But he had heard a lot of music in
London.

By far the most candid portrait of Elgar at this time has been
bequeathed to us by Rosa Burley, who in 1891 became the proprietor
and headmistress of a girls' finishing school in Great Malvern called
The Mount (now a house of Malvern Girls' College). Elgar already
visited the school once a week to give violin lessons. Miss Burley
learnt that the violin lessons were unpopular and that the pupils were
afraid of the violin teacher, who was often bad-tempered and
sometimes spent most of the lesson playing the piano to himself. To
try to thaw him, she decided to have lessons herself and also joined the
Ladies' Orchestral Class which he had formed in Worcester.

She soon discovered that he quickly became bored by teaching the
study of technique and never seemed to be interested in a pupil's
progress. (He told his biographer Basil Maine many years later that he
found teaching like turning a grindstone with a dislocated shoulder.)[5]
At the same time, too, she discovered the strangeness of his character:
'His shyness masked the kind of intense pride with which an unhappy
man attempts to console himself for feelings of frustration and
disappointment . . . He seemed to me to be a man whose emotional
reactions were out of all proportion to the stimulating causes. It was
thus very difficult to be at ease with him since he was so manifestly ill
at ease with himself.'[6] As she probed his reactions she concluded that
he was 'one of the most repressed people possible to imagine . . .
enclosed, as it were, by a haunting fear of innumerable disapprovals.'
He had – and, she states, 'never wholly lost' – a strong Worcestershire
accent but spoke condescendingly of Malvern. He condemned

[5] *Elgar: His Life and Works*, by Basil Maine (London, 1933) Vol. 1, Life, p. 69.
[6] *Edward Elgar: the record of a friendship*, by Rosa Burley and Frank C. Carruthers (London, 1972) p. 23.

Mascagni's *Cavalleria Rusticana* because it was about 'persons in low life'. This determination to divorce himself from the class from which he sprang, though it did not involve the lies and deceptions practised for the same reason by Thomas Hardy, manifested itself in his physical appearance. His heavy moustache suggested a military background, his clothes were those of a country gentleman or of the middle-class professional man who had taken up golf. He avoided carrying a violin case because it gave away that he was a professional musician, which was not a respectable status in 1890. Thirty years later Elgar asked Jelly d'Arányi at a dinner party if it irked her to be introduced as 'Miss d'Arányi the violinist' because when he was younger 'he greatly disliked being introduced as "Mr Elgar the composer". "Mr Elgar, gentleman," he said, would have been enough.'[7] So that chip remained firmly on his shoulder.

Eventually Elgar unburdened himself to Miss Burley about the penalties of his religion. 'He told me of post after post which would have been open to him but for the prejudice against his religion, of golden opportunities snatched from his grasp by inferior men of more acceptable views. It was a subject on which he evidently felt very bitter . . .' This was aggravated by his social class to the point where 'he felt himself branded as something very like a social pariah'. This was the root cause of his deep inner frustration. His only ambition was to write great music, but he knew that teaching and playing would never provide him with the money and leisure he needed to be able to compose. He had further complicated this psychological turmoil by marrying a woman who belonged to the social class which was divided from the tradesman's class by a gulf unimaginable today. Never was there a clearer case of 'if you can't beat 'em, join 'em'. But the result was disastrous for Elgar's psyche. He was hypersensitive and an artist, so he was profoundly hurt. This he covered by an outward jollity and by giving the impression that he was only musical by accident. He was bitter against his father for being a shopkeeper, yet he loved and respected his parents. That Miss Burley did not exaggerate Elgar's sensitivity on this matter is proved by a letter he wrote to F. G. Edwards, a journalist, on 19 September 1900: 'Now – as to the whole "shop" episode – I don't care a d–n! I know it has ruined me & made life impossible until I what you call made a name – I only know I was kept out of everything decent "cos his father keeps a shop" – I believe I'm always introduced so now, that is to say the remark is invariably made in an undertone!'[8] He wanted to be accepted and liked by Alice's Malvern set, but he despised them, knowing them to be in many cases philistines and intellectually inferior to him. He was insecure and this, as it usually

[7] *The Sisters d'Arányi*, by Joseph Macleod (London, 1969), p. 118.
[8] Egerton MS 3090, British Museum.

does, betrayed itself in rudeness, snobbery, and insensitivity to the feelings of others. Even with Alice this darker side sometimes showed in a snappy outburst or a deflating quip. Thus, when she lamented that since her marriage she no longer used the Army and Navy Stores, his comment was, 'No, because I don't make it my business to kill my fellow men'. And when she referred to Hans Sachs, the mediaeval cobbler and poet, as 'a darling old man', Elgar remarked 'Yes, but I expect he blew his nose with his fingers'.

The year 1892 was to hold brighter prospects. The urge to compose returned. He began revising his Three Pieces for strings, calling the result a *Serenade*. Chanot published his *Very Easy Exercises* and his *Etudes caractéristiques*, both for violin. Novello's took his part-song 'Spanish Serenade', to which he added a light orchestral accompaniment on 12 June of that year. In May he resumed work on what, significantly, he called not a cantata but a 'symphony for chorus and orchestra': the setting of *The Black Knight*, Longfellow's translation of Uhland's ballad *Der schwarze Ritter*, which is to be found in *Hyperion*. Here Elgar was turning to words he had known and liked from youth but one wonders, too, if Alice's advice is discernible. No English composer at that date had made a reputation from orchestral music. The ballad was a way to make one's name with the public, but not at the kind of level at which Elgar aimed. If Edward was to succeed, so perhaps she argued, then the festival choral work was the only thing. No one *made* his name at the Crystal Palace, Philharmonic, St James's Hall, or Hallé concerts: it was there that established reputations were maintained or advanced. To attract attention, to gain a hearing from all the critics, with most of the leading lights of English musical life in the audience, it was necessary to have a work performed at one of the Leeds, Birmingham, Sheffield, or Three Choirs Festivals. If Parry, Stanford, and others could go from festival to festival collecting critical encomia, if not general acclaim, why could not Edward? Nothing is more futile than bemoaning the past, wishing things had been otherwise than they are. But this advice, if advice it was, or even if it was Elgar's own reasoning, was only partially successful. He certainly gained the hearing; he probably gained some experience; but it was nevertheless a waste of several years of an orchestral genius's life for him to set these rubbishy lines of Longfellow. The orchestra is plainly his chief interest and the chorus comes off second best: no wonder that when Novello's were reprinting the score in 1897 Jaeger asked for the words to be altered at a point where a chorus he had recently heard 'could not get the words in edgeways'. The music is vital, occasionally characteristic, but generally uneven: it is at its best when light and fanciful, at its worst in strenuous moments. There is no reason to suppose, however, that Elgar was in any way half-hearted in his approach to *The Black Knight*.

It was not in his nature to write anything in which he did not fully believe, and he was certainly trying to get away from the usual deadly 'festival cantata' of the time, in many of which he had played, by giving his example the character of a choral symphony. 'I intended the work to be a sort of symphony in four divisions founded on the poem,' he wrote to Jaeger on 1 March 1898, 'differing to anything, in structure, ever done before, where "the picture" is fixable for a little time the words are repeated – in dramatic parts the words "go on": it's not a proper cantata as the orch: is too important.' It was a stage through which he had to go.

Working on a big undertaking chased Elgar's 'mouldiness' away, at any rate temporarily. Friends helped Alice to cheer him up, notably the Fittons and the Bakers of Hasfield Court, near Gloucester – William Meath Baker and his sister Mary Frances. Miss Baker had been one of Alice's fellow-students of geology and she proved her friendship now by arranging to take the Elgars for a much-needed summer holiday in Germany. They went to stay at Hasfield to discuss it and Elgar took his manuscript-paper with him. Mrs Dora M. Powell – 'Dorabella' of the *Enigma Variations* – has given[9] a charming picture of Elgar that hot summer at Hasfield: 'He used to bring in hedgehogs from the woods and feed them in the house. He sat in the strawberry bed and wished that someone would bring him champagne in a bedroom jug.' They must have left for their holiday in high spirits, because on 11 June Mr Hugh Blair, who had been acting organist at the cathedral since 1889 and with whom Elgar already had a happy musical relationship, called at 'Forli' while Elgar was working and picked up a few sheets of *The Black Knight*. 'If you will finish it, I will produce it at Worcester,' he told Elgar. Abroad, the Elgars visited Beethoven's birthplace in Bonn, heard *Parsifal* twice, *Tristan* and *Meistersinger* in Bayreuth, and spent some time in the Bavarian countryside. They came home through Nuremberg, where they saw *Cavalleria Rusticana*, then only two years old, and Heidelberg, where Elgar, to bring him luck, asked Miss Baker to stamp and post some of *The Black Knight* which he was sending to Novello's to test their opinion.

Elgar loved Bavaria and seems to have been relaxed there, free from the stiff restraints of social life in Malvern and district. He was also, of course, in a predominantly Catholic region. When he wrote to his niece May Grafton and her brothers and sisters on 8 August he made a point of saying: 'Now this is so different to England because it is a Catholic country & in this part there are no protestants: & the church is open all day & you see workmen and workwomen carrying their rosaries & they go into the church as they pass by & say a few prayers (like you do without going to church) & then they come out

[9] *Edward Elgar: Memories of a Variation* (second edition, London 1947), p. 2.

of church & go on with their work . . . Then on one of the roads here
there are (one every 100 yards or so) the Stations of the Cross: doesn't
that seem odd . . . The music in Church is nice but very odd to us.
They have a violin & a hautboy & a clarinet & a trombone which
made such a noise.'

On his return he wrote more songs, including 'Like to the Damask
Rose', and by 26 September he had completed the sketch of *The Black
Knight*. For the next six weeks, while he resumed his round of lessons
and recitals, he awaited a verdict from Novello's. This arrived,
favourable, on 10 November and he began to score the work on
New Year's Eve, completing the task on 25 January 1893. Blair
redeemed his promise on 18 April 1893, when Elgar conducted the
first performance with the Worcester Festival Choral Society. Eleven
days previously, the first performance of the 'Spanish Serenade' had been
given at Hereford, where Elgar often led the local Philharmonic.
The press notices of *The Black Knight* were respectable, but no more.
Encouraged, though, Elgar journeyed to London and on 4 May left
the score for Manns to see. But no performance followed. That
August there was another holiday in Germany, this time to Munich,
where they heard all *The Ring*, *Tannhäuser*, *Meistersinger*, *Tristran*, and
even *Die Feen*. Several of these operas were conducted by Hermann
Levi, then nearing the end of his career (he retired in 1896) and Elgar
was much amused by the sight of him, a small man, leading on a vast
Brünnhilde to take her bow. On this holiday the Elgars were joined
by Rosa Burley and one of her pupils, Alice Davey. Miss Burley
noticed how much happier Elgar was than in Malvern and how
much he enjoyed taking them to a not very subtle but hilarious
parody of *Tannhäuser*.

They had to be home by early September when Elgar was
engaged for the Worcester Festival, the last in which he played in the
orchestra. Was it, I wonder, Parry's *Job* which caused a momentary
return of depression as Elgar contrasted his lot with that of others
and wrote on his festival programme: 'I played 1st violin for the sake
of the fee as I cd. obtain no recognition as a composer'? This was the
man who had recently told one of his violin pupils, Mary Beatrice
Alder: 'Great musicians are things to be ashamed of.'[10]

[10]B.B.C. interview 1973, reprinted as 'Memories of a Pupil' in *An Elgar Companion*
(Ashbourne, 1982), p. 148.

5 Recognition

Recognition, of a kind, was not far away. Novello's accepted another part-song, 'O Happy Eyes', to Mrs Elgar's words, in March 1894, and Elgar composed a ceremonial piece for brass, organ, and strings, *Sursum Corda*, for the Duke of York's visit to Worcester in April. Holidays in Sussex and, for seven weeks, at Garmisch in the Bavarian Highlands, are a sign of more relaxed nerves. But the greatest tonic is success, a sign that one's work is wanted, and the interest shown in Elgar by Hugh Blair, rewarded by the dedication of *The Black Knight* and by orchestrating Blair's *Advent Cantata* for him, was enough to stimulate further creative efforts. In July 1894 Elgar turned again to Longfellow and began work on *Scenes from the Saga of King Olaf*. In doing so, he was not only setting a favourite poet of his and his mother's – while in Heidelberg in 1892 he had sent her a letter describing a students' torchlight procession, adding, 'I must send a line from *here* about which we have read & thought so much . . . it did remind me of Hyperion & the beer scandal etc etc' – but he was, if unconciously, following a fashion for Scandinavian lore which can also be traced in William Morris's Icelandic Sagas, in Delius's *Fennimore and Gerda*, and in Schoenberg's setting of Jacobsen's *Gurrelieder*. At the same time, on returning from Garmisch, he worked on a suite of six part-songs of Bavarian Dances, to words which Alice had written in imitation of Bavarian folk-songs. Each was inspired by a locale in the Bavarian mountains, hence the title 'Scenes'. They were completed on 9 April 1895. As Percy Young has said,[1] these songs represent 'the end of a chapter in the life of the Elgars, signifying a peak in personal fulfilment and mutual happiness, the consummation of the poetic fancy which had lived within Alice since girlhood . . . Perhaps never again did the Elgars return to the pleasure in living and working together . . .'. Alice also wrote the words for two other part-songs which still rank among Elgar's finest creations in this medium, 'The Snow' and 'Fly, singing bird', for women's voices with two violins and pianoforte, though a light orchestral accompaniment was added later. Both poems were interludes in her narrative poem *Isabel Trevithoe*, published in 1878, although *The Snow* had been written in December 1877.

In the winter of 1894 there were two performances of *The Black Knight*, at Hereford and at Walsall. This was what Elgar must have longed for – to attract the attention of the more enterprising

[1] *Alice Elgar*, op. cit., p. 134.

conductors of the flourishing choral societies in the Midlands and the North. He knew only too well that audiences, then as ever, had a built-in resistance to new musical experiences, and, from practical experience, he had a perceptive understanding of the conservative nature and limited technique of many choral conductors. He allowed Novello's to describe *The Black Knight* as a cantata because this 'wd. not frighten the mildest conductor that ever misdirected vocal miscreants whereas the bold statement that it's not a cantata at all might lead to trouble',[2] and when they told him that it was not a success commercially he confided to Jaeger: 'I think it is too artistic for the ordinary conductor of choral societies – I find they are an inordinately ignorant lot of cheesemongering idiots. The chorus & orchestra *go* for my things but the *conductors* always, or nearly always, find them too difficult – to conduct.'[3] At Hereford and Walsall, and again at Wolverhampton in February 1895, the idiots were absent and Alice Elgar recorded in her uninhibited diary that at Wolverhampton there was 'such a reception of E. Mr Adams introduced him saying the B.K. was the work of a genius. Tremendous enthusiasm . . . Wonderful evening.' And no doubt it was, for it can be readily imagined that to choral singers inured to over-familiar classics or to the turgid church cantatas of the 1880s Elgar's exciting new idiom came as a breath of fresh air. We should not find it so today, because we know the later and greater Elgar, and we do not have to make do with the lesser; but to a choir five years before *The Dream of Gerontius* was written, there was enough challenge and adventure in Elgar's early choral works to compensate for the deficiencies of the libretto, provided adequate rehearsal-time was allotted to them. A performance of *The Black Knight* in Birmingham in 1895 nearly came to grief because the work had not been sufficiently prepared.

The attractive opening movement of *The Black Knight* is the first full emergence of the ceremonial style Elgar was to develop to masterly proportions in the *Coronation Ode* ten years later. It is robust and unhaunted by disturbing fancies, the choral writing vigorous and colourful. In the second movement, Elgar's fancy is given wider play in music of pastoral grace – and all the better if the words are inaudible! – and with the 'Spanish' touch he had already applied in *Sevillana*. The third movement is packed with splendid melodies, at least two of which deserve a place in an anthology of Elgar's best tunes, and the finale finally sacrifices chivalric ardour to the lyrical aspects of his muse.

Now Elgar was in full spate creatively – and it should be remembered that at this time he was still having to write his music in the evenings and far into the night, perhaps after expending his

[2] Letter to Jaeger, 9 March 1898.
[3] Letter to Jaeger, 28 May 1899.

energies on a long day's teaching or a choir practice or orchestral rehearsal. In the last week of June 1895 he began to assemble from sketches a major work often overlooked in assessment of his achievement, the Organ Sonata in G. He completed it on 3 July – 'one week's work', he wrote on the score. Since the first performance was given by Hugh Blair at an American Organists' Convention held in Worcester on 8 July, it is equally remarkable that Blair learned the work in the time available. Rosa Burley states that[4] Blair 'made a terrible mess' of the performance, either because he had not learned it 'or else had celebrated the event unwisely'. She would have known of Blair's drinking habits and, in the feline tone of her book, could not resist this innuendo. Elgar, however, defended Blair to her on the obviously reasonable ground that there had not been enough time. The sonata was written for the four-manual Hill organ installed in the Adelaide transept of Worcester Cathedral in 1874, an instrument of classical English design. It is in four strongly contrasted movements and is in Elgar's thoroughly mature style. The alternation between G major and G minor which is the distinguishing feature of the 'Enigma' theme in the *Variations* is present here. In the *Allegro maestoso* first movement, a group of three themes comprises the first subject, the third of them a striking motif in F sharp minor above firm chords. The second subject in 9/8 is *dolce* but in a triplet rhythm which lends it a jaunty air. The most characteristic part of the movement is the withdrawn ruminative section in the development, a passage with a mystical quality. The *Allegretto*, in A–B–A form, is a delicate intermezzo in G minor with the middle section in C. The accompaniment in fourths, fifths and sixths to an ascending chromatic melody is a daring organ effect. The lovely *Andante espressivo* is in B flat, the key of the Violin Concerto slow movement. The lyrical main tune reaches a climax, fades away on an E flat chord and merges into a *tranquillo* section in F sharp which becomes excited before the principal melody returns. This melody recurs in the finale *Presto* (*comodo*), where it provides an oasis of calm amid the virtuoso brilliance of the movement. It has been said that to play this finale well the organist must be a mental and physical athlete. Before its triumphant coda, the listener will have detected more than a hint of the *Enigma Variations*, but of all Elgar's pre-1900 works this sonata is the surest pointer to his eventual success as a symphonist.

Elgar continued work on *King Olaf* in 1895, accepted an invitation to write an oratorio for the 1896 Worcester Festival, and put the finishing touches to *Scenes from the Bavarian Highlands* which was performed for the first time on 21 April 1896, at Worcester. The oratorio, *Lux Christi*, to a libretto by the Rev. Edward Capel-Cure, was produced at Worcester on 10 September 1896. It was composed

[4] *Edward Elgar: the record of a friendship*, op. cit., p. 86.

between January and 6 April 1896 and orchestrated between 16 May and 20 June. Its dedication, to Dr Charles Swinnerton Heap, is of some significance. Heap, who had studied in Leipzig, was forty-nine and the leading choral conductor in the Midlands. He had founded the North Staffordshire Festival at Hanley and persuaded Elgar to conduct the first performance of *King Olaf* at Hanley on 30 October 1896. Elgar's first version of *King Olaf* had been 'through-composed', but Novello's suggested separate numbers. He completed revision on 8 April 1896, telling his publisher, 'I hv excised two recits & a solo besides *many* passages throughout the work'. It was, he said, now shorter by 30 pages of manuscript. Ironically, the success of *King Olaf* caused a temporary rift in his friendship with Heap. The tenor, Edward Lloyd, missed the final rehearsal because of an error over a train. At one point in the performance Lloyd failed to come in at the right moment and Elgar became flustered and lost control. The leader, Willy Hess, saved the situation by conducting with his violin bow and restoring order. Elgar blamed Heap for Lloyd's absence at rehearsal. But on 4 November he wrote to thank him for his 'helping hand'.

With two first performances of big works within eight weeks, Elgar's reputation took a rapid leap forward, though the tone of the critics' notices was still faintly patronizing in its encouragement of the 'Malvern composer'. *Lux Christi* did not attract a large audience. 'It is now clear that Mr Elgar has endowments sufficient for important results,' the *Musical Times* said. 'He is no wayside musician whom we can afford to pass and forget.' The *Times* found *King Olaf* 'a work of high importance . . . which should turn expectant eyes upon its composer'. These are cautious judgements. A reporter in the *Staffordshire Sentinel* quoted an anonymous critic as saying that Elgar was the first contemporary English composer to show 'distinct genius'. True to his usual custom, Elgar at once took the score of *King Olaf* to Manns at Crystal Palace. This time he was rewarded, and the work had its first London performance on Saturday, 3 April 1897. It was favourably received. One critic pointed out that the choir was not at full strength because of the rival attractions that afternoon provided by the Boat Race and an international football match at Sydenham. In the same year the *Bavarian Scenes* were also performed at Sydenham – to the pleasure of Sir George Grove, then seventy-seven, who preferred them to *King Olaf* – but it was still outside London that Elgar's music was most eagerly seized upon. Nicholas Kilburn, of Bishop Auckland, an enthusiastic amateur who became a close friend of Elgar, conducted *King Olaf* in April 1897. Hanley heard it again, so did Worcester. Cowen conducted it in Liverpool and Bradford in 1897 and in Manchester at a Hallé Concert in December 1898. This last performance was the occasion for a notice in the *Manchester Guardian* by Arthur Johnstone, its music critic since 1896, and at thirty-seven the most gifted of the new generation of critics. He found *King Olaf* 'fragmentary and incoherent', mainly because 'he throws away the resources of his remarkable art upon a text that is in places unfit for any kind of musical treatment', but prophesied that something of lasting value would follow when Elgar found the right subject. It is to Johnstone's credit that he was one of the few to recognize 'something of value' when it arrived and to proclaim it as a masterpiece.

It was not *King Olaf* that made Elgar's name in London. Queen Victoria celebrated her Diamond Jubilee in 1897, an occasion for national rejoicing in which Elgar, a monarchist and a Conservative (though with certain radical leanings), wholeheartedly joined. In preparation for the event he sent three preliminary sketches of a choral work, *The Banner of St George*, to Novello's on 30 November 1896 and on 7 December sent a sketch of an *Imperial March*. Both were accepted. The composition sketch of the choral work was completed on 14 February 1897 and orchestration was finished on 15 March. The *March* was composed by 14 January and scored between 1 and 6 February. It was these two works, especially the March, which caught the Londoners' imagination in 1897 and made Elgar's name well known. But Elgar's letter to Novello's of 9 January 1897 shows how insecure his position still was. He hoped it might be of 'material good' if permission were sought to dedicate it to the Queen; he knew Sir Walter Parratt, Master of the Queen's Musick (having met him the previous autumn during London rehearsals of *Lux Christi*) and would ask him, 'unless there is a recognised way unknown to me'. The letter ends: 'I shall be glad to hear your views as to the above points & as to terms: I should not have mentioned the last item, but that the Term will shortly recommence & it will depend entirely upon this matter whether I return to teaching or continue to compose – or try to?' This was still the rub. If it had not been for Alice's small private income things might have been even harder for Elgar, and his natural pride made him ashamed of relying on her money. They spent money on whatever they thought might further Edward's career. He belonged to a London club, for instance, and travelled fairly often to London to attend Covent Garden or Richter and Lamoureux concerts: to hear great music well performed was as essential to him as food and drink. It was essential to Alice, too, to engage two maidservants and she insisted that Edward should always travel first-class. If one looks at the growing number of Elgar performances in 1896–8, one might think that success in a material sense had come to him at last as he entered his forties, but there was little to be made from cantata performances and it still rankled that London had heard so few of his larger works. In 1897 he wrote to the secretary of the Philharmonic Society at whose concerts he was 'naturally anxious to obtain a hearing . . . and should be glad to introduce an orchestral work, not necessarily a long one, during your post-Xmas season'.[5] On being told that any work submitted would receive careful attention, Elgar replied that he did not intend to submit any work of his to a board of directors. At the same time he wrote to Charles Villiers Stanford, whom he had met with Swinnerton Heap in 1896, asking for the chance of a performance by the Bach Choir. Stanford replied that the moment was financially inopportune and added, 'You need not worry over the slowness of societies in London to take up your works. You're better off in the way of performance than many others. . . . Composers' names to attract entrepreneurs must now end in "vitch" or "offski"' – a complaint stemming from the growing interest in London in Russian music, particularly Tchaikovsky's.

If London remained impervious to all except patriotic works, the Three Choirs had asked for another work, for the 1897 meeting at Hereford, and on 15 June Elgar completed a *Te Deum and Benedictus* dedicated to Dr George R. Sinclair, organist of Hereford. Of more significance than the composition itself is that it was this work which first brought Elgar into personal contact with August Johannes Jaeger, nearly three years his junior, who had come to England from Düsseldorf in 1878 and joined Novello's in 1890 as a music reader, when the firm was in Berners Street and controlled by Alfred Henry and Augustus James Littleton. With his continental and cosmopolitan background, Jaeger found himself out of sympathy with the music of Parry and especially with those other composers of songs, anthems, and church cantatas on whose sales among organists and drawing-room ballad singers Novello's largely relied. Consequently for much of the time he was out of sympathy with his employers. At the time of his first contact with Elgar he was publishing office manager and responsible for all the detailed work of putting a general publishing programme into effect. He was never the firm's official adviser on music though in the course of time the soundness of his judgement came to be respected. The advent of Elgar was a revelation, and he recognized his stature at once. 'I am forever pushing, and have pushed since I played through your *fine Black Knight*, Mr Elgar's claim to attention . . . I am conceited enough to think that I can appreciate a good thing and see genius in musicians that are *not* yet dead, or even not yet well known, or Cathedral organists, or Directors of music in colleges for boys . . . Our Editor and other good folk keep on saying very clever, *very* clever etc etc and I say hang your cleverness, *that* won't make *any* music great and "alive".'[6]

[5] Robert Elkin, *Royal Philharmonic* (London, 1947), p. 93.
[6] All extracts are from the Jaeger–Elgar correspondence in the Elgar archives at Worcester and published in *Letters to Nimrod* (London, 1965), ed. Percy Young.

This was a strain which found a ready, perhaps too ready, response in Elgar's nature. To Jaeger he confided his secret hopes and his suppressed anger. When Jaeger first wrote to Elgar on 3 August 1897 about the *Te Deum*, which Novello's had accepted at the end of June – 'Mr Jaeger quite as enthusiastic as he should be over E's music for Hereford', Alice characteristically wrote in her diary – Elgar's reply was revealing. 'You praise my new work too much – but you understand it; – when it is performed will anyone say *any*thing different from what they wd. say over a commercial brutality like the "Flag of England" [a setting of Kipling by Sir Frederick Bridge] for instance: naturally no one will & the thing dies and so do I.' Jaeger's reply 'put new heart' in Elgar who answered: 'Please do not think I am a disappointed person either commercially or artistically. What I feel is the utter want of *sympathy*; they i.e. principally the critics lump me with people I abhor – mechanics.' It is sometimes said that 'in later life' Elgar developed the pose that he was no longer interested in music. In fact it was an attitude he adopted all his life, perhaps as some form of defence mechanism. In early letters to Jaeger in 1897 and 1898, for instance, occur: 'I have no intention of bothering myself with music' and 'I'm really giving up *all music* & am refusing everything – I cannot afford to waste my precious few years of remaining out door life – so I fish etc. Much better than your damned old blasted music.' And this, more seriously (19 October 1897): 'Look here! in two years I have written Lux Xti, King Olaf, Impl. March, S. George, Organ Sonata (big), Te Deum. Recd £86 15. Debtor £100 – after paying my own expenses at two festivals. I feel a d—d fool! . . . for thinking of music at all. No amount of "kind encouragement" can blot out these simple figures.' Nevertheless on 28 October he sent Novello's a piece for violin and piano called *Evensong*, suggesting that the title might be changed to *Vesper*. It was published under the title *Chanson de Nuit*.

These first letters to Jaeger also throw light on Elgar's views, at this time, of his contemporaries and of English musical life. He was no intriguer. In 1893 when a 'plot' was contemplated for removing a local Worcester conductor Elgar wrote to one of the plotters, 'Much as I should love to be at the head of something which might lean to the artistic . . . I feel that the existing order cannot be done away . . . I am too law-abiding (& lazy?) to lead a revolution.' Similarly after London rehearsals of *Caractacus* in September 1898, he wrote to Jaeger: 'I am not really bitter and my heart warms to anything like naturalness and geniality . . . but I detest humbug and sham and can't talk it well. Q's Hall seemed reeking with it. . . .' Again, 'A 3-choir festival always upsets me – the twaddle of it and mutual admiration'. But, provoked by Jaeger's barbs, the resentment he felt against other composers burst out time and again. Jaeger wrote occasional criticism for the *Musical Times* and resented having had to tone down adverse comments on Parry's *Magnificat* (because both the magazine and Parry's music were published by Novello's) although he rightly acknowledged that 'Parry of all men in England is the one who would not take offence at one's opinion if sincerely stated.' 'Parry's Variations are very good,' he wrote to Elgar in 1898, 'but as usual badly scored.' 'I cannot stand Parry's orchestra,' Elgar answered. 'It's dead and is never more than an *organ part arranged*.' (He had not then heard the *Symphonic Variations* and evidently changed his opinion by 1922 for, mistaking Vaughan Williams's comment 'I suppose this ought to be considered bad orchestration' for a criticism of Parry, Elgar turned on him 'almost fiercely' at the Three Choirs Festival that year and said, 'Of course it's not bad orchestration, this music could be scored in no other way.')[7] 'You are wrong in thinking I don't like some "forms" of music,' he told Jaeger in 1898. 'Anything "genuine" and natural pleases me – the stuff I hate and which I know is ruining any chance for good music in England is stuff like Stanford's which is neither fish, flesh, fowl nor good red-herring.' Jaeger often sent him the scores of works by other composers published by Novello. Early in 1898 he sent him some of the music of the American composer Horatio W. Parker (1863–1919). This brought on the following: 'I want to see *S. Christopher* soon but I must work and weep over my own tunes for a little. *Hora Novissima* contains more "music" than any of·your other Englishmen have as yet managed to knock out including Parry Stanford Mackenzie – these great men seem to be busily employed in performing one another's works.'[8] He was ready to help young and struggling composers and recommended Coleridge-Taylor's name to the Gloucester Festival: 'I should *dearly* like to see a clever man get on and upset the little coterie of "3-choir hacks".' He knew what went on in these affairs – 'the disgusting thing is that if two men at the top of the scaffold (I mean *tree* but in their case it shd be gallows) said the word they shd. say, the thing wd be done – but Somervell is the only person they are not afraid of! in the way of honest rivalry.' But Coleridge-Taylor was asked for a work and Elgar hoped he would not write anything 'too startling' – 'of course he will want to show the critics what's in him but the easy going agriculturists who support these things also want a tiny bit of consideration'.

[7] A 'Musical Autobiography', *National Music and Other Essays* (London, 1963), p. 182.
[8] Dr Percy Young, in *Letters to Nimrod*, pp. 8–9, has interpreted this mention of *Hora Novissima* as the first reference in any extant document to *The Dream of Gerontius*, on the grounds presumably of Gerontius's 'Novissima hora est'. But Elgar is clearly referring to Parker's oratorio *Hora Novissima*, written in 1893, as he has just referred also to Parker's *Legend of St Christopher*. *Hora Novissima* was performed at the Worcester Festival in 1899.

Elgar's attitude to Coleridge-Taylor is incidentally symptomatic of
his own vulnerability. In 1899 he could describe the younger man's
music as 'all so *human* and yearning' but by 1900, when Coleridge-
Taylor had had outstanding success with *Hiawatha*, his work becomes
for Elgar 'only "rot"' and 'insincere & cannot do any real good'. By
1903 it is 'a disgrace to any civilised country'. The conclusion is
inescapable that once a younger composer became a potential rival, he
became a target for the dismissive remarks which so often betray
Elgar's insecurity. Arthur Bliss in later years was to suffer the same
fate.

Whatever his views on his colleagues, Elgar was under no illusions
about the public. When Jaeger suggested that he should set the
Jabberwocky poem from *Alice Through the Looking Glass*, he replied,
'The English never take to anything of that sort – treated mock-
heroically – the whole book of "Alice" is now on the stage done by
children – go & see it & weep – I know my twaddly grown up
countrymen & women & am sick of 'em.' He was always on edge
during rehearsals of a new work and perhaps his fiercest outburst
came after preliminary Leeds rehearsals of *Caractacus* in August 1898,
when Alan Gray was also rehearsing a work, *Song of Redemption*, for
the Festival. 'It makes me, an artist, sick to see that fool Gray allowed
as long to rehearse his blasted rot as I am who produce with all its
many faults an attempt at something like a "work".' Nor can he have
endeared himself to his 'rivals' by his reply, reported in the press in
July 1899, to a light-hearted question by the 'Tonic Sol-fa Herald'
about the best way for a professional musician to enjoy his summer
holiday: 'The ordinary professor might study music, if not too
violent a change.'

If these strictures seem mean-spirited and ungenerous, they are also
the measure of Elgar's frustration. He knew that his own music was
better than that written by most of his English contemporaries and he
saw composers, whom as yet he hardly knew, as mediocrities in
professional and university posts, influential in all musical affairs.
Most of the critics reviewing *King Olaf* had again drawn attention to
Elgar's brilliant use of the orchestra, yet *Froissart* had hardly been
played and the *Serenade for Strings* had not yet been professionally
performed in Britain despite its success at Antwerp in 1896 and 1898.
The years of 1898 and 1899 were years in which the *Enigma Variations*
and *The Dream of Gerontius* took shape in his mind. Moreover he was
now in his forties. The tone of the complaints denotes an inferiority
complex, perhaps, the need to assert by denigration, but no one
should underestimate the depth of the wound inflicted on Elgar by
the attitude of his wife's relatives to their marriage and by the failure
of his attempt to settle in London. Nor, as will be seen, should it be
forgotten that with perhaps one exception he bore no grudges. He

could be, and was, magnanimous. But in Jaeger he found a sympathetic outlet for repressed frustrations, and this tempted him very often, I suspect, to dramatize himself in his letters, a tendency that can be noted in some of the earlier letters to Charles Buck. It is a tendency that is sometimes reflected in the music.

At any rate one recognition came his way in December 1897, which should have consoled him: he was invited to write a choral work for the 1898 triennial Leeds Festival, then, with the Birmingham Festival, perhaps the English composer's premier platform. He had suggested another type of work, probably a symphony, but Leeds wanted a cantata, and Elgar had a subject in mind which appealed to him. The idea came from his mother, who described it in a letter to Elgar's sister Pollie. She had been staying in the Malverns and 'I said oh! Ed. look at the lovely old hill, can't we write some *tale* about it. . . . "Do it yourself, Mother," he held my hand with a firm grip. "Do" he said. "No, I can't my day is gone by if I ever could," and so we parted. And in less than a month he told me *Caractacus* was all cut and dried and he had begun to work at it.' So the work was inspired first by Elgar's passionate love of the countryside round Birchwood and by his sense of its history,[9] and partly by the wave of jubilee patriotism. The story of Caractacus, King of Britain, being driven towards Wales by the Romans, seeking advice from druids, being betrayed, defeated and finally pardoned in Rome by Claudius might have made a good libretto in the right hands, but unfortunately Elgar turned again to H. A. Acworth who had made some additions to Longfellow for *King Olaf*. In this case he had the field to himself and, at Elgar's prompting, let himself go at the end in what Sir Arnold Bax called 'a regrettable chorus' for the Romans who see 'glorious ages coming' when the Roman Empire crumbles and is replaced by the British. But it was what Elgar wanted and he began to compose the music at 'Forli' in January 1898. He wrote Scene 2 first, being doubtful if he would provide an overture. Composition was finished on 12 June 1898 and orchestration was begun on 21 June and completed on 21 August. Much of this latter task was done at a rented cottage, Birchwood Lodge, near Storridge, where the Elgars went for weekends or for weeks at a time in the summer to have complete and undisturbed quiet. His terms from Leeds were £100 but he had to provide the chorus and orchestral parts. He felt he was writing well – 'Caractacus frightens me in places,' he told Jaeger on 1 March 1898 – but as usual he was on edge and seven weeks later he was hoping that Sir Frederick Bridge, newly appointed conductor of the Royal Choral

---

[9] He told Jaeger, in August 1898: 'You will see our "woodlands" someday. I made old Caractacus stop as if broken down on p. 168 & choke & say "woodlands" again because I am so madly devoted to my woods.' Birchwood, incidentally, is in Herefordshire.

Society, who was to rehearse the chorus, would not see early proofs: 'If he didn't like it, his remarks, *altho' not unkind*, might prejudice me – for instance if he said (in Aug. or Sept.) that it wd not do for the Albert Hall everybody would hear of that and there would be ructions.' He sent it scene by scene as completed to Novello's and thanked Jaeger 'for not saying *one word* about the work, either for or against, and *please don't yet* or I shall surely die being on edge.' When the first sketch was finished and Elgar began to orchestrate it, Jaeger had plenty to say, and his first target was Acworth's libretto, the final chorus in particular. Elgar's replies are interesting: 'By all means will I ask Acworth to eliminate the "truculent note" in the lines! Any nation but ours is allowed to war-whoop as much as they like but I feel we are too strong to need it – I *did* suggest that we should dabble in patriotism in the Finale, when lo! the *worder* (that's good!) instead of merely paddling his feet goes and gets naked and wallows in it: *now* I don't think he meant by "menial &c" Germany &c, more probably hill tribes and suchlike – jealous evidently, refers to anybody you like.' Three weeks later: 'I knew you wd. laugh at my librettist's patriotism (& mine) never mind: England for the English is all I say – hands off! there's nothing apologetic about me.'[10] It was about this time that he wrote to Joseph Bennett: 'I hope some day to do a great work – a sort of national thing that my fellow Englishmen might take to themselves and love.'

The first choir rehearsals of *Caractacus* were at Leeds on 9 July 1898. Elgar did not look forward to them: 'a day of dread for me,' he wrote to Jaeger. 'I can face any orchestra under the sun, the players always enjoy new effects, but a chorus looks so disgusted if they haven't a shouting four-pt yell from beginning to end.' In view of what was to happen at Birmingham with *Gerontius*, this attitude to choruses, the result of practical experience, is important. Proof-correcting went on throughout July – Elgar, who loved puns, referring to it as 'correct-a-cuss'. In one letter he says: 'As to waiting till after the performance before duplicating the wind, I don't know – I never *have* had to alter anything but I am very dubious about myself when you suggest waiting'; which, besides being a handsome compliment, is a magnificent expression of self-confidence in the certainty of his orchestral effects. More rehearsals at Leeds followed in August, when Elgar met Sullivan, chief conductor of the festival and by now a sick man, and was able to tell him of the 1889 incident when Sullivan took up Elgar's rehearsal-time at Covent Garden. Now the older man made up for that occasion, of which, of course, he

[10] He wrote to Jaeger on 5 November 1899: 'It's no good trying any patriotic caper on in England: we applaud the "sentiment" in other nations but repress it sternly in ourselves: anything like "show" is repugnant to the *real* English – whom you don't know or understand yet nor ever will.'

had been unaware, by refusing to rest while Elgar went through *Caractacus*. Instead he made notes of points which struck him and was generally helpful. Having heard the work again Elgar could write to Jaeger (29 August 1898): 'I will alter no more of C. short of burning the whole thing.'

The first performance was on 5 October. This time the Queen had accepted the dedication. Most of the celebrities of British music were present, and Elgar met Parry for the first time. Cowen was there and, from France, Gabriel Fauré. So too was a cross-section of Elgar's Worcestershire friends, from Lady Mary Lygon, sister of Earl Beauchamp, of Madresfield Court and a pioneer of the musical festival movement, to Dr Sinclair, the Hereford organist, and some Malvern pupils. Nicholas Kilburn came from Bishop Auckland. The soloists were Medora Henson, Edward Lloyd, Andrew Black, and John Browning. All was set for a triumph, but this did not happen. The performance was not as good as it might have been. Rosa Burley, who was present, wrote that the kind of chorus which Elgar had in mind 'did not then exist. . . . The [Leeds] chorus revelled in the straightforward Handelian choruses & were inclined to resent Elgar's music which they found finicking and fidgety. They could not let themselves go, full blast, as they had always done.' The critics were polite. But at least Edward A. Baughan, in the *Musical Standard*, devoted two pages to it. He wrote much of the cantata's 'failures', but about its 'excellent workmanship' he had this to say: 'The elaborate and appropriate use of representative themes has never been approached by any living native composer; the symphonic accompaniment is varied and elastic; the harmony . . . has always the merit of sounding natural and unforced . . .; and the whole texture of the music flows on from note to note with an easy mastery which proclaims Elgar a composer of decided gifts. You may say of him with truth that he writes *music*. . . .'

This delighted Elgar who sent it to his friend the Malvern architect Arthur Troyte Griffith with the comment that it was 'the first to give me the place I've fought for'. *The Times* remarked that the cantata suffered from 'an excess of detail, not from any absence of interest or individuality', and the *Musical Times* detected 'signs of haste in the vocal writing' but found that the score contained 'sufficient material to set up half-a-dozen average composers for life'. Arthur Johnstone, in the *Manchester Guardian*, expressed a hope that Elgar would one day write a genuine music drama, and a few weeks later, when he heard *King Olaf* in Manchester, he declared *Caractacus* to be 'obviously a finer work in every way' than its predecessor. These are hardly bad notices, even if they are not ecstatic, but on his return to Malvern Elgar relapsed, as he usually did after a big work, into his mood of depression and dislike of music, even though he found awaiting him a letter asking for a work for the 1899 Norwich Festival. 'No – I'm not happy at all,' he wrote to Jaeger on 20 October, 'in fact never was more miserable in my life: I don't see that I've done any good at all: if I write a tune you all say it's commonplace – if I don't, you all say it's rot – well I've written *Caractacus*, earning thro' it *15/– a week* doing it, and that's all – *now* if I will write any *easy*, small choral-society work for Birmingham, using the fest. as an advt. – your firm will be "disposed to consider it" – but my own natural bent I must choke off. No thank you.' In the same letter he mentions his idea of a symphony about General Gordon (possibly the work he originally wanted to write for Leeds), a project which Jaeger did everything to encourage. '"Gordon" sym. I like this idée but my *dear* man *why* should I try?? I can't see – I have to earn money somehow & it's *no good* trying this sort of thing even for a "living wage"! and your firm wouldn't give £5 for it – I tell you I am sick of it all! Why can't I be encouraged to do decent stuff & not hounded into triviality.'

Four days after getting this petulant but accurate grumble off his chest, he was reporting to Jaeger that he had been sketching 'a set of Variations on an original theme'. Truly the ways of genius are unaccountable.

At least Elgar's growing fame had given him an even higher standing in Worcester. As far back as October 1897 he had thrown himself heart and soul into the formation with Miss Martina Hyde, a solicitor's daughter and pupil of Elgar, of a new musical society in Worcester, the Worcestershire Philharmonic, with himself as conductor. He saw in it a chance, as he told Jaeger in October 1897, 'to do something novel – in fact if they are not disposed to let young England whoop I shall not take it on'. As the society's motto he chose 'Wach auf' – 'Wake up'. The first concert was on 7 May 1898, with the first performance in England of Humperdinck's *Die Wahlfahrt nach Kevlaar*, sung in German. Winifred Norbury was joint honorary secretary and Lady Mary Lygon a member. Ivor Atkins, Blair's successor as Worcester organist, was a founder member. The society, for which Elgar wrote the programme-notes, played plenty of English works: Cowen's *Idyllic Symphony*, Parry's *The Lotos-Eaters*, Mackenzie's *Dream of Jubal*, Bantock's *Russian Suite*, Stanford's *Last Post*, and music by Percy Pitt, Sullivan, and Walford Davies. There was, for that date, a high proportion of French music: Delibes, Massenet and Chabrier, as well as Gounod and Berlioz (*The Childhood of Christ*, 'a work of real atmosphere & charm', said Elgar). There was some, but not much, Elgar. 'We *must* do things properly whatever the cost' was his approach, and the performances reflected it. He engaged expensive soloists and insisted that all instruments specified by the composer must be used. Rosa Burley's book[11] suggests that Elgar's

---

[11] *Edward Elgar: the record of a friendship*, op. cit., pp. 103–110.

connection with the Society was disastrous from the start because he
had no idea how to deal with its members. These, she said, were
drawn from the very class 'whose social superiority had hurt him . . .
Their easy manners . . . irritated him into extreme impatience with
purely musical feelings . . . His wide vague beat would sometimes
baffle the best of us and in matters of interpretation he seemed
incapable of explaining exactly what he wanted.' The break came in
November 1902 during rehearsals for an exacting programme of
works by Wolf, Berlioz, and Wilhelm Berger. The playing and
singing deteriorated to the point when Elgar flung down his baton,
walked out, and refused to return. He wrote a curt letter to Martina
Hyde describing the chorus as 'extremely ill-prepared this season . . . I
have incessantly warned the members that the future of the society
rested with them, and that I should leave immediately if I thought the
members showed lack of interest: I think the chorus has deteriorated
and is "dull". As I shall be very much occupied next year I do not
propose to offer myself for re-election.' A fortnight of crisis followed
but Elgar would not relent. The concert on 11 December was
conducted by Granville Bantock.

Several of the Elgars' circle of friends have by now entered this
narrative – the Norbury sisters Winifred (who helped to correct the
proofs of *Caractacus*) and Florence, Rosa Burley, Dora Penny, the
Bakers, Troyte Griffith, Lady Mary Lygon, the Fittons. Others saw
him often: Matthew Arnold's son, Richard, and his wife; Father
Bellasis of Birmingham Oratory, Hew Steuart-Powell and Basil
Nevinson, who joined Elgar for chamber music performances in their
homes. Most of them saw a different Elgar from the man revealed in
letters to Jaeger – perhaps only Alice saw his other side ('a woman's
not worth a damn who won't put up with everything except
ineptitude and crime', he confided to Jaeger). His high spirits with
friends were infectious. He loved his 'japes', as he referred to any
'larks'. He went with Dora Penny to watch Wolverhampton
Wanderers play football and set a phrase from the local newspaper's
report – 'he banged the leather for goal' – to a phrase from *Caractacus*.
He played golf, went cycling, beagling, and hunting. He had a passion
for flying kites. Among other hobbies was the intricate and skilled
one, requiring great patience, of poker-work. At Birchwood he killed
snakes in the garden and enjoyed working outside; as he told Jaeger
'I've been cutting a long path thro' the woods like primitive man only
with more clothes'. What, one wonders, did the earnest, sickly little
German at Novello's in Berners Street make of some of the
information casually included in letters from his great English
composer – 'Fox hunting yesterday. No proof-correcting done.'
'There aren't any badgers now – they've gone and deserted the
"earth" near us. Never mind, I'll track 'em further away. I *should* like

to send one in a sack to Berners Street.' 'I'm fishing & have ruminated over your letter.' 'I am . . . sitting in my shirt with my feet in a bucket of water (it's hot) drivelling.' 'I'm just off to the Beagles & shall be away all day – no music like the baying of hounds after all.' 'I had friends coming & my brain (?) has been a fog of Horse talk, Hound jaw, Fox gossip and Game chatter.' 'You live too well for a composer, you lucky fellow', Jaeger retorted.

To his county friends, even the musical ones, Elgar seemed the very reverse of the usual idea of a composer. He was so normal and healthy, and he didn't even *look* like a composer as W. H. Reed, the violinist and intimate friend and biographer of Elgar, discovered as a young man when, in 1898, he played in the orchestral rehearsals in London of *Caractacus* and later left this unforgettable picture:[12] 'A very distinguished-looking English country gentleman, tall, with a large and somewhat aggressive moustache, a prominent but shapely nose and rather deep-set but piercing eyes. It was his eyes perhaps that gave the clue to his real personality: they sparkled with humour, or became grave or gay, bright or misty as each mood in the music revealed itself. His hands, too, gave another clue: they were never still even when he was not conducting; they moved restlessly, turning up the corners of the pages of the score or giving some indication by a gesture of what he wanted . . . but they were always eloquent, always saying something and giving an inkling of the extreme sensitiveness of his mind and character. He looked upstanding, had an almost military bearing . . . The orchestra, it is almost needless to say, adored him . . . He was practical to a degree, he wasted no time . . . He obtained all he wanted from his executants by the movements of his delicate and well-shaped hands, by his eyes, which expressed the whole gamut of emotions, and by his whole facial expression, which lit up in an amazing manner when he got the response he desired and when his music throbbed and seethed as he intended that it should.' From this we may deduce that when working with professionals, Elgar was usually at his best; when working with amateurs, such as those of the Worcestershire Philharmonic, he was at his worst. (In this respect, Benjamin Britten was to resemble him.)

Suppose that Elgar had died in 1898 in his forty-second year, what would his reputation have been? I think he would have now had a position akin to that of George Butterworth, leaving behind in *Froissart* and the *Serenade* two works of accomplishment and even more promise. The cantatas might be heard as curiosities, as they are now; the trifles would have survived, too, as evidence of a delicious melodic charm which never reached maturity. Just to look at the list of his works as completed by 1898 brings back the flavour and taste of a distant epoch – *The Language of Flowers*, *The Wind at Dawn*, *Like to the*

[12]*Elgar*, op. cit., pp. 50–51.

*Damask Rose, Love Alone will Stay, Sérénade Lyrique, Salut d'Amour,
Chanson de Nuit, A Soldier's Song, Sursum Corda, O Happy Eyes, King
Olaf, Imperial March* . . . Elgar dead at forty-two would not rank so
high as Vaughan Williams supposing V.W. to have been killed at
exactly the same age when he enlisted in 1914. Vaughan Williams
would have left the *Songs of Travel, Toward the Unknown Region, On
Wenlock Edge*, the *Five Mystical Songs*, the *Tallis Fantasia*, and the *Sea*
and *London* symphonies as much richer hostages to fortune.

On the whole Elgar's solo songs – as opposed to his part-songs –
deserve most of the unkind words which have been written about
them. Whereas the early violin-and-piano pieces sound like the minor
works of a major composer, the songs could well have come from the
pen of a dozen minor Victorian composers. That it was written
by Elgar at the age of fifteen gives a biographical interest to 'The
Language of Flowers' but, compared with the kind of music
Benjamin Britten was to write at the same age, there is nothing to lead
one to suppose that an important musical journey was beginning.
'Through the long days' and 'Is she not passing fair?' are hidebound
in their conventionality. Only to Alice's words in 'The Wind at
Dawn' did Elgar find the melodic sweep and the boldness of piano-
writing to lift the song out of the common rut. But in later years he
wrote some notable songs. The well-known 'Pleading' (1908) exists
also with orchestral accompaniment, for Elgar later followed
Strauss's example in providing a fuller and richer background than
the piano for certain of his settings. Its passionate lyricism defies the
sneers of those who would class it merely as a superior drawing-room
ballad. Possibly it is, but very superior! More remarkable are the two
songs of Op. 60, 'The Torch' and 'The River', the words being
written by Elgar and passed off as 'Eastern European folk-songs'.
There is a Balkan accent in the music, a wildness which occurs nowhere
else in his output.

It is profitable to look more closely at those early Elgar cantatas for
they did, after all, make his name known as a man of individuality
who was 'always himself'—the phrase occurs several times in the
reviews of those days. Into everything he wrote he poured himself
with uninhibited zest and self-confidence. 'I hold nothing back,' he
said. 'It's jolly good, it *is* a damned fine piece of work,' he told Jaeger
about *Caractacus*, and '*King Olaf* is a mighty work. Wot ye this? . . .
Him wot rote it.' He knew the virtues of the *Serenade*: 'really stringy in
effect'. Of *Froissart* he said 'What jolly *healthy* stuff it is – quite
shameless in its rude young health.' When he heard the Sheffield
chorus in *King Olaf*: 'Never complain of my choral effects again –
they're grand and mighty when properly sung.' 'Anybody with any *real*
feeling (emotion) was quite stricken and overcome by "Lux Xti" –
Albani was quite tearful over the expression of it, so was I. It is naïve

but there is nothing else like it – most of the critics don't think that a good thing but the audience don't care – they love it.' This is not conceit, for it shows how complete an extension of Elgar's personality his music was. In one of his first letters to Jaeger, in 1897, he put the point memorably: 'My music, such as it is, is alive – you say it has heart. I always say to my wife (over any piece or passage of my work that pleases me): "If you cut that it would bleed!" *You* seem to see that but who else does?'[13]

Music came easily to him: he thought music all day long, and he was sometimes too willing to accept what came to him as heaven-sent inspiration. He confessed that he regarded himself as a medium for music, and he did not mind whether the expression of it was lowly (*Salut d'Amour*) or lofty (*Froissart*) provided that it was done with a professional touch, a well-turned-out article. He never wrote a shoddy or untidy note. But a drawback in this willingness to provide music for all sorts and conditions of men and occasions was that he was not always able to sustain the initial enthusiasm: the early works are all uneven and betray their origins as commissions or offerings to festivals. The libretti, for choice of which the composer must bear responsibility, hardly made his task any easier: their material is not such as to set a composer's imagination alight and keep the flame burning.

Nevertheless, in the case of *The Light of Life* – Elgar's original title of *Lux Christi* was thought to be too Catholic for the Worcester Festival[14] – commentators have tended to concentrate on the defects and immaturities rather than on the strengths and virtues. True, the expansion of the biblical text with additions by the Rev. Edward Capel-Cure must have persuaded Elgar that he would be wiser, in the subsequent oratorios, to do the job himself. But the music is another matter. When one has heard *The Light of Life* one should no longer be surprised by the Italianate fluency of the writing for solo tenor in *The Dream of Gerontius*, nor by the assurance with which the orchestra is handled in that later work, nor by the imaginative use of the choir. The score contains several prophetic passages, prophetic of *Gerontius* and *The Apostles* at many points, of the choral writing in the last of his choral works of twenty years later, *The Spirit of England*, and even of the autumnal mellowness of the Cello Concerto. The influences of Wagner and of Verdi's *Requiem* are easily discernible. Also, the spirit of Massenet seems to me to brood beneficially over the score; at such passages as the tenor's 'As a spirit didst thou pass before mine eyes', the music seems to be inviting a libretto for a romantic opera in the

---

[13] This phrase about music 'bleeding' was evidently a favourite with him. It occurs in the Birmingham lectures.

[14] At one point Elgar favoured the title 'The Light that Shineth', erroneously believing that *The Light of Life* had been used by another composer.

style of *Werther*. The orchestral prelude (*Meditation*) contains the work's principal *leitmotive*, the last of them a G major melody (*dolcissimo*) which was to be used again in *The Apostles* and stands for Jesus as the giver of the Light of the World. The opening chorus, 'Seek him that maketh the seven stars', could well have come from *The Apostles* and is a reminder that some themes for these oratorios were sketched as early as the 1880s. For example, the sopranos' theme in triplets, accompanied by clarinets, at the words 'Thou hast borne the sinner's sentence' in the chorus 'Light out of darkness' is the germ of the New Faith theme in *The Kingdom*. Undoubtedly the highlight is the tenor solo 'As a spirit didst thou pass', impassioned and rapturous. Later, when the man who was blind affirms his belief in Christ's divinity, the orchestral writing is an exquisite piece of mature Elgar, and few will be unmoved by Jesus's solo 'I am the good shepherd', with its violin solo. Elgar's musical treatment of Our Lord is straightforward and virile.

King Olaf is also a cornucopia of the future Elgar and is worth hearing on that account, but the libretto is so fatuous and risible that it requires a major effort of willpower to concentrate on the music. This is a pity, because there are striking themes here, colourful, broad melodies, and passages of that dreaming introspection to which Elgar had a secret key. The motif for Odin, slain by Olaf, is harmonically bold and there are some passages of sliding chromatic harmonies where Elgar has gone ahead of Wagner. Typical of Elgar's mood of fantasy is the scherzo-like ballad 'A little bird in the air', and the unaccompanied part-song' 'As torrents in summer' which was somewhat incongruously incorporated into the cantata, and at least shows Elgar beating Sullivan at his own game. Again, however, it is the vivid orchestration which provides the most satisfaction, while the choral writing is imaginative and vigorous, requiring a big virtuoso Northern choir. In the early 1920s Sir Henry Wood visited Elgar, who played *King Olaf* through on the piano and exclaimed 'By Jove, Henry, what jolly fine tunes! I couldn't write them today!'[15] In April 1924, Elgar wrote to Troyte Griffith: 'If I had to set K.O. again I shd. do it just in the same way – the atmosphere is "right" & the technique – I have never done anything like "Dead rides" etc. but you have never heard it with a big Yorks. chorus.'

The point has been well made by Geoffrey Hodgkins[16] that *The Light of Life* and *King Olaf* contain the theme of isolation as the result of religious belief, a theme Elgar understood. In the oratorio the Jewish authorities reject the man who was blind because of his declaration of belief in Christ's divinity; in the saga Olaf is a Christian convert in a pagan country.

[15] *My Life of Music*, by Henry J. Wood (London, 1938), p. 357.
[16] *Providence and Art*, op. cit.

Caractacus is the nearest we can come to hearing how an opera by
Elgar might have sounded. This is not to suggest that it is an opera
manqué. Attempts to stage it, such as that in Liverpool in 1928, have
not been successful, for the characters are not truly operatic, and it is a
hybrid work, half operatic, half dramatic cantata, of the kind English
composers wrote prolifically in the last quarter of the 19th century.
Jaeger, in a letter to Elgar in December 1901, made this shrewd plea:
'Don't cook up *Caractacus* for Covent Garden. It will never do. Write
a real opera, & wait a year or two ... You can't alter a cantata into an
opera, no one can ... I cannot imagine Englishmen or English
women, however operatically fashionable and blasé, enjoying Britons
being shown on the stage under the conqueror's yoke ... I have
studied *Caractacus* again & cannot see anything operatically effective
in it, except the Love Duet & the March with Britons tied captive to
the conqueror's "wheels". DON'T!!!' But it is no surprise to learn that,
in 1898, Elgar was anxious to make an opera from Maurice Hewlett's
The Forest Lovers, published that year. There are forest lovers in
Caractacus and the score is permeated by the sounds and atmosphere
of the forest, for the very good reason that it was the first piece on
which he worked while at Birchwood. Not only is the score full of
woodland music, but its prevalent mood is relaxed and happy – the
dark, complex, moody, restless music of Elgar developed parallel
with the growth of his fame after 1899, as a direct result, it seems, of
the pressures on his personality of the social and artistic life of a
celebrity, the dichotomy between the private 'Birchwood' Elgar and
the nation's laureate.

Acworth's libretto, on which the plot of Bellini's *Norma* seems to
have impinged, is naïve in sentiment but it is no worse, and often a
good deal better, than many of its kind. It provided Elgar with a
Wotan-like hero in Caractacus and with his forest lovers in
Caractacus's historical daughter Eigen and (Acworth's invention)
Orbin, a tenor rôle. A stumbling-block for the squeamish has been
the final chorus 'The clang of arms is over' in which – somewhat
incongruously, in view of the fact that the cantata is about a humbling
British defeat – the end of the Roman Empire is foreseen, to be
supplanted by the evangelistic paternalism of the British Empire. Yet
was it with ironical intent that Elgar based the music of this chorus on
the theme of the Arch-Druid's deliberately false prophecy of
Caractacus's victory? Surely now the text can be considered as much a
period-piece as those of Purcell's *Welcome Odes*. *Caractacus* is a genuine
'patriotic' occasional piece. Far from being pompous and brassy, it is
for most of its course light, delicate, and pastoral, a kind of Elgarian
fantasy-pastiche on the Englishness of English music, with episodes
in madrigalian, ballad, and mock-folk-song style. There are weak
passages, but much more beautiful, vivid, and effective music. There

is, for instance, the 'Woodland Interlude' (Introduction to Scene 3), one of those uniquely Elgarian, fresh-as-dew, bruised-innocence pieces, like *Chanson de Matin*, which defy analysis of their extraordinary capacity to move and delight the listener. It is the quintessence of the Worcestershire Elgar and it is not surprising to discover that it existed in a sketchbook of 1887, where it formed part of an intended suite, and was possibly written even earlier. While designedly a much simpler structure than *King Olaf*, *Caractacus* is more mature as an expression of Elgar's personality. He is in his happiest orchestral vein, with iridescent splashes of colour, endearing fragments of detail, and a continuous pulse of broad lyrical string tone. He had wanted to use four saxophones in the score, but expense ruled them out. Sketches of his rough scoring indicate saxophones in Scenes 1, 2 and 6. Caractacus's first solo is a memorable mixture of Wotan-like nobility and anticipations of Gerontius. There are more *Gerontius* trailers, too, in the orchestral introduction to the Arch-Druid's 'Bard, what read ye' and his 'Go forth, O King', while the Demons' Chorus is suggested by the chorus 'Hence, ere the awful curse is spoke'. Elgar's lighter touch is delightfully illustrated by the irregular rhythms of the Druid maidens' first chorus, in Eigen's beautiful solo 'O'er arched with leaves' (prophetic of 'The sun goeth down' in *The Kingdom*) and in the Sullivanesque 'Come beneath our woodland bow'rs'. The love-duet, as Jaeger acknowledged, is truly operatic. The final scene, beginning with the splendid Triumphal March, is well constructed. Two powerful arias for Caractacus are followed by Claudius's pardon of the three Britons, whose *andantino* trio 'Grace from the Roman!' is a poignant movement. Its triple *piano* final chord is where the work should end, but it would have been unthinkable in 1898 to have closed on such a note, so the notorious but well-written chorus was added. The greatest music in *Caractacus*, however, is in Scene 4 when the King sings his lament 'O my warriors' (in the unusual time-signature of 7/4). This magnificent solo, with choral interjections, is in Elgar's noblest vein, of heroic melancholy.

The faults of these pre-*Gerontius* cantatas are big, just as their virtues are. If Elgar had, at any time of his life, been a selective and 'refined' composer he would have been untrue to his real nature and would certainly have been that much less great and individual a music-maker. These early works reflect the emancipation of provincial musical life from the sacred cantatas of the 1880s to the adventures of the 1900s. Something has already been said about Elgar's musical ancestry, favouring Schumann and Dvořák rather than Brahms and Wagner. I would again stress the French influence, in particular Massenet and Delibes. One has only to listen to the orchestral version of the *Bavarian Dances*, especially the famous 'Lullaby', to appreciate the clarity of the scoring and that Elgar, long

before Thomas Beecham, had perceived the essential grace and style
of the best French light music. Listen to Massenet's *Last Sleep of the
Blessed Virgin*, for strings, and you might almost be listening to an
extra slow movement from Elgar's *Serenade*. This probably also
explains the curious resemblances between Elgar's music and that of
Fauré, his nearest French contemporary. Elgar admitted that a
particularly Wagnerian moment in *Cockaigne* was suggested by a
passage in Delibes's *Sylvia* ballet. He shared with Vaughan Williams
and Stanford a genuine and unfashionable admiration for the music of
Meyerbeer which he knew well. Some of the ceremonial strain in
Elgar owes a debt to Meyerbeer. Wagner of course was an inescapable
influence on every composer of the rising generation in the last
twenty years of the nineteenth century. Elgar spent his savings on
seeing Wagner operas abroad; Vaughan Williams took his wife on
honeymoon to Berlin in 1897 so that he could hear *The Ring* without
cuts; Cecil Sharp and Gustav Holst were Wagner addicts, and so were
many more. That a *Parsifal* atmosphere can be breathed in *Gerontius* is
hardly to be denied, but Gounod and Massenet are there too.
Wagner's influence on Elgar was attributed from *King Olaf* onwards
to Elgar's use of the system of *leitmotive*, or leading (representative)
themes, which dominates *The Ring*. But in the *Musical Times* of
October 1900 he disposed of this theory: 'I became acquainted with
the representative-theme long before I had ever heard a note of
Wagner, or seen one of his scores. My first acquaintance with the
leitmotiv was derived (in my boyhood) from Mendelssohn's *Elijah* and
the system elaborated from that.' He made a neat point to Jaeger who,
at the beginning of their correspondence in 1897, was evidently
talking in Wagnerian similes. 'It is nice to be told I am a sheep,' Elgar
wrote, 'but after all a bell-wether *is* something.'

So, in 1898, Elgar had at last the national fame that was his due. He
was 'in demand' as a festival composer. Norwich wanted a work, and
so did Birmingham (which rejected his suggestion of *St Augustine*, as
he told Joseph Bennett in January 1899). Yet instead of feeling on
the crest of the wave, he was utterly discouraged by the lack of
appreciation of his work by A. H. Littleton of Novello's. He
unburdened himself, just before Christmas, to Jaeger's ready ear:
'For the last six weeks (about) I have been very sick at heart over
music – the whole future seems so hopeless. I wrote to Mr L. –
because I had talked to him of it previously – about the Bir. Fest.
work & he does not reply: also I have asked him how my egregious
debt to the form (K.O. & c) stands and they tell me nothing. Now I
have worked steadily and honestly till I am offered all the festivals &
then the firm seem to have had enough of me. I can quite understand
that my big works don't pay ... but I shd. have hoped that on
artistic grounds the very small remuneration I ask shd. be forthcom-

ing for things which at least interest the better portion of the musical public. No! the only suggestion made is that the Henry VIII dances are the thing – now I can't write that sort of thing & my own heartfelt ideas are not wanted: why K. Olaf should be worthless when it's done often is a mystery to me when things by, say Mackenzie, which are never touched, shd. be good properties. You see I want so little: £300 a year I must make, & that's all. Last year I subsisted on £200. It seems strange that a man who might do good work shd. be absolutely stopped – that's what it means.'

Jaeger evidently sorted out the trouble at Novello's and replied: 'A day's attack of the blues . . . will not drive away your desire, your necessity, which is to exercise those creative faculties which a kind providence has given you. Your time of universal recognition will come. You have virtually achieved more towards that in one year than others of the English composers in a decade.'

Wise, loyal Jaeger. But even he could not yet appreciate the significance of that October evening when Elgar was extemporizing at the piano for his wife. She liked a new theme and asked what it was. 'Nothing,' he replied, 'but something might be made of it. Powell would have done this.' He played another snatch and asked 'Who is that like?' 'I cannot quite say,' Alice replied, 'but it is exactly the way W. M. B. goes out of the room.' She added, with a percipience which was more than just adoring loyalty, 'Surely you are doing something that has never been done before?'

Part II

SUMMIT
1899—1913

'. . . Go, song of mine,
To break the hardness of the heart of man.'

6 'Variations', and the 'Friends pictured within'

In approaching the zenith of Elgar's creative life and the apogee of his national fame, it will be necessary to abandon strict chronological biographical methods and to follow his progress by means of the personal associations and early histories of some of the works, and by a closer study of his relationships with a growing circle of friends and acquaintances – and enemies. Despite his grumbling to Jaeger and his almost neurotic preoccupation with wider public and material recognition – though, as has been seen, he had in some respects a poor opinion of public taste – Elgar was fully aware that it was only in Worcestershire that he was able to work in the concentrated quiet that he needed. The peace and beauty of the countryside were as necessary a creative stimulant to him as they were to Beethoven, and he found them in full measure at the cottage, Birchwood, among the woods and within walking distance of the British Camp and all the other associations with Caractacus. Alice and he first stayed there on 16 May 1898. When he wrote to Jaeger during the summer of 1898, he would put 'Birchwood (once more!)' or 'Birchwood (in peace)' or 'at Forli but just leaving for Birchwood Deo Gratias!' at the head of his letters. But it was from 'Forli', when the woods were 'decidedly damp and rheumaticky – unromantic just now', that on 24 October 1898 he wrote to him: 'Since I've been back [from a visit to London] I have sketched a set of Variations (orkestra) on an original theme: the Variations have amused me because I've labelled 'em with the nicknames of my particular friends – *you* are Nimrod. That is to say I've written the variations each one to represent the mood of the "party" – I've liked to imagine the 'party' writing the var: him (or her) self and have written what I think they wd. have written – if they were asses enough to compose – it's a quaint idea & the result is amusing to those behind the scenes & won't affect the hearer who "nose nuffin". What think you?'

Alice was right. Nothing like this had been done before, except perhaps by Schumann in *Carnaval*, and it is tempting to wonder whence the idea came. Fritz Kreisler, according to his biographer Louis P. Lochner,[1] said that Elgar had told him that the idea for the *Variations* came from listening to Kreisler's transcriptions for violin: a statement, if true, which merely deepens the Enigma.[2] Nearly three weeks after

[1] *Fritz Kreisler* (London, 1951), p. 107.
[2] It is worth noting that the English composer Cipriani Potter (1792–1871) wrote in about 1825 a work for solo piano called '"Enigma" Variations (in the style of 5 eminent artists)'.

that first letter, Elgar on 11 November told Jaeger that the *Variations* 'go on slowly but I shall finish 'em some day'. He said he was possessed by the idea of the Gordon Symphony which Jaeger had suggested but 'I can't write it down yet'. Worcester – 'poor old Worcester' – had asked him for a Festival symphony; he had agreed 'to do the PRINCIPAL novelty for Birmingham' (1900 Festival) and Norwich wanted something new, 'of course', for its festival – 'You see,' the usual complaint followed, 'none of this will pay me a cent! So I am doing hack work – orchestrating a comic opera for another chap! for which I shall be paid. Such is life.' In fact the *Variations* were progressing well. Rosa Burley heard the theme and the first two variations when Elgar visited The Mount 'shortly after the Leeds Festival'. In the succeeding weeks, as each variation was added, she was invited to guess whom it represented. 'The supposed enigmatical significance was not, I think, mentioned at that time'.[3] Mrs Powell (Dorabella) tells us in her book[4] that she first heard the pianoforte version of 'sketches, and in some cases, completed numbers' on 1 November 1898. She mentions C. A. E., R. B. T., W. M. B., Troyte, Nimrod, and her own Dorabella. 'I say – those variations I *like*'em,' he wrote to Jaeger on 5 January 1899. The complete work was orchestrated, according to a note on the manuscript score, between 5 and 19 February 1899. Elgar wrote to Dorabella on 22 February, 'The Variations are finished & yours is the most cheerful . . . I *have* orchestrated you well.' Meanwhile Elgar, on his own initiative, had been in touch with Nathaniel Vert, agent and manager for Dr Hans Richter, whose fame and reputation as a conductor were at their peak. Friend and interpreter of Wagner, Brahms, and Bruckner, Richter had conducted annually in Britain since 1877. Since 1885 he had been conductor of the Birmingham Festival and at this date, February 1899, he was in the final stages of long and complicated negotiations to leave the Vienna Opera and take up the post of conductor of the Hallé Orchestra in Manchester which had been offered to him immediately after Sir Charles Hallé had died in October 1895.[5] Elgar sent a score of the *Variations* to Richter in Vienna, through Vert, on 21 February, having taken Jaeger into his confidence two days earlier: 'You will see my letter to the firm about the Variations I expect; *only* for mercy's sake don't tell *anyone* I pray you about Richter becos' he may refuse. Vert is keen about it & it wd. be just too lovely for anything if R. did an English piece by a man who hasn't appeared yet . . . but I fear R. has been "got at".[6] I have begged for a very early reply from Vienna.'

[3]*Edward Elgar: the record of a friendship*, op. cit., pp. 116–7.
[4]Pp. 12–13.
[5]For a full account of these negotiations see M. Kennedy, *The Hallé Tradition* (Manchester, 1960), pp. 97–126.
[6]Elgar evidently feared or suspected some 'plot' against his work being performed in London. He wrote about this time to Dorabella, 'Richter . . . is to see 'em in Vienna

'A man who hasn't appeared yet.' Elgar still regarded his reputation as regional rather than metropolitan. Novello's were dubious about the *Variations* and it can be deduced from the letters to Jaeger quoted in the previous chapter that Alfred Littleton had in effect rejected them and also the idea of *St. Augustine* as the proposed Birmingham Festival novelty. This, after all, was the period of discouragement to which the self-portraying 14th Variation (E. D. U.) was an answer – 'written at a time when friends were dubious and generally discouraging as to the composer's musical future', Elgar stated. He spent the anxious weeks while Richter studied the score in moving to a new house in Malvern and in revising for publication the score of his *Three Characteristic Pieces* (the 1888 *Suite*), now dedicated to Lady Mary Lygon. Like most husbands, Elgar hated the business of moving house. 'I am awfully worried with this moving & do anything to escape,' he told Jaeger, 'I *flew* out yesterday straight across country to think out my thoughts & to avoid every one.' The house he called Craeg Lea (an anagram of C(arice), E(dward), and A(lice) Elgar) and when he got there he loved it – 'my study is a dream! & the view', he told Jaeger. The view was across Worcestershire, to Edgehill, Worcester Cathedral, the abbeys of Pershore and Tewkesbury, and even the smoke from around Birmingham. They moved in on 21 March and almost simultaneously good news came from Richter. Elgar wrote on 26 March to Dorabella: 'Well: Richter has telegraphed that he will produce the Variations & I think "Dorabella" is to be published *separately* as well (of course) as in the set.' A few days earlier, on 6 March, he had sent Novello's another short work for violin and pianoforte, saying: 'I see from my sketch which I found last week & have since completed that this piece was intended to be a companion to the one you have already . . . so I have suggested calling this "cheerful" piece *Chanson de Matin*.' Elgar sent orchestral versions of both pieces to Novello's on 4 January 1901; in this form they have become extremely popular.

The *Variations* were rehearsed for the first time under Richter in St James's Hall on 3 June 1899. Richter was to conduct the first performance in St. James's Hall on 19 June. He went through the score with Elgar on 16 June, rehearsed the work the next day and again on the morning of the 19th. The first performance was an almost unreserved success. Not only was the music fully appreciated, but the additional interest of the dedication, 'To my friends pictured within', whetted public curiosity. Only the music critic of *The Times* seemed a little peeved by being left out of the secret and wrote that 'it is evidently impossible for the uninitiated to discuss the meaning of the work'. He was guarded in his assessment but conceded that 'on

very soon and – if he is not prevented by certain London – (mystery!) will play you all in the Spring.'

the surface' the music was 'exceedingly clever, often charming and always original, and excellently worked out'. Others were less inhibited. *The Athenaeum* regretted the dedication - 'the *Variations* stand in no need of a programme; as abstract music they fully satisfy' -- but added that the performance was 'perfect' and was 'no mere *succès d'estime*; the *Variations* will, we feel sure, be often heard, and as often admired'. It is, however, to the *Musical Times* (July 1899) that we must turn - naturally! - for the truest appreciation (the writer was Jaeger): 'Here is an English musician who has something to say and knows how to say it in his own individual and beautiful way . . . He writes as he feels, there is no affectation or make-believe. Effortless originality - the only true originality - combined with thorough *savoir-faire* and, most important of all, beauty of theme, warmth and feeling are his credentials, and they should open to him the hearts of all who have faith in the future of our English art and appreciate beautiful music wherever it is met.'

Attention was concentrated on only one of the work's two mysteries: the identities of the dedicatees. These are no longer a mystery, and more ink has since been spent on the name 'Enigma' with which Elgar headed his original theme. In a letter quoted by the writer of the programme-note for the first performance he said: 'The enigma I will not explain - its "dark saying" must be left unguessed, and I warn you that the apparent connection between the Variations and the Theme is often of the slightest texture; further, through and over the whole set another and larger theme "goes", but is not played . . . So the principal Theme never appears, even as in some late dramas - e.g. Maeterlinck's "L'Intruse" and "Les Sept Princesses" - the chief character is never on the stage.'

This is vague enough, though it shows that there are *two* enigmas: the original theme and the unheard theme. Here it should be remembered that Elgar did not use the word 'Enigma' in relation to the *Variations* until a letter to Jaeger on 28 May 1899, three months after the full score was finished. Further, the manuscript full score shows that the word 'Enigma' is written in pencil by someone other

PLATE I

than Elgar. Some time after the first performance Elgar admitted that the 'larger theme' – strange phrase – was a tune to which the Original Theme was a counterpoint. Many friends tried to guess its identity, including Arthur Troyte Griffith ('Troyte'). He asked Elgar if it was *God Save the King* and received the reply 'No, of course not; but it is so well known that it is extraordinary that no one has spotted it'. Elgar told Dorabella he was surprised that 'you of all people' had not guessed it. She adds 'Elgar made it perfectly clear to us when the work was being written that the Enigma was concerned with a tune'. *Auld Lang Syne* has had its adherents including, as recently as 1970, Eric Sams (*Musical Times*, March 1970). When in 1912 Dorabella suggested *Auld Lang Syne* to Elgar, he ended their long friendship.

In his book[7] published in 1971, Ian Parrott put forward two ingenious solutions. Elgar completed the full score on 19 February 1899. He went to church in Malvern on 12 February, Quinquagesima Sunday, when the Epistle was I Corinthians xiii. Verse 12 in the Latin Vulgate reads: 'Videmus nunc per speculum in ænigmate' – 'For now we see through a glass darkly'. Thus the 'dark saying'. As the unheard theme which 'goes', Professor Parrott suggested not a specific tune but the general inspiration of Bach. Another theory, to which I find myself sympathetic because it seems to fit Elgar's sense of humour, was propounded in Holland in 1975 by Theodore van Houten[8]. Briefly, his 'solution' is that the larger theme that 'goes' is 'Britain' and the tune that was Elgar's inspiration was 'Rule, Britannia!', specifically the 'never, never, never' phrase. Thus, 'the chief character is *never* on the stage'; it is 'so well known'; and Dorabella ought to have guessed because her surname was Penny and Britannia was depicted on one side of Victorian pennies. Moreover, in *The Music Makers*, where the 'Enigma' theme is used again, Elgar quotes 'Rule, Britannia!' Professor Parrott's explanation of Elgar's remark to Dora Penny is that as the daughter of a clergyman (her father was Rector of Wolverhampton) she should have known her Bible!

There is more substance to the belief that the first Enigma is Elgar himself. Arthur Johnstone, writing in the *Manchester Guardian* on 9 February 1900, remarked that 'however much the composer may call his theme an enigma . . . one can scarcely escape the impression that it represents the temperament of the artist, through which he sees his subjects; for that, and nothing else, is what forms the connecting link between any series of portraits by the same hand'. This theory is actually confirmed by Elgar in a letter to Dorabella which she prints

[7] *Elgar*, by Ian Parrott (London, 1971).
[8] See *The Enigma – a solution from Holland*, by T. J. L. van Houten, Elgar Society Newsletter January 1976 pp. 28–32; also *You of all People*, by T. J. L. van Houten, *Music Review* May 1976. The *Dies Irae* is put forward by K. Kemsey-Bourne in *The Real Answer to Elgar's Riddle?* in The Elgar Society Journal, September 1986, pp. 9–12.

on p. 38 of her book and the significance of which she and everyone else seem to have overlooked. Writing on 25 October 1901, and chaffing her because she has not been to see him lately, he says: 'I forget if you really are nice or if somebody only imagined you to be. So you must come and tell us whether you are as nice as', and here he quotes two bars of the Dorabella Variation, 'or only as unideal as', and then quotes the opening four notes of the Original Theme. In this context can there be any doubt that he is referring to himself as 'unideal' and therefore identifying himself with that phrase, to which the name Edward Elgar 'goes' in almost natural speech-rhythm? Further confirmation can be found in the score of *The Music Makers*, where the Enigma theme is quoted to illustrate the loneliness of the creative artist, Elgar, 'sitting by desolate streams', just as, in boyhood, he had sat by the Severn. Jaeger, according to W. H. Reed, called the whole thing 'a bit of Elgar's humour'. He, Lady Elgar, and the composer were probably the only people who knew the identity of the 'larger theme'. It really hardly matters any more, since no solution can assuredly be said to be correct. Enigma-solving is a game Elgarians will play to the end of time. The secret, if there is one, died with him. The music itself is much more important. Other mysteries which surrounded the work and its first performances are more easily solved.

One of these concerns the legend that the manuscript score of the *Variations* was sent to Hubert Parry, who was greatly excited by it and, although the night was cold and wet (some versions say foggy), tucked it under his arm and took it to Richter, or to Vert, and insisted that it should be performed soon. This story has been sedulously propagated by Parry's disciples, notably Plunket Greene, Parry's son-in-law, in his life of Stanford[9] and Thomas F. Dunhill in his book on Elgar.[10] it was believed by Vaughan Williams, and Frank Howes[11] states dogmatically that the score was sent by Parry to Richter 'with his enthusiastic commendation'. There is no documentary evidence for this attractive story. It is not mentioned in the official biography of Parry; and there is no reference to it in correspondence between Elgar and Jaeger as assuredly there would have been, for whatever their views of Parry's music both admired and respected the man. In any case the facts undo it. Elgar himself sent the full score in manuscript to Vert who sent it to Richter in Vienna. Jaeger received only a pianoforte score which Elgar despatched from 'Forli' on 13 March 1899, having written three days earlier, 'Shall I send the P.F. arrgt of the variations – now complete – for inspection or wait for the return of the full score?' Their references to this piano score thereafter concern its correcting for publication, which was on 9 June 1899. The

[9] *Charles Villiers Stanford* (London, 1935), p. 157.
[10] *Sir Edward Elgar* (London, 1938), p. 11.
[11] *The English Musical Renaissance* (London, 1966), pp. 178–9.

first time Parry's name is mentioned is in a letter to Jaeger dated 27 June 1899, eight days after the first performance, when in a P.S. Elgar says: 'I have had a nice rapturous letter from C. H. H. P. Most kind of him.'[12] This is further confirmed by Elgar's letter to Parry on 25 January 1900, which begins: 'When Richter produced my Variations you sent me a very kind letter; this, naturally, you will have forgotten – but I have not & never shall – & I also remember that I said I should like to send you a score when printed.'[13] If Parry had played any part at all in bringing about the performance of the *Variations*, it is unthinkable that Elgar would not have acknowledged it in some way or mentioned it in correspondence.

A second performance of the *Variations* was due to be given a month after the first, arranged by Granville Bantock who since 1897 had been director of music at the Tower, New Brighton, a rival to Blackpool. His engagement was to provide ballroom dancing, but aided by one music-loving member of the Tower management committee Bantock promoted concerts of works by Wagner, Dvořák, and other composers. He admired Elgar's music and had chosen an all-Elgar programme for a concert on 16 July, including the *Variations* and the *Three Characteristic Pieces*. Jaeger had written soon after the first performance suggesting amendments to the finale. Elgar (writing on 27 June) was more concerned with other points which show that the Richter performance was not as 'perfect' as the *Athenaeum*'s critic believed: 'I waited until I had thought it out and now decide that the end is good enough for me . . . I always said those celli were – bar one or two – the worst in the world – and a whole heap of passages they have did not come out – including that passage (unheard) on p. 26 (I had forgotten that they actually have it with the bassoon and we never heard it). Again on p. 27 the celli got *no* tone out of those 7ths – I will assist 'em. You won't frighten me into writing a logically developed movement where I don't want one by quoting other people!' He then suggests waiting till after the New Brighton performance before the score is engraved, so that he can 'touch it up'.

[12] Basil Maine in Volume I of *Elgar: His Life and Works* (London, 1933), p. 174, records that Parry said to Landon Ronald on the day after the first performance: 'Yesterday I heard Richter perform the *Enigma Variations* by Mr Elgar, the finest work I have listened to for years. Look out for this man's music; he has something new to say and knows how to say it.'

[13] There is a reminder in this episode of Elgar's precarious financial position. 'A poor man may not do anything gracefully' he wrote to Parry, saying that he hesitated to 'inflict another' score if Parry already had one. He had previously inquired from Jaeger, 'Tell me what you charge *me* for the full score . . . I'm afraid I can't afford it but I shd. like to give one away.' And at this same time he told Jaeger: 'I'm *awfully* hard up just now for a space, but I want to give you a score – can't you take one and put it down to me . . . I've *not* sent a score to Richter . . . I really haven't a brass farden to spare.'

But Jaeger persisted about the finale, saying that Richter had criticized it. Elgar, suspicious as ever of other people's motives, wrote again three days later (30 June): 'As to that finale it's most good of you to be interested & I like to have your opinion – I have my doubts as to some of the rest 'cos it's generally *suggested* to them. Now look here, the movement was designed to be concise – here's the difficulty of lengthening it – I *could* go on with those themes for ½ a day but the *Key* G is exhausted – the principal motive (Enigma) comes in grandioso . . . in the tonic and it *won't do* to bring it in again . . . In deference to you I made a sketch yesterday – but the thing sounds Schubertian in its sticking to one key. I should really like to know *how* you heard that Richter was disappointed – he criticised some of it but not the end – the actual final flourish was spoilt in performance by the insts. going wild. You see there's far too much of this sort of thing said: somebody wants to find fault . . . This sort of thing is of no value to me . . . If I find, after New B., that the end does not satisfy me, I may recast the whole of the last movement but it's not possible to *lengthen* it with any satisfaction I fear.'

By 7 July he was relenting a bit. He wrote 'I am hoping to send you a sketch of a proposed extended finale', and a day or two later, from Birchwood, he wrote 'Aha! I'm here & *at work* in my woodlands. Now: hither comes pp. 1 to 144 end of the Score and *all* the wind &c revised to 76 at this point the Jaerodnimgeresque coda cometh on – I am scoring this prestissimo. Look here – shall I put in *organ* ad lib: just at the end?' Then, on 12 July, 'You're a trump! I'm heartily glad you like the TAIL. *I do* now it's done.' The *Variations* were played at New Brighton in the original version – 'Bantock *is* a brick and *really* understands things' – and the final revision of the coda was sent to Jaeger on 20 July. Dorabella was at Malvern when proofs of the new ending arrived: Elgar played it and roared with laughter adding, 'The old Moss was right' ('Old Mosshead' was one of Elgar's nicknames for Jaeger). But it is beyond doubt that wise and experienced Richter had realized the weakness of the original ending and suggested that such a fine work needed to be more convincingly clinched.[14] Elgar acknowledged this in a letter to Richter on 5 October 1899, saying: 'Following the advice of my friends, and I think your own view, I have added to the Finale making a more sympathetic movement of it. (It only adds *between 2 and 3 minutes* to the length – not more). In place of the original abrupt ending . . . I hope you may approve of the additional music which I feel is an improvement in form.'

[14] According to Arthur Troyte Griffith, Elgar intended the original ending to mean 'Well, we have had a very pleasant evening. I am glad to hear what you all think about it. Good night.' It can be studied in the original (June 1899) piano score. When a ballet was devised by Sir Frederick Ashton on the *Enigma Variations* (Covent Garden, 1968), the original ending was used. A reproduction of it in full score may be seen on p. 27 of the BBC Music Guide *Elgar Orchestral Music* (BBC, 1970).

The third performance, the first with the new ending, was given in Worcester during the Three Choirs Festival in September 1899, Elgar conducting, and Richter repeated it in London on 23 October – 'the 1st time anything by an Englishman has been done twice!!' he jubilantly told Troyte. 'I thought it went well on Monday night,' he wrote to Jaeger on 25 October (from Worcestershire Golf Club), 'but I wanted the finale quicker – the martial pt. anyhow. I hope you liked it all.' Then musical politics intervene: 'I fear the "party" are very sick at its being done again.'[15] The work was soon in frequent demand, but its first performance had nearly been the cause of a complete rift with Novello's during August 1899. As has been seen, it was unusual and fortunate, in those days, in having received three rehearsals before the first performance. Alfred Littleton had asked Richter's agent, Vert, for thirty shillings for hire of the orchestral parts. When this reached Elgar's ears he went to London on 21 August, saw Littleton, had a fierce argument with him, broke his connection with the firm and placed his next work – *Sea Pictures* – with Boosey's. On 1 September he explained the situation to Jaeger:

I have had to write to the firm on one or two matters & have gone on just as of old & they reply: I think we have only one 'thing' between us & that is A. H. L.'s objection to my expression of disgust – this is very real & I can't withdraw it – Vert has lost heaps over the old gang's orchl. attempts & did the work as a favour – an *extra rehearsal* cost him £40 – the letter to the firm containing this information was *not before* A. H. L. – my note to Vert was in reference to the fact that he had *paid* £40 as well as taken the risk of producing an English piece & the publishers 'try it on' to get 30/- more out of him – this certainly aroused my disgust. I would have withdrawn the expression &, if need be, apologised as far as A. H. L. was concerned, *but – this annoyed me more than anything* – he said V. ought to have got the extra rehearsal out of his men for *nothing*!! I was shocked at the sheer brutality of the idea but he repeated it: I confess the prospect of a rich man seriously considering the fleecing of those poor underpaid, overworked devils in the orchestra *quite* prevented me from feeling Xtian. If that is 'business' – well damn your business – I loathe it. Now my dear man, do not worry about me in the least: I have told you over & over again that the state of music in England is simply farcical & depressing & I am well out of the vortex of jealousy, chicanery, fraud & falsehood. I have to thank music for your friendship & for this I am grateful.

This letter, disclosing Elgar's fellow-feeling for professional musicians, also discloses the sheer wonder that an Englishman's music should be given such preparation for a first performance under a great conductor. (It also discloses something of the publisher's difficulties in being able only to charge thirty shillings for hire of parts, though in this case the obstinate Littleton should have had the

[15] By the 'party', Elgar obviously meant the 'academics' whom he so distrusted and disliked.

sense and tact to forget about it.) The episode proves how strongly
Richter believed in the work, for Vert must have acted under his
orders. In February 1900, for instance, Richter conducted performances of it on successive days in Birmingham, Manchester,
Bradford, and Liverpool. Alice Elgar wrote to a friend, 'Dr Richter
is simply devoted to the work.' Elgar's gratitude to Richter never
faded. In 1910, at the height of his fame, he wrote to him: 'The man
you befriended long ago (Variations), be assured this man will never
forget your kindness, your nobility, and the grandeur of your life and
personality.'

The *Variations* are, as every critic has pointed out since the first
performance, completely self-sufficient as absolute music. But
something is added by knowing their biographical origins, and credit
should be given Elgar for a brilliant feat of 'absolute programme-
music' and for the skill with which he assembled his portrait-gallery
from friendships with musical associations or possibilities. The
design of the work is particularly fine: the slow, simple and dignified
theme and first variation (C. A. E.), followed by eight short
thumbnail sketches; the central 'slow movement' of Nimrod, the
emotional pivot of the work; the ballet-like intermezzo of Dorabella;
a scherzo in G. R. S., then building to a climax, three successive
miniature tone-poems, the superb cello variation (B. G. N.), the
mysterious and evocative Romanza, and the self-portraying Finale,
rumbustious, assertive, and recalling C. A. E. and Nimrod before the
final 'grand slam'. It is all carefully balanced. In some notes for
pianola rolls of the *Variations* issued by the Aeolian Company, Elgar
wrote the authoritative account of each variation, carefully and often
significantly phrased. These notes are important not only because of
the light they shed on the *Variations* but because they are another
indication of Elgar's interest in the mechanical reproduction of
music. The pneumatically-driven player-piano, or pianola, operated
by means of a music-roll, was invented in 1897. Elgar had one in his
Hereford home in 1910 and rolls of the First Symphony were made in
that year. The Aeolian Company's 'Duo-Art' performance of the
Variations was issued in 1929 on five rolls in a performance on two
pianos recorded by Freda Whitemore and Dorothy Manley in either
1926 or 1927. Copious descriptive material accompanied the rolls.
Much of this was written by Elgar, but Percy Scholes supplied the
descriptive commentaries on the music.[16] Elgar's notes were written
in 1927 – he refers to 'nearly thirty years' having elapsed since the
Variations were composed, i.e. 1898. These notes were partly

[16] Elgar told Percy Scholes (*The Music Student*, August 1916, p. 346): 'I'm not sure
that the pianola is not our best means of hearing piano works well performed today.
Paderewski and Busoni are not always at hand, but we can domesticate good pianism
in the pianola . . . Properly used the pianola can play with a very beautiful touch.'

republished by Novello's in 1946 as *My Friends Pictured Within* with no indication of when they had been written. Elgar's full manuscript draft may be seen at the Birthplace. He described the Enigma Theme thus:

'The alternation of the two quavers and two crotchets in the first bar and their reversal in the second bar will be noticed; references to this grouping are almost continuous (either melodically or in the accompanying figures – in Variation XIII, beginning at bar 11, for example[17]). The drop of a seventh in the Theme (bars 3 & 4) should be observed. At bar 7 (G major) appears the rising and falling passage in thirds which is used much later, e.g. Variation III, bars. 10–16.'

No. I, 'C. A. E.' is Alice Elgar, 'a prolongation of the theme with what I wished to be romantic and delicate additions'. II, 'H. D. S.-P.' is Hew David Steuart-Powell, one of Elgar's chamber music cronies. 'His characteristic diatonic run over the keys before beginning to play is here humorously travestied in the semiquaver passages; these should suggest a Toccata, but chromatic beyond H. D. S.-P's liking.' III, 'R. B. T.', Richard Baxter Townshend, is a caricature. The Variation 'has a reference to R. B. T.'s presentation of an old man in some amateur theatricals – the low voice flying off occasionally into "soprano" timbre'. Dorabella expands this by dating the incident about 1895 at W. M. Baker's home, Hasfield Court. Townshend had never acted before and did so against his will. She describes him as an amiable eccentric, riding about Oxford on a tricycle with a permanently ringing bell so that people could hear him coming because, being slightly deaf, he could not hear them. 'Elgar has got him with his funny voice and manner – *and* the tricycle! It is all there and is just a huge joke to anyone who knew him well.' But if you did not know him, as Arthur Johnstone of the *Manchester Guardian* did not, you might have agreed with Johnstone's description of this Variation (9 February 1900) as 'a very unsympathetic personality, garrulous, querulous, trivial, meanly egotistic and rather ape-like' – which says rather more for Elgar's powers of musical portraiture even than Dorabella says.

IV, 'W. M. B.' is William Meath Baker of Hasfield Court, 'a country squire, gentleman and scholar. In the days of horses and carriages it was more difficult than in these days of petrol to arrange the carriages for the day to suit a large number of guests. This Variation was written after the host had, with a slip of paper in his hand, forcibly read out the arrangements for the day and hurriedly left the music-room with an inadvertent bang of the door. In bars 15–24 are some suggestions of the teasing attitude of the guests.' He was a devoted Wagnerian. 'R. B. T.' was his brother-in-law, V, 'R. P. A.' is

---

[17] At this point the pattern of quavers and crotchets is reversed.

Matthew Arnold's son Richard, 'a great lover of music which he played (on the pianoforte) in a self-taught manner, evading difficulties but suggesting in a mysterious way the real feeling. His serious conversation was continually broken up by whimsical and witty remarks' – and it is these which are portrayed by the wind instruments, though Dorabella heard his 'funny little nervous laugh' in the same passages. VI, 'Ysobel' is Isabel Fitton, a member of the Malvern music-loving family whom the Elgars knew well. Elgar had dedicated a piano piece, *Presto*, to her on her twenty-first birthday, 8 August, 1889. She was a viola player and the opening bar 'is an "exercise" for crossing the strings – a difficulty for beginners'. The big intervals, according to Dorabella, depict Miss Fitton's tall stature, and the whole movement – 'pensive and, for a moment, romantic', says Elgar – suggests that the composer was fully aware of the charms of the grave statuesque beauty whose steady gaze meets us from her photograph.

VII, 'Troyte'. This is Arthur Troyte Griffith, the Malvern architect who remained a very close friend of Elgar up to Elgar's death. The Variation is not a portrait. It merely records 'maladroit essays to play the pianoforte; later the strong rhythm suggests the attempts of the instructor (E. E.) to make something like order out of chaos, and the final despairing "slam" records that the effort proved to be vain'. Elgar added that 'the boisterous mood is mere banter'. Troyte was a great sharer in 'japes', as Elgar called the lighter side of life. He was outspoken and brusque in his manner, almost to the point of seeming uncouth. Perhaps this, too, is remembered in the music. In any case, it is hard to know why Dunhill found Elgar's account of this Variation 'impossible to believe'. Rosa Burley said Troyte's nickname was 'Ninepin' and she understood the variation was intended to suggest skittles being bowled over.

VIII, 'W. N.' is 'really suggested by an 18th century house': Sherridge, near Malvern, where the Norbury family lived. Both Winifred and Florence Norbury were music-lovers, and Winifred was part-secretary with Miss Hyde of the Worcestershire Philharmonic Society. 'The gracious personalities of the ladies are sedately shown,' Elgar wrote. 'W. N. was more connected with music than others of the family, and her initials head the movement; to justify this position a little suggestion of a characteristic laugh is given.'

IX, 'Nimrod'. Elgar admits that 'something ardent and mercurial, in addition to the slow movement, would have been needed to portray the character and temperament of A. J. Jaeger'. Then follow these important words: 'The Variation ... is the record of a long summer evening talk, when my friend discoursed eloquently on the slow movements of Beethoven, and said that no one could approach Beethoven at his best in this field, a view with which I cordially concurred. It will be noticed that the opening bars are made to suggest the slow movement of the eighth sonata (Pathétique).'

Thus Elgar firmly pins this emotional Variation to a purely musical link between the two men. In her book on the *Variations*, Dorabella recounts in detail (pp. 110–11) a conversation she had with Elgar in 1904 in which, she says, he described the background of 'Nimrod' as 'the story of something that happened'. Briefly, Elgar (says Mrs Powell) was 'down in the dumps'. He wrote to Jaeger and said he was 'sick of music' and was 'going to give it up'. Jaeger wrote a 'screed' in reply, 'all about my ingratitude for my great gifts,' and suggested he should visit Elgar for a talk. They went a long walk and 'he preached me a regular sermon, pointing out that Beethoven, faced with his worries, had written still more beautiful music – "and that is what you must do"'. Either Mrs Powell's memory played her false, or Elgar's memory telescoped several events into one, for the chronological likelihood of this story is impossible. The phrases of Jaeger about 'great gifts' are in the letter quoted in the previous chapter – 'your necessity . . . is to exercise those creative faculties which a kind providence has given you' – and were written in reply to Elgar's outburst about his lack of support from Novello's – 'the whole future seems hopeless' etc. But Elgar's letter was written on 17 December 1898, and Jaeger's on 31 December 1898 – nearly eight weeks *after* Elgar had written to Jaeger (24 October) describing the *Variations* and saying 'You are Nimrod'; and Mrs Powell heard 'Nimrod' on 1 November. Jaeger was married on 22 December 1898, and paid no visits to Malvern. Elgar went to London and saw the couple's new home in January 1899. Probably the occasion to which Elgar referred was as early as August 1897, when he had written about 'never putting pen to paper' and had received a reply 'which has put new heart into me.' They met at the Three Choirs that September and probably it was then that the conversation about Beethoven's adagios occurred. The great piece of music has become a traditional 'requiem' for commemorating the dead; to this use of it there has been some objection, but, in appropriate cases, what could be better than this intimate record of a real friendship? 'I have omitted your outside manner & have only seen the good lovable honest SOUL in the middle of you,' Elgar wrote to him in March 1899. 'The music's not good enough: nevertheless it was an attempt of your E. E.' – and, in November 1900, 'What a jolly fine tune your Variation is: I'd forgotten it & have been playing it thro' – it's just like you – you solemn, wholesome, hearty old dear.' To Joseph Bennett, writing in *The Daily Telegraph* after the first performance, 'Nimrod' sounded a 'suave and meditative character . . . a cheery personage beaming through gold-rimmed spectacles'. At any rate, Elgar eliminated the cheeriness by conducting it himself at a slower tempo and, in 1903, altering the metronome mark in the score from ♩=66 to ♩=52 and changing the direction *moderato* to *adagio*.

X, 'Dorabella' was Elgar's nickname, from *Così fan tutte,* for Dora Penny, daughter of the Rector of Wolverhampton who, as his second wife, married in 1896 Mary Frances Baker, sister of W. M. B. 'The movement suggests a dancelike lightness,' Elgar wrote; and Dorabella herself noticed many years later that he had parodied her youthful stammer. Her enthusiasm, her gifts as a musician, and her merry chatter made her a frequent and welcome guest of the Elgars at Malvern. As can be inferred from her book, she was responsive to Elgar's rapid changes of mood; and he found her a good and intelligent listener. In XI, 'G. R. S.' (Dr G. R. Sinclair, organist of Hereford Cathedral) some injustice is done, for, as Elgar noted, the Variation has 'nothing to do with organs or cathedrals or, except remotely, with G. R. S. The first few bars were suggested by his great bulldog Dan (a well-known character) falling down the steep bank into the River Wye (bar 1); his paddling up stream to find a landing place (bars 2 and 3); and his rejoicing bark on landing (2nd half of bar 5). G. R. S. said "Set that to music". I did; here it is.' Suggestions that this was another of Elgar's deceptions and that the music has nothing

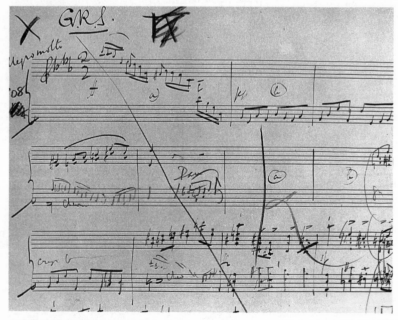

PLATE II. Manuscript of 'G. R. S.' from the 'Enigma' Variations. Elgar has written 'Dan' in bar 5.

It has also been said that bulldogs do not like water – but, as Elgar made clear, Dan fell in, unwillingly. Nothing more needs to be said except that Dan has further claims to immortality. Inscribed by Elgar in Sinclair's visitors' book at Hereford between 1897 and 1903 were several themes representing 'The moods of Dan'. Among them, as will emerge, were themes later to be used in *Gerontius, In the South*, and *The Apostles*.[18] XII, 'B. G. N.' is Basil G. Nevinson an amateur cellist and the third member of the piano trio with Elgar and Steuart-Powell – 'a serious and devoted friend. The Variation is a tribute to a very dear friend whose scientific and artistic attainments, and the wholehearted way they were put at the disposal of his friends, particularly endeared him to the writer.' Elgar stayed often at Nevinson's London home. This glorious Variation is as heartfelt as 'Nimrod' and seems to commemorate Nevinson's faith in Elgar in the days of struggle. It is also a cellist's delight.

About XIII, '***' there has been more mystification. 'The asterisks,' Elgar wrote, 'take the place of the name of a lady who was, at the time of the composition, on a sea voyage. The drums suggest the distant throb of the engines of a liner over which the clarinet quotes a phrase from Mendelssohn's "Calm Sea and Prosperous Voyage".'

The lady was Lady Mary Lygon, sister of Earl Beauchamp, of Madresfield Court, near Malvern. In 1895 she had been appointed a Woman of the Bedchamber to the Duchess of Teck (later Queen Mary) and she accompanied her brother to Australia in 1899 when at the age of twenty-seven he was appointed Governor of New South Wales. Elgar knew her through the Madresfield Festivals of Music and she became friends with him and Alice. In 1905 she married the Hon. W. H. Forbes-Trefusis and, as Lady Mary Trefusis, played an important part in the affairs of the English Folk Dance Society, becoming its first president in 1912. (She had met Cecil Sharp while in Australia.) Sketches for this Variation refer to it as 'L' and sketches for the finale show that Elgar contemplated re-introducing 'L. M. L.' Lady Mary was not in fact on a voyage at the time of composition. (Elgar, writing in 1927, had made a mistake.) The *Variations* were completed by February 1899, and on 24 March of that year Elgar, in writing to Jaeger about the dedication of the *Three Characteristic Pieces*, says 'I want to know if you could get the *title* done *very soon* as Lady Mary is going away & I should like her to see it first . . . She is a most angelic person & I should like to please her.' Elgar then evidently had second thoughts about putting Lady Mary's initials in the published score of the *Variations* and replaced them by asterisks probably

<hr>

[18] Dan died on 1 July 1903. A letter to Elgar from Sinclair on that date says: 'Poor dear old Dan died an hour ago. He was my best friend.' On 6 July Sinclair wrote: 'He has a quiet little grave under the big apple tree.'

because he was superstitious and sensitive about identifying anyone too openly with the thirteenth variation. Lady Mary left for Australia on 11 April 1899. Elgar was in her company four times in the preceding two months and at one of these meetings asked her to accept the dedication of the *Three Characteristic Pieces*. It is obvious that he also mentioned the thirteenth variation to her. In a letter he wrote to her on 25 July 1899 when she was in Sydney, he said: 'The *Variations* (especially No. 13) have been a great triumph for me under Richter. . . .' This is conclusive evidence that she knew about the Variation and disposes of Dora Powell's statement in her book[19] that asterisks were used because a letter asking permission for use of initials had not reached Lady Mary before she sailed. When Elgar published the notes for the pianola rolls, his criterion for disclosing the name of the subject for each variation was if they were dead. Lady Mary was still living. But his manuscript draft for the notes states: 'The asterisks take the place of the name of Lady Mary Lygon. . . .' Thus far the matter is beyond dispute.

But music can mean two things at once, can exist on two levels of feeling. One must therefore pay some heed to Rosa Burley's statement[20] that the 'throbbing and the quotation from *Calm Sea and Prosperous Voyage* . . . bore no reference to the liner and the sea voyage . . . but, as might be expected in a movement called 'Romanza' expressed something very different.' Some of her readers have inferred that she was trying to suggest that she was the lady who Elgar 'clearly and unequivocally told her' was represented and whose name he withheld because 'extremely intimate and personal feelings were concerned'. On the other hand, there is also her remark to one of the other variation subjects, 'I'm not a variation; I'm the theme'.

In addition to Miss Burley's implications there are those of Ernest Newman who, writing in the *Sunday Times* on 18 November 1956, stated: 'There is much expression of personal experiences in his music, but the more tremendous these had been for him the more he resorted to either complete concealment of them from the public eye or to a playful mystification with regard to them. The famous thirteenth variation of the "Enigma" is a cardinal case in point. It is time we heard the last of the old legend that the subject of this variation was Lady Mary Lygon. . . . A present-day listener to the "Enigma" must surely be devoid of all sensibility if he does not see that, whoever the human subject of the No. 13 may have been, it is a poignant brooding upon some personal experience or other that had made a profound and enduring mark on him: to take one feature of it alone, that moving sound-picture of the throbbing of the engines of a great liner and the sad quotation from Mendelssohn's *Calm Sea and*

[19] *Memories of a Variation*, op.cit., p. 115.
[20] *Edward Elgar: the record of a friendship*, op. cit., pp. 125–7.

Prosperous Voyage overture would never have been wrung out of Elgar by the fact that the good lady at Madresfield . . . had chosen to go on a sea trip. A study merely of Elgar's scoring of the variation should make it clear to any person of more than average sensitivity that he was here dwelling in imagination on somebody and something the parting from whom and which had at some time or other torn the very heart out of him.'

Newman claimed that he knew that the real subject of the Romanza was the same as the person whose soul is enshrined in the Violin Concerto (where her identity is concealed not by asterisks but by the use of five dots). On 18 May 1939 he wrote to Alice Stuart-Wortley's daughter Clare: 'I am pretty sure I know the name: the whole facts of the case were given me by a correspondent (unknown to me personally) who was an intimate, long ago, of both Elgar and '. . . . .' I myself had for many years been sceptical about the "Lady Mary Lygon" as the subject of the 13th Variation . . . but I hadn't any information that could give point and body to my suspicion. After receiving the information about the '. . . . .' I asked my correspondent whether the person "enshrined" here was the same as the one covered by the three asterisks: and I was told that they were one and the same (not Lady M. L. of course!) The details are very curious and sad. I'm glad you agree with me that Elgar's secret should not be exposed to profane eyes. Some day, of course, one or other of the three or four people who know it is pretty sure to say something that will get into print, but it won't be *me*!'

Newman let his secret die with him. But one recalls that Helen Weaver sailed for New Zealand in October 1885 with her lungs affected. Several devoted Elgarians insist that the Romanza is nothing but a poignant memory of his former fiancée. But is it putting too great a weight on this delicate miniature tone-poem to suggest that it carries the burden of lost love still longed for? Perhaps Elgar cast a fleeting glance behind him as he thought of separation by sea and land. Perhaps Mary Lygon's journey was merely a pretext, in the only tragic Variation (and the 13th), for using a quotation with Leipzig connections which sounds as much like Schumann's piano concerto as Mendelssohn. The music at any rate, is full of dream-like regret.

The throbbing of the liner's engines is one of several imaginative and inventive strokes of instrumentation in Elgar's music. In the score he specifies that the effect should be obtained by using side-drum sticks for the timpani roll, but most timpanists find that they are too heavy to produce the remote poetic sound Elgar had in mind. When the work was first rehearsed Elgar himself was not satisfied with the result of his directions and the famous timpanist, Charles Henderson, had the brilliant idea, since almost universally adopted, of using two half-crowns near the rim of the drum. But unless a second player is employed, Elgar has left no time for the timpanist to change from coins or sticks to ordinary timpani sticks: he must either cut short his roll or omit the first few strokes of the *naturale* which follows – a rare miscalculation.[21] It is amusing to discover from Elgar's letters to Jaeger that he was on the verge of disguising or deleting the Mendelssohn quotation. 'The pretty Lady is on the sea & far away,' he wrote on 2 May 1899, '& I meant this (originally) as a little quotation from Mendelssohn's Meeresstille u. Glückliche Fahrt – but I did not acknowledge it as the critics – if one mentions anything of the kind – talk of nothing else – so I have now cut out the reference. . . . Tell me what else reminds the critics of something else. I might alter it.' He was extremely sensitive about having his attention called to similarities between his music and other men's. Dorabella once pointed out a place in *Gerontius* which reminded her of Chopin's *Polonaise Fantaisie* and was sharply told: 'I know nothing about pianoforte music. I hate the piano as an instrument and I don't care for Chopin and I never heard the piece you mention.'[22]

XIV, 'E. D. U.' is Elgar himself 'bold and vigorous in general style', but only one side of him, and only the expression of one 'I'll show 'em' mood. E. D. U. is a paraphrase of his wife's name for him, 'Edoo', pronounced as (and no doubt derived from) the German Eduard. Dorabella[23] interestingly points out that the woodwind phrase four bars before rehearsal cue No. 73 in the full score, a phrase which also occurs in C. A. E., is a whistle with which Elgar signalled to Alice his return home or used to attract her attention. In this finale it serves to recall C. A. E. 'Nimrod,' too, is recalled in the revised section upon which he was so insistent, and the work ends in a burst of grandiose assertiveness. (The original ending was just after cue No. 76.) Whether the revised finale was an improvement remains a matter of controversy and a question of taste. It is honest in its blatancy. One does sense that the material after [76] is tacked on and that, being the thinnest in the work, it has (probably for that very reason) the thickest orchestral padding.[24] The 'Nimrod' theme does not really suit the magniloquent treatment it is accorded in the peroration.

Out of such personal characteristics as the whistle, Dorabella's

---

[21] See Percival R. Kirby, *The Kettle-drums* (London, 1930).
[22] *Edward Elgar, Memories of a Variation*, op.cit., p. 52.
[23] *Edward Elgar: Memories of a Variation*, op.cit., p. 116.
[24] There is an interesting letter, dated 23 October 1904, from Elgar to John West of Novello's publishing staff: 'Many thanks for your letter re 2nd bar p 100 of the Variations: yes, it is an error undoubtedly, but on looking at it I *thought* it must be one of those things which *sound* all right to the *timbre* of the insts. I waited until yesterday when I was conducting rehearsal & concert in L'pool and listened to the bar. Do you know it *sounds* all right to me – sort of inverted (perverted) pedal and I don't think we'll alter it.'

stammer, Dan's bark, W. N.'s laugh, R. B. T.'s voice, and R. P. A.'s wit, Elgar concocted a work of art which is all music, through and through, because no knowledge of the work's 'programme' is required for its full appreciation. It is the apotheosis of the miniaturist Elgar. Those who hold that there is no connection between the Elgar of the salon music and the Elgar of the major works overlook the *Variations*, which are *Salut d'Amour* and *Chanson de Matin* raised to a higher degree. Its improvisatory nature is a reminder that the work grew from the kind of piano improvisation which Elgar had been able to invent since childhood, and it is also the last of the 'domestic' works, such as the *Bavarian Highlands* part-songs, associated with his life among friends in Malvern and Worcester. The poetry present in all Elgar's slighter and lighter works pervades every bar of the *Enigma*; and so does his technical skill which in this work amounts to sleight of hand: a perfect canon embedded in W. M. B., subtle and contrasting use of tonality, rhythmical rather than melodic variations of the theme. The theme itself is superb, with the alternation of minor and major emotionally as well as functionally a master-stroke. The late Sir Jack Westrup, in a memorable paper read in April 1960,[25] remarked that its rhythmical structure is unlike Elgar's normal practice and that the melody is organized in a curious fashion. He pointed out that in the sketch the markings over the first two bars were 'even more peculiar. Over the second beat of the first bar (the two quavers B flat and G) is written "pizz." and over the third and fourth beats (the crotchets C and A) "arco". In the second bar "pizz" comes over the crotchets on the second and third beats, and "arco" over the two quavers on the fourth beat.' Westrup thought this alternation of *pizzicato* and *arco* had a suggestion of ballet music.[26] He attached great significance to the G. R. S. and 'Dan' variation and suggested that the Original Theme might have been fashioned later than G. R. S. and 'may be the record of a very personal experience, possibly of an emotional character. That experience may be associated with the River Teme. It may have occurred many years earlier when Elgar was a young man, or it may have happened after he was married. It is even possible that the theme is associated with Elgar's love of animals . . . When we recall Elgar's intense interest in Dan and the use he made of the various interpretations of his moods, it is not wholly fantastic to suggest that the Enigma theme may have had its origin as a lament for the loss of a great happiness' [such as the death of Scap or even Alice's refusal to let Elgar have a dog after their marriage].

The variations themselves are notably free, except, designedly, C. A. E. In 'Dorabella' and the 'Romanza' there is only the slightest

---

[25] 'Elgar's Enigma', *Proceedings of Royal Musical Association, 1959–60*, pp. 79–97.
[26] See Elgar's views on the *Variations* as a ballet, p. 100.

connection with the theme. Those who find Elgar's symphonic methods too diffuse or short-winded can usually admire the *Variations* because of their epigrammatic nature. Each change of mood, each delineation of character or episode is complete in itself, a polished jewel. The orchestration is a perennial delight. As Tovey wrote,[27] 'There is many an ambitious composer of brilliant and revolutionary reputation who ought to be . . . washed in its crystal-clear scoring until he learns the meaning of artistic economy and mastery.' Here, if anywhere, is the Gallic influence on Elgar: its delicacy, fantasy, poetry, and imaginative freedom owe far more to French music, and even to Russian, than they do to Bayreuth or Vienna.[28] It is a moving and intimate work, yet it is perhaps the least subjective of all Elgar's works except the *Introduction and Allegro*; it has passion as well as humour, but it does not have the intense, secret waywardness, in terms of rubato, of the Violin Concerto nor the chromatic splendour of *Gerontius*. It strikes a perfect balance between the classical, the romantic, and the rhapsodic. It is Elgar's orchestral masterpiece and it is, in my opinion, the greatest orchestral work yet written by an Englishman.

For the remainder of 1899 Jaeger and Elgar attended to proofs for the publication of the full score of the *Variations*. Various inquiries about performance of the work were received, among them one from the Scottish Orchestra in Glasgow. This projected performance was abandoned and Elgar wrote (27 December) rather testily, 'When *will* those Vars: (score) be ready? I think my MS must have frightened poor [Max] Bruch at Glasgow – so they have put off the performance & probably, I shall have to thank your firm for another entire loss of performance.' Yet only a month previously he had written: 'I don't mind altering the scores at all: nothing can make me miserable regarding my music, thank you.' Jaeger, in fact, took endless trouble to see that the score and the work were alike perfect. He had been worried still about the ending and after hearing the new finale played at Worcester and in London under Richter in October he wrote: 'I was a little disappointed that the sudden burst into E flat at [82] did not quite come off as explosively and surprisingly as I had anticipated . . . I put it down to the fact that the first fiddlers have not the short quaver rest that many of the other instruments have. They seemed at the performances to glide up to the B flat instead of sharply plunging, hammering on it as with stroke of Thor's war axe! Would it not give

[27] *Essays in Musical Analysis*, v (London, 1936), p. 150.
[28] Towards the end of his life Elgar told Troyte Griffith that if the *Variations* had been written by a Russian they would have 'long ago' been produced as a ballet. He visualized the setting as a banqueting hall, with a veiled dancer as the Enigma. Ashton set his ballet in the garden of Elgar's home, with the 'friends pictured within' visiting him, and Richter's acceptance of the *Variations* as the climax.

you a stronger B flat and a stronger E flat chord and a great surprise if *all* instruments had the crotchet rest before [82]? . . . Excuse my impertinence.' Elgar agreed. 'I've done it to please you (grrhh!) & must put it right in the wind pts when the revision comes if it ever does.'

It was for constructive, helpful, and clear-sighted criticism of this kind that Jaeger was valued by Elgar and other composers. But he played no part in Elgar's op. 37, the *Sea Pictures*, which had gone to Boosey's because of the temporary breach with Novello's. This song-cycle was written for and first performed at the 1899 Norwich Festival on 5 October. Elgar conducted and the contralto soloist was Clara Butt, then aged twenty-seven. ('She dressed like a mermaid,' he told Troyte Griffith, and to Jaeger he wrote 'She sang *really well*.') Elgar's appearance while conducting this performance was memorably described by R. H. Mottram as 'that of a hawk dreaming poetry in captivity'. The songs were a success with the public and the critics. One of them, No. 2, 'In Haven' to words by Alice Elgar, had been written as early as 30 May 1897, when it was called 'Love Alone will Stay' and had been published as 'Lute Song' in *The Dome* in January 1898. The other four had been written at Birchwood in July 1899. Today these songs have only to appear in a programme for someone to castigate the words of the poems Elgar chose to set. In the case of No. 3, Elizabeth Barrett Browning's 'Sabbath Morning at Sea' and No. 5, Adam Lindsay Gordon's 'The Swimmer', the criticism is justified, but the remaining three, Roden Noel's 'Sea-Slumber Song', Alice Elgar's 'In Haven', and Richard Garnett's 'Where Corals Lie' are respectable enough and certainly received the best settings. Once again, however, it is the orchestral part which commands attention, notably in 'Sea-Slumber Song' where the swell of the sea is conveyed by octaves in the strings, harp chords, and the gong struck with a sponge-headed stick. One feels, throughout the cycle, that the words evoked *orchestral* images and tunes and then had to be fitted in willy-nilly. The exception is the delightful and seductive 'Where Corals Lie'. And though Elgar makes an impassioned and convincing climax to Mrs Browning's poem, bringing back the very characteristic violin figure that opened the cycle, he could do little for Gordon's verses except, as Ernest Newman remarked, to preserve faithfully in the musical setting the 'absurdity of rhyme'. The description by the orchestra of a stormy sea is finely done, but the big tune is altogether too rigid for its purpose, and echoes from the first song and from 'Where Corals Lie', while giving the cycle some kind of unity, only throw into relief the poverty of invention in this finale. Whereas Elgar's salon style is sublimated in the *Variations*, this cannot be said of *Sea Pictures*, where three of the songs hover precariously on the edge of drawing-room balladry and are only kept from toppling over by Elgar's orchestral taste and the performance of a sensitive singer. The work as a whole bears signs of being completed in haste to meet a commission, but its best moments have a real kinship with the *Variations* and the scoring throughout is that of a mature master. The songs were performed in London two days after the Norwich performance. On 20 October Ada Crossley sang two of them by Royal command at Balmoral Castle. This was not the first mark of Queen Victoria's favour in that year: on 24 May he had been invited to Windsor by Sir Walter Parratt, Master of the Queen's Musick, to conduct at a concert marking the Queen's eightieth birthday for which madrigals in praise of the Queen (on the lines of *The Triumphes of Oriana* for Elizabeth I and *A Garland for the Queen* for Elizabeth II) had been written by several English composers. Elgar's contribution was 'To Her Beneath Whose Steadfast Star' and his *Chanson de Matin* and *Chanson de Nuit* were also played. On 18 October, in the private chapel at Windsor, ten of Elgar's compositions were given including the *Sword Song* from *Caractacus*. 'I've all sorts of mouldy japes & things to tell you,' Elgar wrote that day to Troyte.

It was the success of the *Variations*, however, that took Elgar to the forefront. Richter's second London performance was a mark of special favour, and he lost no time in including it in his first season as Hallé conductor in Manchester where, on 8 February 1900, as Arthur Johnstone of the *Manchester Guardian* put it the next day, 'the audience seemed rather astonished that a work by a British composer should have had other than a petrifying effect upon them'. Apart from Bantock, Elgar, and Stanford, the first British conductor to take it up was Henry Wood, who put it in a Queen's Hall programme in April 1901. It is a comment on the commercial dictates of the time that a professional British conductor waited so long to perform a British work that had been generally welcomed. As Jaeger said in letters to Dorabella: 'He [Wood] has just written to me "How beautiful the Variations are!" *At last!* . . . I can assure you Wood makes these things hum. I have never heard anything more daringly devilishly brilliant & boisterous than Troyte or G.R.S.. . . .' Henceforward the work was never to suffer neglect; its popularity has increased from year to year. In 1902 it was played in London by the Meiningen Orchestra under Fritz Steinbach, whose comments are illuminating. 'Here', he said,[29] 'is an unexpected genius and pathbreaker in the field of orchestration. Nowadays nearly every composer is content merely to adapt Wagner's innovations, but Elgar, as this work shows, is a real pioneer with a new technique in orchestration, combining entirely original effects with almost unique virtuosity.' Alexander Siloti conducted the first performance in Russia in St Petersburg in 1904 and wrote to Elgar telling him of a 'very great success both with

[29] Edward Speyer, *My Life and Friends* (London, 1937).

the public & with the "musical world" . . . Mr N. Rimsky-Korsakov & Mr A. Glazunov were particularly pleased with them'. A Moscow performance followed.

In a sense the *Enigma Variations* are symbolic: they sum up the world Elgar was leaving for the world into which they took him. In the pages of this score he remembered the scenes and friends of his days of struggle when his world seemed bounded by the Malvern Hills: friendly chamber music, amateur theatricals, local gentry, the cathedral organist, the encouraging friend in the publishing house. In 1899, when the 'friends pictured within' heard themselves in music, new friends' names occur in correspondence and Alice's diary: Frank Schuster, music-loving financier; Alberto Randegger, conductor; Hans Richter; Alfred E. Rodewald, a wealthy Liverpool amateur musician of German descent; Alfred Kalisch, music critic and translator of Richard Strauss opera libretti; Henry Ettling, wine merchant from Mainz and friend of Richter; Adolph Brodsky, violinist, friend of Brahms and Tchaikovsky and since 1895 Principal of the Royal Manchester College of Music.

Of these the closest friends were Schuster and Rodewald. More will be said about Rodewald in a later chapter. Leo Francis Schuster, described by Percy Young[30] as 'a homosexual dilettante whom Alice did not like', was to be a generous friend to Elgar for nearly thirty years. He devoted his wealth to music; his beautiful Thames-side house, 'The Hut', by Monkey Island and three miles from Maidenhead, was a meeting-place for musicians, writers, and painters, as was his London home at 22 Old Queen Street. He was a friend of Gabriel Fauré, who wrote many of his songs while staying at 'The Hut', and for Elgar he had a special and close affection. He had early appreciated Elgar's talent. Writing in August 1903 to Elgar about a concert he had attended in order to hear a work by another contemporary composer he said: 'Don't you seriously think it good of me to go? I do it out of a Conscientious Curiosity, and I may add that but for this C.C. I might never have discovered a certain E.E. perhaps a *little bit* before the ruck!' After he had stayed with the Elgars for the Three Choirs Festival of 1903 he wrote: 'How I enjoyed those walks and talks with you, Edward, and if my speech must have appeared only stupider than my silence, you must make allowances for the fact that I am always, so to speak, paralysed in the presence of genius: in the matter of friendship we are, and I thank God for it, on terms of equality, but try as I may I can never forget that *you* have written a "Gerontius" and I have only listened to it! – the gap *awes* me.'

William McNaught, Charles Stanford, Percy Pitt, Hubert Parry,

[30] *Alice Elgar*, op. cit., p. 157. See also *Siegfried Sassoon Diaries 1920–2* (London, 1981), pp. 293–4.

Alexander Mackenzie, and Edgar Jacques were among the English
musicians whom Elgar met from time to time. Although – and this
must be remembered – he was still teaching in Malvern, he visited
London more often to go to concerts and operas, to see art
exhibitions, to lunch at Pagani's or his club. He even turned up at the
first annual general meeting of the Folk-Song Society. He had
previously taken Lucy Broadwood out to dinner and his interest had
perhaps been awakened momentarily by Kalish and Jacques or even
by Parry. He moved the adoption of the committee's report and with
that gesture both opened and closed his connection with the folk-
song revival. As late as 1929 he was saying in public that inclusion of a
folk-song in a piece of music was a sign that the composer was
shirking his job, and to Troyte he once said: 'I write the folk songs of
this country'.

A new and larger world was opening to him, but perhaps
instinctively he recoiled from some of its implications and, as he
always did, clung more tightly to past memories. As the year 1899
ended, he wrote two letters on 29 December from Craeg Lea. One
was to Charles Buck, with whom Alice and he had spent a few days
after the Sheffield *King Olaf*. 'A patch in the old year which bears
thinking of with pleasure' – the year of the *Enigma* and *Sea Pictures*
triumphs – 'was our little visit to Settle', he wrote. Perhaps his
melancholy mood was induced by his father's illness (William Elgar
was 'just hovering 'twixt this world & the next . . . the end cannot be far
away', but he recovered to live until 30 April 1906). Whatever the
cause, he added a postscript which was to recur frequently: 'Oh! the
mad days'. To Jaeger he sent the old lament: 'All is flat, stale &
unprofitable'. He was in the throes of composing *The Dream of
Gerontius*, and he was following the sequence of moods, so well
observed by Rosa Burley:[31] 'To begin with there would be a period
of great exaltation over the conception of the work and the
commission. . . . This was always followed by a period of black
despair over the intractability of the material and the utter impossibi-
lity of ever getting it into a satisfactory shape. An immense amount
of encouragement, accompanied by assurances that he was the only
person able to do it, and reminders that it must at all costs be done,
had now to be expended in order to shift him into the next phase –
which was one of increasing hope and enthusiasm. Tunes, contrapuntal patterns, and sequences had begun to suggest themselves for
various sections of the work, and would start to build up almost
without his conscious control into something like the completed
whole.'

With *Gerontius* this pattern can be followed stage by stage.

[31] *Edward Elgar: the record of a friendship*, op. cit., p. 89.

7 'Gerontius': Disaster and Triumph

Elgar was asked in November 1898 for a work for the 1900 Birmingham Triennial Festival. He wrote to Littleton of Novello's: 'Now I have to consider the subject, which must be sacred: can you suggest anything? and will your firm want the work? I want to make this my chief work . . .' Littleton did not trouble himself to reply. At first, Elgar considered St Augustine as a subject. He told Joseph Bennett, the critic of *The Daily Telegraph*, in January 1899 that this idea had been rejected as 'too controversial: this is as I feared'.[1] (The controversy can only have related to Augustine's relations with women, not to his theology.) Elgar said he was considering 'a purely scriptural thing, but have not fully decided'. Dorabella says[2] that she heard 'a good deal' of the piano score of *The Dream of Gerontius* while on visits to Craeg Lea and Birchwood in May, June and July 1899, but her dates are wrong and she meant 1900. On one visit she heard the Introduction to Part II and 'Praise to the Holiest' in nearly complete form. When Elgar asked her what she thought of the latter she replied: 'It gives me the impression of great doors opening and shutting.' 'Does it?' Elgar said. 'That's exactly what I mean.'

He had been pondering a setting of Cardinal Newman's poem for many years, perhaps for nearly fifteen, and he had had several discussions with Father Knight about reducing it to a libretto. 'The poem has been soaking in my mind for at least eight years', he told an interviewer in 1900.[3] 'All that time I have been gradually assimilating the thoughts of the author into my own musical promptings.' What became the 'Prayer' theme, first heard in the Prelude at three bars after [2], was inscribed in Sinclair's visitors' book at Hereford on 19 April 1898 was a mood of the bulldog Dan musing on the order to be muzzled. During the Three Choirs meeting at Worcester in September 1899, Alice noted that 'E. walked with Father Bellasis', of Birmingham Oratory. Bellasis had known Newman. It is likely that the discussion was on the subject of permission to use the libretto.

But in November 1899 Elgar sent Jaeger 'Judas & another scrap'. 'Judas' was a theme, later used to introduce the Angel of the Agony in *Gerontius*, which was intended for a work about the Apostles. Possibly at this point he thought still that he might provide Birmingham with 'a scriptural thing', for Jaeger in reply does not refer to *Gerontius* but

---

[1] Letters published in *The Daily Telegraph*, 4 September 1937.
[2] *Memories of a Variation*, op. cit., pp. 17–19.
[3] *Musical Times*, October 1900, p. 648.

says, 'That "Judas" or "night" theme from your new work is a *discovery*! It makes me *shiver* when I think of the effect of soft low brass (Five Tubas, Eh! You'll get them at Bayreuth, but where else?).' It is clear that between late November 1899 and mid-January 1900, the *Gerontius* project was in the melting-pot. On 18 November Elgar wrote to Jaeger: 'I'm glad you like my idea of Judas. I'll send you another wildly expressive bit, but it's very hard to try & write *one's self* out & find that one's soul is not *simple* enough for the British Choral Society.' His next specific reference is on 10 January 1900: 'Judas is dropped! I may have some news for you concerning my works very shortly – but I am sick of the whole thing and wd. never hear, see, write or think of music in shape, form, substance or wraith again.' A letter from Elgar on 5 February 1900, in which he discusses *Gerontius*, establishes beyond doubt that the sketches he was sending to Jaeger in November 1899 were *not* in their *Gerontius* form: 'I say, that Judas theme will *have* to be used up for death and despair in this work, so don't peach.'

Littleton of Novello's was dubious about *Gerontius* for Birmingham not on theological grounds alone, but because it contained no rôle for the leading oratorio singer of the day, Mme. Albani, whose participation in a new festival work was considered essential to success. This kind of discouragement, combined with his perpetual pleading of poverty, caused Elgar (as he told Jaeger on 5 February 1900) to 'give up' the Birmingham commission, 'as I really could not afford to go on writing'. On New Year's Day 1900 G. H. Johnstone, chairman of the festival committee, and Mrs Johnstone went to lunch with the Elgars in Malvern and, in Alice Elgar's words, 'arranged for E.'s work Birm. Fest. Deo gratias'. Johnstone offered to relieve Elgar 'of all trouble in the matter rather than lose me' and, the next day, Elgar sent a telegram accepting the terms and 'began again at former libretto'. The terms were £200 for the work, then a royalty of 4d per copy on the sale of vocal scores payable only when initial costs had been recovered. 'All goes slowly here,' Elgar wrote to Jaeger on 4 January. 'I'm working like a — fool & get kicked for my pains &/or pleasures – I don't know which they are.'

On 12 January Elgar visited Birmingham Oratory to see Fr Bellasis again, and set to work revising and orchestrating. To Jaeger he continued in a vein of melancholy – 'I am sick of music and all that's connected with it & long for Birchwood & pigs & cattle'. . . . 'Music is a trade and I am no tradesman' – and he also kept up a mystifying secrecy about *Gerontius*: 'I am working away at my thing for Birmingham . . . but I have nothing to do with the publishing this time & must not talk about it even to you.' Why not, asked Jaeger, understandably, adding: 'So you are "sick of music" eh? Papperlapapp! That's what Wagner said . . . so I take it your "blues" are a good sign.' Elgar then explained the arrangements with Birmingham and that he had heard from 'nice good Mr Alfred' Littleton on 23 January that Novello's were to publish the work. 'I am setting Newman's "Dream of Gerontius" awfully solemn & mystic. . . . Now I must go on to my Devils' chorus – good!'

Rosa Burley's account[4] of the composition of *Gerontius* is reliable evidence. Elgar was afraid that 'the strong Catholic flavour of the poem and its insistence on the doctrine of purgatory would be prejudicial to success . . . He told me in fact that Dvořák, who had planned a setting of the work for the 1888 Festival, had been discouraged from making it for this very reason . . . Throughout the early months of 1900 we simply lived *Gerontius*. We talked of little else on our walks and Edward seemed to think of nothing else. Again and again manuscript fragments would be brought to The Mount on the lesson days, tried over and discussed . . .'

On 2 March Elgar sent forty-four pages of the manuscript score to Jaeger, with the typical injunction, 'Deal tenderly with it it's the *only* copy there is – I can't yet afford a copyist – poor divvil.' On 20 March he sent fifty-five more pages, up to the end of Part I. 'The final chos. is godly effective &, I think, not quite cheap . . . As soon as this "Dream" (nightmare) is done – I'll write such a lot of things for Ysaiah – & all the profits – I *should* dearly love to get out some of my chamber music!' This last punning remark was in reply to a suggestion from Jaeger that he should write 'a big fiddle piece' for Ysaÿe.

Proofs of the vocal score began to arrive at Malvern from 3 April.[5] Now also began the remarkable series of criticisms and suggestions about the work made by Jaeger to Elgar. Of few established masterpieces have the birth-pangs been so fully recorded, nor in such racy language. Jaeger had already (25 March) written, 'By Jove! What a task for you. Yet I feel sure you will be equal to it . . . the greater the difficulty the more surely you will rise to it.' On 8 April Elgar copied out the Angel's song 'for your own Angel to sing' – this being Mrs Jaeger who was expecting a child very shortly. Jaeger found the song 'uncanny, because it has a character unlike anything else in music as far as I know. Simple as it is, its very simplicity is its wonder, for it is a kind of simplicity I have never met with before, so aloof from things mundane, so haunting and strangely fascinating.' He had studied again Part I in proof 'and have been tremendously stirred by it. . . . Since *Parsifal* nothing of this mystic, religious kind of music has appeared to my knowledge that displays the same power

---

[4] *Edward Elgar: the record of a friendship*, op. cit., pp. 134–135.
[5] Dorabella, on p. 21 of her book, says that 'Gerontius proofs were arriving in batches every few days' in November 1899, but she has confused these with the final proofs of the *Variations*.

and beauty. . . . I am now most curious and anxious to know how you will deal with that part of the poem where the soul goes within the Presence of the Almighty. *There* is a subject for you! Whatever else you may do, don't be *theatrical*.'

To this Elgar replied, 'Please remember that none of the "action" takes place in the *presence* of God: I would not have tried *that* neither did Newman. The Soul says "I go before my God" but *we* don't, we stand outside – I've thrown over all the "machinery" for celestial music, harps etc.' In reply to an apology from Elgar for trouble he was causing by his continual revisions, Jaeger wrote on 27 April: 'Go on "troubling" me, my dear friend, I love to do all I can for one whom one loves as a man & friend and admires sincerely, greatly, as an artist, a weaver of most wondrous sounds, whose genius, moreover, I had the happiness to appreciate and extol before almost any one of my colleagues!' On 29 April Elgar's letter to Jaeger contains a hint of anxiety about the need for the chorus at Birmingham to have their parts to learn as soon as possible: 'I want you to push on the printing of what I sent and shall send today or tomorrow. Then if the Birm. people like, they can have copies up to the end of the Demons' chorus. The end of the work requires some consideration & I don't want to send the MS until I've been thro' it (as usual) again – again – again – again & after that once more!'

It will perhaps be easier to follow the course of the discussions henceforward if they are set out in the form of a dramatic dialogue:

ELGAR (7 May): I want you to look very carefully at Pt. II of Gerontius as it comes from the printer and tell me if you think those conversations between the Angel and the Soul are wearisome. . . . I know the poem too well and you (as an outsider as it were) might see if you would further curtail it. Between ourselves this is the only part of the work that I fear or even think twice about. If the words are sufficiently interesting the music will do. . . . I wanted the Angel's song & two or three other in tempo portions to stand out.

JAEGER (22 May): Oh! I am half undone and I tremble after the tremendous exaltation I have gone through. . . . I have not seen or heard anything since *Parsifal* that has stirred me and spoken to me with the trumpet tongue of genius as has this part of your latest, and *by far* greatest work. . . . Your wonderful music is inexpressibly and most wonderfully elevating, 'aloof', mystic and heart-moving, as by the force of a great compassion. . . . That solo of the 'Angel of the Agony' is overpowering. . . . Those poignant melodies, those heart-piercing *beautiful* harmonies! I recognise the chief theme as having belonged to 'Judas'. Nobody could dream that it was not originally *inspired* by *these very words of Newman's*. You must not, *cannot*, expect this work of yours to be appreciated by the ordinary amateur (*or* critic!) after one hearing. You will have to rest content, as other great men had to before you, if a few friends and enthusiasts hail it as a work of genius. . . . Goodnight, my friend, and go on with your magnum opus to the joy and benefit of us poor ordinary mortals and ad majorem dei gloriam! Much love!

Alice Elgar's diary records on 21, 22, and 23 May: 'E. writing hard'. On 25 May 'E. very engrossed last chorus Gerontius'. On 29 May 'Very hard at last chorus', 30th 'Nearly finished great chorus'.

ELGAR (31 May): By this post comes the great Blaze [Praise to the Holiest]. . . . There's still some more MS to come but not much. I can't tell you how much good your letter has done me: I *do* dearly like to be *understood*.

On 6 June, four days after Elgar's forty-third birthday, Alice entered these words: 'E. finished the Dream of Gerontius. Deo gratias. Rather poorly.'

ELGAR (7 June): God bless you, Minrod.[6] Here's the end.

JAEGER (8 June): The more I study the work the more I marvel. It is wonderful. Come & discuss some little points with me.

In a letter to Dorabella on 9 June Jaeger said, 'E.E. has sent the completion of his blessed Gerontius. The work undoes me utterly if I am in the mood. [That reservation is important.] . . . The Chorus Parts will not be in the hands of the B'ham singers for another 3 weeks or more; so your honoured aunt must possess her soul in patience. . . . The majority of the B'ham audience will not be able to appreciate Gerontius first time; too subtle & original & too mystic & beautiful. . . .'

Already it was becoming clear that the chorus, of whom Dorabella's aunt, Mrs Hodgson, was a member, and indeed the soloists, would have their work cut out to learn the work in time for the first performance on 3 October.

ELGAR (14 June): Plunket Greene [who was to sing the Priest and the Angel of the Agony] leaves middle of July & wd. like to squint at his part previous. Will the rough 8vo. copies be ready by the end of this month? . . .

JAEGER (14 June): There is a lot of *Joseph* and *Mary* about the work; very proper for a Roman Catholic lying at death's door to sing about, but likely to frighten *some* d—d fools of Protestants. I had a long talk to the Secretary of one of the big Glasgow Societies yesterday and showed him proofs. . . . He *at once*, on reading the words, spoke of the 'Roman Catholic element' being so prominent!! 'Tommy rot' you say: *ditto*, says I, who am rather an Agnostic than anything else. But alas! one must deal with people as one finds them, and if, without bowdlerising a superb poem, one can remove Mary and Joseph to a more distant background, it may not be a bad thing.

ELGAR (15 June): . . . Of course it will frighten the Low Church party but the poem must on no account be touched! . . . Them as don't like it can be damned in their own way – not ours. It's awfully curious the attitude

---

[6] Not, as usually quoted, Nimrod. Elgar liked to vary his nicknames.

(towards sacred things) of the narrow English mind: it puts me in memory of the man who said, when he saw another crossing himself 'Oh, this *devilish crossing*'. There's a nice confused idea for you.

JAEGER (16 June): *I* have often said 'Oh this *devilish crossing*' and yet I am not bigoted. There is one outside our shop . . . where I have often been all but killed! Otherwise I agree with you. . . . My wife's Irish (Roman Catholic) nurse nearly had a fit when she saw in my wife's bedroom a picture of *Martin Luther*! 'Religion' (*Dogma*) is a damnable thing at times and responsible for more misery and cruelty and general badness than any other thing the devil ever invented.

(15 June): There is one page [159 of vocal score, containing the Soul's 'Take me away'] I can make nothing of, i.e. nothing adequate to Newman's words or the situation, though I have played and sung it over and over again. . . . But all the rest is *most beautiful, exquisite, ethereal.* That lovely contrapuntal movement beginning at [rehearsal cue number] [126] [the *Andante tranquillo* orchestral theme, leading into the Angel's Farewell] has gone straight to my heart and burned itself into my brain. I fancy I have not seen any such lovely writing of a quiet soothing character since *Die Meistersinger*! . . . It almost seems a dream *to me*, for with all my appreciation of English music I did not expect such a work to come out of this tight little island, and I felt quite sure it would not – much as I admired him – come out of E.E.! All the greater seems the marvel and all the intenser my *delight*!!

(16 June): . . . Page 159 I have tried and tried and tried, but it seems to me the *weakest* page in the work! Do re-write it! Surely you want something more dramatic *here*!! It seems mere weak whining to me and not at all impressive. As I have said, *all* the rest of the finale is wonderful. Yes, even page 161, with a return (for a while) to the music of page 159 is beautiful! . . . That passage 'I ever had believed' (page 63) I *cannot* take, too. I fancy that against that most solemn Judgment theme, the voice in *monotone* would sound *much more* impressive. Here we require no 'tune' in the voice, surely. At any rate, that rise to E on 'had', and the accent on 'on the moment' grate on me, also the voice moving in thirds with the theme at 'forthwith it fell' I *'can't abide'*. Again, what about 'that now thou dost *not* fear'? (page 64) Think of something more important to pierce one's brain and *stick there*!

ELGAR (19 June): I was awfully glad to get your letter about the end. I'm so sick of the whole thing: 'cos why? 'Cos every ass I meet says 'I suppose' or 'I hope' you're going to keep to the old A. & M tune 'Praise to the Holiest'!!!! Blast the B.P. [British Public] – they have no souls, hearts or minds worth a thought. . . .

(20 June): . . . I've been through all your suggestions for which a heap of thanks: I'm truly glad you like the thing cos I've written it out of my insidest inside. Some of your remarks are just & I've endeavoured to meet them: Some I can't see the force of & will be pigheaded & sit tight. . . . P. 64 I enclose revised: the accent on 'had' must be for sense; the rest is mere talking. . . . A tenor's monotone is never effective I feel – contraltos & baritones can do it, but sops. & tenors squeak & hum. . . . P. 159. You

must read the poem; I cannot rewrite this: the Soul is shrivelled up & voiceless & I only want on this page a musing murmur & I've got it – it wakes up later – but I can't do this better if I try for fifty years. . . . I don't think you appreciate the situation – the soul has for an instant seen its God – it is from that momentary glance shrivelled, parched and effete, powerless & finished, & it is condemned to Purgatory for punishment or purging – he sighs &, if you prefer it, whines. I've given him some of his aspiratory tunes in the middle but the situation is as sad as can be – deepest dejection & sorrow . . . therefore my final cadence, which is good, then comes the Angel, peaceful & soothing. . . . I can't see how you can ask for the Soul to have a dramatic song here: he is in the most dejected condition & sighs 'Take me away anywhere out of sight'. No, I can't alter that.

JAEGER (27 June): Don't think you have convinced me. . . . I had read the poem well, and appreciated the situation at the end (Soul after seeing God) well. But, surely, the first sensations the Soul would experience would be an awful, overwhelming agitation; a whirlwind of sensations of the acutest kind . . . a bewilderment of fear, excitation, crushing, over-mastering hopelessness etc. etc. . . . *Your* treatment shirks all that . . . *your* view, as expressed in the music, suggests to me nothing so much as an 'Oh lor, is that all. What a poor show, take me away, it gives me the *miserables*'. Yes, a whine I called it. . . . Wagner would have made this the *climax* of *expression* in the work, especially in the orchestra. . . . I *don't* want your 'Soul' to sing a dramatic '*Song*'. Heavens! But what is your gorgeous orchestra for? and why should you be dull and sentimental at such a *supremest* moment? . . . Here is your *greatest* chance of proving yourself *poet*, seer, and do-er of *impossible* things and you shirk it. Bah! . . . Did I not hold your splendid powers in such reverence and admiration, and were the rest of the work less superb, I should hold my peace and be *content* with a 'mere English cantata'! But you 'can't alter that passage', and so I will merely sing to *myself* 'my sad perpetual strain'.

ELGAR (27 June): . . . I've kept back p. 159 for consideration but all the time know I'm right & that you're wrong. However I'll see – one thing does annoy me. You say I've 'shirked' it – now I've shirked nothing – I've only set the thing as I feel & see it, which is not shirking at all, at all.

JAEGER (30 June): So that poem of N's has beaten you after all at its supremest climax! and you are *no* Wagner! . . . Anyhow, you have improved the whine summat and that's summat to your credit. But sure-ly, that alteration at just before 126 is *no* improvement . . . No, please don't alter it as per the MS you have sent. It takes away the *surprise*, and the dramatically appropriate 'gliding in' of the new, *lovely* peaceful theme. *Please* don't alter that if you can't alter it any better way than as per your MS. . . . I know *you* don't like the new way better than the old, do you? . . . I wanted you to suggest, in a *few* gloriously great and effulgent orchestral chords, given out by the whole force of the orchestra in its most glorious key, the momentary *vision* of the Almighty. A few chords! . . . and then for a few bars the Soul's overwhelming agitation with a quasi-choked, suppressed 'Take me away', *molto agitato*, and *then* as miserable a whine as you like. . . . No, it need not have been done 'theatrically' at all, at all! And to suggest the *glory* of the momentary vision need not have been blasphemous either. But, I grant you, it wanted a Wagner or R. Strauss to do that, nobody else would dare attempt it. No! as I know now, not even E.E.

ELGAR (1 July): Very well; here's what I thought of at *first* – I've copied it out & sent it – of course it's biggity-big. . . . The following alterations will have to be made: viz: the *souls* chorus[7] will *follow* the 'Take me away'. That is to say: I enclose p. 157 – the top of it is all right & I've attached the Judgment theme, (I can't get it in the rushing string passages!) at end of second p. (of my M.S. enclosed) the Solo 'Take me away' comes in, as it stands in type. Now enclosed I send the *end* of the solo which *must join* on to the *Souls* chorus. It is in type. And again the Souls Chorus joins on to the end (last) movement – this 'join' I also enclose. . . . I hope you'll like the emendation.

So those commentators who have assumed that Elgar's 'I can't alter that' was his last word have not taken into account this letter of 1 July. From the evidence above, we can deduce that the Souls in Purgatory chorus of 'Lord, Thou hast been our refuge' was placed immediately before the Soul of Gerontius's 'Take me away': hence Elgar's reference in his 20 June letter to wanting only 'a musing murmur – it wakes up later' on this page (159) of the score. When he removed this chorus to its present position at cue no. 125 he replaced it with the marvellous orchestral passage which now stands at cue nos. 118–19, presumably in response to Jaeger's suggestion of 'a few chords'. A later passage in the letter shows that the final cadence of the Soul's 'Take me away' (now p. 163 of V.S. rehearsal cues nos. 124–5) was immediately followed by the Angel's Farewell beginning at 126. The Souls in Purgatory's interjections during the Angel's solo at 129 (p. 167 V.S.) are apparently the other 'join' to which Elgar refers. Elgar refers to this matter – which he again stresses was his original intention – in a letter of 11 July when he returned the last proofs:

'You are as usual a brute to me – will those bars do? You don't say. I can tell you one thing, old Mosshead, you might ask—, or—, or—, to turn you out a few bars like that in vain! Never mind. I'm glad I did it after all. I had in my original sketch marked it out so, but I thought it too much for the fat mind of the filistine. We shall see.'

Once again, Elgar feared that the 'stupid' British public might not follow his trend of thought and also that British choral societies and orchestras would not appreciate the poetical subtlety of this work. He was to be proved right. But Jaeger still hankered after something more at 'Take me away'. It is strange that so sensitive an Elgarian failed to appreciate the stroke of genius of that blinding flash on the

[7]Chorus (Souls in Purgatory) 'Lord, Thou hast been our refuge', p. 163 V.S.

orchestra as Gerontius sees his God. On 17 July Elgar wrote to him:
'I *won't* alter p. 159 & be darned to you . . . – at 120 for *one semi-quaver*
value ffffffzzzz is the one glimpse into the Unexpressible – then it (the
Music) dies down into the sort of blissful Heaven theme which of
course fades away into nothing.' That really was the last word. Jaeger
let the matter drop except for pointing out that Edward Lloyd would
run out of breath on 'Take'.

Throughout the July and August of the glorious summer of 1900
Elgar worked at Birchwood on correcting proofs of the chorus parts
and on copying out the full score. As usual the effort of composition
had left him physically weak – he had stopped work in April for a
fortnight because of a cold – and now he relaxed with country
pursuits. He learned to ride a bicycle, took to felling and sawing trees,
and learned about growing potatoes – 'What names: "Beauties of
Abram", (they mean Hebron!), Adirondacks etc, etc'. Birchwood
always induced an idyllic mood. On 11 July he headed his letter to
Jaeger with a quotation from the Woodland interlude in *Caractacus*,
adding: 'This is what I hear all day – the trees are singing my music –
or have I sung theirs? I suppose I have? It's too lovely here.' He loved
the view from his study window – 'a lot of young hawks flying about
– plovers also – 150 rabbits under the window & the blackbirds eating
cherries like mad'. His letters for those seven weeks are peppered with
references of this sort. 'Felling one tree in view – blasting another &
learning to bicycle & fifty 1000 nice things to do & all the time I have
to be writing new bars to please an old duffer who won't
acknowledge 'em.' . . . 'The heat has been really awful & upsetting
everyone – I don't like to say a word about these woods for fear you
shd. feel envious but it is godlike in the shade with the snakes & other
cool creatures walking about as I write my miserable music' . . . 'I was
out all yesterday with a sawmill, sawing timber into joists, planks,
posts, rafters, boarding yea! boarding with feather edge: how little ye
townsmen know of real life. Anyhow I got a chill over my exertions.
. . . Now to come down to the *damned* music.' He finished the full
score on 3 August and he wrote on it 'Birchwood. In summer'.
Knowing that he had created a masterpiece, he also wrote this
quotation from John Ruskin's *Sesame and Lilies*:

This is the best of me; for the rest, I ate, and drank, and slept, loved and
hated, like another: my life was as the vapour and is not; but *this* I saw and
knew; this, if anything of mine, is worth your memory.

On that same day Alice wrote to her friend Mrs Nicholas Kilburn:
'We have both been learning to bicycle. E. can now go beautifully and
I am just beginning. Our landlord friend and neighbour [Mr Littler]
has been unweariedly patient in teaching us . . . E. has today finished
his orchestration. He has written his Dream of G. from his very *soul*.'

Also on 3 August a friend, William Eller, bicycled over to Birchwood from Ledbury for lunch with Elgar. 'In those days I seldom went abroad without my camera. On arrival at the cottage I was shown up into Elgar's workroom, where he sat at a huge table absolutely covered with musical MSS ... His first words after the usual greetings were to the effect that he was greatly relieved at having that instant written his name under the score of the last bar ... indeed the ink was not yet dry ... I begged Elgar to remain just as he was while I went down and fetched my camera ... He told me some things about the work ... finally he declared with the greatest possible emphasis "I do not know what fate has in store for this work, but this much I can tell you, it is GOOD".'[8]

It had been decided that Jaeger should write an analysis (extended programme-note) of the new work so that the public could study it beforehand: few English works had had this helpful attention, although Joseph Bennett had written one of *King Olaf*. Jaeger sent it to Elgar for approval and from comments on it written in August 1900 we learn much that is of interest about the composer's attitude to *Gerontius*. Jaeger picked out from the Prelude the various *leitmotive*, giving them names such as 'Prayer', 'Sleep', 'Judgment', 'Ruin'. Elgar challenged 'Sleep', then added:

I suppose after all 'Sleep' will be right – I meant 'to be lying down weary & distressed' with your poor head buzzing & weak & – have you ever been really ill? Sleep will do but it's the ghastly troubled sleep of a sick man. Look here: I imagined Gerontius to be a man like us and not a priest or a saint, but a *sinner*, a repentant one of course but still no end of a *worldly man* in his life, & now brought to book. Therefore I've not filled *his* part with Church tunes & rubbish but a good, healthy, full-blooded romantic, remembered worldliness, so to speak. It is, I imagine, much more difficult to tear one's self away from a well-to-do world than from a cloister. Your No. 6 might be Anguish but Despair will do ... I didn't give this 'prayer' theme to Gerontius too plainly – solidly – as he *wanders*: rather – if he'd been a priest he wd. have sung or said it as a climax but as he represents ME when ill he doesn't – he remembers his little Churchy prayey music in little snatches – see? He's of the world – or was & is going thro' a bad time, even if quite repentant etc. ... My wife fears you may be inclined to lay too great stress on the *leitmotiven* plan because I really do it without thought – intuitively, I mean. For instance, I did not perceive till long after it was in print that 'In Thine own agony' & the appalling chords I last bar p. 150 II 3rd line, bar 2, p. 154 introducing & dismissing the *Angel of the Agony* were akin but they are, aren't they?

Referring to the theme used in various guises in the orchestra in Part II (where Gerontius sings 'I see not those false spirits', where the Angel tells him 'Thy judgment now is near' and at Gerontius's 'I go

[8] *The Music Student*, August 1916, p. 350.

before my Judge'), Elgar said he meant to describe 'an indefinable feeling that there's more around you than you know: have you ever been in a pitch dark room & have *felt* the presence of people when you have no proof or knowledge that anyone is there. I *have* & it feels like that. Yah! don't bother me about music. I ride a Bicycle.'

Even after the analysis was published and the work had been performed Elgar asked Jaeger to eliminate the term 'Ruin': 'the idea is quite right – but the word is *heavy* – too direct – the "sense of ruin" is the thing & that's too long a title – but I fear the outsider will scoff inwardly & outwardly at that little theme being supposed to represent RUIN. I intended all this peaceful music (start of Part II) to be "the memory (remembrance) of the soul" – an utter childish (childlike) peace – as described in an unset portion of the poem – the word *flight* wd lead the ASS to think of *rapid* movement – rapid movement *did* (or rather) *was* taking place but the Soul was not conscious of it exactly. Twig?'

Elgar was deeply touched that his friend should devote so much time and labour to the analysis. Jaeger worked on it after office hours and on Sundays, making himself tired and nervy. Novello's offered to pay him five guineas for it, although Elgar had suggested ten guineas to Littleton. Elgar was furious when he heard about it: 'You must stick out for more. . . . Your firm is enough to make one disgusted with one's fellow creatures forever. I will not say what I think, but all other publishers are so different and nice and pleasant to do with even if things are not smooth, and all others are reasonable and obliging and considerate. . . . Boosey wd. fly rather than ask *me* to arrange about the libretto in order to save himself a possible fee, but your firm is incomprehensibly—.' Elgar made his own gesture of thanks to his analyst. On 27 September he sent him his two 'very first' sketches of *Gerontius*: 'If you don't want 'em throw 'em in w.p.b. I am not getting conceited (don't fear) and think my scrawl worth having – ciel! but somehow I couldn't tear up these two bits and I'm an ass.'

. . . . .

The first performance of *The Dream of Gerontius* on 3 October 1900 (the day before polling day in a general election)[9] is the most famous, or notorious, bad performance in the history of English music. It is well, if contradictorily, documented and it is impossible to blame one man or one factor for that disastrous Wednesday morning in Birmingham. The basic cause was the haphazard condition of English music-making at that date. The performance was heading for trouble from the start. One major contributory cause was the short time the

[9] This week was to prove doubly important in English life. *Gerontius* was performed for the first time and Winston Churchill was returned to Parliament for the first time. Neither event was then appreciated at its full significance.

chorus had in which to learn the work which, as they (or some of them) realized as soon as they saw the score, broke new ground. This was not *Judith* or *Job* or *The Dream of Jubal*. Dorabella, in an article in the *Musical Times*,[10] blames Elgar for 'being dilatory in getting the chorus parts corrected and returned to the printers'. Presumably she had not seen Elgar's letters to Jaeger or she would never have committed herself to this opinion. He delivered Part I to Novello's on 2 March and Part II on 20 March. Proofs of Part I arrived at Malvern on 3 April. By mid-May he was getting revisions of his corrections, some of them muddled by the printer. By 20 June he had dealt with all he had received. On 24 June he complained 'I've had a proof of the finale for *ten* days and no *read* proof or MS yet! Where the divvle is it? Aren't we wasting time sadly? . . . Thanks for sending Plunket Greene his "songs". Now he'll be happy.' On 5 July he returned another batch of proofs, adding 'I am very anxious to get all the Chorus copies out now, & a voc. sc. as *soon* as possible, 'cos I must consult the Birmingham people early about semi-ch. etc.' On 11 July he returned the last proofs. The alterations he had made caused some delay. '*Your*! confounded alterations have left me with nothing to work with – for instance the new bar on p. 64 (old paging) I've no copy at all & haven't an idea what I put in. Do send me this quick. . . . Now, dear man, do keep the thing going & let's have those chorus parts ready.' He had wanted long bar lines in the vocal parts but expense had precluded it. Copies of the vocal score were available by 21 July and the orchestral parts and full score were corrected during August: running it close, but this was hardly Elgar's fault. He was agitating for them to be ready by September so that he could go through it with Richter, who was to conduct.

The chorus had their parts in August. There is a note for the 24th in Alice's diary: 'Heard chorus were delighted with Dream of Gerontius'. This was to prove an over-optimistic piece of hearsay and probably came from Dorabella's aunt, Mrs Hodgson, wife of an archdeacon. She was a soprano and a fine sight-reader and said to her niece: 'How lovely this music is! but shall we *ever* learn it in time?' The answer was no, and a chief reason for it – and perhaps the biggest single blow to the performance – was the death in June at the age of fifty-three of Swinnerton Heap, the chorus-master who had so brilliantly trained the North Staffordshire Festival choir for *King Olaf* in 1896. He knew Elgar's secret of writing the kind of music Midlands choirs thoroughly understood. His sudden death before a copy of *Gerontius* had been seen by the chorus might not have sealed the work's fate if the festival committee had been able to call on his equal as a substitute. But at the tenth hour this was impossible and they called Stockley, who was now seventy, out of retirement. He was not

[10] February 1959, pp. 78–79.

in sympathy with the way his former orchestral violinist had developed and, as a nonconformist, he was not in sympathy with the Roman Catholicism of Newman and Elgar. In any case he now no longer had the energy and control needed to instil not only *Gerontius* but other new or unfamiliar works into the chorus in the comparatively short time at his disposal. Besides the Elgar, the festival included Parry's *De Profundis*, which was also very poorly performed, and Coleridge-Taylor's *Hiawatha's Departure* (first produced in London the previous spring). W. T. Edgley, a tenor in the chorus, told Dorabella[11] that, because the chorus were supplied only with single-voice parts, 'one section of the choir had no idea what the others were doing (or not doing)'. Some of the tenors practised *Gerontius* at home and knew their parts well; the basses did not know their parts at all and there was some 'buffoonery' in that section of the chorus. It is not true that Elgar attended only the final rehearsal on Saturday, 29 September, or that Stockley, because of his lack of sympathy, did not invite him before then. Elgar went to a rehearsal at Birmingham on 12 September as is proved not only by Alice's diary entry but by Elgar's letter to Jaeger of 13 September: 'I sent a wire this a.m. on my return from Birmingham'. As late as 20 September Elgar was still correcting the orchestral parts. Jaeger had written on the 18th, 'For God's sake return all *proofs* at once or we shall get landed in a fine quandary.' Elgar went to London on 21 September for an orchestral rehearsal at Queen's Hall and wrote to Jaeger afterwards: 'Somehow, after thinking of the rehearsal, I feel very much ashamed of myself as author of "Gerontius" – a sort of criminal – and wonder if I shall ever get up sufficient courage to go to Birmingham at all'.

At the final joint choral and orchestral rehearsal at Birmingham on the Saturday (29 September), Elgar realized how very far short of his intentions the reality was likely to prove in this performance. The 'best of him', the ideal tapestry of music which he had imagined while he worked amid the sounds of summer at Birchwood, was now presented to him as an unpalatable piece of work by a choir that had very little interest in the vision he had created. As will perhaps have been gathered by now, he was not the man to rise above disappointment with a blithe spirit: he was either up or down, there was no level-headed medium mood. He sat next to Richter, explaining what he wanted and indicating tempi. 'Things got very chaotic,' Edgley says, 'and everyone worked up to a high pitch and unfortunately E.E. more than anyone, naturally. He seemed desperate, with whom I cannot remember, but it was not all "the choir" as most people think.' Be that as it may, Richter invited Elgar to address the choir. Instead of exhorting them to do better, Elgar

[11] See Diana McVeagh: *Edward Elgar: His Life and Music* (London, 1955), pp. 30–31.

ticked them off from the front of the orchestra, using the words 'It is no better than a drawing-room ballad.' This was much resented. 'Chorus dull and wretched,' Alice wrote in her diary that evening, echoing Elgar's opinion. That same day, Jaeger wrote to Dorabella: 'Richter likes the work as much as I do.' Richter, too, was horrified by the choir's inability to grasp the implications of the music, and realized that he himself had underestimated the novelty and magnitude of the work, that it required far more insight than the *Variations* and a close knitting-together of choir and orchestra. He tried to salvage the situation. He called an extra rehearsal for the Monday and spent the weekend pacing up and down his hotel room with the score propped on the mantelpiece, learning its every nuance so that he could impart his own knowledge and enthusiasm to the choir. He was too late. The six hours' rehearsal on the Monday over-strained the chorus, who thus began the festival on Tuesday tired and stale. Other composers suffered, too. The critic of the *Sunday Times* was 'rudely awakened' in Parry's *De Profundis* 'to the fact that something was wrong'. Bach's *St Matthew Passion* was given a performance 'worthy of a fourth-rate provincial choral society'. *Gerontius* had the place of honour on the Wednesday morning. Richter went to the chorus's dressing-rooms, and according to one of the sopranos, 'with unforgettable voice and gesture besought us to do our very best for "the work of this English genius".'[12] His words fell on a majority of deaf and resentful ears.

Not only were the conductor and choir ill-equipped to do justice to a masterpiece; the soloists (if the best then available) were inadequate to their task. Edward Lloyd was fifty-five and within two months of retirement. He had had a successful career for the previous thirty years in oratorios and songs, and had sung in several previous Elgar first performances. Gerontius was the last major rôle he undertook. A fine singer of Handel arias and drawing-room ballads was Dorabella's verdict. He sang Gerontius, according to Vaughan Williams who was present, 'like a Stainer anthem, in the correct tenor attitude with one foot slightly withdrawn'.[13] At the end of Part I, in the great 'Go forth' chorus, the choir sang flat and during the interval, Ferruccio Bonavia said, 'Richter, bitterly disappointed, paced the artists' room like a caged tiger. The second part, begun in an atmosphere of apprehension, did nothing to change the fortunes of the day.'[14] Plunket Greene sang the bass rôles. He began the Angel of the Agony's solo in Part II a semitone flat and stuck to it till the bitter end. Only the Wagnerian mezzo-soprano, Marie Brema, as the Angel, appears to have redeemed the affair. Dorabella says that she 'saved the situation in

[12] *Birmingham Post*, 8 March 1934.
[13] M. Kennedy, *The Works of Ralph Vaughan Williams* (London, 1964), p. 389.
[14] In 'Elgar', *The Music Masters*, iii, op. cit., p. 144.

Part II several times' and W. H. Reed speaks of 'complete mastery and understanding'. Vaughan Williams, on the other hand, in stating that Greene had 'lost his voice', added that Miss Brema 'had none to lose'. In a letter to her dated 24 April 1903 Elgar wrote, 'I have, of course, in memory your fine and intellectual creation of the part; and, although I never thought the "tessitura" suited you well, as the magnificent artist you are, you *made* it go very finely'; a tactful evasion rather than a heart-felt compliment. The cool detachment of this letter lends credibility to the claim[15] that the part of the Angel was intended for Clara Butt and composed with her voice in mind. Certainly Jaeger, discussing an aspect of the rôle of the Angel, wrote to Elgar on 13 April 1900: 'I hope Clara Butt will suit you in this respect. I fear much singing of "shop songs" may ere long spoil her completely for *artistic* work'. Elgar had much admired her in *Sea Pictures*. In 1900, however, she was still only 26 and at the start of her career; it is unlikely that the Festival committee would have engaged a comparative newcomer for a work already fraught with risk.

Elgar told Arnold Bax in 1901: 'The fact is neither the choir nor Richter knew the score.'[16] Henry Wood in *My Life of Music* writes: 'I shall never believe he [Richter] was to blame for its failure.' Ultimately of course, responsibility must lie with the conductor and Richter's fault lay in his failure, when he first saw the score, to appreciate its subtlety and the need, therefore, for him to supervise every rehearsal from the start. Elgar did not hold it against him, though he conducted most of his own first performances thenceforward. He blamed a higher authority than Richter. Six days after the performance – not in the trough of reaction on the next morning – he poured out his bitterness to Jaeger in perhaps the most astonishing letter he ever wrote:

I have not seen the papers yet except one or two bits which exuberant friends insisted on my reading and I don't know or care what they say or do. As far as I'm concerned music in England is dead – I shall always write what I have in me of course.

I have worked hard for forty years & at the last, Providence denies me a decent hearing of my work: so I submit – I always said God was against art and I still believe it. Anything obscene or trivial is blessed in this world and has a reward – I ask for no reward – only to live & to hear my work. I still hear it in my heart and in my head so I must be content. Still it is curious to be treated by the old fashioned people as a criminal because my thoughts and ways are beyond them. [A hit, presumably, at Stockley.]

I am very well and what is called 'fit'! I had my golf in good style yesterday & am not ill or pessimistic – don't think it, but I have allowed my heart to open once – it is now shut against every religious feeling and every soft, gentle impulse *for ever*.

[15] *Clara Butt, her life story*, by Winifred Ponder (London, 1928).
[16] Sir Arnold Bax, *Farewell, My Youth* (London, 1943), p. 30.

While at Birmingham the Elgars received news of a financial loss and Alice had a slight operation performed on her throat. In a second letter to Jaeger, on 12 October, Elgar claimed that these were what had upset him. No doubt they aggravated his disappointment but there is no disguising the calculated disillusion which he was expressing so eloquently if incoherently: 'I'm rather pleased with my work – privately – but it is annoying – whatever *you* may think, to know that it's *no good* commercially, and that with *one* exception (your own good self) all my best friends including the highest thinkers only made one remark during my "exaltation", "now you must write a few popular songs" instead of a word of appreciation, in its best sense, fifty times, by the men even who had promised to finance my work, during the week, nay on the very moment of performance did they drum it into my poor ears "now a popular song or two will make up for this" – my wife ill, and our money gone. Damn Gerontius: I'd really forgotten it when I wrote to you last.'

There is a significant postscript to these outpourings which proves how deeply the Birmingham experience wounded Elgar, whatever he pretended to Jaeger. In 1924, at the Hereford Festival, Adrian Boult, a conductor whom Elgar admired and whose career he had helped, told him of his intention to conduct *The Dream of Gerontius* at Birmingham (where he was conductor of the City of Birmingham Symphony Orchestra) with a reduced body of woodwind because of expense. Elgar was horrified. Boult himself then paid for the extra players, but Elgar was unforgiving and scarcely spoke to one of his most devoted interpreters for nearly seven years. Eventually, in 1931, when Boult was B.B.C. Director of Music and conductor of the Corporation's new symphony orchestra, W. H. Reed intervened to heal the breach. Elgar wrote to Boult from Marl Bank on 12 April 1931: 'I will refer to the ancient matter for one moment now & never again. My feelings were acute: I have never had a real success in life – commercially never: so all I had (& have now) was the feeling that I had written *one* score which satisfied R. Strauss, Richter & many others; it was the discovery that no one in that very wealthy city – which always pretended to be proud of the production of *Gerontius* – cared a straw whether the work was presented as I wrote it or not: *there* at least I hoped to be recognised. Now let us forget it.'[17]

But what was the reaction of others at Birmingham in 1900 to the music and the performance? The wife of W. M. B. of the *Variations* perhaps summed it up in her remark to Dorabella, 'A very poor performance but what a wonderful work!' Mrs Stanford left the hall with Vaughan Williams and said to him 'Is not that a fine work!' A correspondent of the *Observer* was at the rehearsal on 29 September

[17] *Music & Friends, Letters to Adrian Boult*, ed. by Jerrold Northrop Moore (London, 1979), pp. 96–97.

and reported that one of the musicians present – Parry, Stanford, or Manns – 'roundly asserted *Gerontius* to be the finest work yet written by a British musician'. Yet dissentient voices spoke out too, some of them to Jaeger who wrote to Dorabella on 14 October: 'I have been . . . "pitched into" . . . for being enthusiastic over *Gerontius*. I don't mind a bit. It was *lack* of enthusiasm both in the performers & amongst the critics which riled me at B'ham & afterwards, when I read the critiques. Now you Englishers *have* a composer *at last*. You might be excused if you waxed enthusiastic over him for once in a way. But oh dear no! If this were only a wretched new opera or a dull new oratorio by Mascagni or Perosi, the papers would have had *columns* of gossip & gush about those 2 frauds. But it's only an English *musician* (not an actress or a jockey or a Batsman) and he is treated like a very ordinary nobody. Oh you unpatriotic creatures. I won't say a word about the performance but I suffered purgatory!! . . . old Stockley the choir-mess-ter ought to be boiled & served on toast. . . . Dear E.E. sent me quite a depressing letter last week. I told him it was *weak* & *wicked* to write like that. . . .'

Do the critics deserve the obloquy they have received for their notices of *Gerontius*? Some were disturbed by the subject, one commiserated with Novello's 'whose philanthropy had risked overloading their shelves with more useless copies'. Fuller Maitland in *The Times* could summon up nothing less fence-sitting than 'a remarkable and in some ways a beautiful work'. He described the tenor rôle as 'seldom either grateful to the singer or very attractive to the average hearer. . . . How to write a long and dramatic soliloquy with no lack of melodic beauty or affecting expression has been shown in Sir Hubert Parry's *Job* and it is only necessary to allude to this in order to point the vast difference that exists between the two composers in this regard. . . . If only he [Elgar] would more often yield to the instinct for melodic beauty . . . the new composition would merit very high rank indeed.'

This was Olympian damning with faint praise, but if one reads through all the other many and lengthy notices of the first performance, one discovers that every critic almost without exception acclaimed the work as one of the most remarkable, beautiful, and impressive ever written by an English composer and castigated Birmingham for the wretched performance. Herbert Thompson, of the *Yorkshire Post*, for instance, called it 'the most powerful and profound utterance of one of the most individual composers'. Charles L. Graves, in the *Spectator*, spoke of its creating 'a deep impression by its beauty, its earnestness, and its distinction' despite the 'imperfections' of the performance. Arthur Johnstone in the *Manchester Guardian* on 4 October drew an unconventional parallel: 'A comparison with Berlioz is simply inevitable – for

Edward Elgar's dramatic power admits of comparison with the great masters. . . . Elgar's music, like parts of the poem, fairly merits the epithet "Dantesque". . . .'

Nor, I should have thought, could any composer less thin-skinned than Elgar reasonably have complained of the column-long notice on 4 October in *The Daily Telegraph* whose critic, Joseph Bennett, dealt fairly with the theological aspect: 'I must confess inability to see quite clearly that a subject so awful, and as regards each individual of us so profoundly intimate, belongs to those which should be decked in musical trappings for the delectation of a festival crowd. Such things properly belong to the Church. . . .'

Bennett's opinion of the music, though raising a smile today, was expressed dogmatically but with dignity: 'What he has written he has honestly written, and his critics, who are inclined to condemn, must do so with all respect. . . . I do not complain of a free harmonic method as such, provided its effect be good, but it is not given to me to say why in the present case the ear is almost continuously assailed by chromatic phrases and chords, which none can accuse of being beautiful. . . . But against this must be set precious pages in which the conditions have forced Mr Elgar to take up other ground and sing the song of that in music which is naturally expressive. . . . [It is] a work possible only to the highest gifts of imagination, feeling and skill. . . . "The Dream of Gerontius" advances its composer's claim to rank amongst the musicians of whom the country should be proudest. It is with sincere regret that I speak of the performance as inadequate to the claims of the work and the importance of the festival. . . . True the music was difficult but there had been time to prepare it. . . . It is not my business to discover why the chorus could not sing six lightly accompanied bars without losing the pitch or why all the concerted music was rendered in a hesitating and pointless fashion.'

The Birmingham fiasco did not, of course, kill *Gerontius* but it might have done. No other choir rushed to do justice to it, for the rumour had gone round that it was formidably difficult. Richter, however, was determined to make amends. In Manchester, where the Hallé Choir had R. H. Wilson as chorus-master, he worked for several years to bring orchestra and choir to a pitch where he could perform *Gerontius* really well. 'All the night,' he told Wilson, 'I have a gimlet that bores into my forehead, and that gimlet is *Gerontius*.' When the soloists and conductor signed Elgar's manuscript score on 3 October 1900, Richter, whose command of English was erratic but forthright, wrote: 'Let drop the Chorus. Let drop everybody! but let NOT drop the wings of your original genius.' He knew what sort of work it was, and if Germany had not forestalled him, there is no doubt that Richter's Manchester performances would have rehabilitated it within five years. Luckily Elgar did not know, though he may have guessed, what Novello's attitude was to *Gerontius*. Littleton wrote to Johnstone of the Birmingham Festival on 6 November 1900: 'I have been much blamed by my co-directors for agreeing to pay so large a sum. Unfortunately for us the work is a commercial failure & we have no anticipation of ever realising our initial expenses'. Retaliating, Johnstone called it 'one of the greatest works ever written by an Englishman.'

Elgar returned to Malvern deeply anxious about his financial position and proceeded to write the overture *Cockaigne: In London Town* – 'It's cheerful and Londony: "stout and steaky"' he told Jaeger. To Richter he described it as 'extremely cheerful like a miserable unsuccessful man ought to write'. It had been requested by the Philharmonic Society, and at the end of his manuscript he wrote, from *Piers Plowman*: 'Meteless and moneless on Malverne Hills'.

The P. won't pay anything [letter to Jaeger, 26 October]. Now look at this:

To copying parts	12. 0. 0.
Rehearsal ex.	3. 0. 0.
Do. & concert	6. 0. 0.
net loss	21. 0. 0.

Now what's the good of it? Nobody else will perform the thing. . . . I really cannot afford it and am at the end of my financial tether. Don't go and tell anyone but I *must* earn money somehow – I *will not* go back to teaching & I think I must try some trade – coal agency or houses – I really wish I were dead over & over again but I dare not, for the sake of my relatives, do the job myself. Well we shall see – I've not read the papers yet re *Gerontius* & never shall now. I'm sorry you've been bothered over it – just like my influence on everything & everybody – always evil!

More self-dramatization? Or was he genuinely haunted by the 'sense of ruin' he had expressed with such vivid truth in his masterpiece? Ernest Newman met Elgar for the first time in October 1901 in Liverpool, and recalling the occasion over fifty years later he wrote: 'He gave me even then the impression of an exceptionally nervous, self-divided and secretly unhappy man; in the light of all we came to know of him in later life I can see now that he was at that time rather bewildered and nervous at the half-realisation that his days of spiritual privacy – always so dear to him – were probably coming to an end; while no doubt gratified by his rapidly growing fame he was in his heart of hearts afraid of the future. I remember distinctly a dinner . . . at which Mrs Elgar tactfully steered the conversation away from the topic of suicide that had suddenly arisen; she whispered to me that Edward was always talking of making an end of himself.'[18]

It is as hard to understand a man's mind as it is to relate art to life – *Cockaigne* after financial loss and the failure of *Gerontius* has the

[18] *Sunday Times*, 23 October 1955.

incongruity of the Beethoven last quartets in the midst of frenzied bickering with relatives. Art is not the product or result of its creator's daily life, but of his inner life; and to that only he holds a key. Elgar for most of the time disguised his unhappiness and his sense of ruin and inferiority, as well as his sense of scorn, beneath the extrovert exterior known to the Malvern locals or beneath the studied jocularity of his letters to Jaeger. To Jaeger alone at this time he revealed himself consciously or sub-consciously – 'I do want to see you or somebody as knows suffin – I am bored to death with commonplace ass-music down here – the bucolics are all right when they don't attempt more than eat, drink & sleep but beyond those things they fail'; and: 'It's raining piteously here and all is dull except the heart of E.E. which beats time to most marvellous music – unwritten alas! and ever to be so.' He checked the published score of *Froissart*, and spent what might seem an extravagant amount of time on the pianoforte version of 'Dorabella' until one remembers that Novello's paid him royalties only on the sale of arrangements other than orchestral. (By 1904 he reckoned that the *Enigma Variations* had made him about £8.)[19] He spent the winter months of 1900–1 preparing the *Prelude and Angel's Farewell* from *Gerontius* for separate publication and performance for orchestra alone, with solo voice or in its original form. He took care with it, but he must have been depressed by the prospect of this of all works existing only in the form of concert extracts. The first performance of the two excerpts was given at Bradford in the orchestral version, with Elgar conducting, on 16 February 1901. Four days later Henry Wood conducted them at Queen's Hall with Kirkby Lunn singing the Angel. As will be related in a later chapter, other works were brewing at this time – 'In haste & joyful (Gosh! man I've got a tune in my head),' he wrote to Jaeger on 12 January – but here we are concerned with the future of *Gerontius*.

Jaeger, to his eternal credit, did all he could speedily to bring about a second performance. On 27 December 1900, he wrote to Dorabella, 'I'm still trying hard to get *Gerontius* performed in London, but it is almost hopeless. I still hope Wood will do it.' But at least Wood conducted the two extracts and Jaeger was delighted. 'It is the highest thing in English art (musical art),' he told Dorabella. '. . . Wood conducted it with loving care; spent 1½ hours on it & the result was a performance which completely put Richter's in the shade.' With Jaeger at the Birmingham performance were Professor Julius Buths, musical director of the city of Düsseldorf since 1890 and conductor of the Lower Rhine Festivals there since 1893, and Otto Lessman, editor of the *Allgemeine Musik-Zeitung*. They perceived the magnitude of *Gerontius* and that it was in the mainstream of European nineteenth-century music. 'Directly it was over,' Jaeger wrote to Dorabella,

[19] Letter to Jaeger, 10 August 1904.

'Buths grasped my hand (coram publico) & blurted out: "A wonderful work; it's the most beautiful work I know" etc. etc.' Lessman's eulogistic review was sent to Elgar by Richter's friend Ettling to whom Elgar replied on 30 October 1900: 'My wife has translated the articles to me and I am – I need not say – intensely gratified at being taken seriously & being understood. I wish my own countrymen could do this – but alas! in England this can never be – & I know it.' What he resented was the English critics' appraisal of *Gerontius* solely within the context of English music, whereas he knew that it merited international assessment. Rimsky-Korsakov had told him the *Variations* were 'the best since Brahms' and Richter thought the crescendo in 'Nimrod' better than Wagner's in the *Die Meistersinger* overture. But the English, excepting Johnstone, compared him only with Parry and Stanford or accused him of subservience to Wagner's methods. It was Jaeger who had suggested to Novello's in the summer of 1900 that Buths, 'one of the ultra-moderns of Germany, great propagandist for Richard Strauss', should be invited to Birmingham to hear some English music. The invitation went, it is said, on the strength of *Hiawatha's Departure*. But Jaeger followed it up with a score of the *Variations*. In acknowledging them Buths wrote of their 'aristocratic character . . . sensitive, thoughtful and full of feeling. . . . "Hats off" to such artistry.' Buths, who was forty-nine, took the score of *Gerontius* back to Düsseldorf and at once began to translate the poem into German. In the meantime he conducted the *Variations*, their first performance in Germany, on 7 February 1901. 'A great and genuine success,' he told Jaeger. During April Elgar was anxiously inquiring about progress with the German translation as he had heard that other towns there might undertake a performance. Though he was working, the failure of *Gerontius* was still at the front of his mind: 'I know nothing of *any* festivals,' he wrote to Jaeger, '& fully conclude my countrymen do not want me any more – they want something which they can do without having to see the score & they can't read mine!' Alice wrote to him too: 'When are we going to hear those wonderful sounds again, the sooner you can tell us so the better for my dear Dr!'s spirits & consequently for his work.'[20]

In fact the wonderful sounds were next heard in Elgar's own Worcester, on 9 May, in an abbreviated performance by the Philharmonic Society, whose gesture of confidence in their conductor and his music is too often overlooked.[21] William Green sang

[20] Elgar had received the honorary doctorate of music at Cambridge University on 22 November 1900.
[21] The omissions were pp. 68–94, 112–55, and 163–4 of the vocal score. This is authenticated from the records of G. S. Chignell, assistant conductor and accompanist to the Society. (See letter from his son, W. R. Chignell, published in *Musical Times*, March 1956, pp. 146–7.)

Gerontius, Hélène Valma the Angel, and F. Lightowler, of Worcester, the bass rôles. Evidently Elgar had been as edgy with the chorus during rehearsals as he had been at Birmingham for, after the performance, he wrote a congratulatory note combined with an apology: 'I was, a month or two ago, very much hurt at what I felt (erroneously, it seems) to be a want of interest in the practices. I know now that this was a mistake on my part.' The *Prelude and Angel's Farewell* were included in the Gloucester Festival programme in September, when *The Times*, in approving this 'effective selection', ominously added the rider 'Even if we cannot hope for frequent revivals of the whole oratorio'. But by then, early in July, Elgar had received news of the date of Buths's performance at Düsseldorf. 'I note with joy & tears Dec. 19th,' he wrote to Jaeger, 'my devotion to Buths.'

Two incidents of the summer of 1901 illustrate Elgar's generosity and kindness to his friends. Although he was busy at this period with several new works in various stages of gestation,[22] he offered to help in the orchestration of the cantata *Emmaus*, which Dr Herbert Brewer, who had succeeded Lee Williams as organist of Gloucester in 1897, had composed for the Three Choirs meeting there in September. Work had been delayed by illness and Brewer offered to withdraw. Elgar told Jaeger on 26 June that he was arranging to assist Brewer '& hope it will relieve his mind & perhaps his wife's – oh, these wives of musicians – what they go through – & *suffer* – my heart bleeds for them sometimes, we MEN can buck up & fight, but the others – . . . Brewer always says how can he "*re*pay me" & you said "pay me" – I don't want any pay or return – I only want *them* to sleep a little in peace instead of lying awake o' nights.' He had not forgotten his own struggles. Then, when the Elgars moved to Birchwood in July ('in the intense quiet & solitude which I love') they lent Craeg Lea to the Jaegers, who could otherwise not afford a holiday, and to Buths and his daughter. Elgar already had his fears about Düsseldorf: 'I *hope* it will be a success for your sake and Buths' but it (being English) cannot be & will only be another millstone round the neck of me – for which I shall be expected to write polki or something to pay for the blasted expense.' (He had arranged some of the *Gerontius* choruses for S.A.T.B. and had then been asked by Novello's 'for more Ladies' trios'.) Nine days later he was telling Jaeger: 'Remember (Private) that your countrymen never approach an English work with even a semblance of interest or respect – it is only something "pour rire" after all & I cannot hope that my work will fare better than Sullivan's etc.'

The Elgars went to Düsseldorf, arriving there on 16 December. Their departure had been delayed by Alice's cold and by more eye

[22] For details see Chapter 12.

trouble of Elgar's – 'the doctor wants me to give up as much music writing as possible!' he told Jaeger. 'So do the publishers & the critix – and the public – and the other composers & so does Ed: Elgar.' There are two vivid accounts of the performance of *Gerontius* on 19 December, one by Elgar in a letter to Littleton of Novello's and the other by Jaeger in a letter to Dorabella. The Gerontius was Ludwig Wüllner – 'splendid', said Elgar, 'not in voice but intelligence *genius* – he carried everyone away and made Gerontius a real personage – we never had a singer in England with so much brain – even here he is exceptional'. The Angel was sung by Antonie Beel, who failed, and the bass – 'fine', said Elgar – was Willy Metzmacher. The chorus, the Städtische Musikverein, was, again according to Elgar, 'very fine and had only commenced work on 11 November. This disproves the idea fostered at Birmingham that my work is *too difficult*. The personnel of the chorus here is largely amateur, and in no way, except in intelligence and the fact that they have a capable conductor, can they (or it) be considered superior to any good English choral society. . . . Professor Buths was unsurpassable as conductor and took *infinite* pains to make everything "go". . . .'

Jaeger fills in the details of the rehearsals. The orchestra numbered over eighty, 'not like Wood's 110 for reading powers or tone, but they answered every purpose. . . . Buths . . . is not a great "interpreter" – I mean *co-creator* and there were many passages of which more might have been made. . . . But directly Wüllner opened his mouth to sing "Jesus, Maria, meine Stunde Kam" we said that man has *Brains*. . . . Next morning there was another orchestral rehearsal when E. interfered more frequently to secure readings more in accordance with his conceptions. Then in the evening, *the* Event. The Hall was crammed full though it was a beastly night. . . . We (E., Mrs E., A. Johnstone of the *Manchester Guardian*, & yours truly) sat in the third row of the balcony right facing the orchestra and we heard marvellously well. . . . The Chorus was perfect, there is no other word for it. . . . That masterful piece (Demons' Chorus) which was so completely ruined at B'ham, was given with perfect ease & yet with strenuous dramatic force. . . . Wüllner did not seem in very good voice & he made one serious blunder. . . . In Part 2 Wüllner was *great*, especially in the "Take me away". The big chorus "Praise to the Holiest", which astonished the German musicians by its monumental architecture, was a masterly performance & the Finale, that wonderful Finale, was another revelation to those who heard it only at B'ham. Unfortunately the Angel was anything but angelically perfect . . . the audience could not have realised, thanks to Buths' alertness, how dangerously near collapse the performance came once or twice through this d— Angel's shortcomings. . . . Well, at the end E. was enthusiastically called, & though he had to fight his way through thronging crowds of people down the stairs & to the front, the applause & shouts were kept up until . . . he reached the podium. . . . I rushed out . . . & wired 400 words to *The Times* . . . another wire which I sent to the Central News was much mutilated by that agency & only a few papers thought the event of sufficient importance to give the 8 or nine lines to it. . . . If this had been Dan Leno's first appearance in Germany there would have been *columns* in all the English papers. Ye Gods! You have a lot to do yet to be considered a musical nation.'

Elgar was fêted and honoured, dined and wined by Düsseldorf musicians and painters – this, it should be remembered, at a time of fierce anglophobia in Germany. He visited Franz Wüllner, director of the Cologne Conservatoire, and father of Ludwig, who said he might include *Gerontius* in his next season. He returned to London on 1 January 1902, to lunch at Pagani's with the Henry Woods and to attend part of a Queen's Hall concert. Awaiting him were the words of a hymn – 'O mightiest of the mighty' – which he was to set for Edward VII's Coronation. The contrast was too much: 'the horrible musical atmosphere I plunged into at once in this benighted country nearly suffocated me – I *wish* it had completely,' he wrote to Jaeger from Malvern on 3 January. Six days later he was asking if any money was due to him ('Mazurka, Violin arrangement for instance. I should be glad to have it as it is an awkward time of year financially'). He had influenza by mid-January, but his chronic pessimism, rather than influenzal depression, accounts for the by now familiar lament in a letter written on 13 January in reply to Jaeger's good news that Buths was to repeat *Gerontius* at the Lower Rhine Festival at Düsseldorf in May: 'I am glad to hear about *Gerontius* at the Fest – more for your sake than my own. I am dead to these wonders . . . My things are successful among musicians but the public don't buy them . . . My music does not arrange well for the piano & consequently is of no commercial value. If I had a free mind I shd like to write my chamber music, & symphony etc etc, on all of which forms of art providence has laid the curse of poverty. Bless it! . . . Providence, as I've often told you, is against all art so there's a satisfactory end.'

The second Düsseldorf performance was on 19 May. Wüllner again sang Gerontius, Johannes Messchaert was the bass, and the Angel's music was for the first time sung to true and beautiful effect by the English contralto Muriel Foster. The Lower Rhine Music Festivals had been a triennial Whitsuntide event, held since early in the nineteenth century successively in Düsseldorf, Aachen, and Cologne. Mendelssohn had conducted them, and some of his successors had been Joachim, Anton Rubinstein, Brahms, Richter, Richard Strauss, and Steinbach. Buths had been responsible for the Düsseldorf event since 1893, and his services to English music included not only his Elgar performances but also performances of works by Delius, notably *A Mass of Life*. Again, Elgar's eye trouble delayed his departure for the festival, but he and Alice arrived there on 16 May and listened to rehearsals in company with Rodewald from Liverpool, Johnstone of the *Manchester Guardian*, Henry Wood, and Alfred Kalisch. Wood writes[23] of the chorus having been rehearsed 'for nearly two years', which is patently nonsense. Elgar, he said, 'was recalled 20 times after the end of the first part. I have never seen an audience so excited nor a composer so spontaneously acclaimed; certainly not an Englishman – unless, perhaps, Sullivan after the first performance of *The Golden Legend*.' Johnstone's report in the *Manchester Guardian* states that 'full justice was done to the instrumental part of the work by the magnificent Festival orchestra of 127 performers . . . The part of the Angel was given by Miss Muriel Foster with the wonderfully beautiful and genuine voice that has long been recognised as her most remarkable gift, and with considerably greater and more expressive eloquence than any previous experience might have led one to expect from her. . . . The semi-chorus, seated in a line before the orchestra, acquitted themselves almost to perfection in the delicate task that they have to perform throughout the death-bed scene.' Next day, at a dinner in honour of Elgar, Richard Strauss proposed the toast 'to the welfare and success of the first English progressivist, Meister Edward Elgar, and of the young progressive school of English composers'. Writing from Germany on 23 May to Littleton at Novello's, Elgar said: 'Richard Strauss, who never speechifies if he can help it, made a really noble oration over *Gerontius* – I wish you could have heard it – & it was worth some years of anguish – now I trust over – to hear him call me Meister!' He commented further on another aspect of this speech in a letter to Jaeger on 11 June 1902: 'What a fuss about Strauss's speech! too ridiculous & nobody seems in the least to know what he said or meant. I always said British musicians were several kinds of fool & ignoramus – but this is worse than usual from them.' He was referring here to Strauss's survey of British composers in which he said that Arne was somewhat less than Handel, Sterndale Bennett than Mendelssohn, and some Englishmen of later day 'not quite so great as Brahms'. Elgar pointed out in one of his Birmingham lectures a few years later that these words were 'purposely misunderstood' in some quarters.

It is perhaps, an over-dramatic simplification to say that this Düsseldorf triumph secured the future of *Gerontius*, though no doubt it encouraged choirs to tackle it. In Berlin, six months after Düsseldorf, the *Prelude* and *Angel's Farewell* were included in a concert

[23] *My Life of Music* (London, 1938), pp. 324–5.

conducted by Busoni and were afterwards described as 'the most barren piece of senseless music-fabrication that has been heard for a long time'. But performances in 1903 of the complete work in Danzig and Darmstadt were successful, and this seems to be an appropriate place in which to give some account of the Elgar 'boom' on the Continent which followed Buth's advocacy.[24] Steinbach's opinion of the *Variations* has already been quoted. Fritz Volbach, musical director at Mainz, conducted *Gerontius* and *The Apostles* in 1903 and 1904. Felix Weingartner became an ardent Elgarian at this period on the strength of the *Variations* and *Cockaigne*. Richter, who once told Ettling he preferred Elgar's music to Brahms's and Tchaikovsky's, wrote to Elgar in 1902 about Wilhelm Backhaus: 'He is a grand player and he plays your March in D, some Gerontius etc. by heart, wonderfully well'. Richter, Backhaus, and Adolph Brodsky were all working in Manchester simultaneously, and each vied with the other in admiration of Elgar. Ettling introduced *Cockaigne* to Paderewski, about whom Schuster, in a letter to Elgar dated 26 November 1902, told one of the best of all Elgar stories. Paderewski, at a ducal party, asked where Elgar studied. 'Nowhere.' Then who taught him? 'Le Bon Dieu,' was the reply. In June 1904, Ettling wrote of visiting Fritz Kreisler and finding him at the piano 'deep in *The Dream of Gerontius*, he told me full of enthusiasm for you, whether it is true you once wrote a violin concerto & if so, he would feel happy if you would trust it to him'. These were all Continental musicians of a certain type who would immediately recognise the cosmopolitan backbone of Elgar's music, the saturation of its orchestral sound with the influences, to their ears, of Brahms, Wagner, Dvořák, and Schumann. This was meat and drink to them. This was recognized at the time by Johnstone in his perceptive account of the May Düsseldorf performance of *Gerontius* in noting that the festival gave 'only the most typically excellent of newer compositions, and of older compositions only those upon which it is felt that contemporary genius had been more particularly nourished'. The 1902 festival included Liszt's *Faust Symphony*; nor, said Johnstone, 'is it accidental that the preference is given to Strauss among German and Elgar among English composers. For those are the men who really carry the torch, and the Germans are not to be deceived in such matters.' But eighty years later we can be warned by the word 'progressivist' in Strauss's toast. If we seek an explanation of the short-lived nature of Continental enthusiasm for Elgar's music it is to be found in the

---

[24] It had repercussions for others, too. Parry's *Blest Pair of Sirens* had a great success at the Duisburg Festival in May 1903. Jaeger accompanied him, and Elgar's comment to him in a letter was: 'Duisburg isn't a Lower Rhine Fest. after all – I suppose you'll all try to make out it's a bigger thing.' But on their return Elgar wrote: 'I . . . rejoice that dear old Parry had a good time with his "Sirens".'

musical personalities of his Continental enthusiasts. He came at the end of an epoch in European music, at the dawn of a renaissance in England. Already, disruptive and revolutionary forces were at work. However, you will not find in the careers of Richter, Brodsky, Kreisler, Steinbach, and Weingartner evidence of special 'progressivist' sympathy with the symphonies of Mahler or the early works of Schoenberg. To Richter, the music of Debussy and Franck was anathema. The 'European mainstream' to which Elgar belonged was, in the first ten years of the twentieth century, to branch out into many stimulating tributaries. Europe, always preoccupied with novelty, thereafter found time, amid new claims on its attention, to interest itself still in Brahms and Wagner; it had no time for Elgar, who stood in their shadows, and who seemed, after first acquaintance with his serious and substantial manner, to be a contradictory English gentleman, slightly pompous, disturbing in his mixture of extroversion and introspection, not quite romantic enough, and not even remotely erotic. So his claim to a place in the company of Berlioz, Liszt, and Brahms – where choral music was concerned – ceased to exercise the European musician's curiosity, especially after the political and national disruptions of the 1914–18 war.

But this was in the future. If Elgar had felt the contrast between German and English musical life after his first Düsseldorf success, he must have been again painfully conscious of the puritanical provincialism of the English attitude to art at the time of his second visit, which he prolonged with trips to Kassel, Eisenach (Bach's birthplace), and Leipzig. *Gerontius* was to be launched in the Worcester Three Choirs Festival of 1902, but in April the festival committee had doubts about the 'propriety' of performing such a Roman Catholic work in an Anglican cathedral.[25] The Bishop, Dr Gore, was a prime mover, but somebody had 'put him up to it'. Elgar wrote to Jaeger on 9 May: 'The whole objection now is manufactured by one man with the express purpose of (as he thinks) ruining the work and me.' Who this was is not at all clear. Can it have been Dr Davidson, Archbishop of Canterbury, who four years later was to express public disapproval of the new *English Hymnal* on the grounds of its alleged Anglo-Catholic bias? According to Sir Steuart Wilson,[26] Elgar told him that Bishop Gore wrote to Dean Forrest forbidding the performance and that, owing to the Trollopian relations between a bishop and a dean, it became an obligation on the Dean to see that the performance happened. Later Elgar received a handsome retraction from the Bishop. It is interesting that Elgar, so often

[25] Bigotry was not the sole cause of such stupidities at that time. The Dean and Chapter of St Paul's Cathedral held out against Parry's *Blest Pair of Sirens* for many years because of the implications of the word 'sirens'.
[26] *Musical Times*, June 1957, p. 304.

referred to as a 'devout Catholic', was not in any way offended by suggestions for 'de-Romanizing' the libretto. He wanted the music to be heard, and the composer outweighed the Catholic. He asked Fr Bellasis if textual alterations would be permitted, and it was proposed to omit the passage in Part I between cues [29] and [32] – the litany of saints – to substitute 'Jesus', 'Lord', or 'Saviour' for 'Mary' and 'Joseph' and to substitute 'prayers' for 'masses' in the Angel's farewell. 'It's a dreadful mix-up,' said Elgar, 'and as usual in these petty things they all seem to hide somewhere and expect me to "play the man!" I am only anxious to do what is sensible.'[27] Elgar conducted the performance, with Muriel Foster, John Coates, and Plunket Greene as soloists: a letter inviting Jaeger to come and hear the work suggests that the composer had still not heard the music as he had imagined it – 'You must come to Worcester & hear what Gerontius *might* be – the building will do it.' Three weeks later, he conducted it again at the Sheffield Festival, with John Coates, David Ffrangcon-Davies, and Muriel Foster, but again a curse seemed to be on the work, for the choir made their first entry a semitone flat. There were no further performances until March 1903, when two on successive evenings at last established it as performable without mishap.

On 12 March, at a Hallé concert in Manchester, Richter atoned for Birmingham. Johnstone of the *Manchester Guardian*, the English critic who had heard more *Gerontius* performances than anyone else and who thoroughly understood Elgar's music, wrote that it had been 'possible to hope that the Manchester performance of his great oratorio would be a striking success, and perhaps even throw a new light on the merits of the composition; and it can scarcely be questioned that the experience . . . fulfilled those hopes. It was doubtless the most carefully prepared of the performances that have been given thus far in this country. Dr Richter was, for various reasons, peculiarly anxious that it should go well.' It was 'a rendering that sounded spontaneous and unembarrassed, as though the singers were sure of the notes and could give nearly all their attention to phrasing, expression and dynamic adjustments. In the highest degree remarkable, too, was the orchestral performance . . . Experience of all the complete performances yet given induces us to think that the difference between thorough success and ordinary half-success with this oratorio depends more on the semi-chorus than on any other point, and this is where the pre-eminence of last night's rendering, among all yet given in this country, is most unquestionable . . .'

John Coates, Marie Brema (Johnstone admired her 'nobly

[27] *The Daily Telegraph* critic's comment on the suppressions was: 'Surely it is time for the cathedral clergy to recognize that if a work of art cannot be performed in its integrity it should not be produced at all. . . . Great is the mystery of some godliness.'

expressive style'), and Andrew Black were the soloists. Elgar did not hear this performance. It had been postponed for a week because of Coates's illness and was given the evening before the performance he was himself to conduct at Hanley. Adolph Brodsky wrote to him: 'We [he and his wife, Anna] just came home from the concert. It was an ideal and overwhelming performance. The impression we have from this work: greatness and sincerity; and then only you begin to realise that it is also a great master work from the technical point of view. Only a genius & a pure practical soul could have created such a work.' Rodewald wrote in equally enthusiastic terms. The Hallé Orchestra, who played again in the Hanley performance, arrived for the rehearsal 'absolutely beaming', as Alice described the occasion in a letter to Dorabella. Again, as with *King Olaf*, the North Staffordshire Chorus did full justice to Elgar's music and was selected to sing the first London performance in the uncompleted Westminster Cathedral on 6 June. Novello's had written to Elgar on 12 November 1902, saying that 'we believe that Mr Allen Gill intends giving a performance of the work in the spring,' but nothing came of this proposal. A great amount of publicity preceded the cathedral performance when at last the English capital heard this great English music several weeks after both Chicago and New York had presented it. But the critics' reception was still cautious: they were badly placed, the acoustics were unsatisfactory and they did not like Wüllner as Gerontius. Muriel Foster and David Ffrangcon-Davies were the other soloists. The event was a fashionable and controversial occasion. It had been organized by Lady Edmund Talbot, sister-in-law of the Duke of Norfolk. She had been introduced to Elgar by Alice Stuart-Wortley. At one time the Concertgebouw Orchestra of Amsterdam was to take part in the performance but withdrew six weeks beforehand. What Elgar conducted on that Saturday afternoon was described merely as 'Full Orchestra'. The notice by the critic of *The Times*, J. A. Fuller Maitland, tells us all we need to know about the attitude to *The Dream of Gerontius* by a particular section of English musical opinion. He referred sarcastically to 'the lavish praise that was bestowed on it by Herr Richard Strauss ... no doubt speaking with an authority based on an exhaustive knowledge of the whole of British music.' Because of this praise 'many who would not venture to express a favourable opinion of anything English on their own account have the satisfaction of feeling that they have the right to admire what has been so warmly praised in Germany.' If *Gerontius* had not thereby become a 'prime favourite', there was 'no reason to doubt whether the oratorio would not meet the fate of many better works and be put straightway on the shelf.' No further London performance was given until February 1904. Thereafter the work took its rightful place as a classic of the time. It was performed in Brussels (in French)

on 26 March 1905. The first Vienna performance was conducted by
Franz Schalk on 16 November 1905 when the bass solos were sung by
Richard Mayr, later to be the most famous Baron Ochs in Strauss's
Der Rosenkavalier. It was even performed in Paris in 1906 when Claire
Croiza sang the part of the Angel. This performance was brought
about by Fauré, to whom the score had been sent by Schuster. Every
British provincial choral society took it up; it was given eighteen
times at Three Choirs Festivals in the composer's lifetime and has
been performed there at many festivals since his death; Richter
conducted it several more times in Manchester, where Johnstone
wrote in the *Manchester Guardian* that 'to hear the Gerontius music is
to become acquainted with by far the most remarkable and original
personality that has arisen in musical Britain since the days of Purcell.'

So much space has been devoted to the genesis of *The Dream of
Gerontius* not only because of the intrinsic interest of a kind of
adventure story but because of the work's historical importance in the
development of English music. It remains a unique contribution to
English choral music because it broke new ground. Even so sensitive
a critic as Johnstone loosely called it an oratorio, whereas the whole
point of the work is that it cannot be fitted into such a category. It is
simply what Elgar called it on the title-page: a setting to music of a
poem. Elgar loved a 'tale'. He had hoped to find an English epic in
Caractacus, but his mature genius was fired to its highest imaginative
point by the most personal and mysterious of all stories, the journey
of a man's soul from this world to whatever lies hereafter. Jaeger's
reference to it as a 'sacred cantata' offended Elgar – 'don't perpetuate
that dreadful term unless we're obliged,' he wrote.[28] *Gerontius* has
retained the mystique with which its early misadventures endowed it.
Reputations have been won in the singing of the solo rôles, which
have been distinguished by several notable interpreters. Those with
long enough memories like to argue the relative merits of Gervase
Elwes, John Coates, Heddle Nash, and Steuart Wilson. In later years
Richard Lewis and Ronald Dowd have become identified with the
work. Elgar himself, according to Basil Maine, rated Wüllner and
Coates highest, and also admired Elwes. None of these three had what
in purely vocal terms could be called a great tenor voice, yet it is clear
from all that one reads that they were great interpreters of this rôle.
Gerontius, as Jaeger rightly wrote, requires brains as well as voice;
within my own experience I recall Parry Jones as one of the most
moving and impressive singers of Gerontius although the voice itself
was not of the first order. Among the most distinguished singers of
the Angel's music are numbered Muriel Foster, Clara Butt, Astra

---

[28] Elgar gave his approval to the inclusion of *Gerontius* in the oratorio section of
Novello's catalogue, adding in a letter to Jaeger on 23 August 1904, 'there's no word
invented yet to describe it'.

Desmond, Gladys Ripley, Kathleen Ferrier, and Janet Baker: a royal line of succession. The bass rôles have fared less well, despite the distinctive contributions of Harold Williams, Norman Walker, and Dennis Noble. Elgar's bass parts are written for a richer, deeper bass than England usually produces. Foreign interpreters of the parts of the Priest and the Angel of the Agony sometimes have the vocal equipment but can never master the English vowels and phrase-rhythms. To this day, therefore, the music awaits its ideal trio of singers.

There are some to whom the combination of John Henry Newman's Catholicism and Edward Elgar's chromaticism is so abhorrent on aesthetic grounds that they cannot hear *The Dream of Gerontius* without acute mental, and even physical, discomfort. For them nothing can be done. For the vast majority not afflicted in this way the work is a musical masterpiece of the highest calibre, and a spiritual and artistic experience which repeated hearings do not lessen in power. One reason for its success is the skilful way in which Elgar adapted the poem, some might say improving on Newman in the process, tautening it and rejecting unerringly the parts unsuitable for musical setting.[29] The marvellous opening of the Prelude, *lento mistico*, scored for muted violas, clarinets, and bassoons with the cor anglais entering unforgettably at the fifth bar, takes the responsive listener at once into the world of Elgar's imagination, and vividly into the sick-room. We follow Gerontius's progress from death to the threshold of eternity with the attention that supreme art compels. Never before in English choral music had the orchestra sounded so expressive, so detailed in its illustrative imaginativeness. Point after point in the text is etched into the memory by the scoring. One thinks immediately of the low flute crescendo in the Demons' Chorus for the 'low hideous purring', the compassionate oboe at 'manhood crucified', the extraordinary writing for strings at 'the emptying out of each constituent' and to illustrate the 'strange innermost abandonment', the hollow chord at the word 'terrible' in 'The thought of death and judgment was to me most terrible', the use of the harp as the Angel sings 'Farewell', the sense of timelessness in the strings' rarefied opening to Part II, the pre-echoes in the orchestra of the Angel's first song, and the splendidly brazen brass snarls in the Demons' Chorus. Yet there is a tendency sometimes to write of *Gerontius* as if the orchestration, marvellous as it is, was the whole story. This is, after all, a major choral work and the writing for the

---

[29] A detail in Gerontius's part in Part II has puzzled many listeners and performers and also puzzled Elgar, who wrote to Novello's on 4 April 1902: 'I am writing to the Oratory [Birmingham] to ask if they have any views as to 'My soul is in *thy* hand' – it's of course not right sense but, as it is *my* in the big authoritative edition of the Cardinal's work, I hesitate to alter it.'

voices, soloists and choir, is that of a master, and its originality and brilliance should not be overlooked. Two aspects in particular are outstanding. First is Elgar's use of a semi-chorus to represent, in Part I, the Priest's Assistants at Gerontius's death-bed. Their first entry with 'Kyrie eleison', unaccompanied, could only have been written by a man who thoroughly understood choral singing and who had lived among choirs and cathedrals, as Elgar had. 'The building will do it', he told Jaeger; and to hear the voices steal in at this point during a performance in Worcester Cathedral or York Minster is to realize the completeness of Elgar's conception. He had strong views about the semi-chorus which he thought should be limited to eighteen voices (five sopranos, five contraltos, four tenors, and four basses), 'pure and "sweet" without the slightest hardness of tone'. This he wrote to Nicholas Kilburn in October 1902, in reply to a series of questions about the choral effects in *Gerontius*. 'At Düsseldorf,' he wrote, 'they were placed *between* the soloist & the orchestra & I recommend this plan in the printed full score.'

The other specially notable feature is the extremely fluent type of recitative, a true melodic speech-rhythm, which characterizes the part of Gerontius. This is very marked in the beginning of Part II, where the Soul of Gerontius sings of the liberation from the body: 'I feel in me an inexpressive lightness . . . I hear no more the busy beat of time . . . This silence pours a solitariness into the very essence of my soul . . . And hark! I hear a singing; yet in sooth I cannot of that music rightly say whether I hear or touch or taste the tones . . .' These words, and many other examples from Part I, especially the great opening 'Thou art calling me', are set so inevitably and rightly that once heard it is impossible to divorce them from the music: they have become one and indivisible. There are the usual blemishes in Elgar's word-setting, where the music takes hold and the words must fend for themselves – 'Within his ample palm' is one ugly moment, and there are several in the Angel's part, 'Softly and gently' being a particularly jarring example – but for the greater part of the work the union of voice and verse is perfect. It need not be thought that Elgar was unaware of the rhythmic stresses of his native tongue and disregarded them to suit his purpose. He had pronounced views, as expressed in a letter to Jaeger written on 26 April 1908: 'I hold that *short* syllables may be sustained occasionally for the sake of effect just as an actor does. There is one dear good man against who I wd. not *think anything* . . . & that is Parry. But he almost if not quite annoys me in the way he sets the words which swarm in our English – two syllables, both short, the first accented, e.g. petal. Set in an ordinary way a poem sounds like reading a newspaper paragraph. I remember insisting on doing[30] a poem of Tennyson (Lotos Eaters!) by P. I liked it & studied

[30] At Worcestershire Philharmonic, 10 May 1902.

it with the chorus for months & had great difficulty in getting them to *take* to it . . . After the concert a very well educated lady . . . said to me "We have done our best to please & I am sorry you insisted: I shall never read the poem again with any enjoyment". This of course simply on account of the *driven* accents . . . Only the other day one of your best chorus-masters said I know nothing of writing for the voice *or* choral effect – asked why, he pointed to a ff on a C for sopranos: this sort of thing is annoying as it shews what idiots we write for. If the clown had an ounce of artistic sense he wd. have seen that the note was to help the contraltos & to lead into a *diminuendo* impossible to obtain in any other way.'[31]

The massed choral effects in *Gerontius* are nearly all splendid. He hardly ever excelled the finale of Part I, 'Go forth in the name of angels and archangels,' for poetry combined with grandiloquence. The climax of 'Praise to the Holiest' is thrilling to sing and to hear, and its brilliance drives from the mind some rather less inspired pages a little earlier. Here again, the first sounds of 'Praise to the Holiest', coming from afar, are choral writing *par excellence*. The Demons' Chorus has been the butt of critics taking a lead from Ernest Newman's 1905 book in which he referred to 'pantomime demons'. But if it is properly rehearsed and sung incisively it does convey the composer's sardonic and sarcastic intentions. Sir Henry Coward and Sir John Barbirolli found the way to interpret this section correctly, and so perhaps did Richter, for Arthur Johnstone wrote of 'a welter of infernal but most eloquent sound' at the 1903 Hallé performance. Elgar's use of fugue in this chorus is expressive and free, a startling contrast to the fugue in *Lux Christi* which he said he wrote because he felt it was expected of him – and it sounds like it. The Demons' fugue is tremendous stuff, and it wears its academic dress with a rakish indifference to fashion, as do all the finest choral passages in *Gerontius*. 'You know, Billy,' Elgar said to W. H. Reed after a Lincoln performance of the work, 'I believe there is a lot of double counterpoint, or whatever they call it, in that' – so anxious was he to be free from any suggestion of academic methods or techniques, though of course he knew them inside out. He was also anxious that the work should always sound dramatic (as records of his own conducting of parts of it testify). Thus, he preferred John Coates's robust singing of Gerontius to that of Gervase Elwes. Even though – or perhaps because – Elwes was a devout Catholic, his interpretation was, for Elgar, 'too saintly'. In 1927 when he coached Steuart Wilson

---

[31] This occurrence bears a striking resemblance to a story, told by Reed and others and transposed to the orchestra, that an academic-minded musician asked Elgar why a bass clarinet passage was marked *pp* against the rest of the orchestra's *ff* when it could not possibly be heard. Elgar is said to have pointed to a solo passage for the instrument a few pages later for which the earlier bars were a 'warming up'. Possibly the passage concerned is nine bars after cue 31, 1st movement, 1st Symphony.

in the part and they came to 'Sanctus fortis' Elgar looked up from the piano and said, 'Verdi wouldn't have been ashamed to write that tune!'

In *Gerontius*, we find the fullest expression of all Elgar's many-sided gifts. It is his finest work. Part I is practically flawless; tension sometimes slackens in Part II but is skilfully built up again at the end for the Angel of the Agony's aria, Gerontius's 'Take me away' and the Angel's tender and compassionate Farewell. Anyone can pick out the weaker moments: far more important is the work's impregnable strength as an impassioned human document. Not only did Elgar bring Newman's poem to life and give expression to his religious beliefs at that time; he expressed unforgettably the darker side of his own nature: the 'sense of ruin' pervades the music, and in Gerontius's anguished cries on his bed of pain can be recognized the tormented spirit discernible in Elgar's letters. The day he completed *Gerontius* he wrote to Nicholas Kilburn: 'I think you will find Gerontius far beyond anything I have yet done – I *like* it – . . . on our hillside night after night looking across our "illimitable" horizon (pleonasm!) I've seen in thought the Soul go up & have written my own heart's blood into the score.' Thus from his deepest experience, Elgar created the last great artistic monument of the reign of Queen Victoria and the last of the nineteenth century.

8 Friends and Relations

After the second Düsseldorf *Dream of Gerontius*, Alice Elgar wrote an account of the performance and of Strauss's tribute for her mother-in-law, who had barely three months more to live. No reply survives, but one written in 1899 still applied. From the music-shop home in Worcester High Street, Ann Elgar had said: 'What can I say to him the dear one – I feel that he is some great historic person – I cannot claim a little bit of him now he belongs to the big world.'

In these moving words are an ironic tribute, for though he *was* an historic person belonging to the big world, the dichotomy of his life in the years to follow was the conflict and contrast of Elgar the Historic Person with Elgar of Worcester. The London Elgar and the Country Elgar were very nearly two different people except that the personality at the heart of both was complex, so that parts of one mixed with the other, not always to happy effect. The results show plainly in his music. His creative life is usually divided for convenience into three periods: the early but unsatisfactory works up to 1899, the masterpieces from 1899 to 1919, then the twilight and virtually silent last fourteen years. But this is an over-simplification, because the 1899–1919 period is strongly sub-divisible. The *Variations* and *Gerontius* stand apart as the most artistically and psychologically complete of all his works. The mainly orchestral works produced from 1908 to 1913 are technically and psychologically far more complicated and diffuse. There can be little doubt that these fascinating nuances reflect the composer's personality and outlook to a larger degree than in most composers' works. Though his creations were his private kingdom, Elgar was constitutionally unable to seal them off from other facets of his mind.

Rosa Burley's memoirs of Elgar in the period after the first performance of *The Dream of Gerontius* stress the manifestations of these inner tensions.[1] They spent much time together cycling in the lanes within a twenty-mile radius of Malvern. 'He was very difficult and one never quite knew what would be the mood of the afternoon . . . I found that he was particularly touched by birdsong and that he loved and knew all the little creatures that darted in and out of the hedges.' As their outings grew more numerous he told her more about the 'misery which clouded a large part of his life' and of the 'ungovernable resentment' he felt – against the 'academics' who were

[1] *Edward Elgar: the record of a friendship*, op.cit., pp. 145–9.

jealous of him; because he was financially hard-pressed (still giving violin lessons at her school, for instance); because recognition had come 'too late'; and, most bitterly of all, because he was a tradesman's son and had been brought up in a shop. The social handicap of his upbringing could not be understood, he maintained, by anyone who had not experienced it. Even his marriage into a higher class had not helped; because Alice, even though she resented her relatives' attitude to her husband, still accepted their caste system and found it almost impossible to have much contact with his parents, brothers and sisters. There is a well-attested story of his last-minute withdrawal from a dinner-party at one of the homes of the 'gentry' in Worcestershire – this was when he was already famous – because, as he said in a note to his hostess, 'you will not wish your table to be disgraced by the son of a piano-tuner.' In the early years of the twentieth century, as he became a celebrity, a knight, and a friend of royalty, he found it increasingly difficult, because of the defect in his pyschological make-up, to cope with the strains on his personality. All his life, as his daughter told me, he could never quite believe that he, Ted Elgar from Broadheath and 10, High Street, was a member of what we should today call the Establishment. If one studies the conflicting accounts of Elgar's personality, one discovers a consistent pattern: with those seriously engaged in the business of professional music-making, such as W. H. Reed and orchestral players generally or Fred Gaisberg and the gramophone people, he was usually friendly, even lovable, outgoing, and humorous; with non-musicians, especially those of the upper middle-class, he was often prickly, boorish, and rude – on the defensive. In this latter case, too, his attitude was further complicated by what must surely have been the most 'ungovernable resentment' of all – against the philistinism of British musical life. His resentment of his financial state was not merely petty grumbling over petty cash; he was embittered because composers were poorly rewarded commercially compared with writers and painters. As will have been noticed, a persistent theme in his letters was his scorn for the British public. He knew that at bottom the British did not regard music as an indispensable part of their lives and he never forgave them, indeed it often seems that he hated them. This hatred was frequently vented on some hapless representative of the public who happened to encounter Elgar in one of his moods of despondency and gall.

To come nearer to understanding these complexities, it is perhaps a help to look at some of his personal relationships at this period of his life. When his mother died in the late summer of 1902 he lost the first moulding influence on his mind, for it was she who had stimulated his love of literature and the world of nature around him. Although, like all children, he had sometimes felt misunderstood by his parents,

Elgar had an abiding love and respect for the 'two honest old burghers' as he called them to Troyte Griffith. After his father died in 1906, Elgar sought Troyte's aid (as an architect) in designing a suitable gravestone. 'I do not feel drawn towards the stonemason monumental-artist sort of thing,' he wrote.[2] 'As we bear an old Saxon name wd. it be too fanciful, if practicable, to take some Saxon thing for a model or rather type?' He was immensely proud to show his parents the proofs of his success. The day after the robes of his Cambridge doctorate arrived at his home (on 3 December 1901), he took them to Worcester to show them to William and Anne. When he was knighted his first thought was to go to tell his father, then an old and ailing widower; but perhaps most fitting and moving of all was his gesture, in September 1905, when he walked in procession along High Street, Worcester, on his way to receive the honorary freedom of the city. As he passed Elgar Brothers' shop he bared his head in salute to his father, who watched the scene from an upper window.

In 1902 Edward and Alice Elgar had been married for thirteen years. To say that she was the greatest influence on his life is no exaggeration, for no other interpretation is possible. She was eight years older; and if any amateur psycho-analyst chooses to notice that Elgar's wife and many of his women friends were older than he and to deduce that he preferred a maternal relationship, no one can stop him, though he will get little encouragement from me. It would be much nearer the mark to say that in Alice, Elgar found wife, mother, friend, mentor, and spur. It is possible to look askance at certain aspects of their life together – in which marriage is it not possible? – but any attempt to 'debunk' the legend of their relationship is doomed to failure from the facts of Elgar's words, his reaction to her death, and the disinterested testimony of others who were by no means blind to Alice's faults. Psychologists would no doubt also have a field-day with those notes and entries in Alice's diary written in a private language of baby-talk which she and Elgar kept up throughout their marriage. Thus, on a love-poem she had written before their marriage, she later scribbled: 'I spec this is to E's own souse Braut wopse' ('I expect this is to E's own self. Bride ?? . . .'). In 1892, when she wrote a poem for him, she added at the foot: 'For my Beloved's booful music. Pease not beat. Will dis do?' Elgar would reply in a similar style, commenting 'Vessy nice.' He once wrote in the margin of her typescript 'If zu smells sis, zu'll find it's not fesh! grrh!' It is easy to ridicule this idiom unless one realizes that it was the practice of the Victorian English upper class – 'people of breeding', as it used to be said – to have three forms of spoken expression: intimate for God and for beloveds such as humans and pets; formal for social occasions

[2] 25 October 1907.

and for dealings with tradesmen; and natural for relatives and friends. In the working classes there were two forms, the 'proper' style of address to their employers and landlords, and a vernacular (often with the old 'thee' and 'thou') for everyone else. The intimate mode of talk for humans and pets was highly personalized and often comprised mispronunciations and faulty grammar from early childhood, invented words, bits of the liturgy, and even quotations from songs. It was meant for only the most intimate circle and was embarrassing to anyone who was not in that circle. Most families today still have some variety of private language. It is in this context that the Elgars' intimate words should be read.

There must have been great stresses in the 1890s for a patrician lady who married a lower-middle-class shopkeeper's son, a man whose social graces were acquired rather than inherited, and who ran the risk of being suspected of having married 'above him' for the reason that his wife had a small private income. That they shared literary and artistic tastes would merely be counted against them as an even odder cause for matrimony. That Elgar should have felt gratitude to Alice for her courage is obvious. She, for her part, marrying beneath her at forty, would be suspected of a wish to be 'off the shelf' at any cost. That she had married for love of a man in whom she had rightly perceived the quality of genius would hardly have occurred to some of the gentry of late Victorian Worcestershire. So when her choice was justified, when her talented local composer became the acknowledged leader of his profession, friend of kings and marquesses, it is understandable that she rubbed it in, although one may feel that a little less zest would have assisted Edward more. For there were no half-measures, as some extracts already quoted from her diary will have shown. She had never doubted Edward's supremacy and never would:

Parratt quite carried away with enthusiasm for E's great music [*Lux Christi*] . . . Glorious *King Olaf* a magnificent triumph. D.G. . . . Dear Bavarians [*Scenes from the Bavarian Highlands*] first time. Immense enthusiasm. . . . Great success. D.G. [*Variations*] . . . It was said there had never been such a triumph in Mainz [*The Apostles*]. . . . E. lectured most splendidly, held his audience breathless (Birmingham, 1905). . . . Orch. & large part of audience simply rose, people *wept*. E. looked very *apart* and beautiful being recalled again & again [London first performance of A flat symphony]. . . . This is a day to be marked. E. finished his Symphony [No. 2]. It seems one of his very greatest works, vast in design & supremely beautiful. It is really sublime. . . . Wertheim [piano soloist in Saint-Saëns piano concerto which Elgar conducted] agitating as he left out 1/2 bars. Required a genius to keep it right.

She declared war on any discourtesy, such as this at a rehearsal of *The Music Makers*: 'Most annoying . . . people moving & going in &

out & H. Wood quite unbearable even shutting door noisily.' One
evening she was engaged in conversation about the Nobel Peace Prize
and confided to her diary, 'Pray it may be given to E.' Attending a
wartime concert at which Stanford's 'common' *Songs of the Sea*
preceded a work by Elgar she noted: 'The great music began – E.
looked like the High Priest of Art.' It was Alice's faith which was
really sublime, however indulgently we may smile and perhaps feel
that the Almighty, too, was being congratulated on His good taste.
Had these effusions been limited to private entries in a diary – even
with one eye on posterity – no harm would have been done. But they
were not. Arnold Bax was at the age of seventeen taken to meet Elgar
at Birchwood in 1901. 'The composer's wife, a pleasant-looking fair-
haired lady, with – it struck me – rather an anxious manner, welcomed
us very kindly in her gentle, slightly hesitant voice. Almost at once
she began to speak enthusiastically and a little extravagantly about her
wonderful husband and his work.'[3] Vaughan Williams, seated next to
Alice at a Three Choirs rehearsal of the Second Symphony in 1912,
was nudged during the slow movement and persistently asked 'Isn't it
lovely?' She was unable to realize that the adoration of the Malvern
group of intimate friends was shared at a less intense level elsewhere.
Even Jaeger sometimes found it too much. Describing to Dorabella
the first Düsseldorf full rehearsal of *Gerontius*, he wrote: 'As for dear
Mrs. E., you can imagine her state of seventh-heaven-beatitude, with
eyebrow lifting, neck twisting, forget-me-not glances towards the
invisible Heavens! Don't think I am making fun of her! I am not; but
you know her signs of deep emotion over the Dr's music, don't you?'

Indeed she did, for one of the best pictures of the domestic life of
Edward and Alice is contained in Dorabella's book, a picture that,
though sometimes feline, is both warm-hearted and shrewd. It tells
much 'between the lines'. Though Alice's loyalty was never strained,
life was not a bed of roses and it would be wrong to draw a portrait of
her as a pliant creature, fondly waiting to worship the latest
emanation of her husband's genius. She was an inexorable manager,
of a type that Elgar needed. Schuster in a letter to Elgar in 1903
referred to her as an 'indefatigable hostess and *marvellous* manager'.
Elgar was lazy and uninterested in business matters, but Alice insisted
that they were attended to. 'One can so easily understand how the
anxiety and worry of it all would get on her nerves,' Dorabella wrote
in her book.[4] 'Letters unanswered and promises &c. unfulfilled, and
even the possibility that contracts might be broken.' That Elgar
realized her value to him in this respect is evident from the letter from
a member of the Baker family at Hasfield Court which Dorabella also
quotes,[5] in which the writer recalled an occasion when Elgar was

[3] *Farewell, My Youth*, pp. 29–30.
[4] *Edward Elgar: Memories of a Variation*, op. cit., p. 83.   [5] Op. cit., p. 102.

leaving the house at Hasfield to play in the garden with the children. The afternoon post had arrived and Alice held out a packet of letters to him. 'But I'm going out now,' he said, and threw them on the floor, where one of the children picked them up. 'Oh, Edward, that *was* naughty,' said she, adding, 'These must be answered *at once*.' 'With a shout of ribald laughter he took them from her and went straight back upstairs, without another word.' Alice knew, too, the hardship of days when he was deep in writing a new work and she would leave a tray of food outside his study, though often it remained there uneaten. Then, if he came to a meal – one such as Dorabella describes when *The Kingdom* was being written – he would sit, tense and silent, looking pale and drawn, and returning at the first possible minute to his study. Perhaps after midnight he would emerge, the battle won, ready, when the others were tired and sleepy, for conversation and to be amused. On other occasions he was the life and soul of the party. 'He kept up a running fire of absurd remarks, comments, chaff and repartee,' says Dorabella.[6] 'I often laughed so much that I could hardly eat and was positively afraid to drink. Also it did not help matters to have the Lady [Dorabella always referred to Alice in this way] at the bottom of the table – not always completely approving, particularly if Carice was present – putting in remarks to try to check the flow: "Oh, Edward dear, how *can* you?" or "Oh, Edward, *really*!" "Cheer up Chicky" was all she got for her pains.' Sometimes Alice would apologize to visitors for her husband's behaviour: 'Oh *please* don't mind him. Edward dear, how *can* you?'

No one knew better than Alice that this kind of schoolboyish exuberance would be followed by a mood of dispirited, morose boredom when Elgar needed distraction, and she unerringly picked the people who would cheer him up. Life was complicated, too, for the cheerers-up, as Dorabella found: 'It needed a good deal of tact and care to think of the right things to say or the right line to take; particularly when one found that a person who had been lauded to the skies on a former visit was now flung to earth – though seldom by *him*.'[7] He was not the easiest of men with whom to live, as his outbursts of sulky temper at rehearsals must have made clear to other people. He paid dearly for his abuse of the choir at the Birmingham *Gerontius*, and W. H. Reed has recorded similar examples, notably one at the 1902 Worcester *Gerontius* rehearsal, for instance, when the timpanist made a bad mistake in the orchestral climax before 'Take me away' and Elgar 'stopped the rehearsal, his face a picture of horror – he gazed long and intently at the unfortunate drummer, and then said almost with terror in his voice: "Why – why did you do that?"'[8] Nevertheless, Alice's criticisms of his music were accepted in a

[6]*Edward Elgar: Memories of a Variation*, op.cit., pp. 25–6.
[7]*Edward Elgar: Memories of a Variation*, op.cit., p. 27.   [8]*Elgar*, op.cit., p. 68.

generous spirit. Though not a technical musician, her claim to the title of 'the first Elgarian' is indisputable: she understood his work and he knew she did. Reed recounts Elgar's words on this subject: 'I played some of the music [the ending of the Violin Concerto] I had written that day, and she nodded her head appreciatively, except over one passage, at which she sat up rather grimly, I thought. However, I went to bed leaving it as it was; but I got up as soon as it was light and went down to look over what I had written. I found it as I had left it, except that there was a little piece of paper, pinned over the offending bars, on which was written "All of it is beautiful and just right, except this ending. Don't you think, dear Edward, that this end is just a little . . . ?" Well, Billy, I scrapped that end.'

He scrapped other things, too, that did not win the nod of approval. In 1903 he was planning a ballet on the subject of Rabelais and had gone so far as to speak to Henry Higgins, chairman of the Grand Opera Syndicate which administered Covent Garden. He wrote to Troyte about this on 19 November 1903: 'He is keen to produce "Rabelais" on the lines I suggested! New costumes & everything – "like a shot". We'll have some fun one day.' But people less broadminded than Troyte, Alice among them, were not at all happy that the writer of Coronation odes and of The Apostles, should turn to the subject of Rabelais. So he abandoned the sketches, although he got his own back by adapting one of the tunes as the introductory Maestoso section of his Coronation March for George V. If it seems extraordinary that such an attitude should have prevailed, one has only to turn to Falstaff and to Elgar's depiction of the 'honest gentlewoman' – Doll Tearsheet, Mrs Quickly, and company – and then to quote another phrase from a letter to Troyte: 'Alice is horrified I fear with my honest gentlewomen – of course they must be in – do you think I have overdone them?' No one could possibly think he had, for their musical representation is genteel and bowdlerized. Bearing this in mind, it would be unwise' to spring to arms and cry, 'with all the emancipated frankness of today, that the Philistine, narrow-minded, patrician ladies of Malvern had deprived the world of a lusty, rumbustious ballet suite in Rabelais. The likelihood is that Elgar would have been quite unable to transpose the world of Pantagruel into music, and no doubt he knew it. An artist is not so easily discouraged if he wants to create something. Alice's disapproval of the subject probably had something to do with the abandonment of Rabelais; but the real reason, we may be sure, is that Elgar knew it 'would not work'. He was, in any case, toying with several ideas which came to naught at about that date. The incident is valuable, however, in throwing some light on points where these marriage partners, ideally matched in most ways, found themselves reminded of their different backgrounds. It is unlikely that Alice, gently as she remonstrated, could at all share Elgar's noisy, practical-joke type of humour or that she understood the side of him illustrated by this letter to Jaeger in June 1902: 'I *hate* coming to town – shall miss the haymaking I fear. Had 50 miles ride (on a bicycle) yesterday amongst the Avon country – Shakespeare etc. etc. Oh! so lovely but solus 'cos I can't find anybody here foolheaded enough to eat bread & cheese & drink beer – they've all got livers & apparently live in the country 'cos they can't afford to be swells in a town. Oh! Lor!'

But even if she could not share this part of her husband, Alice knew its importance for him. She had made a great sacrifice in giving up her literary pretensions to devote herself wholly to him and there are some rather pathetic glimpses of her in later life showing immense pleasure when anyone expressed interest in her writings. She also tolerated – perhaps did not even deign to recognize – Elgar's relationships with several women friends, such as Rosa Burley, Dora Penny, Alice Stuart-Wortley, and Lalla Vandervelde. Whatever she thought, suspected, or knew about these friendships – *amitiés amoureuses* of a kind particularly prevalent in that era – she kept to herself and put no obstacles in the way of his meeting them or inviting them to his home. On a less heroic level she ministered to his hypochondria, worrying herself over every detail of his comfort and, as their daughter remembered, never able to settle until she heard he had arrived safely at a destination. An amusing description of her solicitude has been given by Granville Bantock's daughter.[9] The Elgars were staying with the Bantocks in 1898: 'Elgar's wife . . . surrounded her husband with a ring-fence of attention and care which was almost pathetic. The composer himself depended upon his wife to a surprising extent . . . my newly-wed mother was, I am sure, awed by Mrs Elgar, with her array of rugs, shawls and cushions, extra body-belts and knitted bedsocks for Edward's comfort. One evening Helena noted with astonishment no fewer than seven hot water-bottles being filled for his bed on the occasion of Elgar's complaining of a slight chill!'

For his part Elgar tolerated her liking for society, her predilection for the nobility and for outward and visible signs of distinction, even if he sometimes found the company of the 'great' more than a little oppressive. A letter to Schuster in July 1910, when he was staying in Cornwall with the 13th of the Variations. Mary Lygon, by now Lady Mary Trefusis, tells much: 'It is heavenly etc. here! but I would like to choose my company as you allow me to do at The Hut. . . . Lady M. is as of old and always very "nice" & dear & rather severe. Of the rest I will tell you . . . Alice is radiantly happy. . . . I wish you and . . .! and . . .!! and . . .!!! were here. . . .' His natural inclination was to refuse

[9] In *Elgar and Granville Bantock* by Gareth H. Lewis, Elgar Society Journal, Vol. 1, no. 5, May 1980, p. 11.

honours, but he accepted them because they meant much to Alice and he owed much to her. When she died, he placed his Court Sword in her coffin, and it is buried with her.[10] Not too much should be made of Dorabella's veiled hints[11] about suppressions by Alice: that, apart from one incident, she never heard horse-racing, one of Elgar's interests, mentioned in the household in her fifteen years of close acquaintance with it. His racing interests were strong enough for him to note, on the day of the first performance of *The Apostles*, that Grey Tick had won the Cesarewich at 20 to 1.

One evening in 1914 Alice read aloud to Elgar from one of her own writings. That night, in her diary, she allowed herself some regrets for her abandoned literary ambitions. But she added: 'The care of a genius is enough of a life work for any woman.' It was as simple as that. We may think she was a snob, we may find oppressive her undiluted, blinkered enthusiasm for her husband's music. But were she to return today and see the position Elgar still occupies, the number of broadcast and concert-hall performances and the growing collection of superb recordings, she could say: 'All this you owe to me.' And she would be right.

. . . . .

The other profound influence of the crucial years in Elgar's life was August Jaeger. He made his appearance on the scene in 1897 at the very moment when Elgar knew that, given the chance, he could have the world at his feet. His friendship acted like a catalyst on Elgar, releasing in him the scorn and derision he felt for his English contemporaries. Jaeger, who shared these views, played him along and one has the sensation, reading their early correspondence, that each was using the other as an outlet, each administering to the other's 'chip'. Later, as has been seen and will again be seen in later chapters, Elgar came to respect his German friend's opinions, to take criticism from him in a tolerant spirit, often to accept his advice, and eventually to sustain a deep affection for him. The letters to Jaeger, many of which have been and will be quoted, are an indispensable guide to Elgar the composer. They also illustrate, more vividly than any other of his letters, even those to Troyte, Elgar's quirky humour, his extraordinary love of puns and plays on words, an aspect of him so integral to a full portrait that it cannot be set on one side as mere decoration. Jaeger, whose native tongue was not English, must have been flattered to be the principal target for these shafts of his strange unpredictable friend. Such spellings as 'orkestration' were com-

---

[10] F. Bonavia has written that 'all' Elgar's honours were buried with Lady Elgar, and Dorabella gives a supposedly authentic list. Mrs. Elgar Blake assured me that only the sword was buried. When her father became Master of the King's Musick he obtained a new one which is now at the Birthplace at Broadheath.

[11] On p. 8 of *Memories of a Variation*.

monplace. When Elgar dropped the formal 'Dear Mr. Jaeger' for 'My
dear Jaeger' he added 'The mister-y is soluted'. 'I say nuffin', 'those
two daze', 'Indeks', 'Direxshuns', 'Him wot rote it', 'a Joon
programme' – these were obvious extensions of the private language
of Edward and Alice. But whenever his inner despair broke out in
letters to Jaeger, the jocular tone was dropped and conventional
spelling was used. He also took pleasure in punning, an acquired
taste, and had a crossword-puzzle-addict delight in transposing
letters, such as the rather charming 'Cueen's Qopy' and his
conversational 'Look, bung yirds' to Dorabella whenever he saw
young birds. He played a game with the word 'score', making it more
and more unrecognizable to Jaeger, from 'skore' to 'skoughre' to
'ssczowoughohr' and even wilder permutations. He once spelt
anxious as 'angkschzsuszcs', and he enjoyed variations of the names
Jaeger and Nimrod – 'Jägerer', 'Jaegerissimo', 'Jaggs', 'Jay',
'Jaerodnimgeresque', 'Jagpot'. Occasionally, in the later years, he
was 'Augustus' or 'Nimrod' or 'Mosshead'. This kind of playfulness
sometimes became slightly barbed. In August of 1903 Jaeger
confessed that a progression in *The Apostles* set his teeth on edge. 'If I
found that in a work by a beginner, I should laugh & say "poor chap,
how crude".' (The offending passage is in the voice parts at bars 3 and
4, p. 109 of the vocal score.) Elgar took this kind of thing very much
to heart. 'Try it ppp & dolce – I fear your heavy thumb & melodious
forefinger are rather stiff, old Boy.' He signed this letter, written on 2
August, 'Edward of the *crude* (you old toad) progression'. The next
letter, on 5 August, has a similar signature. 'Edward the Crude', with
a drawing of himself cocking a snook and saying 'Yah!' was on a
letter on 7 August. By 16 August it was 'Yours Crooder than ever', on
20 August 'Your groping old crudity', and by 20 September a P.S.
'You haven't called me crooood lately – I breathe again.' No wonder
he hadn't; by then the point was no doubt well taken. Of course it was
all good clean fun, but ... Occasionally these verbal fantasies
achieved real and penetrating wit, as for instance in the letter of 14
November 1900, preceding his departure to Cambridge to receive an
honorary degree. This was signed 'Yours gownily' and included the
sentence 'I feel Gibbonsy, Croftish, Byrdlich & foolish all over.'
There was also the delightful letter which Jaeger, as 'Dear Augustus',
received at Christmas 1902:

a regular Yule-loggy puddingy, Brandy-saucious letter. . . . I have had Xmas
presents – all Wagner's prose works (translated) 8 vols & & & & & & the

Encyc. Brit & the bookcase!!!! a present (£42). Behold in me a learned prig:
prig mark you – I know the height of Arrarat (But don't know how to spell
it) & all sorts of japes. Look 'ere: I'm learned now & no base Nimrodkin

(Hebraic plural) shall look down on me: is not my learning vast in 35 volumes & in a revolving bookcase – my head too revolves with delight. I can tell you who was Aaron's mother-in-law's first cousin's bootblack & infinitesimal Calculus etc. etc. I charge 6d. to enter the study now. I say, I have a lively fine specimen of a Vanessa – pish! I shd say to one unwise a peacock butterfly who is helping the Apostles & lives in this study. I feed him – no, drink him on sugar & water & he lives in a Chrysanthemum – it's lovely & Japanesy & pastoral – I'm sure the beast is a familiar spirit – Angel Gabriel or Simon Magus, or Helen of Tyre or somebody – just fancy sitting in this study surrounded with flowers & a <u>live</u> butterfly at Xmas – this music's going to be good I can tell you. . . . Your austere & learned friend (34 vols & a bookcase) Paracelsus Elgar (with a pain in his stomach) Mince pizon.[12]

To Jaeger the years from 1898 to 1904, when he was midwife to works he knew to be masterpieces, must have seemed, for all their trials, a golden age. And when kings and noblemen fêted his protégé at the Elgar Festival of 1904 he began to fear, for two reasons: selfishly though understandably that his own day was done, and that the demands of being a celebrity might harm Elgar as a creative artist. He wrote a warning note: 'Don't let 'em spoil you, you "dear innocent, guileless Child" as dear old Hans [Richter] calls you in his fatherly loving way.' The guileless child of forty-six replied from a Manchester hotel, beginning the letter formally in a mock-serious vein: 'The position I now hold – greatly owing to your exertions & friendship – warrants me in throwing you over. . . . Now, you old Moss, read the other side.' On the opposite page he wrote: 'Dearie Moss . . . Whenever anything of mine is to be done you beg me not to be conceited & not to forget old friends etc. You are an old PIG & deserve some such letter as the unfinished one on the other side. . . . Don't bother me about conceit again – I haven't any except that I always resent any familiarity from outsiders & I *do* stand up for the *dignity* of our art – not profession.' Nevertheless from 1905 onwards the correspondence diminished. Jaeger was away from Novello's at Davos, hoping to cure his tuberculosis, and so there were fewer musical matters for Elgar to write to him about. Elgar himself was ill about that time and Lady Elgar took over much of his correspondence. In 1907 and 1908 the Elgars spent a good deal of time out of England and by then Jaeger was dying. To Dorabella in 1908 he wrote: 'I say, what *is* Elgar composing now? . . . He never tells me now, the wretch.' A year earlier he had written 'I have worked *terribly* hard for E. E. and ruined my health over it very likely. . . . I have never loved & admired a man more, made myself more a slave for any man out of sheer enthusiasm.' He lived to hear the symphony for

[12]A similar letter, signed 'Isaac Newton Elgar', went on the same day to Dorabella (or, on this occasion, Dorabellissima). She records that the bookcase was soon 'sent away' by Alice as Elgar 'would turn it round so'.

which he had hoped since 1898 and to write about its effect on him to 'My dear, great Edward'. But this will be told in a later chapter. The beneficial effects of Jaeger's friendship are obvious. Less salutary was his by no means inadvertent stoking of Elgar's resentment of the academic hierarchy represented by Stanford and Mackenzie. For example, in October 1899, after reading a favourable magazine review of Elgar's music he wrote, 'I should have liked to watch Stanford's face as he read it.' But, in fairness, it did not need a Jaeger to create bad blood between Stanford and Elgar. The characters of the two men made a clash inevitable; and , sure enough, it came, though not from the petty kind of jealousy ascribed by Jaeger (and Elgar) to Stanford of which, indeed, Stanford was incapable.

. . . . .

Charles Villiers Stanford was five years older than Elgar. He was an Irish Protestant, educated in Dublin and at Cambridge University. His academic career was brilliant, and he was also a fine practical musician as conductor and organist. When he was thirty-one he was appointed to the staff of the new Royal College of Music, at thirty-three he was conductor of the London Bach Choir, and at thirty-five he succeeded Macfarren as Professor of Music at Cambridge. When he was twenty-five he had a work performed at the Three Choirs Festival, Richter and Manns conducted his music in London, and he had a Birmingham Festival commission when he was thirty, a year after his first opera had been produced in Hanover. By the 1890s he occupied a commanding position in English musical life as teacher, conductor, and composer. He was warm-hearted, generous, and irascible: his bark was worse than his bite, but not everybody realized it. Some of his pupils (Vaughan Williams was an outstanding example) stood up to him and gave him affectionate respect. Others fled from his tongue to find another teacher. By some critics his achievements were regarded with awe,[13] others led by Bernard Shaw found his music excessively influenced by Brahms, Verdi, and other greater figures. Today his exquisite songs and part-songs, his Irish arrangements, his church music and such excellent choral works as the *Songs of the Fleet* keep his name alive. During his lifetime he quarrelled with most people and his relationship with Cambridge was decidedly prickly. It was a law of nature that Stanford the tactless and Elgar the thin-skinned would disagree. Their first meeting in 1896, already recounted, was friendly enough, and it was in that year, as Sir Alexander Mackenzie recalled in his book *A Musician's Narrative*, that Stanford, after hearing *King Olaf*, 'enthusiastically drew my attention

[13] Jaeger, writing to Elgar in March 1898, after he had written an unfavourable notice of a Stanford concert for the *Musical Times*, said: 'Really one gets quite disgusted and wants to say something nasty when one sees those critic friends of composers & conductors use only eulogisms to describe whatever the latter do.'

to the almost unknown new-comer's splendid gifts.' The next year Elgar asked for Stanford's opinion of, of all things, *The Banner of St. George*, and Stanford, forgetting that he was dealing with a sensitive fellow-artist and not a student's composition exercise, replied that 'it's all very well having fine raiment, but there must be a fine body to put it on'. Coolness lasted for about two years, but on 18 January 1900, Elgar conducted *Sea Pictures* at a Hallé concert the rest of which Stanford conducted. He mentioned to Jaeger ten days later: 'We are quite as before . . . we smoked & supped together.' This rapprochement resulted in Stanford's inclusion of the *Sea Pictures* in a R.C.M. concert on 15 March with Muriel Foster as the soloist, although in the event Parry conducted because Stanford was ill. Elgar made Stanford an honorary member of the Worcestershire Philharmonic Society and performed his *The Last Post* at one of its concerts. Whatever Elgar may have thought of Stanford's music, Stanford genuinely admired Elgar's. His attitude to *Gerontius* was double-edged; the musician in him appreciated it, the Protestant was repelled. He told Herbert Howells that he would have 'given his head' to have written Part I. To T. F. Dunhill he remarked that 'it stinks of incense'. The latter remark got back to Elgar, though when it was made is not known. Nevertheless Stanford had unqualified admiration for the *Variations*, and it was he who, on the strength of that work, urged Cambridge to make Elgar an honorary Doctor of Music. The letter containing the invitation was received at Malvern on 17 October 1900, exactly a fortnight after the Birmingham *Gerontius* fiasco. Alice was delighted; Elgar's first inclination was to refuse. He said he could not afford the robes, and a deeper-seated reason was his dislike of being in any way associated with the 'academic' musicians he despised. Miss Rosa Burley, in a note quoted by Dr Percy Young in *Letters to Nimrod*,[14] says that she reminded him that this was a recognition of *Gerontius* and that he could hire the robes. Next day he notified Cambridge of his acceptance and chose St Cecilia's Day, 22 November 1900, for the ceremony. The story told by Basil Maine[15] that Alice was so anxious for him to accept that she persuaded Rodewald to travel from Liverpool to plead with him is therefore obviously untrue. Cowen was to be similarly 'doctored' and Elgar was sufficiently proud of the honour to write to Jaeger: 'Edwards [F. G. Edwards, then editor of the *Musical Times*] ought to give a list of the people on whom it has been conferred . . . the general public don't know the difference between "it" & the stupid Canterbury commercial transaction.' Stanford was not present at the conferment because he had to be in Leeds for talks about the 1901 festival. If he was avoiding anyone that day, as has been suggested, it would have been Cowen, not Elgar, for there was intrigue at that time over the conductorship of the Leeds

[14] Pp. 111–12.   [15] *Elgar: His Life and Works*, op.cit., i, p. 118.

Festival, in which Cowen was deeply involved. He contributed to a subscription list for Elgar's robes sent round by Bantock. Others who helped provide the necessary £45 were Parry, Jaeger, Wood, Plunket Greene, Pitt, Kilburn, Kalisch, and friends of earlier days. It was Rodewald who travelled to Malvern a year later on 8 November 1901 '& announced to me the great surprise about the Robes – I don't know what to make of you all & am in a fit of the *blues* thinking of the kindness of you all for which I have done nothing to deserve – it's very odd & dreamlike & I don't know who I am. . . .'[16]

Stanford's admiration was practical as well as emotional at this time. He insisted that the *Variations* should be played at the 1901 Leeds Festival, where Elgar conducted them at his invitation. He wrote to Elgar appreciatively of the *Cockaigne* overture and the first two *Pomp and Circumstance* marches – 'they both came off like blazes, and are uncommon fine stuff' – and he conducted the *Variations* at the R.C.M. on 13 December 1901 – 'I liked them better every time'. In a postscript to this letter he said: 'Will you do me a great kindness? Give us [the College] the première of an orchestral thing some day. There's cheek. I only ask it because I could give such a thing a dozen rehearsals; and that tells. And I'd like a big thing, a Symphony please. I'll pledge my conscience to make them play it right for you.' And in April 1902 Stanford sought permission to have Elgar nominated for the Athenaeum Club. Again, the thought of the entrance fee of 30 guineas made Elgar doubtful about accepting, but Stanford advised him to write a couple of songs, as he had done, and pay the fee with advance royalties. Elgar was elected under Rule 2 on 8 May 1903, and his sponsors were Parry and Stanford.

For *Gerontius*, too, Stanford was a champion. He had his own troubles with the Leeds Philharmonic Society[17] Committee principally because of their failure or unwillingness to consult him. He had wanted *Gerontius* in the 1901–2 season, but the committee had curtly rejected the idea and the following March he wrote to J. H. Green, secretary of the Society:[18] 'A work which is the first English composition to be given at a Lower Rhine Festival (in consequence of which Sheffield upsets its programme to include it) is not a work to be simply dismissed because A or B don't personally care for it. It is the duty of a great choral society in a great town to let its public form their own judgment on such an important composition which has even reached with success Germany in its most Anglophobic temper. . . . Surely it is for a choral society such as yours to lead and not follow.' He genuinely hoped for the success of this work in London and was so concerned about the proposal to perform it there

[16] Letter to Jaeger, 9 November 1901.
[17] Stanford had been conductor of this famous Northern chorus since 1898.
[18] This and other letters are quoted from Plunket Greene's *Charles Villiers Stanford*.

for the first time in Westminster Cathedral, of which he had had unhappy experience in regard to his own work, that he went to Malvern in April 1903 to warn Elgar (rightly, as it happened) whose reaction, expressed on 20 April in a letter to Littleton, was typically edgy: '*Stanford* has been here and *deeply* commiserated with me on the cathedral performance: thinks it is a *great pity* for *my* sake etc. etc. all on account of the deadly bad acoustics of the building etc. etc. *Is* there anything in all this? . . . I quite appreciate Stanford's kindness in pointing out that the performance *must* be disastrous – they say that about anything I do or compose. . . . The fact is if anything can be *said* not done to throw cold water on the thing it will be done.'

Stanford also comes well out of the muddle Elgar created over a symphony for the 1904 Leeds Festival. Frederick Spark, the cantankerous and autocratic secretary of the festival, invited Elgar on 27 October 1902 to compose a work for October 1904. Elgar accepted but gave no indication of the type of work he had in mind. So on 18 December Spark commissioned a symphony for 50 guineas. This figure did not satisfy Elgar, who substituted a choral work. However, three months later, he said he could not produce a choral work and Spark raised the fee for a symphony to £100, to which Elgar agreed. Seven months later Elgar, who was low in health and spirits, withdrew the offer of a symphony because, he said, it would preclude his writing a large choral work for the festival in the future. The real reason he told to Troyte Griffith in a letter written on 26 December 1903: 'The history of the Leeds Symphony is this: I always promised the *dedication* to Richter: early this year (I think) I promised the first performance at Leeds; at the Birmingham Festival time I learnt that R. was counting upon conducting the *first performance* – so I withdrew it from Leeds & gave it to him – *if it's ever ready*. That's all.'

But Leeds knew nothing of this. From their point of view, Elgar was prevaricating; and matters were made worse when, after the work had been withdrawn, they read an announcement of an Elgar Festival at Covent Garden to be held the following March, conducted by Richter, and to include 'a new orchestral work' which, the *Daily News* confidently but erroneously proclaimed, was 'the symphony announced for Leeds'. (It was *In the South*.) The committee decided to omit Elgar from the 1904 festival entirely, after a final attempt to get a short choral work from him. The affair, Stanford told Elgar, was 'evidently a sore subject with them'. He wrote in January 1904 to W. S. Hannam, chairman of the committee, reporting Parry's comment that their decision was 'a fatal mistake' and 'simply impossible'. Stanford continued: 'What earthly harm can it do to play *Cockaigne* at the end of the Wednesday evening programme . . .? Fair play, old chap, and a man's artistic work ought to rank independently of his personality. If it had not been that Hans von Bülow had taken this view of Wagner, the Bayreuth theatre would not be standing now.' Eventually the committee thought better of the matter and included *In the South* in the Festival programme.

So, apart from the squally passage in the late 1890s, Elgar and Stanford maintained reasonably cordial relations up to 1904. But on 27 December 1904, according to Alice's diary, Elgar received 'an odious letter from Stanford – sent most gentle & courteous reply'. No one knows what it was about but Stanford thereafter avoided his company and they did not speak to each other for nearly twenty years. I am convinced that the subject of the letter was the Birmingham professorship, about which there had at this time been much newspaper publicity. This conviction is fortified by a letter written by Elgar to Littleton of Novello's two days later, on 29 December, in which he said 'Many *disagreeables* arise from a certain quarter over my new appointment which seems to have caused bitter irritation'. The 'certain quarter' must refer to Stanford. When, in his Birmingham lectures in 1905, Elgar mocked at some of the English music written since 1880 and at the writers of rhapsodies, Stanford took it as a personal attack. It may have been intended personally; it was certainly tactless. 'Some of us', he said in his first lecture, speaking as one who had played in orchestras in the 1880s, 'felt that something at last was going to be done in the way of composition by the English school. . . . It is saddening to those who hoped for so much from these early days to find that . . . we had inherited an art which has no hold on the affections of our own people and is held in no respect abroad. . . . Many respectable and effective works have been written during the twenty years 1880–1900. To me they represent more or less . . . such a phase of art as in another way was represented by Lord Leighton. There you had a winning personality, a highly educated man, a complete artist, technically complete, but the result was cold and left the world unmoved. The musical works produced in the period named leave me in exactly the same way: I am amazed at the dexterity displayed in the finish of the works, but there is absolutely nothing new. . . . Twenty, twenty-five years ago some of the rhapsodies of Liszt became very popular. I think every Englishman since has called some work a rhapsody. To rhapsodize is one thing Englishmen cannot do. . . . It points a moral showing how the Englishman always prefers to imitate'.

W. H. Reed admitted that Elgar scorned the subterfuges of diplomacy and tact 'and went straight to the point, hitting out right and left when he got worked up by his own eloquence. He had an unhappy knack of doing this at times; even in an ordinary short speech he would let a word or a phrase drop which . . . if he had stopped to consider it, he might have left unsaid.'[19]

[19]*Elgar*, op.cit., p. 89.

Elgar and Stanford avoided each other thenceforward. In July 1910, when Parry, Stanford, Mackenzie, and Elgar were all at Bournemouth, Stanford 'fled when he saw E.', Alice noted in her diary, though they appeared together later in a photograph, seated at extreme ends of the group. At Cambridge in February 1912 Elgar conducted Stanford's new Seventh Symphony and was 'amused' to do so. Yet the breach was not healed. But Reed, in a letter to Plunket Greene reprinted in the Stanford biography,[20] recalled how, as Lady Elgar's coffin was being taken from St Wulstan's Church, Little Malvern, to the graveside after her funeral service on 10 April 1920, he was surprised to see Stanford standing at the back. 'He impulsively caught hold of my arm and said "Tell Elgar I *had* to come. I daren't go to the graveside as the doctor has absolutely forbidden me to stand in the open air without a hat, but tell him how sorry I am and that I just felt I *must* come." He was far from well and I firmly believe that he had toiled all the way from Great Malvern contrary to the doctor's orders.' Elgar did not discover that Stanford had been present until after the ceremony. He wrote on 18 April to Schuster: 'I only regard it as a cruel piece of impertinence. For years (?16) he has not spoken to me and has never let me know why. . . . His presence last Saturday was a very clever "trick" to make it appear that, after all, he is really a decent fellow etc., and that I am the culprit – that the fault (if any) of our difference (which only exists by his manufacture) is wholly *mine* and not his. As to his wanting to show respect and the like, I do not believe a word of it and never shall do: it was a mere political trick. He is an old friend of yours, older than I am and probably more trusted but that cannot alter my opinion. For the good things he has done in the past I still hold respect.'

During the Gloucester Festival of 1922 a memorial tablet to Parry, who had died in 1918, was unveiled. Afterwards, on the lawn of Herbert Brewer's home, Elgar and Stanford were brought together by Granville Bantock. Stanford, holding out his hand, said: 'Let's forget all about it.' Elgar, taken aback and professing still not to know what had to be forgotten, responded. Another event at the same time tells us much more about these two men. A photograph was taken to mark the Parry occasion. In the group were Elgar and Stanford, Bantock and Hugh Allen, Henry Hadow and Brewer. Before they assembled, the bluff Hugh Allen called out: 'Now then, Elgar, don't have your coat all buttoned up like that.' Elgar's reply was devastating. 'Ah,' he said, 'I always keep *everything* buttoned up when I am in *this* company.'[21] Again the old suspicion of the 'academic' establishment. The remark shows how precariously healed was the wound to Elgar's mind delivered by his years of struggle,

[20] *Charles Villiers Stanford*, op.cit., p. 158.
[21] *Elgar As I Knew Him*, op.cit., p. 94.

alone and unrecognized. It would be easy to explain the differences
with Stanford on this score alone, but it would be wrong. Elgar held
no grudge against Parry. Quarrels of the depth to which this one went
are usually personal and often petty. Elgar's letter to Schuster shows
how little he wanted to admit, even to himself, that he had given a
fellow-artist cause for complaint by his remarks at Birmingham in
1905. For one so thin-skinned himself as Elgar, it was an
extraordinarily insensitive blunder; the whole Birmingham lecture
experience was an unpleasant memory to him, and he probably
wanted to put it out of his mind as much as possible. The only
possible cause of the embittered outburst after Alice's funeral can
have lain in whatever was written in the 'odious' letter of 1904.
Elgar's last reference to the whole matter was in a slightly
disingenuous letter he wrote, but did not send, to the *Sunday Times* in
July 1933, when the publication of Basil Maine's book provoked
comment on the relationship of the two composers. He objected to
use of the word 'disagreements' in a letter from the *Yorkshire Post*
music critic Herbert Thompson which the paper had published on 2
July 1933. 'There could be no "disagreements" [he wrote]. Stanford
(Mr, Dr and Knight) at various times thought it well to avoid
speaking to me for periods varying very considerably in length. It was
a matter for comment that such periods of silence invariably began
when some work of mine was produced. [This was untrue.] I never
refused to "shake hands" after these silences although the reason for
them was never disclosed; three men whom Stanford asked to
"approach" me with a view to a renewal on his part of ordinary
civilities were A. E. Rodewald, Hubert Parry and, last of all,
Granville Bantock. On every occasion I hoped that the reason for
"cutting" me might be told: Stanford only said "We (!) have been
under a cloud". I shook hands without comment but I am still
without knowledge of the reason for Stanford's somewhat eccentric
silences.'

None of this would be of any account today if it were not that some
of Stanford's disciples, who were not such big men as C. V .S.
himself, were responsible in the 1920s and 1930s for ensuring a cold
climate for Elgar's music in circles where they had influence.

Like attracts like, even if the basic reason for the attraction could
not be given by either party. Elgar and Stanford were not alike except
in some superficial ways. Stanford's buccaneering and irascible
manner may have concealed a warm heart but this did not endear him
to Elgar. Yet he was as enthusiastic an advocate of Elgar's music as
Parry was, so that this is no explanation of the care which Elgar took
not to implicate Parry in his criticisms of Stanford. Elgar went out of
his way in his inaugural Birmingham lecture to pay a warm tribute to
Parry, 'the head of our art in this country'. One cannot explain Elgar's

liking for Parry by saying that Parry was an early enthusiast for the
Variations: so was Stanford. In fact Stanford, as an able and
industrious conductor, did more for Elgar practically than Parry did.
Parry was, of course, the more likeable man, outwardly the perfect
English gentleman and squire. Yet this is a very superficial picture;
and it seems likely that Elgar instinctively recognized the idealist
artist inside Parry, the radical free thinker who often found himself, as
he said, in a minority of one, who felt ill at ease among the hunting,
shooting gentry of his native Gloucestershire, who had bouts of black
depression and had had to overcome the prejudice of his family
against music as a profession. It is significant that Elgar responded
wholeheartedly to the agnostic idealism of Parry's cantata *A Vision of
Life*,[22] to the composer's own libretto. 'I say,' he wrote to Jaeger on 8
October 1907, after a Leeds Festival performance, 'that "Vision" of
Parry's is *fine stuff* & the poem is literature: you *must* hear it some day.'
(How Jaeger must have smiled ruefully.) To Parry, in 1909, he wrote:
'I am so delighted we are to have *Job* in Hereford Cathedral. Your
Cardiff "Vision" was, I conclude, too strong for the Church, but I
hope we may have it soon. It's really strong bracing stuff, and, like
your Odes, some of us love it and love you for giving us these things.'

When, in 1905, the Manchester University Press published selected
music criticisms by Arthur Johnstone who had died after an
operation at the age of forty-three on 16 December 1904, Elgar, of
whose music Johnstone was so percipient a critic, was asked to write a
preface. He agreed, but when he found that the book was to include
Johnstone's review of J. A. Fuller Maitland's book *English Music in
the 19th Century* in which Johnstone strongly contradicted Fuller
Maitland's eulogistic view of Parry's music, he withdrew because he
did not wish it to be thought that he was lending his name to support
of such opinions. And when in 1920, in the first issue of *Music and
Letters*, Bernard Shaw, in an equally eulogistic appraisal of Elgar,
referred to 'the little clique of devoted musicians with the late Hubert
Parry as its centre' and their 'initial incredulity as to his genius', Elgar
wrote a letter, published in the second issue, repudiating Shaw and
emphasizing that Parry, far from slighting him, had shown him
'ungrudging kindness' and had advised and encouraged him on
'many occasions'. Elgar sent Shaw a copy of the letter, which G. B. S.
described (8 March 1920) as 'quite the right thing'. He then had the
last word: 'P. was a d—d nice chap; and if he had been a little less nice
he would also have been a little less d—d. I hope you didn't take his
advice as well as his encouragement.'

With the third of the 'academic' trio, Sir Alexander Mackenzie,
Elgar maintained polite but frigid relations. They had little in

---

[22] First performed Cardiff Festival, September 1907.

common. Mackenzie was a notable wit, and Elgar's feelings for him would not have been improved by an occasion when they were dining at adjacent tables at a London club where Elgar was a new and ill-at-ease member. When Elgar was offered the cheese-board, Mackenzie leaned across and said: 'Why don't you try the Port-Salut?' adding quietly 'Salut d'Amour'. Jaeger wrote to Elgar in 1903: 'I'm told that Mackenzie foams at the mouth when you say Apostles to him.' But in later years, when Mackenzie had retired and his music was nearly forgotten, Elgar sent him boxes of flowers and vegetables from his Worcestershire garden and in 1933 persuaded Boult to revive Mackenzie's violin concerto. This was another example of the streak of warm-hearted generosity which characterized Elgar. When Jaeger had eye trouble, Elgar sent him to a specialist and paid the bill. In 1903, when Jaeger took up bicycling to get fresh air, Elgar made him a present of his old bicycle, and in 1905 he arranged for Schuster to send a fur coat to Jaeger in which he could lie outdoors in Davos.

No discussion of Elgar's friendships at this period of his life would be adequate without fuller mention of a name that has already occurred several times: Alfred E. Rodewald, 'dear Rodey', of Liverpool, who was perhaps the nearest to Elgar's heart of all his many friends. Rodewald, a textile magnate, born in Liverpool and educated at Charterhouse, lived for music. He was a gifted conductor and played the double bass. He was a friend of Richter (the conductor's only pupil) and he made the mainly amateur Liverpool Orchestral Society good enough to play the works of Elgar, Strauss, Wagner, and Tchaikovsky. He was a great supporter (and, probably, subsidizer) of Bantock's New Brighton enterprise and it was probably at the Elgar concert there in July 1899 that he first met Elgar. Thereafter, whenever Elgar visited Liverpool for performances of his works he stayed with Rodewald at his home at 66 Huskisson Street or at his cottage at Saughall, near Chester.[23] He gave Rodewald and his players the first performance of the first two *Pomp and Circumstance* marches, on 19 October 1901, four days before the first London performance. No. 1 is dedicated to Rodewald and the Liverpool Orchestral Society. Rodewald's letters to Elgar reveal a sunny personality and a great warmth of heart. They usually began 'Dear old cocky' and were full of jokes and merriment. He genuinely loved Elgar and his music. 'Ah! my dear boy,' he wrote to him after hearing *Cockaigne*, 'you write from the heart and not from the brain, there's the secret.' It was Rodewald who organized the collection of money to buy Elgar his Cambridge robes and who offered to commission a symphony from him. Like many North-Western businessmen, Rodewald also had a cottage in Wales, at Bettws-y-coed. For most of July 1903, when Elgar had

[23] This 'cottage' is now the vicarage at Saughall.

finished *The Apostles*, he stayed there with Rodewald and they were
joined for part of the time by Jaeger – 'it is quite free and easy here,'
Elgar told him, 'you dress as you like & do exactly what you please –
no formality or any nonsense.' On 7 November 1903, when
Rodewald was forty-three, news of his being mortally ill was received
in Malvern. Elgar wrote to Jaeger: 'I am writing now to tell you
about our poor dear friend Rodewald: it came as the most awful
shock to me yesterday a.m. – he is quite unconscious & four doctors
say he cannot possibly recover – I had a cheerful card from him on
Wedy morning last – & now – it is too awful & my heart is quite
broken. On the card he says I shd meet you there on the 14th – alas!
alas! Yours ever Edwd. He thought he had influenza & said he was
over the fever & hoped to be soon all right.'

Two more letters to Jaeger tell the rest of the story, the first on 9
November from the North Western Hotel, Liverpool: 'Too late. I
stood it as long as I could & rushed up here – our dear, dear, good
friend passed away quietly at 12.30. I am heartbroken & cannot
believe it. God bless him. He was the dearest, kindest, *best* friend I
ever had. I don't know how I write or what I've written – forgive me.
I am utterly broken up.' The second was from Malvern, 11
November:

> I could not rest so went up on Monday: did not go to the house but called
> at a friend's in the same street[24] – they told me – I broke down & went out –
> *and it was night* to me. What I did, God knows. I know I walked for miles in
> strange ways – I know I had some coffee somewhere – where I cannot tell. I
> know I went & looked at the Exchange where he had taken me – but it was
> all dark, dark to me although light enough to the busy folk around. I thought
> I wd. go home – but could not – so I stayed at the hotel. Now, had I been less
> stricken I shd. not have eaten – but in a dazed way I ordered dinner & wine &
> I believe ate all thro' the menu – I know not – it probably saved my life I
> think – but I lived on as an automaton – & did everything without thought –
> then I went to my room & wept for hours – yesterday I came home without
> seeing anyone & am now a wreck & a broken-hearted man. Do not send me
> any more score [of *The Apostles*] – yet. I used to pass him every sheet as I
> finished it at Bettws & heard his criticisms & altered passages to please him,
> God bless him! . . . I can't say what I feel but I have lost my best & dearest – I
> thank heaven we all had that bit of time together in Wales: you know a little
> of what he was.

He wrote in the same vein to Schuster and to Ernest Newman,
whom he had met at Rodewald's house. To modern eyes there seems
to be an exhibitionist note about the carefully observed 'incoherence'
of his own reactions to deep and genuine personal sorrow. No doubt
it was the safety valve of the strength of his emotions: we shall see

[24] Adrian Mignot, tobacco merchant, of 80 Huskisson Street, President of Liverpool
Orchestral Society at this time.

other examples in due course. More important is that a few months later he made sketches of what seven years thence was to become the great Larghetto of the Second Symphony, the movement in which Alice heard a 'lament for dear Rodey and all human feeling'. So Rodewald was another friend 'pictured within'.

Two other women besides Alice had a strong influence on Elgar's life: the American Julia Worthington, and Alice Stuart-Wortley (1862–1936), daughter of the painter Sir John Millais and second wife of Charles Stuart-Wortley (later Lord Stuart of Wortley), Conservative M.P. for the Hallam division of Sheffield for many years. Not much is known about the friendship with Mrs Worthington, since few letters survive. According to Dorabella, quoting Alice Elgar as her authority, hers is the 'soul' enshrined in the Violin Concerto. But despite this categorical statement, for which no other evidence is offered, all documentary evidence points to Alice Stuart-Wortley as the inspiration of this work and of parts of the Second Symphony. In letters to her he refers to 'our own concerto' and 'your symphony'. She was a good pianist, devoted to Elgar's music,[25] deeply artistic, and she shared with Elgar a love of the countryside. He idealized women and beauty in a Froissart-like way, and Alice Stuart-Wortley evoked a strong response from the 'fey' side of his nature. He called her 'Windflower', after his themes, her daughter believed, not his themes after her. When her husband was created a peer at the end of 1916 Elgar wrote to her: 'The Windflower can never become wholly a "conservatory plant", can it? It will sometimes remember its woods.' While composing the Violin Concerto early in 1910 he wrote to her on 27 April: 'I have been working hard at the windflower themes – but all stands still until you come and approve!' And, the next day: 'The tunes stick and are not windflowerish – at present.' In a letter to Schuster in 1910 Elgar referred to Alice Stuart-Wortley and then added: 'I want to end that concerto but I do not see my way very clearly to the end so you had best invite its stepmother to The Hut too. Do.' He makes it clear again and again how much he wants her to like the work and, before the first performance, referring to a spare ticket, he wrote: 'I wish I could use it and you might conduct – but you *will* be conducting the concerto wherever you are.' It is impossible not to infer from these statements that hers was the 'soul' of the work especially when one discovers, on a sheet of her notepaper, the Spanish quotation which heads the work – 'Aquí está encerrada el alma de. . . . . ('Here is enshrined the soul of. . . . .') in Elgar's writing with the date 22 September 1910.[26] The five dots stand for Alice or for her initials A. S. C. S.-W. Their relationship

[25]She was influential in arranging the Westminster Cathedral *Gerontius*.
[26]See Chapter 6. I appreciate Helen Weaver's significance, but remain convinced that the 'soul' is Windflower's.

was based on her sensitive response to Elgar's music and its highly personal idiom: he warmed to such appreciation. He often quoted to his friends a line from a poem by Sir John Davies (1569–1626) – 'Musicians thinke our soules are harmonies', an idea similar to the theme of *The Music Makers*. Edward Elgar and Alice Stuart-Wortley were souls in harmony as far as his music was concerned, and this understanding was one of deep affection involving no disloyalty or infidelity to either of the other marriage partners. Indeed, the four people concerned were firm friends (Elgar gave Charles Stuart-Wortley some of the early sketches of the Violin Concerto, and Alice Elgar wrote affectionate letters to 'my dearest namesake'). To a man of Elgar's poetic and sensitive imagination, such a relationship was a strong emotional stimulus, and it is one more example of Alice Elgar's noble character that where lesser women might have harboured groundless jealousies, she interpreted the situation correctly because she understood her husband's nature. She, after all, was his reality.

Elgar met Alice Stuart-Wortley in 1902, when he was forty-five and she was forty, and their friendship ripened from formality in March 1909.[27] She and her husband lived at 7 Cheyne Walk, Chelsea, where Elgar and his wife frequently visited them. She played through many of his works to him. 'I *love* to hear you play,' he wrote in 1911. 'One reason why so many people cordially dislike me is that I cannot stand their music whether written or performed & I pay no compliments & I never ask anyone to play unless it gives me pleasure. I do not like piano solo players' playing but I love yours – you will understand the difference. I am not going to praise you now because you are quite vain enough! but you *must* play when I ask & I would not think of asking you to play to ordinary people who wd. not understand what poetical playing really is.' She encouraged him to write a piano concerto, and his uncompleted work in that form would probably have been dedicated to her. In February 1917, when he was writing *The Sanguine Fan* ballet music he told her: 'I thought of using *your piano concerto*! (Labour exchange!) but you would not allow that would you?' In the same letter he said: 'Where are you? I wanted to tell you that the theme and *every note* must be approved by you (bless you!) before anything can be done. Oh! why are you so far away and so difficult to get at??' His letters over the years do not conceal his affection for her. Thus, shortly after a rehearsal for the second performance of the Violin Concerto in Queen's Hall in 1910: 'The concerto at 9 a.m. in the dark was divine – all seats empty but a spirit hovering in Block A.' And again in October 1915: 'I missed you at Q's Hall but I thought of you and my eyes wandered to empty Block A.' Even more touching is a letter he wrote on 27 April 1916, after she

[27] Elgar addressed her in a letter on 25 March 1909 as 'my dear Carrie', the diminutive of Caroline by which Schuster and others knew her. Thereafter it was 'Alice'. The first 'Windflower' letter was 21 March 1910.

had been unable to attend an evening of private music-making at Elgar's London home, Severn House: 'The things sounded lovely & the room is divine for a small orchestra – only the goddess of the feast was not there. . . . It was nice to hear Reed's eager voice asking disappointedly "*Where* is Mrs. W.?" & later Landon "*Where on earth* is Mrs. W. in all this music?" I said *to myself* "Everywhere – and alas! nowhere". But you see they all thought it was nothing without you & so did I.' To her he confided his innermost feelings about his own works. In three of the hundreds of letters he wrote to her we obtain vivid glimpses of the man as few knew him. Two date from 1912, shortly after he had finished *The Music Makers*. On 19 July, he wrote from Hampstead: 'Yesterday was the most *awful* day which inevitably occurs when I have completed a work: it has *always* been so: but this time I promised myself "a day!" – I should be crowned – it wd be lovely weather – I should have open air & sympathy & everything to mark the end of the work – to get away from the *labour* part & dream over it happily. Yes: I was to be crowned for the first time in my life. But – I sent the last page to the printer. Alice & Carice were away for the day & I wandered alone on the heath – it was bitterly cold – I wrapped myself in a thick overcoat & sat for two minutes, tears streaming out of my cold eyes and loathed the world, came back to the house – empty and cold – how I hated having written anything: so I wandered out again & shivered & longed to destroy the work of my hands – all wasted. And this was to have been the one real day in my artistic life – sympathy at the end of work. "World losers & world forsakers for ever & ever." How true it is.'

A few weeks later, on 1 September 1912, when he went to Hereford for the Three Choirs Festival, he went back to Plâs Gwyn, the house he had recently left, 'to see if the swallows are still cared for. Alas! the new tenants are "tidy" people – the loft is repainted . . . and the windows closed tight – so my companions of eight years found no welcome this year & have had to seek new homes – we had seen and known them & I resented their disturbance very much.' At Christmas 1914 he wrote: 'I cannot buy you pearls of untold worth . . . so I send you a little scrap of my old, old lonely life *in which no one shared*; I had my dreams &, I suppose, ambitions & I send you one of the little school-books which lightened my entire loneliness'.

The lonely composer walking on the heath, the poet who felt a companionship with the swallows, the romantic artist who drew 'inspiration' from the friendship of beautiful women: this is the true and secret Elgar, and the best of his music reflects this side of the many-sided man.

9 Nobilmente

Elgar's music is inextricably associated with the Edwardian era, a period which has attained a mythical aura. From a distance of over half a century it appears as a golden age – a glittering social scene; Covent Garden at its most opulent; literature and the theatre adorned by Hardy, Wells, Kipling, Bennett, Pinero, Beerbohm Tree, Shaw, and Barrie; the cricket field peopled by giants; the political world of Asquith, Balfour, the young Churchill, and Lloyd George; the zenith of the country-house party. Yet there was another side – poverty, unemployment, violent industrial strikes, the threat of war, the spread of subversive and revolutionary doctrines in politics and religion, the agitation of the suffragettes. Much like any other age, indeed, as we are reminded by Jaeger's words in his analysis of *The Apostles* when he referred in 1903 to the music's message of beauty and peace 'in these days of unprecedented stress and complexity.' Our age's superficial nostalgia for the imagined Eden of Edward VII's reign has become attached to Elgar's music. But the nostalgia Elgar expresses is not our nostalgia. He wanted to escape from his present as much as we do from ours; it is the perennial desire of the Romantic artist. Elgar in the late 1890s and early 1900s is a parallel case to the Pre-Raphaelites of a generation earlier. Just as they escaped from the harshness of the real world into a mock-mediaeval earthly paradise, so he fled to the historical past of Caractacus, the literary past of Falstaff, the chivalry of Froissart. Later, as will be seen, the world of his childhood, the wand of youth, beckoned irresistibly. There is a distinction to be made between what we recognise in Elgar's music as representative of the spirit of his time and his own unconscious reflection of its precarious hollow features so that now, like contemporaneous works by Mahler and Strauss, it seems to foretell its own impending Götterdämmerung. The greatness of his music sprang from the unceasing tension between, at one level, his need for solitude and his desire for recognition, and, at another, his Catholic need to hope and to believe and his personal tendency to despair. Gradually, his faith crumbled, his hope dwindled, and he saw that the reality of life and of human behaviour conflicted totally with what he had been led to believe.

Like most creative artists, Elgar was a man of swift and ready emotional response rather than a deep thinker. He was romantic, chivalrous, patriotic, and loyal – it was the conventional mood of the time. Moreover, he was a great craftsman who thought naturally in musical terms. Like Purcell, Handel, and Bach he turned events of any kind into music without questioning their ethical or political, sociological or humanitarian basis. 'I like to look on the composer's vocation as the old troubadours or bards did. In those days it was no disgrace for a man to be turned on to step in front of an army and inspire them with a song. For my part, I know that there are a lot of people who like to celebrate events with music. To these people I have given tunes. Is that wrong? Why should I write a fugue or something which won't appeal to anyone, when the people yearn for things which can stir them?'[1]

Elgar, of course, well knew that some people were stirred by a fugue, but in this context he was thinking of truly popular music which, he considered, could also be good music. All that he did was to write music for certain national occasions: he did not advocate war, aggression, or oppression. Yet because he chose the superb title *Pomp and Circumstance*[2] for a set of marches and because the tune of one of them was fitted to words glorifying Britain at the zenith of her imperial power, writers and journalists have equated Elgar's name with a political condition of which they disapproved. The Edwardian age, the Elgarian age: both sound alike, both are usually intended as opprobrious phrases. But, for many people, it was also a good time to be alive, a time of and for greatness, and it was far easier to produce art which had a confident foundation. Elgar as a man responded to the thrill and pageantry of the peacetime military parade or ceremonial function; Elgar as a composer had the knack of writing colourful, tuneful music of a kind that caught the ear of the populace. He was under no illusion that he was producing something lasting: these were occasional pieces, and of all Elgar's laureate music, only two or at the most three tunes have survived the occasions which brought them into being. The *Pomp and Circumstance* marches are quite separate; a purely musical exercise. 'I did not see why the ordinary quick march should not be treated on a large scale, in the way that the waltz, the old-fashioned slow march and even the polka have been treated by the great composers; yet all marches on the symphonic scale are so slow that people can't march to them. I have some of the soldier instinct in me and so I have written two marches of which, so far from being ashamed, I am proud.'[3]

It has been said many times that Elgar's 'ceremonial' manner in some way 'infected' his bigger, more serious works. Of course it did,

---

[1] *Strand Magazine*, May 1904.
[2] The title was taken from Shakespeare's *Othello*, Act III, Sc. 3, when Othello says:
    'Farewell the neighing steed and the shrill trump,
    The spirit-stirring drum, the ear-piercing fife,
    The royal banner, and all quality,
    Pride, pomp, and circumstance of glorious war!'
[3] *Strand Magazine*, May 1904, when only Nos. 1 and 2 had appeared.

because it was an essential part of the man. He was not divided into self-sealing units. But the ceremonial manner itself has been only superficially examined. It ought to be clear by now that Elgar was subject to a profound melancholy and that he lacked confidence to an almost pathological degree. He at no time imagined that everything was for the best in the best of all possible worlds. He perceived the emptiness behind the façade; and though he expressed this unforgettably in his larger symphonic works, it is present, whether he himself was fully aware of it, in some of the lesser music in his *nobilmente* manner. It was not to be expected that his contemporaries would penetrate to this side of Elgar's music: the outer surface was the more obvious and this was their only concern. But Elgar the laureate and courtier was never at ease with Elgar the dreamer and the lower-middle-class provincial. He was a conservative, the natural result of his upbringing in a family which had relied on royal and squirearchical patronage. In this respect he was the opposite of Parry, born into the landed gentry, who despised conservatism. Yet Elgar too, had the radical streak: he was an artist, a 'dreamer of dreams' in a materialist society. He wanted his music to be widely appreciated, yet part of him despised the public for its narrow and restricted taste. His natural pride in his achievements clashed with the demands made upon him by the upholding of his position of fame. Before discussing some of the ceremonial music, it is essential to probe more deeply into the circumstances of its composition, the changes that its success involved, and their effect on the man himself.

As already related, Elgar had a success in the diamond jubilee year of Victoria's reign with the *Imperial March* and the *Banner of St George*. Neither of these works is the jingoistic tub-thump of inter-wars mythology. The march, though brilliantly scored, is relatively sombre and restrained in its trio and at no point is it blatantly militaristic. *The Banner of St George*, its text apart, does not deserve the obloquy squandered on it. The lyrical elements in *The Black Knight* are again to the fore, the music's principal character being hymn-like and asseverative rather than emptily boastful. Even in the designedly grandiose penultimate section, the broad melody's progress is threatened by disruptive salvoes of percussion, as in the coda of the First Symphony of over a decade later. The work, with its effective soprano solo, points the way to the more ambitious *Coronation Ode*. The final chorus, 'It comes from the misty ages', is not the clinching finale the work needs and is mainly to blame for the impression that this cantata is too long to sustain its initial momentum.

The jubilee mood spilled over into the final chorus of *Caractacus*, dedicated to the queen-empress. Acceptance of the dedication was the first sign of royal favour, greatly prized by a man who always felt that in Britain music was the least acknowledged of the arts. Two concerts

at Windsor, not attended by Victoria, in 1899, the year of the queen's
eightieth birthday, included music by Elgar, one of them no fewer
than ten items. But two of the *Sea Pictures* were sung by Ada Crossley
at Balmoral by royal command. Although the march and the *Banner*
gave him a national reputation, they did not earn Elgar much money.
In 1899 and 1900 he was preoccupied with the *Variations* and
Gerontius. On 22 January 1901 Queen Victoria died. The only
references to this event in Elgar's letters to Jaeger are a cheery 'God
save the King' at the end of a piece of mundane business
correspondence on 27 January and a wish expressed three days later
that the title-page of the full score of *Froissart* 'didn't look so like the
newspapers' borders over the death of our beloved Queen.' Edward
VII was on the throne at last – 'fat vulgar Edward' to the intellectuals,
'good old Teddy' to the people, an enigmatic man still, and one, it
appears, of irresistible charm. The twenty-six-year-old Winston
Churchill, writing to his mother from Winnipeg in January 1901,
summed up Society's views on the new reign.[4] 'I am curious to know
about the King. Will it entirely revolutionise his way of life? Will he
sell his horses and scatter his Jews or will Reuben Sassoon be
enshrined among the crown jewels and other regalia? Will he become
desperately serious? . . . Will the Keppel be appointed 1st Lady of the
Bedchamber?'

It was through the equivalents of Edward VII's Sassoons that
Edward Elgar achieved his rapid rise to social distinction. The Elgars
already had a friend at court in Lady Mary Lygon, but it was through
the Speyers and the Schusters, wealthy patrons of all the arts, who
'knew everybody', who took up each new prominent 'name', that
they moved rapidly into circles where Alice considered herself to be
in the right element and where Elgar was pleased but apprehensive to
be. But whatever may be said of the wealthy upper and upper-middle-
class strata of Edward VII's reign, a strong section of them, a
minority but an influential minority, was anything but philistine and
uncultured, and it was in this milieu that Elgar found friends, patrons,
and admirers. Schuster and Edgar Speyer brought Richard Strauss
and Elgar into friendship; Schuster introduced Elgar to Herbert
Beerbohm Tree and J. S. Sargent. Among the aristocracy, the Elgars
came to know the Marquess of Northampton, an amateur musician
who was competent enough to be able to play Bach fugues in piano
duet with Elgar when he went to stay in Hereford; Lady Maud
Warrender, daughter of the Earl of Shaftesbury, who sang the solo
part in *The Music Makers* on at least one occasion; the Duke of
Norfolk and other prominent Roman Catholics such as Lady
Winefride Elwes and her husband Gervase, beginning his career as a

[4] Randolph S. Churchill, *Winston S. Churchill*, i (London, 1966), p. 545.

singer. Conducting at Sheffield, Elgar was invited to lunch with Lady
Alice Fitzwilliam (though apparently he was on one occasion 'not
pleased with the company or food & excused himself & went off'). It
was she who introduced him to the Stuart-Wortleys. This was a
group of people brought together by a love of artistic matters, not by
any political affiliation, the kind of civilized gathering that has always
existed in English society. There is, in any case, no reason why a great
composer should have fashionably or even unfashionably progressive
views. As Lionel Trilling has somewhere written, no literary figure of
the front rank in the first thirty years of the twentieth century was
liberal or radical in his ideas: they left these things to the second rankers and went on with their work. The same applies to
Elgar. Schuster himself was a Liberal-Radical and after the crushing
1906 defeat of the Conservatives Elgar wrote to him: 'You are a
disappointing *toad* & a Radical. All the same my heart warms to
you. . . . Having turned out the respectable Hotel Cecil and having
installed the Waiters in place of the gentlemen, you will probably
have to drop music & musicians to seem respectable among the
artistic governing body.'

Credit should be given to Elgar that he relished this patronage, and
the royal favour that followed, not because of self-aggrandisement
but because it was an official recognition by the 'ruling class' of the
growing importance of music. 'I always stand up for the dignity of
our art,' as he had told Jaeger. It annoyed him to see the wealth and
position achieved by painters. Speaking in July 1904, about the new
Musical Copyright Bill he complained that

while the world of fashion as well as the middle classes – the *real* supporters
of music – honoured the art at Covent Garden, legislators were heaping
indignities on it, whittling down the . . . Bill by inserting clauses which will
make it inoperative. Why of all the arts should music be supposed to have no
rights? . . . We composers are not *genuine* artists if we as much as hint that the
work of our brains is worth something. . . . The whole attitude of the world
of England is nothing less than an indignity to our art. Wagner was derided
because he wore a silk vest and velvet cap and surrounded himself with such
luxuries as he could afford. But our second-rate painters may build
themselves magnificent houses and indulge in all sorts of eccentric luxuries
and no one has a word to say against them.[5] The public cannot reconcile
music with any other human activity.

Bernard Shaw remembered Elgar talking about music at a lunch
and Roger Fry remarking: 'After all there is only one art: all the arts
are the same.' 'I heard no more,' Shaw wrote. 'My attention was taken
by a growl from the other side of the table. It was Elgar, with his
fangs bared and all his hackles bristling, in an appalling rage.

[5] He was perhaps remembering that Sir John Millais, at the peak of his career, earned
over £25,000 a year, a colossal sum at that time.

"Music," he spluttered, "is written on the skies for you to note down. And you compare that to a DAMNED imitation." [6]

In an after-dinner speech in Aberdeen in honour of Sanford Terry in 1910, Elgar uttered these prophetic but revolutionary words: 'If we educate young people to be first-class players . . . what is to become of them afterwards? . . . I would like you to think seriously whether the humanising sphere of music could not be enlarged by municipal aid – by assisting choral societies and orchestras from the rates. . . . Düsseldorf is not a very beautiful town, but many people go to reside there on account of the music; the town looks upon that orchestra as a valuable asset, and the municipality takes the responsibility of any loss that may arise. . . . The time is coming when all towns must be able to give the people the good music they want.'

These are not the words and outlook of a complacent and reactionary diehard, lulled by association with the 'establishment' into euphoria. They are common sense. True, the keynote of Elgar's greatest music is a regret for the good things – and people – that are gone, but he lived in hope – sometimes against hope – that there were good things still to come. When he lost the hope he ceased to write music.

In November 1900 Elgar began to sketch his gayest orchestral work, the overture *Cockaigne* which contains a passage where a military procession passes along the streets of London. So it is not surprising that this was also the period of composition of the first two of a proposed set of six military marches, one of which was intended for a soldier's funeral. Four of the marches appeared between 1901 and 1907, a fifth in 1930. A sixth was left in short score – Alice's diary for 6 October 1910 records 'E. working at Pomp & Circ. March – not vesy well and raser depressed' – and sketches exist for others. None is funereal. On 10 May 1901, the day after the Worcestershire Philharmonic's *Gerontius*, Elgar called Dorabella into his study and said 'I've got a tune that will knock 'em – knock 'em flat.' He then played the D major *Pomp and Circumstance* March No. 1. He had written to Jaeger on 12 January 1901, 'In haste and joyful (Gosh! man I've got a tune in my head),' and there is little doubt that the tune he meant is the Trio section of this march, better known as 'Land of Hope and Glory'. By August 1901 Nos. 1 and 2 were completed and sent to Boosey's for publication – a result of the coolness with Novello's after the *Variations* and *Gerontius*. Boosey had been given *Cockaigne* as well. (Jaeger wrote to Elgar in October 1901, about a cantata commissioned for the 1905 Norwich Festival of which no trace remains: 'Now, you *will* send that to us won't you? . . . We shall pay you just as well as Boosey's . . . I have had another long talk about

[6] Letter to Virginia Woolf quoted in *Beginning Again* (London, 1964), p. 126, by Leonard Woolf.

you to Messrs. A. & A. L. & you need fear no worries in future. They
have had an eye-opener over the Leeds Festival & I'm sure they'll
meet you in every way in future.') After the first Liverpool
performance of the two marches, they were performed in London at a
Queen's Hall Promenade Concert under Henry Wood on 22 October.
Elgar was not present. 'I shall never forget the scene at the close of the
first of them – the one in D major,' Wood wrote.[7] 'The people simply
rose and yelled. I had to play it again – with the same result; in fact
they refused to let me get on with the programme. . . . I went off and
fetched Harry Dearth who was to sing *Hiawatha's Vision* but they
would not listen. Merely to restore order, I played the march a third
time.' Jaeger sent Elgar a postcard that night: 'Your splendid
marches were the greatest success I have ever witnessed over a
novelty at any concert. The hall was only half full alas! (though the
Promenade was pretty crowded) but the people made such a row &
kept it up for so long. . . .' Wood, with a sense of showmanship,
reversed the order of the marches and played the A minor (No. 2) first
and the D major (No. 1) second. So that when Stanford wrote to
Elgar that he found himself 'in a minority' at Wood's concert in
preferring the first march he was referring to No. 2 in A minor. The
critic of *The Daily Telegraph* thought that the marches suggested not
the orderliness of the Guards but 'the irregular advance of an army of
glittering barbarians'.

The success of the D major march was no doubt associated with
Boer War nationalist fervour. I think the audience also immediately
recognized that they had heard one of the great melodies of the world,
a tune that is at once memorable, stirring, disturbing, and singable.
Even before the success of this music, Elgar had had an approach
from Henry Higgins with a commission from the Grand Opera
Syndicate for a work to be performed at a State performance at
Covent Garden on the eve of Edward VII's Coronation on 26 June
1902. Although he was thinking about a symphony for Richter, he
put everything aside, as he explained to Jaeger on 12 November 1901:
'Manchester as you say can & will wait – not so Coving Garden &
several 100 other things.' He added that his Cambridge robes had not
yet arrived: 'I *want* 'em now to appear at Court.' Probably it was at
that meeting with his sovereign that an historic suggestion was made
to Elgar, as he stated years later in a letter to Clara Butt (21 November
1927): 'King Edward was the first to suggest that the air from the
Pomp and Circumstance March should be sung and eventually the song
as now known was evolved, via the *Coronation Ode.* . . .' Elgar
evidently conveyed the idea to Jaeger, who did not think much of it (6
December 1901): 'I say, you will have to write another tune for the

---

[7] *My Life of Music*, op. cit., pp. 203–4.

Ode in place of the March in D tune (Trio). I have been trying much to fit words to it. That drop to E & bigger drop afterwards are quite impossible in singing *any* words to them, they sound downright vulgar. Just try it. The effect is fatal. No, you must write a new tune to the words & not fit the words to this tune. Consider this carefully & give no choir a chance of scooping down. It will sound horrible. Try it. . . .'

So Jaeger was the first to make a valid criticism that has been repeated many times since. But Elgar, never one to bother too much about whether the words fitted his tunes if he thought his tunes good enough, ignored him, and four days later he received from the librettist the first draft of 'Land of Hope and Glory'. In any case the Ode was not intended for Novello's. They had to be content with the ceremonial arrangement of 'God Save the King' for soprano, chorus, and orchestra, and Elgar took particular care over the score of this work, wanting the English names for the instruments and being annoyed when the printers altered 'clarionets' to 'clarinets' 'in our ignorance', as they explained. 'I wanted in this particular score everything to be "plain English",' he wrote to Jaeger on 9 May 1902. '. . . The names of the instruments . . . look *very nice* in English I think & *Kettledrums* is a good Handelian-looking word: see West's query as to *Haut-boys* – I feel that Oboes wd. spoil the whole thing – but I don't want to be faddy or silly, only English – which after all may be both !'

The *Coronation Ode*, with words by A. C. Benson about which poet and composer had corresponded since March 1901, was ready by 1 April 1902. Three days before the Coronation, the King was taken ill and operated on for appendicitis. All festivities were cancelled. Elgar's letter to Jaeger on 24 June may be surprising to those who have accepted only a superficial view of his 'laureate' character: 'Don't for heaven's sake *sympathise* with me – I don't care a tinker's damn! It gives me three blessed sunny days in my own country . . . instead of stewing in town. *My* own interest in the thing ceased as usual when I had finished the MS – since when I have been thinking mighty things! [*The Apostles.*] I was biking out in Herefordsh: yesterday & the news reached me at a little roadside pub. I said "Give me another pint of cider." I'm deadly sorry for the King but that's all.'

It is amusing to compare this reaction of England's great composer of royal music with the scene at the Westminster Abbey Coronation rehearsal as described in Parry's diary:[8] 'The Bishop of London stepped on to the dais . . . and, addressing mainly the performers . . . announced the necessity of the King's undergoing an operation . . . ending with an appeal to all to join in a Litany. . . . The choir joined in with a most superb tone and produced an effect I have never

[8] C. L. Graves, *Hubert Parry*, ii (London, 1926), pp. 28–29.

experienced before – so solemn and pathetic. A few kneeling figures
on the floor of the Chancel.'

'Land of Hope and Glory', arranged as a song with words different
from those in the *Ode*, was sung by Clara Butt in London in June
1902. The *Ode* had its first performance at the Sheffield Festival on 2
October, some compensation to the chorus who had been selected for
the cancelled Coronation performance. Elgar conducted and Muriel
Foster was the contralto soloist. Johnstone wrote in the *Manchester
Guardian* next day: 'It is popular music of a kind that has not been
made for a long time in this country – scarcely at all since Dibdin's
time. At least one may say that of the best parts, such as the bass solo
and chorus, "Britain, Ask of Thyself", and the contralto solo and
chorus, "Land of Hope and Glory". The former is ringing martial
music, the latter a sort of church parade song having the breadth of a
national hymn. It is the melody which occurs as second principal
theme of the longer Pomp and Circumstance march, which I beg to
suggest is as broad as "God Save the King", "Rule Britannia" and
"See the Conquering Hero", and is perhaps the broadest open-air
tune since Beethoven's "Freude Schöner Götterfunken". Moreover,
it is distinctively British – at once breezy and beefy. It is astonishing to
hear people finding fault with Elgar for using this tune in two different
compositions. I find it most natural in a composer, to whom music is a
language in which, desiring to say exactly the same thing again, one
has no choice but to say it in the same notes. Besides, such tunes are
composed less frequently than once in 50 years. How then can one
blame Elgar for not composing two in six months? The chorus
enjoyed themselves over it and so did the audience.'

This surely is the commonsense view. It is perfectly true, as Ernest
Newman said,[9] that the vocal version of the march tune can 'hardly be
called a success, either here or in the song-arrangement. . . . It is
married to the words much against its own will . . . it really will not
bear the attempt to make it look heroic. It is dignified in just the right
kind of way in its proper place in the march, but when it is dressed up
in the pompous sentiments of the *Coronation Ode* its clothes seem
several sizes too large for it.' But it is a great tune which people who
care little for the niceties of word-setting like to sing, ignoring the
correct accentuations. It swept the country in 1902 and became
a second national anthem. Attempts to change the words have met
with little success, because only the squeamish worry about them any
more. It is a fine community song, along with 'Abide with me' and
others; as Johnstone recognized, it has the slight ecclesiastical flavour
which endears a tune to the sentimental British crowd; and nothing
will kill it now. When audiences saw its composer, military in bearing

[9] *Elgar* (London, 1905), p. 48.

and often mistaken for the Duke of Connaught, it no doubt reassured them that music was not necessarily written by eccentric and possibly immoral hermits. If they saw him in the Malvern countryside, in tweeds and riding boots, as Arnold Bax did, they too might have 'expected him to sling a gun from his back and drop a brace of pheasants to the ground'.[10] Unlike Bax, they could not see in this 'typical' figure a 'morbidly highly strung artist'. Nor could they hear in the tune of the March in D major the note of recessional, the heroic melancholy, which, rather than self-confident assertiveness, we see as its true character if we strip ourselves of the accumulated extra-musical associations. Elgar revelled in 'the glories of our blood and state', but he knew the next line and it is the shadows, as well as the substantial things, that haunt his music.

The 'pompous sentiments' Newman found in Benson's text for the *Coronation Ode* are not reflected in the music of what is a large-scale and highly successful choral work. But even the words are aware of threats and violence and are anything but complacent; prayers for peace recur. The opening 'Crown the King' movement is in Elgar's noblest and most elaborate style, magnificently orchestrated and expansive, its coda based poetically on 'Land of Hope and Glory'. It is followed by 'Daughter of Ancient Kings', written and composed on 4 April 1902 when the rest of the work was finished because it was realised there was no reference to Queen Alexandra. (In 1911, for the Coronation of King George V, Elgar provided an alternative chorus at this point, 'The Queen', in honour of Queen Mary.) The martial bass solo 'Britain, Ask of Thyself' is followed by an exquisite serenade to the art of music, 'Hark, upon the Hallowed Air', for soprano and tenor with light accompaniment, its tranquillity continuing into the devotional quartet 'Only Let the Heart be Pure'. This poetic and lyrical mood – the reverse of the superficial idea of Elgar's ceremonial music – is maintained in 'Peace, Gentle Peace' for the soloists and small orchestra and the chorus unaccompanied. So, after three meditative movements, the stage is set for the finale, 'Land of Hope and Glory', with a text which contains no mention of 'wider still and wider shall thy bounds be set' or 'God who made thee mighty make thee mightier yet'. Instead, 'Truth and Right and Freedom, each a holy gem, Stars of solemn brightness, weave thy diadem', unexceptionable sentiments at any period. The work is a master-piece.

The success of the *Coronation Ode* set the seal on Elgar's 'official' status. He received honours such as no previous English musician had accumulated in so short a time: Durham and Leeds gave him honorary degrees in 1904, Oxford (where Parry spoke generously) and Yale in 1905, Aberdeen, Pennsylvania, and Birmingham in 1906

[10] *Farewell, My Youth*, op. cit., p. 30.

and 1907. He was knighted in the summer of 1904, a few weeks after what was perhaps the greatest honour a living English composer had been accorded, a three-day festival of his works at Covent Garden on 14, 15, and 16 March. The first two concerts were attended by the King and Queen and the third by the Queen. It had been planned to give a series of Elgar concerts in Manchester, but a compromise was reached whereby Richter and the Hallé Orchestra played at Covent Garden. The idea originated from Alice, who said at a social function 'Why not have an Elgar festival?' and Schuster agreed with her. The King, with whom Elgar had by now wined and dined, held a levée at the Palace on the 14th to which Elgar was invited. On 5 July Elgar returned to receive the accolade, the King saying to him afterwards 'Good sport to your fishing', a reference to Elgar's new home, Plâs Gwyn (Welsh for White House), in Hampton Park Road on the outskirts of Hereford and near to the Wye. They had moved in on 1 July. It was large and imposing but they liked it, particularly Alice. It was a home fit for knighted genius. 'I think *great* music can be written here, dear Dora, don't you?' she said to Dorabella. Carice, Elgar's daughter, then aged fourteen, remarked to a parlourmaid that she was glad her father had been knighted 'because, you see, it puts Mother back where she was before they married'.

Elgar's life at this point was as *nobilmente* as his music. In the autumn of 1905 he and Schuster sailed on a month's Mediterranean cruise with the Royal Navy in H.M.S. *Surprise*. In Athens they were entertained by Schuster's friend Admiral Lord Charles Beresford, C-in-C Mediterranean since May, an ebullient, extrovert personality, with the Waterford hunt in full cry tattooed across his back and usually accompanied everywhere he went, like George Sinclair, by a bulldog. He was a son of the Marquess of Waterford and was twice returned to Westminster for English constituencies. An advocate of naval strength, he was a bitter adversary of Admiral Lord Fisher. He had been a companion of the Prince of Wales's wild youth in the 1860s, but their friendship had been disrupted by a violent quarrel over personal (and feminine) affairs in 1891. Also there were Lady Maud Warrender and her husband Sir George, and Lady Charles Beresford. At a reception given by the British Ambassador in Turkey Lady Maud sang some of the *Sea Pictures*; while Elgar dined with Lord Charles aboard his flagship *Bulwark* the band played *Salut d'Amour* and the *Sérénade Lyrique*. Following the Akaba crisis, tension between Britain and Turkey was acute, and Elgar was able to see at first-hand how Britannia ruled the waves. On 1 October the holiday party went ashore in Smyrna. It was 'very, very hot & sirocco blowing', Elgar wrote in his diary. They 'drove to the Mosque of dancing dervishes . . . Music by five or six people very strange & some of it quite beautiful – incessant drums & cymbals (small) thro' the quick movements . . .' This experience led to an entry in his sketchbook headed 'In Smyrna (In the Mosque)'. Later he completed the impressive and exotic piano piece *In Smyrna*. It was published in a charity anthology and not made widely available until 1976. It is a notable example of the improvisatory quality of Elgar's piano writing, like the exquisite miniature *Skizze*, written in 1901 for Julius Buths and not published in Britain until 1976. He had needed such a holiday to recover from the strain he imposed upon himself by ill-advised acceptance of an honour from Birmingham University where Richard Peyton had offered £10,000 for the endowment of a Chair of Music on condition that 'it should in the first instance be offered to and accepted by Sir Edward Elgar, Mus. Doc., LL.D.' Peyton's wealth came from his family firm of manufacturing chemists. He retired early to pursue a munificent career as patron of the arts, particularly music. Many of the eminent artists who appeared at the Birmingham triennial festival were engaged as the result of Peyton's journeys (at his own expense) to the Continent to negotiate with them.[11] His offer to Birmingham put Elgar on the spot: he disliked teaching, but, if he refused, Birmingham would lose its Chair of Music. On the other hand, he had as recently as April 1904 rejected a generous offer from his friend Adolph Brodsky of the professorship of composition at the Royal Manchester College of Music[12] and Manchester University. Brodsky had said: 'As little as we would expect Franz Liszt to be a piano teacher, as little we are expecting from you to be a "teacher" in the common sense of the word. It is your great personality we want to secure . . . The both institutions can offer you £400 a year. You will have at your disposal all the time you happen to want for composing your immortal works'. To say 'yes' to Birmingham after refusing that must have worried Elgar. He spent nearly a month in worrying indecision but, on 25 November, provisionally accepted, the condition being that he could resign after three years if it interfered with his composing.

The inaugural lecture, 'A Future for English Music', was fixed for 16 March 1905, and attracted a large press. As the date approached Elgar became more apprehensive, and his spirits were further damped eight days beforehand by the cool reception given to the first performance of the *Introduction and Allegro for Strings*. The first lecture, which contains much common sense and advanced thinking, provoked a storm of controversy because, as has already been shown, some of the comments on British music of 1880–1900 were tactless, if true. 'I must go and buy some strychnine. This is the end for me,'

[11] Full details about this episode, with the texts of Elgar's lectures, may be found in *A Future for English Music* by Edward Elgar, ed. Percy M. Young (London, 1968).
[12] See *The History of the Royal Manchester College of Music*, by Michael Kennedy (Manchester, 1971) pp. 29–31.

Elgar said as he left the platform. But worse followed. In succeeding lectures he attacked every sacred British cow in sight.

The second lecture 'English Composers' was not given until 1 November 1905, eight months later, and provoked a letter to *The Times* from Stanford (3 November) in refutation of the assertion that 'our art has no hold on the affections of the people and is held in no respect abroad'. Elgar had asked: 'How are we to account for the apathy of the public when English music is performed?' and to some extent he still awaits an answer. He was dubious about the real feeling for music among the middle-classes: 'it exists but fitfully and easily expires'. This was a preliminary to a plea for municipal aid for music. He wanted 'simplicity, manhood, clearness and melody from the coming generation of composers'. A week later, on 8 November, he spoke on 'Brahms's Third Symphony', and his championship of it as 'absolute music' led to a retort in the *Manchester Guardian* of 9 November by Ernest Newman in which he asked why, if absolute music was music at its best, Elgar had written so much descriptive music. The fourth Lecture, on 29 November, was on 'English Executants' – 'some brainless singers are amongst us still', he said, with feeling. He said that Northern choral singers were trained – 'perhaps over-trained' – to a perfection of finish and attack never before attempted 'but often there is something wanting: an understanding of the subject sung about.' He cited German choirs as 'superior in education' and also blamed the Northern choirs for their tendency to sing flat. He blamed solo instrumentalists for 'nervousness and tension'. British orchestral players were 'the finest in the world', but concerning English conductors 'we can in no way indulge in very contented feelings. We have heard of snakes in Ireland and we have heard of English conductors.' (He excluded Wood – 'himself a giant' – from his strictures.) He spoke of the conductors of his early youth as 'men who treated an orchestral work like a problem of Euclid and thrashed it out without sympathy, without love and without hate.' 'It is all very well to say "conductors are born not made", but have we ever seriously attempted to make them?' The only drawback to orchestral players from British academic institutions was that 'they lack fire; they have to be whipped to enthusiasm . . . This is the fault of studying under an uninspiring conductor.' Our solo singers – with named exceptions including Lloyd, Santley, Coates, and Muriel Foster – lacked dramatic instinct because there was 'no drama in England . . . dressed-up dolls and dummies fill the stage at most of our theatres . . . These people cannot act.'

The subject on 6 December was 'Critics', in which he paid warm tribute to the late Arthur Johnstone and said of Shaw's writing on music that 'there was always a substratum of practical matter, or to put it chemically to [*sic*] volatile and pellucid fluid, held in solution, matter which was precipitated into obvious solid fact by the introduction of the reader's own common sense.' He urged the foundation of 'a periodical devoting itself to the consideration of music and matters bearing upon music apart from concert-giving or concert-going.' On 13 December, in 'Retrospect', he answered some of the criticisms and attacks which his lectures – in those days of much fuller reporting – had provoked. In this lecture he said again that 'the symphony without a programme is the highest development of art ... It seems to me that because the greatest genius of our days, Richard Strauss, recognises the symphonic-poem as a fit vehicle for his splendid achievements, some writers are inclined to be positive that the symphony is dead. Perhaps the form is somewhat battered by the ill-usage of some of its admirers, although some modern symphonies will testify to its vitality; but when the looked-for genius comes, it may be absolutely revived ... Let me say definitely that when I see one of my own works by the side of, say, the Fifth Symphony, I feel like a tinker may do when surveying the Forth Bridge.' He pleaded for a higher standard at 'people's concerts' – 'English working-men are intelligent: they do not want treating sentimentally, we must give them the real thing, we must give them of the best because we want them to have it' – and urged better concert-halls and a National Opera.

Parenthetically it is interesting to note here the number of admiring references to Richard Strauss made by Elgar during the lectures. After Düsseldorf the two composers met again at a dinner party at the Speyers' five days before a London performance (10 December 1902) of *Ein Heldenleben*. Elgar is said, by Rosa Burley, to have suggested in reply to Strauss's request for advice, that Strauss should consider a work based on the Book of Job and to have been astonished that Strauss had never read it (he could not have known of Strauss's violent anti-religious opinions). After the *Heldenleben* performance, Elgar wrote to 'Richard Coeur de Lion': 'I must tell you ... how tremendously I felt your music & how I rejoiced to see & hear how the audience appreciated your gigantic work & your genius. I regret more than ever that I cannot speak to you in your own tongue; I want to say so much – *all* of which wd. be in praise & thankfulness for your work.'

Elgar was deeply upset by the controversy which followed his first lecture. 'I have been very unwell but am better now', he wrote to Jaeger on 3 April 1905. 'It really makes me disgusted with English musical life to see the way everybody (except Kalisch who heard me speak) misquotes me! I set a high ideal for the younger men ...' Then, on 6 June, came a by now familiar tone of voice: 'I don't hear anything of music now or rather of *music* I hear much, of musicians, little: they are always quarrelling ... I have no news of myself as I have for ever lost interest in that person – he ceased to exist on a certain day when his friends interfered & insisted on his – It is very sad.' Even his first voyage to the United States later that month and the ceremony at Yale failed to rouse his spirits. He was ill again on the voyage home. His letters around this time are full of complaints about illness and of 'the cook who can't cook' and other domestic afflictions. He had been ill during a holiday in Italy in January 1904. In spite of the honour of the Elgar Festival two months later, its preparation involved him in the kind of business work he disliked. Stress led to headaches, and three days beforehand, when Schuster gave a magnificent dinner at his Old Queen Street home in his friend's honour – 'he had even', Henry Wood says,[13] 'conceived a series of emblematic decorations on the panels of his dining-room referring to various phases of Elgar's work' – Elgar had spent all day in bed. After Schuster had proposed his health ('with his heart in his voice', Alice wrote), Elgar made no response but went on talking to his neighbour. 'I have not been well,' he wrote to Nicholas Kilburn in August 1904, in reply to congratulations, and to Schuster on 3 September: 'I am still very low & see nothing in the future but a black stone wall against which I am longing to dash my head – and that's all: a pitiful end for a "promising" youth.'

There is little doubt that the strain of being a celebrity and of not having the solitude to compose severely affected Elgar in 1904–6, and took their toll of the largest composition of the period, *The Kingdom*. How he must have sighed for the days at Craeg Lea and Birchwood. Peace and quiet were a necessity to him. He decided in 1903 to leave Craeg Lea because new building development was spoiling the view and bringing noise and less privacy. He had already given up Birchwood because of 'the difficulty of keeping it aired etc'. But, as he told Jaeger,[14] 'I would like to end my days there – only it's too remote for my wife & Carice is now growing up! & must be in the loathèd world. Alas! Alas!' He inquired if Birchwood was for sale, but it was not. It was a deeper blow to him than he ever admitted to his family. To Jaeger he confided:[15] 'You saw my dear place & I hate having to give it up. My life is one continual giving up of little things which I love, & only great ones, I'm told, come into it, & I loathe them. I do like my *little* toys.' But Arnold Bax, who had first met him there, sensitively perceived what the cottage meant to Elgar. In 1910 Bax was invited to submit a work for a Promenade Concert and Wood told him it was Elgar who had recommended Bax's work – 'It seems that he never forgot my visit to Birchwood (I think his days there counted as the happiest in his tormented life, and he kept a special regard for anyone who had seen him in those surroundings).'[16]

[13] *My Life of Music*, op. cit., pp. 235–6.   [15] Letter, 27 August 1903.
[14] 29 August 1903.   [16] *Farewell, My Youth*, op. cit., pp. 31–32.

For an artist who required solitude the months following the 1904 Festival at Covent Garden must certainly have been a torment for which Rodewald's death and the disputes with the Leeds Festival committee were unhelpful preparation. Knighthood in July 1904, the Three Choirs Festival, the Leeds Festival, worry over accepting the Birmingham post; then in 1905, the Oxford doctorate, first performance of a new work, the lectures, visits to Hanley, Leeds, and York for performances of his works, the visit to America, the Worcester Festival and the freedom ceremony, the Mediterranean cruise, straight back to the Norwich Festival, and then in November – no doubt because Plâs Gwyn was a drain on the pocket – he took the London Symphony Orchestra on its first provincial tour, conducting his own and others' works in Birmingham, Manchester, Sheffield, Glasgow, Newcastle upon Tyne, and Bradford. Travelling tired Elgar and gave him headaches. He became 'frightfully sick of the tour'. Also, as he wrote to Schuster, more lectures were due in December – 'I am killed with the University'. Alice's diary at the end of 1905 records: 'E. oppressed with the Birmingham Prof. & quite unable to write music', though E. himself wrote to Walford Davies on 31 December to say 'I am working away & some of the themes are not bad'. This refers to the Prelude to *The Kingdom*.

But the prospect of further lectures in 1906 depressed him as the time to deliver them drew near. On 1 November he spoke about 'Orchestration' and on 8 November about 'Mozart's G minor Symphony'. Alice rescued him from his predicament. She proposed to the dean of the arts faculty that the Professor of Music should merely take the chair at lectures given by others. This became the pattern for 1907. On 29 August 1908, Elgar resigned and Granville Bantock succeeded him. Richard Peyton's written comment to the university secretary was, 'I am pleased to think that there will be now a prospect of some satisfactory results attending the existence of a musical professorship in the university . . . The actual result & virtual waste of time has, I need not say, been a great disappointment to me.'

If Elgar gained much *réclame* from his elevation to popular fame, he gave much, too, of the most precious commodity any artist possesses: his time. It is true he was working largely on behalf of his own music, conducting it here, there, and everywhere, and not, as Parry was, devoting time to students and administrative bodies. But the hard fact remains: he needed the money. An author could live on his books in the Edwardian age, but a composer could not live on his music. And, since his music was in demand, he was fulfilling a proper purpose in presenting it in the most favourable manner. It was not yet the age of the British conductor, with the exception of Wood, and Elgar knew that he himself conducted his own music better than anyone, though he might have excepted Richter. What he suffered at others' hands he put in a letter to Jaeger on 1 July 1903: 'When they [his works] go as I like – elastically and mystically – people grumble – when they are conducted squarely and sound like a wooden box these people are pleased to say it's better. It's a curious thing that the performances which I have hated & loathed as being caricatures of my thoughts are the very ones held up as patterns!'

It is not easy to guess at whom these remarks were directed. As early as 1903 Richter, Bantock, Buths, Steinbach, Cowen, Stanford, Wood, and Elgar himself had been the chief conductors of his music.

The effect of Elgar's national prestige upon the compositions of 1903–13 will be considered in the two following chapters. We are concerned here with the over-stressed 'laureate' works. In fact, after the *Coronation Ode*, except for two more of the *Pomp and Circumstance* Marches (No. 3 in C minor, 1905, and No. 4 in G, 1907) there is little further in this line in King Edward's reign except for two part-songs, a 'Marching Song' for the Empire Concert in 1908 and a further setting of Newman, 'They are at rest' for the anniversary in 1910 of Queen Victoria's death. The accession of King George V brought a *Coronation March* and a short choral work 'O hearken thou', sung at the Abbey ceremony. The *Coronation March* is the greatest of Elgar's orchestral 'laureate' works. Its *maestoso* opening theme was originally intended for the Rabelais ballet and other ideas were sketched in Rome for an Italian processional. But this is no hasty assemblage of discarded ideas. Nearly eleven minutes long, it is on an imposing scale, like a concert-overture or the finale of a symphony. This is a march written for an abbey, not for the streets of London, sombre and stately, and suggesting in some of its sections an heroic tragedy. The orchestration is brilliant but the undertones are often melancholy, and the trio· is of special tenderness, as if the dead King was being remembered while the new one was crowned. It is an astounding piece, successful at several levels. In 1912, to mark the royal visit to India and to pay some of the bills incurred by a move into a Hampstead mansion, Elgar composed an 'Imperial Masque', *The Crown of India*, for Oswald Stoll's London Coliseum. Elgar found some of Henry Hamilton's libretto difficult to stomach – 'there is *far too much* of the political business' – and deleted the worst lines. He had a month in which to undertake the commission so he fell back on a theme written in 1903 to illustrate the 'sinful growth' of the bulldog Dan and on other sketches of earlier works which had come to naught. *The Crown of India* was assembled from early notes for a work about Falstaff, abandoned ideas from the 1903–4 sketches for a symphony, left-overs from *The Apostles* and from a contemplated second *Cockaigne* overture. The 1914–18 war brought forth the famous *Carillon* recitation for speaker and orchestra, a pot-pourri called *Polonia* and dedicated to Paderewski, two further attempts to equal the success of *Carillon*, and the finest of all his laureate works, *The Spirit of England*, a setting for tenor or soprano solo, chorus, and orchestra of three poems by Laurence Binyon, which can rank with the finest of his choral works in the nobility of its utterance. For one theme he drew on another 'Mood of Dan' inscribed in July 1902 in Sinclair's visitors' book to illustrate 'Dan wistful, outside the cathedral'. The first movement, 'The Fourth of August', begins with a typical rising-and-falling Elgarian sequence which is to run through the whole movement. Compassion and dignity are the keynotes, with a radiant ecstasy for the soloist. When the horror of war is described, 'the barren creed of blood and iron', the orchestra quotes from the Demons' Chorus of *Gerontius*. 'To Women' is a noble and beautiful setting in which Elgar's harmonic idiom takes on an impressionistic quality quite new to it. The onomatopoeia of war are expressed with a musical truth and vividness not again approached until Britten's *War Requiem* of 1962, but it is the deep sadness in the voices that makes this movement so haunting. It ends with a quotation from the main theme from 'The Fourth of August', whereas 'For the Fallen' begins by quoting from 'To Women' – its first lines likening England to a mother mourning for her children. Other themes are recalled in the orchestral prelude to this finale which is in the shape of a funeral march (the *cantabile* theme is Dan's wistfulness). This movement has the heaviest burden of personal anguish and regret yet it is never threatened by self-indulgence. The section 'They went with songs to the battle' contrasts a wistful gaiety of rhythm (*pp* and *dolce*) with desolate diminished fifths in the harmony and a lamenting oboe, insistent and heart-rending. For the poem's most often quoted verse 'They shall grow not old . . .'[17] Elgar's music is restrained, sad beyond all words to describe, and with a wonderful falling cadence at 'At the going down of the sun.' At 'To the innermost heart of their own land', the dead march returns and the opening is recapitulated. Throughout the whole work, the listener will sense near-quotations and sometimes direct quotations from *The Dream of Gerontius* (at 'but not to fail!' in 'To Women', for example) as if the sorrows of war had reawakened in the disillusioned Elgar all that 'sense of ruin which is worse than pain' that lies at the core of his greatest religious masterpiece.

A wounded officer wrote to Schuster on 9 May 1916, castigating 'all the people writing about war & soldiers when they haven't a notion of either. Sensible people like Yeats keep quiet, or express the feelings of non-combatants in the most touching & poignant forms imaginable, as Elgar & Binyon. How often the sad last phrases of Elgar's 'For the Fallen' echo despairingly & yet somehow

[17] Although this is Binyon's phrase, Elgar set 'They shall not grow old'.

victoriously in my head.' And Britten, writing in the Aldeburgh
Festival programme-book for 1969, said of 'For the Fallen': '[It] has
always seemed to me to have in its opening bars a personal tenderness
and grief, in the grotesque march an agony of distortion, and in the
final sequences a ring of genuine splendour.'

The success of *Carillon* overwhelmed the other two wartime
recitations with orchestra, rather unfairly. *Le drapeau belge* (1917) is
short but touching and shares its main theme and its mood of resigned
mourning with *The Spirit of England*. But the most elaborate work of
the three is the magnificent *Une Voix dans le Désert*, its drums and bare
string harmonies establishing a chilling mood to which poignant
contrast is provided by the exquisite solo soprano song, 'Quand nos
bourgeons se rouvriront' – the voice of the shepherdess in the desert
of war and death – an outstanding example of elegiac Elgarian poetry,
both in its vocal writing and in the expressive orchestral accompaniment. To detach the song from its context would be to violate Elgar's
artistic concept; and even though that concept belongs ineluctably to
1915, the piece is far too good to be abandoned on that account. It
would still provide a moving centrepiece for a Remembrance Day
ceremony.

In 1924, for performance during the British Empire Exhibition at
Wembley, he produced an *Empire March* and eight songs, *Pageant of
Empire*, to words by Alfred Noyes. Sir Walter Parratt, Master of the
King's Musick since 1893, had died the previous month and there had
been rumours that the office would be allowed to lapse. In a letter to
Lady Stuart of Wortley, on 16 April, he refers to this:

'I wrote to Stamfordham[18] urging that the Master of the King's
Music shd. be retained – its suppression wd. have a very bad effect
abroad where the effacement of the last shred of connection of the
Court with the Art wd. not be understood. It is not S's dept so it was
turned over to F. Ponsonby.[19] He wrote to me that it was one of the
offices which it was (long ago) proposed (scheduled) to cease. I wrote
again offering myself (honorary) – *anything* rather than that it shd. be
publicly announced that the old office was abolished. No reply.
Colebrooke[20] wrote to the Ld. Chamberlain – but as far as I can make
out the three depts. simply quarrel over these things: no grit, no
imagination – *no music*. No nothing except boxing, football & racing
so it is. I have had no further reply & I believe the matter is to drop
tacitly.'

But in May, Elgar was appointed to the vacant post, one that he
graced and in the hearts of his countrymen had occupied in effect for

[18] Lord Stamfordham (1849–1931), the King's Private Secretary.
[19] Sir Frederick Ponsonby (1867–1935), later Lord Sysonby, Treasurer to King
George V.
[20] Lord Colebrooke (1861–1939), a Lord-in-Waiting.

twenty-seven years. He coveted it simply for its historical and romantic associations, not for any special feelings of loyalty. The same letter to Lady Stuart included this: 'Everything seems so hopelessly & irredeemably *vulgar* at Court.' It also refers to talk of a peerage for Elgar. 'I fear it is hopeless but it wd. please me,' he wrote; and it would have pleased him because it would have honoured music, as Tennyson's had honoured literature. He wrote to Lady Stuart, who was influential in these matters, in 1926: 'Of course, I should love to have the *offer* but it is impossible for me to suggest in the remotest way that I want it: this sort of thing I have never done and although I know well that it *is* done . . . I cannot think of it: so adieu! to all my greatness.' On 24 December 1927 he wrote to her: 'H.M. has offered me the wretched *K.C.V.O.*(!!!) which awful thing I must accept! Alas!'

He had been made a member of the Order of Merit in the Coronation Honours List of 1911 – 'the one thing which really delights him,' Alice wrote to Troyte. Curiously, King Edward, who had instituted the Order, had not conferred it upon his friend. Elgar himself was a little concerned that the Worcestershire people did not attach enough significance to the honour, for it had only been in existence nine years and had not yet acquired the almost mystical significance it holds today. He wrote to Troyte in July 1911: 'I wish you wd. write to the Worcester paper & say a little what the Order of M really is! Some . . . think it is a sort of degradation & quite unworthy of me. . . . At the Investiture Sir G. Trevelyan & I were marshalled next G.C.B. & *before* G.C.M.G. (which is Ld. Beauchamp's highest distinction!) & of course before G.C.S.I. etc. It was very nice.'

He was made K.C.V.O. in 1928, a baronet ('of Broadheath') in 1931, and G.C.V.O. in 1933, years when such honours ceased to matter for him, because although they showed official recognition of his position in musical life, they did nothing to combat the neglect of his music which had by then occurred. He accepted them, no doubt, because through him they honoured English music and, perhaps, because it pleased his vanity to know that he, once an outsider, had won his right to exact this tribute from the kind of people who had resented his ascent to the head of his profession. If this can be explained as further proof of his essential insecurity, as in the case of Tennyson, it is also understandable. The professional honour which gives English musicians cause for the deepest personal pleasure and pride, the Gold Medal of the Royal Philharmonic Society, was denied him until 1925, when he was sixty-eight, and awarded to him some months after it had gone to Delius. (It is said that a peerage for Elgar was contemplated in 1933 but was withheld as a 'waste' when news of his fatal illness was known.)

'In Elgar', wrote Constant Lambert in *Music, Ho!* 'we get an example of a composer, in touch with both his audience and his period, expressing himself nationally in an international language.' Arthur Johnstone, thirty years before, had found 'Land of Hope and Glory' to be 'distinctively British' because it was 'beefy and breezy', which is true enough of the song though not of the tune in its orchestral dress. But is there any justification for the assumption that Elgar was a nationalist, a typically English composer, apart from the extra-musical associations of his work with typically English state occasions? It is time the whole concept of music as a national language was swept away. There is no English music, only music by Englishmen. Elgar, as Lambert realized, could and wanted to 'put himself across' to his fellow-countrymen, but there was nothing specifically English in the way that he did it, nothing that can be linked with folk-song or the Tudor composers or Purcell. To account for what is called the 'English quality' of Elgar's music can be done only by explaining it as a response to his expression of some national sub-conscious, 'the echo of the echo of a sigh', as in the Welsh tune of the *Introduction and Allegro*, the Adagio of the First Symphony and the slow movement of the Violin Concerto. The music distils a national mood by a deeply personal transmuting of emotion. All the virtues and failings of Elgar's work are traceable to the man himself, not to the fact that he was an Englishman alive in the period of England's imperial noonday. He may or may not have accepted the age in which he lived – he certainly did not rebel against it, but there are degrees of acceptance. The issue is irrelevant: the diversity of the music written in the first fourteen years of the twentieth century is sufficient in itself to explode any theories about the artist's relationship to the time in which he lives. That is why the 'Edwardianism' of Elgar's music is an outdated label which was never accurate. Elgar's world was the world of music, of Strauss's *Heldenleben*, Puccini's *La Bohème*, Schoenberg's *Gurrelieder*. The faults of taste, the descents into triteness and triviality, afflict them and others – Sibelius, for example, and Mahler – as much as they afflict Elgar; they are the faults of big men undertaking big tasks. They have nothing to do with the sun's never setting on the British Empire, even if Stanford did say to Elgar, about the D major March, 'You have translated Master Rudyard Kipling into Music . . . and said "blooming beggar" in quite his style.'

Whether this was the first association of the names Kipling and Elgar, and hence an automatic association of both with 'jingoism', it has proved a lasting one that would have been more accurate if it had been less superficial. Just as the detractors of Kipling's popular style forget the darker, mysterious side of his work,[21] and overlook the

[21] In this connection, it is interesting to read in Elgar's letter to Frank Webb on 27 March 1892: '*Do* I know Kipling's works? *rather*: & like the tales very much though

1897 'Recessional' about navies melting away, so the detractors of Elgar forget that what people turn to most often in Elgar's music is not the swagger and blare of the extrovert works, but the sweet, tender melancholy that is far and away the predominant characteristic of his work, one that is heightened because in his major compositions the miniature Elgar is integrated into the symphonic Elgar. He did not need to keep one style apart from the other, as Sibelius did; he was incapable of doing so – 'I hold nothing back.' The style was the man, which was only what H. C. Colles meant when, in *The Times* of 1 April 1939, he wrote: 'His whole output is a series of variations on one melody which was the essence of his being.' The exquisite *Chanson de Nuit* and the eloquent *Sospiri* are in the same world as the Adagio of the First Symphony. The tune of the first *Pomp and Circumstance* march is but one of a family: the opening theme of the First Symphony, the chorus 'Go forth' in *Gerontius*, the slow movements of the *Serenade*, the symphonies and the concertos, 'Nimrod', and the Angel's Farewell. The march-like opening of the First Symphony is dismissed by exhilaration akin to the quick sections of the marches, with the off-beat thumps that also highlight brilliantly effective episodes in the slow movement of the Second Symphony, in the Boar's Head and Coronation scenes of *Falstaff*, in parts of the Violin Concerto and in the finale of the Cello Concerto. Episodes which disturb some listeners, where there is incongruity between the jubilee-procession style and its context, can sometimes be traced to the relative poverty of the invention – the last bars of the *Variations*, for example, and several passages in the two oratorios. It is the fault of exuberance, of a flamboyant generosity which had no room for anaemic half measures.

He indirectly answered his critics in his first Birmingham lecture in 1905. Some people, he said, deplored vulgarity. But he deplored the commonplace much more. 'Vulgarity in the course of time may be refined. Vulgarity often goes with inventiveness, and it can take the place of initiative – in a rude and misguided way, no doubt – but after all it does something, and can be and has been refined. But the commonplace mind can never be anything but commonplace, and no amount of education, no polish of a university, can eradicate the stain from the low type of mind which is the English commonplace. English music is white and evades everything. . . . What I want to see coming into being is something that shall grow out of our own soul.'

These sentiments echoed some expressed three years earlier by one of the younger group of composers, Ralph Vaughan Williams, in an

---

some are too awful to ever have been written . . . In the last book (name forgotten) there are two excruciatingly horrible: one about a leper & the other about the orang-utang'. (The book was *Life's Handicap*, 1891, and the stories are 'The Mark of the Beast' and 'Bertram and Bimi'.)

article headed 'Good Taste'.[22] 'The truth is that the young Englishman is too musicianly. The "musicianly" composer . . . has found out all the mechanical means by which beautiful music is produced. . . . Many a young composer has stifled his natural impulses in the desire to be musicianly. . . . If a composer is naturally vulgar, let him be frank and write vulgar music instead of hedging himself about with an artificial barrier of good taste. . . . If every composer will be himself, his music will at all events be genuine.'

'English' music is not an identifiable product. It is, simply and obviously, music written by Englishmen out of genuine creative endeavour or, to use Elgar's more romantic term, 'their own souls'. How the best of English composers found their own souls differs widely. Elgar and Vaughan Williams found theirs by completely varying ways, but being men of strong and original character they produced music of strong and original character, and their art has been called 'typically English'. This phrase is almost meaningless. Where is there such a person as the 'typical Englishman'? Elgar, certainly, was not one, a man so emotional that, as Compton Mackenzie has described, he trembled all over and veins and beads of sweat stood out alarmingly on his head with the excitement of listening to the 'March to the Scaffold' from Berlioz's *Fantastic Symphony*.[23]

I have used the word 'superficial' to describe the accepted response to Elgar's *nobilmente* style and to his comparison with Kipling. A more striking parallel is with Tennyson – both were countrymen always ill at ease in cities, both liable to fits of almost demented grief over the death of friends, both outsiders who had no reason to think highly of society's conduct (Tennyson's father had been excluded from his inheritance, Elgar's wife had been penalized financially for 'marrying beneath' her), both married to women who tried to protect them from the inconveniences of the world, both needing the admiring approval of friends and colleagues, both acutely sensitive to unfavourable criticism, both pessimistic about the lasting quality of their own work, both regarded as spokesmen for the country through their art, both at their best in elegiac, wistful, intimate moods, both attacked as representative Victorian and representative Edwardian rather than as poet and musician. It is perhaps significant of the personal qualities in Elgar's music that it was at its first peak of popularity when Britain's greatness was uncontested and people did not need to look below the surface, that it fell into disfavour while the Empire began to crumble,

[22] Published in Vol. I, No. 2 of *The Vocalist* (May 1902).
[23] 'Dorabella' (Mrs Dora Powell) in her *Edward Elgar: Memories of a Variation* (Second Edition, London, 1946), p. 5, says that his concert-hall neighbours became used to being elbowed or clutched by Elgar when he was excited by music and knew What it was 'to have an arm black and blue with bruises next day . . ., with practice one learnt to shift imperceptibly . . . so that the position of the grip varied.'

and that it won a new and more perceptive audience when Britain had ceased to be a great Power, when the Empire had disintegrated, and when people heard in the music what had always been there to hear: the funeral march of a civilization, of a spiritual and artistic way of life which was decaying.

Elgar transcended the time in which he lived. Nervous energy and what he himself called 'stately sorrow' are the moods of the symphonies and concertos. The so-called 'complacent' tone of the music – the Trio tune of the D major March is the example usually cited – is not complacent at all. There is, as I have already suggested, a note of resignation in this melody, emphasized, as in the Larghetto of the Second Symphony, by the sepulchral scoring (horns, bassoons, clarinets in their low register). The outbursts of extrovert grandiloquence in the symphonies are always followed by withdrawn, cloistered passages of tender lyricism, the general effect, as in Mahler, emphasizing the instability of the full conception. This can be traced musically to the constant shiftings of tonality and harmony. Nowhere can this fusion of the 'laureate' and the 'mystic' Elgar – or the 'London pride' and the 'windflower' Elgar – be more profitably studied than in the pages preceding the coda of the first movement of the First Symphony and the tragic contrast in the Second Symphony's first movement between the energetic exposition and its collapse into the withdrawn, ghostly mood of the development section. This elegiac side of Elgar's music has its origins in a nostalgia for childhood – 'oh, the mad days' – as was the case with Mahler, and it is not surprising that movements like the poignant and fanciful trio in the second movement of the First Symphony have a strong connection with the mood of the *Wand of Youth* suites. There is a restraint – this, at any rate, is typically English – which perhaps half-conceals the truth, and certainly makes the music doubly effective. Elgar did not wallow; his expressions of nostalgia, excepting the Cello Concerto, have a unique, unself-pitying quality all the more remarkable because the man himself was not free from self-indulgence in the matter of 'the days that are no more'.

It is only in recent years, when Mahler's symphonies have at last become a main contour on the musical map of Britain, that comparisons between Elgar and Mahler have become obvious, if misleading. Both composed their autobiographies in music, with many references to external events and many internal cross-references between works. Elgar's Second Symphony, first played six days after Mahler's death, has a psychological programme not unlike Mahler's Ninth, with a complex, volatile first movement, a funeral march, a wild and sinister scherzo episode, and a finale in which the ultimate mood is one of resignation and sadness. Elgar made less use than Mahler and Strauss of commonplace ingredients absorbed into the symphonic scheme, but he shares Mahler's vulnerability. The Austrian is more daring and progressive in technical and harmonic means, the Englishman finer-grained. Both, by sheer musical sensibility, can sustain a long, seemingly fragmented structure as a coherent, narrative whole.

As for the *Pomp and Circumstance* marches themselves, for every ten people who know the much-performed Nos. 1 and 4, perhaps one or two know the full set. Their pre-eminence in their field is for the obvious reason that no one has yet approached Elgar in the sheer musical effectiveness of his ceremonial manner. Any other marches, whether by Walton, Ireland, Bliss, or Eric Coates, are but pale imitations. It is likely, too, that most of those whose lips curl at the mention of *Pomp and Circumstance* have rarely, if ever, listened to the marches as music and as a whole. If they had, they would recognize that Nos. 1 and 4 are superb in their own right, especially when played as Elgar wrote them and without overblown sentiments not implicit in the music. As for Nos. 2, 3, and 5, they blow the 'jingoist' jibe sky-high. They are less fruity melodically than Nos. 1 and 4, totally lacking in rhetoric and pomposity. No. 2, for example, in A minor is a nervously restless piece in Elgar's symphonic manner, scored rather like a Schubertian *marche militaire* or a theatrical entr'acte. No. 3, like No. 2 also in the minor, is a subtle work, with a hint of mystery in its opening bars, and a trio section of lyrical and quite un-military charm. No. 5, written in 1930 but probably sketched much earlier, is jovial, with more than a touch of self-parodying, tongue-in-cheek humour in its final pages. The complete set, played one after the other, comprise a kind of suite, devoid of monotony except for the actual march form, consistently exciting rhythmically and scored with all Elgar's command of thrilling and poetic instrumental colour.

They are great popular music. There is nothing inferior about them, and it is because he was able to transfer their 'popular' elements to his larger-scale works that Elgar remains indispensable for an expression of national sorrow or rejoicing: the death of a King, the death of a hero like Churchill, or the crowning of a Queen. Not because of pomp or circumstance, but because, as Parry perceived, his essential and real message reaches the hearts of the people: that the transience of human life overwhelms all ceremony, that 'golden lads and girls all must, as chimney sweepers, come to dust'. And also because the music carries in itself the seeds of its personal and human origins, not as the celebration or commemoration of an epoch or an ideology, but as a memory of a summer-evening talk with a friend about Beethoven, the enshrinement of the soul of a woman, the remembrance of a man snatched away, as Rodewald was, in the prime of life, the fears of a man on his death-bed, apprehensive about what lies ahead – 'no end of a worldly man, and now brought to book'.

10 Unfinished Trilogy

This was Elgar's position in 1901–2: he was nearing forty-five, he had had a success with the *Variations*, a failure with *The Dream of Gerontius*. He had had riotous success with two *Pomp and Circumstance* marches and the *Cockaigne* overture. At a time when choral singing in Britain was at its zenith, it was his orchestral works which had taken him to the top. *King Olaf* remained the most frequently performed of his choral music, *The Black Knight* had never established itself. As Jaeger wrote to him in 1901, it 'doesn't move much for some reason or other, chiefly no doubt because the subject is a bit gruesome & the music ends poetically pp. I have thought that if we could do something with the work for orchestra alone, we might make it better known. . . .' All of which seems to contradict the theory that Elgar was prevented from writing the orchestral music that really interested him because the taste of the time was for choral works, religious if possible. Elgar himself supported the theory when, in 1933, he told Delius that he wrote his choral works because it was 'the penalty of my environment'. This may have been true in the mid-1890s, the period of *Lux Christi* and *The Black Knight*. But by 1902 Elgar had established a new situation whereby the public acclaimed him as an orchestral composer. Yet, after beginning several instrumental projects during 1901–2, he turned aside from them to begin a large-scale oratorio. It helped Elgar in his pecuniary difficulties to know that a Birmingham Festival commission was available to him, but there is no merit in pretending that *The Apostles* and *The Kingdom* are potboilers, written against Elgar's better judgement in order to make ends meet. He wrote them because he wanted to. There is documentary proof to support his statement that it had long been his wish to write an oratorio on the subject of the work of Christ's Apostles, a wish prompted by a schoolmaster's casual remark in a scripture lesson.

Elgar conceived his project as a trilogy dealing with the beginnings of Christianity, Christ's call to the disciples, the years of teaching in Jerusalem, the mission to the Gentiles and, finally but never accomplished, the Church Universal. Themes for this vast work had accumulated in his sketchbooks since the 1880s though some had been used up for *Lux Christi*. Some sketches are dated 1896. It has already been seen that he was preoccupied with the idea of Judas Iscariot in the winter of 1899, and that his 'Judas theme' became the Angel of the Agony in *Gerontius*. In November 1901 he wrote the Morning Psalm section; and music that eventually found its way into

The Kingdom was written early in 1902, notably the setting of the Lord's Prayer. To carry out his ambition he had, of course, to provide his own libretto. He worked on it throughout the late summer of 1902, collecting material and reading several commentaries on the New Testament. Another source was Longfellow's poem *The Divine Tragedy*. Despite the theological study which went into it, despite the novel and sympathetic approach to the character of Judas, the text lacks a focal point of issue of the kind that makes *Gerontius* compelling. Whereas the music of *Gerontius* seems to spring unbidden from the poem, some of *The Apostles* sounds very consciously 'set to music'.

Work on the music in the summer of 1902 was hindered by Elgar's old eye trouble – 'My eyes are bad and I must write no more,' he wrote in May to Jaeger who had by now been told of the work. There was still some doubt whether Novello's would publish it – *Gerontius*, it must be remembered, had still not been performed in London despite its success at Düsseldorf. Littleton wrote to Elgar on 11 July: 'I have been in correspondence with Mr Johnstone (Birmingham Festival) about *The Apostles*. He places such a high commercial value on the work that I fear there is no chance of our coming to terms. . . . I have tried hard to do my part in helping *Gerontius* and should have liked to have continued to do my best for other works.' In July Elgar went to Bayreuth where he heard *Parsifal* and *The Ring*. This seemed to provide the spur he needed – a sacred equivalent to Wagner's tetralogy. He was also inspired by the example of Handel's *Messiah* – 'the greatest figure in religious music' was his opinion of Handel, 'for he had a sense of beauty & humanity which belonged so much to himself'. On 3 August Elgar wrote to Jaeger from Craeg Lea: 'My eyes are better, I think, & I'm working at the Apostles – which you will not like – it's too philosophical for your *cheap publisher's side* of your mind, but just the thing for the *real* A.J.J.' He was ill again before Christmas – 'I have *liver*: you know what that means!' – but on New Year's Day 1903, Alice noted that he was 'keen on his work' and the next day was 'very busy with his booful music'. Jaeger went to Malvern to hear some of it on 4 January. Johnstone of the Birmingham Festival paid a visit to discuss Novello's terms for its production in October. (These were £500 on receipt of the manuscript, £500 after the sale of 10,000 vocal scores – achieved in February 1906 – and thereafter the royalty of 6d on sales of each vocal score.) Then on 12 January Hans Richter came and was played parts of the *Coronation Ode*[1] and *The Apostles*. Later that month, on the 21st, Elgar began to let Jaeger have sections of the score for printing, although the work was by no means completed, and was again delayed by a chill on the liver – 'it stops *all* work', he wrote to

[1] In preparation for a Hallé performance in Manchester.

Littleton, '. . . I have been quite disillusioned as to the musical world for some years and so I say farewell to it without the slightest regret.' Despite this depression, he completed the first scene in early February, received early proofs on the 17th and a few days later sent off the manuscript of the second scene, 'By the Wayside' – 'quite new and different from anything else', said Alice, who took each parcel to the post office, as she had done for every work since they were married. The third scene, 'By the Sea of Galilee', was finished on 23 March, and by then Elgar was beginning to be anxious for more proofs, no doubt remembering the last-minute rush which had affected *Gerontius*. On 19 March he wrote to Jaeger: 'You promised me I shd. have plenty (of copies that is). You know I am not a *proper composer* & I know I ought not to try – but! well I must. Now – I prefer *revises* of course & I like to send 'em to three or four friends whose judgment I rely on (for phrasing etc. etc.) – vocalists & *sich* – that takes one copy. My wife wants one for *scoring* purposes, i.e. making the skeleton for me – that takes another & I like to have one by me to refer to, phrasing, &c. . . . don't *laugh at me for my silly ways* because I'm clever at some things but *not* at composing.' Elgar always objected to the word 'composed' on the title-pages of his scores and asked Jaeger on 20 March to make it simply 'by Edward Elgar'. (He had explained to him, on 21 June 1898, that 'this word always brings up a vision of a man scratching the back of his head with a pen – if I *do* scratch (which heaven forbid!) it's not for ideas.') 'Send along revises – anything else,' he added. 'Lumbago better, rheumatism bad, temper evil, disposition venomous, mind – vacant.' The Judas death scene was composed on 24 and 25 April.

A crisis arose at the end of May when Elgar upset Novello's engraver, Brause, by sending seventeen pages of a new chorus – 'Turn you to the stronghold' – to be inserted at the end of Part I. Elgar was unrepentant and told Jaeger on 28 May: 'I have been obliged to recast on acct. of the difficulty in finding a Judas to my mind & particularly wanted these sheets as I have to travel & try vocalists – now here I am, through confounded stupidity, without any copy at all. Even if the Judas sc: cd. not be proceeded with – I suppose everybody layed him down & wept & forgot all about such things as revises. I am absolutely vexed! for once. Tell me is Messchaert singing well?'

Elgar had realized that he needed really impressive singers for the parts of Peter, who was gradually to assume a commanding rôle, and Judas. Worried by this and by further eye trouble he radically altered the design of the whole work. What we now know as *The Kingdom*, much of which was already written ('O sacrum convivium', for instance, was written at Rodewald's house in Liverpool in December 1902), was planned as Part III of *The Apostles*. In June he wrote to

Littleton: 'My eyes are again in trouble – he [the doctor] forbids more work. Now I propose to the B'ham people that they produce Pts I and II of *The Apostles* – this portion is complete in itself and may well stand alone. . . . The concluding portion of the work (Pt III to round it off), much of which was written first – you can have any time later.'

A rough score of Judas's part was sent to the Dutch baritone Anton van Rooy who had been singing Wotan under Richter in *The Ring* at Covent Garden during May. Jaeger warned Elgar of the possible effects of 'foreigner's English' on the part. On returning home from the first London performance of *Gerontius*, Elgar worked at the score until 21 June when Alice's diary entry reads: 'Finished – all but the very end.' The Elgars then went to London and were presented to the King. Back at Craeg Lea, Elgar wrote on 1 July to Jaeger: 'I was bothered in town by a heap of people – principally trying to find singers *with brains* – now I have to put up with a – caste of English – I won't go into the disappointments – oh! these singers – *where* are their *brains*?. . . . I have some full score ready for you but will hold it for a space. . . . The only way out of the singer business was to omit "Peter" – who shines forth in Pt III & let Black[2] do Judas – It's pitiful but there are really no *good* singers beyond three & one (Bispham[3]) we can't have!' He wrote another letter on the same day in reply to a worried one from Jaeger: 'I'm not ill! & it is of no use to postpone the work as I shall *never* get English vocalists – a complete caste that is – to do my work. Pt. III was written first & most of it is ready to print – but I can find no singers.'

He was, in any case, hard on his singers in both *The Apostles* and *The Kingdom*. To a soloist who protested that he could not make himself heard over the large orchestral sound Elgar was encouraging from the rostrum, Elgar replied that it did not matter: the voice was used at the particular point 'as a vehicle to carry on the words' and the orchestra was more important.

For the rest of July he went to Rodewald's cottage at Bettws-y-Coed where he worked on the orchestration, a process which took from 28 June to 17 August. He also wrote several long letters to Canon Charles V. Gorton whom he had met earlier in 1903 at Morecambe while adjudicating at the music festival of which Gorton was chairman. The Canon had read through the text of *The Apostles* from a theological viewpoint and made several criticisms which Elgar answered. He also wrote a commentary on the text, published in the *Musical Times* of October 1903.

'Of course *we* know that the Resurrection was the climax,' Elgar wrote, 'but I was trying to look at it from the point of view of the weak man of the time. . . . The garden scene has been done too much

[2] Andrew Black (1859–1920). [3] David Bispham (1857–1921).

already. . . . Thomas also was impossible on account of bringing in another principal. . . . I have endeavoured to suggest that forgiveness is for *all who repent*. To my mind *Judas'* crime & sin was *despair* (Ibsen etc. etc.); not only the betrayal which was done for a worldly purpose. In these days, when every "modern" person seems to think "suicide" is the actual way out of everything my plan, if explained, may do some good. . . . The music explains – by means of leitmotifs & general treatment – much of the "interdependence" of the words.'

In August Jaeger was examining the work in detail – the episode of the 'crude progression' has already been mentioned. He was also working on an analysis, as he had done for *Gerontius*. 'I say,' he wrote, '*do* give us a less jolly tune for Christ's "The Keys of the Kingdom", p. 102.[4] The words themselves *jingle*; *do* make the music a little more stately, dignified & monotonous (in the true sense of the word), & on p. 83 at "Ye shall lie down" you have the *notes* of "God save the King". Don't sneer at me; these things will jar on one. Simply take out the E on "lie" & there you are. . . . Your work grows on me tremendously & by leaps & bounds. It's great stuff & quite wonderfully original & beautiful. Bless you, this is your finest work so far & your greatest.'

Elgar replied: 'The "Keys" are all right, if sung intelligently – the *Keys* do not need emphasising – but the result in the next two sentences – no one but you wd. try to sing it in time, Moss. p. 83. Shan't alter it on any account – put a pause over the E.' Elgar was annoyed over the terms the Birmingham Festival were offering Jaeger for use of his analysis and told Johnstone what he thought. 'Curse the Festival,' he said to Jaeger. 'I really think the more one has to do with the practical side of music the more awful this life becomes. I am so sick of it all! Birmingham is the worst Festival programme I have ever seen, I think (talk about the 3 choirs!) Elijah! Messiah!! Legend!!! I *can't* invite any decent folk for such a week.'

Jaeger jibbed at certain points in the score, notably on p. 135 where the chorus thrice repeat the word 'cometh' in 'a band of men and officers cometh with lanterns and torches and weapons', and, two pages later, where Elgar wanted an octave leap from B to high B on the 'Hold' of 'Hold him fast'. 'There is no objection to the repetition of cometh 3 times,' Elgar replied on 9 August, 'if done with any dramatic instinct as a good actor would do, & as a chorus, to be considered good, *must* do some day. To repeat "with lanterns" wd. be silly. It is unfortunate that all choral music shd. be affected by dull church music & by comic opera but so it is. If you could have heard van Rooy sing "Hold" you wd. not have criticised it – it is useless to try & explain to you my ideas so put "Hold him fast" [with 'Hold' on high D tied across the bar line].'

[4] Vocal score page reference.

'Yah!' Jaeger replied, 'I *can* imagine an artist like van Rooy & Wüllner singing "Hold him fast" with A.1 effect. Alas, where is *your* van Rooy & Wüllner amongst English oratorio singers! If Black *can* do it as you *imagined* it, leave it for Gawd's sake. Perhaps he can be taught not to be comic. That Judas part is superb & worthy of the biggest artist living.'

By 12 August Elgar was beginning to tire. He was within a few days of completing the full score and told Jaeger, 'I want to be *quite free* for a little time – Bike touring belike – & could not undertake to do anything, *except* to revise MS pts. with the score.' Composers today should note that Elgar, with the aid of a friend, John Austin, of Worcester, worked on all the individual orchestral parts himself. He sent Jaeger various theological treatises that had helped him in his approach to his theme – by the Rev Professor A. B. Davidson, by Richard Whately, and by the Rev F. L. Cohen – and explained the significance of certain *leitmotive*. On the 17th he completed the score and Jaeger wrote to him: 'The beauty of the music moves me to tears. . . . The Apostles are certainly your maturest & greatest work; the certainty of touch & style displayed throughout is wonderful. . . . But it is all so original, so individual & subjective that it will take the British Public 10 years to let it soak into its pachydermal mind; unless, of course, the story, being known by everybody, will carry the work along. . . . As for the poor critics (the dullest among them I mean) they will be bewildered I fear. . . . I believe that by the time you have completed Part III you will have given to the world the greatest oratorio since the Messiah. . . .'

Elgar was touched: 'I feel I can only say "non sum dignus". Never mind the B.P. – they must wait; so long as my intimate friends – friends I have gathered round me because of their hearts and brains – are satisfied, nay even only *interested* in my work, I have my reward. . . . The weather is awful & has upset all plans for rest & change. . . .'

He eventually got his rest by staying for a few days at Hereford with G. R. Sinclair. Schuster and Rodewald stayed with Elgar for the Three Choirs Festival there. By 15 September he was agitating for parts to correct. For the rest of the month he worked on them, becoming irritated, as he usually did, with Novello's. 'I'm sorry the parts worry you,' he wrote to Jaeger. 'I can't think *why*. Your men must be jolly slow.' He wrote to Schuster on 27 September: 'I am *dead* with fatigue correcting proofs for orchestra – *three*, yes three! copyists have become ill, insane & useless & have given up work wrestling with the complications of the score & I have to sit here (and did sit also in London) & wearily plod over their stuff.' Elgar began orchestral rehearsals with the Hallé Orchestra in Manchester on 5 October. Choir rehearsals were happier affairs than in 1900. 'I heard the chorus at Birmingham,' Elgar wrote to Canon Gorton on 23

September, '& it is fine – &, in all fear and trembling, I am not yet disappointed with my work.' Stanford attended one of the rehearsals and, according to Elgar, was 'enthusiastic over the Apostles: telling people all around (Albani etc. etc.) of its or their glory'. Albani was one of the six soloists in the first performance on 14 October. The others were Muriel Foster, John Coates, Kennerley Rumford, Andrew Black, and David Ffrangcon-Davies. There was a very different atmosphere from that which had prevailed at the first performance of *The Dream of Gerontius*, as Johnstone noted in the *Manchester Guardian* of 15 October: 'Vague hostility towards the unusual and the unknown has given way almost universally to the recognition that he is one of the great originals in the musical world of today; and he thus compels attention even in those who instinctively dislike both his particular methods and the kind of general atmosphere into which his religious art transports the listener.'

The critic of *The Daily Telegraph* called the occasion 'unique' in his experience of the Birmingham Festival. 'It has never happened that the whole musical world, not only in this country but also abroad, has gathered more or less closely around the production of an Englishman. . . . Though sturdily independent, courting nobody, he now occupies the position of a man with whom most people are determined to be pleased.'

This time there was no disaster. The critics acclaimed the work. 'Perhaps the most remarkable work of the present century', the *Telegraph* said. 'The composer is at his best in rendering the music of the heavenly choir', said Johnstone, whose notice did not commit itself as irrevocably in the work's favour as that of *Gerontius* had done; comparing the two works he wrote of *The Apostles* as 'of greater depth and significance but less perfectly finished' than *Gerontius*. Jaeger had gone to Birmingham for the final rehearsal and the first performance but had collapsed and stayed in his hotel bed. This time he received no embittered letter from Elgar, merely commiseration and the happy P.S. 'I am getting conceited now'. So the composer was evidently satisfied. Ferruccio Bonavia, however, who played in the orchestra, has written[5] that Elgar seemed 'nervous and ill at ease' during rehearsals and that while 'there was actually no obvious failing in the performance . . . the public was as far as ever from grasping all that the oratorio stood for'. The inference to be drawn is that it was a *succès d'estime*, but it did not trouble Elgar, who wrote in a sketch-book: 'On leaving Birmingham after the Festival we (Alice and I) went into St Philip's Church, walked up it to see the stained glass and on turning round were struck by Burne-Jones's "Ascension", the sun shining through it. Very impressive ending to our glorious week.'

[5] In 'Elgar', *The Music Masters*, iii, op.cit., p. 84.

But by 23 October Elgar was 'not very well & much worried with finance side of new work & disappointed at that side' (Alice's diary). The public's reaction to *The Apostles* was respectful but it never seized their imaginations as *Gerontius* had. After Richter's first Manchester performance in February 1904, Arthur Johnstone noted that there was 'no scene of great enthusiasm' such as had greeted *Gerontius* at the Hallé. Some thought this was because of the solemnity of the subject; Johnstone was not to be deluded, however, and added: 'The *Apostles* being unquestionably much more austere and difficult to understand than *Gerontius*, we are inclined to accept the simpler explanation that the audience did not like it so well.'

A few days after the first performance, Schuster had given Elgar a hint that Alice's idea of an Elgar Festival might very well materialize at Covent Garden – 'As to your lovely scheme,' Elgar wrote to Schuster on 22 October, 'I can say nothing now save thanks: it is just like you to think of it: but plans!' Jaeger, too, was able to report good news on 30 October: Fritz Steinbach wanted to conduct *The Apostles* at the Lower Rhine Festival at Cologne at Whitsun 1904, 'crooood passages, ugly bits, awkward points & all'. Elgar was sceptical if this would occur in reality, but all elation was shattered for him a few days later by Rodewald's death. He went to Manchester to conduct in mid-November, by which time he knew that the festival would be held in March of the following year, and then, with Alice, he went to Italy in the hope of regaining his full health and of escaping the cold and damp of the English winter. Neither ambition was adequately fulfilled, and his letters from Italy are a curious mixture of high and low spirits. They spent the first ten days at Bordighera – 'lovely but too cockney for me,' he told Schuster. 'I want something more Italian or *more* civilised & would prefer to be virtuous at Alassio or wildly wicked at Monte Carlo to being betwixt & between here. . . . Alice & I have been out *with a donkey* all day up in the woods & mountains – donkey's name is "Grisia" – a lovely beast. . . . Bought some figs today – did not know the name so asked for "frutti, per habilmenti d'Adam ed Eva". I got 'em. . . . Oh! that donkey. She's a love. I am going to buy her & ride her from here to Alassio! . . . We are both riotously well & shall never come home. We go to Alassio on Thursday.'

Just before Christmas they were joined by their daughter Carice with Rosa Burley (whose school, The Mount, Carice attended until its financial collapse in 1906). Rosa again noted how Elgar's spirits rose when he was away from England. They were staying in the Villa San Giovanni in Alassio. One afternoon Elgar went for a walk and recorded how he strolled among 'streams, flowers, hills: the distant snow mountains in one direction and the blue Mediterranean in the other. I was by the side of an old Roman way. A peasant shepherd stood by an old ruin, and in a flash it all came to me – the conflict of armies in that very spot long ago, where now I stood – the contrast of the ruin and the shepherd – and then, all of a sudden, I came back to reality. In that time I had "composed" the overture – the rest was merely writing it down.' So *In the South* was born, one of his most exuberant and colourful works. Yet just before he had left for Italy, Elgar had written to Ivor Atkins in Worcester: 'I've been into the Cathedral, which I have known since I was four, and said farewell. I wanted to see you. I am sad at heart and feel I shall never return.'

From Alassio a few days later he wrote to Troyte Griffith: 'The *view* at Bordighera is the great thing, but the whole *place* is English & the folk ½ French – also it feels like Malvern & the roads are full of English nurserymaids & old English women & children.' To Jaeger he was even more explicit: 'This place is jolly – real Italian & no nursemaids calling out "Now, Master Johnny!" – like that anglicised paradise Bordighera! pff! . . . Do come out – it seems *so easy* to come & so difficult to go back. . . . What matters the Mediterranean being rough & grey? What matters rain in torrents? Who cares for gales? *Tramontana!* We have such meals! such wine! *Gosh!* . . . We are at last living a life. The Mosquitoes are a trial & I am stung because I refused to believe in 'em & wd. not pull down the mosquito curtains at night round my bed. . . . I can't believe all these great Germans are doing my music: is it true? I think it's a dream. I hope you are pleased, old boy, anyway.'

Over Christmas he was at work on the concert overture *In the South* (which was completed on 21 February 1904) and concerned with plans for the Covent Garden festival. Clara Butt's terms for *Gerontius* were said to be 'prohibitive' and Higgins had written on 19 December to say that Muriel Foster would be in America and unable to sing the Angel. 'I had naturally thought of Brema but I am told on the very best authority that on the last two or three occasions on which she sang it was almost painful.' He proposed Kirkby Lunn as a substitute, adding: 'I am fully aware of her lack of poetic feeling . . . at the same time I cannot help thinking that no amount of poetic feeling will compensate for a raucous voice.' The weather was cold and by 3 January 1904, Elgar was writing to Jaeger in yet another mood: 'This visit has been, is, artistically a complete *failure* & I can do nothing. We have been *perished* with cold, rain & gales. Five fine days have we had & three of those were perforce spent in the train. . . . You must understand that when a wind *does* come – & it is apparently *always* on – it is no bearable, kindly east wind of England – but a tearing, piercing, lacerating *devil* of a wind: one step outside the door & I am cut in two numbed & speechless: I have never regretted anything more than this horribly disappointing journey: wasting time, money & temper.'

Jaeger was able to tell him that *The Apostles* would be performed in

Cologne on 22 May, in New York and Manchester (under Richter) in February, and in London in March (during the festival). The Elgars had planned to stay in Italy until the end of February but an invitation to dine with Edward VII at Marlborough House early in February provided a welcome excuse to return to Malvern. 'You ask why we return,' Elgar wrote to Schuster, 'simply on account of the weather which has been mostly *unbearable* – eleven days in the house with bitter east winds is too much away from one's books & everything one works with etc. etc. I have had crippling rheumatism & colds & have had the doctor for days. . . . Next week was a convenient time to either give up the house or take it on & the King's pleasant wish to me "clinched" our determination, which was wavering, to fly home. . . . You see I *only* want to go home to finish my work. I cannot work anywhere else.'

No previous English composer had been accorded such a tribute as Elgar received on 14, 15 and 16 March 1904, at the Royal Opera House, Covent Garden. Richter, the Hallé Orchestra and Choir were the performers. On the opening night, *The Dream of Gerontius* was performed (Kirkby Lunn, John Coates, Ffrangcon-Davies), on the second *The Apostles* (Agnes Nicholls, Kirkby Lunn, John Coates, Ffrangcon-Davies, Kennerley Rumford, and Andrew Black) and on the third evening the concert was

> Overture, *Froissart*
> Selections from *Caractacus* (Suzanne Adams, Lloyd Chandos,
>   and Charles Clark)
> *Enigma Variations*
> *In the South* (first performance; conducted by Elgar)
> *Sea Pictures* (Clara Butt)
> *Pomp and Circumstance* Marches Nos. 1 and 2

The theatre was filled on each evening despite the high prices. Jaeger[6] described the festival to Dorabella, who was unable to attend: 'The new overture is *beautiful* & new, & shows a surer touch than almost anything else I know of E.E.'s. *The Apostles* impressed me tremendously though nothing "came off" as the composer meant it. The acoustic defects of the theatre were too great. . . . Elgar had a *rare* time and everything was splendid. Ask dear little Mrs E. She must have been in the 7th Heaven of Happiness. *Such* swells they met, from the Queen downwards. A great time for E.E., & some of us who have believed in him & fought for him (I had to fight hard for him at Novello's) are happy. . . .' Elgar was almost filial in his thanks 'from

---

[6] A reminder of Jaeger's comparative poverty is contained in his letter to Elgar on 24 February 1904: 'I say, *if* the C.G. people give you any tickets which you *can't* do with remember poor "Nim". I really can't afford to pay & I *should* like to hear at least the *Overture* (*In the South*). You have no poorer friend than yours ever Moss.'

my heart' to Richter: 'Without you the thing could not have been done at all, and with you it was a great artistic success and your presence gave it a *dignity* which would otherwise have been wanting.'

The festival, election to the Athenaeum, friendship with his Sovereign, knighthood, acclaim at home and abroad – 1904 was surely Elgar's *annus mirabilis*. 'We really have a composer who, while being recognized by musicians as a master-mind, a man of the highest ideals, and one who does not swerve one inch from his appointed path for the sake of popular favour, can yet command it sufficiently to fill Covent Garden on three nights in succession with people anxious to hear his most serious work,' said a writer in *The World*. It was less than six years since Elgar had found London still unwilling to lend an ear to his serious work and just under five since Richter had introduced the *Variations*. Even now he found a grudging attitude to his work among the London critics, and he was aware that he was looked at askance by his colleagues because busts and plaquettes of him were on sale (some showing him 'conducting his new overture *In the South*') and because he let his name be used in advertisements for pianos and pianolas. Outwardly all was sunlight and glitter: inwardly the same uncertainties, doubts, and misgivings governed his life. Something of 1898-ish petulance is contained in a letter replying to one from Jaeger about the forthcoming Cologne performance of *The Apostles*: 'I don't know *anything* about Köln – except they've asked me to go. I am quite tired of being supposed to "Bless" performances of my things which are not "coached" by me or my advice is asked when it is too late to make any change: but if I *must* go I must – only I don't want to go at all.' He and Alice went on 19 May. On the 21st the soloists failed to arrive for a rehearsal and Elgar, according to Alice's diary, showed his annoyance. He 'wd. not come up and be seen – agitation of the Steinbachs'. But the performance was 'gorgeous' (and others followed at Mainz in November and Rotterdam in December). At the end of July 1904, a month after moving into Plâs Gwyn at Hereford, Jaeger received a letter of a kind he had often had before: 'Everything is dull & goes slowly: & I am tried very much liverwise & am wofully short of money. I really think I must take some violin pupils again: only, as I have not touched it for so long, I should have to begin once more with elementary ones! Such is life & I hate, loathe & detest it.' A week later: 'It's all very well to talk to me about doing Sextetts & Symphonies & all the things I *want* to do, but tell me what & who is going to keep a roof over our heads? nobody thinks of that.'

He wrote in the same vein to Lord Northampton, whose reply from Compton Wynyates on 15 August deserves quotation: 'I don't at all like what you say of yourself. Of course you know best whether you are making progress and whether you are gloomy; and you might possibly be for the moment "flat, stale and unprofitable",[7] but you say "*as ever* unprofitable" and that I have good reason to know is absolutely untrue from the artistic side. You *must* realize that you have in you a special power of bringing upon others the strongest influence for good. You have already used that power in a most remarkable degree. You have moved men's souls to the highest truths of Christianity and then you say in a fit of depression "as ever unprofitable". I can only think of you as a musical apostle, given one of God's greatest gifts.'

Already Elgar was concerned about completing the second part of *The Apostles* trilogy for Birmingham's 1906 festival, for which it was expected. Some as we know was already written and he worked on it in part of 1904. But the need for money was paramount: his new home, his social obligations, his visits to London, all these took money and time. Throughout the winter of 1904 he was low in spirits, although he completed the *Pomp and Circumstance* March No. 3 on 20 November. 'I am better but jolly down,' he told Jaeger in August. At Christmas he wrote to Schuster: 'One line at this time (I *hate* it) because Alice says it's "nice". Oh! Lord. Well! I wish you everything nice and good – all, in short, everything I want and haven't got. I think that's about it. Everything here is flat, stale and distinctly unprofitable. . . . It is foggy and cold and I want to be in Italy. Oh! this dreadful life, if one could but slough it off and *end*, mark you! I don't want to live in any frightful other world – I am so sick of this.'

As I mentioned in the previous chapter, 1905 was a bad year for Elgar. The *Introduction and Allegro for Strings* was written and was a failure. The Birmingham lecture fiasco followed, and then the visit to the United States, undertaken, as he explained to Littleton, because 'my pocket gapes'. While there he was ill because of the excessive heat. In the autumn the Three Choirs Festival, the Mediterranean cruise and the tour with the L.S.O. left little time for creative work, but Alice noted on 29 October that he was 'playing new tunes' and in November and December 1905 he was again writing the oratorio. The whole period was punctuated by 'colds, rheumatism and liver' which occur with such regularity whenever Elgar was disturbed creatively or by trying to live two lives at once that it is clear they stemmed from some psychological hypochondriac cause. On New Year's Eve 1905, he had written to Walford Davies: 'I am the same depressed (musically) being & the same very much alive (chemically & every other 'ally) mortal; keen for everything except my vocation, which I feel is not my vocation by a long tract of desert: I am working away & some of the themes are not bad.' Jaeger, who had spent a large part of 1905 in Switzerland and had been away from Novello's

---

[7] This adaptation of a line from *Hamlet* was one of Elgar's favourite quotations applied to himself.

all year, had voiced his fears in a letter before he went to Davos in January 1905: 'I worry over your *muse*, for I fear greatly we shall get less & less out of you. This is the danger of success artistic & social! (especially social of course). I grieve over it & so do all those who most sincerely love & admire you. We know you *must live* but England *ruins* all *artists*.'[8] Elgar ignored this in his reply but he gave indirect confirmation of its accuracy the following August: 'I know nothing about Apostles pt. 2 or any analysis: if it is ever finished I imagined you might take on the analysis *if* properly recompensed: my life now is one incessant answering of letters & music is fading away.' Nevertheless a few days later he sent to Novello's his part-song *Evening Scene*, to words by Coventry Patmore. This was written in memory of R. G. H. Howson, the bank manager who conducted choirs at the Morecambe festivals – 'the musical soul of the Morecambe affair', as Elgar described him. It was 'my best bit of landscape so far in that line,' he told Jaeger (24 August). 'You won't make anything of it on the P.F. – Morecambe is the place to hear it.' Jaeger found it a 'perfect gem'. It reminded him of Schubert and Goetz, and one can hear what he meant.

Work on what was now known as *The Kingdom* continued over the New Year period of 1906. He was at work on the Prelude from 28 December 1905. Alice's diary a fortnight into the year 1906 records: 'E. not well & depressed. Turning against his work. A. very sad.' His gloom was increased by the Liberals' crushing victory in the general election – 'E. expressed pessimistic views.' By 9 February Alice was writing in this vein: 'Shows distinct traces of trials gone through. Less vivacious and more self-assertive in opinions, etc.' This was the period when Elgar's religious views were undergoing a change from orthodox Catholicism (of a kind) to some kind of humanism. The embittered note of anguish in his letters is more than just his usual theatrical complaining, it is genuine misery of soul. In the margin of his scripture books he wrote comments such as 'Contempt is our lot here'. Although he attended mass more regularly in the first years at Plâs Gwyn than he had at Malvern, this was because Alice hired a taxi to take them and because he liked the priest. But gradually, over the next few years, he went less frequently, though he kept up appearances during Three Choirs weeks.

The beginnings of *The Kingdom* were sent to Novello's by mid-January 1906. Novello's thoughtfully sent a set of proofs to the sick Jaeger and Elgar wrote to him on 26 January: '*Heart Friend*: I have been very evil in not writing to you but I had not the heart to do so. *Today* we hear from Mrs Jaeger that you are seeing the proofs of my new thing: I did not dare to suggest that you *should* see them & I dare

[8] Gustav Holst thought similarly. 'Every artist ought to pray that he may not be a "success",' he wrote to Clifford Bax.

not send my own sheets, so – I could not write. I am so delighted that
the firm send the stuff on to you. So far it is the best thing I've done *I
know*: remember it's not piano music & won't sound well on a tin
kettle.' The chorus 'O ye priests' was written in February and March.

Because of Jaeger's illness and Elgar's depression and his work
against time, there are fewer letters about the genesis of *The Kingdom*.
Jaeger was unfortunate enough to have one of his usual frank
expressions of criticism answered, on 17 March 1906, by Alice in her
most Mrs Proudie-like mood; 'I think yr. surroundings must have
depressed you when you wrote – It is curious that that chorus ['O ye
priests'] did not fire you, it works up all who have heard it to a great
pitch of excitement – & I think you might have given E. some credit
for his fine literary taste & poetic feeling in his selection of words – If
you cannot feel sacerdotalism of any Church, there is the eternal
priestdom of elect souls in all ages, who have stood above the lower
minds & dragged them up. . . . Wait to judge of the new work, &
especially to *remark* to anyone on it till you have heard E. play it – all
those who have, & all those have been real musicians, think it the
most original & greatest thing he has done. . . . He is better, I am
thankful to say, but the strain of the work is very great for him &
makes him very easily worried. . . .'

Elgar answered the next letter in the vein to which Jaeger was more
accustomed: 'Your remarks about those *two* bars in the Intro. were
quite right & they were *never intended* to go in – they are altered now. It
is easy(!) enough to write a melody – except the last two bars: I am
sure it is the difficulty of avoiding a "barn door" ending that has kept
the modern school from symmetrical melody. Meyerbeer is, of
course, notorious for bad endings & Mendelssohn is almost as bad –
or quite as bad in another way.'

In April the Elgars paid their second visit to America where
Edward conducted *Gerontius* and *The Apostles* at the Cincinnati
Festival. While there he continued to work on *The Kingdom*, but his
return to England was saddened by his father's death while he was
away. He was again ill and depressed, and a doctor ordered complete
change. So they went for a holiday to New Radnor where he worked
hard – 'I hear a lovely *tune*,' Alice wrote to Jaeger. 'He has worried so
much over it so it is better not to write about it to him.' The holiday
came to an abrupt end when Elgar slipped on some wet stones and
twisted his knee. He was in pain and became so depressed that he
wrote to Birmingham to ask if they would be prepared to accept half
the work. Luckily he recovered quickly, and he worked at a great
pace completing the composition. The soprano's beautiful aria 'The
sun goeth down' was written during June and July of 1906 ('*very* fine
& wonderful', Alice noted).

'My work nears completion & will send it to you as soon as it is ready', he wrote on 17 July to Rosa Burley, who was now teaching in Portugal. 'I can get about again but have not cycled yet. *I have no one to cycle with.* The world seems very old to me now and all [so] changed . . . I seem *tired* – oh! so tired. Everything is senseless. I was away when your trying time at Malvern came & it is a grief to me to know that I was unable to do anything . . . You know I wish you everything good now & always.'

On 21 July he wrote to Jaeger: 'I am just completing the final revision of my notes & sketches: the whole thing is intentionally less mystic than the A.: the *men* are alive & working & the atmosphere is meant to be more direct & simple.' Composition was finished on 23 July, and the orchestration, begun on 29 July, was completed at an amazing pace: 'I scored 70 pages in the week,' he told Jaeger on 7 August. By 24 August all was finished, and he devoted himself to the Three Choirs Festival at Hereford. At the end of September he went to Manchester for orchestral rehearsals of *The Kingdom* by the Hallé, who were to play at Birmingham, and to choir rehearsals in Birmingham. Jaeger was ordered abroad again and was desolate at missing the first performance. This, on 3 October, was conducted by Elgar, with Agnes Nicholls, Muriel Foster, John Coates, and William Higley as soloists. The hall was packed and standing-room cost a guinea, so great was the interest. Every Elgar first performance was now an Occasion, drawing every leading musician in the land to hear it. *The Kingdom* was successfully received. A report in the *Birmingham Mail* next morning said that, while conducting, 'Sir Edward Elgar's emotions were so stirred by his own wonderful work that, according to the observation of the choristers, tears were streaming down his face several times during the oratorio'. The first London performance was given in November. There was to be no major work for another two years. There were to be no more oratorios.

· · · · ·

Why was Part III of the trilogy never completed? Some, but not much, was written, as he had told Jaeger, and it would have been called *The Last Judgement, The Saints,* or *The Fulfilment.*[9] He wrote to Alfred Littleton on 3 December 1907 that he had given up the idea 'definitely and finally'; 'I am sadly disappointed with the commercial results of the last oratorios, and for the sake of my people must not waste more time in attempting to write high "felt" music.' He wrote to Jaeger in June 1908 in a similar vein: 'I have no intention of completing my oratorio cycle or whatever it is – I am not allowed to beg a dispensation of a benevolent providence who objects to the

[9] In a letter outlining the trilogy, he wrote on 28 October 1903 to Littleton: 'III. The Church of God (or Civitas Dei)! Last Judgment & the next world as in Revelations: each work to be complete in itself.'

world being saved or purified or improved by a mere musician. Of course I have the thing – the biggest of all – sketched but I cannot afford for the sake of others to waste any time on it. Alas!' Schuster and Lord Northampton pleaded with him to complete the trilogy. The latter wrote to him on 16 September 1910: 'I can quite understand that you may foresee a difficulty in getting your great work completed by next year in time for the Birmingham Festival but that does not and cannot mean that you "abandon" the wish to write the third part of the Apostles. . . . The Apostles are part of you and it is complete in you.' Finance was a constant grumble, but there must have been artistic reasons for the abandonment of the scheme. I think there can be little doubt, as he had hinted to Northampton, that he felt this vein was exhausted, and he was probably discouraged, too, by the lack of singers able to fulfil his intentions. Also, as Geoffrey Hodgkins has pointed out,[10] the libretto for the third oratorio was to be taken from the later chapters of the Acts and from *Revelations*, in neither of which is there much dialogue and even fewer dramatic situations. Bonavia, in his essay on Elgar from which I have previously quoted, draws on his experience as critic and player to make a penetrating point about *The Apostles*: 'Except at the Three Choirs Festivals, we have never heard a performance of this work that could be called adequate, while some performances, even when conducted by Elgar himself, fell far short of mere adequacy. It was pitiful to see him sometimes conduct forces utterly incapable of doing justice to his music or to his direction. With the Englishman's dislike of a fuss he would say nothing, but one can well imagine what his feelings must have been and the reason why he often complained to his friends that it was useless to write music that nobody wanted.'

There were fitful efforts at resuming work on the trilogy, usually at the prompting of Henry Embleton, patron of the Leeds Choral Union, the choir Sir Henry Coward conducted. Embleton organized an Elgar festival in Leeds in 1909 and set his heart on obtaining the third oratorio. He asked for it first in June 1914, speaking first to Lady Elgar 'in such a beautiful & delicate way like a friend who really loved E. and his work. E. had a talk when he came in & they clasped hands at parting, E. consenting. A feeling of great quiet joy settled down on us.' Perhaps, if the war had not intervened, the mood might have lasted, but it is dubious. When a movement from *The Spirit of England* was sung in Leeds in 1916, Embleton asked again for Part III, even suggesting March 1918 for the first performance. After Lady Elgar's death in 1920, Embleton and W. H. Reed both urged completion of the trilogy as a means of taking Elgar's mind off his grief. For a time it looked as if they might have some success. In May 1921 Elgar asked Troyte Griffith if he could find him a house in

[10] *Providence and Art*, op. cit., p. 15.

Malvern. 'It is possible that I may be finishing the III part of *The Apostles* & I want to be quiet and uninterrupted *generally*. . . . What I feel now is that I am not young! and I want to complete the great work; – that I want to be near my dearest one's grave; – & that I want you not too far off.' About this time Reed records that 'after much persuasion' Elgar would take a few sheets of music from a cupboard and play them 'grunting away as he played and explaining that the motif used for the "Shofar" in *The Apostles* was going to be used again for the "Last Trump".' But the mood passed again. Nothing new was written. He looked at it again in 1926 but in June 1927 he told Embleton that there was little likelihood of its ever being written. This was the month of his seventieth birthday, and he had seen Queen's Hall half empty for the celebratory concert.

.   .   .   .   .   .

Much has been written elsewhere about the comparative failure of both *The Apostles* and *The Kingdom* to match the success of *The Dream of Gerontius*. There are many practical reasons. Both works, *The Apostles* in particular, are difficult and expensive to perform. For many years Novello's handicapped them by a kind of levy on every performance. They make great demands on the intelligence of performers and listeners. Much of the supreme appeal of *Gerontius* lies in its singleness of idea, its unified and complete dramatic purpose. Neither *The Apostles* nor *The Kingdom* is complete in itself. Both, too, are peculiarly composite. The number of *leitmotive* used is itself an indication of Elgar's preoccupation with the literary side of his work, a dangerous procedure in a work of musical art. His letters to Canon Gorton and to Jaeger reinforce this view. He was excited about his presentation of the characters of Judas, Mary Magdalene, and Peter, but he was an optimist if he thought that an audience would be as absorbed as he was, theologically and intellectually, by such abstruse matters. 'If the words are sufficiently interesting, the music will do,' he had told Jaeger: an extraordinarily fallacious doctrine for a composer to hold. Elgar's comments on Jaeger's analysis of *The Apostles* betray his preoccupation with the structure of the work:

[10 August 1903] I meant to suggest the Earthly Kingdom on p. 36. Here it is (see score also) – the germ – . I really meant to make it feel as if it *grew* out of Peter's first speech (1st bar p. 35) or rather first tune – the Apostles' first ardent feeling. You will find a weak (very) version of the theme (in small notes viola) at 185 & on p. 163 (small notes) by which you learn that the Earthly Kingdom turned out rather badly.

[14 September 1903] Your Judas is splendid – I should have liked a reference to the way a proud sinner at last confronted with the result of his sin is swayed by all sorts of feelings – prompted or suggested by the Psalm he knows so well – ending in blasphemy & despair. I don't like *plot* – it (that theme) figures more the man of action – & it staggers about at the end in a ghastly way.

A major flaw in both oratorios is that they lack that compelling, unifying, poetic impetus which makes *The Dream of Gerontius* such a powerful experience. To borrow a vulgar phrase, we can see the wheels go round in *The Apostles* and *The Kingdom*. The audience cares about Gerontius's drama because Elgar gives him life. Of the Apostles he gives only Judas much life, and in fact Judas dominates the second part of *The Apostles* to the extent that his fate pushes the Crucifixion into the background. It was the human sinner who fascinated Elgar. He saw in Judas another Gerontius, a 'worldly man brought to book'. This was why he accepted Archbishop Whately's portrayal of Judas[11] as a zealot who overreached himself: Elgar was much better at depicting virtue than vice, as he exemplified in the Mary Magdalene episodes of *The Apostles* – Mary's compassionate soliloquy is exquisite, but the chorus's interjectory invocations to 'costly wine' and crowns of rosebuds suggest a naughty escapade at Malvern Girls' School. It is worth pondering that some of the most characteristic Elgarian music in *The Apostles* illustrates Judas's Iago-like 'credo': 'We shall be hereafter as though we had never been . . . our spirit shall vanish as the soft air, and our name shall be forgotten in time.' 'Judas was the clever man-of-the-world type,' Elgar wrote to Thomas Dunhill.[12] 'I have made him . . . a man with brains. Notice his first speech in "By the Wayside"; the simple people say, "He setteth the poor on high", &c. Judas can see just a little farther – the certain result of such a change, "He poureth contempt upon princes".' Elgar's conservatism evidently also favoured this interpretation. Nobody really cares about Elgar's scheme of an oratorio about the Apostles' 'Calling, their Teaching and their Mission' unless the music compels us to care. As he said to Jaeger 'It's what I feel'. These oratorios are at their best when he was 'feeling' and not when he was pasting together his *leitmotive* and his extracts from the Bible and the Apocrypha. It is this latter element, when secular vigour is sharply contrasted with the sensuous appeal of the lyrical passages, that causes the works to sound episodic.

And yet . . . Those who love Elgar's music and are rash enough to try to express their love by the printed word write often of its endless fascination. He is one of a handful of composers whose music can be likened to a crystal on which the sunlight plays so that its shape, its colours, its intensity, seem constantly to vary. The persistent listener to Elgar will understand this metaphor: the notes of the music are fixed, but the listener's reception of them may differ in detail from

[11] *Lectures on the Characters of Our Lord's Apostles*, Richard Whately, Archbishop of Dublin (London, 1893).
[12] Quoted in Dunhill's *Sir Edward Elgar*, p. 200.

year to year, even day to day. The music is so alive – it lives, as a critic wrote years ago, in a perpetual change – that it demands that our response should never be stereotyped and fixed but should be as fluid and flexible as the music itself. It is particularly hazardous to take a prepared position about *The Apostles* and *The Kingdom*. Familiarity with them such as is now possible through recordings breeds not contempt but deeper understanding, increased affection and an intensification of admiration for Elgar's achievement. Is it really valid to complain of the lack of emotional unity in *The Apostles*? Was it meant to be there? The subject demanded treatment different from that accorded to Newman's poem about a dramatic single event, a man's journey into the after-life, and invited music of concentrated illustrative power, even though the musical structure is episodic. The weak passages are those from which Elgar was absent autobiographically. Thus, he was more successful with Judas's anguish than with Mary Magdalene's repentance. There is a parallel here with the comparative feebleness of the 'honest gentlewomen's' theme in *Falstaff* and the perceptiveness of Falstaff's music, yet another self-portrait.

Paradoxically, notwithstanding the thoroughness and serious study which Elgar brought to his task, *The Apostles* may be enjoyed simply as beautiful, often glorious, music without too much concern about its theology or even its 'plot'. Vaughan Williams was mistaken when he wrote to me that he felt that, in *The Apostles*, Elgar was 'oppressed by the fact that he was writing for the Church of England'. In setting the verses from St Matthew upon which the papacy founds its claim to infallibility – 'Thou art Peter, and upon this rock I will build My church' – he knew he was stating a Catholic belief.

The solemn opening phrases of *The Apostles* (belonging harmonically more to the twentieth than to the nineteenth century) foretell the size and grandeur of Elgar's ambitious design: they launch us on a long and eventful journey which is enhanced by the vivid musical depiction of the landscapes we pass: night and dawn in Jerusalem; the stormy Sea of Galilee; darkness at noon. But this is incidental to the spiritual and emotional power of the music as it overwhelms the listener with its compassion, insight and radiance. Orchestrally it is Elgar at his most colourful. *Cockaigne* had just been written, *In the South* and the *Introduction and Allegro* were round the next corner, the symphonies not far away. In addition to a full complement of the 'normal' orchestra, he included bass clarinet, double bassoon, an important part for organ, and, among the percussion, small and large gongs, antique cymbals, glockenspiel, tambourine and triangle.

Judas's aria in Scene 4 is Elgar's greatest single dramatic episode, the text brilliantly compiled at this point. At a time when we know Elgar to have been afflicted by thoughts of suicide, there is extra poignancy in the delicate and beautiful accompaniment to the words 'the breath in our nostrils is as smoke' and the suggestion of the fragility of grasp on life at 'the little spark in the moving of our heart'. When Judas rushes out to kill himself, the chords on the muted horns are of Mahlerian strength and intensity. But if this is the oratorio's zenith, it should not divert our admiration from the harmonic splendour and daring of the opening chorus 'The Spirit of the Lord'; the oriental brightness and exoticism of the sunrise over Jerusalem, no whit inferior in virtuosity of scoring to similar passages in Strauss, Debussy or Ravel; the 'Woodland Interlude' intimacy and conversational style of the Beatitudes; Mary Magdalene's touching 'Hide not thy face from me', with clarinet, flute, and oboe tracing their path amid her words; the fervent prayer of 'Turn you to the stronghold'; the Fauré-like limpidity of the Sepulchre scene; and the elaborate and wholly successful finale, with its glowing new theme for 'Give us one heart', its broad and powerful *nobilmente* climax for the full chorus, and the sublimely tender Alleluias as the four soloists sing of redemption to the phrase of Gerontius's 'Thou art calling me' and the last E flat major chord swells out as if a cathedral acoustic was one of its constituents. Elgar wrote most of this work in favourite Worcestershire haunts to which he had cycled. 'In Longdon Marsh', he wrote on the score and added lines from William Morris's *The Earthly Paradise*:

> To what a Heaven the Earth might grow
> If fear beneath the earth were laid,
> If hope failed not, nor love decayed.

Once again that insistence on hope, but hope was failing him as he worked on *The Kingdom*. This second part of *The Apostles*, as it originally was, is less complex and more consistent in style than its predecessor, and shares several themes with it. The choral writing is even finer than that in the earlier work and plays a greater part in the design of the oratorio. The expressive range of Elgar's writing for voices in *The Kingdom* is perhaps its greatest glory and overshadows the marvellously apt orchestral writing which one tends by now to take for granted. But the choral passages have the strength and sweetness which was Elgar's hallmark and which lift him, even in his conventional moments, head and shoulders above his contemporaries. Only the diehard anti-Elgarian would be unmoved by the Mystic Chorus's 'When the great Lord will', by the splendour of 'O ye priests' and its unexpected and effective dying fall, by the brilliance of the scene in the Upper Room, with the grand striding theme 'He who walketh upon the wings of the wind' and the later agitated questionings of the people 'What meaneth this? These men are full of new wine'. Then there are the duet for the two Marys 'At the Beautiful Gate', a passage of exquisite sensitivity; the noble solo for the bass (Peter) in Part III with its 'Your young men shall see visions and your old men shall dream dreams', a passage as moving as its counterpart in *The Music Makers*; the fervent setting of the Lord's Prayer; and, of course, the soprano's 'The sun goeth down', which begins as a self-communing of peculiar intimacy and rises to a passionate declamation of faith, a dramatic scena on an operatic scale. The oratorio also has an extended Prelude, a fine example of Elgar's ability to create an atmosphere, as he did in *The Dream of Gerontius*, by his orchestral scoring. It is in the Prelude that we first hear – *andante, dolce e solenne* – the aspiring and consolatory theme known as the New Faith with which, two hours later, the oratorio peacefully ends.

Both oratorios are likely to continue to be eclipsed by *The Dream of Gerontius*. But hear them sympathetically performed in their right setting in Gloucester, Worcester, or Hereford, and the predominant impression can be not of their failings but of their beauties, the brilliance and colour of the orchestral writing, the superb understanding of choral sound. Whether one accepts them as a series of musical frescoes, almost pre-Raphaelite in detail, or is stirred simply by the Elgarian-ness of the music, one is likely to agree with Ernest Newman that 'time after time we feel that we are in the presence of a musical gift of the first order'. Arthur Johnstone considered some of the music in *The Apostles* to be 'greater' than that in *Gerontius*, and Samuel Langford wrote that although *The Kingdom* had not the unity of *Gerontius* 'as music it is certainly better', and went on to express the wish that Elgar would 'set himself once more to write living music to a living poem'. Both these judgements seem incomprehensible today, but one can understand how they came to be passed. On the other hand, so distinguished and knowledgeable an Elgarian as Sir Adrian Boult regards *The Kingdom* as a finer work than *Gerontius*, and he has written[13] how he remembered Schuster's saying to him: '*Gerontius* is the work of a raw amateur beside *The Kingdom*.'

These two oratorios marked the end of a tradition. Elgar tried, by a symphonic blood transfusion, to revivify the form and he succeeded only because he was Elgar and could not help pouring great music into whatever design he selected. Perhaps he cogitated the scheme too long so that, as in the similar case of Vaughan Williams's Morality *The Pilgrim's Progress*, he was able to identify himself wholly with his plan but unable, because of this intensity, to give it the objectivity of presentation which *Gerontius*, for all its seeming fluency, possesses to a notable degree. It is significant that devotees of Elgar and Vaughan Williams find in these 'problem works' so much of the essence of the composers that they can ignore the defects, whereas to the

[13] Note by Sir Adrian Boult accompanying H.M.V. recording of *The Kingdom*.

unconverted the obstacles erected by the composers themselves prove unsurmountable. The last two oratorios are the music of a great composer, but they are not consistently great music. When Elgar heard *The Kingdom* in King's College, Cambridge, in June 1907 he told A. C. Benson that 'it was so far behind what he had dreamed of – it only caused him shame & sorrow ...'. Elgar, Benson wrote in his diary, 'seemed all strung on wires ...'. Ernest Newman was remarkably prescient, writing in December 1901, when he suggested that Elgar should abandon choral writing and concentrate on his true medium, the orchestra. *Gerontius* was 'the real Elgar' because the composer had found 'a poem peculiarly fitted to stimulate and become part of him. I very much doubt whether he will be so fortunate again.' After *The Kingdom* had been performed, Newman urged[14] Elgar to abandon the projected third oratorio and to 'turn his mind to other themes ... at present he is simply riding post-haste along the road that leads to nowhere'.

The Kingdom ends with what Diana McVeagh calls 'gentle, drooping chords of acceptance'. These chords are the end of Elgar's religious choral music, and it is tempting to describe the two oratorios as a swan-song. But were they? Did they not show the way to other composers? Elgar gave to sacred choral music the limitless advantage of orchestral virtuosity, with the chorus playing a more subtle rôle, sometimes prominent, sometimes fragmentary, sometimes as commentators. His lesson was not lost on his contemporary juniors. Vaughan Williams, Holst, Walton, even Britten and Tippett, have consciously or unconsciously sown their seeds in the furrow which Elgar ploughed and which he abandoned when he realized that he had exhausted his capacity for inspiration by religious themes.

[14]*Birmingham Post*, 22 March 1907.

11 Full Orchestra

Elgar's mature orchestral output after the *Variations*, its origins, and its varying reception by the public, is best looked at as a whole. But, in returning to the year after the failure of *Gerontius* at Birmingham, it is salutary to recall that not everybody reacted to his music as recalcitrantly as the majority of that festival audience. Bernard Shaw, in his famous *Music and Letters* essay in 1920, remembered his own scepticism 'when the excitement about *Gerontius* began. . . . But when I heard the *Variations* (which had not attracted me to the concert) I sat up and said "Whew!". I knew we had got it at last.' Arnold Bax, in his teens, became an admirer on the strength of the vocal scores of *King Olaf* and *Caractacus*. 'Two years later to this admiration was added reverence, for *The Dream of Gerontius* took utter possession of what religious sense I have.'[1] Ralph Vaughan Williams also first heard the *Variations* at a concert to which some other work had attracted him. When he was in his early thirties he asked Elgar for lessons in orchestration but was told, by Alice, that Elgar did not take pupils. So he studied the scores of the *Variations* and *Gerontius*. 'The results', he wrote years later in his 'Musical Autobiography', 'are obvious in the opening pages of the finale of my *Sea Symphony*', and in another article he cited Gerontius's 'Thou art calling me' as the phrase which influenced him most, in both the *Sea* and *London Symphonies*, adding: 'I am astonished . . . to find on looking back on my own earlier works how much I cribbed from him, probably when I thought I was being most original.' Holst, too, wanted to 'victimize Elgar – bicycle to Worcester to see him a lot'. That was in 1903. The young men of English music recognized his genius from the start. Elgar was, of course, incapable of teaching composition or orchestration, and they would have been sadly disillusioned, and probably snubbed outright, if they had tried to engage him in technical discussions. Shaw's article quoted above recounts the occasion when someone tried to describe to Elgar a phrase of Wagner's by a reference to the chord of the supertonic. 'Elgar opened his eyes wide, and, with an awe which was at least very well acted, asked, "What on earth is the chord of the supertonic?" And then, after a pause, "What *is* the supertonic? I never heard of it".' W. H. Reed, at his first meeting with Elgar in 1902, asked him if he gave lessons in harmony and counterpoint, to be told: 'My dear boy, I don't know anything about those things.'[2]

---

[1] *Farewell, My Youth*, op. cit., p. 29.   [2] *Elgar As I Knew Him*, op. cit., p. 21.

Contrary man! Yet his contrariness was his very nature, and accounts for his ability, despite the embittered despair of his letters to Jaeger in the days after *Gerontius*, to turn directly to the composition of one of his cheeriest orchestral works, the overture *Cockaigne* (*In London Town*). He wrote that it was suggested to him 'one dark day in the Guildhall: looking at the memorials of the city's great past & knowing well the history of its unending charity, I seemed to hear far away in the dim roof a theme, an echo of some noble melody . . .' He completed it on 24 March 1901, and it was first played on 20 June 1901, at a concert of the Philharmonic Society, who had commissioned it. Because it was published by Boosey, during the quarrel with Novello's, Jaeger had not seen it before the first performance and evidently he disliked it because on 26 June Elgar wrote to him 'Never mind about Cockaigne – I think you'll find it all right some day.' Other Germans liked it, notably Felix Weingartner who called it 'a marvellous work' and conducted several early performances in Europe. Richter soon took it up in Manchester and it was an immediate success in America. Arthur Johnstone compared it with the *Meistersinger* overture after what must have been a very fine performance by the Hallé on 24 October 1901, for Elgar wrote to Jaeger: 'Orchestra the finest I ever heard: not so big as Leeds but gorgeous. I conducted Cockayne ar Rehearsal yesterday at Richter's request' and, later, 'Cockaigne was golorious last night under Richter. I don't think any of you London Johnnies know what orchestral playing is until you hear the Manchester orchestra (*in Manchester* that is, their own room). Coriolan was colossal & Brahms's No. 3 Sym. overpoweringly fine.' This, as every provincial knows, is not the thing to write to a Londoner, and his enthusiasm for Richter won him a cool response when in a letter to Canon Gorton after the Morecambe Festival of 1903 – a letter published in the *Musical Times* – he made this observation: 'It is rather a shock to find Brahms's part-songs appreciated & among the daily fare of a district apparently unknown to the sleepy London Press: people who talk of the spread of music in England & the increasing love of it rarely seem to know where the growth of the art is really strong and properly fostered. Some day the Press will awake to the fact, already known abroad and to some few of us in England, that the living centre of music in Great Britain is not London, but somewhere farther North.' Honest, but tactless.

Elgar had sent the score of *Cockaigne* (dedicated 'to my many friends the members of British orchestras') to Richter in August 1901, saying: 'Here is nothing deep or melancholy – it is intended to be honest, healthy, humorous and strong but not vulgar.' The day after the performance in Manchester, writing from Rodewald's house in Liverpool, Elgar thanked Richter for his interpretation, adding 'but it has taught me that I am not satisfied with my music and must do, or rather try to do, something better and nobler. I hope the Symphony I am trying to write will answer to these higher ideals and if I find I am more satisfied with it than my present compositions I shall hope to be allowed to dedicate it to my honoured friend Hans Richter: but I have much to do to it yet.'

Elgar's slender output in 1901 and 1902 – *Cockaigne* and two *Pomp and Circumstance* marches were the bulk of it, apart from the *Coronation Ode* – is partly explained by this reference to a symphony. It was not the only project on which he was engaged. A Norwich Festival cantata was a possibility. Sketches for a work about Falstaff were made in 1902. In 1901 he wrote a *Concert Allegro* for piano for Fanny Davies who played it at St James's Hall, London, on 2 December of that year. Richter described it as 'like a marriage between Bach and Liszt'. Miss Davies had hoped for a concerto but was content, until one should arrive, with 'just a nice "little Elgar"'. After her recital (all of English music), she returned the manuscript to Elgar with pencilled comments and suggestions for making the music lie more easily for the fingers. After each comment she added 'Humbly. F.D.' She borrowed back the manuscript in 1906 for several performances, including one in Manchester where Richter heard it. In the intervening five years Elgar had evidently made some cuts and revisions and had thought of turning it into a piece with orchestra. But he never did, and the manuscript disappeared until 1968 when it was discovered among the papers of the conductor, the late Anthony Bernard. It was edited by Diana McVeagh and John Ogdon for performance (and later recording) by Mr Ogdon on 2 February 1969. While not wholly satisfactory or satisfying, it is recognisably Elgar's work. The virtuoso introduction is typical in its contrast of a bold energetic theme with a tender one. But the principal theme is a passage of two-part invention (hence Richter's Bach comparison) and the second subject (*cantabile*) is what probably suggested Liszt to the conductor.

Schuster had introduced Elgar to Herbert Beerbohm Tree and this led to an invitation to compose incidental music for Stephen Phillips's play *Ulysses*. But this scheme foundered when Elgar, after arranging to visit Phillips at his home at Ashford, travelled there only to find that the playwright had gone out. 'I admire P. as you know,' he wrote to Schuster, 'but I do regret his manners.' In August of 1901, the Elgars went for a week's holiday to South Wales to stay in a cottage rented by Rosa Burley at the Dylan-Thomas-sounding village of Llangranog, Cardiganshire. Here, one day, as Elgar wrote in a programme-note four years later, 'on the cliff, between blue sea and blue sky, thinking out my theme, there came up to me the sound of singing. The songs were too far away to reach me distinctly, but one point common to all was impressed upon me, and led me to think perhaps wrongly, that it was a real Welsh idiom – I mean the fall of a third . . .' He thereupon wrote a tune which he planned as part of a 'Welsh Overture'. But the memory of the singing found its way four years later into the *Introduction and Allegro for Strings*, and other sketches were used for *The Apostles*. Elgar, as will by now be readily appreciated, was an impulsive, responsive man, setting down uninhibitedly in his letters the reaction of the moment. But as a composer he was as cool-headed and as long-sighted as Beethoven. The strength of his music is that it is emotion recollected in tranquillity. Like Beethoven he would store up a musical idea for years until it found its right form, its right setting, and its right perspective. It has already been seen how ideas for *The Apostles* were sketched years before work began in earnest. The various 'Moods of Dan', Sinclair's bulldog, inscribed between 1897 and 1903 in Sinclair's visitors' book are in themselves proof of the long gestation of certain ideas: themes for *Gerontius* written in 1898, the opening of *In the South* in 1899, part of *Crown of India* in 1903 and of 'For the Fallen' in 1902. Themes from Powick asylum days occur in mature works. Nearly all Elgar's major works grew slowly, and nowhere is this more evident than in the case of the Second Symphony. Moreover he was an economical composer and never let good ideas go to waste if they could not be accommodated in the context for which they were first planned. Possibly this, rather than any atavistic desire to keep the *Salut d'Amour* fires burning, accounts for the continued appearance throughout his career of short pieces for orchestra. The two *Dream Children* idylls of 1902, for example. Were they perhaps discarded fragments of the 'Gordon' symphony or of some other abandoned project? They are of a particular touching intensity, like *Chanson de Nuit*, and have a personal intimacy. The title is from Charles Lamb's essay, from which Elgar quoted a passage in the score:

And while I stood gazing, both the children gradually grew fainter to my view, receding, and still receding till nothing at last but two mournful features were seen in the uppermost distance which, without speech, strangely impressed upon me the effects of speech; 'We are not of Alice, nor of thee, nor are we children at all . . . We are nothing; less than nothing, and dreams. We are only what might have been . . .

Rosa Burley remarks that the use of 'Alice' gave the passage a special significance for Elgar and says that the two pieces were to be dedicated 'to a certain lady who was a friend of the Elgars'. She meant Alice Stuart-Wortley. But Elgar, perhaps for obvious reasons, put no dedication on this score.

The first signs of an Elgar symphony date from 1898 when he considered a kind of 'Eroica' based on General Gordon. 'The thing possesses me,' he had told Jaeger, 'but I can't write it down yet.' By February 1899 he was 'making a shot at it' and in November of that year admitted to having 'written a *theme*'. Early in 1901, Alice Elgar wrote to Jaeger that 'there could be no *nobler* music than the symphony. I long for it to be finished & have to exist on scraps – Do write & hurry him, it always does *some* good.' Rodewald had also tried to hurry him by offering to relieve Elgar of financial responsibility during its composition, but Elgar would not be hurried – he knew better than to think he could hurry a symphony, and in any case he was too proud to accept money from friends. In the autumn of 1901 Jaeger was telling him how anxious Henry Wood was to conduct the symphony at the Leeds Festival but Elgar replied that 'there's not the slightest chance of my doing it, I fear', though rashly saying 'the festival shall have it, of course'. This was the beginning of the muddle and acrimony with the Leeds authorities which has already been described. From Alassio in January 1904, when there were rumours that the symphony was to be played in Essen, Elgar wrote to Jaeger: 'I wish my friends wd. not gossip about me: Ettling wrote from *Weingartner* asking for first German perfce. of sym. promising Munich Berlin etc. So I wrote to *W*. saying it wd. not be ready for him this season etc. etc. Then apparently Ettling writes off to Pitt! Bless us all!' He elucidated this a few weeks later when he said that he had had 'chiding and angry' letters because 'somebody suggested that the future Symphony might be produced at *Essen!*' He was tempted by the idea of a Weingartner first German performance in Berlin or Munich – 'I suppose no introduction *cd.* be better possibly' – but he ruled out a first performance for Essen because of his long-standing promise to Richter. Just how much of a symphony was written by 1904 it is not possible to know. Dorabella saw a fat note-book labelled 'Symphony' at Craeg Lea in 1901, and was played 'scraps' of it. Her book gives no clue to the identity of the scraps, and she may have been inaccurate in her recollection of the date. But a letter from Elgar to Richter on 11 October 1903 ends '. . . we had a peaceful & happy journey & all the incidents are being worked into the Symphony in E flat dedicated to Hans Richter . . .' An early version of an important theme in the finale of the Second Symphony

Ex.6

dated about 1903–4 is marked 'Hans himself!' Parts of the slow movement of No. 2 date from May 1904, while Elgar's mind was still full of the shock of Rodewald's death six months earlier. These sketches are parallel with some for a projected second *Cockaigne* overture, in C minor, sub-titled 'City of dreadful night'.

For a while, too, in 1901 Elgar mentioned to Jaeger work on a string sextet, but this was soon lost among such remarks as 'Oh! my string Sextett – & I have to write rot & *can* do better things'. If by 'rot' he meant his music for the play *Grania and Diarmid* by W. B. Yeats and George Moore he was doing himself an injustice. This began with a request from Moore, who had heard Elgar's music at a Leeds Festival, for a horn-call to be used in the play which Frank Benson was to produce at the Gaiety, Dublin, in the autumn of 1901. Eventually Elgar wrote the horn-call, incidental music (37 bars), and a magnificent funeral march which is scored with eerie resonances. 'I've been awfully busy writing,' he wrote to Jaeger on 1 October 1901, '& have finished the short incidental music to that Irish play: there's a funeral march which you wd. like & it sounds big and weird – not deep in the orchl. whirlwind sense.' He thought he might use the music later for an opera, but nothing came of the idea. He hoped, too, that the march might become a best-seller and asked Novello's through Jaeger for £100 for it. It would, he said, 'arrange in every possible way & there's now room for a new dead march, I think'. Perhaps with one eye on the commercial aspect he dedicated the score to Henry Wood, and he conducted it himself in several cities, including Liverpool where, he told Jaeger on 30 December 1902, it 'made a tremendous impression. . . . *When* is it to be published?' He knew he had written something good. The march is a noble, elegiac piece, with a central trio of symphonic cast, and there is a song to a poem by Yeats, 'There are seven that pull the thread', which is as delicate and atmospheric as anything he wrote, with his familiar poetic use of the clarinet and a phrase that is another obvious clue to work progressing on sketches for the Second Symphony. When in 1903 Elgar asked Yeats's permission to publish the song, the poet agreed 'with great pleasure' and described the *Grania* music as 'wonderful in its heroic melancholy'. When George Moore heard the march at rehearsal he wrote: 'Elgar must have seen the primeval forest as he wrote, and the tribe moving among the falling leaves – oak leaves, hazel leaves, for the world began with oak and hazel.'

Insufficient interest has been shown in the knowledge that Weingartner, Steinbach, and other German conductors of the day took up *Cockaigne* so promptly, a work that is generally regarded as thoroughly 'English' in atmosphere, especially in its evocation of brass bands and military bands marching through London streets. (Its reflection of that peculiar strain in Londoners which finds an outlet in their devotion to pearly kings and queens is not the least of its pictorial virtues.) Did they see deeper into it than did the English music critics and even, perhaps, Elgar himself? With their European background and their knowledge, if not appreciation, of Mahler's early symphonies, did they, even subconsciously, realize what is obvious today: that there is a Mahlerian contrast of banality (some would say vulgarity) and philosophy in *Cockaigne*? The particular is given a universal vision. The military band approaches and recedes, and as it does so, as the march rhythm in the bass fades, we hear not just a vivid sound-picture of London at the turn of the century but the fading of a world. The strings weave mysteries and the horn is the spirit of romance. The music exists at two levels.[3] When it came to *In the South* in 1904 they showed similar interest, though there the shadow of Richard Strauss was probably what they recognized. When the Elgar Festival of 1904 was planned there was still hope that its focal point would be a symphony. But when he himself realized this was impossible, Elgar also realized that such a unique and important occasion ought to be able to boast a new work. So from Alassio in January 1904 we find him writing to Schuster: 'I have had to write to Higgins etc. & say that the symphony is impossible – I have partly promised a concert overture for the festival, "In the South" or some better title if you can suggest one.' The score was finished when Elgar returned to Plâs Gwyn. The last pages went to Jaeger on 21 February and Richter rehearsed it in Manchester on 9 March. That evening Elgar wrote to Jaeger: 'That Overture is *good* & the Roman section absolutely *knocking over*. They [the Hallé Orchestra] read it like angels & the thing *goes* with tremendous energy & life. . . .' Later in the year he again wrote: 'I *love* it: it's alive!' He had dedicated it to Schuster, in gratitude for the materialization of the Elgar Festival. There is a letter from Elgar to Schuster's sister Adela, written after his death in 1927, in which Elgar says that he had failed to find something 'radiant, bright, and uplifting for dear Frank's memorial stone' but adding: 'I have said in music . . . what I felt long ago – in F.'s own overture *In the South* and again in the final section of the Second Symphony – both in the key he loved most I believe (E♭), warm and joyous with a grave radiating serenity'.

In the South is certainly all that Elgar intended. It was a success at its first performance, and after Richter had conducted it later in Manchester Arthur Johnstone referred to 'a kind of graphic power, arising from far-reaching play of the imagination. In thematic originality it is perhaps more strongly stamped with Elgar's originality than any other work. Its whole tone, atmosphere, and colouring are something essentially new in music. . . . The *grandioso* theme [the "Roman section"] . . . is a most extraordinary piece of musical expression of a kind scarcely ever foreshadowed by any other composer, except once or twice by Beethoven. . . .' Other critics

[3] Mahler conducted the *Variations* and *Sea Pictures* (except no. 5) in New York, 1910–11.

pointed out the resemblances to Strauss's *Aus Italien* and to both
composers' use of divided strings. The resemblance is too obvious for
the point to be worth making; but if *In the South* is in the Straussian
mould – and there is no denying that it is, though it is Strauss very
much à la Elgar[4] – it is *Don Juan* that seems to be the model both in
exuberance and reflectiveness. It is another example of the potent
effect of landscape and historical suggestion on Elgar's musical
imagination. He admitted that the idea for the work – which he ought
to have called a tone-poem instead of an 'overture', misleading
conductors to expect an eight-minute piece – came from the 'thoughts
and sensations of one beautiful afternoon in the Vale of Andora'. On
the manuscript he wrote several poetic quotations: from Tennyson's
The Daisy:

> What hours were thine and mine
> In lands of palm, and southern pine
> In lands of palm, of orange-blossom
> Of olive, aloe, and maize and vine.

From Byron's *Childe Harold*:

> . . . a land
> Which *was* the mightiest in its old command
> And *is* the loveliest . . .
> Wherein were cast . . .
> . . . the men of Rome!
> Thou art the garden of the world.

In the section dealing with the past glories of Rome he 'endeavoured
to paint the relentless and domineering onward force of the ancient
day, and to give a sound-picture of the strife and wars, the "drums
and tramplings" of a later time', and again quotes Tennyson:

> What Roman strength Turbia show'd
> In ruin, by the mountain road.

In the South is the most richly, colourfully, and glamorously scored
of all Elgar's works, rivalling Strauss in its arrogant mastery of every
kind of orchestral effect. It is, in effect, a tone-poem, as *Cockaigne* is,
and its comparative neglect for many years was always incomprehensible, for conductors and orchestras love a relatively short
work which demands both executive virtuosity and interpretative
insight. Nothing in Elgar is more thrilling and uplifting than the
leaping opening – sketched in July 1899 as 'Dan triumphant (after a
fight)' – divided strings and brass crowning all. This effervescent start

---

[4] Elgar wrote to Jaeger on 13 August 1904, à propos Jaeger's analysis of the overture:
'I do not think I should put that about Strauss at the beginning – not necessary – S.
puts music in a very low position when he suggests it must hang on some
commonplace absurdity for its very life.'

is followed by a reflective pastoral episode in which the shepherd's piping (clarinet) is answered by an *espressivo* phrase suggested to him by the name of the town Moglio, which amused him and Carice. Then follows the agitated, lumbering episode of the ancient Romans, *grandioso* and A flat minor, containing some of Elgar's boldest harmonic excursions as he recalls past grandeur together with the 'drums and tramplings'. Elgar builds a very brilliant passage in this striding theme before it merges, on muted strings, into the *Canto popolare* episode. This haunting melody (original and so Elgarian, but Italian in spirit) is given to the solo viola as a salute to Berlioz from 'Edward in Italy'. It sounds even more romantic as a horn solo before its return, over a drumroll, on the viola. But it is suddenly cut off as the brilliance of the opening returns. The end is sheer poetry. The *nobilmente* theme from the introduction is transformed into a moving 6/4 melody and gradually grows more impassioned until it is worked up to a final climax on strings, brass and glockenspiel in the ascendant, crowned by triumphant brass.

A postscript to the initial success of *In the South* in 1904 was that Elgar was asked by Novello's later that year to make various arrangements of the *Canto popolare* section. So it appeared, subtitled *In Moonlight*, for small orchestra and in versions for organ, piano, piano with violin or viola or cello or clarinet, and piano trio. There was a song also called *In Moonlight*, for high or medium voice, for which Elgar fitted lines from a poem (1822) by Shelley, 'An Ariette for Music', starting at the line 'As the moon's soft splendour'.

When Herbert Howells asked Elgar for the secret of his understanding of the strings, he was told: 'Study old Handel. I went to him for help ages ago.' This understanding supremely distinguished his next major orchestral work, the *Introduction and Allegro for Strings* of 1905, although its opus number, 47, is three earlier than that of *In the South*. His 'Welsh tune', noted during that 1901 Cardigan Bay holiday, had been brought back to his mind in 1904 'by hearing, far down our own Valley of the Wye, a song similar to those so pleasantly heard on Ynys Lochtyn. The singer of the Wye unknowingly reminded me of my sketch. . . . Although there may be (and I hope there is) a Welsh feeling in the one theme – to quote Shakespeare again: "All the waters in Wye cannot wash the Welsh blood out of its body" – the work is really a tribute to that sweet borderland where I have made my home.' On 28 October 1904, Jaeger wrote to Elgar suggesting that he should write a short new work for the recently formed London Symphony Orchestra. 'Why not a *brilliant* quick String Scherzo, or something for those fine strings only? a real bring down the house *torrent* of a thing such as Bach could write. . . . You might even write a *modern Fugue* for strings, or *strings & organ*! That would sell like cakes.' Elgar was abroad at the end of November 1904, visiting Mainz to hear Fritz Volbach conduct *The Apostles* and Cologne where Steinbach conducted *In the South*.[5] Then he went to Rotterdam for a performance of *The Apostles* on 2 December. Jaeger, writing from Davos in January 1905, prodded him for an orchestral work for Julius Buths – 'But it must be a Uraufführung, see? First production anywhere. Now, seeing what B. has done for your fame, I think you ought to see whether you can't do something. But it must be of your *Best* entre nous, because you will be matched with Mahler whose 3rd symphony with chorus will form an important part of the Fest. most likely.' (The Lower Rhine Festival, June 1905. Mahler's Second Symphony was played.) Elgar ignored this request, but Alice noted on 22 January 'E. trying string orch. piece'. Elgar replied to Jaeger on 26 January: 'I'm doing that string thing in time for the Sym. Orch. concert. Intro: & Allegro – no *working-out* part but a devil of a fugue instead. G major & the sd. divvel in G minor with all sorts of japes & counterpoint.' The L.S.O. concert was to be on 8 March. As usual when composing Elgar protested ill-health – 'I am at my wits' end to know how to do anything & have been having one liver chill after another,' he wrote to Schuster on 13 February (the day he completed the *Introduction and Allegro*) but added 'The new Pomp and C. is a devil & the string thing most brilliant with a real tune in it however.' Schuster, most loyal and generous of all Elgar's patrons, had had a hand in promotion of the concert, which was an Elgar programme: *In the South*, the *Grania* Funeral March, *Sea Pictures* (Ada Crossley), the first performance of the third *Pomp and Circumstance* march, *Cockaigne*, the first performance of the *Introduction and Allegro*, and the *Variations*. Elgar conducted. Alice told Jaeger that 'many people think it [the *Introduction and Allegro*] the finest thing he has written, the 4t. comes in with so beautiful an effect, the peroration towards the end *is* fine. The new March is *thrilling* – the most pacific friends were ready to fight! The critics – some of them – of course were frightened at it, but happily the audiences judge for themselves.'

The *Introduction and Allegro* was repeated at Queen's Hall on 19 March, but was coolly received. When Dorabella visited Plâs Gwyn in April and asked when the new work was to be played again, she was met with what she called Alice's 'stony image' look and the reply: 'Nothing has been settled yet. I think you had better not ask.' Elgar told her: 'That's good stuff. Nothing better for strings has ever been done – and they don't like it.' Arthur Johnstone's untimely death in December 1904 had deprived Elgar of his most under- standing and perceptive critic, but Johnstone's successor in Manchester was Ernest Newman, then at work on a book on Elgar. It is from his notice in the *Manchester Guardian* of Richter's first Hallé

5 Sir Donald Tovey in his analytical note on *In the South* disclosed that Steinbach had thought the work 'patchy'.

performance (7 December 1905) of the work that we know of a remarkable incident that tells us not only that audiences were slow to respond to the music but that Richter was quick to appreciate its qualities, although he 'treated it more staidly [than Elgar] without the lithe flexible convolutions of the melody. . . . There was a moderate amount of applause, probably intended for the orchestra. . . . Dr Richter, however, jumped at the applause and, to everyone's astonishment, played the whole thing through again. It was more than a good many people had bargained for. . . .' Good for Dr Richter. But the work stayed out of Hallé and other orchestras' programmes for many years. For instance, after a performance at a Philharmonic concert in 1906 it was not played in the Society's programmes until Beecham conducted it in November 1937. It was the rise in standards of orchestral playing and rehearsal achieved after the outbreak of the Second World War that enabled this masterly work to gain the position it now holds, when it is generally regarded, even by those not otherwise favourably disposed towards Elgar, as one of the three or four greatest compositions for strings. Dunhill, in his book published in 1938, acclaimed it as a masterpiece yet ended his discussion of it with the words 'It deserves to be far more widely known than it is.' Fortunately such a statement is no longer necessary. It is one of Elgar's finest creations, spacious, elusive, lyrical. The majestic opening, which as in all of Elgar's works goes straight to the point without any preliminaries, is as strong an utterance as he ever made, and is perfectly contrasted with the next, gentler, rising and falling theme (the basis of the Allegro section) over which in the manuscript Elgar wrote (from *Cymbeline*) 'Smiling with a sigh'. Then comes the 'Welsh tune', for solo viola, characterized by a falling third. Instead of a development section Elgar wrote a fugue, but it is a wayward, exciting fugue, far removed from any academic con- notations, a romantic, emotional fugue which Bach would not have been ashamed to own. The weaving of the thematic material, the brilliant building-up of tension and the equally masterly relaxation of it so that the music slides gently back into the Allegro section, these are the hallmarks of a master-composer who was able to exploit every possibility of the medium he had selected. Strings had rarely sounded so sonorous, capable of such variety of expression and colour, until this work was written. It was the forerunner of many works of a similar kind and served as the model (string quartet and string orchestra) for another English masterpiece written five years later, Vaughan Williams's *Tallis Fantasia*. The subtle contrast and interplay of quartet and full strings go far beyond the concerto grosso: they opened up possibilities in the employment of string tone which have had their influence on most English music written since this superb piece was first heard.

When the anxiety of the first performance of *The Kingdom* was over, Elgar's health and morale were low. He was too sensitive a mortal to be fitted for the rôle of controversialist, and the arguments in the newspapers and journals about his Birmingham lectures depressed him and jangled his nerves. Only a week after the first performance of the oratorio Elgar wrote to Schuster: 'I don't seem to realise that I have written anything & am trying to forget all about it & myself.' He could not settle to any creative work. With Alice he went in December to Llandrindod Wells and after Christmas, despite anxiety about the financial aspect, to Capri, Naples, and Rome for most of the first two months of 1907. Canon Gorton travelled with them and they were joined by Schuster. For the first weeks Elgar was ill and worried about money. He visited Axel Munthe on Capri and it was there, at Quisisana, on 15 January, that he sketched an *Andantino* for violin, mandoline, and guitar, the amusing origin of which was described by Alice in a letter: 'This morning E. went over to the barber's to have his hair cut, the barber was always playing the mandoline so E. took up a violin and they performed a duet, then a guitarist arrived and they performed a trio brilliantly to a delighted audience. E. so gay and amused. I do trust it will do him good being here.'

In Rome Elgar was pleased to be fussed over by the Italian composers Perosi and Sgambati. Perosi showed him through the Vatican and St Peter's. While in Rome Elgar wrote the four part-songs of op. 53 to words by Tennyson, Byron, Shelley, and Elgar himself. These were successors to the op. 45 set of *Five Part-Songs from the Greek Anthology*, for male voices, first sung in London in April 1904, both works being the direct result of his connection with the fine competition choirs at the Morecambe Festival. Elgar's part-songs are as good as most of his solo songs are inferior. The *Greek Anthology* pieces are among his best, with a strong feeling for the words and many arresting features of colour and humour. The delicious asides of 'It's oh! to be a wild wind' are a contrast to the vigour of 'Yea, cast me from heights' and the vividness of 'After many a dusty mile'. It will be found that in all his part-songs – notably the beautiful 'My love dwelt in a Northern Land' of 1889, the elaborate test-piece for male voices 'The Reveille' of 1907, the unearthly 'Owls' of 1907, and the richly wrought 'Go, Song of Mine' of 1909 – the authentic accent and tone of Elgar are to be heard.

One of the part-songs of op. 53 was to Byron's words

> Deep in my soul that tender secret dwells,
> Lonely and lost to light for evermore,
> Save when to thine my heart responsive swells,
> Then trembles into silence as before.

This song was dedicated to Mrs Julia Worthington, an American whom the Elgars had met in New York in 1905 and who had visited England in the following two summers. She was wealthy and unhappily married, with a villa in Italy, and was a leading American hostess – 'a sort of Duchess . . . socially clever and a friend to all the distinguished people', J. B. Yeats described her in a letter to his son the poet, adding: 'She is an intimate friend of the musician Elgar.' The Elgars returned from Italy to Hereford on 26 February and four days later Elgar left for his third visit to America. Alice stayed behind. He conducted *The Apostles* and *The Kingdom* in New York and then went to conduct in Chicago, Cincinnati, and Pittsburgh. 'After our sweet & delightful time in Capri it is a hideous change to be in western America,' he wrote to Mrs Gorton, wife of the Canon. While in New York, he told Delius many years later, he refused a request to lead a meeting to pray for the failure of Richard Strauss's *Salome*! He sailed for home on 20 April. He had no big work on hand but he wrote his two single and two double chants on 24 May and completed the fourth *Pomp and Circumstance* March on 7 June. He had looked out the music he had written for his brothers and sisters when he was twelve and they had performed their play 'The Wand of Youth'. He had re-scored some of it for Powick in 1879–80, but now he worked on it again. He wrote to Jaeger, who was in Germany in another attempt to regain his strength, on 28 May: 'I shall be fifty next week so they tell me, but I don't know it. I have my pipe & the bicycle & a heavenly country to ride in – so an end. I take no interest whatever in music now & just "edit" a few old boyish MSS – music is off.'

A few days later he added a P.S. to a letter from Alice to Jaeger: 'I'm busy & must not use my eyes much so I am doing trifles: poor things but mine own boyish thoughts. I wax old but not infirm. . . . The first pt. of the 4th march is good: the middle *rot* but pleasing to march to.' During this May he also composed the part-song 'How calmly the evening'. On the day of his fiftieth birthday, 2 June, he composed the part-song *Love*. Its second verse may be interpreted as a tender tribute to Alice herself:

> In my time of outer gloom
> Thou didst come, a tender lure;
> Thou, when life was but a tomb,
> Beamedst pure.

Alice noted in her diary that the birthday was 'trying to him, as usual'. All summer his eyes gave him trouble, but the work on *The Wand of Youth* seemed to reawaken deeper impulses and by 27 June Alice was able to write in her diary that 'E.' was 'playing great beautiful tune': the opening of a symphony, not the symphony he had 'tinkered' with for eight years, but something new. It is not fanciful to deduce that this was sparked into being by the 'boyish MSS' of *The Wand of Youth*.

He found he could re-charge his batteries, as it were, by re-living the days of his boyhood when he dreamed of music and thought in music. The delicate and fantastic mood of the exquisite 'Fairy Pipers' is related to the Adagio of the First Symphony; in the 'Sun Dance' and 'Serenade' the symphony's second movement stirs in the womb. On 2 August, Alice recorded, he 'wrote lovely river piece. You cd. hear the wind in the rushes by the water.' The 'Sunbeam Dance' was orchestrated on 8 August and the first suite completed three days later. On 22 September, when Littleton visited Plâs Gwyn, he played him what Alice called his 'gorgeous new tune' and some ideas for a violin concerto for which Fritz Kreisler had asked him in 1906. He also worked from 26 October to 9 November on a string quartet for Brodsky. Then, as was the usual pattern with Elgar's composing, he seemed to 'dry up' and come to a halt. So he became depressed again. 'I see nothing ahead,' he wrote to 'Windflower'. He attended the festivals at Gloucester, Cardiff, and Leeds, then decided to spend the winter in Rome, not as an extravagance but because it was cheaper to rent a villa in Italy and live quietly there than to meet the obligations in England of being Sir Edward Elgar. He told Jaeger he hoped to see him while passing through London 'on my way to economize "in the South"' and from Rome he wrote to Troyte: 'One thing that gives me a little satisfaction over our exile (for it is that although "meant pleasant") is that you will be sorry we are gone.' But before he and Alice left, on 5 November, he made a kindly gesture to Jaeger, whose end was obviously not far away, racked as he was by fits of coughing and physically changed so that it distressed Elgar to see him. 'I have today,' he wrote to 'my very dear Nim' on 25 October, 'asked Messrs. Novello to transfer all rights & royalties in the Analyses of Gerontius, Kingdom & Apostles to you from the last making up of the accounts. I am very much "wanted" by my poor relations, just now more than ever [his brother-in-law Will Grafton was dying] so I apologize to you for not making the transaction retrospective: this I wished to do but *cannot*. So forgive your friend & please accept the little I can do.'

In Rome they rented 38A Via Gregoriana. 'Here is my Mecca & I love it *all*', he wrote to Schuster at Christmas. 'Note the fact that I am pagan not Xtian at present & I love the pinocchi & the food & the wine! . . . Yes, I am trying to write music, but the bitterness is that it pays not at all & I must write & arrange what my soul loathes to permit me to write what *you* like & I like. So I curse the power that gave me gifts & loathe them now & ever. I told you a year ago I could see no future: now I see it & am a changed man & a *dour* creature. But not to you dear Frank, not to you. Bless you.'

What his soul loathed at this time, December 1907, must have been *A Christmas Greeting*, to Alice's words, written for Sinclair's choristers at Hereford Cathedral and quoting from the 'Pastoral Symphony' in *Messiah*, and a setting of Bret Harte's *The Reveille*, a part-song for the Blackpool Musical Festival of 1908. Yet in this month he sketched the first movement of the symphony, telling Littleton that he doubted if the work would be finished, it was too noisy to work in Rome. They were entertained by the British Ambassador at the Embassy, where the Brodsky Quartet played, and by the American composer John Alden Carpenter. Elgar had French lessons and went to the theatre with Julia Worthington. In February he had influenza, but before leaving Italy in May he went several times to the opera and visited Florence. They were in Rome during a two-day general strike after police had fired on crowds in the Piazza di Gesù who used the funeral of an Italian workman as the pretext for a Socialist demonstration. Elgar and his daughter walked to the piazza afterwards. 'Bright sun that a.m. found the streets occupied in every direction with troops, bayonets & loaded rifles,' he wrote home to his niece May Grafton. 'Bloody "war". I saw the poor human stains on the stones & the bullet marks on the walls. . . . It was wonderful to walk over that great empty square with soldiers ready for the fray all round. And all the horses of the cavalry picketed on one side.' He also visited Sgambati, 'dear man', who showed him some historic possessions given him by Liszt. He told Jaeger about them: 'The first copy of the score *Siegfried Idyll* sent by Wagner to Liszt in Rome with a little writing on the title. Also the *first* exemplar of *Faust* (Berlioz) sent by B. to Liszt! & above all (1868) the full score *Meistersinger* sent by W. to L. with words & the title "De profundis clamavi!" at the top, a date etc. below & *Richard*. How wonderful to see and touch.'

But this same letter, dated 26 April, dealt with more personal matters in a way with which poor Jaeger was only too familiar after ten years: 'I have made a sort of name by writing some big things & can only get *commissions* to write rot – ah! ha! I must *talk* to you some day about my avoiding work on big things – I have too many people *now* alas! (& the clog gets heavier every day) to allow me to think of anything I would wish to do: it is painful but it is the only reward I get . . . I cannot afford to get a *quiet* studio where I might have worked & my whole winter has been wasted for the want of a few more pounds: it seems odd that any rapscallion of a painter can find a place for his "genius" to work in when a poor devil like me who after all *has* done something shd. find himself in a hell of noise & no possible escape! I resent it bitterly but can do nothing. It is just the same now at Hereford, noise has developed in the neighbourhood – I dodged it doing the *Kingdom* at great expense by going to Wales, but I can't do it again: my lovely works do not pay the rent of a studio!'

Rome itself, he told Walford Davies,[6] had deeply interested him

[6] Letter dated 15 July 1908.

III Elgar aged 23

IVa Birchwood, in summer

IVb On the Wells Road, Malvern.
Elgar with his daughter Carice, and
Troyte

V 'My dear Nimrod'. Letters
between Elgar and Jaeger (below)
about *The Dream of Gerontius*,
1900

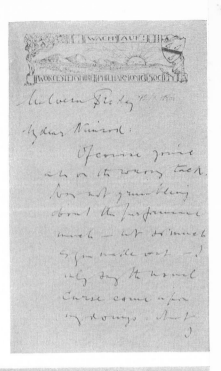

VI Elgar's early Champions

VIa Augustus Jaeger at Bettws y
Coed, 1903

VIb Hans Richter, photographed
by Elgar at Bayreuth in 1902

VIc Alfred Rodewald, with 'Sam',
at Bettws, 1903

VII Alice Elgar

VIII Edwardian afternoon at The Hut, Bray. Elgar with Frank Schuster, two unidentified ladies and Lord Northampton (right)

IX Gloucester Festival, 1922. Left to right: Herbert Brewer, Elgar, Lord Gladstone, Henry Hadow, Hugh Allen, Stanford

X Alice Stuart-Wortley. Windflower, the 'soul' of Elgar's
Violin Concerto. A portrait by her father, Sir John Millais

XIa 'Brinkwells', the cottage near Fittleworth, Sussex

XIb The Music Room at Severn House, Hampstead

XII Elgar's 'first idea' for *The Dream of Gerontius*

XIIIa With W. H. Reed

XIIIb With Bernard Shaw

XIII Elgar in the 1920s.

XIV Elgar conducting massed choirs in Parry's *Jerusalem* at the opening of the British Empire Exhibition, Wembley, April 1924

XV Elgar with his brother Frank at the Gloucester Festival, 1922

XVI With Marco

and he longed to return, 'but I could not reconstruct the ancient period or the renaissance: I could only efface the present by peopling the place with folk living from 1650 to 1800. Evelyn, Horace Walpole etc. etc. I felt a classic failure but learned much & want to learn more. Music was practically out of being . . . they asked me to conduct a concert & in fact advertised my name but I heard the orchestra & fled. . . . I am trying to work & am covering sheets of paper to no good end.' But this was not true. From 13 June, a month after the return from Italy, he was hard at work on the symphony. 'E. writing Symphony', Alice wrote in her diary, adding 'E. deep in his musics. Lovely weather'. Elgar wrote to Jaeger: 'I can't answer your letter at this moment. I can't say I have anything more *important* to do but it must be done & done now. Oh! such a tune.' And of course Alice agreed and wrote to their old and ailing friend two days later 'E. sends his love . . . & wants to say to you the "Sym. is A.1"'. It is *gorgeous*, steeped in beauty.' He worked through July, interrupting himself only with bicycle rides, bird-watching and tending his daughter Carice's rabbits. He worked on the Scherzo on 4 and 5 August, then went to Ostend for five days to conduct his own works and to London for a Promenade Concert of his music. On 22 August Alice's diary says: 'E. playing *La Tosca* and going on orchestrating slow movement'. The Adagio was completed on 23 August and the finale sketched on 27 and 28 August. For relaxation he went back to an interest of his teens, chemistry, and turned part of an outhouse into a laboratory which he called 'The Ark'. There he would lose himself among phials and test tubes. He enjoyed 'experiments' and blew up a water butt with one of his concoctions. He made soap and he invented a 'sulphuretted hydrogen machine' which was patented as the Elgar S.H. Apparatus. And on 25 September he finished the symphony, and collapsed with nervous exhaustion. It was dedicated, as he had always promised it would be, 'to Hans Richter, Mus. Doc. True artist and true friend'. 'You *will* like some of my latest phase,' he wrote to Schuster, 'so do I.'

The first rehearsal of the Symphony was in Queen's Hall on 23 November. It was played for the first time at a Hallé concert in the Free Trade Hall, Manchester, on 3 December 1908. Jaeger was too ill so the programme-note was written by Ernest Newman, and Walford Davies also wrote a preliminary article about it. Elgar told him: 'There is no programme beyond a wide experience of human life with a great charity (love) and a *massive* hope in the future'. But he sent a pianoforte arrangement of the score to Jaeger and, a week before the first performance, received a letter which must have deeply moved him as his mind went back to *Gerontius* and the years before it:

My dear, great Edward,
    I was allowed to come down today for the first time for a month and I

spent some happy quarter hours on your Adagio in the Symphony. . . . My dear friend, that is not only one of the very greatest slow movements since Beethoven, but I consider it *worthy of that master*. How original, how *pure*, noble etc. . . . It's the greatest thing you have done. . . . I detected one or two places where the great adagio of the Choral Symphony was recalled to my memory, nothing in the way of a reminiscence (the Satz is *quite* your own), but just the feeling of nobility of sentiment. At [104] we are brought near Heaven.

To another friend he wrote: 'Elgar's symphony has been a perfect godsend to me, for it has made me forget for a few happy hours that I am a doomed man.'

Jaeger's views were generally shared. This was not only Elgar's first symphony, it was England's. Samuel Langford, writing in the *Manchester Guardian* on the day of the first performance, declared: 'That the work is the noblest ever penned for instruments by an English composer we are quite certain.' After the slow movement the Manchester audience burst into applause. 'Dr Richter is not inclined to break up a composition,' Langford wrote, 'and the fact that he encouraged the composer to come on to the platform and acknowledge the applause . . . may be taken as a sure sign that he felt there was in this movement something peculiarly deserving of recognition, something supremely beautiful.' He ended his notice: 'When the music ceased we felt that we had listened to one of the works which help music onward.' The critic of *The Daily Telegraph* described the excitement of the evening and the effect of the music. Interestingly, he found a return to 'simpler ways and a simpler expression than he [Elgar] employed in his later oratorios. Here we have much more of the language, or rather the idiom, of *Caractacus* and of *The Dream of Gerontius* than of *The Kingdom* and of *The Apostles*. . . . Whatever the poetic basis, whatever the mental foundation of the symphony, the composer has maintained from the first setting-down of the central theme to its final exposition in the last pages of his score the sway of beauty. . . . After the extremely beautiful and poignantly expressive slow movement the composer was called on to the platform to bow several times by a crowd that was almost beside itself with enthusiasm. Again this scene was repeated at the close, and from none was the applause more hearty than from the orchestral players themselves, who rose as one man and cheered Elgar to the echo.' No English work had ever before received such rapturous and immediate acclaim. In the audience on that historic evening was a twenty-year-old Manchester youth, Neville Cardus, who many years later put into words the significance of the event:

Those of us who were students were excited to hear at last an English composer addressing us in a spacious way, speaking a language which was European and not provincial. No English symphony existed then, at least not big enough to make a show of comparison with a symphony by Beethoven or Brahms and go in the programme of a concert side by side with the acknowledged masterpieces, and not be dwarfed at once into insignificance. . . . I cannot hope, at this time of day, to describe the pride taken in Elgar by young English students of that far-away epoch.[7]

Four days later the symphony had its first London performance at Queen's Hall, with Richter conducting the London Symphony Orchestra. Fauré, invited by Schuster, and the young Adrian Boult were among those present. 'Gentlemen,' said Richter to the players, 'let us now rehearse the greatest symphony of modern times, *and not only in this country*'; and when he came to the Adagio he echoed Jaeger's words and said 'Ah! this is a *real* Adagio such as Beethoven would have written.' Jaeger attended the triumphant Queen's Hall performance. Three days previously he had written his last letter to Elgar. 'It's a great and masterly work and will place you higher among the world's masters than anything you have done. Ill as I am (& I feel so ill tonight that I want to go to the nearest Ry Station & throw myself under a Train to end my misery) I hope to go next Monday . . .' He described the scene in Queen's Hall to Dorabella: 'I never in all my experience saw the like. The Hall was *packed* . . . The atmosphere was electric . . . After the first movement E.E. was called out; again, several times, after the third, and then came the great moment. After that superb Coda (Finale) the audience seemed to rise at E. when he appeared. I *never* heard such frantic applause after any novelty nor such shouting. Five times he had to appear before they were pacified. People stood up and even *on* their seats to get a view . . .'

The great work was recognized as such from the day of its birth. In 1909 it received eighty-two performances – seventeen in London and the rest in America, Manchester, Vienna, Berlin, Bonn, Leipzig, St Petersburg, and Sydney, among other places. In just over a year after the Manchester first performance it was played a hundred times, an amazing record especially when one remembers that there was no broadcasting to aid the spread of its fame. Here at last, in overflowing measure, was the recognition he had craved ten years before. He accepted the change with wry humour: 'The Symphony . . . is making a very wild career,' he wrote to Schuster's sister Adela on Christmas Day 1908, '& I receive heaps of letters from persons known & unknown telling me how it uplifts them: I wish it uplifted me – I have just paid rent, Land Tax, Income Tax & a variety of other things due today & there are children yapping at the door. "Christians awake! Salute the 'yappy' morn". I saluted it about seven o'clock, quite dark, made a fire in the Ark & mused on the future of a bad cold in my head & how far a carol could get out of the key & still be a carol: resolve

[7] *Ten Composers* (London, 1945), p. 146.

me this last.' Yet on the same day he wrote to Alice Stuart-Wortley, 'That symphony *is* a new world, isn't it?'

The *Daily Telegraph*'s critic, in a further article after the Manchester performance, tried to explain why the audience 'let itself go' over this particular work. He decided that its 'intense humaneness' was one reason, also its 'robustness, sincerity, power, conviction and individuality'. Those words hold good today. But perhaps the most moving personal reaction to the symphony was that of Lord Northampton, whose admiration for the personality and music of 'my most dear friend', as he always addressed Elgar in his letters, was very deep.[8] Writing after a performance in January 1910, he said: 'I hardly know what to think and certainly not what to write. That you, a mortal with whom I had just talked, had out of yourself given the world *that* . . . it is almost terrifying in its greatness.'

Elgar opened 1909 by conducting the symphony at Queen's Hall on New Year's Day. Alice thought he 'looked nobilmente as if he were his music'. By this date other English conductors besides Wood were making their name in the concert-hall. Landon Ronald was one who conducted the new work in 1909, and another was Thomas Beecham, who did not share the widespread adulation of Elgar's music. At this time he was touring the country with his own New Symphony Orchestra and he included the A flat symphony in his programmes. His scandalous treatment of it was noticed in Hanley by the composer Havergal Brian, who exposed what was going on in a letter to the *Musical Times*: 'The first movement was cut down one half: part of the "exposition" & the whole of the "development" were cut out, & some minutes were sacrificed in the succeeding movements. Those who know the symphony will be astonished to hear that the actual time occupied in its performance was only 38 minutes! [instead of approximately 55]. It was an insult to the composer. . . .' Beecham later described the work as 'neo-Gothic, the equivalent of the towers of St Pancras Station'. This did not stop him writing to Elgar in July 1909 to inquire if he had an opera 'either grand or light, short or long, that I could produce'.

Elgar did little except conduct and play at chemistry in the first months of 1909. But in April he went, via Paris, to Italy where he and Alice stayed at Careggi, near Florence, with Julia Worthington at the Villa Silli. They visited Venice, and ideas began to stir again. As usual, Elgar was stimulated by a place, in this case St Mark's. It was during this visit that he wrote his biggest part-song, 'Go, Song of Mine,' to D. G. Rossetti's translation of Calvacanti (a work whose dying fall anticipates the Second Symphony), and a smaller one, 'The Angelus'.

[8] Inviting Elgar to stay with him he once wrote: 'As long as we keep off politics we are not likely to fight.'

The latter was dedicated to Alice Stuart-Wortley to whom he wrote: 'I was afraid the simple words might be too papistical for you – or for your family!' It is a delightful work, but 'Go, Song of Mine' is superb, closely linked thematically and emotionally to the Second Symphony and the Violin Concerto. A sketchbook is headed 'Opera in Three Acts – Edward Elgar – Careggi – May 1909' and another sketchbook, bought in Florence, contains a rough drawing of a stage set. About this time, too, are dated sketches which matured in *Falstaff*.

Carice left a touching description[9] of this holiday. Elgar, she remembered, 'spent much time at the piano, improvising & playing his favourite music. I shall never forget his playing of the *Coriolan* Overture, he had a gift of making the piano sound as though the whole orchestra was there . . . In Venice . . . he was disappointed because you could not see the beauty for the people; with the result that we were up at five one morning so as to walk round without interference'. They returned home by way of their favourite old haunts in the Bavarian Highlands – 'rather spoilt with a lot of building since they were there in the nineties' – and called on Richard Strauss at Garmisch. 'We were amused when Strauss wanted to show my father some score or paper of interest, he called out to Frau Strauss who produced a bunch of keys from her underskirt, & duly locked it all up again when they had finished.'

But it was only back at home, at Hereford, that he could work properly. On 19 August Alice wrote in her diary: 'E. possessed with his music for the Vl. Concerto'. Dorabella stayed at Plâs Gwyn that month and heard the sketches. She describes in her book an evening when, after watering the garden with the hose, they sat outside until it was dark. Then, 'when the windows were wide open and the curtains drawn back, and lovely scents came in from the garden,' Elgar played the themes of the concerto. On 3 October, he looked over his old 1903 – 4 symphony sketches, and his sketches written in Italy, and perhaps the remnants of the 'Gordon' symphony, and was 'quite inspired with Symphony No. 2'. But work on both projects was interrupted by the pressures of public life: the Three Choirs Festival in September, another tour as conductor of the London Symphony Orchestra in October, and an Elgar Festival organized by Embleton and the Leeds Choral Union in November. Another 'official' occasion towards the end of September was a visit to Liverpool for the three-day festival of the short-lived Music League, one of several ventures for the promotion of English music. Elgar was president and spoke at a mayoral banquet. Arnold Bax, who was one of the young composers represented, remembered him on this occasion 'in high spirits and his most genial temper . . . At dinner he startled me by

[9] *Alice Elgar*, op. cit., pp. 164–5.

shouting down the table, "Mr Bax! Was it you who told me the story of the two-and-ninepenny crab?" '[10] On 24 January 1910 he conducted his three new songs with orchestra (op. 59) at the memorial concert for Jaeger, who had died in the previous May. These were the only songs written as part of a projected cycle of six orchestral settings of poems by Sir Gilbert Parker (1862–1932), a popular Canadian-born writer of imperialistic fiction whose poetry, in contrast, was sentimental. For some unknown reason the cycle was left incomplete, the three songs completed being numbered 3, 5, and 6. 'Was it some golden star?' and 'O, soft was the song' are Elgar in his happiest vein of fantasy and romance, and there is a strong reminder in 'Twilight' of the intimate musing on 'what might have been' which characterises the Violin Concerto. Elgar had completed orchestration of them on 5 January. Five days later he was 'very busy with the [Violin] Concerto and bassoon piece [the *Romance*]'.

Early in 1910, when staying with Schuster at 'The Hut' and with the Edward Speyers at their home, Ridgehurst in Hertfordshire, he continued work on the Violin Concerto. Lady (Edgar) Speyer was a professional violinist, Leonora von Stosch, and she played parts of the work at 'The Hut'. Elgar became despondent about it, but the Speyers and Stuart-Wortleys encouraged him to persevere. 'I am not sure about that Andante,' he wrote to Mrs Stuart-Wortley on 7 February, 'and shall put it away for a long time before I decide its fate.' He and Alice were thinking of living in London and in the same letter he tells his friend that he would find London 'too lonely' – 'I think a decent obscurity in the country is all I can attain to – there is really no place for me here as I do not conduct or in fact do anything & I am made to feel in many ways I am not wanted'. But from 7 March, they took a flat (No. 7) in 58, New Cavendish Street.[11] There he asked his old friend Hugh Blair to hear what he had written, and one spring day in Regent Street he met the L.S.O. violinist W. H. Reed and asked him if he would go to the flat to help him with the arrangement of passage-work, bowings, and fingerings and to play over passages in different ways. Elgar's close friendship with Reed dates from these meetings. 'On my arrival in the morning', Reed wrote,[12] 'I found Sir Edward striding about with a number of loose pieces of MSS which he was arranging in different parts of the room. Some were already pinned on the backs of chairs, or fixed up on the mantelpiece ready for me to play . . .' Reed also went to Schuster's home at Bray where much of the slow movement was sketched and

---

[10] *Farewell, My Youth*, op. cit., p. 31.

[11] This building, known as Kingsley Lodge, was demolished in 1971. The Elgars occupied this flat only until 2 June 1910. They then had a service flat in Queen Anne's Mansions, S.W.1. (demolished in 1972) from July 1910 until early in 1911. From May to July 1911 they lived in 76, Gloucester Place, W.1.

[12] *Music and Letters* (January 1935), pp. 30–6.

re-written. 'As I saw it,' he wrote, 'in that early spring, with all the young green on the trees and the swans lazily floating by on the river, so the vision comes to me again with the music that was written there, music that depicts with such fidelity the poetry and beauty of the scene.' But still the new symphony, begun (or re-begun) in Venice, occupied some of Elgar's thoughts. From 1–10 April he was on a motoring tour of Devon, Cornwall, and Wiltshire with Schuster, visiting Tintagel on 3 April. The two place names Venice and Tintagel are on the printed score of the Second Symphony. At first Tintagel, where the Stuart-Wortleys were staying, had been omitted from the itinerary. Elgar wrote to Alice Stuart-Wortley: 'I am with Frank and his sister and tomorrow commence a motor tour "round" Cornwall avoiding Tintagel, it seems, but I am not *director* or dictator or Heaven knows what wd. happen to you or to Tintagel . . . Love, Windflower, Yours, E.' He returned to London and to a round of theatre-going – plays by Galsworthy, Shaw, Barrie, and Granville Barker – and to more work on the concerto. He was in the capital when Edward VII died on 6 May. 'These times are too cruel & gloomy,' he wrote to Schuster. 'It is awful to be here now – that dear sweet-tempered King-Man was always so "pleasant" to me. I have the Concerto well in hand & have played(?) it thro' on the p.f. & it's *good*! awfully emotional! too emotional but I love it: Ist movement finished & the IIIrd well on – these *are* times for composition. I have a cold & cannot face the winds – so I did not venture to Bray today although I ventured to Cough . . . We are dismally gay – walk like ghosts & eat like ghouls. Oh! it is terribly sad.'

At 'The Hut' on 16 June, he wrote to Mrs Stuart-Wortley: 'I have made the end serious & grand I hope & have brought in the real inspired themes from the 1st movement. Frank approves. I did it this morning . . . the music sings of memories & hope,' But back at Plâs Gwyn a week later he wrote to her: 'I am appalled at the last movement & cannot get on – it is growing so large – too large, I fear.' He and Reed worked on it together. Reed played through the finale and Elgar became excited about the cadenza. 'We played each of the passages in every imaginable way, and the lento between [105] and [106] nearly moved him to tears as he repeated it again and yet again, dwelling on certain notes and marking them "tenuto", "espress", "animato" or "molto accel," as he realized step by step exactly what he sought to express.' On 13 July Elgar told Mrs Stuart-Wortley: 'All radiance again'. Early in July Alice had taken him to Cornwall to stay with Lady Mary Trefusis. Before they left Hereford he wrote to Schuster that he had been working too hard. 'The world has changed a little since I saw you I think – it is difficult to say how but it's either larger or smaller or something . . . This Concerto is *full* of romantic feeling – I should have been a philanthropist if I had been a rich man –

I *know* the feeling is human and right – vainglory! . . . You will like the cadenza which is on a novel plan I think – accompanied very softly by a few insts. & – it comes at the end of the last movement – it sadly thinks over the 1st movement.' The concerto had always been promised to Kreisler. In an interview the great violinist gave in November 1909, quoted in his biography,[13] he told a reporter: 'Sir Edward Elgar promised me a concerto three years ago. When he writes one it will be a labour of love rather than profit. But I can't get the first note out of him.' Now, by July 1910, he had been shown the work. 'That last movement is good stuff!' Elgar wrote to Schuster, 'Kreisler saw it on Friday & is delighted.' In the earlier letter (29 June) to Schuster, quoted above, Elgar had written: 'There are fine rows going on over the 1st performance & I am desperately annoyed at several things.' The first performance had been promised to the Philharmonic Society, but Novello's, on 24 June, sent proofs of the first two movements to Robert Newman, manager of the Queen's Hall Orchestra, to show to Kreisler. Newman began to negotiate for the first performance for his own orchestra, with the support of Novello's and Kreisler. The latter, according to Sir Henry Wood,[14] also favoured a first performance with Richter in Manchester, but the Hallé Concerts Society missed their chance by saying they could not engage Kreisler until the 1910–11 season, although Richter had written to Elgar from abroad on 14 July 1910, saying: 'As conductor of the Hallé Concerts I feel obliged to ask you whether we could have the first performance of the Concerto; as *friend* I should not venture to be importunate.' Interest in the concerto among violinists was intense. On 24 August Elgar wrote to Novello's, 'All questions of performance other than Kreisler's must wait until I have seen K. on Sept. 2nd – if K. is enamoured of the work he may want to play it in US & in Germany in which case it will not do to let a third-rate artist have it first. If Mr [Frederick] Stock [cond. of the Chicago Symphony Orchestra] should be speaking to you before the 2nd Septr. – you might ask him what soloist he proposes: it will never do to have it hacked about by the sort of creatures who play in the States!' He finished the concerto during August. Kreisler played through it on 8 and 9 September, telling Elgar 'You have written an immortal work'. He played it again on 15 and 17 October, Alice remarking that it was 'wonderful, quite different from previous time – really magnificent'.

On the Sunday preceding the Three Choirs Festival at Gloucester, Schuster organized a small private party at the house Elgar had taken for the week. That evening W. H. Reed, with Elgar at the piano, played the concerto to the privileged audience, which included Julia Worthington and Alice Stuart-Wortley. 'You are not going to leave

[13] *Fritz Kreisler*, op. cit., p. 105.
[14] *My Life of Music*, op. cit., p. 226.

me all alone in the tuttis are you?' Elgar whispered to Reed before they began. The Gloucester Festival of 1910 was an historic week for English music: the first hearing, albeit private, of Elgar's magnificent concerto followed two days later by his conducting of *Gerontius* preceded by a new work for strings by Vaughan Williams, the *Fantasia on a Theme by Thomas Tallis*. 'Bliss was it in that dawn to be alive . . .'

The concerto had its first performance at the Philharmonic Society concert in Queen's Hall on 10 November 1910. On the evening of the 9th Schuster was Elgar's host at another of his lavish and generous parties. And on that day Elgar wrote to Richter:

My dear Hans . . . I have feared that you may have felt a little annoyed over the first performance of the Concerto being given here, but things were not quite in my own hands regarding this, and some day I will explain . . . It is wonderful to me to know that I have your real friendship; perhaps, no not perhaps, that I have your love. My dear friend, you have from me all the love and reverence one man can feel for another. I feel a very small person when I am in your company, you who are so great and have been intimate with the greatest. I meet now many men, and I want you to know that I look to you as my greatest and most genuine friend in the world. I revere and love you . . . Now forgive me for sending this letter, which is about nothing, and yet is about everything, because it is about you. The man you befriended long ago (Variations), be assured this man will never forget your kindness, your nobility, and the grandeur of your life and personality. Love. Yours ever, Edward.'

But Richter was nearing the end of his career. His eyesight was failing and three months later he announced his retirement. He never conducted the concerto. The first performance nearly repeated the success of the symphony. 'The place was simply packed,' Dorabella recalled. 'Kreisler came on looking as white as a sheet . . . but he played superbly. E.E. was also, obviously, very much strung up, but all went well and the ovation at the end was tremendous. Kreisler and E.E. shook hands for quite a long time . . . Finally they came in arm-in-arm.' It was as well that Elgar could not look into the future, for this was the last time a big work of his was to receive immediate and uninhibited public acclaim. It was dedicated to Kreisler, but the inscription on the score, already discussed in Chapter 8, provided the public with yet another Elgarian enigma: 'Aquí está encerrada el alma de . . . . .' (The quotation is from Lesage's *Gil Blas*.[15]) Elgar translated it in a letter to Nicholas Kilburn on 5 November 1910: 'Here, or more emphatically *in here*, is enshrined or simply enclosed – buried is

[15] The full quotation is 'Aquí está encerrada el alma del licenciado Pedro Garcias'. It was quoted by Oliver Wendell Holmes in his *The Autocrat of the Breakfast Table*, in a chapter about childhood and youth and a love affair with a schoolmistress. The Holmes book appeared in the Everyman Library in 1906.

perhaps too definite – *the soul of.....*? The final "de" leaves it indefinite as to sex or rather gender. Now guess.' Ernest Newman said in a *Sunday Times* article[16] that Elgar had told Basil Maine that the 'soul' was feminine. Elgar, whose knowledge of printer's procedure was extremely detailed, knew that three 'points' are the usual indication of an omitted passage; his use of five was obviously significant. The Violin Concerto is Elgar's most intimate and personal work; it is among the most memorable compliments ever paid to a woman, and its mood of tenderness and of wistful regret is unequivocal testimony to Elgar's feelings. On 25 October 1910 he wrote to Alice Stuart-Wortley: 'I have also been making a little progress with Symphony No. 2 and am sitting at my table weaving strange and wonderful memories into very poor music I fear. What a wonderful year it has been! With all the sad things in the great public life – the King's death downwards – the radiance in a poor, little, private man's soul has been wonderful and new and the concerto has come!' A week earlier he had sent her the telling letter shown in Plate XI, with quotations from the concerto.

It is said that Elgar and Kreisler were not too happy with each other at the first performance of the concerto, but they repeated it at the Queen's Hall on 30 November. Kreisler gave the third London performance with Henry Wood conducting on 28 December and the fourth, with Elgar, on 16 January 1911 – which other new work by a British composer has had four London performances within ten weeks? Kreisler played the concerto in every major concert-hall of the land during a tour with the Queen's Hall Orchestra and Wood, and Elgar conducted it for him in Liverpool. (He also performed it in St Petersburg, with Koussevitzky conducting, in February 1913.) Kreisler's fee for the first two performances was £200; Elgar received £100 for each performance he conducted. Kreisler himself declared to his biographer that the greatest performance he ever heard was that given by Eugène Ysaÿe in Berlin in 1912. This is supported by Vladimir Cernikoff in his book *Humour and Harmony*: 'He had a way of playing the cadenza in that very beautiful work in such a detached manner that, for once, the expression "Music from Heaven" seemed inadequate.'

In Brussels in March 1911, Elgar conducted the First Symphony, in which Ysaÿe acted as leader of the orchestra he usually conducted. Ysaÿe wanted to play the concerto in London but he and other violinists such as Michael Zacharewitsch quarrelled with Novello's about the high performing fee which he claimed they demanded. He did not wish to pay any fee, and had borrowed parts for his continental performances. So the concerto dropped from his repertoire and England never heard him play it. Once again Elgar had

[16] 21 May 1939.

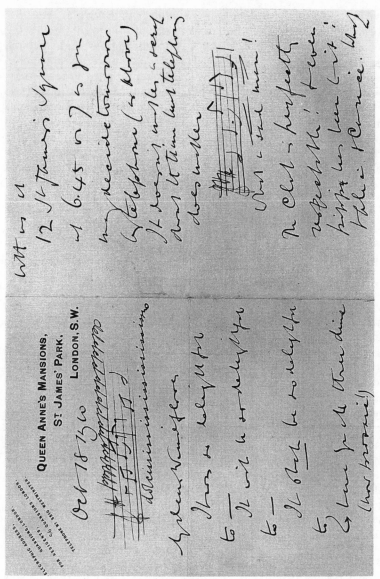

PLATE XVII

good reason to detest 'the business side' of music. Novello's, however, denied Ysaÿe's allegation, pointing out that the fee never exceeded ten guineas and the usual fee was 7½ guineas including loan of the music. Elgar wanted Novello's to give way to Ysaÿe but Ysaÿe called off the London concert and another in Norwich. Novello's eventually dropped the fee in July 1914.

After helping Ivor Atkins in an edition of Bach's *St. Matthew Passion*, Elgar devoted the first two months of 1911 to completing the Second Symphony. He took only a fortnight to finish and score the first movement from his sketches. He eventually gave all the sketches of the symphony (they are now at Broadheath) to Alice Stuart-Wortley, whose friendship with him is one of the motivations of the work. To her he wrote on 29 January: 'I have recorded last year in the first movement to which I put the last note in the score a moment ago and I must tell you this: I have worked at fever heat and the thing is tremendous in energy.' On 30 January he was, Alice recorded, 'trying to think of 2nd movement.' To Frances Colvin, wife of Sidney Colvin, Keeper of Prints and Drawings at the British Museum and a distinguished *littérateur* and friend of R. L. Stevenson, he wrote on 1 February: 'I am too busy with the "Spirit of Delight" symphony.' He then quoted some further lines of Shelley, from *Julian and Maddalo*, a poem which records, like the symphony, a visit to Venice:

> I do but hide
> Under these notes, like embers, every spark
> *Of that which has consumed me*

A week later the slow movement was ready and Lady Elgar noted in her diary: 'Very great and impressive. A. [herself] hears lament for King Edward and dear Rodey in it, and all human feeling. E. wrote it all from his sketches in one week.' The third movement was done by 16 February. On that day Elgar wrote to Alice Stuart-Wortley: 'I have just put the last note to the IIIrd movement and very wild and headstrong it is with soothing pastoral strains in between and very brilliant. I bring it tomorrow and then for the great serene movement.' On the 28th Alice could write: 'E. finished his Symphony. It seems one of his very greatest works, vast in design and supremely beautiful . . . It is really sublime . . . It resumes our human life, delight, regrets, farewell, the saddest mood & then the strong man's triumph.' Alice posted the score to Novello's and, after his visit to Brussels, Elgar went to the United States and Canada where he was to conduct the Sheffield choir during their Coronation year tour of the New World. He had never liked America and now that his friend Professor Sanford of Yale was dead there was little to which to look forward there. To Sidney Colvin he wrote: 'I know I ought to be glad that perhaps I shall earn some money, but I would rather starve . . . Truly parts of the world are beastly!' His every nerve was 'shattered by some angularity, vulgarity, and general horror'. From Cincinnati, 'this awful desert', he wrote to Alice Stuart-Wortley: 'It is sweet to hear of Tintagel & our own land . . . I loathe & detest every minute of my life here! but I have lovely things to think of & shall soon be back & hope to see you. All I can do is to count the days . . . it is so raw &

silly out here ... I am sure you are better in Tintagel – I am selfish
enough to be thankful that you can think of me there & you will not
forget Frank's car taking us to Boscastle & you will not forget the
road home – how lovely it was – a year ago! ... I long to be back &
forget this worse than nightmare.' While he was away, his wife was
looking at houses in London, for they had decided to live there, a
decision which must have cost Elgar much heart-searching, torn as he
was between his passionate love of the West Country and the
demands made on his time by engagements which necessitated his
presence in London, as well as his liking for the West End theatre, his
clubs and the capital's nearness to Schuster at Maidenhead. While he
was away, too, he worked on music for King George V's Coronation
– a march and an *Offertorium* – and accepted an invitation from the
London Symphony Orchestra to be its permanent conductor for the
1911–12 season now that Richter had retired.

While he was in New York, Elgar on 13 April had responded to
Littleton's request for information about the Second Symphony with
a detailed description. The letter began as analytical guidance for the
writer of the programme-note for the first performance but it turned
into something self-revelatory and of considerable significance:

> '(Motto) Rarely, rarely, comest thou,
>   Spirit of delight ...
>   *Shelley.*

To get near the mood of the Symphony the whole of Shelley's poem may be
read, but the music does not illustrate the whole of the poem, neither does
the poem entirely elucidate the music.

The germ of the work is in the opening bars – these in a modified form are
heard for the last time in the closing bars of the last movement. The early part
of the 1st movement consists of an assemblage of themes. I wish the theme at
[11] to be considered (& labelled) as the second principal theme.

The spirit of the whole work is intended to be high & pure joy: there are
retrospective passages of sadness but the whole of the sorrow is smoothed
out & ennobled in the last movement, which ends in a calm &, *I hope &
intend,* elevated mood. N.B. private. The second movement formed part of
the original scheme – before the death of King Edward – it is elegiac but has
nothing to do with any funeral march & is a 'reflection' suggested by the
poem! The Rondo was sketched on the Piazza of S. Mark, Venice: I took
down the rhythm of the opening bars from some itinerant musicians who
seemed to take a grave satisfaction in the broken accent of the first four bars.

The last movement speaks for itself, I think: a broad, sonorous, rolling
movement throughout – in an elevated mood.

The reappearances of the first theme are obvious & I need not point them
out. Please note the new 'atmosphere' at [27] (suggested at [24]) with the
added cello solo at [28] – remote & drawing someone else out of the
everyday world: note the *feminine* voice of the oboe, answering or joining in,
two bars before [30], note the happiness at [30] – real (remote) peace: note at

[33] the atmosphere broken in upon & the dream 'shattered' by the inevitable march of the Trombones & Tuba pp. In the 2nd movement at [78] the feminine voice *laments* over the broad manly 1st theme – and may not [87] be like a woman dropping a flower on the man's grave?'

The Symphony was first played in Queen's Hall at the London Musical Festival on 24 May 1911. The composer conducted. It was high summer in an epoch of brilliance and wealth, London in its glory with the excitement of a Coronation less than a month away. And the work unfolded to a by no means full hall on that May night was mainly elegiac in mood and ended quietly, almost resignedly. There was no roaring ovation such as had greeted the First Symphony, no one stood on the seats to acclaim the composer-conductor. Henry Wood was at the side of the platform as Elgar walked off. 'Henry, they don't like it,' he said, 'they don't like it.'[17] To the leader, W. H. Reed, he said: 'What's the matter with them, Billy? They sit there like a lot of stuffed pigs.'[18] The comparative failure of that first performance, if failure it was, can be explained by its obvious contrast with the mood of the occasion: a fashionable audience, ready to acclaim a new king and a new reign of hope and glory and expecting Elgar to celebrate the glories of our blood and state, heard instead a restless work, full of enigmatic passages and containing a funeral elegy inspired, as they thought, by the death of the king they had mourned a year ago. Subconsciously they were perhaps disturbed by the setting-sun finale; and if any lines of poetry were in their minds that evening besides Shelley's 'Rarely, rarely, comest thou, spirit of delight' (inscribed by Elgar on the score) then they were probably from Kipling's 'Recessional':

> Lo, all our pomps of yesterday
> Are one with Nineveh and Tyre.

It is not the sort of music to provoke, on first hearing, an ovation such as had greeted the First Symphony. But Richard Capell, then the critic of the *Daily Mail*, described the response as 'unhesitating' and spoke of 'most cordial warmth'. He told me many years later that the hall was not full because of the very high prices of admission and that there were two other composer-conducted first performances in the programme, of Walford Davies's *Parthenia* Suite and Bantock's *Dante and Beatrice*.[19] Moreover, Elgar's view of the audience's response is contradicted by *The Daily Telegraph* report the next day which spoke of the exhilaration of the closing pages 'which roused the audience to much enthusiasm'. The *Telegraph* critic unhesitatingly declared the work to be superior to the First Symphony – 'there seems to be a

---

[17]*My Life of Music,* op. cit., p. 326.   [18]*Elgar,* op. cit., p. 105.
[19]The concert also included Monteverdi's *Lamento d'Arianna,* sung by Julia Culp, so it was not exactly a 'box-office' programme!

firmer grip, not only of the symphonic form, but of the substance expressed within its confines'. He was puzzled by 'the psychology' of the Rondo, but his most interesting comment was reserved for the Larghetto. He called its description by the programme-analyst as a 'funeral march' a 'strange misnomer. Far more is it suggestive of a deeply, poignantly-felt Lament, in its elegiac pathos and Elgarian introspection. . . . Intimate and immensely solemn, it brings up memories of the earlier Elgar more than any other of the four movements.' This wholly accurate piece of perception seems to show that Elgar's Edwardian contemporaries were not solely preoccupied, as modern caricature has it, with the panoply of regal tribute. Late in the notice the writer again speaks of a 'very warm reception', adding 'there are heights here that hitherto even Elgar himself had not touched, but we are doubtful if the greater public will realise the fact immediately.' The critics generally were divided over the work's merits and stature, the slow movement receiving most criticism. *The Times* (which said the symphony was 'received with much favour though with rather less enthusiasm than usual') surprisingly described it as 'much shorter than its predecessor', and another writer said that 'no small amount of it seems to speak of pessimism and rebellion.' When it was repeated at a London Symphony Orchestra concert on 8 June the audience was described as 'miserably small'. The symphony did not come into its own until after the First World War. One wonders how well or badly it was played in 1911–14 and suspects the worst. It should be remembered that there was still only a handful of really brilliant conductors working in England. In Elgar's music, Elgar himself could evoke a good performance if the orchestra responded to him. Otherwise the best conductor was Landon Ronald. Henry Wood rarely had enough rehearsal, Beecham would not look at the work. Richter had retired. The rest were choral conductors who would have been baffled by a score of this complexity. Thus even so Elgar-minded an orchestra as the Hallé, playing the symphony under Elgar on 23 November 1911,[20] could only persuade Samuel Langford to this view in the *Manchester Guardian* next day: 'Elgar's original charm and his power of surprising us into wonder have diminished rather than grown as his craftsmanship and subtlety of fantastic variation have increased. In this symphony he vitalises the imagination of his hearer in listening to multitudinous transformations of a very sparse supply of melody. . . . We can hardly say that the work contains any melody in the full sense of the word. Neither can we say with confidence that it quite vanquishes the impression of coldness and hardness that will

[20]The first American performances were given in Cincinnati on 24 and 25 November 1911 by the Cincinnati Symphony Orchestra conducted by Leopold Stokowski. The work was not appreciated.

remain mixed with all our admiration of Elgar's music, despite its glowing orchestral colour.' Grudging indeed. No melody. Coldness. Hardness. What sort of performance can it have been? Three weeks beforehand Langford had also called the Violin Concerto 'short-winded in melody'. It is an interesting contemporary view. The symphony was not played again for fifteen years by the Hallé, which of all English orchestras at that time had the strongest Elgar tradition thanks to Richter, Brodsky, and the composer. It was not played at a concert of the Royal Philharmonic Society (as it became in 1912) until 1916 and not after that until 1923.

He was despondent after the first performance; not even the award of the O.M. wholly lifted his spirits. The obligations of an unofficial laureate weighed heavily on him, as Jaeger had feared. Elgar wrote to Canon Gorton on 16 July: 'I have had really no time for anything except "official" (more or less) work: now the "tumult & the shouting dies" & the net gain is little. I have my Star (which you shall see) & that is something, but troubles manifold dog me & it is *by no means* in sunshine that I walk – quite the reverse, alas!' On 27 June he ended his agreement with Novello's because of disappointment with his royalty account and performing fees. Three days later he wrote to Littleton: 'I have never deceived myself as to my true commercial value & see that everything of mine, as I have often said, dies a natural death; if you look at the concerts you will see that a new thing of mine "lasts" about a year & then dies & is buried in the mass of English music. I am now well on in years & have to consider a "move" & make a new home – under the depressing state of my music I have to reconsider this entirely & shall probably go abroad or to a cottage in the country & leave the musical world entirely.' In September there was the Three Choirs at Worcester, followed by the Norwich Festival, and in October a visit to Turin to conduct some of his own works, including the concerto (soloist Zacharewitsch) at the international exhibition. The orchestra was Toscanini's, and the *Introduction and Allegro* was already in its regular repertory. Back in England there was a series of L.S.O. concerts for his début as its permanent conductor, and on New Year's Day 1912 he and Alice moved into the imposing mansion in Hampstead which Alice Stuart-Wortley had found for them and which they had decided to call Severn House.

This was No. 42, Netherhall Gardens. Hampstead was then still rural, with farms, cattle, sheep and tree-lined Finchley Road.[21] Netherhall Gardens, off Fitzjohns Avenue, was an area of 'carriage folk'. John McCormack, the tenor, lived there and had a Rolls-Royce. The Elgars' house was named 'Kelston' and had been designed in

[21]For much information about Elgar and Hampstead I am indebted to *Elgar: the Hampstead Scene*, by Dr Louie Eickhoff.

1888 by Norman Shaw for the painter Edwin Long R.A. It was the last and grandest of Shaw's Queen Anne-type studio homes – brass front doors, Roman mosaic in the vestibule, Spanish mosaic in the bathroom, a gallery 60 ft long, studio, ceremonial staircase, and stables. There were separate entrances for servants and for the artist's models. The garden was 'small but pretty'. To buy the house on mortgage, Alice had to go to law to break a trust set up under her mother's will. Today we should call its acquisition a 'status symbol'. For Alice 'E's own house' represented a victory over the attitude which had driven them from London in the first years of their marriage, a demonstration that her faith in her Edward's genius and ultimate success had been triumphantly justified, and a proclamation to all concerned that an English composer could live in style. The purchase was completed in December 1911. She wrote to a friend: 'The whole house appeals to him in every way – the quiet is so wonderful and healing . . . it is so lovely to see E. so happy and in a setting which seems to have been waiting for him.' Elgar himself had more modest tastes – Birchwood remained his idea of a home – but he knew what was due to Alice and he liked the house. 'I ape royal state, under my wife's kindly direction', he wrote to Canon Gorton. There was the additional attraction, which must have weighed with him, that it had been built for a painter. 'Our second-rate painters may build themselves magnificent houses. . .' he had said in 1904. Now a first-rate musician was to live in a painter's house. He must have relished the *volte-face* as a snook cocked at the public he despised; and perhaps he remembered what he had written so sarcastically to Jaeger three years earlier, on 3 June 1908: 'What an object lesson is poor dear Madame Albani: one of the best of women. She has sung to these delightful English their own *oratorios* and sacred things for years – her husband loses all their money – she has to advertise for pupils! Now look at a battered old w—e like Melba & Co: – !!! My beloved countrymen & women wd. & will subscribe anything to help her if necessary – it makes my head boil – where is providence? *Nothing.*'

There was never any question but that Severn House would be a drain on Elgar's pocket. Friends rallied round. Edward Speyer had the small room off the music-room fitted with cupboards and shelves to make Elgar a study and library. Schuster furnished the drawing-room with Empire furniture, and Muriel Foster and her husband gave a settee. Elgar, to Alice's dismay, sold his old violin so that he could buy a billiard-table. Three days after moving in he wrote to Mrs Stuart-Wortley: 'The house is divine, so quiet, quieter than Hereford even, where we heard trains. The heating apparatus we can't manage yet & get too hot. (I think, entre nous, it was designed for the comfort of Long's nude ladies!)' Severn House was a practical materialization of the perpetual conflict within Elgar, a conflict which had intensified at this time when he no longer attended mass. He showed the house to Rosa Burley, who shrewdly perceived[22] that, while he was proud of its palatial appearance, he also wanted to make it clear to her that 'success meant nothing to him and that there was always some lovely thing in life which had completely eluded him . . . he also told me . . . that even now he never conducted his music without finding that his mind had slipped back to summer days on the Malvern Hills, to Birchwood or to the drowsy peace of Longdon Marsh.' When 'Dorabella' saw Severn House and remarked that he must be in clover, he replied: 'I don't know about the clover – I've left that behind in Hereford.'[23] So did the retreat into the past continue, and it was to manifest itself in his music in his taking-up of abandoned earlier projects, such as *The Music Makers* and *Falstaff*, the orchestration of Alice's and his early song *The Wind at Dawn*, and the use of themes from his wind quintet and Powick works in *Cantique* and *Crown of India*.

His own need for money was still great. Yet he would only make money by the sweat of his brow, as it were. When Sir Edgar Speyer sent him a cheque, the result of shares speculation undertaken for Elgar, he returned it on moral grounds. He conducted the L.S.O. for nothing because their funds were in low water. Yet this is the man who is sometimes represented as the laureate of complacency and the established order. He was willing only to profit from the composition of such a work as the masque *Crown of India*, and it is apparent from a letter to Frances Colvin that he intended his stay in London only to be short: 'My labour will soon be over and then for the country lanes and the wind sighing in the reeds by Severn side again and God bless the music halls!' You did not have to scratch far below the surface of Sir Edward Elgar, O.M. (as he became on 17 June 1911) to find Ted Elgar of Worcestershire. *Crown of India* has a 'March of the Mogul Emperors' and a 'Dance of the Nautch Girls' but this music, so often dismissed as trumpery, is full of the real Elgar, the dreamer by the Severn, the man who loved the birds in the hedgerows. The 'India' part is a façade behind which the poet stands, violin in hand.

. . . . .

The two symphonies and the Violin Concerto represent the midsummer of Elgar's art. They have been excellently dissected and analysed in thematic detail in other books on the composer and on the sleeves of long-playing gramophone records, so it is not proposed to add further analyses here. But something may still be said about these three works, especially the symphonies, which are masterpieces of romantic music, using the modern symphony orchestra to glorious

---

[22] *Edward Elgar: the record of a friendship*, op. cit., pp. 191–2.
[23] *Memories of a Variation*, op. cit., p. 98.

effect. Some deep puritanical strain in English criticism of the arts has often shown in a horror of the uninhibited use of colour and full-blooded emotional expression by painters, writers, and musicians. The adjectives 'gaudy' and 'vulgar' occur too frequently to allow of any other interpretation. The virtuosity of Elgar's orchestration, the acrobatic ease with which he deployed his instrumental forces, understanding to the last note the capacity of each instrument, these were regarded in his lifetime and for a time afterwards with grave suspicion. The cliché gained a hold that although the scoring was opulent in its use of tone-colour, the content of the music was empty, rhetorical, and rhapsodically uncontrolled. Because Symphony No. 1 begins with a march-tread in the basses and No. 2 is dedicated to the memory of Edward VII after having been 'designed as a loyal tribute', it was an easy step for writers in the 1920s and 1930s such as Cecil Gray and Constant Lambert to display their superficial knowledge of the works by a glib assumption that they reflected the spirit of a vulgar and complacent age. Lambert in his brilliant book *Music Ho!*[24] wrote: 'The aggressive Edwardian prosperity that lends so comfortable a background to Elgar's finales is now (1934) as strange to us as the England that produced *Greensleeves*. . . . Much of Elgar's music, through no fault of its own, has for the present generation an almost intolerable air of smugness, self-assurance and autocratic benevolence.'

Langford, living in Edwardian England, heard coldness and even austerity in that same music! In any case the Edwardians themselves regarded their own period as 'feverish'. But the predominant Elgarian mood, as was pointed out in Chapter 9, is noble, melancholy, wistful, and elegiac lyricism. It passes belief how anyone who listens attentively to the Elgar symphonies can fail to hear that, far from being smug and self-assured, they express a sense of unease and an awareness of human tragedy. Whatever they may or may not reflect of the time in which they were composed, they reflect far more of Elgar's personality. He described No. 2 as 'the passionate pilgrimage of a soul', and in both works can be heard the musical expression of the contrasts and conflicts in his make-up with which the reader will by now be familiar: exuberance followed by depression; restless gregariousness followed by loneliness and withdrawal; optimism giving way to a resigned fatalism and distrust of 'providence'; a deep nostalgia for the vanished days. No. 1 in A flat is perhaps emotionally less complex than No. 2 and its triumphant ending is one of the reasons Lambert's generation felt uneasy about it. And, of course, they equated its long opening theme with 'Land of Hope and Glory', applying political and sociological associations to what should be approached in a musical context. There again, like the trio of the first

[24](Third Edition, London 1966), p. 240.

Pomp and Circumstance march, this tune is hymn-like rather than military or martial; it is basically melancholy and it becomes heroic. To call such a long melody a 'motto-theme' is slightly ridiculous: it is more of a presence, and for Elgar it represented a moral virtue, the 'charity' mentioned in his letter to Walford Davies. This tune undergoes many transformations and vicissitudes before it emerges with banners flying fifty minutes later. Every development in the symphony can be traced to some element of this great *idée fixe*, which appears in many moods: calm, spectral, foreboding, and triumphant. Where is the 'confidence' in the first movement? Once the theme has been fully expounded the music switches violently to D minor, the key furthest from the tonic A flat major, and becomes restless and agitated. Here is a semi-military tune, obviously the villain of the piece, violent and disruptive, and with two consolatory pendant themes. The battle that rages between them is anything but complacent; the effect is of constant turbulence, of nerves on edge. When the A flat melody returns in full, after various mysterious and tentative appearances, a determined effort to crush it ends with great brass chords which have that hollow, doom-laden sound that is peculiar to Elgar. The movement ends quietly, with harps, solo violin, and clarinet contributing to the tenderness which – again it must be said – is conveyed by Elgar in music as by no one else. The second movement is also animated and nervy, with short phrases and broken rhythms for the allegro molto section and, in a central episode in B flat major, a gracefully scored, fantastic vein that belongs to the poignant world of *Dream Children* and *The Wand of Youth*. This is Elgar's nostalgia for youth, for its innocence perhaps and also for its solitude. Solo violin and woodwind repeat the main theme of this section just before the music disintegrates in broken phrases and subsides into the compassionate and heartfelt Adagio. It is the apotheosis of the withdrawn, tender side of Elgar, and to subject such emotional music to technical discussion would almost be to do it a physical injury. To borrow Vaughan Williams's words,[25] it 'has that peculiar kind of beauty which gives us, his fellow countrymen, a sense of something familiar – the intimate and personal beauty of our own fields and lanes. . . . It falls to the lot of very few composers, and to them not often, to achieve this bond of unity with their countrymen. Elgar has achieved this more often than most, and be it noted, not when he is being deliberately "popular" . . . but at those moments when he seems to have retired into the solitude of his own sanctuary.' This Adagio is certainly a sanctuary. When we reach this tune,

Ex. 7

Molto espressivo e sostenuto

etc.

pp   *f*

[25]'What Have We Learnt from Elgar?' in *Music and Letters* (January 1935), pp. 15–16.

we can agree with Jaeger that we are brought near to Heaven – and it is another manifestation of the opening march tune. The finale reverts to the restless mood of the earlier part of the symphony. The *pizzicato* theme in crotchets which stalks into the finale on the cellos (supported by bassoons) is later transformed into a radiant augmented version in G flat – which serves to emphasize the truly symphonic thematic unity and interrelationship of the whole work, for this is yet another derivation of the 'motto-theme'. It is all a preparation for the return of the A flat tune, but when it does return, in the panoply of Elgar's most glittering orchestration, it is not a rhetorical gesture nor does it have an easy passage. During this peroration note how the accompaniment tries to disrupt the flow of the theme with irregular crashes. The end is victory but it has not been easily achieved – 'a massive hope for the future'. Hope, not assurance, and hope under continual threat.

The Second Symphony is a very much more complicated structure, technically and emotionally. In places it shows signs of its long gestation; its best moments are unequalled elsewhere in Elgar's output. As every Elgarian knows, two lines by Shelley preface the printed score

> Rarely, rarely, comest thou,
> Spirit of Delight.

In the original manuscript this quotation was written by Elgar at the *end* of the finale, after his signature and the place names Careggi, The Hut, Tintagel and Plâs Gwyn. Not only is this quotation Elgar's clue to the romantic and tragic nature of the symphony, it is a broad hint that in the rest of Shelley's poem will be found other identifications with the music and the personality of its composer: the love of the countryside, for example, and the tendency to misanthropy.

> I love all that thou lovest,
> Spirit of Delight:
> The fresh earth in new leaves dressed
> And the starry night;
> Autumn evening, and the morn
> When the golden mists are born . . .
> Everything almost
> Which is Nature's, and may be
> Untainted by man's misery.
> I love tranquil solitude
> And such society
> As is quiet, wise and good, . . .
> Thou art Love and life! Oh, come,
> Make once more my heart thy home.

The first movement is on an enormous scale, huge in its breadth and

its command of orchestral resource, a supreme example of the power
and originality of Elgar's symphonic style, which combines a kind of
'fragmentation' method – particles of themes are shown in new and
unexpected guises – with the ability to move in large paragraphs,
telescoping conventional development and exposition passages.
Listen, for instance, to the start of the first movement, when violins
and cellos play their repeated B flats, followed by an upward swoop of
a sixth. The tempo quickens almost at once as another two-bar theme
appears, to be followed by two more equally short motifs. The second
and third bars of the movement contain a descending phrase which
may be taken as representing the rarity of the Spirit of Delight. This
exuberant opening rarely fails to thrill the sympathetic listener with
its effect as of a dam bursting. After this energy has spent itself, the
group of 'second subject' themes, beginning with a long cello theme,
again clearly indicates that a struggle for ascendancy between
stridency and lyricism is to occur. No Mahler movement is more
obviously a battleground for conflicting emotions and nervous
tensions than this by Elgar – and where is the comfortable Edwardian
opulence in these pounding basses, shrilling edge-of-hysteria brass, in
the muted strings, the eight hollow-sounding notes on the harp, the
strange throbbing of the timpani while the cellos, in their highest
registers, sing some unearthly lament for the ideal that is always out of
reach? It is this passage which Elgar was describing when, after
completing this movement on 29 January 1911, he wrote to Mrs
Stuart-Wortley: 'I have written the *most extraordinary* passage I have
ever heard – a sort of malign influence wandering thro' the summer
night in the garden'. (Writing to Ernest Newman on the same day, he
described this episode with a significant difference: 'There's one
passage . . . which might be a love scene in a garden at night when the
ghost of some memories comes *through* it; – it makes me shiver'.) At
the height of the movement, the 'spirit of delight' phrase is hammered
home with more climactic blows from the timpani supported by
trombones and, after a dramatic pause, the music seems to dive back
into the hurly-burly as if to escape – what is this but tragic art of deep
intensity? The slow movement is unrivalled as a national elegy, yet its
origins, as we now know, lay in the shock of Rodewald's death in
1903. It is personal as well as ceremonial and it contains, in the passage
where the oboe sings a lament in free counterpoint to the solemn
tread of the funeral march, one of Elgar's most powerful strokes of
imagination. Its climax, at [86], when the strings seem to be straining
to express the inexpressible in grief, has a paradoxically consolatory
exaltation like the sun suddenly breaking through the clouds; and
nothing is more touching than the final bars, which shuffle to a close
as if overpowered by the solemnity of death. The Rondo (third)
movement recaptures the exhilaration of the opening of the

symphony. Elgar described it as 'wild and headstrong with soothing pastoral strains in between and very brilliant'. The pastoral strain – at cue 106 – is a haunting little phrase for woodwind, ending with a drop from F sharp to C. On the sketch of this theme Elgar wrote the name 'Windflower'. The rather forced gaiety of the robust principal theme is suddenly obliterated by the enigmatic and extraordinary passage when, above a steady pulsing on E flat, the cello tune from the first movement returns – the 'malign influence in the summer night' – and the percussion, with a steady and relentless hammering, overwhelms the rest of the orchestra while the brass tear the heart out of the once-lyrical tune. The storm subsides as suddenly as it arose, but what does it mean, for some extramusical idea must have been its inspiration? W. H. Reed is among those who have noted a kinship between the theme that gives rise to this pandemonium and one written many years later for 'The Wagon Passes' in the *Nursery Suite*, and this leads to the deduction that there was some mental image for Elgar in the idea of wheels and hoofs, especially when it is known that he told Canon W. H. T. Gairdner that he associated this passage in the symphony with these lines from Tennyson's *Maud*:

> Dead, long dead,
>   Long dead!
> And my heart is a handful of dust
> And the wheels go over my head.
> And my bones are shaken with pain,
> For into a shallow grave they are thrust,
> Only a yard beneath the street,
> And the hoofs of the horses beat, beat
> The hoofs of the horses beat,
> Beat into my scalp and brain.

Elgar said in his letter to Littleton that this movement had an Italian origin, but he was referring to its light-hearted opening. Perhaps this nightmare episode has a link with the death of the demonstrator during the Italian two-day general strike while Elgar was in Rome. It seems certain that the music is intended to convey the agonized reaction of Elgar to sudden death, and it is the musical parallel to his letter to Jaeger after Rodewald's death. Some further lines from *Maud* may well have haunted Elgar:

> But up and down and to and fro
> Ever about me the dead men go.

He told orchestras when he rehearsed this section of the Rondo: 'I want you to imagine that this hammering is like that horrible throbbing in the head during some fever. It seems gradually to blot out every atom of thought in your brain and nearly drives you mad.'[26]

[26] Bernard Shore, *Sixteen Symphonies* (London, 1949), p. 279.

The last movement begins gently and with stately dignity. The rolling theme might even be called leisurely – until after a very short course it is subjected to fidgety and nervous embellishment by woodwind and strings: short broken-winded sequential passages, restless and unsure. Even the important *nobilmente* theme soon gives way to a fugal section – a weak passage of marking time – and more frenzy, with a top B for the trumpet[27] piercing the texture and, as in the First Symphony, an attempt by syncopated off-beats to upset the course of the first subject when it returns. The ending is famous: a long elegiac farewell based on the 'spirit of delight' theme, radiant, tender, compassionate, full of secret regret but consolatory and hopeful. Anything but complacent. The pilgrimage is over, the passion spent.

I make no apology for describing these works in such language. Elgar 'felt' his music; and if one cannot 'feel' it emotionally no amount of probing into its innards will do any good. Yet, of course, both can be appreciated on a purely technical level as masterly examples of symphonic construction. The old label of 'rhapsodic' hardly stands up to analysis, for both are extremely tightly and closely organized thematic compositions. Their restlessness is accounted for by the curious tonality, which is constantly and violently switched about. In both works theme after theme is found to stem from a common source: the ingenuity, whether conscious or sub-conscious, is of a kind that only a composer of the highest, Beethovenian calibre commands. I do not mean only the more obvious transformations, such as (in the First Symphony) the scherzo theme into the adagio theme and the staccato march of the finale into a broad, truly Elgarian melody. There are literally dozens of examples in both works of a fragment of melody being expanded or transformed into a new theme which again generates another. It is a kind of fission process, and it proves that although the music sounds spontaneous, Elgar (to adapt Shaw's phrase) had paid his price in headwork to achieve his effect. What Diana McVeagh has brilliantly described as his 'mosaic method of construction' indicates the sheer power of concentrated ingenuity in the interlocking of his material and also its source in a single germinal idea. He himself told C. Sanford Terry that all the themes for a particular work came 'from the same oven' and that often it was the climax of a movement that he settled first. His modulations are nearly always inspired, and perhaps the outstanding technical feature of his work is the fluent and original use of counterpoint which binds every movement together and is the basic cause of the thematic relationships. The symphonies and the Violin Concerto are a complex interwoven pattern of contrapuntal strands, and it is the poetic use of

[27] When Ernest Hall, the principal trumpet of the B.B.C. Symphony Orchestra, held this note over two bars, Elgar was so delighted that he authorized the innovation.

counterpoint that accounts for some of the most memorable moments in the works. They are filled with his melodic, harmonic, and rhythmical characteristics – rising sevenths often combined with a falling sixth; frequent 'leaps' to accented passing-notes, giving a sense of urgency; strongly accented metrical patterns; and the use of elementary diatonic effects to achieve a startling simplicity. To regard Elgar as merely a supreme improviser is to misunderstand him utterly. He was both architect and interior decorator. Westrup, in his paper from which I have already quoted, singles out Elgar's method of 'composition from isolated scraps' – surely a further derivation from his natural bent for improvisation. 'His autograph sketches', Westrup said, 'confirm the picture. It is difficult for anyone looking at them now to imagine how such an apparently disorderly mass of material came to be welded into works which seem to have a compelling unity. But this was Elgar's method . . . Anything that might be useful was jotted down, and then when the time came there was a process of assembling and rejecting the raw material. Few of us could produce a work like *Gerontius* by this method; but with Elgar it worked wonders, over and over again. It is only when it failed that we notice the seams.'[28]

In both symphonies the orchestral scoring is of a richness and subtlety that still sound remarkable and must, from an English composer in the early 1900s, have sounded superhuman. I could fill pages with descriptions of particular passages – the end of the Adagio of the A flat symphony is paramount – but I presume that my readers will know the works and, if they do not, the music itself is its own best advocate and they should seek it out. But on this subject of Elgar's orchestration it is worth quoting the views of an orchestral player and of another composer. First, Bernard Shore, for many years principal viola of the B.B.C. Symphony Orchestra and one of England's most experienced and distinguished practitioners: 'In one respect no composer has ever matched Elgar. None other has fully exploited all the orchestral instruments and at the same time written nothing impossible. In this latter respect Strauss frequently sins, and so did Wagner. . . . Elgar was unerring.'[29]

And Vaughan Williams, who was also a conductor and knew the problems of working with amateurs when 'extra' instruments were not available and either had to be omitted or written in for another instrument: 'I have found that with Wagner the extra instruments could almost always be dispensed with altogether, with a little loss of colour it is true, but with no damage to the texture. But when it came to Elgar the case was quite different. Even in the accompaniments to choral movements there was hardly anything that could be left out

[28]'Elgar's Enigma', op. cit., p. 90.
[29]*Sixteen Symphonies*, op. cit., p. 258.

without leaving a "hole" in the texture.'[30]

It is invidious to decide which is the finer of the symphonies. Much depends on the listener's mood at the time, as well, of course, as on the quality of interpretation and performance. The First Symphony contains, in the Adagio, the best single movement, and the variations between its heights and depths are less than in No. 2. But the E flat has moments when it attains the loftiest heights. It is more difficult to play and to conduct, and there are days when even a sympathetic listener can be exhausted by its quixotic moodiness. If it receives an unconvinced interpretation, one can understand why some people find it attitudinizing music, rather self-consciously aware of its place in the history of the epic symphony, and one can sympathize with the criticism that the notes imply more than they actually convey. But when it is played and interpreted well, all doubts are swept away and it is one of the most thrilling, moving, and enduring experiences that music can provide.

The symphonies' companion-piece, the Violin Concerto, is of a more intimate nature although it is on an equally imposing scale. It is nearly as long as the symphonies, but none of these works is too long because their material justifies the length at which it is treated and sustains the interest in its treatment. The concerto is Elgar's most personal work, a self-communing and a declaration of secret love. Yet it is elaborate and spacious in conception and execution. No matter whose soul it enshrines, it enshrines the soul of the violin and of the composer. It depends for its perfect interpretation on a close and intuitive understanding of the subtleties of rubato, fractional variations of tempo, infinitesimally fluctuating nuances of expression, little hesitations and catches of the breath that bestrew the soloist's part. Above all it must be played with a full and singing tone, for the writing for violin is almost vocal, and operatically vocal, in its curving intensity. It needs stamina, too, and the ability to dominate a large orchestra. In short it is a great violin concerto for great violinists. The thematic material is copious but again is shown throughout the work to be closely related, and the structure of the first movement, in which the development section is replaced by a free fantasia on the themes, is bold in its originality. There are two outstanding passages, the first entry of the violin, which remains a moving and surprising moment no matter how many times one hears it because of the way the orchestra plays the first two bars of the principal theme leaving the soloist to complete it, and the accompanied cadenza in the finale when, over an accompaniment of strings *pizzicato tremolando* ('thrummed' was Elgar's description) and occasionally the full orchestra, the soloist recalls themes from the

[30]'What Have We Learnt from Elgar?' op. cit., p. 15.

earlier movements, caresses them, lingers lovingly over them and finally bids them a regretful farewell. The first subject of the first movement becomes the final theme of the cadenza, its ardour changed to wistfulness. It is a theme from the essential Elgar, a tune from his childhood which can be heard in its earlier form in the overture to the first *Wand of Youth* Suite. All Elgar's love and understanding of his favourite instrument is in this concerto and especially in this cadenza which is the most poetic cadenza in the world, for it not only displays the instrument's technical range but enables it to show its unrivalled capacity for emotional expression. The 'thrumming' was suggested to Elgar by the sound of the Aeolian harp which he had fixed outside a window at Plâs Gwyn. This concerto is sensuous music, colourful, rich, uninhibited, for even the restraint of the Andante is soon swept by gusts of passion. The slow movement is unequalled in Elgar's work as an expression of passionate regret. No soloist and conductor who does not relish the concerto for these qualities should ever approach it. It is not music for faint hearts nor for the austere. It requires devotion, but it must not sound devout. Elgar wrote of 'philanthropy' in connection with this concerto, and generosity above all else, notably in the grandiose parts of the finale, is what it needs from its interpreters.

.   .   .   .   .

Installed in Hampstead, Elgar began 1912 in busy fashion, conducting the L.S.O. in London and taking them on tour. W. H. Reed, who to Elgar's delight was now leader of the orchestra, says that these tours 'did him a world of good, as they took him out of himself. . . . He was on the best of terms with the orchestra and never tired of telling them he was "one of them" . . .' While travelling by rail Elgar regaled the impresario Percy Harrison 'and those with him in his reserved saloon carriage with endless stories of his youth, the country people, and his travels abroad . . . rubbing his hands together gleefully, entirely forgetting the pessimistic moods and the despondency that sometimes overtook him'.[31] (To the end of his life he enjoyed the company of orchestral players. He understood their quirks and humour. While the orchestra were tuning up at a Queen's Hall concert to which he went with Adrian Boult in the 1920s, he said: 'Adrian, just listen to what that trumpeter is doing. Now if I'd written that, he'd say it was unplayable.') While they were in Leeds, the Festival committee asked Elgar to conduct at the 1913 festival and to compose a new work. The animosities of 1904 were forgotten. In January and February he was deep in his music for the masque *The*

[31] *Elgar As I Knew Him*, op. cit., pp. 107–8.

Crown of India, which he soon 'cooked up' from discarded sketches. He viewed it quite frankly as a potboiler. As he told Frances Colvin: 'When I write a big serious work e.g. *Gerontius*, we have had to starve and go without fires for twelve months as a reward: this small effort allows me to buy scientific works I have yearned for and I spend my time between the Coliseum and the old bookshops. . . . I found a lovely old volume *Tracts Against Popery* – I appeased Alice by saying I bought it to prevent other people seeing it – but it wd. make a cat laugh.'

He was still physically unwell. He had ear trouble and gout. 'I have been very very dreary,' he wrote to Mrs. Stuart-Wortley in April 1912, '& have felt this terrible Titanic disaster acutely & I have been lonely. . . . Welcome home.' Another mood is described in a letter to Frances Colvin of 27 April: 'I took a walk again this p.m. & saw a flock of sheep – bless them – talking a language I have known since I was two years old – then two *excellent* anti-Socialist lectures on the heath – & last but most effective the Hampstead *prize band* playing uproarious selections also on the heath: I heard & subscribed to this mild attempt at a continental Sabbath . . . & was very happy.' But he was homesick for Worcestershire – 'I long for a sight of my own country', he told Canon Gorton. It was this escapist mood that impelled him to complete the setting of Arthur O'Shaughnessy's poem *The Music Makers* on which he had been working intermittently since about 1903. (Jaeger referred to it once in a 1904 letter as 'The Dreamers'.) Elgar had first inquired about obtaining permission to set the poem (published in a volume called 'Music and Moonlight') in September 1907 and this was obtained a year later. On 23 May 1912, Alice Elgar's diary states, he was 'not very happy' about his progress with the music – 'not "lit up" yet'. But it was completed by mid-July and fully scored by 21 August. He had composed some of the music while fishing the Wye at his favourite spot, Mordiford Bridge, and this in itself is a clue to the obsessively personal and 'secret' nature of the music. His 'spiritual home' at Hampstead, he told Alice Stuart-Wortley, was the tree-lined Judge's Walk, and he wrote its name under the opening section of the work, which contains the melody that is perhaps the most Elgarian expression of yearning in all his music and at the same time seems to symbolize inspiration itself. The poem, with its stress on the 'apartness' of the creative artist, appealed strongly to Elgar. In a note he wrote in July 1912 he spoke of the music as 'mainly sad' but added: 'There are moments of enthusiasm and bursts of joy occasionally approaching frenzy: moods which the creative artist suffers in creating or in contemplation of the unending influence of his creation. Yes, suffers – this is the only word I dare to use, for even the highest ecstasy of "making" is mixed with the consciousness of the sombre dignity of the eternity of the artist's responsibility.' Yet perhaps the clue to *The Music Makers* is also a major clue to Elgar himself – its original title *The Dreamers*. Elgar's music is the music of dreams; not the haunted nocturnal fancies of Britten's music, but daydreams of a world beyond reach. The word runs through his music: *The Dream of Gerontius*, *Dream Children*; in the Piers Plowman quotation which partly inspired *Cockaigne* there is the line 'I have no care of dreams if I see them fail'; the part-song 'Serenade', composed in 1914, begins and ends with the words 'Dreams all too brief, dreams without grief, Once they are broken come not again' (this part-song is sub-titled 'Hadley Green', an area near Barnet to which Elgar was often taken by Alice Stuart-Wortley); and the last movement of the *Nursery Suite* was to be called 'Dreaming'. Criticism of the music has often resolved into criticism of O'Shaughnessy's poem, but though not great verse it is no worse than many another chosen by musicians. The other major criticism of *The Music Makers* has always been of Elgar's use of quotations from his other works, though why this should be reprehensible *per se* is not clear. Composers whose music is powerfully and essentially Romantic have always made skilful and valid use of quotations and self-quotations, for example Mahler, Strauss, and Shostakovich. To read most commentators on *The Music Makers*, one would think that the music was one long quotation whereas the references to previous works occupy only a small percentage (see p. 360). I think they are recalled with deeply moving effect and perfect taste. When the Nimrod theme is given to the voices it is slightly varied melodically, so that it becomes a free counterpoint to the orchestral statement of the tune. The effect is wonderful. The Enigma theme dominates the orchestral introduction, a plain indication of the autobiographical nature of the work. Elgar said: 'I have used the . . . theme because it expressed when written (in 1898) my sense of the loneliness of the artist as described in the first six lines of the ode and, to me, it still embodies that sense. At the end of the full score of the *Variations* I wrote: "Bramo assai, poco spero, nulla chieggio" (Tasso) ["I long for much, I hope for little, I ask for nothing"]. This was true in 1898 and might be written with equal truth at the end of this work in 1912.' 'The dreamers of dreams' introduces a fragment of *Gerontius*; there is a further reference to the Enigma and to the Violin Concerto at 'we dwell in our dreaming and singing a little apart'; 'wand'ring by lone sea breakers' evokes *Sea Pictures*; fragments of the symphonies are heard; at 'on one man's soul it hath broken a light that doth not depart' the Nimrod theme pays further tribute to Jaeger's encouragement. 'I do not mean to convey his was the only word or look that "wrought flame in another man's heart",' Elgar wrote, 'but I do convey that amongst all the inept writing and wrangling about music his voice was clear, ennobling, sober and sane.' It was, perhaps, again of Jaeger that Elgar was thinking when he recalled 'Novissima hora est' for 'a dreamer who slumbers and a singer who sings no more'. The choral writing is as good as any he achieved, and there are even anticipations of themes later to be used in the Cello Concerto. The small contralto part, written for Muriel Foster, requires an intensity which she must have been well able to bring to it. 'Tinsel' and 'tawdry' have been the pejorative words applied to this cantata, but rather than finding it 'under-composed', I find it an original treatment of the poem, and one of Elgar's most endearing and unjustly under-rated works. If the words stirred personal memories, why should he not have linked them to the musical embodiment of those memories? Rather than showing a lack of inventive resource, this weaving of fragments from the past into the texture of what is a declaration of the artist's standpoint is, in my opinion, a most original and imaginative solution of the creator's problem of lending significance to his own 'passionate pilgrimage' in art. In the poem he found the roots of his own motivation as a composer, and it was natural, therefore, to treat it musically by showing what had grown from the roots. To the unsympathetic, the work will certainly be repellent because it so accurately reflects the subjective, self-centred, self-aware side of Elgar that is illustrated by his strange letter to Alice Stuart-Wortley (quoted in Chapter 8) about his walk on Hampstead Heath after he had finished setting the Ode. Of its importance to him as an artist one is left in no doubt by this extract from another letter to Mrs Stuart-Wortley (29 August 1912): 'I have written out my soul in the concerto, Sym. II & the Ode & you know it . . . in these three works I have *shewn* myself.' Also, he had enshrined the souls of Nimrod, Schuster and Windflower in the Ode, as the quotations imply.

To add to its personal significance for him, he dedicated *The Music Makers* to Nicholas Kilburn who lost no time in performing it, with his Bishop Auckland Music Society, a few months after the first performance at the Birmingham Festival on 1 October 1912. Kilburn wrote to Elgar putting into words something of what he felt of music's, and especially Elgar's music's, moral force. The reply he received (written on 26 March 1913) must have startled him:

You talk mystically as becomes you & your northern atmosphere. I cannot follow you. I could have done a few years back – but the whole thing (no matter how one fights & avoids it) is merely commercial – this is forced into every fibre of me every moment. Not long ago one could occasionally shake this off & forget, but an all-foolish providence takes care that it shall not be unremembered for a moment & so – & so?? You say 'we must look up'. To what? to whom? Why? The mind bold and independent, the purpose free must not think, must not hope – yet it seems sad that the only quotation I can find to fit my life comes from the Demons' chorus! a fanciful summing up!

To what – to whom – why? The 'dreamer of dreams' was a deeply divided, unhappy man. He had lost his faith in God and now he had no faith in man's redemption. He could not easily settle to composing in London: there were too many distractions. Alice held court at Severn House – the Paderewskis, Siegfried Wagner, Siloti, Hamilton Harty, Chaliapin (whose first London *Boris* Elgar saw and liked): all were entertained. There were the Royal Academy dinner, the Academy Private View, the games of billiards with friends, sitting for a portrait, news of performances of the Violin Concerto in Russia. Returning to the land which had stimulated Elgar's creative faculties on previous occasions, they went in January 1913 to Naples and Capri. The trick worked, and Elgar decided that his work for Leeds should be a symphonic study of Falstaff, a project he had considered eleven years before. But before they left for home in February they heard that Julia Worthington was dying of cancer in New York. On his return to London Elgar was depressed and ill. He sketched bits of *Falstaff*, but could not concentrate. He went alone to Llandrindod Wells for a 'cure' and then to his sister's in Worcestershire. He worked on the new score in earnest in May, but the deaths within a few days of each other of Lord Northampton and Mrs Worthington – 'our dear dear Pippa', Alice called her – depressed him. By cruel coincidence, the news of Julia Worthington's death came on the day of a London performance of *The Music Makers*. But he finished *Falstaff* in June and July, stirred by memories awakened by letters from Rosa Burley. 'My dear Rosa', he wrote in July, 'Yes I remember all the sweetness of it – the syringa, then the beans and the limes. I suppose I shall never see it all again or cycle over the old place. How lovely the Marsh must be – I envy you your seeing it and living in it all again. During the two moments I have spent in M.[alvern] all the people seem to disappear & only the eternal hills and all the memories of the old loveliness remains'. At this time, too, his pride was hurt when he was told by the London Symphony Orchestra that they were not renewing his engagement as principal conductor. He put the last notes to the score of *Falstaff* early on 5 August. Alice's diary paints a touching picture: 'E. down at 4 a.m. A. made him tea &c. &c. & he finished his great work *Falstaff*'.

He corrected early proofs of *Falstaff* and wrote an analytical note for *Musical Times* while on holiday at Penmaenmawr, North Wales, in August. 'Falstaff is immense,' he had written to Troyte in July, 'it lasts 20 minutes [sic!] & you will like it only it wants a gigantesque orchestra.' Other large projects were also in his mind. He wrote to Sidney Colvin on 22 July: 'Chaliapin has been here & talking over many schemes for a great part for himself "Lear"! for instance: you have seen him, I suppose – a splendid *man* – figure and mind – & the finest artist I have ever heard. But there is also a scheme for an allegorical affair on a huge scale – these two things may hold me musically for some time but I shall keep in mind the Hardy ideas [for an opera] & if my half-promises for the other two things are not wanted to be kept I will at once plunge into the Hardy work if it can be arranged.'

Elgar conducted the first performance of *Falstaff* at Leeds on 2 October 1913. It was badly placed in a long programme and was received with cold respect. Lady Elgar's diary comment was: 'E. rather hurried it & some of the lovely melodies were a little smothered but it made its mark & place. E. changed, very depressed after'. Robin Legge in *The Daily Telegraph* wished that a greater conductor than Elgar had conducted, 'for much of the wondrous maze of detail in this score did not become audible at all to me'. He called it a 'masterpiece' but urged Elgar to cut the score by five or more minutes. And he noticed the music's principal defect: 'I have not yet fathomed the (to me) mystery as to why what I believe is called in theatrical language the "fat" of the music is applied to other folk and their doings, or to description, and not to the protagonist himself.' When it was played in London under Landon Ronald[32] a few weeks later, on 3 November, Legge rebuked the capital's public because there was 'only a beggarly row of half-empty benches'. At the first Manchester performance on 27 November, the reception by the Hallé audience was described by Langford as 'hardly enthusiastic' It was a bad performance and the music emerged as 'disjointed and broken'. Elgar was missing the attentions of a master-conductor like Richter. He sent his old friend the score on 24 November with the words 'How I wish you were going to conduct this work!' Two and a half years earlier, just after Richter's retirement, Elgar had sent him the score of the Second Symphony saying 'it was meant for you to like'. It is interesting to speculate on Richter's interpretations of the Violin Concerto, the E flat symphony, and *Falstaff*. A thousand pities that these works came too late for him. *Falstaff* certainly came too early for it to be a success with the 1913 public. It is a long and complex work, swift-moving and episodic. The detail and learning in Elgar's programme-note would daunt any audience at a first hearing. It had no chance in the orchestral conditions of those days when very few rehearsals were possible. For an orchestra to play *Falstaff* well, it must not only master the notes, it must know the music thoroughly and intimately, have the score in its head, not its head in the score.

According to Eric Fenby,[33] Elgar regarded *Falstaff* as his best work. From the viewpoint of virtuosity, of complete command of instrumental effect and colour, this is undoubtedly true. Every point

[32]It is dedicated to Ronald. In the 1920s the young Barbirolli remarked to him what a wonderful work it was, to receive the reply: 'I can't make head or tail of it.'
[33]*Delius As I Knew Him* (London, 1936, 2nd ed. 1966), p. 115.

is made. It is musicians' music. I rate it below the symphonies, the Violin Concerto, and the *Variations*. There is an air of midnight oil and of literary knowledge about the work that is foreign to Elgar's usual spontaneity and expressiveness. He had loved Shakespeare since his talks with Ned Spiers in the room above his father's shop in High Street, Worcester, and he was something of a Shakespearean authority; it is evident from his analysis that he had read all the leading commentaries on the character of Falstaff and had determined to vindicate the Falstaff of *Henry IV* rather than the buffoon of *The Merry Wives of Windsor*, something easier to do in prose than in music. So we get a Falstaff in C minor, almost a tragic figure who uncannily resembles Elgar himself! Elgar's Falstaff yearns nostalgically for his days in the 'Wand of Youth' when he was page to the Duke of Norfolk; he dies not only babbling of green fields but almost like a Gerontius with memories of the anthems he has sung in a West Country cathedral; he is more likely to idealize the women in the Boar's Head than pinch their bottoms. In other words Elgar chose those aspects, as he saw them, of Falstaff which appealed to his musical style. The Falstaff theme, as apt for variation as the Enigma, lacks any suggestion of coarseness and it is hardly surprising that Tovey, in his analysis of the work, attributed a variant of it to the phrase 'blown up like a bladder with sighing and grief' when Elgar's intention was to depict 'a goodly portly man, of a cheerful look, a pleasing eye, and a most noble carriage'. Prince Hal, of course, comes out of it more simply: his theme lacks the real note of nobility, and, in fact, is not marked *nobilmente*. It has been suggested to me by a composer that this theme is outstandingly inventive because it shows that Elgar is telling us from the start that Hal will treat Falstaff shabbily at the end. I wonder if Elgar was ever tempted to call the work 'Henry the Fifth' as Verdi was once tempted to call *Otello* 'Iago'. For a tone-poem on this scale to succeed, the music must be so vivid that no explanation is necessary, or it must be thematically so distinguished that no explanation matters, the listener is quite happy anyway. This is where *Falstaff* several times fails – I hasten to add, once again, in my opinion. Of course when a listener has done his homework – and these days it is much easier to do so – it is obvious that all the scurrying and rustling represent the episode at Gads Hill, and the struggle for the twice-stolen booty 'got with much ease', and that one of the themes when treated in an energetic fugal manner illustrates the discomfiture of the thieves. But without that knowledge the music, I submit, is not very interesting in itself and once the knowledge is gained the passage soon palls and becomes something to be endured until the imagination is stirred again. Harmonically and contrapuntally it is magnificent and one appreciates why Tovey the analyst and professor gloated over the score at this point. I always wish Elgar's estimate to Troyte that *Falstaff* lasted twenty minutes had proved accurate, for then we should have had an unflawed masterpiece that out-Straussed Strauss, because Elgar demonstrates in the best parts of the score that he is Strauss's equal in depicting events in music and his superior in the matter of emotional expressiveness. Like *In the South, Falstaff* has two self-contained interludes which interrupt the main flow but paradoxically give it a binding unity. These two interludes are the finest parts of the score, indeed they are among the finest parts of Elgar, perfect examples of the miniature Elgar done with supreme taste. The first is unmistakably introduced by Falstaff (bassoon), drunk on sack, falling to sleep behind the arras. He drifts into sleep – has this state of mind ever been conveyed in music so exactly ?[34] – and as he sleeps he dreams of his youth in music of the most tender nostalgic fragrance, untouched by any trace of self-indulgence. As in the Violin Concerto, a solo violin muses on what might have been. The music henceforward is programme-music of the highest order. The ramshackle recruits whom Falstaff commands are recognizable without reference to any analysis, as they slouch along, and so is the battle scene. After the battle we have another of Elgar's masterly theme transformations which justifies the word symphonic in the work's title. The ramshackle gait of the scarecrow army:

Ex. 8

becomes this songful, blithe tune as they approach the orchards of the West Country

Ex. 9

just as Elgar's heart must have lifted every time he returned from London to Worcestershire. It is moments such as this which one cherishes in *Falstaff*. The second interlude, Shallow's Orchard, juxtaposes a rustic tabor and pipe tune with a sleepy melody which must represent the peace of being in the countryside. After the interlude has obviously ended, this motive tries to continue but is brushed aside by the violins introducing Harry's theme, now that he is King, and Falstaff in augmentation as he sees himself at the King's right hand. The last ten minutes of the work are magnificent. No one

---

[34] A similar passage in Elgar's music, which it is interesting to compare, is the link between the second and third movements of the First Symphony.

but Elgar could so vividly have evoked – so that we can almost see them – the excited crowds round the Abbey, peering on tiptoe for a sight of the King's procession, throwing their hats in the air and cheering. (Note the little solo for side-drum of which Elgar himself was very proud.) The King arrives, *grandioso*, and banishes Falstaff, whose collapse is expressed in a nonplussed, bewildered breaking-up of his theme. His death scene is very great music. The music to which he fell asleep to dream of his youth returns, but we can sense that this is the prelude to eternal sleep. Themes from the past are recalled, some sharply, some hazily, as his mind wanders. The prince's theme becomes wonderfully tender, an idealization of their friendship. Elgar uses the clarinet for the last moments, the King's imperious shadow falls coldly across the picture, there is a roll of drums, and all is over. If the first part of the work was on a similar artistic level, then *Falstaff* could be declared its creator's noblest achievement. As it is, it contains some of his greatest music. It is a work that repays the closest study of its score, which is a miracle of ingenuity and skill.[35] The nation that has produced a composer capable of writing *Falstaff* can hold its head high. For all its Shakespearean learning, *Falstaff* is wholly Elgarian. To Ernest Newman, Elgar wrote: '*Falstaff* . . . is the name, but Shakespeare – the whole of human life – is the theme'.[36]

The start of the year 1914 found Elgar at Severn House working over some of his old pieces from sketchbooks – *Carissima*, for example – and writing the splendid and much under-rated part-songs of op. 71, 72, and 73. These were all completed by 3 February. Two of them, 'The Shower' and 'The Fountain' bear the inscriptions 'At Mill Hill' and 'At Totteridge', places he had visited with Alice Stuart-Wortley. He sent them to Novello's, naming his fee. The firm's new chairman, Augustus Littleton, (1854–1942, brother of Alfred) writing from Cannes to the company secretary Henry Clayton, called Elgar's terms 'high amounting to extortion but . . . other houses would jump at the stuff at the price . . . I don't want any more Elgar symphonies or concertos, but am ready to take as many part-songs as he can produce, even at extortionate rates.' Comment, even if coherent, would perhaps be superfluous! On 21 January Elgar conducted *Carissima* for a gramophone recording, its first performance and his first contact with a medium in which he took an increasing and practical interest. He looked again at his sketches for a piano concerto but his heart was not in it. He was easily distracted by the operas and concerts of the London season, and, restless as ever, he

---

[35]In a letter to Novello's about *Falstaff*, Elgar wrote on 7 November 1913: 'I wrote the 3 trombone parts for the new seven-valved insts. – they have these low notes (bless them!)'.

[36]Letter from Elgar to Newman, 26 September 1913.

went to Stratford for the Shakespeare birthday and to the Isle of Man
to adjudicate at a festival. He painted heraldic shields in the billiard-
room of Severn House and built a workshop above the stables. He
collected prints of old Worcester to hang in his study. An odd episode
is recounted in a letter to Alice Stuart-Wortley dated 3 May 1914:
'After all I did not dine at the R.A. – I went in, found they had *omitted*
my O.M. & put me with a crowd of nobodies in the lowest place of all
– the bottom table – I see no reason why I should *endure* insults – I can
understand their being offered to me. Love & thanks for all your kind
troubles: all wasted. I left at once and came here [the Athenaeum] &
had a herring.' (He had made a similar impulsive decision in June
1911 when he refused to attend George V's Coronation and forbade
Alice to go, thus hurting her deeply.) In June he conducted the
Leeds Choral Union in *The Apostles* in Canterbury Cathedral; it was
after this performance, as mentioned in Chapter 10, that Embleton
persuaded him to think again about the third part of the trilogy of
oratorios. Their holiday in July was spent in Scotland, in Ross,
where they could look across to Skye and where Elgar and his
daughter could take a boat out to sea to fish. 'The wild birds feed
their young within 30 yards of this window – gannets, oyster-
catchers and divers and a dozen others', he wrote to Mrs Stuart-
Wortley. His wife thought it the most beautiful place they had
visited except Bavaria. Six days after Alice wrote those words,
Bavaria was part of enemy territory. The Elgars watched the troop
trains pass through Inverness and Edinburgh as they made their way
back to London. 'The spirit of the men is splendid', he wrote on 6
August to Alice Stuart-Wortley, to whom he had earlier telegraphed
for information about the rumours reaching Scotland in the days of
no radio and slow delivery of newspapers, 'the Seaforths went first,
later in the week the mounted Lovats Scouts rode through – were
given a sort of tea meal here [Gairloch Hotel] by the manageress &
rode off in the moonlight by the side of the loch & disappeared into
the mountains. . . . I *wish* I could go to the front but they may find
some menial occupation for a worthless person.' He went to the first
Promenade Concert on 15 August. The audience was wildly enthusiastic about the patriotic music Henry Wood conducted. Yet in the
same concert was the first performance of a new Elgar work, *Sospiri*,
for strings and harp, a little masterpiece dedicated to W. H. Reed and
completed the previous February. How out of place it must have
sounded in an atmosphere of 'Now God be thanked who has
matched us with His hour' and 'Pack up your troubles' and 'Wider
still and wider'. For it is, though short, a major work of grave
beauty, an epitome of Elgar's ability to express nostalgic regret. The
earlier *Elegy* for strings (1909) is a formal expression of condolence
compared with the wounded heart-cry of *Sospiri*. Its dedication to

Reed was presumably in gratitude for his work on the concerto. It was written after the death of Julia Worthington, so the personal nature of its sorrow is understandable. But the brooding tragedy of the music, its Mahlerian intensity, suggest that these 'sighs' are for something known only to Elgar in, as he once put it, his 'insidest inside'. To that war-excited audience as yet unbaptized by fire it must have sounded out of key. If they could have looked six years ahead to the Cello Concerto, they would have recognized the note of desolate agony. A sketch for *Sospiri* is headed 'Absence'. Both here and in *The Music Makers* Elgar made nostalgia almost tangible, just as he had in the 'what-might-have-been' vein of the Violin Concerto. As Jerrold Northrop Moore has said, he had to find in his memories a richness, a poetry, and a heartache that only time could put there. The past, however, was becoming never-never-land.

To Schuster on 25 August 1914, Elgar wrote:

Concerning the war I say nothing – the only thing that wrings my heart & soul is the thought of the horses – oh! my beloved animals – the men and women can go to hell – but my horses; I walk round & round this room cursing God for allowing dumb beasts to be tortured – let Him kill his human beings but – how CAN he? Oh, my horses.[37]

What manner of man was this, who had composed the death of Falstaff and the cadenza of the Violin Concerto and could consign human being in wartime to hell? Before the war was over, one of the singers of his music, the baritone Charles Mott, was to write to Elgar: 'There is one thing that "puts the wind up me" very badly & that is of my being wiped out & thus miss the dear harmonies of your wonderful works.' A few hours later, Mott was wiped out.[38]

[37] A similar passage occurs in Robert Graves's autobiography *Goodbye to All That* when he describes the Western Front: 'I was shocked by the dead horses and mules; human corpses were all very well, but it seemed wrong for animals to be dragged into the war like this.' (Penguin edn., p. 173).
[38] Mott died of wounds in France, 12 May 1918.

Part III

DECLINE

1914–1934

'The bright day is done and we are for the dark'

12 War

Ernest Newman, writing in the *Musical Times* of September 1914 on 'The War and the Future of Music', remarked that in England Elgar was still 'the one figure of impressive stature'. It was nearly fifteen years since the *Variations* had first been played and the English musical scene in that time had been transformed. Yet much remained the same. Parry was still director of the Royal College of Music, Stanford still taught there and was still Professor at Cambridge, Mackenzie was still Principal of the Royal Academy of Music, Brodsky was still Principal of the Royal Manchester College of Music and still active enough as a soloist to have played the Violin Concerto in Vienna in 1913 under Franz Schalk. But Elgar's name and fame surpassed them all. He stood aloof from 'schools' of music, he had no academic position, he exerted no direct influence on the young. He had seen new names come into prominence but none challenged his supremacy. Bantock had his admirers, Josef Holbrooke enjoyed a brief spell of attention, and Delius was regarded almost as a foreign composer. Of a younger group the most successful and admired was Vaughan Williams, whose *A London Symphony*, first played in March 1914, owed something to Elgar's example. His friend Gustav Holst was known only to a restricted circle. Ethel Smyth, J. B. McEwen, Frank Bridge, Arnold Bax, Cyril Scott, York Bowen, Percy Grainger – all had work to their credit but some had yet to make their mark and others, though they did not realize it, had already made what mark was within their capacity. One thing was common to all the younger men: they could face the world of music bravely and confidently, and this they owed, as much as to anything, to the vantage-point won for them by Elgar.

When he returned to Severn House in August 1914, he joined the special constabulary in Hampstead and became a staff inspector. 'One does what one can,' he wrote to Schuster. 'It's a pity I am too old to be a soldier. I am so active. Everything is at a standstill & we have nothing left in the world – absolute financial ruin – but we are cheerful & I will die a man if not a musician.' Schuster played up to him and asked for a special constable to be posted at 'The Hut' for an indefinite period. Elgar, whose number in the force was 0015014, replied: 'State what feminine society The Hut will provide for No. 0015014. On receiving your reply the matter shall be proceeded with at once.'[1] But

[1] In 1915 Elgar resigned from the Special Constabulary and joined the Hampstead Volunteer Reserve, the First World War equivalent of the Home Guard.

it was soon apparent that this was not to be a war for 'japes'. His friend and patron, Sir Edgar Speyer, was bitterly attacked in the press for his alleged pro-German sympathies and even accused of signalling to German submarines from his Norfolk home. Elgar stood by him and received a letter written on 24 October 1914, saying how much Speyer and his wife had been 'touched by your kind letter and we appreciate this friendly greeting and mark of confidence at a time when sense of fairness and proportion and logic seem to have forsaken a section of the people.' Belgium was over-run and news of supposed German atrocities horrified the British people. A patriotic poem called *Carillon* by the Belgian Emile Cammaerts stirred Elgar deeply and he provided it with a musical background. It was first performed at Queen's Hall on 7 December 1914, recited by the poet's wife, Tita Brand, who was the daughter of the first *Gerontius* Angel, Marie Brema. Early in 1915 Elgar took the L.S.O. on a provincial tour performing *Carillon* in every town, with Constance Collier and sometimes Cammaerts himself as reciter. The work caught the mood of the moment. The patriotic fervour of the words, matched by fiery and where necessary gentle music, excited audiences to white-heat and, according to Dunhill, 'created a sensation in the concert-hall the like of which London can never have witnessed either before or since'. Henry Ainley and Réjane were among those who declaimed it. So, at private gatherings, were Schuster and Lalla Vandervelde, daughter of Edward Speyer and wife of a Belgian minister. It was at one of these private performances that Alice was reminded that England still had some way to go before it could call itself musical. She found the audience 'like old county family people who knew *nothing* of music. Old Lady Lurgan said occasionally "That is pretty".' The breed is not yet extinct. *Carillon* was so closely bound to the mood of the hour that its expectation of life was obviously short, although it was revived, with new words by Laurence Binyon, in the Second World War. But nothing could revive the spirit of 1914–15. Later in the war Elgar tried but failed to repeat the success of *Carillon* with two other Cammaerts recitations, *Une Voix dans le Désert* and *Le drapeau belge*. The former was conducted (after its first performance) by Beecham whom Alice described as 'very phantasmagoric, & not appealing to us *at all*'. He drank water and wanted to be called Thomas. It seems hardly believable.

After the war had lasted for a year, the mood had turned sour and bitter. The war was horrible, torturing, brutal. Casualty figures were sickening; London was raided almost nightly by Zeppelins. To Elgar it was the epitomization of the despair in his soul. He looked back with increasingly rosy gaze on the peacefulness of his childhood in the provincial solitude of the 1860s. He was ripe, on 10 November 1915, for the proposal for incidental music brought to him, at the critic

Robin Legge's suggestion, by the actress Lena Ashwell (1872–1957). She had known him for over five years and probably knew about *The Wand of Youth* play he had written with his brothers and sisters in 1867. She wanted to produce an adaptation by Violet Pearn of an Algernon Blackwood novel, *A Prisoner in Fairyland*, under the title *The Starlight Express*.[2] Its theme was the same as *The Wand of Youth* – children had vision, grown-ups were obstructive. Briefly, the children of an English family living in a village in the Jura mountains are misunderstood by the adults. They form a secret society in which each member is a star or a constellation. They believe that while they are asleep their spirits play among the stars and collect stardust (sympathy). It sticks to them and makes them shiny. It collects in star caves, into which anyone who hopes to accomplish anything useful in life must go. The children's ambition is to get their confused ('wumbled') parents out of their bodies and into a star cave. They are helped by Cousin Henry and the figures of his own imaginative childhood, a Tramp, a Gardener, a Lamplighter, a Dustman and the Laugher. He has brought them from his English childhood in the Starlight Express, a train of thought. Eventually the parents and other adults are 'saved' and the earth remembers it is a star. The play ends with the Star of Bethlehem shining.

This piece of whimsy owes much to Barrie and is of particular interest because it is one more example of the late-Victorian escape into an imagined golden age of childhood – the English literature and poetry of the period can show many similar examples. Elgar was immediately attracted and, encouraged by Alice Stuart-Wortley, agreed to write a score. By 13 November he had decided to adapt his *Wand of Youth* music again – 'Fairies and Giants' had originally been his 'Humoreske, Broadheath 1867' – and had drawn tears from Lena Ashwell by his playing of the 'Fountain Dance'. Two days later he met and liked Blackwood and one evening after dinner at Severn House he, Alice, and Blackwood had a 'nice out-of-the-world talk late round the fire'. As he worked, Elgar found that the score was growing. It was not just an adaptation of the old tunes; there were new ones. Novello's were not interested in publishing it; Landon Ronald arranged for Elkin to do so. Throughout December Elgar worked absorbedly, helped by Alice ruling the bar-lines, writing in the instruments' names, and the words of the songs. There were consultations with Julius Harrison, who was to conduct it in the theatre, and his assistant Anthony Bernard. All was sweetness and light, befitting the play, until Elgar went to the Kingsway Theatre on 27 December, two days before the première, and saw the settings. He was furious. To a friend of the designer he wrote: 'Your friend has

[2] Elgar was not the first choice as composer of *The Starlight Express*. As early as March 1914, Clive Carey had been approached, with Violet Pearn's approval.

entirely misused any chance this play had of success – he's an ignorant silly crank with no knowledge of the stage . . . He ought to be put in a home!' He refused to conduct the first performance and did not even go to see it. But he relented and attended several performances. It was not a success, though, and was taken off on 29 January 1916. '*Lovely* play & music *enchanting* – killed by bad setting &c.,' Alice loyally recorded. Blackwood also disliked the settings; he described them in a letter to Elgar as 'suburban, arts and crafts pretentious rubbish.'

It *is* enchanting music. More than that, it is a major score for the theatre. The songs are a revelation of what Elgar might have achieved in a light opera and the ending, with a setting of 'The First Nowell', is touching. But it is the closely-woven, intoxicatingly scored orchestral music which, as a modern complete recording has shown, entitles it to a high place among Elgar's evocations of a world beyond recall. The use of *The Wand of Youth* tunes is poignant, and, in the world of 1915, must have seemed well-nigh unbearable. For Elgar had by now become one of his own Dream Children – 'we are nothing; less than nothing, and dreams. We are only what might have been.' What can have been his thoughts, this man who believed no one wanted his music, when, after records of extracts from *The Starlight Express* had been issued by the Gramophone Company in 1916, he received a letter from an army officer in the trenches: 'Though unknown to you, I feel I must write to you tonight. We possess a fairly good gramophone in our mess, and I have bought your record *Starlight Express*: "Hearts must be soft-shiny dressed" being played for the twelfth time now. The gramophone . . . is the only means of bringing back to us the days that are gone, and helping me through the "Ivory Gate" that leads to Fairyland, or Heaven, whatever one likes to call it. And it is a curious thing, even those who only go for Ragtime revues, all care for your music . . . Music is all that we have to help us carry on.'[3]

Elgar had found pleasure in London in his friendship with Colvin and Laurence Binyon, both of the British Museum staff. His lifelong passion for books, especially the esoteric, endeared them to him and him to them. As we know from his letters to Jaeger, he liked the oddities of language and inventing words. He was delighted when Troyte Griffith told him of the cobbler's word 'unsqueaken' and even more pleased when Colvin passed it on to E. V. Lucas who used it in the novel *London Lavender*. Binyon gave Elgar a copy of his poems *The Winnowing Fan* which included the now famous 'For the Fallen'. He began work on three of the poems ('The Fourth of August', 'To Women', and 'For the Fallen') in 1915, but one evening at Queen's Hall, in casual conversation with the Cambridge composer Cyril B. Rootham, he discovered that Rootham was setting 'For the Fallen'

[3] *The Voice*, November 1917, p. 9.

and that Novello's had agreed to publish his setting. He wrote to Binyon on 24 March: 'I cannot tell you how sad I am about your poems: I feel I cannot proceed with the set as at first proposed & which I still desire to complete: but I saw Dr Rootham, who merely wished to thank me for my "generous attitude" etc. & said very nice things about my offer to withdraw – but his utter disappointment, not expressed but shewn unconsciously, has upset me & I must decide against completing "For the Fallen". I have battled with the feeling for nearly a week but the sight of the other man comes sadly between me & my music. . . . I am going into the country & will see if I can make the other settings acceptable without the great climax.' Typically, to Alice Stuart-Wortley, he added the comment 'After all, nobody *wants* any real music.'

Binyon was bitterly disappointed and pleaded with Elgar, but Elgar was unmoved: 'There is only one publisher for choral music in England: Dr Rootham was in touch with Novello first – my proposal made his MS waste paper & I could not go on – that's exactly a bald statement of the case.' Sidney Colvin took the line that Elgar was being unfair to Binyon and also received the comment that 'no one wants my music'. Colvin was having none of that. 'I think you take far too censorious and jaundiced a view of your countrymen,' he replied on 13 April. 'You cannot in your heart fail to believe that there is a big minority passionately sensitive to art, to whom your work makes all the difference in their lives.' Elgar replied to this with typical asperity: 'Some of my dear friends appeal to me to work in order that the people – musical people – may have something really good (that is complimentary to me and, inferentially, to the B.P. [British Public] – something they really want – well, they do not want me & never did. If I work at all it is not for them.' He consoled himself by concocting *Polonia*, a 'symphonic prelude' in which some colourful original Elgar was united with quotations from Chopin, Paderewski, and the Polish national anthem. This was written for the conductor Emil Mlynarski. The proceeds of *Carillon* and *Polonia* went to Belgian and Polish charities, so that Elgar made nothing from the success of the former. So many friends urged him to continue with 'For the Fallen' that by July he was at work on it again, though still deeply disturbed by the thought of Rootham. In the meantime, however, Rootham's setting was published. Elgar therefore felt himself at liberty to continue with his own work and its completion was announced in *The Times* in March 1916. Rootham was offended. He no longer had any right to be, but undoubtedly salt was rubbed in the wound when Elgar detached 'For the Fallen' and 'To Women' from the complete set and allowed them to be performed separately, with Agnes Nicholls as a soloist, at Leeds on 3 May 1916. On 8 May 'For the Fallen' had the first of six consecutive performances at Queen's Hall, when Agnes

Nicholls, in aid of the Red Cross, sang in this each evening as a prelude to *The Dream of Gerontius* – with Clara Butt and Gervase Elwes.

Elgar worked hard for music in these first years of the war. In addition to conducting in London, he offered his services to the Hallé in Manchester, saying: 'I am not a rich man but what you can give me, give me.' Visits to Manchester must have given him a foretaste of the great change that had come over the world.[4] Richter, retired and old in Germany, had renounced his British honours. Brodsky was interned in Vienna (though he was later released and returned to Manchester). It is said that when someone asked Beecham at a Royal Philharmonic meeting where all Elgar's friends had gone, Sir Thomas replied: 'They're all interned.' It was not wholly true, but true enough. Even so it is not correct to blame the end of Elgar's fame in Germany on the war. The conductors who had liked his music were of an older generation and had retired or died. There were new suns in the sky and Buths's success with *Gerontius* was a thing of the past. But in England no cloud as yet dimmed his reputation.

In January 1917 'Windflower' went to Severn House to try to interest Elgar in composing music for a short ballet to be given as part of a Chelsea matinée to take place in March in aid of war charities. The ballet was devised by Mrs Ina Lowther and was based on a fan design drawn in sanguine by the Chelsea artist Charles Conder. The fan was owned by Mrs John Lane, wife of the publisher and a member of the matinée committee. It showed Pan and Echo with eighteenth century figures in the background. This was another pastoral, escapist theme calculated to appeal to Elgar at this time, and he wrote the music within a month. *The Sanguine Fan* was performed in the revue called 'Chelsea on Tip-toe' on 20 March. In the cast were Fay Compton, Ina Lowther (as Echo), Gerald du Maurier, and Ernest Thesiger. Elgar conducted. Three days later he added a shepherd's dance to the score and a second performance was given during another charity miscellany on 22 May. Alice's diary comment was: 'A *very* heavy, dull audience – why shd. Philanthropy make ladies so oppressively stupid. . . . E. rather depressed, such a dull house to hear that perfect work.' In 1920 Elgar recorded some extracts from what is a relatively short score (barely 17 minutes) and after that the music was forgotten until 1973 when Sir Adrian Boult recorded it. It is not, *pace* Alice's spirit, a perfect work but it is exceedingly pleasing, its opening theme a very happy invention, and its nostalgic wistfulness seems borrowed from the *Falstaff* interludes. Indeed echoes from earlier works flit in

[4] He seems, for some reason, to have been less fond of Liverpool after the Rodewald years. Writing to Littleton of Novello's on 12 December 1911 when he was trying to avoid a conducting engagement offered him by Liverpool Philharmonic Society, he commented: 'I *hate* the Society & the audience is the most vulgar & uneducated in Europe!'

and out, teasing the ear while enslaving it. The scoring is pellucid, and the whole piece exudes the atmosphere of the theatre; there can be little doubt when one hears Elgar's incidental music that he had every qualification to make him a great opera-composer.

'I cannot do any real work with the awful shadow over us', he said in 1917, but no sooner was *The Sanguine Fan* finished than he set to work on four Kipling poems for four baritones and orchestra. These he called *The Fringes of the Fleet*, dedicated them to Lord Beresford,[5] and suggested that they should form part of the 'show' at the London Coliseum. They were a success and he toured the British provincial music-halls conducting them during August, September, October, and November. They returned to the Coliseum where the 'act' came to an abrupt end when Kipling rather belatedly objected to his poetry being performed in this way. 'He is perfectly stupid in his attitude,' Elgar wrote to Alice Stuart-Wortley. 'If I do happen to write something that "goes" with the public and by which I look like benefiting financially, some perverse fate always intervenes and stops it immediately.' In the early part of 1917 he had at last completed the Binyon settings, which he called *The Spirit of England*. 'I fear I have been a very long time,' he wrote to Binyon on 12 April, 'but the difficulty over the one poem last year put me off somewhat & it has taken me all this time to overtake the first care*ful* rapture.' The first complete performance was given at the Royal Albert Hall on 24 November 1917, with Agnes Nicholls as the soloist. 'Here in truth is the very voice of England,' Newman wrote.

This was Elgar's outward and 'official' life during the war. Privately he was deeply unhappy and frequently ill. As often as he could he escaped to Worcestershire or to the Lake District. In Worcestershire he stayed with his sister Pollie (Mrs Grafton) at Stoke Prior, near Bromsgrove, and from there in November 1914 he wrote to Alice Stuart-Wortley: 'Yesterday [12 November] I went to Worcester & had the joy of sitting in the old library in the cathedral amongst the MSS I have often told you of – the view down the river across to the hills just as the monks saw it & as I have seen it for so many years – it seems so curious, dear, to feel that I played about among the tombs & in the cloisters when I cd. scarcely walk & now the Dean and canons are so polite & shew me everything new, alterations, discoveries etc. etc. It is a sweet old place, especially, to me, the library into which so few go. I will take you in one day.' Mrs Stuart-Wortley evidently tried to alleviate Elgar's nostalgia for his native city, for Lady Elgar's diary for 14 April 1916 records that 'A.S.W. came & brought E. the fragments of King John's tomb'. 'I am sick of towns,' he wrote to Schuster in 1916. He wanted to be away from London 'for a long

[5] The admiral was created an English peer on 1 January 1916.

time'. The constant entertaining at Severn House, however acceptable the company, was a drain on his strength. He wilted, but Alice thrived. ('So nice to be in London again after Bradford's very local atmosphere,' she wrote in her diary after staying with the Behrens family.) News of deaths – of Steinbach and Richter in 1916, of his Uncle Henry in 1917, and of George Sinclair – depressed him, and so did the war news. He kept Sinclair's last letter on the desk before him.[6] It had been obvious since April 1916, when Elgar was taken ill on a train and spent three days in a nursing-home, that his nerves were strained to breaking-point. He was unwell for the rest of the year, the physical cause of his depression, illness, and occasional dizziness being attributed to Menière's disease of the ear which had been diagnosed first in 1912. He was also worried about the state of his finances. He was confined to bed in December 1916, when Alice Stuart-Wortley's husband Charles was raised to the peerage and became Lord Stuart of Wortley. 'I am out of bed,' he wrote to her on 20 December, 'and I use the first minute to send you love & congratulations on the event – I gave you a coronet long ago – the best I had but you may have forgotten it – now you will have a real one, bless you! . . . I feel afraid of you & wonder in a vague sort of way what will be the difference? But you are still the windflower I think & hope. . . . Everything pleasant & promising in my life is dead – I have the happiness of my friends to console me as I had fifty years ago. I feel that life has gone back as far when I was alone & there was no one to stand between me & disaster – health or finance – now that has come back & I am more alone and the prey of circumstances than ever before.' It is sad to think that he found no consolation in such a letter as the following, written by Schuster after a wartime bereavement, when he had attended a performance of the A flat Symphony:

As long as I have *it* [Elgar's music] I can bear my losses, although I thought when I went into the hall today that I *couldn't*. I felt then as I never have but as you, I fear, sometimes do – that life was not worth the living & I would not be sorry to lose it. Then came your symphony – and in a moment I knew I was wrong. In it is *all love* – and love makes life possible. I wonder if you realise when you feel despondent & embittered what your music is to me – and therefore to countless others? You may not care to be of use to those who live after you – but surely it must be *something* to you to know you are giving happiness & hope & consolation to your fellow creatures? Bless you for it anyway.

Elgar's letters to Alice Stuart-Wortley in the spring and summer of

[6] This letter, dated 5 February 1917, begins: 'My dear Edward. I want to tell you about a wonderful viola player who played at my recital last Thursday. I never heard anyone to approach him. . . . His name is Lionel Tertis. It would be splendid if you could write something for him to play. . . .'

1917 reveal the extent of his spiritual bleakness and his growing nostalgia for Worcestershire and an irrecoverable and perhaps imaginary past. On 5 March he wrote: 'I was dreaming yesterday of woods & fields &, perhaps, a little drive round Harrogate – or a little play journey to Fountains or some lovely remembrance of long ago idylls, & now deep snow! Well, I have put it all in my music, & also much more that has never happened.' Alice Stuart-Wortley had been visiting his old haunts and he wrote: 'So you have been to B[roadheath]. I fear you did not find the cottage [his birthplace] – it is nearer the clump of scotch firs – I can smell them now – in the hot sun. Oh! how cruel that I was not there – there, *nothing between* that infancy & *now* and I *want* to see it. The flowers are lovely – I knew you wd. like the heath. I could have shewn you such lovely lanes.' Later: 'I am glad you "feel" Stoke [Prior]. That is a place where I see & *hear* (yes!) you. A. has not been there since *1888* & does not care to go & no one of my friends has ever been but you. No one has seen my fields & my "common" and my trees, only the Windflower, and I found her namesakes growing there – aborigines I'm sure – real pure sweet forest folk. Bless you.' In Chatham in September 1917, on tour with *The Fringes of the Fleet*, he wrote to her again: 'Alice & I are here – no performance last night. Terrible gun-firing, raid etc. etc. . . . I am not well and the place is so noisy & I do not sleep. The guns are the quietest things here. I long for the country & Stoke. I think all the time of it – and you. I have been thinking also so much of our lost festivals – no more music. . . . Everything good & nice & clean & fresh & sweet is far away – never to return.'

Alice Elgar realized that his need to recapture the peace and solitude of Birchwood was paramount. She and Carice found an oak-beamed cottage, Brinkwells, near Fittleworth in Sussex, which answered the need. They first went there in May 1917, just before his sixtieth birthday. 'It's *divine*,' Elgar wrote to Schuster, 'simple thatched cottage . . . with wonderful view.' There was a studio in the garden in which he could work and, best of all, there were woods in which he could walk for hours. The cottage was small and isolated, on a hill overlooking the Arun and the South Downs. Like Gladstone, he found delight in chopping wood, and he learned to make hoops for barrels. Back in London early in 1918 he was again ill. He went to the theatre, and Lalla Vandervelde introduced him to Bernard Shaw – no doubt the occasion of the outburst to Roger Fry[7] – but his old throat trouble was now seriously aggravating him. In March a septic tonsil was removed, an operation which caused pain and discomfort.[8] The day he left the nursing-home he asked for pencil and paper and wrote what was to become the opening theme of the Cello Concerto.[9]

[7] See p. 167.   [8] After this operation, the ear trouble vanished.
[9] *Alice Elgar*, op. cit., p. 180.

Both before and after the operation he turned for relaxation to books and wrote to Troyte Griffith in Malvern who shared his passion for reading. Passages from these letters give us some idea of Elgar's voracious and wide-ranging literary appetite: 'I have always avoided Lafcadio Hearn but have read his Lectures on Literature with the greatest joy. . . . Now I have the Life and Letters which also interest me hugely. As to the many Japanese books by Hearn I cannot stand 'em: I feel like E. V. Lucas about Tagore. He says that some people admire the poems but adds, "Me, they, for the most part, stump". I think the contempt conveyed by this purposely contorted sentence is really juicy. . . . Colvin's Life of Keats is of course new and first class. Morley's Reminiscences, or whatever they are, first vol. good, second vol. too Indiany and dull. "Some Hawarden Letters" are interesting as shewing the hopeless mutual-admiration of the Gladstone party: some of the letters are really beneath contempt; Balfour-Browne has pubd. a book of Rems. also; not much good; slipshod sort of arrgt. . . .' 'I have read "South Wind" and enjoyed it; he N. Douglas is really clever and I regret that he doesn't write more carefully, the book is so slipshod and with talent like his so much more might be done. Get his book about "Calabria" and say what you think. . . .'

In the month before his tonsils operation a new friendship began. The 28-year-old conductor Adrian Boult had already met Elgar at Schuster's house. He planned on 18 February 1918 to precede a performance of Vaughan Williams's *A London Symphony* with *In the South* and the previous day he went to Hampstead to tea to go through the score. Alice duly recorded: 'Quite a nice quiet man . . . He seemed really to understand'. Her verdict on the concert was 'too few strings but reading of it really good'.

After convalescing for a few days in April at Schuster's, Elgar went for most of the rest of 1918 to Brinkwells. There he rapidly regained strength. He enjoyed the isolation and the peaceful routine which he described in a letter to Lady Stuart of Wortley written on 12 May 1918: I rise about *seven* work till 8-15 – then dress, breakfast – pipe (I smoke again all day!) work till 12-30 lunch (pipe) – rest an hour – work till tea (pipe) – then work till 7-30 – change, dinner at 8. Bed at 10 – every day practically goes thus. . . . We go lovely walks . . . the woods are full of flowers, wonderful. . . . We will order the pony for you & I shall be at the station of course . . . the only thing to remember is that it is difficult to alter the pony arrgts. for conveyance as he – it – is in request. I am looking forward to your coming with acute joy: it really is lovely here – food good & plentiful – *much beer!* – but *do not mention it.*' A few days later he wrote again: 'The woods are still carpeted with bluebells but the heavy rain of three days ago tried them severely and they look rather faded: I have been down the wood & told them you are coming & asked them to remain for your loved visit. . . . You need bring very little of anything but if quite convenient some dry biscuits *might* be a joy as the stock in these villages . . . has run out for days: but the thing is to bring yourself & rest: there will be a full moon & all lovely & nightingales.' He was glad to hear the Allied advances had freed Percy Hull, who from 1896 (when he was eighteen) had been assistant to George Sinclair at Hereford until 1914 when he was interned while on a walking tour. 'You have had a dreadful time with those appalling Yahoos the Prussians,' Elgar wrote to him, 'and it is a mercy you have been allowed to leave their unsavoury clutches. . . . We shall welcome you home again with enthusiasm and I trust the post of organist in your own cathedral will be yours. I was only too glad to do what I could to further your claims, which I believe are generally recognised, but I do not pretend to understand the corkscrew minds of one at least of the people at Hereford.' A month later (1 July) he wrote to Schuster: 'High summer ! and divine warmth which I know you enjoy with me. . . . I am better but not fit for the world & don't seem to want it – I get a few fish & read & *smoke* (praise be!) but there are only about six people I want to see & you are one – number one I mean, the rest follow. . . .'

In fact he was at work again. Elgar's creative spells followed a pattern. They were usually preceded by a period of acute depression. The *Variations* and *Gerontius* followed one such period; the bleak and despondent 1907 was followed by a burst of activity which produced two symphonies and a concerto; now, five years after *Falstaff* during which time he had written nothing comparable in scope and had withdrawn into solitude, the fires blazed up in him for the last time. While in the nursing-home for his operation he began to make sketches for the chamber music he had long wanted to write. On returning home he began a string quartet and a sonata, and then began a piano quintet too. At Brinkwells, Reed was a frequent visitor during the summer, and Elgar got him to play through the works as they proceeded. Alice was overjoyed. 'E. writing wonderful new music, different from anything else of his,' she wrote in her diary. 'A. calls it wood magic. So elusive and delicate.' The sonata was completed first (on 15 September 1918) and dedicated to Marie Joshua, an old friend of the Elgars. She died four days after he had inscribed her name on the score and he inserted a reminiscence of the slow movement before the coda of the finale in tribute to her memory. The work also contains other personal allusions. Alice Stuart of Wortley had broken her leg while at Tintagel in the late summer of 1918 and Elgar sent her some sketches of the sonata with this letter (11 September): 'The first movement is bold & vigorous, then a fantastic, curious movement with a very expressive middle section: a melody for the violin – they say it is as good as or better than anything I have done in the expressive way: this I wrote just after your telegram about the accident came &

I send you the pencil notes as first made at that sad moment. . . . The last movement is very broad & *soothing* like the last movement of the IInd symphony. I have been sketching other things which are full of old times.' These 'other things' were the quartet and quintet on which work progressed in the intervals of woodcutting and bonfires. Alice's diary entries for 15 and 16 September are especially valuable in regard to the quintet: 'Wonderful weird beginning – same atmosphere as "Owls"[9] – evidently reminiscence of sinister trees & impression of Flexham Park . . .' 'Sad "dispossessed" trees & their dance & unstilled regret for their evil fate – or rather curse – wh. brought it on . . .' 'The sinister trees & their strange dance in it – then a wail for their sin – wonderful'. Flexham Park was near Fittleworth, but it seems likely that the group of dead trees was at Bedham Copse. The name Bedham occurs at the end of the first movement in the published score. Just what the trees' sin was nobody knows. It used to be said that there was a local legend that the trees were the forms of Spanish monks who had been struck by lightning while practising black magic. Research[10] has shown that no such legend was known in Fittleworth and that there was never a Spanish monastic settlement in Sussex, only Spanish chestnut trees. Possibly Elgar linked the trees with a local community of Augustinian canons about whom he would have read in the county history. Or there may be the strongest clue of all in Alice's diary, which recorded on 18 July 1918 that Elgar had taken Algernon Blackwood to see the trees. Blackwood wrote ghost stories and was fascinated by the occult. Two months later Alice linked the quintet with Edward Bulwer-Lytton's novel *A Strange Story*. Writing in the *Sunday Times* on 11 October 1931, Ernest Newman, dedicatee of the quintet, referred to a 'quasi-programme that lies at the base of the work'. When the first movement was completed, Elgar had written to him on 5 January 1919, 'it is strange music I think & I like it – but – it's ghostly stuff'. Whatever the nature of that programme, Elgar was fascinated by trees, as we know from *Caractacus* and his exultant phrase to Jaeger, 'The trees are singing my music – or have I sung theirs?'. W. H. Reed described the 'haunted' trees: 'with gnarled and twisted branches, bare of bark or leaves – a ghastly sight in the evening, when the branches seem to be beckoning and holding up gaunt arms in derision . . . Their influence is also apparent in the Sonata (second movement) and the finale of the Quartet, in which there is a striking ponticello effect'.[11]

[9] 'Owls' to words by Elgar, is No. 4 of the op. 53 part-songs written in Italy in 1907. Describing it to Jaeger (26 April 1908), Elgar wrote: 'It is only a fantasy & means nothing. It is in a wood at night evidently & the recurring "Nothing" is only an *owlish* sound.'
[10] Introduction by Michael Pope to Eulenburg edition (1971) of the Piano Quintet.
[11] Article on Elgar's chamber music in Cobbett's *Cyclopaedic Survey of Chamber Music* (Second Edition, London, 1963).

Sussex in its autumn uncertainty held Elgar in thrall, just as Worcestershire did. 'Here we have had much bad weather', he wrote to Colvin, 'but the sunrises have been wonderful & quite made up for a lot of rain & gales: I have never seen anything so wonderful as the sun climbing over our view in golden mist. I see now where Turner found such sights as Norham Castle, etc.' That was written on 26 September. The following day Alice's diary refers to 'wonderful new music, real wood sounds & another lament wh. shd. be in a war symphony'. This new music was the slow movement of the Quintet. A fortnight later he was composing the slow movement of the Quartet.

In October 1918 the Elgars attended Parry's funeral in St Paul's Cathedral. On 15 October, Reed and Elgar played the Sonata to Schuster, Muriel Foster, the Colvins, Landon Ronald, and others. Writing for the piano had made him look again at the Piano Concerto and he showed it to Irene Scharrer, promising her the first performance. The war was obviously drawing to an end and Colvin and Binyon tried to interest him in setting an ode about peace which Binyon had written. Elgar's letter to Binyon on 5 November 1918 is of prime importance in a consideration of the mood in which he began work on the Cello Concerto: 'I think your poem beautiful exceedingly – but I do not feel drawn to write peace music somehow – I thought long months ago that I could feel that way & if anything could draw me your poem would, but the whole atmosphere is too full of complexities for me to feel music to it: not the atmosphere of the poem but of the time I mean. The last two divisions VI and VII are splendid altho' I regret the appeal to the Heavenly Spirit which is cruelly obtuse to the individual sorrow & sacrifice – a cruelty I resent bitterly & disappointedly.'

Later Elgar reconsidered the ode and wanted to set it, but he never did. He returned to Brinkwells on Armistice Day and showed Reed the early sketches of the Cello Concerto. He and Alice were both rather forlorn figures at this time. Alice had not been well after a minor operation. 'My poor dear Alice is better now,' he wrote to Colvin on 21 November. ' . . . I have commenced music again & hope to proceed: the axe however claims me & I make huge fires in the wood, meanly delighting in the fact that I can burn more than anyone I know – a frame of mind I am ashamed of in the cold hours.' The parallel with Millais must inescapably be drawn, the Millais of 'Autumn Leaves' and his saying about bonfires: 'Nothing brings back sweeter memories of the days that are gone; it is the incense offered by departing summer to the sky.' The Elgars' summer had departed. At the end of the year they returned to Hampstead for a run-through of parts of the Quartet and Quintet but the prospect did not please Elgar. 'It means another interruption,' he told Schuster, '& the future is *dark* as A. poor dear is not well & of course is bored to death here while I am in the seventh heaven of delight: so we may only return here to clear up – we shall see. But it seems that if I have to live again at Hampstead composition is "off" – not the house or the place but *London* – telephone etc. all day and night drives me mad.'

But it was not merely the telephone ringing that had caused him to say of Severn House 'This is no home for me'. In November 1918, while they were at Brinkwells, it was burgled. Alice, still convalescent, left Elgar at the cottage and went to the station in a dogcart on a cold night to catch the train to London to find out the extent of their loss – most of Elgar's clothes and even his braces.[12] But the night he returned to Severn House he sketched a further part of the Cello Concerto, marking the theme 'Very full, sweet & sonorous'. Alice now acknowledged that the house was beyond their means. No one else in Netherhall Gardens would have painted their own staircase, as Elgar did, nor themselves have planted the bulbs in the garden, as he and Alice did. The post-war fuel shortage drove Alice to Hampstead town hall in January 1919 to try to melt a bureaucrat's heart with her picture of Sir Edward 'sitting in the ice-cold studio with no food' and her plea for an increased coal ration. Later, with her own hands, she stowed away logs, cheaper than coal. That summer they returned from Brinkwells to find that a neighbour had felled some trees and was building a garage 'under the music-room windows'. She consulted her solicitor cousin, William Raikes, but nothing could be done. On 2 September she put the house on the market.

·   ·   ·   ·   ·   ·

The first performance of the Sonata was given by Reed and Anthony Bernard at a meeting on 13 March 1919 of the British Music Society, yet another organization to promote British music. It had been formed in June 1918 by Arthur Eaglefield Hull, and E. J. Dent and Bernard Shaw were prominent participators. The first public performance was on 21 March, by Reed and Landon Ronald, at the Aeolian Hall. Elgar had not liked the music at the morning rehearsal and was with difficulty persuaded to attend the concert. The critics' response was cautious and reserved. But before this there had been private performances of the Quintet, one of which Shaw had attended. He wrote to Elgar afterwards (8 March 1919), and it was after this that their acquaintance turned into firm friendship. 'The Quintet knocked me over at once,' he wrote. 'I said to myself, with

[12] The two burglars, wearing Elgar's suits, were caught on 13 July 1919. They were both policemen, who turned to their advantage the fact that they were keeping an eye on premises left empty by owners who had notified the police. Between 12 and 15 December 1918 they burgled several houses (Elgar's was the fifteenth), and they were found guilty and sentenced to five years' hard labour.

the old critic's habit of making phrases for publication, that this was the finest thing of its kind since *Coriolan*. I don't know why I associated the two; but I did: there was the same quality – the same vein. Of course you went your own way presently. There are some piano embroideries on a pedal point that didn't sound like a piano or anything else in the world, but quite beautiful, and I have my doubts whether any regular shop pianist will produce them: they require a touch which is peculiar to yourself, and which struck me the first time I ever heard you larking about with a piano.'[13]

Shaw also entered a 'solemn protest' about the fugue: 'You cannot begin a movement in such a magical way as you have begun the Quintet and then suddenly relapse into the expected.' There is a considerably mollified reminder in this letter of the Corno di Bassetto whose writings in the 1880s and 1890s Elgar had enjoyed and remembered: the astuteness in spotting the weakness of the fugal section and the unconventional, though not entirely unpianistic, writing for the pianoforte. At any rate this work and the Quartet were warmly received when they were first played in public at a Wigmore Hall concert (in which the Sonata was included) on 21 May 1919, given by William Murdoch (piano) with the British String Quartet (Albert Sammons, W. H. Reed, Raymond Jeremy, and Felix Salmond). Elgar had invited Salmond to give the first performance of the Cello Concerto and asked him down to Brinkwells that summer to work with him. 'I am frantically busy writing,' he wrote to Colvin on 26 June, '& have nearly completed a Concerto for Violoncello – a real large work & I think *good* & alive. It is impossible to say when it will appear or be heard – probably next winter. Would Frances & you allow me to put on the title page To Sidney and Frances Colvin? Your friendship is such a real & precious thing that I should like to leave some record of it; I cannot say the music is worthy of you both (or either!) but our three names wd. be in print together even if the music is dull & of the kind which perisheth.' On 23 July he wrote to Alice Stuart: 'I am arranging the next bit of the violoncello concerto for piano & writing it out fair – which I detest.' On 3 August he told her that Salmond and he had 'polished' the concerto and he added: 'I want to finish or rather commence the piano concerto which *must* be windflowerish so I hope you will come but somehow I know you will not.' He delivered the Cello Concerto to Novello's on 8 August.

The first rehearsal of the Cello Concerto was in Mortimer Hall on 26 October. Elgar was to conduct it. The rest of the concert – Scriabin's *Poème de l'Extase* and Borodin's Second Symphony – was conducted by Albert Coates. The events at the rehearsal were a

---

[13] Writing to Lady Stuart of Wortley about the Sonata, Elgar said (1 October 1918): 'I have *struggled* hard to make my piano passages fit other fingers – & I wanted help in this direction.'

permanent disgrace to British music. Coates was at that time fervently championing Scriabin's cause, and he continued rehearsing for an hour after the time when it had been agreed that Elgar should take over the rostrum. The greatest English composer of his age was kept waiting as he had been thirty years before when he was unknown. If he had not put Salmond's reputation first, Elgar might have withdrawn from the concert. Members of the orchestra, which included a nineteen-year-old cellist, John Barbirolli, would not have blamed him if he had walked out. In her diary Alice wrote: 'An insult to E. from that brutal selfish ill-mannered bounder Coates'. At next day's Queen's Hall rehearsal on the morning of the performance, Coates was no more helpful. The performance was a disaster and the audience's response politely cordial. Alfred Kalisch, who had heard all the major Elgar first performances, wrote in the *Musical Times* of December 1919 '... an important new work by our foremost living composer ... did not suffice to fill the hall to overflowing, and ... was obviously under-rehearsed'. *The Daily Telegraph* dismissed the occasion in a few lines, complaining of 'a lack of exaltation' and lack of surprise. A 'godsend to players on the violoncello' was the best the writer could muster. Ernest Newman fixed the blame where it belonged, writing that the orchestra 'made a lamentable public exhibition of itself'. Alice's rage was still blazing in her diary entry for 28 October: 'Still furious about rehearsals – *shameful*. Hope never to speak to that brutal Coates again'.

It is, of course, understandable that the public should have been puzzled by the contrast between the pre-war Elgar of the symphonies and Violin Concerto and the end-of-war Elgar of the three chamber works and the Cello Concerto. Autumn had indeed followed high summer. The colours are muted in these four late masterpieces, three of which are in the key of E minor. The Sonata and the String Quartet continue the mood of *The Sanguine Fan* in that they re-explore, with the wisdom and understanding of maturity, the days of youth. The idiom is conservative but academic rules are broken, as they always were by Elgar. The first movement of the Sonata begins in A minor and takes most of its length to establish the tonic key of E minor, the second subject being in B flat major, always an Elgarian favourite for poetic musing. There is a typical restlessness about this movement, for all its outward show of placidity, and it is this unexpected deployment of tonality which imparts it. The slow movement, 'Romance', is the Elgar of the exquisite, small, lighter pieces which he wrote in such profusion in his youth – his published Opus 1 was called *Romance*. It is as if he were looking back to *Sevillana* or the part-song *Spanish Serenade*. This 'Spanish' element, with its chromatic descents, lazy rhythms, and harped chords, frequently recurs in Elgar's music. Here, in his maturity, he found a new, creative way of expressing a primary source of his inventiveness.

The Quartet also recaptures the early Elgar but with such profundity that one is reminded of Wordsworth's comparable achievement in *The Prelude*. The first movement is unusual in Elgar in the terseness and subtlety of its form; the mood is plaintive and restless but curiously subdued in its expression. The opening theme is in a hesitant 12/8 rhythm which is halted by a series of mysteriously harmonized chords before the broad and confident second subject is played. The rest of the movement is constructed from these features, each theme being shown in transformations of tone-colour, the interplay of the instruments displaying something of the concentrated intimacy of mature Beethoven. A climax is reached but the end is restrained. Lady Elgar was particularly fond of the C major slow movement (it was played at her funeral service). The beautiful, simple (and simply beautiful) opening melody

Ex. 10

Piacevole (poco Andante)

p dolce
2nd Violin

is one of those apparently artless tunes which enshrine a world of lost innocence. It is introduced by the second violin over a counterpoint by viola and cello. The leader does not enter until the twenty-third bar, an octave above his colleague. The theme is repeated in richer harmony and there are episodes of repetitions of a one-bar motif, dreamlike in effect. At the reprise the first violin plays what sounds almost like a quotation from *Chanson de Matin*, as if to emphasise this movement's quality of dewy freshness, so easy to hear but so difficult to compose. In the finale, Elgar recaptured the brilliance and energy of his pre-1914 orchestral works with the rhythmically exciting first theme. The second subject is vague in its tonality (perhaps A major), its lyricism qualified by the viola's minatory semiquavers motif, with its three repeated notes in groups of four and its changing accentuation. The second subject is recapitulated out of conventional order and the coda is based on both main themes. The work ends triumphantly, but there is a moment of sinister portent when the lower strings play *sul ponticello* and a cloud passes over the sun. The work is autobiographical, no doubt, but in the outer movements at any rate Elgar is telling us about himself as a composer rather than as a man. Few of his movements are more intricately, imaginatively, and originally constructed than the first, with its remarkable dovetailing of themes into an iridescent texture.

The Piano Quintet is the most ambitious of the chamber works, unlike the Quartet in character, being impulsive and exuberant.

Again in only three movements, it is of large design, with an air of magniloquence that almost recalls the music of ten years before. Its mysterious and romantic opening is arresting, foretelling richness to come. The first four notes of the piano part at the very start of the work, played in octaves, are identical with the plainsong antiphon 'Salve Regina'. They are followed by a wail of grief on the strings, the contrast suggesting the programmatic basis which Newman hoped the composer might reveal as a guide to performers and listeners. The second subject also has the 'Spanish' flavour of the Sonata, and perhaps the undisclosed programme explains the fugato passage in this movement which worried Shaw. It is also worth noting that the motif in the piano which first occurs seven bars before Fig. 1 and is repeated at the end of the movement and in the Adagio is also used at a highly emotional moment in the Cello Concerto (second bar of 66). Throughout the work there is a tinge of bitterness, even steeliness, which gives it strength and derives from its tonic key of A minor. It is designed on a grand scale, expansive and concerto-like in ensemble passages. The piano writing is fluent, Brahmsian, and well integrated. Inevitably Franck is recalled by the unifying use of cyclic form, but no one but Elgar could have written the sublime Adagio, with its ripe and eloquent viola melody and a cello part which hints broadly at the larger rôle for this instrument that was shortly to follow. The finale is mainly vigorous but has a memorable passage when the prevailing mood of confidence gives way to some ghostly memory from the past. The Quintet certainly ranks among Elgar's major achievements, but while one is tempted to call it the finest of the three chamber works, that distinction, it increasingly seems to me, belongs to the String Quartet, a composition of rare subtlety, consummate craftsmanship, and still under-rated magnitude in the genre. It is in every sense a deeply Romantic work, and another Elgarian enigma.

The Cello Concerto, of all Elgar's orchestral works, is the most elusive and withdrawn, the most subdued in its orchestral dress. The rhetorical flourish for the soloist with which it opens – a moment akin to the opening of the *Introduction and Allegro* – soon subsides into a long, deceptively simple tune which needs as skilful a judgement of its tempo as does the opening of Brahms's Fourth Symphony if it is not to sound merely weary instead of numbed with despair. This is overpoweringly the music of wood smoke and autumn bonfires, of the evening of life; sadness and disillusion are dominant and the music comes perilously close to what Jaeger would have called a 'whine' of self-pity. As in the symphonies, this emotional element is conveyed by shifts of tonality and in addition by a certain harmonic austerity. The scherzo's brightness of mood sounds forced ('the heart dances, but not for joy'): there is an air of unreality and fantasy about the cello's tessitura, the use of pizzicato, and the woodwind scoring. In the very lovely adagio there is no attempt to disguise the melancholy: a short, sustained, songful lamentation, the music of a broken heart. And although the finale rattles the skeleton of the old, swaggering, rumbustious Elgar, the high spirits are short-lived. Chromatic string harmonies make the tragedy unequivocal. Following Dvořák's pattern, Elgar recalls a theme from the slow movement, and the music assumes a nihilist note that is unequalled in intensity elsewhere in his output, surpassing even the note of agony and ruin in *Gerontius*. The opening recitative returns, plunges to the depths and the work ends in almost indecent haste as if too much has been revealed. It is sometimes said that this Concerto is Elgar's war requiem but the phrase, accurate in some respects, needs clarification. He was an egocentric artist, and the requiem here is not so much for the dead in Flanders fields as for the destruction of a way of life. With an artist's vision, he saw that 1918 was the end of a civilization. Here, rather than in the finale of the Second Symphony, is the elegy for an age. The slaughter of war, whether of men or horses, had grieved Elgar, but this requiem is not a cosmic utterance on behalf of mankind, it is wholly personal, the musical expression of his bitterness about the providence that was 'against great art' and the Heavenly Spirit that was 'cruelly obtuse' to individual sorrow and sacrifice. There is no 'massive hope for the future' in this music, only the voice of an ageing, desolate man, a valediction to an era and to the powers of music that he knew were dying within him. For the paradox is that whereas this Cello Concerto bears some marks of faltering inspiration, this very uncertainty of invention is used to advantage to create a marvellous impression of a relaxed and epigrammatic change of style. With his superb technical resource and, once again, perfect understanding of the instrument, Elgar created one of the great cello works of the world, surpassed only by Dvořák's for its exploitation of the instrument's capacity for expressive melody and surpassing it in exploration of its more bizarre and playful characteristics. The orchestra used is the same size as that employed for the Violin Concerto but it is scaled down to allow the cello always to dominate the score. To all intents and purposes this concerto was Elgar's last word. It was a word of resignation, a farewell to beauty in music of poignant pathos. Of *Gerontius* he had written: 'This is the best of me.' Now, after entering details of the concerto in his personal catalogue of his works, he wrote: 'Finis. R.I.P.'.

The cry of anguish that rends the finale of the Concerto might almost have been a moment of vision. Only Mahler, with the hammer-blows of destiny in his Sixth Symphony, has foretold so accurately in music his own immediate fate. After the first performance Elgar went to conduct his own works with

Mengelberg's Concertgebouw Orchestra in Amsterdam. Thence he went to Brussels where Lalla Vandervelde's husband had arranged that he should be honoured in gratitude for *Carillon*. He was shown the battlefields and the new buildings – 'shoddy ugly & degraded', he described the latter to Troyte. 'The suburbs of, say, Wigan are noble compared to these atrocities. The Belgians swagger & do nothing but eat & drink – have forgotten the war. . . .' He returned in mid-November to find that Alice was ordered by the doctor (his physician, Sir Maurice Abbot Anderson) to stay indoors. She had been ill, he told Binyon, since 2 November, but it was not considered serious. He left her in Hampstead while he went north to conduct Kilburn's choir. But she was up and about again on 21 December and they spent Christmas 'all by their loneses', a 'quiet and happy day'. She summed up 1919 as 'the year in many ways as regards disturbances, strikes, trials, finance, a serious one! Fear not much fizz in it for E. except in writing his wonderful music'.

After Christmas Elgar was irritated by prospective buyers who came to look over Severn House. 'Every ring of the bell plunged poor Elgar into melancholy,' Reed recorded,[14] 'and if he heard the ring followed by the shuffling of strange feet . . . he ran out of the house incontinently by a side-door that had been used by the previous tenant [Edwin Long] as an entrance and exit for his models.' They hoped they might be able to buy, instead of rent, Brinkwells. He was looking over his sketches for the third oratorio but he had no real work on hand. He might have been expected to contribute to the ceremony for the unveiling of the Cenotaph in Whitehall but he took no part. 'I fear (private) the Cenotaph affair will not include me,' he told Alice Stuart of Wortley in January 1920. 'The *present* proposals are vulgar & commonplace to the *last degree*. I really cannot appear in it!' The same letter refers to Alice having 'a fresh cold & is a notably poor thing – it is very wearing'. 'My poor dear A. does not rid of the tiresome cough,' he told Colvin on 5 February when he wrote to express his delight at being elected to the select membership of the Literary Society (probably on the strength of his remarkable and erudite long letter on the 'Quadruple Alliance' of Horace Walpole, Gray, West, and Ashton published in *The Times Literary Supplement* of 4 September 1919). Other honours came at this time: membership of the Accademia in Florence and of the French Académie des Beaux-Arts; he was elected to the Council of the Royal College of Music. These were compensations for Alice in her disappointment over Severn House.

There was compensation, too, in the way in which she and Edward had drawn closer in these last years, sharing simple pleasures such as going by bus to the new cinema followed by tea at a Lyons café or

[14] *Elgar*, op. cit., p. 129.

enjoying the black puddings Edward had bought in a shop in Fleet Street. Though her heart was failing – pulmonary oedema was the cause of that worrying cough – they would walk up Finchley Road from the bus-stop and look for signs of spring. Providence, which Elgar believed was against art, arranged a last and immense pleasure for them both when Adrian Boult decided to conduct the Second Symphony in London on 16 March. It had had relatively few performances since the unhappy first one in 1911. Elgar, with Carice, went to the rehearsal – 'don't be afraid to let the first movement go & the celli in the opening of the finale might play *out free* almost – *mf*', he wrote in a note to Boult. The performance itself was vividly described in Alice's diary: 'Wonderful performance of the Symphony. From beginning to end it seemed absolutely to penetrate the audience's mind & heart. After 1st movement great applause & *shouts*, rarely heard till end, & great applause all through. Adrian was wonderful – At end frantic enthusiasm & they dragged out E., who looked very overcome, hand in hand with Adrian at least 3 times. E. was so happy & pleased.'

The next day Elgar wrote to Boult: 'My dear Adrian: With the sounds ringing in my ears I send a word of thanks for your splendid conducting of the Sym: I am most grateful to you for your affectionate care of it & I feel that my reputation in the future is in your safe hands. It was a wonderful series of sounds. Bless you!' He added a characteristic postscript: 'The "Boys" *will* take very long bows when the thing flows violin-wise – I wish we cd. mark the parts as some old fiddle books were with a bow & pricks shewing the *part* of the bow to be used' (a drawing stressed his point). Alice, too, wrote to 'Dear Mr Adrian Boult' thanking him from her heart.

A week later Alice went to hear the three chamber works. Elgar had begun, after thirty years, to keep a diary and that night he wrote: 'Thoughts of the 30 (weary fighting) years of her help and devotion.' He, too, must have noticed, like Reed, that she was getting 'mysteriously smaller and more fragile. She seemed to be fading away before one's very eyes.' On 25 March she took to her bed and next day was showing signs of uraemia. Her last visitor was Muriel Foster. On 27 March Elgar pencilled his last note to her, using their intimate language. He addressed it to 'Lady Elgar', folded it in three, and left it for her to see when she awoke. He wrote: 'Darling wife. I thought you wd. rather I went to my lunch so I have started: you was asleep. I shall be back very quick. I kissed your paws (bofe). Your own Edou.' On 6 April, Elgar wrote to Schuster, 'I tried to be frivolous yesterday but I am heartbroken: our poor little dear one is inarticulate and can understand nothing. It is too awful. Pity *us* more than her even.' Only then did the doctor call in a specialist. On 7 April the Last Rites were administered at 3.30 p.m. and at 6.10 p.m. Alice Elgar died in her Edward's arms. She was seventy-one.

Elgar was stunned. He was so withdrawn that no one dared approach him when the undertaker had to be interviewed. It needed Rosa Burley gently to persuade him to face reality. But Rosa's incautious remark to Elgar that she would now be Carice's mother and run the household ended thirty years of friendship. Landon Ronald went to stay with him; Schuster and Carice made the arrangements for the funeral at St Wulstan's, Little Malvern, and asked Reed's string quartet to play the slow movement of the Quartet at the service. Elgar stayed for the rest of the month in Worcestershire, at Little Malvern and at Stoke Prior. In letters to Schuster he poured out his woe:

[12 April] . . . We can see the little grave in the distance & nothing cd. be sweeter & lovelier, only birds singing & all *remote* peace brought closely to us. I cannot thank you for the quartet – it was exactly right & just what she wd. have loved . . . the boys played like angels. . . . The place she chose long years ago is too sweet – the blossoms are white all round it & the illimitable plain. . . .

[17 April] I am doing my best here . . . Juno seems to know that something is wrong & never leaves me – such wonderful things are dogs. Here [Stoke Prior] my dear A. never came so I can bear the sight of the roads & fields. . . . After 37 years my poor old sister may have to turn out – everything being sold – & although the 70 acres or so of land has been let with anr. farm for more than 200 years the new rich refuse to sell the house & paddock separately – after 200 years! . . . So I am in a sad house. The same fate is due on May 1 for my poor old *eldest* sister – stone deaf etc. her little house has been bought 'over their heads' & she is turned out – nowhere to go! So you see I am unhappy. You write to me of my music, etc. like the good fellow you are. . . . Don't talk to me of achievement. I drank spider juice for my mother's sake, went thro' penurious times to buy my dear wife a car for her old age – I failed of course. . . . But Juno's nose presses against me & says a walk is near.

He returned to Severn House at the beginning of May, and wrote to Walford Davies: 'All I have done was owing to her and I am at present a sad and broken man – just stunned. . . . I cry out "Leave me with my dead" – and creatures have to come in and count over her pretty valueless little rings and the most private things to see what they are worth – it drives me to distraction, and I am no fit company for human beings.' After his death, among his papers was found a sheet of notepaper on which he had written the date of Alice's death and these lines by Swinburne:

> Let us go hence, my songs; she will not hear,
> Let us go hence together without fear;
> Keep silence now, for singing-time is over,
> And over all old things and all things dear.

His friend Ernest Newman, to whom he had dedicated the Piano Quintet, commented on Elgar's bereavement in a letter to his wife Vera on 7 April 1920.[15] 'I am sad today over the death of Lady Elgar,' he wrote. 'I am very fond of Edward, and I know that, whatever people may say, to a man of his fine and sensitive nature, the severance of a long tie like this must inevitably mean much bitterness and suffering, much dwelling in the past and self-reproach. We always seem heavy debtors to the dead: we feel they have not had their chance and that life has given us an unfair advantage over them. . . .'

Perhaps Elgar's most moving tribute to Alice was contained in a letter he wrote to Ivor Atkins on 30 December 1922. After looking through the score of *King Olaf*, he said: 'It seems strange that the strong (it is *that*) characteristic stuff shd. have been conceived & written (by a poor wretch teaching all day) with a splitting headache after dinner, at odd sustained moments – but the spirit & will was there in spite of the malevolence of the Creator of all things . . . But thro' it all shines the radiant mind & soul of my dearest departed one: she travelled to London (I was grinding at the High School) & became bound for one hundred pounds so that my work might be printed – bless her! You, who like some of my work, must thank *her* for all of it – not me. *I* should have destroyed it all & joined Job's wife in the congenial task of cursing God'.

[15] Vera Newman, *Ernest Newman: A Memoir* (London, 1963), p. 18.

13 Submission

The last fourteen years of Elgar's life are a long and slow diminuendo. Towards the end, the old energy tried to reassert itself but it was too late: by then, not only the mind but the body was tired. He did not retreat from the world and shut himself away after Alice's death, but her departure from the scene had deprived him of a prime motivation. As he wrote to Boult on 5 August from Brinkwells: 'I am lonely now & do not see music in the old way & cannot believe I shall *complete* any new work – sketches I still make but there is no inducement to finish anything; – ambition I have none . . .' When he returned to 'cold and empty' Severn House he found interest and amusement in his microscopes and in games of billiards with his old friend and benefactor, Hugh Blair, whom he had never deserted in the hard times which had come upon him. Elgar's life from now onwards could almost take as its motto the passage from *Antony and Cleopatra*: ' "The music, ho!" "Let it alone; let's to billiards".' There was no one to encourage him to work, to rule the barlines, to post the manuscript to the publishers, to remind him by her devotion of her faith in his music. Yet the decline of interest in his work which was to add its discouraging force to the other pressures upon him had not in 1920 gathered momentum. The reverse was true. Shaw's article in the first issue of *Music and Letters* had given him a rare accolade: 'Elgar is carrying on Beethoven's business. . . . Elgar alone is for Westminster Abbey.' In the same number a critic and composer of the younger generation, Philip Heseltine (Peter Warlock), praised the symphonies and called for more performances. Boult's performance of No. 2 had been a major event, and Elgar himself was due to conduct it at Cardiff in the South Wales Festival organized by Lord Howard de Walden and Cyril Jenkins, a pupil of Stanford and composer of some choral works which Elgar thought 'very good'. He decided to keep the engagement, as he had also kept one to conduct *The Apostles* at Newcastle upon Tyne. Fortunately the *Manchester Guardian* sent Langford to Cardiff, so that we have a contemporary view of the occasion by one who had signally failed to respond to the symphony in 1911.[1] Now things were changed: 'Small as the audience was, the composer could not have had a more enthusiastic or more cordial reception. His recent bereavement gave also an additional note of solemnity, and the appropriateness could not but be felt with the beauty of each passing movement. . . . In the experimental

[1] See Chapter 11.

performances before the war the thing would not rise, and though the players laboured with it the result remained heavy and comparatively lifeless. How different today. The music really seems to inhabit the air. . . . Harshness there was none. We learn afresh, from such a work, to prize our emotions of beauty. The composer has not set himself to be austere, but the lines of beauty are so clearly conceived that the music shines, the sun glistening on its wings as it passes with a touch so light that the intensity of our delight is as quick as tears.'

The First Symphony was included in a London concert in June 1920, given by the New York Philharmonic Orchestra conducted by Walter Damrosch. Elgar did not attend, but Damrosch wrote to tell him that the applause was so tumultuous that he had lifted the score from the desk and pointed to it 'to show to whom the real tribute was due'. Yet these plaudits had a hollow sound for Elgar. He was looking for a purchaser for Severn House; the landlord of Brinkwells had changed his mind and decided not to sell the cottage to him; Alice's estate was being settled, with Schuster's ready help as a trustee. 'C[arice]. & I have now a comfortable two hundred a year! and anything I can make – but that cannot be much now; my race is run,' he wrote to Schuster on 2 July. But to Alice Stuart of Wortley he confided (18 July): 'Frank gives a rosy picture of our finances as he had to sign some papers being a trustee but (as I told him) he knows *nothing* of the affairs (money left dear A. for life) outside the one trust he is in: I fear he is unwittingly making out things much better than they are. My friends always remind me of the gillie who said to Dr Johnson (when he was nearly dead riding over the moors) by way of encouraging & amusing him "Oh! such pretty goats!" That's about all they say.' This same letter, from Brinkwells, gives a frank self-portrait of Elgar at this time: ill and lonely. 'I have had *three* more slight attacks [of dizziness] & do not like the outlook at all: I take no notice of the conditions only I have to lie down for a day or two. . . . Music I loathe – I did get out some paper, but it's all dead. . . . The old life is over & everything seems blotted out. . . . It seems odd that Stoke [his sister Pollie's farm at Stoke Prior] was advertised last Saturday week (the sale) – the *same* day Birchwood Lodge (our old Worcester cottage) advertised & *sold* – I wanted it, & then in *Country Life same day*!! all the Wye fishing where I used to lie & fish & write & dream & where you & I walked once. Does it not seem strange that the *three* only havens of rest, to which in my busy life I have always fled for comfort & rest, should all be sold in the same week? Strange such a clean sweep of my old life. . . . I am "numb", I could not have borne the many memories but they have cut down the woods [near Brinkwells] so much & made a road etc. which alters the look of the place but of course dear A. *made* it & it is full of remembrances – too too sad for words. One odd thing I must tell you: in the shelter which

Mark [a handyman] built for her & which I do not allow anyone else to use, touch or look at, a wren has built a nest just where A.'s head used to touch the roof-twigs. Muriel [Foster] always called her the Little Wren so it seems pitifully curious. Now, my dear W. do not think we are gloomy – far from it; but everything in life has changed – I, to all intents and purposes, am an invalid – you see the stronger I get (& I am fairly well) the worse my ear is – if I am low in health & unable to get about, my ear is less troublesome; so there it is – in a vicious circle.'

He went for a short visit to his old friends the Speyers at Ridgehurst but things were changed there too. 'I cannot say that I appreciate the influx of *Germans*,' he told Alice Stuart. 'The –s (now Americans) came over & Frank, also some extraordinary females, friends of the youth whom F. introduces as his *nephew* – are we all mad! After this, *what*? Then at Ridgehurst we had a German lady & her daughter who sang to the Germans in Brussels!!!... About Stoke – I asked a millionaire friend – I descended so low – & begged he wd. save it: he sympathised & sent an agent who reported it wd. only *pay four per cent* – so my friend cd. not entertain it!!! That is the end: the public have my best work for nothing & I have not one single friend who cares – except you! My whole past is wiped out & I am quite alone.... I am glad you played the Cello Concerto – I have forgotten it ... there is absolutely nothing left in the world for me.... It is useless to pretend to a real friend – In the midst of it all I am not really depressed – only I see the inevitable.... I hear nothing of anyone & do not write at all – in fact I have "gone out" – & like it.'

The coolness with Schuster implied above was not a passing whim, as a letter from Schuster to Boult[2] on 3 September 1921 makes plain. Schuster had been in Europe and rushed back to London for a Promenade concert on 1 September at which Elgar conducted *Falstaff* and the Violin Concerto. Because of a customs muddle over his luggage, he arrived in the Queen's Hall after the concerto had begun. 'Edward had a tremendous reception (perhaps bigger *before* [*Falstaff*] than *after* it?) & took his calls with that appearance of sulkiness which would *do* for any composer of less commanding genius. I could have slapped him (& very nearly did) when I went round to tell him what I had done & encountered to be present & was greeted with the *coldest* of handshakes!'

W. H. Reed gave him companionship and Elgar wrote many letters to Troyte whom he had asked to design a headstone for Alice's grave: 'I fear the arms must be on a lozenge; Boutell says "A Lozenge takes the place of a shield to bear the arms of Ladies, *with the sole exception of the Sovereign*". That seems conclusive.... Could the motto "Fortiter

et fide" go in:[3] it suited dear A. so well.' When Schuster first visited
the grave in 1923 and wrote his approval of the stone, on which the
inscription begins 'Pray for the soul of Lady Elgar . . .', Elgar replied
(23 September): 'I know quite well that it is incorrect to put *Lady* – it
should be Dame but in these days polluted by all sorts of awful
women now *Dames* I would not let myself put the desecrated word.
My God! Clara B. and Melba in the same world, either this or the
next, with Alice!!'

He went to Worcester in September 1920 for the first post-war
Three Choirs Festival, staying quietly in the house in the Cathedral
precincts where his Uncle Henry had lived for many years until his
death in 1917. This saddened him and he shunned social gatherings.
He conducted *Gerontius*, 'For the Fallen', *The Music Makers*, and the
Introduction and Allegro. Not only was his mind full of his nearest loss:
Parry and Sinclair were commemorated, too, and the war dead. 'A
glorious week', he called it to Schuster, and afterwards to Alice Stuart
he wrote: 'I like to think of the Worcester days & you & the flowers
& the fruit & the warm sun & my cathedral & the music: but it *is*
lonely.' To the Colvins he confided his memories of a happy past at
Brinkwells – 'a past gone, shattered. I am . . . a sad, sad man & not fit
for company. I could not see you two dears – Kreisler came & I went
out to see him but no more, I felt that I was no longer "in" the world,
or rather that the old artistic "striving" world exists for me no more
so my one short attempt at life was a failure. . . . Inscrutable nature
goes on just the same – young larks, six, in a nest on the lawn, & many
other birds; nightingales sing; but I miss the littlest gentlest presence
& I cannot go on.'

Christmas in 1920 was especially trying – 'this horrible season of
Christmas – I always loathed it,' he wrote to Frances Colvin on 30
December. He had stayed at Kempsey and had taken his relatives to
lunch at an hotel at Stratford upon Avon that he used to know. What
he found disgusted him, he told Lady Colvin – 'under new
management, *U.S.A.* I believe. A three weeks carnival at Christmas, a
Jazz Band specially engaged – dances every night – the whole place
"booked-up" with an abandoned set of filthy wretches! I have known
S-on-A since 1869 and wish it cd. have been spared – we did not
honour Shakespeare in this way in those sweet old years. Think of a
Jazz Band.' Describing the same events to Alice Stuart, with whom
he had often had lunch at the hotel, he added: 'Thus goes another (I
think the last) of my peaceful poetic old haunts.'

But if he would not go to the world, the world went to him. He
was host to several musicians and composers, among them the
brilliant young violinist Jascha Heifetz, for whom he polished up a

[3]This was the family motto of her father, Maj.-Gen. Roberts. 'Bravely and
faithfully.'

very early violin study 'for strengthening the third finger'. He now saw more of Ernest Newman, whom he and his daughter very much liked but who had been *persona non grata* with Alice until the war years because of his criticisms of the oratorios. He went to conduct in Amsterdam and Brussels (where he was made a member of the Belgian Ordre de la Couronne by King Albert) and he spoke at a London banquet for Landon Ronald. He was introduced by Robert Nichols to Siegfried Sassoon and to Arnold Bennett who was later to describe him as 'a disgruntled old man'. On 20 November 1920 he conducted *Falstaff*, the Cello Concerto, and the Second Symphony at the inaugural concert of the City of Birmingham Symphony Orchestra, a project towards which he had supported Bantock's endeavours since 1907. The hall was by no means full. But Elgar's mind went back thirty-five years to Stockley's Orchestra. 'I almost expected to see myself come on with the fiddle!' he told a local journalist.

In January 1921 he sustained the 'ghastly shock' of Gervase Elwes's tragic death when he accidentally fell beneath a train at Boston, Massachusetts. As he told Percy Hull, 'apart from the acute sorrow at losing so good & great a gentleman & so great an artist, we must both feel that his loss is a severe thing for the festival . . . my personal loss is greater than I can bear to think upon but this is nothing – or I must call it so – compared to the general artistic loss – a gap impossible to fill – in the musical world'. This was the time when he felt he might complete the trilogy, but he never went beyond playing over his old sketches. On the first anniversary of Alice's death he wrote to Frances Colvin, 'Yes, it is a year ago; I have tried everything but with no result save that I can do no more and, for the first time in my life, I am "running away"!' 'I have tried to take up the old life,' he wrote to Colvin from Brinkwells in July, 'but it will not do and so there's an end. I feel like these woods – all aglow – a spark wd. start a flame – but no human spark comes.' And a month later, in another letter to Colvin, he said: 'There is no work left for me to do: my active creative period began under the most tender care and it ended with that care. All my friends, dear though they may be, seem rough, violent, and in most cases *coarse* in comparison – no more.' He joined gleefully with Troyte in deriding an article Troyte had sent him in which Hope Bagenal wrote about the effect of church acoustics on choral music: 'I shewed the art: to Hull & we both laughed at the notion of the brass being more "harsh" – the effect of the large nave, especially Worc. & Glouc: cathedrals is to enhance the "round" tone; if the writer had heard Beethoven's *Engedi* he wd. perhaps have learnt something.' He wrote another learned letter to the *Times Literary Supplement* about references to Shakespeare in Scott's novels. He was delighted by Norman Allin's singing of Judas at a run-through of *The Apostles* in preparation for the 1921 Hereford Festival.

Such artistry compensated for an opinion he had expressed a month earlier in a letter to William Starmer, conductor and organist at Tunbridge Wells: 'I am not a song writer . . . my best songs are not sung for the reason that they require *"breath"* – the modern singers seem to emulate young terriers and prefer a staccato falsetto bark which is not pleasing to me – so I think you may safely avoid my productions.' He took a delight in the success of Percy Hull's first Three Choirs Festival as Hereford conductor, but it was during a rehearsal of *The Apostles* that 'Elgar walked on to the platform and took up the baton without even looking at the chorus, much less giving them any sort of greeting. He announced the number at which he wanted us to start in such a quiet voice that no one could hear him and there was an embarrassed silence. He repeated the number but no louder and no one had the courage to ask him to "speak up" as his whole manner was forbidding in the extreme . . . By this time the chorus was thoroughly jittery, their entries were tentative and, in addition to this, they began to sing flat. One encouraging lift of that wonderful left hand of his would perhaps have saved the situation but none came and . . . he walked off saying "You don't appear to know anything of the work".'[4] An hour later at a tea-party he was 'chatting away most genially, making jokes and generally being the life and soul of the party with those wonderful keen eyes blinking and twinkling as they always did when he was enjoying himself.'

Elgar had recommended Holst's *Hymn of Jesus* to Hull for the 1921 festival and hoped the choice was financially justified – 'we all detest the Box Office but we all have to bow down to it even if we cannot worship it'. He was always warmed to life by friendship and devotion, and these he received from Hull. He was warmed, too, by his growing closeness to Shaw who had heard *Falstaff* for the first time and had written to him enthusiastically: 'Talk of *Till Eulenspiegel* or *Don Quixote*! This ought to be played three times to their once. Composing operas is mere piffle to a man who can do *that*.' 'I don't think we should have "liked" Aristophanes personally,' Elgar wrote to Colvin on 13 December 1921, 'or Voltaire (perhaps) but I cannot do without their works. G.B.S.'s politics are to me appalling but he is the kindest-hearted, gentlest man I have met outside the charmed circle which includes you.' He orchestrated Bach's Fugue in C minor, telling Eugène Goossens that he depended on 'people like John Sebastian' for inspiration now that his wife was dead and he could not be original. He finished the score on 22 May 1921, telling Lady Stuart: 'I think it is *brilliant* – a word I wanted in connection with Bach, who, in arrangements, is made "pretty" etc. etc.' The Fugue had arisen from a lunch in 1920, probably at Schuster's, at which Richard Strauss

[4] Letter from Lady Hull, Elgar Society Newsletter, May 1975, pp. 8–9.

had been present. Elgar and he discussed the orchestration of Bach's organ music. Strauss promised to transcribe the Fantasia in C minor and Elgar the Fugue. Elgar had soon held out the hand of friendship to Strauss after the war. When Boult was going to Munich in the late summer of 1920 Elgar asked him to give Strauss 'warm greetings . . . It is difficult to know how feelings have stood the wear & strain of the last few years, it may be that S. will not be too "receptive", anyhow it will be kind to *me* if you can assure him of my continued admiration &, if he will, friendship. I have followed, as well as broken communications could allow, his later compositions; I cannot expect him to be interested in mine – he has probably forgotten the good old days when he was named (by me) Richard Coeur de Lion, but I hope not.'[5]

During August 1921 he left Brinkwells for the last time and in September prepared to leave Severn House[6] and 'go forth into the world alone as I did forty-three years ago – only I am disillusioned and old'. He took a flat in 37 St James's Place, W.1., and also became a member of Brooks's, which he liked because it was 'real XVIII century & full of memories of Fox etc. etc.'. On 15 October he wrote one of his last letters from Severn House to Alice Stuart, who had been instrumental in finding it for him. 'I could not help feeling until about really I think a few weeks ago that my dear A. wd. be sure to come back & take charge of things. I cannot explain but I never touched anything without feeling – I cannot say *thinking*, one doesn't think – that I was responsible to her for every movement. Now I feel the desolation & hopelessness of it all & curiously, feel more satisfied – not happy but *calmer* over the situation. It must be. With all my artistic stupidity I have always been in other peoples' troubles the strong man – but I failed for myself & no one did anything to help. Selah! The end of Severn House was more *radiant* than the beginning.' To Troyte Griffith he wrote, 'Now I know & submit.'

.   .   .   .   .

'I submit.' Was this an echo of the letter to Jaeger after the failure of *Gerontius*? In this case, however, the reaction was not an original piece of music like *Cockaigne*. Five days after he wrote to Troyte, his transcription of the Bach fugue was conducted at Queen's Hall by Eugène Goossens. ('The conductor sat a little heavily on it – no champagne,' he told Alice Stuart.) Its free-ranging and romantic approach caused some controversy. Neo-classicism was in the air; a purer, more authentic approach to Bach was gaining ground. It was a significant pointer. Goossens was one of two composers whom Elgar

recommended in December 1920 to Herbert Brewer in response to
Brewer's request for advice about young British composers who
might provide new works for the 1922 Gloucester Festival. The other
recommendation was Arthur Bliss,[7] whose early string quartet Alice
had heard and liked in 1916. 'It would be a first-class thing for the
festivals to get in real new blood and away from the heavy dullness of
the – well, you know,' he wrote to Brewer. 'Whatever they do has
some vitality and grip. . . . These young men will . . . do away with
the remnant of the notion that everything must be a sort of Ch. of E.
propaganda.' Brewer hoped for a new work from Elgar, too, but was
disappointed. 'I only regret the appearance of my own name so often,'
was his comment on the inclusion of *The Apostles*, *The Kingdom*, and
'For the Fallen'. 'I cannot yet see my way to writing. The upset in my
life has been too great.' All that Brewer got from him was the full
transcription of the Bach C minor *Fantasia and Fugue*. Elgar had
completed the *Fugue* on 22 May 1921 and he orchestrated the *Fantasia*
by June of 1922, though he said he had begun the latter before the
Fugue and then 'dropped' it, perhaps because he then still hoped that
Strauss would fulfil his side of the bargain. The young men he helped
were grateful. Bliss wrote to him of 'the fine and rare encouragement
your presence is' and Bax dedicated a string quartet to him, but he
never went to hear it. How interested he really was in their music is
problematical. He did not, as Vaughan Williams did when he attained
a similar pre-eminence in English music, attend almost every first
performance of a new English work. The truth is that, like Delius, he
was not very interested in the work of his contemporaries and juniors.
He helped people he liked as men rather than as musicians, as in the
case of Bantock, or because he thought they had had a raw deal, like
Holbrooke. In 1898 he had been a generous champion of Coleridge-
Taylor, but by January 1900 he was writing to Jaeger: 'I think you are
right about C. Taylor – I was cruelly disillusioned by the overture to
Hiawatha which I think really only "rot" . . . his later work is
insincere & cannot do any real good.' The only really enthusiastic
compliments he ever paid to other English composers were to
Edward German and, in his last months, to Delius. His relationship
with Bliss was typical. They had met in 1912 at Severn House when
Bliss was at Cambridge. Elgar sent him a miniature score of *Cockaigne*
in 1916 while he was fighting on the Somme. Bliss was invited in 1919
to one of the private performances of Elgar's Violin Sonata (which he
did not like) and in the following year the Gloucester commission
materialized. Something happened after the 1922 performance of
Bliss's *Colour Symphony* – in his autobiography, Bliss wrote of being
hurt by Elgar's 'biting tongue'. There was an estrangement until 1928

[7] The works concerned in 1922 were Bliss's *Colour Symphony* and Goossens's *Silence*.

when Bliss wrote to him and received a candid reply: 'Frankly, I was greatly disappointed with the way you progressed from years ago. There was so much "press" of a type I dislike and newspaper nonsense. I can easily believe you were responsible for little or none of this but it rankled a great deal because I had great hopes for you: I had affection. It will seem vulgar to you if I add that commercially you have (I believe or was led to believe) no concern with the success of your works – an unfortunate side of art which we penniless people have always with us and try to ignore. I hoped you were going to give us something very great in quite modern music, the progress of which is very dear to me; and then you seemed to become a mere "paragraphist". I am probably wrong and trust I was.' Bliss then dedicated his Pastoral *Lie strewn the white flocks* to Elgar, who liked the work. It is apparent that the coolness is another example of Elgar's jealousy of the artistic and financial success of a younger man.

As 1921 drew to its end he seemed to be reviving. He was able to tell Schuster in January 1922 that he had been to hear Thibaud and Cortot play his Sonata, had taken Edith Evans out to dinner, and had 'brought the house down' with his remark at a social gathering that 'It seems if you scratch the Russian Ballet you get the Tartar emetic.' Did he know Ambrose Bierce's definition of a Russian – 'a person with a Caucasian body and a Mongolian soul. A Tartar emetic'? In January 1922, his daughter Carice was married to Samuel Blake, and he spent more of his time in his clubs, where he entertained the theatre folk – Squire Bancroft, Seymour Hicks, Granville Barker – whose company he found so agreeable, particularly that of Norman Forbes, brother of Sir Johnston Forbes-Robertson. He went to Leeds in March to conduct *The Apostles*, where, as he recounted ruefully to Lady Stuart, 'my friend ... was too busy looking after five young soldiers to pay any attention to me! It does seem rather odd & shews what adulation is worth that the composer & conductor should be left *alone* to find his way on foot thro' dark streets!! What an odd world it is. I rather like the complete isolation, but it seems odd.'

That he was as susceptible as ever to the charms of women is illustrated by a curious episode involving the talented and very attractive Hungarian violinist Jelly d'Arányi. At her second London recital in Wigmore Hall in May 1919, when she was 25, she and George Reeves played Elgar's Violin Sonata. The composer was delighted by the performance and wrote her a note of thanks. In February 1920 she played the sonata at Severn House for Lady Elgar. A year or so later, according to Jelly d'Arányi's biography,[8] Elgar conceived a 'violent affection' for her and addressed her as 'My darling Tenth Muse'. He took her to lunch in Pall Mall and one day,

[8] *The Sisters d'Arányi*, op. cit., pp. 118–19.

when she went to Severn House for a book he wanted to give her, 'a little scene took place which ended in Jelly ensconced in a taxi "cursing old men"'.

He hankered after the country. He would often go to visit his ailing sister and brother in Worcestershire, and he was always glad to unburden himself to Troyte. He invoked his aid in an unsuccessful attempt to prevent Worcester buying his portrait by Philip Burne-Jones which now hangs in the Guildhall there. 'Weak-kneed' he called it. 'Phil is a good creature but is feeble & makes me stand like himself.' And the same letter contains comments on the Playfair production of *The Beggar's Opera* that have a tang of the Elgar–Jaeger correspondence: 'The Beggar's Opera is amusing & awfully improper – a jingle of songs & one great proof – if an added one is needed – that the English are entirely unmusical – this burlesque is about as far as their intelligence can go & its amazing long run is unthinkable in any other country.'

This sentence is characteristically Elgarian, as many other letters I have quoted will have shown. But perhaps its sour mood was engendered by personal disappointment because the public were beginning to ignore his great works. When the Leeds Choral Union sang *The Apostles* at Queen's Hall in June 1922 the audience was so small that Shaw wrote to the *Daily News* to apologize to Elgar 'for London society, and for all the other recreants to English culture' and to posterity 'for living in a country where the capacity and tastes of schoolboys and sporting coster-mongers are the measure of metropolitan culture'. Although a June afternoon is not the most sensible day on which to perform an oratorio, it was just about this time that a strong reaction against Elgar's music began to be obvious. The outward mood of the twenties was not sympathetic to the nobility of an Elgar; it was either brittle or experimental, or looked back to an earlier age. Stravinsky, Milhaud, Honegger, Lord Berners, and Walton's *Façade*: these were one side of the musical twenties; Vaughan Williams's *Shepherds of the Delectable Mountains* and *Pastoral Symphony* were another; the songs of Warlock were a third. These composers were producing new music: Elgar was silent. More hurtful to him than the change of public mood was the change he detected among his friends. A few days after the London performance, the Leeds choir sang *The Apostles* in Canterbury Cathedral – a memorable occasion – and Elgar received one letter after the Queen's Hall performance and one (from Alice Stuart) after Canterbury. To Lady Stuart he wrote on 14 June: 'I have *seen* no one, *no one* has written or taken the slightest notice & I have read nothing & seen no papers: truly I *am* a lonely person if I liked to think so – but my "friends"!!! where, oh, where! are they? Silence profound. I was talking to Claude [Phillips] last week & he said "Don't be a Timon". I am not – but do these horrible frauds expect me to continually "attend" them when they happen to want me?' In the same vein he had written to her in 1923: 'My barren honours are dust. Not a single friend has shewn any sign of life, except your house, for years. . . . I only feel with the D. of Wellington that I only hope that they do not think I am (or rather *was*) such a d—d fool as to believe them.'

The year 1923 brought from him only some slight incidental music to Binyon's play *Arthur* for Lilian Baylis's Old Vic production. It was in 1923 that he said to Compton Mackenzie, who had just founded the magazine *The Gramophone*, that he supposed all the young critics of the paper would be sneering at him. 'Not that I care,' he added, 'I take no more interest in music. . . . The secret of happiness for an artist when he grows old is to have a passion that can take the place of his art. I have discovered the joy that diatoms can give me. This miraculous world of beauty under the ocean revealed by the microscope is beyond music.'[9] He defended himself from the indifference of those who were not in sympathy with his music by taking the offensive – 'I take no interest in music', or, as he said to Vaughan Williams at the Three Choirs Festival in 1923 after a rehearsal of the Cello Concerto, 'I am surprised that you come to hear this vulgar music.' His other contributions to the 1923 festival were the provision of orchestral accompaniments to anthems by Wesley and Battishill and the orchestration of Handel's Overture in D minor. Writing from Kempsey to Clayton of Novello's on 16 July 1923 he said: 'I had known the overture from the old two-stave organ arrangement since I was a little boy & always wanted it to be heard in a large form – the weighty structure is (to me) so good – epic.'

The end of Elgar's composing career is mainly explained by Alice's death, but there is more to it than that. After the first grief, such a loss might have inspired him to some memorial effort, but his flame was extinguished. When he said 'I have gone out, and I like it', he never spoke truer words. Alice's death and the feelings of guilt with which it was inevitably accompanied were merely the temporal manifestation of his increasing spiritual disenchantment with the England which had brought forth his music. The gulf between the world of late Victorian Worcestershire and post-1918 Britain was so wide that it is now almost impossible to imagine it. But it is significant that the bitterness about the early struggles and snubs in the Worcester and Malvern of 1885 receded from Elgar's letters after 1914 and was replaced by a longing to re-live and recapture what he now saw as an ideal world. He did not want the world of the 1920s, with what he had described to Binyon as 'the complexities of the time', and he would not waste his 'lovely music' on it.

Two encounters with 'the commercial side' also particularly

[9] *The Gramophone* (June 1957), p. 1.

distressed him. In June 1921 Clayton of Novello's was embarrassed to tell him that his total revenue from all his works from the previous five years amounted to just over £256, of which the sales of the pianoforte solo and duet versions of the *Enigma Variations* accounted for a little under £6. Elgar replied on 12 June: 'It makes sorry reading but I have never permitted myself any illusions & have none now . . . I wish the firm could see its way to buy me out entirely; I never really belonged to the musical world – I detest my slightest necessary connection with it & should be glad to have done with it and get back to my (deceased) dogs and horses'. Two years later, in July 1923, he asked Novello's for 100 guineas for two male-voice part-songs, *The Wanderer* and *Zut, Zut, Zut*. The firm's John E. West, in a report to the chairman, criticized both works, describing *The Wanderer* as 'rather ordinary' and *Zut, Zut, Zut* as 'cheap without being sufficiently interesting . . . Is the composer falling off in the value of his ideas?' Novello's offered to publish them as Elgar's own property. Elgar wrote to Clayton on 11 August: 'I am too old to begin altering the method of publication I have been accustomed to &, after due thought, will not ask you to print the PtSongs as "author's property". Just tear up the MSS – or return them to me & I can do so'. To this Clayton replied: 'Neither I nor anyone else here wd. wantonly destroy an Elgar MS, so if that is to be the fate of your two partsongs for men's voices, you must apply the finishing touch yourself.' He offered fifty guineas for the two – half what Elgar wanted – and explained that 'the whole difficulty about these two compositions is that we never do, and never can, sell partsongs for men's voices in large quantities. Send us something effective for mixed voices or for women's voices & the whole situation will be changed at once'. Elgar accepted the fifty guineas. The final break with Novello's came in July 1924.

He was appalled and repelled by the rise of Socialism. Already lonely without his wife, he grew lonelier and more aloof. 'I have . . . settled into servile slipperdom very easily,' he wrote to Colvin from Kempsey on 27 May 1923, 'and wonder why I ever worked. What fools we were to have tried to do anything decent – I regret everything good I have ever done.' To strangers this attitude took an unfortunate form. In 1904, at a party at Schuster's, at which Adrian Boult was present, the contralto Edith Clegg was among the guests. Schuster opened her music-case and took out an Elgar song, calling across the room 'Edward, you must come and meet Miss Clegg. She's going to sing *After* for us.' Elgar heaved himself off a settee, went over to the singer and said 'Good evening, Miss Clegg. You've spoiled my evening for me,' and turned his back. One's condemnation of such boorish conduct is tempered by compassion that so great a composer could be so lacking in assurance.

He thawed only to those who shared his memories of his heyday.

Thus to Alice Stuart after the 1923 Worcester Festival, he was able to say: 'I am so delighted you were there & liked the dear old things – they sounded well in the cathedral but I cannot see the future – Where are the new soloists?... *The Kingdom, Gerontius* & "For the Fallen" are not bad; I think I deserve my *peerage* now when these are compared with the new works!!!' He remained the outsider. If the young men like Bax and Bliss liked to salute him as their leader, that was very kind of them, but he did not seek to be a figurehead and he played no active part in any post-war scheme for the propagation of English music. He believed an artist had his personal view to state and that was all there was to it. He played his part in healing the wounds of war: he renewed his friendship with Kreisler and he extended a welcome to Richard Strauss when Strauss visited England in 1922. But he excused himself from a reception for Sibelius and in later years did not attend receptions for Schoenberg and Ravel. He had had enough of London; in April 1923 he took a summer lease of Napleton Grange at Kempsey, five miles from Worcester towards Tewkesbury, so that his sister, who had been ill, could stay with him there. On his visits to London he spent most of his time at the theatre, although he rarely enjoyed the plays. 'I have been to *12* theatres since I returned,' he told Lady Stuart, 'I am so desperately lonely & turn in to see anything.' A play by Conrad he described to her as 'the most amateurish, childish, drivelling imbecile futile rubbish you ever saw'. He also said he could not 'stand' Galsworthy, though later he admired the Forsyte novels. He was determined, he wrote, not to be old-fashioned, adding: 'I am only old-fashioned in loving you.' In the autumn of 1923, perhaps remembering that a change of scenery used to stir him to new endeavour, he went on a cruise to South America and travelled 1,000 miles up the Amazon. But nothing came out of the journey except, according to Reed, that he was impressed by the importance of the opera house in South American towns. On his return he wrote his music for the Wembley Exhibition which opened on 23 April. He wrote his *Empire March* at Perryfield, Bromsgrove, in January 1924. Sending a sketch of the opening to Lady Stuart he added, 'It should rouse people up – I *could* rouse Brazilians but not English.' The rehearsals, he told Lady Stuart, tried his patience, 'overwhelmed with etiquette & red tape... the K. insists on Land of Hope & there were some ludicrous suggestions of which I will tell you – if we ever meet. But everything seems so hopelessly & irredeemably *vulgar* at Court.... I was standing alone (criticising) in the middle of the enormous stadium.... 17,000 men, hammering, loudspeakers, amplifiers, four aeroplanes circling over etc. etc. – all mechanical & horrible – no soul & no romance & no imagination. Here had been played the great football match[10] – even the turf, which

[10] The first Wembley Cup Final.

is good, was not their [sic] as turf but for football – but at my feet I saw a group of real *daisies*. Something wet rolled down my cheek – & I am not ashamed of it: I had recovered my equanimity when the aides came to learn my views – Damn everything except the daisy – I was back in something sane, wholesome & *gentlemanly* but only for two minutes.'

His pessimistic outlook extended, of course, to the world of music: he prophesied (as Beecham and Harty also did) that there would be no orchestral concerts because 'broadcasting is killing all the concert rooms'. Most surprising of all, the same letter contains a distasteful piece of gossip about his most loyal friend, Schuster: 'This afternoon he was sitting in the back of a smart car . . . driving with an *odd looking* – I hate to say it – "*bit of fluff*"!! in flamboyant *pink* on the front seat. All laughing loudly; they did not see me & I was glad for I shd. have been thoroughly ashamed.' Since Elgar must have known that similar conclusions were drawn, however wrongly, about his own friendships with women, it is strange that he was not more charitable to a man who had helped him so much. But even at Schuster's home he had found evidence of change: nothing was the same. He disapproved of some members of Frank's household. 'You cd. not say the one word to F. as usual,' he wrote to Alice Stuart after a visit to 'The Hut' in October 1922. 'I tried to write but the effect has been that all idea of composition is "choked off" so we will forget my little delusion about taking up music again: that is over.' A year later, after another visit to Schuster's he wrote to her: 'I cd. not enjoy it:—and— were there but – poor dear old Frank.' He grew further away from even his oldest friends when in 1923 he in effect retired to the life of a country gentleman in Worcester. He took to race-going; he surrounded himself with dogs; he became passionate about cars. 'I am in the throes – & have decided on the newest Lea Francis – I think,' he wrote to Percy Hull in the autumn of 1924. 'We all went to Coventry & wallowed in cars. I bought an *Austin 7* a fortnight ago for my sister who loves it.' He was reconciled to the continual snapping of links with the past. In 1924 Kilburn died and Stanford. Sir Walter Parratt, too, and late in the year Fauré. 'His chamber music never had a chance here in the old Joachim days,' he wrote to Schuster. 'I may be wrong but I feel that it was "held up" to our loss. . . . As far as I can resent anything – which is not far – I resented such neglect.' Schuster tried to persuade Elgar to support a Fauré memorial concert. 'I suppose he only wants a pound for a ticket!' he wrote to Alice Stuart. 'I am tired of the world which never notices my existence except to ask for a pound.' Nevertheless, he tried to persuade Brewer to perform Fauré's *Requiem* at the 1925 Gloucester Festival, but this exquisite work was still considered too risky at the box-office. (He had himself sought Lady Stuart's influence in 1923 for a knighthood for Brewer: 'I fear he has not the goodwill of the R.C.M. – quite unnecessary but those sort of people pull only their own strings & not being content to do that cut other people's.' Brewer was knighted three years later.) A few weeks earlier Puccini had died. 'I thought the notices [obituaries] of Puccini dreadfully inadequate,' he told Schuster, having characteristically prefaced this with 'I fear you will have nothing more from "my pen" – but if that's all to look forward to you will not miss much. Music is dying fast in this country.' Yet on 15 June 1925, he was telling Alice Stuart: 'I *am* doing the piano concerto but do not tell anyone as I may switch off at any moment – as is usual.' Family illnesses and deaths also beset him. 'I am here in the midst of invalids, operations, deaths & nursing homes for my relatives,' he wrote to Schuster on 4 November 1925, 'This has been going on for a year & I do not trouble my friends with letters in consequence – there is really nothing to say apart from macabre festivities.' Some weeks later, just before Christmas 1925, he himself went into a nursing-home for three weeks for an operation, his last entreaty to his daughter Carice being to 'be sure the cows in the field don't get into the garden'. At this period of his life he spent hours travelling round Worcestershire with W. H. Reed, revisiting old haunts and pointing out to his companion places he loved. Reed, in *Elgar As I Knew Him*, remarks that Elgar 'seemed to know every inch' of his native county and Herefordshire and the Severn and Wye. 'He never tired of talking of them, exploring and re-exploring them.' This close knowledge of places he liked extended beyond the West Country. In a letter to Lady Stuart he mentions a Lake District journey which Percy Anderson and Frank Schuster had made together, adding: 'They must have driven over the bridge and under the castle which they never saw and also they went thro' Gosforth and never saw the cross. Oh! these motorists.' His knowledge of architecture, history, and folklore was characteristic of the agile mind of the truly self-educated man – all his life he read, absorbed and retained knowledge.

His presence as a resident of Worcestershire naturally made itself felt at this period at the Three Choirs Festivals. His music had always had a principal place in the programmes, but now his eminence, his age, and his powers as his own interpreter conferred a special accolade on the concerts. It is forgotten that he was not a 'Three Choirs' composer in the fullest sense. None of his major works had a first performance there (those that did were *Froissart*, *Lux Christi*, the second *Wand of Youth* suite, the suite from *Crown of India* and 'Go, Song of Mine'). The three biggest choral works had held a regular place, but it is surprising to discover that the *Variations* were not played there between 1903 and 1926, nor the Violin Concerto between 1911 and 1927, the First Symphony between 1910 and 1925

and the Second between 1913 and 1927, *Cockaigne* between 1909 and
1927, and *In the South* between 1904 and 1930. Under his baton and
with his devoted Billy Reed leading the orchestra, Elgar's music at the
Three Choirs between 1920 and 1933 was performed with unchallengeable authority.[11] Langford, in the *Manchester Guardian* in
September 1924, summed it up: 'The very walls [of Worcester] cry
out to us from the same romantic past that has bred his music. His
music, heard within them, is redolent of England in the complete
sense which in other places may fail it.' Not that everything always
went well. Elgar had to feel that the performance was 'alive' or he lost
interest, and, so deep was the wound from *Gerontius*, he could not
tolerate a lack of interest among the performers. Bernard Shore
recalls[12] a rehearsal of *Falstaff* when the side-drummer came in late at
the moment of Falstaff's death. He made the same error in the
performance. 'We were horrified to see a spasm of anger on Elgar's
face. He stopped conducting and made no attempt to control things
again.' Perhaps the most celebrated similar occasion was at a Three
Choirs performance of *The Kingdom* in 1924 which Sir Adrian Boult
has vividly described.[13] 'It was at once apparent that the choir were
perhaps resting too much on last year's laurels. . . . Bad intonation
was evident near the start, and I felt that Sir Edward was losing
interest, as he began to drive the performance, getting faster and
faster as if the one thing he wanted was to get out of the Cathedral and
forget about music. We endured this for nearly an hour when we
came to the wonderful scena "The sun goeth down", which was
written for that great soprano, Agnes Nicholls. She had, if I
remember rightly, practically retired at that time, but returned at
short notice to take over the part which she had made her own many
years before. I shall never forget the intense concentration with which
she began that gentle opening phrase, and the way the orchestra
seemed instantly to spring to life and, immediately after, the
disgruntled composer's interest quickened, and from that moment
the performance returned to the extraordinary beauty of the year
before.'

How much this kind of singing must have meant to the old
composer can be gauged from an extract from a letter to Schuster
written a month after that performance: 'There is not a single voice
coming on in the solo world & young people have given up choral
work & the distressingly *thin* physique of the modern boys & girls
who *do* try to sing makes their voices so frail & metallic that the
general tone is miserable.'

[11] For details of Elgar's conducting of his own works at Three Choirs Festivals, see
M. Kennedy's 'Elgar and the Festivals', in 'Two Hundred and Fifty Years of the
Three Choirs Festival' (ed. B. Still, 1977), pp. 31–6.
[12] *Sixteen Symphonies*, op. cit., p. 262.
[13] *Elgar Centenary Sketches* (London, 1957), pp. 9–10.

Elgar's conducting was described by Sir John Barbirolli, who
played in the orchestra under him in London and at the Three Choirs,
as 'not great by the highest professional standards' but 'it was
extraordinary how he could make you feel exactly what he wanted if
you were in sympathy with him.'[14] Sir Adrian supported this view:
'His nervous, electric beat unfailingly added a tension and a lustre
which produced a tone quality one came to recognise as highly
personal. . . . Musicians who heard Elgar conduct are getting fewer in
number, but I think they will all agree that if they could make a list of
the finest performances they had ever heard of Elgar's works, nearly,
if not all of them would turn out to have been conducted by Elgar
himself.' Bernard Shore is more detailed: 'It was his face and certain
expressive gestures of his left hand that would sometimes lighten up a
page.'[15] Elgar re-lived his music as he conducted it and, says Mr
Shore, 'invariably clouded' the climax of the first movement of the
Second Symphony at one bar after [42]. 'The silent break . . . never
came off to perfection . . . His eye would fail to hold us and his usually
clear beat became fluffy.' One important point is also made by Mr
Shore: ' Jog-trot, humdrum conducting is the death of this emotional,
highly-strung music . . . Elgar's own tempos were always fluctuating.' This last statement was confirmed to me by Sir Adrian, who said
that he noted Elgar's own treatment of certain passages in his works
and would discover, when he went to another Elgar-conducted
performance a year later, that the treatment of the same passages was
varied. It supports Elgar's own preference, expressed to Jaeger, for
elasticity in performances of his music. It is imperative that this
should be realized for, although Elgar was the first great composer to
record most of his own music for the gramophone, it would be a
mistake for any conductor rigidly to follow Elgar's interpretations as
definitive.[16] The recordings are fascinating and historic, but had he
made them again a year or two later, they might have differed
considerably – indeed, in the case of his two recordings of the Second
Symphony, the earlier is the more emotional and 'elastic'. It is music
of changing moods, acutely responsive to atmosphere and occasion.
'I *feel* & don't invent'. That is the key.

Although he told Schuster that 'my influence at the 3 choirs is nil',
it became the focal-point of his year and he in his turn became the
focal-point of the 'twaddle and mutual admiration' he had scorned in
1898. Wearing the robes of his doctorate or Court dress with orders,
he was a magnificent and striking figure except to those who found

[14] *A Personal Note*, in LP recording of *Gerontius*, E.M.I. 1965.
[15] *Sixteen Symphonies*, op. cit., p. 261.
[16] His published orchestral scores contain detailed markings of tempi, bowing,
phrasing, and nuances of expression. In vocal music, he told McNaught of Novello's
in 1908, 'I overdo this sort of thing (necessary in orchestral stuff) as I put down all my
feelings as I write and then haven't the heart to take 'em out'.

his delight in dressing up merely a pompous affectation. Even so admiring a friend as Schuster, who disliked the atmosphere of the cathedral cities and always stayed elsewhere, called him 'the pouter pigeon'. At his house parties Elgar was dandyishly dressed, often in a white summer suit. He was portly now, his hair white, his moustache luxuriant. He carried a stick as he grew older and as his ominous 'sciatica' began to trouble him. He made several small musical contributions to the festivals' atmosphere, in 1911 arranging two Bach chorales for brass so that they could be performed from the tower of Worcester Cathedral, writing a Civic Fanfare[17] for Hereford in 1927, and in 1923 orchestrating accompaniments to motets by S. S. Wesley, Battishill, and Purcell. He even took issue in the local paper in 1926 with a canon of Worcester who appeared to be objecting to a proposal to perform parts of *Parsifal* at the Three Choirs because Wagner was a sensualist. This was too much for Elgar, who quoted John Donne to the canon and added: 'If the Canon really believes that such emotions in early life debar a man from taking part in the services of the church in riper years he should at once resign his canonry and any other spiritual offices he is paid to hold.'

But there were still grudging voices. As late as 1922 the neurologist Sir Henry Head described Elgar to Siegfried Sassoon[18] as 'that little provincial music-master'. Sassoon, who was in Schuster's circle, formed a priggishly unflattering view of Elgar and his 'baritonal garrulity'—'a very self-centred and inconsiderate man ... always pretending and disguising his feelings ... He prides himself on his conventional appearance. I have often heard him use the phrase a "Great Gentleman". It is his sublimity of encomium ... No doubt he sublimates himself as a G. G.—the Duc d'Elgar'. He described an incident at The Hut on 6 June 1922 when Elgar attacked Lady Maud Warrender on the subject of Queen Mary's Doll's House. In a 'crescendo climax of rudeness', Elgar said: 'We all know that the King and Queen are incapable of appreciating anything artistic; they have never asked for the full score of my Second Symphony to be added to the Library at Windsor. But as the crown of my career I'm asked to contribute to—a *Doll's House* for the Queen! I've been a monkey-on-a-stick for you people long enough. Now I'm getting off the stick. I wrote and said that I hoped they wouldn't have the impertinence to press the matter on me any further. I consider it an insult for an artist to be asked to mix himself up in such nonsense.' A doctor who examined him in 1925 found him to be 'a neurotic, who most of all wanted reassurance'.

[17] The fanfare was written for the entry of the mayoral party at the opening service on 4 September 1927. Elgar began the fanfare promptly at 3 p.m., but the mayor was late, so the second performance was given a few minutes later! The occasion was recorded.
[18] *Siegfried Sassoon Diaries 1920–2*, op. cit. Sassoon found him to be at times a 'club bore'.

14 Finale

In 1927 Elgar was seventy. The anniversary coincided with one of the lowest points that his reputation among the arbiters of fashion had reached. A birthday concert at Queen's Hall was given to a hall no more than half full. 'I have had some satisfaction & even pleasure in my life,' he wrote to Charles Volkert who had been head of Schott's London branch when Elgar was in London in the 1880s, 'but have no pleasant memories connected with music.' It is a terrifying and tiresome statement, for surely even that year he must have had pleasure from a concert in Manchester on 20 January when, to salute him in his seventieth year, Adolph Brodsky, then seventy-five, had returned to the Hallé platform to play the Violin Concerto? Elgar conducted. *Froissart*, *In the South*, *Sea Pictures*, and the *Variations* were also in the programme. Memories of Richter's heyday in Manchester and of his own triumphs there, the presence of Brodsky symbolizing the interest of a European generation in his work: was there nothing pleasant in the occasion? On 26 June Schuster, himself now seventy-five, performed his last generous act of homage to his friend, arranging performances of the three chamber works at 'The Hut' (by then re-named the 'Long White Cloud') by Sammons, Murdoch, Reed, and others. As it had always been, Schuster's home was a focal point for artistic people of all generations and outlooks. Among the audience on that Sunday were Siegfried Sassoon, Arnold Bennett, William Walton, and Sacheverell and Osbert Sitwell. Elgar described the day to Lady Stuart of Wortley, who had not been present: 'You were sadly missed last Sunday at The Hut – or rather at the new place as the Hut atmosphere has gone never to return. Dear old Frank was radiant &, as usual, a perfect host. . . . I *hope* I behaved as becomes an old visitor. . . . I *wish* you could have heard the things which seem to me to be of my best & the Quintet is not of this world; but you know more of this than I do.' Sir Osbert Sitwell has written, in *Laughter in the Next Room*,[1] an ironic and unsympathetic account of the occasion, omitting to mention that it was a seventieth birthday concert and admitting that he found Elgar's music 'in spite of its genius . . . obnoxious, so full of English humour and the spirit of compulsory games,' whatever that may mean.

I seem to recall [he wrote] that we saw from the edge of the river, on a smooth green lawn opposite, above an embankment, and through an

---

[1] (London, 1949).

hallucinatory mist born of the rain that had now ceased, the plump wraith of
Sir Edward Elgar, who with his grey moustache, grey hair, grey top hat and
frock coat looked every inch a personification of Colonel Bogey, walking
with Frank Schuster. . . . In the main the audience was drawn from the
composer's passionately devout but to me anonymous partisans. . . . It is
true that these surviving early adherents to Elgar's genius seemed to be
endowed with an unusual longevity, but even allowing for this, it was plain,
looking round, that in the ordinary course of nature their lives must be
drawing to an end. One could almost hear, through the music, the whirr of
the wings of the Angel of Death: he hovered very surely in the air that day,
among the floccose herds of good-time Edwardian ghosts, with trousers
thus beautifully pressed and suits of the best material, carrying panama hats
or glossy bowlers, or decked and loaded with fur and feather. And though
the principal lived on until 1934, most of them knew, I apprehend, as they
listened so intently to the prosperous music of the Master, and looked
forward to tea and hot buttered scones (for it was rather cold, as well as being
damp), and to all kinds of little sandwiches and cakes, that this would prove
their last outing of this sort. The glossy motors waited outside to carry them
home, like the vans drawn up to take the fine beasts away from an
agricultural show. Some of the motors were large and glassy as a hearse.

This evocative passage is a prototype for the superficial view of
Elgar. He did look like a retired general, he was something of a
dandy. But Sitwell and others like him saw only what they wanted to
see – the military bearing. They did not notice the troubled and
withdrawn eyes. They heard only what they wanted to hear, the pomp
and circumstance; they did not listen to the note of resignation, nor
realize that Elgar ten years earlier had seen the hearses drawn up. No
doubt Sitwell was oppressed by the atmosphere, for even W. H. Reed
refers slightly in *Elgar As I Knew Him* to feminine 'Elgar
worshippers'. He was accurate in one respect. Death was claiming
Elgar's friends. Lord Stuart of Wortley had died on 24 April 1926,
two days before Elgar conducted the L.S.O. in the *Variations* and the
First Symphony. 'It was a great ordeal,' he told Alice Stuart, '& I
missed something too great to express – I looked at the familiar seats
& my eyes filled.' Colvin died in 1927 and Schuster on 26 December
of that year, Herbert Brewer in 1928. 'Only his most intimate friends
could realize how easily that sensitive soul was lacerated,' Elgar said
of Schuster in a letter to Adela Schuster on 24 January 1928. Schuster
might well have said the same of him. Even after death this loyal
friend's devotion was proclaimed. He left Elgar £7,000 because he
had saved England from the reproach of having produced no
composer 'worthy of rank with the great masters'. The loss of his
friend and confidant was a heavy blow to Elgar. 'He was always the
most loving, strongest and wisest friend man ever had,' he wrote to
Adela Schuster on 8 January, 'I seem dazed – to have lost a limb, to
have grown older, suddenly.' To Alice Stuart he was able to speak his

whole mind: 'It is a dispensation of whoever controls us that in remembering childish holidays we recollect always the *fine* days – the bad ones do not come back so easily; in the passing of friends it is somewhat the same: the radiant happy & sunny Frank I have before me as I write & the small temporary little irritations which worried me at the time are gone & forgotten for ever.' The death of his brother Frank in 1928, after years of illness, was another blow.

Elgar had left Napleton Grange, Kempsey, in the autumn of 1927 and from 7 November to 7 April 1928 rented Battenhall Manor, Worcester, from Mrs Claire Sybil Buckle. He then moved to Tiddington House, Stratford-upon-Avon, home of Sir Gerard and Lady Muntz, where he stayed until December 1929. It is tempting to think that he was enjoying the irony of now living in the kind of houses to which his father, as a tradesman, had taken Elgar to improvise on the gentry's pianos. At Tiddington House he could indulge his old love of Shakespeare by visits to Bridges Adams's company at the memorial theatre. He spoke of writing incidental music; not Shakespeare but a playwright named Bertram P. Matthews was the recipient of music for his play *Beau Brummel*, produced by Gerald Lawrence at Birmingham in November 1928. Elgar conducted on the first night; he still fulfilled many engagements to conduct his own works,[2] but his life was now centred on his dogs – on his 1929 Christmas card he quoted Whitman's 'I think I could turn and live with animals. . . . They do not make me sick discussing their duty to God.' His sentimentality over dogs had been growing since Alice's death. She had not liked dogs and used Elgar's and her frequent absences from home as an excuse for not keeping one. But he loved them, and in the fourteen years after Alice's death he made up for the deprivations of the previous thirty. The death of his sister's Juno had upset him and when in 1923 his daughter's dog had been killed by a car he wrote to Lady Stuart: 'I cannot keep back my tears & am not ashamed.' When his spaniel Marco was ill in 1925 he abandoned his London engagements, telling Lady Stuart: 'He is now the only thing left in the world to me – and he's ill & looking for me everywhere'. Marco and the cairn terrier Mina, both of whom survived him and are buried in the garden of his birthplace, were treated as if they were humans and had seats on either side of him at table. It was symbolic that his last published orchestral work should be called *Mina*, a haunting, halting morsel of nostalgic charm. 'Noble Marco & funny little wistful Mina,' was Ernest Newman's description of 'a lovable pair'.

Elgar was not well at this time – 'it is my *ear* which has failed (& is painful) after threatening for years,' he told Lady Stuart in May 1929.

[2] But he cancelled an engagement at Bristol in 1928 because the orchestra was to be reduced in numbers.

But at the end of the year he made a spirited attack in letters to the press on a Labour M.P.'s proposed Musical Copyright Bill, which could have forbidden a composer to charge more than twopence for the perpetual right of public performance of a work – 'the most serious blow ever aimed at the unfortunate art of English music', he called it. Ironically a year later he was trying to sell his original full scores and told Lady Stuart: 'Last year . . . the copyright of *The Dream* had to be renewed in U.S.A. & it was seriously questioned if it was worth while to pay the fee – two dollars. I said "I suppose Gerontius is merely waste paper", & the official answer was "yes" – but I risked the two dollars which [neither] I nor my heirs will ever see again. Such things are really humorous.'

.   .   .   .   .

At this point a major diversion from the main path of the narrative will be taken so that justice can be done to a part of Elgar's life which has only been disclosed in its full importance by the devoted researches of Jerrold Northrop Moore. This is his long association with the gramophone recording industry. Publication in 1974 of Elgar's complete correspondence with the Gramophone Company (His Master's Voice)[3] fills a gap in our knowledge of the composer and shows him in his late years in a mood very different from the moroseness with which the reader will by now be over-familiar. Here is a warm, witty, playful, optimistic Elgar. In none of these letters is there the note of self-pity; instead a becoming modesty and genuine humility are discernible. The reason is not far to seek – as was suggested earlier, when Elgar was making music with professionals he was no longer troubled by his insecurities and inadequacies. This was his territory; and, since he was fascinated by mechanical and scientific devices, he was willing to listen to and learn from the experts. Also, he realized the importance of the gramophone as a branch of music, its importance to posterity, and its capabilities. The result is that we have a heritage of his interpretations of many of his major works which are never less than instructive and are in some cases unexcelled.

Elgar was introduced to H.M.V. in 1914 by Landon Ronald, who had been associated with the Gramophone Company as adviser since 1900. On 21 January 1914, at the H.M.V. studio at Hayes, Middlesex, and with an orchestra of just over thirty players, Elgar conducted the very first performance of a new short piece, *Carissima*. At the session he met two American brothers who had pioneered recording in Europe, Fred Gaisberg (1873–1951) and his brother Will (1878–1918). On 16 May he signed an exclusive contract and in the wartime years conducted several of his works for recordings, including the

[3] *Elgar on Record: the composer and the gramophone*, by J. N. Moore, London, 1974.

topically popular *Carillon*, with Henry Ainley as reciter, extracts from *The Starlight Express* with Agnes Nicholls and Charles Mott as soprano and baritone soloists and a very abridged version of the Violin Concerto (four short-playing sides). The last was in rivalry to a Columbia version, also abridged, by Albert Sammons and Sir Henry Wood which had already appeared. Elgar's soloist was Marie Hall, to whom he had given lessons at Malvern Link in 1895. Elgar himself made the abridgement, reducing each movement to fit on a four-minute side and leaving the fourth side for an almost complete recording of the cadenza. To help the balance in the primitive studio conditions of the time, he wrote a harp part to replace the fuller accompaniment (there is no harp in the full score). This was done in November 1916 and the recording was made on 16 December. In 1917, Elgar recorded a *Gerontius* extract and his new *The Fringes of the Fleet* with the original baritone soloists. *Polonia* was recorded in 1919. It is noteworthy that H.M.V. were courageously anxious to record his newest works as soon as they could; also, as early as 1918 they were investigating the possibility of a complete *Gerontius*. The Cello Concerto, heavily cut in the first and last movements and slightly in the second movement, was recorded just before Christmas 1919. The soloist, Beatrice Harrison, learned the work specially for this occasion and became one of its finest interpreters. In February 1920 selections from *The Sanguine Fan* and more of the recordings of *Enigma Variations* and *The Wand of Youth*, begun the previous year, were completed, but Lady Elgar's death and its aftermath kept him out of the studio until November 1920 when a 're-take' of the *Adagio* of the Cello Concerto was made.

In 1921 Elgar opened the company's new premises in Oxford Street, London. In his speech he urged that a gramophone 'with a first-class selection of records' should be placed in every school in Britain. At the end of the year renewal of his contract was due and he had received 'tempting offers' from another company. But he told H.M.V. he was happy with them and would accept another contract whether his fee was increased or remained the same. The new contract, for three years, was for a retainer of £500 a year for a minimum of four sessions a year. In 1923 his recent arrangements of Handel and Bach were recorded, but the most ambitious project to date was begun in March 1924 when the Second Symphony was recorded with the Royal Albert Hall Orchestra. This was made under the 'acoustical' system; in 1925 electrical recording was introduced. Elgar called it 'the greatest discovery made up to that time in the history of the gramophone'.[4] His contract was again renewed at the end of 1925 (£500 a year, with a £500 bonus on signature) and his first recordings under the new process were of *Cockaigne*, *Pomp and*

[4] *The Voice*, December 1927, p. 5.

Circumstance Marches Nos 1 and 2, and *Chanson de Nuit*. Elgar's recordings now came under the International Artists Department, administered by Trevor Osmond Williams, who at this date was forty-one and, like Fred Gaisberg, became a close friend of Elgar. He was a director of the Covent Garden Opera syndicate and a prime force in the affairs of the Covent Garden touring company. Bernard Wratten, a member of the department, has described[5] Elgar's extremely 'correct' relationship with the recording executives. 'When he came to a recording session he was stiffly reserved and at first tended to conduct with the minimum of movement and (so it appeared) of interest.[6] But we always tried to get together much the same contingent of orchestral players . . . and we almost invariably had Willy Reed at the first desk. Surrounded by musicians he knew and who were, some of them, his friends, Elgar would gradually thaw and eventually, if all went reasonably well, he unbent a little. Sometimes, though not always, he would become caught up in his own music and he was then oblivious of his surroundings.'

In 1926 Osmond Williams made his first attempt to persuade Kreisler to record the Violin Concerto but nothing came of it. On 26 February extracts from *The Dream of Gerontius* were recorded at a live performance in the Royal Albert Hall which Elgar conducted. Four sides of these were issued (some rejected matrices have since been transferred to a long-playing disc). Elgar's comment to Gaisberg was 'the coughing is a sad disaster'. The performance, as we can hear, was often flawed, but the preserved incandescence of the closing pages under the composer's direction is in itself sufficient justification for this experiment. The next major plan was for the re-recording of the Second Symphony to be issued for Elgar's seventieth birthday. This was made in two sessions on 1 April 1927 in the Queen's Hall, where the *Enigma Variations* had been recorded in April 1926. The symphony was available to the public in time for 2 June 1927 but on 15 July Elgar conducted a re-take of the first side of the third movement for substitution in later sets. He briefly rehearsed the London Symphony Orchestra in the passage and, without his knowledge, the engineers recorded his voice. On this record, which was not issued until nearly fifty years later, he says:

At 92 I should have asked the clarinets to phrase – in fact all the woodwind – ta-ta-*tum*: play that almost *forte* or you can't hear it, you see? At 92 . . . Ninety-two and *forte*, please, gentlemen! . . . I want the double-basses to

[5] Letter to J. N. Moore, 20 October 1972, quoted in *Elgar on Record*, op. cit., pp. 58–9.
[6] For example, on 7 November 1929, when Elgar was to record a selection of his short pieces such as *Rosemary*, Wratten said that having to deal with him that day 'was rather like trying to make friends with a large and distant mastiff which gazes steadfastly into the middle distance whatever overtures one makes' (letter to J. N. Moore quoted in *Elgar on Record*, op. cit., p. 100.

pizzicato firmly because there's nothing else to keep the rhythm after 92 – when you get to the *forte*, please. I think you'd better play those three octave Gs . . . I'm going to ask – I was going to ask for those semiquavers, but you *did* it . . . six semiquavers before 93. Don't rush it too much. Nice – ah, what is it? *Yeh*-ta-ta-ta-ta-ta-ta: without holding it back, but *clear*. Now 92 . . . That doesn't sound warm at all . . . *fortissimo* without any tone. Can't you get it to go: *Oh* – ee-*da*-dum? – the last quaver not starved . . . Now 93: for *goodness'* sake sonorously but not *fast* . . . *That's* it! . . . Now . . .

When he was told about it, Elgar was pleased, and a disc was cut specially for him.

A further effort at recording 'live' was made at the 1927 Hereford Festival. The first and second performances of the new *Civic Fanfare* were recorded, as were extracts from *Gerontius* and parts of *The Music Makers* (those involving the soloist, Olga Haley, had to be omitted because she was under contract to another company). Although the records were seriously flawed, Gaisberg, supported by Elgar, ensured that the waxes and matrices were preserved. In 1927, too, H.M.V. put on the market an electrical gramophone which impressed Elgar so much that he agreed to speak at the press reception held by the company to promote sales. 'The student of today can hear the finest orchestra perform the work of his choice as often as he pleases', he pointed out.

In 1928 he and Beatrice Harrison re-recorded the Cello Concerto and Osmond Williams began negotiations to record the Violin Concerto with Kreisler in Berlin. 'We would go over together and make a big thing of it,' he wrote to Elgar on 26 March. On 3 August Elgar wrote to Lady Stuart of Wortley: 'I am to go to Berlin to make records of the Violin Concerto with Kreisler, but it is not quite settled.' It was still not settled by 17 June 1929, when Trevor Osmond Williams wrote to Kreisler in Berlin asking him to record the concerto in London in the following September. Kreisler replied that it would give him pleasure, but unfortunately he would be in America in September. Some other time. Gaisberg returned to the fray in August 1931, hoping to mark Elgar's 75th birthday in 1932 with a recording of the concerto. But again there was no response.

In 1928 and 1929 the two *Wand of Youth* suites were recorded in Kingsway Hall and in November 1929 he recorded several of his small pieces. At the same time he was recorded playing five improvisations at the piano, a fascinating document which was not published until 1975. Elgar was deeply distressed by the sudden death of Trevor Osmond Williams in Vienna in July 1930. Writing to Alfred Clark, chairman of the Gramophone Company, nearly three months later, on 7 October, he said: 'I cannot yet feel I can write about dear Trevor (Osmond) Williams: – I think you know what I feel – I cannot get over the loss.' And on 13 January 1931 he wrote again to Clark: 'On looking over the year just closed, I find the greatest (and bitterest) sensation was the death of Trevor Osmond Williams; his going has left a blank in my life and a pain which nothing can soften. He had become my greatest friend. At my age old acquaintances fail and depart with appalling rapidity and young friends are not easy to find. Trevor was always ready to look after me – a dinner, lunch, theatre – anything pleasant and helpful. You knew his charm and most delightful company and can realise what a loss his death made . . . But he has gone and I am lonely'.

Elgar's recordings in 1930 were of the *Crown of India* Suite, *In the South*,[7] the First Symphony, and the new *Pomp and Circumstance* March No. 5. The recording of the March on 18 September was its first performance; the first public performance was given two days later. Gaisberg during this period supplied Elgar with other recordings from the H.M.V. catalogue in which he showed interest. Elgar was delighted with the complete Verdi *Requiem*, a work 'I have always worshipped; always means since I played 1st fiddle in one of the earliest performances in England 1880 about . . . I write now to ask you to tell me about the basso, Pinza. His phrasing is the finest I have heard. Where is he? etc'. Gaisberg sent him four of Ezio Pinza's opera recordings.

. . . . . .

It will be seen that the friendships with Osmond Williams and Gaisberg warmed Elgar's old age. Another friendship which meant much to him was with Bernard Shaw. One letter from Shaw, dated 4 April 1928, refers to Schuster's bequest to Elgar which was subject to death duty of £700: 'Schuster really deserves to be buried in the Abbey, though he overlooked ME. I grudge Churchill [then Chancellor of the Exchequer] his share. Why don't they make us duty-free instead of giving us O.M.s and the like long after we have conferred them on ourselves?' Elgar opened a Shaw exhibition at the 1929 Malvern Festival, when Shaw publicly stated that Elgar was a greater man than he. This was the year of *The Apple Cart*, for which Barry Jackson, the festival director, had entertained hopes of an overture by Elgar, 'but', Shaw wrote to Elgar, 'on obtaining from Boult a rough estimate of the cost of an Elgar orchestra, and letting his imagination play on the composer's fee, he went mournfully to his accountants. . . . My own view was that six bars of yours would extinguish (or upset) the A.C. and turn the Shaw festival into an Elgar one; but that it would be a jolly good thing so. . . .' Shaw returned the

---

[7] The first recording of *In the South*, though only a brief extract, was made in 1909, five years after it was written, by the La Scala Symphony Orchestra, conducted by Carlo Sabajno. It is included in the Elgar Society's record 'Elgar's Interpreters on Record' (1980).

compliment by becoming a regular attender of the Three Choirs Festivals where, at Worcester in 1929, Sir Neville Cardus remembered seeing him listening to the First Symphony, 'moved to his foundations'. In 1930 Elgar acceded to requests for a test piece for the National Brass Band Championship and wrote the *Severn Suite*, much of it derived (as does all the later music) from old sketchbooks. The Minuet, for example, borrows its themes from wind quintet pieces written in 1878 and 1879. He wrote only a piano score and the work was orchestrated for brass band, not entirely satisfactorily, by Henry Geehl. At the time this was a well-kept secret, but Geehl later gave his own account of this somewhat uncomfortable 'collaboration': '. . . I was in continuous consultation with the composer, who provided me with a very sketchy piano part with figured bass and a kind of skeleton orchestral score, mostly in two or three parts, with an indication of the sort of counterpoint he desired me to add; the rest of the score he left to my discretion. Elgar was not an easy man to work with. He had many pre-conceived ideas on brass treatment – usually unworkable – which he tried very hard to get me to adopt, and it took a great deal of argument on my part to convince him that his ideas were just not possible. I remember particularly a "bad" afternoon when I endeavoured to persuade him to omit the mutes in the Minuet, well knowing that the sound would be entirely different from what he imagined. But all to no purpose! So the somewhat banal sound of the muted trombones will be handed down to posterity! I did, however, get my own ideas adopted in several instances, but these were always conceded rather grudgingly.'[8] Elgar dedicated the *Severn Suite* to Shaw who said it would 'ensure my immortality when all my plays are dead and damned and forgotten. . . . The Salvation Army bands and Besses o' the Barn should be taught by you how to score.' Shaw went to the brass band competition at the Crystal Palace on 27 September, hearing the suite eight times. 'If there is a new edition of the score I think it would be well to drop the old Italian indications and use the language of the bandsmen,' he wrote to the composer. 'For instance. Remember that a minuet is a dance and not a bloody hymn; or steady up for artillery attack; or NOW – like Hell. I think that would help some of the modest beginners. . . . The scoring is, as usual, infallible. You should have heard the curiously pleasant oboe quality of the muted flugels picking up after the cornets. The held note of the soprano cornet *in excelsis* was enormous. These chaps have iron lips. . . . Nobody would have guessed from looking at the score and thinking of the thing as a toccata for brass band how beautiful and

---

[8] H. Geehl: 'The Unrecognised Arranger', *The Bandsman*, April 1961, pp. 3 and 8. The article also describes how he quarrelled with Holst and that he worked best with Ireland, who admitted he knew nothing about brass bands and adopted all Geehl's suggestions.

serious the work is as abstract music'. The winning band was Foden's Motor Works, conducted by Fred Mortimer. Elgar orchestrated the suite for normal orchestra and conducted the first public performance of this version at the Worcester Festival of 1932, having already recorded it for H.M.V.

Elgar had not attended the Crystal Palace with Shaw because of an attack of sciatica: a warning sign of his fatal illness. He had been in pain while conducting at the 1930 Hereford Festival but, Reed says, 'made his usual witty and pleasant remarks *sotto voce* as he was being helped on and off the platform'. Since 3 December 1929 he had been living again in Worcester, having bought a house called Marl Bank on Rainbow Hill. (He had earlier rented it for the 1929 Worcester Festival.) It was large with a large garden, but Elgar told Adela Schuster that it was 'a very little house'. He had, he said, to reduce all possible outlay 'owing to the extraordinary state of music in this country.' He was 'retiring . . . the rest is silence'. In fact he was more productive at this period than he had been for years. In early November 1929, as Master of the King's Musick, he had written a short 'carol' to mark King George V's recovery from a severe illness. Then came the *Severn Suite* and the fifth *Pomp and Circumstance* march, the completion of one sketched many years earlier and now dedicated to Percy Hull. He wrote a song and dedicated it to Joan Elwes, a soprano whose voice had caught his fancy and to whose ability he drew Gaisberg's attention. He sketched an oboe work for Léon Goossens. He began another suite, the result also of looking over the sketches of his youth and his days at Powick. This was a much more successful effort than the *Severn Suite*, probably because it looked back nostalgically yet with piquant humour to the days of *The Wand of Youth*. Called the *Nursery Suite*, Elgar dedicated it to the Duchess of York and her two daughters, the Princesses Elizabeth and Margaret Rose. It was the birth of Princess Margaret in August 1930 which had given him the impetus to start work on the music.

It is a measure of Elgar's affection for and gratitude to the recording company that he should again have allowed the first performance of a new work to be given in the recording studio. On 23 May 1931, in the Kingsway Hall, he conducted the L.S.O. and all but the last side was recorded[9] though the whole work was played. Herbert Hughes, who was present for the *Daily Telegraph*, wrote on 25 May that the music was 'the sublimation of eternal youth. There is a philosophy, a metaphysic, in this music that comes from one of the subtlest intellects of our time.' On 4 June, the day after Elgar's elevation to the baronetcy, the whole suite was played again at the Kingsway Hall in the presence of the Duke and Duchess of York

[9] Time ran out on the last side, for which the music was 10 seconds too long.

(later King George VI and Queen Elizabeth) and other invited guests. This time the last side was fitted in. This re-visiting of old sketches by the practised hand resulted in a masterpiece with all the freshness and wistful charm of *The Wand of Youth*. It is a moving testament of old age, fresh as spring in the opening Aubade, which quotes a hymn-tune, 'Hear Thy Children', that Elgar had written in his youth, and hitting off with uncanny musical accuracy the difference between a serious and a sad doll, the latter with a recognizable echo of *Gerontius*. The famous fifth movement, 'The Wagon Passes' is a vignette immediately vivid and attractive, but with a slightly sinister reminder of the Rondo of the Second Symphony and the 'hooves that beat into the brain'. Finally, in 'Dreaming (Envoy)' he recaptures the atmosphere of the Adagio of the First Symphony. For the last time, the old composer calls upon his favourite instrument, the violin, to interrupt the dreaming with cadenzas. It is not sentimental to imagine that he was seeing himself again as the young fiddler giving recitals in Malvern and Worcester.

The recording session was a pleasant aspect of being Master of the King's Musick. But something of the old asperity showed through in a letter on another royal matter which he wrote to the Dean of Worcester, Dr W. E. Moore Ede, on 12 June 1931: 'I have heard from Mr Bernard Shaw that some anonymous versifier has sent you a version of a stanza in the National Anthem with a view to a substitution at the Three Choirs Meeting. I have no views: – the old "Confound their politics" in this National address to the Almighty would have the effect – if the Almighty ever took any notice of anything, which of course he never did, does, or will do – of putting the whole Government in Hell with MacDonald in the lowest place – so from my point of view it does not matter what is said, sung, or otherwise delivered. In any case the words would not come before me officially – the music might do so, but as there could be no alteration required, that is improbable . . .'

The *Nursery Suite* had an immediate success after its first public performance at the Promenade Concerts in August, but the year generally was clouded by a return of the enmities of a quarter of a century earlier. This arose from an article on modern English music contributed by Edward J. Dent, professor of music at Cambridge University since 1926, to Adler's *Handbuch der Musikgeschichte* (Second Edition, 1930), in which Dent referred to Elgar's music as 'to English ears . . . too emotional and not quite free from vulgarity. His orchestral works . . . are vivid in colour but pompous in style and with an affected nobility of expression.' The chamber music was dismissed as 'dry and academic'. This last remark is all the more surprising when one discovers that on 30 April 1919 Dent had written to Elgar in these terms: 'I hope I may write a line to say how deeply I

FINALE 317

was impressed with your quartet and quintet on Saturday afternoon. They are both intensely characteristic of yourself, especially in the slow movements. . . . I rejoice that you have taken to chamber music. . . . I hope you will go on writing more. . . .' Even more complacently damning was the assertion in the article that Elgar 'possessed little of the literary culture of Parry and Stanford'. As far as his compositions are concerned, that might have been to his advantage; but, in fact, as has been amply demonstrated, Elgar was probably one of the most widely read men of his time, with a brilliantly retentive memory. The literary allusions and quotations in his Birmingham lectures would do credit to a professor of English literature. Dent's article displayed an intellectual arrogance which might have been lessened had he not taken it upon himself to speak 'for English ears' instead of for E. J. Dent's ears when, of course, such opinions would have been irreproachable, although a handbook is a dangerous place in which to give permanence to such deeply felt prejudices. Dent devoted 16 lines to Elgar, 66 to Parry and 41 to Stanford. The controversy that he provoked raged in the musical journals, where some of Elgar's defenders (as is usual on these occasions) showed themselves in no better a light than those they were attacking. A letter signed by eighteen people[10] was sent to editors in England and Germany protesting against Dent's 'unjust and inadequate treatment' of Elgar. It would, perhaps, have been better had they taken the view that the article, which would probably have reached only a very select minority, would be better ignored. But no doubt it was only the tip of the iceberg. Someone else dredged up another contribution by Dent to an Italian periodical in 1925 in which he linked Elgar not very accurately with Liszt (as he did in the later article) and added that Elgar was 'repugnant to many English musicians by reason precisely of that chevalieresque rhetoric which badly covers up his intrinsic vulgarity'. In England, Dent said, 'the best musicians have a real horror of Liszt' – and, by implication, of Elgar. It was an intolerably narrow and smug attitude. Dr Percy Young, writing from personal experience, ascribed the episode to 'the Stanford cult which was practised and preached in Cambridge at that time, and of the fashion of withholding approval from all living English composers who failed in showing a knowledge of the 16th century and, second, a desire to embellish folk song. There was an obligation on the part of Cambridge music students then to avoid all mention of Elgar. The name appeared to suggest something slightly indecent. . . .'[11] This

---

[10] The signatories were: Emile Cammaerts, John Goss, Harvey Grace, Beatrice Harrison, Hamilton Harty, Leslie Heward, John Ireland, Augustus John, Robert Lorenz, E. J. Moeran, André Mangeot, Philip Page, Landon Ronald, Albert Sammons, Bernard Shaw, Richard Terry, William Walton, and Peter Warlock.
[11] *Elgar O.M.*, op. cit., p. 235.

was no exaggeration. Anybody who has experienced the later manifestation of this supercilious attitude, even on the fringe, will know that Elgar's name provoked an automatic curl of the lip from those who failed to resist the influences of the Stanford-Dent-Allen brigade. A hint of this approach, in lesser, more rationalized form, was noticeable in the music criticism of *The Times* after the Second World War, as Bernard Shaw perceived when he wrote in 1949: 'The critics are getting tired of his music. There is a very marked reaction in *The Times*.' An atavistic puritanism in some English musical criticism has never been able to reconcile the Elgar of *Gerontius* with the Elgar of *Salut d'Amour*. Much ink and space have been devoted to regrets that a man of his ability could stoop to salon music. No apology was necessary. The light music has been beneficial in its influence on its *genre*, as the work of Eric Coates testifies. It is beautifully scored and always melodically distinctive. The only pity is that it never earned the composer performing fees proportionate to the harmless pleasure it has given to thousands. It remains to say that Dent was violently anti-Catholic and to record the pleasing irony that the organist at his cremation in 1957 played the Angel's Farewell from *The Dream of Gerontius*.

There was a happier end to 1931 when H.M.V. opened its new recording studios in Abbey Road, St John's Wood, at the same time as it merged with Columbia to become Electric and Musical Industries Ltd (E.M.I.). The studios were inaugurated musically by Elgar's *Falstaff* on 11 and 12 November, one of his finest recordings. Elgar was in high spirits throughout, and when on the morning of 12 November Pathé newsreel filmed the occasion, he conducted the L.S.O. in the *Pomp and Circumstance* March No. 1 and greeted them with 'Good morning, gentlemen. Very light programme this morning! Please play this as if you had never heard it before.'

For Elgar, at seventy-four, the unhappy Dent affair meant that life had come full circle. He was back in Worcester, a baronet now and a local celebrity as he had been fifty years before. The names of Parry, Stanford, and Mackenzie clashed with his in the columns of the London musical press. No wonder that when his boyhood friend Hubert Leicester wrote a book called *Forgotten Worcester* and asked him to write a preface, he took the opportunity to hit back at the resurgence of the old academic snobbery which had beset his years of struggle: 'From among the crudities which one of the many – why are there so many? – unbrilliant university men has used in reference to myself, the following comes to mind. I am said to have "left the humdrum atmosphere of Worcester for" – etc. I object to this. I deny that any atmosphere could be exactly humdrum while Hubert Leicester and myself were of it and in it; it might well have been disagreeable, but that is another matter. . . .' The gibe was unworthy of him, but one may sympathize with him for making it.

Since 1927 he had kept trying to persuade Lady Stuart of Wortley to buy a gramophone. 'I have just been playing over your symphony [No. 2],' he wrote, '& most of it sounds divine'. His letters to her for the next six years mention the gramophone as his 'one joy' and he speaks of his particular pleasure in records of the Brahms symphonies and of Wagner's *Siegfried Idyll*. Every spring he sent her the first windflowers, provided they were growing wild. He retreated further into the past, revisiting Birchwood with Billy Reed. Together they played sonatas by Rubinstein, concertos by Spohr, and a suite by Ries – all works he had played as a youth and which led him into spoken reminiscence of 'the old days'. As throughout his life, he hated the winter and each year longed for the coming of spring and the return of warmth, never failing to gather the first wild windflowers to send to 'Windflower' or sending her news of his doings, adding, at Christmas 1929, that his card 'brings my love or rather a remembrance of it since 1897 – thirty-two years accumulation.' He still enjoyed motoring round the Worcester lanes and going to the races – Neville Cardus found him elated in the Hereford Club after a performance of *Gerontius* because he had backed the winner of the St Leger – he still enjoyed going to the theatre; he still liked meeting his fellow-composers at the Three Choirs. He still basked in the flattery of attractive young women. (One of his domestic staff later described him as a 'naughty old man', though what degree of naughtiness was implied would be difficult to assess.) The last of his feminine muses was Vera Hockman, a young orchestral violinist, who caught his fancy during a *Gerontius* rehearsal in Croydon in November 1931. He monopolized her at a party after the performance and she stayed close to him for his remaining two years. They played his sonata – it was now 'our sonata' – and he told her: 'We are together, I am so happy.' He gave her the copy of *Hyperion* that had belonged to his mother. 'With you', he said, 'that most perfect threefold relationship is possible – so rare on earth: guardian, child, lover.' 'And friend as well', she added.

He was by now on amiable terms with Ralph Vaughan Williams, realizing that V. W., despite his connections with the anti-Elgarians, was not a man for cliques but a man who could share friendships without sharing opinions. He admired Vaughan Williams's *Sancta Civitas*, telling the composer that the work had completed his own trilogy for him, and he introduced him to the poetry of Skelton, saying 'One day you must make an oratorio out of Elinor Rumming.' The result was that Vaughan Williams wrote the *Five Tudor Portraits*. Yet, for all this gregariousness and outward jollity, he was on the defensive. He tried to deter Basil Maine from writing a book about him by saying 'The interest in my music is too slight and evanescent to be worth such concentration as you propose to devote to it.' Yet

after conducting the Second Symphony in London in the autumn of
1931 he wrote to Lady Stuart: 'The Sym: scarcely sounded 20 years
old – oh, that awful first performance.' He took delight in playing his
Falstaff recording to any visitor to Marl Bank. After the second
interlude he told Basil Maine 'That's what I call music', and, to John
Barbirolli, after the exuberant little solo for side-drum he said 'Well,
that's a good bit, anyway.' Reed remembered the joy that 'suffused his
face' when he conducted this passage.

   The year of his seventy-fifth birthday was almost like a return of an
annus mirabilis such as 1910. It was a busy year, for he conducted his
works in many towns, some of these occasions being sentimental
journeys – that, for example, to Hanley when he conducted *King Olaf*
in the Victoria Hall where he had conducted its first performance in
1896. Perhaps he thought of the quarrel with Swinnerton Heap on
that day, for he was, as always, deeply conscious of the past and some
of the friendships from those days were still fresh. Dr Charles Buck of
Settle was still alive (though he had only a few months to live) and
Elgar wrote to him: 'I have thought much of you and the dear old
days lately . . . it is just fifty (!!) years since you were here [Worcester]
& played in the orch: what a lovely time we had, the first of many
adventures. In this August weather I always live over again the
holidays I had with you & the taste of potted Ribble Trout comes
with ineffaceable relish: nothing so good in eating or company has
occurred to me since 1882.' And Rosa Burley – he had abruptly ended
his contacts with her after Alice's death and had ignored her when
they met at festivals. Yet in 1932 she was surprised to receive a
Christmas card, posted in London, and inscribed 'from Edward'. She
wrote to him saying she did not wish to resume the relationship.

   On one occasion at the H.M.V. studios in February 1932, Elgar
was thrilled to hear that Gracie Fields was making records upstairs. 'I
wish I could see her at work', he said to W. L. Streeton, the artist's
manager. They crept into the studio and watched Miss Fields rehearse
a song with Ray Noble's orchestra.[12] Afterwards he chatted to her and
congratulated Ray Noble on his orchestral arrangements. But
Gaisberg had more serious recording projects up his sleeve. He had
put the new [1930] BBC Symphony Orchestra under contract.
Someone at E.M.I. thought there should be a new orchestral
transcription of the Funeral March from Chopin's Piano Sonata in B
flat minor and that Elgar should be asked to write it for Boult and the
BBC orchestra to record. Boult, no doubt prompted by Gaisberg,
wrote to Elgar, who accepted the suggestion. He sent off the

[12] Elgar enjoyed much of the 'dance music' of this period. He told Shaw how much he
liked 'Monah' by Jay Wilbur and his Band – 'sheer delight'. He went to a Jack
Hulbert – Cicely Courtneidge revue twelve times because he like 'the little tinkling
tunes'.

manuscript on 31 March and the recording was made on 30 May, with Elgar and Carice at the session. (The opening of the march is appropriately funereal, but the trio section sounds disconcertingly like a Tchaikovsky ballet waltz!) Gaisberg, meanwhile, was bringing another scheme to fruition. He was still anxious to record the Violin Concerto as a seventy-fifth birthday tribute and having abandoned Kreisler as hopeless, he chose as soloist the boy prodigy Yehudi Menuhin. When the suggestion was put to him in November 1931, Elgar was enthusiastic and added a few marks to a copy of the score, which Gaisberg sent to Menuhin for him to study. On 12 July Gaisberg took Elgar to the Grosvenor House Hotel for a rehearsal at which the sixteen-year-old Menuhin was accompanied by Ivor Newton. Accounts conflict of what really happened. According to Menuhin, Elgar listened only to a few bars, declared himself perfectly happy, and went to the races. But Newton, in his autobiography,[13] says that they played 'right through the concerto except for the *tuttis* ... Menuhin and Elgar discussed the music like equals.' He describes in detail a conversation between composer and soloist over a difficult passage in the finale and says that Elgar went off to Newmarket when it was time for lunch. Whichever account is accurate, it is still a remarkable story and the recording sessions at Abbey Road on 14 and 15 July resulted in a gramophone classic. 'I hope our work pleases you', Elgar wrote on 19 July to Gaisberg (whom he had now nicknamed 'Barbarossa'), 'we did our best: of course *Yehudi* is wonderful & will be splendid'. Writing to Novello's on 20 July he described Menuhin as 'the most wonderful artist I have ever heard'. In November Menuhin performed the concerto in the Royal Albert Hall with Elgar conducting. 'Yehudi was marvellous', Elgar wrote to Gaisberg on 22 November, '& I am sure would never have heard of the Concerto if you had not set the thing in motion ... It is only one of the many kindnesses you have done for me.'

During the year, he attended the first performance at Sadler's Wells of Ninette de Valois's ballet of the *Nursery Suite*. Constant Lambert conducted and remarked that when Elgar came on to the stage to acknowledge the applause it was as if one of the great masters from the past had materialized into the modern age. At the Three Choirs at Worcester he conducted *Gerontius*, 'For the Fallen', the *Severn Suite*, *The Music Makers*, and the First Symphony. It was at this festival that he met William Walton, whose *Belshazzar's Feast* had been a sensation at Leeds in 1931 and had been acclaimed as the most important English choral work since *The Dream of Gerontius*. His Viola Concerto was to be played by Lionel Tertis in the same programme as Elgar conducted 'For the Fallen'. Elgar would not talk about music with

[13] *At the Piano* (London 1960), pp. 185–7.

Walton, only about racing. He hated the younger man's concerto, sad to say, and paced up and down behind the orchestral gallery during the performance deploring that such music should be thought fit for a stringed instrument.

It was about this time that he went to conduct Alan Kirby's Croydon choir in *The Apostles*. He became, Kirby wrote,[14] 'more and more lost in the music. A slow smile came over his face, and he almost stopped conducting; his spirit seemed to have taken wings. . . . When Elgar left the rostrum it was obvious that he was greatly moved.' Yet the quirkiness remained, to flash out in certain company. After a concert at Queen's Hall in 1930 at which Toscanini had conducted the *Variations*, Bax and Harriet Cohen found Elgar at the Savoy Grill 'characteristically surrounded by actors, Norman Forbes and Allan Aynesworth amongst them. Harriet, of whom Elgar was really very fond, rushed up to him and began vivaciously and charmingly to congratulate him upon . . . the evening's wonderful music. With – as I thought – rather ridiculous affectation and ungraciousness, the old composer turned to his actor friends and spread out his hands in mock-mystification, exclaimed "What on earth *are* these people talking about?" '[15]

But he can perhaps be forgiven, for he had known Toscanini's[16] interpretation for twenty-five years, just as he had known Steinbach's and Nikisch's. Foreign views of his music were no novelty to him, and he was irritated by the attitude of some English critics who, while denying him wholehearted approval, seemed at the same time determined to keep him exclusively English property and warned intruders to 'keep of the grass'. Musicians like Bax and Malcolm Sargent were thrilled to their foundations by Toscanini's conducting of the *Variations*, but critics – even Ernest Newman – complained of its lack of an 'English' quality. Well as the English violinist Albert Sammons played the concerto – and he played it unforgettably well – there was room for other interpretations, but no foreign violinist was allowed to feel that he had succeeded in the work which was created by the Austrian, Kreisler. And when Pablo Casals, the Spaniard, revealed the true qualities of the Cello Concerto, which languished in semi-obscurity for several years, he too was accused of playing it *too* beautifully, *too* intimately, with too much care for phrasing and not enough 'austerity' and 'gruffness'. Well might Elgar ruefully have remembered his 1905 lecture: 'English music is white, it evades everything.' Elgar liked Toscanini's, Menuhin's, and Casals's

[14] *Centenary Sketches*, p. 26.
[15] Arnold Bax, *Farewell, My Youth*, op.cit., p. 32. Bax dates this episode in 1933 but Forbes died in September 1932.
[16] Toscanini asked for a full score of the Violin Concerto in December 1932, but he never conducted it.

interpretations of his music: all he wanted, he told Neville Cardus, was
that it should sound stylish, well written, and colourful; he did not
compose 'in sackcloth'. As far back as 1899 he had written to Jaeger: 'I
wish the critics had a little more imagination when British music in
concerned: if it's cut and dried they sneer at it, and if we do show a bit of
real feeling and emotion they laugh at it'.

The climax of the birthday year was an Elgar Festival in London on
30 November, 7 and 14 December. The three concerts in the Queen's
Hall were played by the BBC Symphony Orchestra and were
broadcast. Elgar conducted *Cockaigne*, the Violin Concerto (with
Sammons), and the Second Symphony; Boult conducted the
Introduction and Allegro, the *Enigma Variations* and *The Kingdom*;
Ronald conducted the First Symphony. In writing his thanks to
Boult, Elgar recalled the 1920 revival of the Second Symphony as
'one of the happiest events of my life and I thank you'. After the last
rehearsal of *The Kingdom*, Elgar insisted on addressing the orchestra
and thanking them for their support and friendship.

'The orchestra gave him everything it had,' Bernard Shore wrote.[17]
'. . . It was something like the attachment felt by passionately loyal
subjects to a monarch.' Elgar, for his part, was generous enough to
write to the young Menuhin: 'Your friendship . . . has given me a
new zest in life. . . Nothing in late years has given me so much artistic
joy as your playing of the Concerto.'

Yehudi Menuhin's father arranged for a Paris performance of the
Violin Concerto at the Salle Pleyel on 31 May 1933. It was a notable
occasion but the shrewd Gaisberg 'felt that it had not just made the
impression that was its due'. Elgar went to France and back by
aeroplane, his first flight. He was thrilled. The man who had
welcomed the bicycle and the motor-car also welcomed the
aeroplane. To Adela Schuster, who was perturbed about this
adventure, he wrote: 'The risk, according to the insurance people, is
at the same rate as railway travelling which shows that the commercial
people are not afraid. . . . It is wonderful to avoid changes, oily-
smelling boats & the hundred other troubles of the channel crossing.'
Yet to Shaw he struck a deeper note: 'I wd. love to have a reassuring
word from you & Charlotte before my final departure – I somehow
feel I shall not return.' With him went his valet, Richard Mountford,
and Gaisberg. Elgar completed a crossword puzzle during the flight
from Croydon to Le Bourget (which took two and a quarter hours).
In planning his visit, Elgar had expressed the wish to Gaisberg that
they should try to visit Delius at Grez-sur-Loing. They drove there in
a Paris taxi. He and the partially paralysed Delius were soon talking
animatedly about music, literature, and flying. Elgar described flying

as rather like Delius's music – 'a little intangible sometimes, but always very beautiful. I should have liked to stay there for ever. The descent is like our old age – peaceful, even serene.'

The two great English composers, both with barely a year of life left to them, liked one another, rather, one suspects, to their surprise. They were survivors of an alien culture. Both had written in 1899 orchestral works (the *Variations* and *Paris*) which showed that English music had come of age. Little though they had in common, except a romantic nostalgia very differently expressed, they had both owed their first fame to German acclaim. And now, in the spring of 1933, Elgar was writing to Adela Schuster: 'I am in a maze regarding events in Germany – what are they doing? In this morning's paper it is said that the great conductor Bruno Walter &, stranger still, Einstein, are ostracised: are we all mad? The Jews have always been my best & kindest friends – the pain of these news is unbearable & I do not know what it really means.'

The BBC Elgar Festival had ended with the announcement by Sir Landon Ronald at a dinner in Guildhall that the BBC had commissioned a third symphony (for £1,000 and £250 a quarter payable in arrears while he was at work on it – or for a year, whichever was the shorter period). This had been engineered by Shaw, who had written to Elgar at the beginning of the year 'Why don't you make the BBC order a new symphony? It can afford it.' Shaw himself took the matter further, with the help of Sir Landon Ronald, and Elgar was 'overwhelmed' by his friend's 'lofty idea'. Elgar had shown a jocular postcard from Shaw about a new symphony to Gaisberg, who also became busy behind the scenes on the matter. He even suggested to Elgar (29 June 1933) that the BBC Symphony Orchestra should record the work before the first concert performance, which would be 'good publicity for us, and give the critics time to study the work . . .' Elgar had conducted this orchestra in the recording studio in the *Pomp and Circumstance* Marches Nos 1 and 2 in October 1932 and in *Cockaigne* and other works in April 1933. He had also recorded *Froissart* in February 1933 with Beecham's new London Philharmonic Orchestra. Hearing the test-pressings in March he wrote to Gaisberg: 'It is difficult to believe that I wrote it in 1890! – it sounds so brilliant & fresh . . . Leon G's [Goossens's] oboe passages . . . are divine – what an artist!'

Ironically, after the long years of virtual silence, Elgar was also at work on another major scheme, an opera. Over the years he had toyed with several ideas for operatic subjects. On 7 June 1904 he promised an opera to Novello's '*if* A. C. Benson finds the libretto'. Then there was the opera plot worked out at Careggi in 1909; and in 1910 Elgar told Littleton that 'Volkert (Schott) is convinced that *Caractacus* would make a bold, brilliant opera – so am I – only we want the

libretto altered & where's the MAN to do it?' In 1913 Colvin had
brought Thomas Hardy and Elgar together as potential col-
laborators. Hardy had written on 28 July of that year saying that the
first consideration was 'whether it should be a production in the
grand style based on "The Dynasts" or a romantic or tragic Wessex
opera based on one of my best known stories . . . I have thought "A
Pair of Blue Eyes" would be good for music, as it would furnish all
the voices and has a distinct and central heroine, with a wild
background of cliffs and sea.' The war put paid to the idea, and Elgar
later complained to Walford Davies that he had always wanted
'something heroic and noble' but had only been offered 'blood and
lust' as libretti. Now his friendship with Barry Jackson of the
Malvern Festival had induced him to think over a plan he had
formulated years before for turning Ben Jonson's *The Devil is an Ass*
into an opera. 'My difficulty in trying to "plan" it years ago,' he wrote
to Jackson in September 1932, 'was the end – the actual wind-up – this
you may be able to "see" – I don't know if clubs were "raided" at the
time of B. J. – but that wd. make a tremendous scrambling finale – last
ensemble.' Jackson agreed to act as librettist and by the beginning of
1933 Elgar had started writing the music, though writing is perhaps
too strong a word. As can be seen from Dr Young's detailed account
of the sketches,[18] most of the music is a tentative re-working of old
sketches from as far back as 1879 and the 'Shed Books', with bits of
discarded material from the oratorios, *Crown of India* and works that
came to naught. He told Jackson that the work would be on 'a
grandiose scale'. He devised a better title – *The Spanish Lady* – and sent
for Reed to play the sketches to him, excitedly interrupting the music
with descriptions of the stage action and making drawings of the
settings. Then he would switch to the symphony, which was in
scrappy sketch-form, and, getting tired, would take the dogs for a
walk. Was he happy, feeling that he was at work, or did he know that
it was all a charade, that his inspiration was fitful, if not wholly
extinct? He continued to dwell much on the past, constantly talking
about his youth and telling the romantic story of his own career. Part
of this *recherche du temps perdu* may have been the actual business of
having work in progress, a reminder of the days at Craeg Lea and
Birchwood. We can never know. 'Just my luck', he exclaimed when
he learned that Richard Strauss was also at work on a libretto adapted
from Ben Jonson by Stefan Zweig, which became *Die schweigsame
Frau.*

Rumours about the progress of the Third Symphony filtered
through to the newspapers. A chance remark by Elgar at the 1932
Worcester Festival – that it was 'written' but that it would not be
worth his while to complete the full score because no one wanted his

[18] *Elgar O.M.*, op. cit., pp. 363–73.

music – was taken up by the *Daily Mail*. Yet a few days earlier he had written to Walter Legge of H.M.V. to say that 'there is nothing to say about the Mythical Symphony for some time – probably a long time – possibly no time – never'. In February 1933 Elgar wrote to John Reith, Director-General of the BBC, to say he hoped to begin scoring the symphony 'very shortly ... up to the present the symphony is the *strongest* thing I have put on paper'.[19] In August 1933 Elgar conducted the Second Symphony at a Promenade Concert. Gaisberg met him at the Langham Hotel to discuss a projected recording of the Piano Quintet with Harriet Cohen, but he was really anxious to know about the symphony. Elgar was evidently in expansive and reminiscent mood: 'When I write music I am all of a tremble, as if I was in the hands of another person'. He referred to the 'wonderful melody' of his own *Serenade* – 'as though speaking of someone other than himself', Gaisberg wrote. He compared himself with Strauss: 'although seven years older he said he was turning out fresher and more inspired music than Richard'. The symphony, he declared, was 'practically complete'. Gaisberg diagnosed that 'vanity kept him going ... Shaw's new plays at Malvern each year and Richard Strauss's *Arabella* are the incentives that kept him screwed up.' But a letter to Gaisberg a few days later was warier: 'whether you will ever hear more of Sym.III or E.E. remains to be seen.' Later that month Gaisberg went to Marl Bank to stay with Elgar. On Sunday 27 August Elgar, 'in fine humour', played parts of the opera and then bits of the symphony. Gaisberg described extracts from four movements[20] and thought the music 'youthful and fresh – 100% Elgar without a trace of decay ... In his own mind he is enthusiastically satisfied with it and says it is his best work. He pretends he does not want to complete it.... His Secretary Miss Clifford says he has not done much recently on the Sym. and seems to prefer to work on his opera. I think he misses the inspiration and driving force of Lady Elgar.... He complains of the drudgery of scoring....' Elgar also played parts of the work to other friends, including Bernard Shaw and his biographer Basil Maine. The latter wrote: 'He relied partly on the sketches (so disjointed and disordered as to be a kind of jigsaw puzzle), partly on memory, partly I imagine on extemporization. During the improvised (or memorised) passages, it was possible to think that one was beginning to share Elgar's vision, but the experience was so clouded and so fleeting that

[19] Quoted in 'Elgar and the B.B.C.' by Humphrey Burton, a paper read to the Royal Society of Arts, 13 December 1978, *Journal of the Royal Society of Arts*, March 1979, pp. 224–36.
[20] Gaisberg described the second movement as 'slow and tender' and the third as 'an ingenious scherzo', but the sketches show that Elgar's final intention was for the second movement to be *Allegretto (scherzo)* and the third *Adagio*.

it could not possibly be recaptured by means of the sketches alone.'[21]

Gaisberg's report has since led to speculation that the symphony really was completed, but that is untrue. All that remains is the folio of 42 pages of sketches in the British Library. Most of these are in short score, for example the exposition of the first movement is complete in this form. There are some pages of full score, most notably the first two pages of the symphony and the end of the exposition. Each page is marked 'Sym.III'. A sketch of a first-movement theme is inscribed 'V.H.'s [Vera's] own theme'.

The facsimiles of the sketches published by W. H. Reed in *The Listener* in 1935 and in his book *Elgar as I knew him* are only about a third of the total material. Of the material in the British Museum folio, about a quarter was composed during the 1930s. The rest was drawn from various unfinished works. These were the incidental music to the play *Arthur* (1923), the third oratorio *The Last Judgement*, the piano concerto, a proposed setting (1905) of Matthew Arnold's *Callicles*, and a work called *Arden*. A period of thirty years was thus involved. Christopher Kent's examination of the complete material[22] revealed that the development section of the first movement is merely unconnected fragments, as are the recapitulation and coda; the second movement, which drew largely on *Arthur* (a superb score), is undecided as to key; there is little development of the third movement (drawn from *The Last Judgement*), the end of which Reed mistook for the end of the symphony; the finale, which contains most new material, only reached the exposition stage.

The existence of the pages of full score has encouraged groundless speculation that other pages existed and have been unreasonably suppressed or destroyed (by whom and why? No one who had access to them would have committed such a crime). Unlike most other composers, Elgar would frequently put short passages into full score if he was satisfied with a particular section long before other parts of the same movement were even sketched. He would also write out sections for, perhaps, the violin, often in several forms so that they could be played over for him to decide which he preferred (as was the case with the Violin Concerto). In his improvisatory way of composing, he would arrive at a final version from some rhythmic hint or melodic nuance. For example, he told Sir John Barbirolli that the stately theme which opens the finale of the Second Symphony was evolved from its quicker rhythmical form later in the movement. No one, therefore, can know what direction the Third Symphony material would eventually have taken.

He would also play over on the pianoforte whichever parts he had written, often extemporizing at length to fill the gaps. In this way he

[21]Basil Maine: *Elgar: His Life and Music*, London, G. Bell & Sons, 1933, vol. 2, p. 101.
[22]'Elgar and the B.B.C.', op. cit., p. 234.

persuaded Gaisberg that the symphony was much further advanced than it was, whereas Basil Maine was not taken in. There is no possibility of any reconstruction of the Elgar symphony on the lines of Deryck Cooke's performing version of Mahler's Tenth Symphony. Such a task not only should not but could not be undertaken. The Mahler was found to be virtually a completely composed short score. What remains of Elgar's Third Symphony amounts to sketches of a sketch for a sketch. It is a further affirmation of his creative sterility after 1920 – the state of having 'gone out'. None of the works published as 'new' after 1920 had a bar of new invention in them. Themes were developed and orchestrated, but the material all came from sketchbooks, some of them going back nearly fifty years. In the case of an enormous project like a symphony, Elgar in 1932–3 was over seventy-five, in the early stages of cancer, and clearly no longer able to bring the mental concentration to bear on the labour involved.

In any case the activity was to be short-lived. Just before the visit to Paris Elgar had had another bout of sciatica. He recovered and conducted his last recordings, of the youthful *Serenade for Strings* and the *Elegy* on 29 August 1933. But at the Hereford Festival in September Reed found him 'more than usually tired' between his cathedral appearances. He conducted *Gerontius* and *The Kingdom* and Lionel Tertis's transcription of the Cello Concerto for viola (to which he had given his blessing when Tertis played it to him at Tiddington House on 20 June 1929). He had taken a house for the week and sat in the garden talking to Vera and friends and proved to Shaw, by use of the full score of *Elijah*, that Mendelssohn was a fine orchestrator.

In October he was taken to the South Bank nursing-home, Worcester, for an operation. The 'sciatica' was found to be a malignant tumour pressing on the sciatic nerve. There was no hope for him. He suffered bouts of intense pain, followed by remissions when it was possible to hope for recovery. But always the pain returned. His thoughts turned to his oldest friends: to Hubert Leicester, to whom he wrote 'We have had some good times', and to Florence Norbury. To her he said: 'I lie here hour after hour, thinking of our beloved Teme – surely the most beautiful river that ever was and it belongs to you too – I love it more than any other – some day we will have a day together there – on it? by it? You shall choose the place – I shall come & see you as soon as possible but it will be sad to return in winter – it would have been nicer to get better in spring.'

He expressed a wish that he should be buried at the confluence of Severn and Teme, without religious ceremony. He had for many years avoided going to church and while dying and still lucid he refused to see a priest, none other than the son of Gervase Elwes. He objected to the church's 'mumbo-jumbo', he said. His consultant, Arthur Thomson, was impressed by his 'magnificent courage'. Elgar told him he had 'no faith whatever in an afterlife. I believe there is nothing but complete oblivion.' There was only one thing he really loved in life, he said, the Golden Valley of the Teme, especially a place below Knightsford bridge where he composed much of *Gerontius*. In the intervals of consciousness his mind was full of his unfinished symphony. He wrote four bars on a piece of music paper and handed them to Reed, 'fighting back the tears which were choking him as he said: "Billy, this is the end".'[23] To Ernest Newman, over Christmas 1933, he sent some quotations from the Adagio, writing in the margin: 'I send you my stately sorrow; naturally what follows brings hope.'[24] He asked Reed to promise that no one should ever attempt to complete, or 'tinker with' the symphony: 'all bits and pieces ... no one would understand ... I think you had better burn it.'[25] There was a bizarre episode when B.B.C. officials went to Worcester to ask the doctors whether anything could be done to relieve Elgar's pain yet leave his mind clear to finish the symphony. His friends did their best to ease and brighten his last days. Shaw sent him *Too True to be Good* and a letter telling him to 'trust to your mighty Life Force and damn the doctors'. Thanking him, Elgar could not respond to the mood – 'I am still in the depths of pain ... I am low in mind.' Gaisberg arranged that Harriet Cohen and the Stratton Quartet should record the chamber music, and he went down to Worcester with the records and a new gramophone. The dying man played them again and again. 'Such was his growing weakness,' Reed wrote, 'that he could not refrain from weeping whenever the slow movement [of the Quintet] was reached.'[26]

In November he had collapsed, and, while unconscious, had been given the Last Rites. But he rallied and on New Year's Day 1934 returned to Marl Bank. He grew weaker, but he made one final contact with his own music. Gaisberg arranged a recording of extracts from *Caractacus*, conducted by Lawrance Collingwood, and with the co-operation of the G.P.O., a microphone connected Elgar's bedroom with the recording studio in London. In the morning of 22 January Elgar was half-conscious but he rallied in the afternoon. At 4 p.m. he made a little speech to the orchestra, listened to the first recording session for the *Triumphal March*, and made some criticisms which were clearly heard in the studio. When recording of the second part of the March began he said to Gaisberg: 'I say, Fred, isn't that a gorgeous melody? Who could have written such a beautiful melody?'[27] At the end he specially asked for the *Woodland Interlude* to be played and repeated twice, that music inspired by the Hereford-

[23] *Elgar As I Knew Him*, op. cit., pp. 146–7.
[24] *The Listener*, 11 March, 1954, p. 422.
[25] 'Elgar's Third Symphony', by W. H. Reed, *The Listener*, 28 August 1935, Supplement p. 1.
[26] *Elgar As I Knew Him*, op. cit., p. 145.
[27] *Music on Record*, by Fred Gaisberg (London, 1946), pp. 249–51.

shire countryside around Birchwood, the music he had heard the trees singing. Early in February he asked for Ernest Newman to come to see him. Newman described the meeting in the *Sunday Times* many years later:

> He had altered tragically since I had seen him a little while before; and he obviously knew his end was near . . . he spoke despondently of his fear that his music would not live after him. . . . Then, after a brief silence, he made a single short remark about himself which I have never disclosed to anyone and have no intention of ever disclosing, for it would lend itself too easily to the crudest of misinterpretations. . . . It explains a good deal in him that has always been obscure or puzzling to us; it has a particular bearing, I am convinced, on that passion of his for public mystification of which the most remarkable outward expressions were his two 'enigmas' – that of the *Variations* and that of the 'Soul' enshrined in the violin concerto.[28]

His final days were dreadful indeed. On one of them Father Gibb, S. J., was admitted to his room and told Carice afterwards that her father had reaffirmed his adherence to the Roman Catholic faith.[29] At the end the pain left him. . . and he died at 7.45 a.m. on 23 February 1934, aged seventy-six years and eight months. He was buried three days later, at Alice's side, at Little Malvern. There was no music and no mourning. Simultaneously, at St George's, Worcester, a Low Mass was said at which the *Pie Jesu* he had composed in memory of William Allen in 1887 was sung. He is commemorated in Worcester Cathedral by a window on the subject of *The Dream of Gerontius*. Beneath it is a tablet bearing the words of the Priest at Gerontius's death-bed: 'Proficiscere anima Christiana de hoc mundo.'

During his last weeks, his sister Pollie had sent accounts of his illness to Alice Stuart of Wortley, 'for I know you love him'. After Elgar's death, from her Chelsea home, Little Cheyne House, 'Windflower' wrote to Carice: 'Eulogies pour in on every side, tributes to his genius, life, and character, but he has written his own biography as no other man can ever do. He is our Shakespeare of music, born and died on the soil in the heart and soul of England with his love of his country, its music, and its meaning in his own heart and soul. I think of you all today as the prayers of England go with him as you give him back to that soil, and whilst we cannot go with him, he remains with us in all his wonder-works.'

---

[28] *Sunday Times*, 6 November 1955. In a letter to Dr Gerald Abraham, quoted in *The Listener* of 23 July 1959, Newman said: 'Elgar's distressing remark consisted of only five words, but the scope they would give to a "reading" of him is infinite, so I am determined to keep them to myself: they are too tragic for the ear of the mob.'

[29] Mrs Elgar Blake said to me in 1969 that she doubted if her father was conscious at this time, but the priest's statement absolved her of further responsibility in 'the difficult business of carrying out his wishes to be buried by the river'.

15 Coda

Anybody who spends some time among the great collection of letters to Elgar preserved at Worcester will come away with an overwhelming impression of the respect and affection with which he was surrounded and which he and his music inspired. Yet throughout his life, as we have seen, he remained lonely and unsure. When he was old and full of honours, a young couple with Worcester connections spent an evening with him. He was brimming with humour and good stories. He played them records of his music, striding about the room humming. When they had gone, he asked his niece: 'Do you think they *really* loved my music?' Many, like A. H. Fox Strangways, knew him only as a man with an 'endless curiosity about everyday things and his power of finding fun in chance people and ordinary incidents'. They would never have suspected the dark side of his soul that was bared to Jaeger and Lord Northampton. The intellectuals who despised his patriotism and emotion and found his liking for the racing fraternity an incomprehensible aberration could never have realized the sensitivity that the mask of worldliness concealed. Langford said of Mahler's music: 'With his lighter hand he draws us to and with his heavier thrusts us from him.' These words could equally be applied to Elgar's personality. It seems almost perverse of him to have maintained in the face of all the devotion and admiration he received that music meant nothing to him, that he regretted every good thing he had ever done, that his influence on everything and everybody was 'evil', that it was better to enjoy a 'jape' than to enjoy *The Apostles*. It can be explained only by the sense of inferiority and hurt and humiliation that he carried with him from the struggles of his youth. He resented to his last breath that he had reached his fifth decade before he achieved the recognition he felt was his due and could concentrate on the works he wanted to write instead of on teaching and playing. Sending to Lady Stuart in 1929 a cutting of an article he had written in a Malvern paper in 1887, he added: 'I feel that I really was something apart from the ordinary country violin teacher even then.' He resented the class of society which had dominated the Worcester social scene in his youth, and this resentment took the form of a strange mixture of dislike and respect in his attitude to them in later life. The indelible stain of an inferiority complex is to be found in his constant expectation that he would be slighted, his music disliked, and his intentions misunderstood. Not all the adulation of an era, not all the devotion and homage of great men and musicians, could wash it away. Somewhere in his past something or somebody wounded him so deeply, so irreparably, that he never fully recovered. Though he revealed so much about himself in his letters, he buried the secret of his wounds in his heart. It showed itself only in the anguish and solitude of certain passages in his music.

Although he desired popular appreciation, he also regarded himself as a 'dweller apart'. The lack of professionalism in English music-making annoyed him. His Birmingham lectures reveal him as a progressive in his time, conscious of the narrowness of outlook in English musical life, of its deficiencies and of the possibilities of improvement. He who is supposed to be a 'typical Edwardian', accepting the *status quo*, saw clearly the sham of much English artistic life. He despised the standards of acting and production in the theatre of the early 1900s; he knew from bitter experience the shortcomings of performers; he held a poor opinion of public taste. As he grew older, he became disillusioned because the more things changed, the more they remained the same or, in his view, became worse. He hated the vulgarity of the 1920s and 1930s. When he saw the new Memorial Theatre at Stratford-upon-Avon he withdrew his support in protest against its ugliness. When Ramsay MacDonald was elected to the Athenaeum he sent in his resignation. Though for Alice's sake and his own sense of enjoyment and material fulfilment he had been prepared to live the life of a *grand seigneur* in Hampstead, he soon fled from it, and though he kept one foot in the door in his later years he did so in the rôle of country-gentleman-about-town. He never satisfactorily resolved the conflict within him between the desire for worldly success and acclaim and the equally strong desire for the withdrawn, solitary life of the artist. His own veering from 'japes' and gregariousness to sudden black despair were the outward signs of the conflict; the inner signs are writ large across the music, especially the Second Symphony. There is, through his whole life, a discontent with circumstances; certainly he experienced penuriousness but never real poverty. Though he ought to have been treated better by publishers, he was always able to live in comfort, indulging his fancies and hobbies, keeping a manservant, living in fine houses. Many another struggling composer must have envied him and his domestic peace in Malvern and Hereford.

.   .   .   .   .   .

After Elgar's death, Fox Strangways, editor of *Music and Letters*, wrote:[1] 'More than one who was present at the six BBC concerts of British music in January [1934] was struck by the way in which Elgar's A flat symphony stood out head and shoulders above all the

[1] *Music and Letters* (April 1934), p. 109.

'rest. . . . As we listened, it suddenly came across us: this is mastery.'
His mastery, the success with which he achieved his musical
purpose, is unchallengeable. 'It is within his limitations that the
master finds himself,' Goethe said; and Elgar knew his limitations,
worked within them, and created a distinctive and distinguished
personal idiom. His influence on other English composers can easily
be traced but he remains what he always was: an unexpected,
unheralded phenomenon. It required a musician who had settled in
Britain as Jaeger had done to point out that the English belief in
Elgar's insularity and lack of appeal to the Continent was partly a
'group delusion'. 'There are far more Elgar performances on the
Continent than the English think,' wrote Hans Keller,[2] who then
stimulatingly argued that 'the conservative Elgar's manner is still a
little too new for the broad Continental public. . . . The stunning
effect of the Schoenbergian revolution has made itself felt, and the
Continent is far too busy assimilating the changes thus wrought in its
own musical tradition to appreciate the full significance of Elgar's
conservative progressiveness.' Since 1957, the centenary of his birth,
a resurgence of interest in Elgar has spread to some of the greatest
conductors and interpreters on the international scene.

His truest qualities remain unique and inimitable. 'Music is in the
air all around you, you just take as much of it as you want,' he said in
1904, and in his work – 'peculiarly composite', as Langford wrote in
1924 – we hear the music that was all around Elgar: Franck, Brahms,
Schumann, Dvořák, Wagner, Delibes. He took what he wanted, and
changed it by his own personality and technique into something rich
and strange. He had a poet's perception of the fleeting moment: the
wagon passing, the excitement of a Coronation crowd, the veil that
comes over the eyes as the vanished past is recalled. He believed in
inspiration ('Music is written on the skies') and saw himself as the
vessel into which music was poured from he knew not where. More
prosaically, he called himself an 'incubator'. Oscar Wilde's son
Vyvyan Holland, whom the Elgars befriended in Plâs Gwyn in 1909,
remembered walking with him along the banks of the Wye while
Elgar, humming to himself, jotted down themes on small sheets of
music paper. 'He once told me that he had musical day-dreams in the
same way that other people had day-dreams of heroism and
adventure, and that he could express almost any thought that came
into his head in terms of music.'[3] Like the romantic poets and artists
of the mid-nineteenth century he was acutely responsive to landscape
and to travel. The place names inscribed on his scores all had a special
significance for him – Venice and Tintagel in the Second Symphony,
Alassio in *In the South*, 'Birchwood – in summer' in *Gerontius* and 'In

[2] *Music and Musicians* (June 1957), p. 17.
[3] Vyvyan Holland, *Time Remembered* (London, 1966), p. 20.

Longdon Marsh' in *The Apostles*, Judge's Walk ('my spiritual home for many years', he told Alice Stuart-Wortley) in *The Music Makers*. He told Barry Jackson: 'If ever after I'm dead you hear someone whistling this tune [from the Cello Concerto] on the Malvern Hills, don't be alarmed, it's only me.' Of a wooded country road called Wadborough near Drakes Broughton, off the road from Worcester to Pershore, he said to a friend: 'I shall come back to haunt this place'. Trees were part of the inspiration of the chamber music and of *Gerontius*: 'the summer wind among the lofty pines'. On a postcard showing the Via Appia Antica he wrote the first three bars of the First Symphony, adding: 'Here it was!' And at the very last, when music was dead within his dying body, his thoughts were of the Teme, 'Severn's wild sweet daughter, a wayward child', as Francis Brett Young described it. Always, through his life and music, there runs this motif of the river – 'I am at heart the child on Severn side' . . . 'What the reeds were saying' . . . 'Like something you hear down by the river'. By some alchemy he put this into his music, a fresh wistful quality, whenever his thoughts went back to his youth, to the land of lost content, alone by the river.

'A man's attitude to life' was how he described the broken-hearted Cello Concerto. This directly personal appeal is the secret of his music. The technical expertise is but the means by which he speaks to the hearts of large numbers of his fellow-beings. What his message is will vary with each listener – perhaps he did not fully comprehend it himself. In *Gerontius*, the symphonies, *The Music Makers*, most of all in the Violin Concerto, are a human soul's hopes and regrets, disappointments and beliefs, universally shared experiences, strengths and weaknesses, faults and foibles. For those who love his music, it has a curious quality which transcends mere crotchets and quavers. It becomes part of one's chemistry. It gathers personal associations which become poignant with the passage of time, and when the poignancy seems almost unbearable, the music becomes a renewing stream of solace. That he was a great master of the art and fabric of music is only one aspect of the final portrait of Elgar as one of those rare beings who make men dream dreams and see visions. In all his music, whatever and whoever may have been the sources of his inspiration, there is but one soul enshrined, the sad soul of Edward Elgar.

APPENDIX I   Chronological List of Works

c. **1867**   'Humoreske Broadheath' and other music for Elgar children's play *The Wand of Youth* (see **1907**).

c. **1870**   *Fugue in G minor* for organ (unfinished). Reproduced in *The Music Student*, August 1916, p. 346.

1872   Song, *The Language of Flowers* (James Gates Percival, 1795–1856). Dedication: To my sister Lucy on her birthday. Composed 29 May 1872. Unpublished.
Chantant, pianoforte solo.

1874   Anthem, arranged for strings with original introduction. Performed at All Saints' Church, Worcester, 1874.

1876   *Vocal*:
Salve Regina. Composed 16 September 1876. First performance: St George's Church, Worcester, 6 June 1880.
Tantum Ergo. Composed 27 November 1876. First performance: St George's Church, Worcester, 29 June 1879.

1877   *Study for strengthening the third finger*. (Re-copied 1920 and dedicated to Jascha Heifetz.)
Reminiscences, for violin and pianoforte. Composed 16 March 1877. Dedication: Oswin Grainger.

1878   *Arrangements*:
Adeste fideles arr. for orchestra.
Beethoven, *Violin Sonata* op. 23, finale, arr. for wind quintet.
Corelli, *'Christmas' Concerto*, arr. for wind quintet.
Handel, Overture *Ariodante*, arr. for small orchestra.
Weber, *Oberon*, 'O 'tis a glorious sight', arr. 'for Mr. F. G. Pedley'.
Chamber music:
Fantasia for violin and pianoforte (unfinished).
String Quartet in D minor (unfinished).
String Quartet in B flat (unfinished).
String Trio in C (unfinished).
Trio for 2 violins and pianoforte (unfinished).
Harmony Music ('Shed') for wind quintet (2 flutes, oboe, clarinet, bassoon), No. 1, allegro molto. Completed 4 April 1878. Dedication: 'Professor' Exton; No. 2 ('Nelly Shed', Nelly being Helen Weaver). Dedication: W. Leicester; No. 3, incomplete. Dedication: Frank Elgar; No. 4, Allegretto. Publisher: Belwin-Mills Music, 1978.
Promenades for wind quintet: 1. Moderato e molto maestoso; 2.

Moderato ('Madame Tussaud's' [*sic*]; 3. Presto; Andante ('Somniferous'); 5. Allegro molto; 6. Allegro maestoso ('Hell and Tommy'). Publisher: Belwin-Mills Music, 1978. No. 5, Allegro molto adapted as Scherzando of Minuet in *Severn Suite*, **1930**.

Andante con variazioni ('Evesham andante') for wind quintet. Composed May 1878. Dedication: H.A.L. (Hubert Leicester). Publisher: Belwin-Mills Music, 1978.

Allegro for oboe, violin, viola, and violoncello (unfinished).

Romance, for violin and pianoforte. Opus 1. First performance: Worcester, 20 October 1885. Dedication: Oswin Grainger. Publisher: Schott, 1885

Orchestral:

Menuetto (scherzo) dated 1 October 1878 (re-copied 1930).

Symphony in G minor after Mozart (parts of first and third movements exist).

Introductory Overture for Christy Minstrels for flute, cornet, strings. First performance: Worcester, 12 June 1878, cond. by E.E.

Minuet-grazioso. Composed 21 December 1878. Performed at Worcester, 22 January 1879. Lost.

Vocal:

Domine Salvam fac. Composed 1878–9. First performance: St George's Church, Worcester, 29 June 1879.

Hymn Tune in G major.

Hymn Tune in F major. Published as Drakes Broughton, No. 151 in *Westminster Hymnal*, 1898 and 1912. Also used in *Nursery Suite*, Aubade, **1931**.

Song, *If She Love Me* (Temple Bar Rondeau).

1879 *Chamber music:*

Polonaise in D minor; *Polonaise* in F major for violin and pianoforte (unfinished; MS dated 7 March 1879). Dedication: For J. H. with esteem. First performance (in edns by J. Parry): Doncaster, 15 May 1974, Paul Collins (violin) and John Parry (piano).

Four Dances, for wind quintet: 1. Menuetto-allegretto; 2. Gavotte ('The Alphonsa'); 3. Sarabande-Largo (re-copied **1933** for *The Spanish Lady*); 4. Gigue-allegretto. Publisher: Belwin-Mills Music, 1978.

Harmony Music ('*Shed*') No. 5 ('The Mission') for wind quintet. 1. Allegro moderato; 2. Minuet and Trio; 3. Andante ('Noah's Ark'); 4. Finale. Completed 4 May 1879. Publisher: Belwin-Mills Music, 1978. Minuet adapted for Minuet of *Severn Suite* **1930**.

Harmony Music ('*Shed*') No. 6 for wind quintet. 1. Allegro molto; 2. Andante arioso.

Intermezzos for wind quintet, completed 5 May 1879. 1. Allegretto ('Nancy'); 2. Adagio solenne ('Mrs & Miss Howell'); 3. Allegro molto ('The Farm Yard'); 4. *Andante con moto*; 5. Allegretto. No. 2 also used in *Cantique*, op. 3, arr. for organ and for orch., **1912**. Publisher: Belwin-Mills Music, 1978.

Adagio cantabile ('Mrs Winslow's Soothing Syrup') for wind quintet. Publisher: Belwin-Mills Music, 1978.

Orchestral:

Music written for Worcester City and County Pauper Lunatic Asylum, Powick, and scored for piccolo, flute, clarinet, 2 cornets, euphonium, 2 violins, viola, cello, bass, and pianoforte:
Five Quadrilles, La Brunette. Dedication: Geo. Jenkins (asylum clerk).
Five Quadrilles or Caledonians, Die junge Kokotte. Composed 19 May 1879. Dedication: Miss J. Holloway (pianist and organist).
Five Quadrilles, L'Assommoir. Composed 11 September 1879. (No. 5 also occurs as sixth movement of *Wand of Youth Suite No. 2,* **1908**).

Vocal:

Easter anthem, *Brother, For Thee He Died.*

1880   *Arrangements (c.* 1880):

Mozart, *Violin Sonata in F* (K.547), Allegro, arr. as Gloria for St George's Church, Worcester.
Beethoven, Themes from *Symphonies Nos 5, 7, and 9,* arr. as Credo by 'Bernhard Pappenheim' (E.E.) for St George's Church.
Schumann, *Scherzo,* from *Overture, Scherzo and Finale,* op. 52, arr. for pianoforte solo.

Orchestral: (Music for Powick).

Five Lancers (The Valentine). Composed 14 February 1880.
Polka (Maud)
Five Quadrilles, Paris. Composed 17 October 1880. 1. Chatelet; 2. L'Hippodrome; 3. Alcazar d'Eté (Champs Elysées); 4. Là! Suzanne!; 5. Café des Ambassadeurs: La femme d'emballeur. Dedication: Miss J. Holloway.

Vocal:

O Salutaris hostia (four-part chorus). Publisher: Cary, 1888.
Credo in E minor.

1881   *Chamber music:*

Fantasia on Irish Airs for violin and pianoforte (unfinished).
Fugue in F sharp minor (unfinished – incorporated into *The Spanish Lady*).
Harmony Music ('Shed') No. 7 for wind quintet (see **1879**). Allegro; scherzo – allegro giusto.

Orchestral:

March – Pas Redoublé (No. 1). First performance: Worcester Glee Club, 1 March 1881.
Air de Ballet. First performance: Worcester, 17 May 1881. Worcester Amateur Instrumental Society, cond. by A. J. Caldicott.
Polka (Nelly) for Powick band. Composed October 1881 (Nelly was Helen Weaver).

1882   *Orchestral:*

March – Pas Redoublé (No. 2) (later incorporated into *The Spanish Lady* and into *Suite in D* – see below). Composed 1881–2. First performance: Worcester Amateur Instrumental Society, cond. by A. J. Caldicott, 20 February 1882.

Air de Ballet. Performed: Worcester, 16 August 1882. MS. in private possession.

Polka (La Blonde) for Powick band. Composed 15 October 1882.

Rosemary for pianoforte solo (composed at Settle, Yorks., 4 September 1882), then scored for piano trio. Originally entitled *Douce Pensée*. Scored for small orchestra; published 1915 by Elkin.

Suite in D for small orchestra; 1. Mazurka; 2. Intermezzo – Sérénade Mauresque; 3. Fantasia gavotte; 4. March – Pas redoublé. No. 2 was first performed at Worcester, 4 April 1883, cond. by Rev E. Vine Hall, and No. 4 at Worcester, 20 February 1882. Suite first performed complete at Birmingham, 1 March 1888, cond. by W. C. Stockley. Nos 1 and 3 may not have been written until 1883 or 1884. No. 2 composed March 1883.

Suite revised **1899** as *Three Characteristic Pieces*, op. 10. 1. Mazurka; 2. Sérénade Mauresque; 3. Contrasts: The Gavotte A.D. 1700 and 1900. Dedication: Lady Mary Lygon. Publisher: Novello, 1899.

Vocal:

O Salutaris hostia, bass solo. (Incomplete but edited by Dr Percy Young.)

Four Litanies for the Blessed Virgin Mary (a capella choir). Dedication: Fr. T. Knight, S. J. Publisher: Cary, 1888.

1883 *Arrangement:*

Wagner, *Tannhäuser*, Act II, Entry of the Minstrels, arr. for pianoforte.

Chamber music:

Pastourelle, op. 4, No. 2, for violin and pianoforte. Dedication: Miss Hilda Fitton, Malvern. Publisher: Swan, 1906; Novello, 1912.

Virelai, op. 4, No. 3, for violin and pianoforte. Dedication: Frank W. Webb. Publisher: Swan, 1906; Novello, 1912.

Fugue in D minor, for oboe and violin.

Orchestral:

Polka (Helcia) for Powick band. Composed 1 October 1883.

1884 *Orchestral:*

Polka (Blumine) for Powick band.

Sevillana, op. 7. First performance: Worcester Philharmonic Society, cond. by Dr W. Done, 1 May 1884. First London performance, Crystal Palace, cond. by August Manns, 12 May 1884. Dedication: W. C. Stockley. Publisher: Tuckwood, 1884. Revised version of 1889 published by Ascherberg, 1895.

Vocal:

A Soldier's Song (C. Flavell Hayward). First performance: Worcester Glee Club (Crown Hotel, Broad Street), 17 March 1884. Dedication: F. G. P., Worcester (F. G. Pedley). Published: *Magazine of Music*, 1890. Re-named *A War Song* and re-published by Boosey, 1903, and sung at Royal Albert Hall, 1 October 1903.

Instrumental:

Une Idylle, op. 4, No. 1, for violin and pianoforte. Dedication: E.E., Inverness. Publisher: Ashdown, 1910, and by Beare in 1885.

Griffinesque, for pianoforte. Composed 17 February 1884.
Publisher: Novello, 1981.

1885 *Arrangements:*
Maud Valerie White, *Absent and Present*. Cello obbligato. C. H.
Dolby, *Out on the Rocks*. Cello obbligato. C. W. Buck, *Melody*.
Pianoforte accompaniment.

Chamber music:
Gavotte for violin and pianoforte. Dedication: Dr C. W. Buck.
Publisher: Schott, 1886.
Allegretto on G E D G E for violin and pianoforte. Dedication:
The Misses Gedge, Malvern. First performance: Wells House,
Malvern, 22 December 1885. Publisher: Schott, 1889.

Orchestral:
Overture, *The Lakes*. MS. lost.
Scottish Overture. MS. lost.

Vocal:
Song, *Through the Long Days* (John Hay). Composed at Settle,
August, 1885. Dedication: Rev E. Vine Hall. First performance:
London, St James's Hall, 25 February 1897. Charles Phillips
(baritone). Publisher: Stanley Lucas, 1887; Ascherberg, 1890;
in *Seven Lieder of Edward Elgar*, Ascherberg, 1907, op. 16,
No. 2.

1886 *Chamber music:*
Trio for violin, violoncello, and pianoforte. 75 bars only of first
movement. Re-copied 21 September 1920. Performed complete
by John Parry, Doncaster, 15 May 1974.

Vocal:
Song, *Is she not passing fair?* (Charles, Duc d'Orléans, *tr.* L. S.
Costello). Publisher: Boosey, 1908.

1887 *Chamber music:*
String Quartet, op. 8. MS. destroyed.
Sonata for violin and pianoforte, op. 9. MS. destroyed.
Duett for trombone and double bass.

Vocal:
Pie Jesu, in memory of William Allen. Re-arranged in 1902 as *Ave,
Verum Corpus* (Jesu, Word of God Incarnate), op. 2, No. 1.
Dedication: In mem. W. A. Publisher: Novello, 1902.
Ave Maria (Jesu, Lord of Life and Glory), revised 1907 as op. 2,
No. 2. Dedication: Mrs H. A. Leicester. Publisher: Novello,
1907.
Ave Maris Stella (Jesu, Meek and Lowly), revised 1907 as op. 2,
No. 3. Dedication: Rev Canon Dolman, O.S.B., Hereford.
Publisher: Novello, 1907.

Vocal:
Song, *Queen Mary's Song* (Tennyson). Composed 1887, rev. 1889.
Dedication: J. H. Meredith (honorary member, Worcester Ama-
teur Instrumental Society). Publisher: Orsborn and Tuckwood,
1889; Ascherberg, 1892. Re-published in *Seven Lieder of Edward
Elgar*, Ascherberg, 1907.

Song, *As I Laye a-thinking* (Richard Barham, 'Thomas Ingoldsby'). Composed late 1887. Publisher: Beare, 1888.

1888   *Chamber music:*
String Quartet in D (unfinished: 3rd movement, Intermezzo, used as No. 3 of *Eleven Vesper Voluntaries*, see **1889**.)
Orchestral:
Three Pieces for String Orchestra. MS. lost, but probably revised as the *Serenade in E minor.* 1. Spring Song, allegro; 2. Elegy, adagio; 3. Finale, presto. First performance: Worcestershire Musical Union, cond. by the Rev E. Vine Hall, 7 May 1888. See **1892**.
Salut d'Amour (Liebesgruss), op. 12 (written as pianoforte solo and orchestrated). First performance: London, Crystal Palace, cond. by August Manns, 11 November 1889. Dedication: à Carice.[1] Publisher: Schott, 1889 (also for violin and pianoforte and in other arrangements).
Vocal:
Ecce sacerdos magnus for chorus and organ. First performance: St George's Church, Worcester, 9 October 1888. Dedication: Hubert Leicester. Publisher: Cary, 1888.
Song, *The Wind at Dawn* (C. Alice Roberts). Dedication: Dr Ludwig Wüllner. Publisher: *Magazine of Music*, 1888; Boosey, 1907 (with dedication added). Orchestrated by Elgar, 1912.

1889   *Chamber music:*
Mot d'Amour (Liebesahnung) for violin and pianoforte, op. 13, No. 1. Publisher: Orsborn and Tuckwood; Ascherberg, 1890.
Bizarrerie for violin and pianoforte, op. 13, No. 2. Publisher: Orsborn and Tuckwood; Ascherberg, 1890.
Organ:
Eleven Vesper Voluntaries for organ, op. 14. (No. 3 is from unfinished string quartet of 1888.) Dedication: Mrs W. A. Raikes. Publisher: Orsborn and Tuckwood, 1891; Ascherberg, 1891.
Pianoforte:
Sonatina in two movements, 'composed expressly for May Grafton by her affectionate Uncle, Edward Elgar, Jany. 4: 1889'. See **1932**.
Presto. Composed at 'Saetermo', Malvern, 8 August 1889. Dedication: 'To Miss Isabel Fitton Aug. 8; 1889' [her twenty-first birthday]. Publisher: Novello, 1981.
Vocal:
Part-Song (S.A.T.B.) *O happy eyes* (C. A. Elgar), op. 18, No. 1. Publisher: Novello, 1896. For *Love*, op. 18, No. 2, see **1907**.
Part-Song (S.A.T.B.), *My Love dwelt in a Northern Land* (Andrew Lang). First performance: Tenbury Musical Society, 13 November 1890. Dedication: Rev J. Hampton, M.A., Warden of St Michael's College, Tenbury. Published: Novello, 1890.

1890   *Orchestral:*
Violin Concerto, destroyed during 1890.
Concert Overture, *Froissart*, op. 19. (Written at 51 Avonmore

---

[1]Carice in this case is Elgar's wife, not his daughter.

Road, West Kensington, between 6 April and a date in July.) First performance: Worcester Festival, Public Hall, 9 September 1890, cond. by E.E. First performance in London: St James's Hall, 16 November 1900, cond. by Frederic Cowen. Publisher: Novello, 1901.

Vocal:
Folk-Song arrangement, *Clapham Town End*, for voice and pianoforte.

1891 *Chamber music:*
La Capricieuse for violin and pianoforte, op. 17. Dedication: Fred Ward (a Worcester pupil of Elgar). Publisher: Breitkopf and Härtel, 1893.

Vocal:
Part-Song (s.a.t.b. with 2 violins and pianoforte), *Spanish Serenade (Stars of the Summer Night)* (Longfellow), op. 23. Orchestral accompaniment added 12 June 1892. First performance: Herefordshire Philharmonic Society, cond. by the Rev. J. Hampton, 7 April 1893. Publisher: Novello, 1892.

1892 *Chamber music:*
Very Easy Melodious Exercises in the First Position for solo violin, op. 22. Dedication: May Grafton (Elgar's niece). Publisher: Chanot, 1892; Laudy, 1927.
Etudes Caractéristiques pour violon seul, op. 24. Dedication: Adolphe Pollitzer. Publisher: Chanot, 1892. (No. 4 is known to have been written on 30 April 1882, the rest were composed in 1877.

Orchestral:
Serenade in E minor for string orchestra, op. 20. 1. Allegro piacevole; 2. Larghetto; 3. Allegretto. First performance: Worcester Ladies' Orchestral Class, cond. by E.E., at some time in 1892; Larghetto only, Hereford, 7 April 1893, cond. by Rev. J. Hampton, and in London, St Andrew's Hall, 19 June 1894. First professional public performance of complete work, Antwerp, 23 July 1896; in England, New Brighton, cond. by E.E., 16 July 1899; in London, Bechstein Hall, 5 March 1905, cond. by E.E. Dedication: W. H. Whinfield. Publisher: Breitkopf and Härtel, 1893. (See also **1888**, *Three Pieces for Strings.*)

Choral and vocal:
The Black Knight, symphony for chorus and orchestra, op. 25. (Poem by Uhland, tr. H. W. Longfellow.) Begun 1889. First performance: Worcester Festival Choral Society, cond. by E.E., 18 April 1893; in London, March 1895. Dedication: To my friend Hugh Blair, M.A., Mus. B. Publisher: Novello, 1893.
Song, *A spear, a sword* (C. A. Elgar) August 1892.
Song, *1588: Loose, loose the sails* (C. A. Elgar).
Songs, *The Mill Wheel* (C. A. Elgar): 1. *Winter*; 2. *May (a Rhapsody)*. December 1892.
Song, *Like to the Damask Rose* (Simon Wastell). First performance: London, St James's Hall, 25 February 1897, Charles Phillips (baritone). Publisher: Tuckwood, Ascherberg, 1893. Republished in *Seven Lieder of Edward Elgar*, Ascherberg, 1907.

Song, *The Poet's Life* (Ellen Burroughs). Composed in 1892. Published in *Seven Lieder of Edward Elgar*, Ascherberg, 1907.

Song, *A Song of Autumn* (Adam Lindsay Gordon). Dedication: Miss Marshall. Publisher: Orsborn and Tuckwood; Ascherberg, 1892. Re-published in *Seven Lieder of Edward Elgar,* Ascherberg, 1907.

Song, *Shepherd's Song* ('Barry Pain'), op. 16, No. 1. Publisher: Tuckwood, 1895; Ascherberg, 1896. Re-published in *Seven Lieder of Edward Elgar*, Ascherberg, 1907.

1894   *Arrangement:*

Wagner, *Parsifal,* Good Friday Music, arr. for small orchestra for Worcester Girls' High School, 13 June 1894.

Orchestral:

Sursum Corda for strings, brass, and organ, op. 11. Theme taken from abandoned Violin Sonata 1887, re-shaped 1893 as *Andante religioso*. First performance: Worcester Cathedral, cond. by Hugh Blair, 9 April 1894. Dedication: H. D. Acland. Publisher: Schott, 1901.

Vocal:

Part-songs (s.s.a. with 2 violins and pianoforte), *The Snow* and *Fly, Singing Bird* (C. A. Elgar), op. 26, Nos 1 and 2. Dedication: Mrs E. B. Fitton, Malvern. Publisher: Novello, 1895. Orchestration added December 1903; first performance of this version, London, Queen's Hall, 12 March 1904.

Song, *The Wave* (C. A. Elgar).

Song, *Muleteer's Song* (C. A. Elgar).

Song, *Rondel* (Longfellow, from *Froissart*), op. 16, No. 3. First performance: London, St James's Hall, 7 December 1897. Publisher: Ascherberg, 1896. Re-published in *Seven Lieder of Edward Elgar*, Ascherberg, 1907.

1895   *Sonata in G* for organ, op. 28. First performance: Worcester Cathedral, 8 July 1895, Hugh Blair. Dedication: C. Swinnerton Heap, Mus. D. Publisher: Breitkopf and Härtel, 1896.

Cadenza for C. H. Lloyd's Organ Concerto in F minor, played by G. R. Sinclair, Gloucester Festival, 1895.

Choral and vocal:

Scenes from the Bavarian Highlands. Six choral songs with pianoforte (1895) or orchestral (1896) accompaniment, op. 27. (Bavarian folksongs adapted by C. A. Elgar.) 1. The Dance; 2. False Love; 3. Lullaby; 4. Aspiration; 5. On the Alm; 6. The Marksman. First performance: Worcester Festival Choral Society cond. by E.E., 21 April 1896. Orchestral version of Nos 1, 3, and 6 first performed in London, Crystal Palace, 23 October 1897, cond. by August Manns. Dedication: Mr and Mrs Henry Slingsby Bethell, Garmisch, Bavaria. Publisher: J. Williams, 1896; orchestral versions, (*Three Bavarian Dances*) Novello, 1907.

Song, *After* (P. B. Marston), for voice and pianoforte, op. 31, No. 1. Composed 21 June 1895. First performance: London, St James's Hall, 2 March 1900. H. Plunket Greene (baritone). Publisher: Boosey, 1900.

Song, *A Song of Flight* (C. Rossetti), for voice and pianoforte, op. 31. No. 2. First performance and Publisher as for *After*.

1896 *Choral and vocal:*

Oratorio, *The Light of Life* (*Lux Christi*), for soprano, contralto, tenor, and bass soloists, chorus, and orchestra, op. 29. (Libretto written and arranged by the Rev. E. Capel-Cure.) First performance: Worcester Festival, 10 September 1896, Anna Williams, Jessie King, Edward Lloyd, Watkin Mills, cond. by E.E. Dedication: C. Swinnerton Heap, Mus. D. Publisher: Novello, 1896.

Scenes from the Saga of King Olaf, cantata for soprano, tenor, and bass soloists, chorus, and orchestra, op. 30. (Libretto by Longfellow and H. A. Acworth.) Work was begun 15 July 1894, revised version completed August 1896. First performance: North Staffordshire Music Festival, Hanley, 30 October 1896, Medora Henson, Edward Lloyd, David Ffrangcon-Davies, cond. by E.E.; first performance in London, Crystal Palace, 3 April 1897, cond. by August Manns. Publisher: Novello, 1896. Extract available in separate form, Part-song (s.a.t.b.) *As torrents in summer*.

1897 *Instrumental and orchestral:*

Minuet for pianoforte (also for small orchestra, op. 21). Orch. version 1898. First performance: New Brighton, 16 July 1899, cond. by Granville Bantock (orchestral version). Dedication: Paul Kilburn. Publisher: *The Dome* and J. Williams, 1897 (pfte.); J. Williams, 1899 (orch.).

Chanson de Nuit for violin and pianoforte and for orchestra, op. 15, No. 1. First performance (orch.): London, Queen's Hall, cond. by Henry J. Wood, 14 September 1901. Dedication: F. Ehrke, M.D. (violinist in Worcestershire Philharmonic). Publisher: Novello, 1897 (vn. & pfte.), 1899 (orch.). Composed 1897 as *Evensong*. For op. 15, No. 2 see **1899**.

Imperial March for orchestra, op. 32. First performance: London, Crystal Palace, 19 April 1897, cond. by August Manns. Publisher: Novello, 1897.

Choral and vocal:

The Banner of St George, ballad for chorus and orchestra, op. 33 (Shapcott Wensley). First performance: London, St Cuthbert's Hall Choral Society, cond. by Cyril Miller, 18 May 1897. Publisher: Novello, 1897.

Te Deum & Benedictus for chorus and orch. or organ, op. 34. First performance: Hereford Festival, 12 September 1897, cond. by Dr G. R. Sinclair. Dedication: G. R. Sinclair. Publisher: Novello, 1897.

Part-song, *Grete Malverne on a Rock*. Private Christmas card, 1897. Published in 1909 as the carol *Lo, Christ the Lord is born*.

Song, *Rondel: The Little Eyes that Never Knew Light* (Swinburne). First performance: Worcester Musical Union, 26 April 1897, Gertrude Walker, acc. by E.E.

Song, *Love Alone Will Stay* (*Lute Song*) (C. A. Elgar), for voice and pianoforte. Written 30 May 1897. Publisher: *The Dome*, 1898.

Revised, orchestrated, and incorporated into *Sea Pictures*, op. 37, No. 2, 1899 as *In Haven (Capri)*. See **1899**.

1898 *Arrangement:*
The Holly and The Ivy for chorus and orchestra, for Worcestershire Philharmonic Society, 9 January 1899, cond. by E.E.
Orchestral:
Festival March in C. First performance: London, Crystal Palace, 14 October 1898, cond. by August Manns. Fragment only remains.
Choral and vocal:
Caractacus, cantata for soprano, tenor, baritone, and bass soloists, chorus, and orchestra, op. 35 (H. A. Acworth). First performance: Leeds Festival, 5 October 1898, Medora Henson, Edward Lloyd, Andrew Black, John Browning, cond. by E.E. First London performance: Royal Albert Hall, 20 April 1899, Medora Henson (soprano), Edward Lloyd (tenor), Douglas Powell (baritone), Andrew Black (bass), Royal Choral Society and orchestra, cond. by E.E. Dedication: H.M. Queen Victoria. Publisher: Novello, 1898.
Extract available separately, part-song s.a.t.b., *The Sword Song*.
O Salutaris hostia, in Tozer's *Benediction Manual*, No. 47. Publisher: Cary, 1898.

1899 *Instrumental and orchestral:*
Chanson de Matin for violin and pianoforte and for orchestra, op. 15, No. 2. Completed 6 March 1899. First performance (orch.): London, Queen's Hall, cond. by Henry J. Wood, 14 September 1901. Publisher: Novello, 1899 (vn. & pfte.), 1900 (orch.).
Variations on an Original Theme (Enigma) for orchestra, op. 36. Theme (Enigma) (andante); Var. 1. C.A.E. (andante); 2. H.D.S.-P. (allegro); 3. R. B. T. (allegretto); 4. W. M. B. (allegro di molto); 5. R. P. A. (moderato); 6. Ysobel (andantino); 7. Troyte (presto); 8. W. N. (allegretto); 9. Nimrod (adagio); 10. Intermezzo, Dorabella (allegretto); 11. G. R. S. (allegro di molto); 12. B. G. N. (andante); 13. Romanza (* * *) (moderato); 14. Finale, E. D. U. (allegro). First performance: London, St James's Hall, 19 June 1899, cond. by Dr Hans Richter; first performance of version with revised finale: Worcester Festival, 13 September 1899, cond. by E.E. Dedication: To my friends pictured within. Publisher: Novello, 1899.
Vocal:
Part-song (s.a.t.b.), *To Her Beneath Whose Steadfast Star* (F. W. H. Myers). Composed 7 February 1899. First performance: Windsor Castle, 24 May 1899, as one of a group of songs dedicated to Queen Victoria in the manner of *The Triumphes of Oriana*. Publisher: Macmillan, 1899.
Song, *Dry Those Fair, Those Crystal Eyes* (Henry King). First performance: London, Royal Albert Hall, 21 June 1899. Publisher: Souvenir of Charing Cross Hospital Bazaar, 1899.
Song-cycle, *Sea-Pictures*, for contralto or mezzo-soprano and

orchestra, op. 37. 1. Sea-Slumber Song (Roden Noel); 2. In Haven (Capri) (C. A. Elgar); 3. Sabbath Morning at Sea (E. B. Browning); 4. Where Corals Lie (Richard Garnett); 5. The Swimmer (Adam Lindsay Gordon). Composed July 1899 at Birchwood, with exception of No. 2 (see **1897**, *Love Alone Will Stay*). First performance: Norwich Festival, 5 October 1899, Clara Butt, cond. by E.E. First London performance: 7 October 1899, Clara Butt, with E.E. as pianist (4 songs only). Publisher: Boosey, 1900.

1900 *Orchestral:*
Sérénade Lyrique for small orchestra. First performance: London, St James's Hall, 27 November 1900. Dedication: Composed for Ivan Caryll's Orchestra. Publisher: Chappell, 1899.

Choral and vocal:
The Dream of Gerontius (Cardinal Newman) for mezzo-soprano, tenor, and bass soloists, chorus, and orchestra, op. 38. Composed 1900 (vocal score finished 6 June 1900, orchestration finished 3 August 1900). First performance: Birmingham Festival, 3 October 1900, Marie Brema, Edward Lloyd, H. Plunket Greene, cond. by Dr Hans Richter. First London performance: Westminster Cathedral, 6 June 1903, cond. by E.E. with Muriel Foster, Ludwig Wüllner, and David Ffrangcon-Davies, and North Staffordshire Festival Chorus. Dedication: A.M.D.G. (Ad Majorem Dei Gloriam). Publisher: Novello, 1900.
Song, *Pipes of Pan* (Adrian Ross). First performance: London, Crystal Palace, 30 April 1900, Miss Blouvelt; Queen's Hall, 12 May 1900, Andrew Black (bass). Publisher: Boosey, 1900.

1901 *Instrumental:*
May Song for pianoforte and for violin and pianoforte (both completed 2 March 1901) Dedication of violin and pianoforte version: 'Inscribed to Mrs T. Garmston Hyde'. Publisher: W. H. Broome, 1901; Morrice Music Publishing Co., 1901; orchestrated 1928 (Elkin, 1928).
Concert Allegro for pianoforte, op. 41. First performance: London, St James's Hall, 2 December 1901, by Fanny Davies. Dedication: For Fanny Davies. MS. rediscovered in 1968 and published by Novello, 1973 (edited by John Ogdon and Diana McVeagh).
Dramatic:
Incidental Music for *Grania and Diarmid* (W. B. Yeats and George Moore) op. 42. 1. Incidental music; 2. Funeral March; 3. Song, *There are seven that pull the thread.* First performance: Dublin, Gaiety Theatre, 21 October 1901. *Funeral March* performed London, Queen's Hall, 18 January 1902 cond. by Sir Henry J. Wood. Dedication: Henry J. Wood. Publisher: Novello, 1902.
Orchestral:
Military Marches, *Pomp and Circumstance*, op. 39, No. 1 in D major and No. 2 in A minor. First performance: Liverpool Orchestral Society, cond. by A. E. Rodewald, 19 October 1901; first London performance: Queen's Hall, 22 October 1901, cond. by Henry J.

Wood. Dedication: No. 1 – A. E. Rodewald and the members of the Liverpool Orchestral Society; No. 2 – Granville Bantock. Publisher: Boosey, 1902. See also *Land of Hope and Glory*, **1902**. For March No. 3 see **1904**; No. 4, **1907**; No. 5, **1930**.

Concert Overture, *Cockaigne (In London Town)*, op. 40. First performance: London, Queen's Hall, Philharmonic Society, 20 June 1901, cond. by E.E. Dedication: To my many friends the members of British orchestras. Publisher: Boosey, 1901.

Orchestration of *Emmaus*, by H. A. Brewer. Publisher: Novello, 1901. (All copies destroyed in 1959.)

Vocal:

Song, *Come, gentle night* (Clifton Bingham). Publisher: Boosey, 1901.

Song, *Always and Everywhere* (Krasinski, tr. F. E. Fortey). Publisher: Boosey, 1901.

1902   *Arrangement:*

God Save the King for soprano solo, chorus, and orchestra. Publisher: Novello, 1902.

Orchestral:

Dream Children, two pieces for small orchestra (or for pianoforte), op. 43, after Charles Lamb. First performance: London, Queen's Hall, cond. by Arthur W. Payne, 4 September 1902. Publisher: J. Williams, 1902; Schott, 1913.

Choral and vocal:

Coronation Ode (A. C. Benson), for soprano, contralto, tenor, and bass soloists, chorus, and orchestra, op. 44. 1. *Crown the King with Life*, soloists and chorus; 2. *Daughter of Ancient Kings*, for chorus; 3. *Britain, Ask of Thyself*, bass and men's chorus; 4. *Hark upon the hallowed air*, soprano and tenor soloists; 5. *Only let the heart be pure*, S.A.T.B. soloists; 6. *Peace, gentle peace*, S.A.T.B. soloists and chorus unaccompanied; 7. Finale, *Land of Hope and Glory*,[2] contralto solo, chorus, and orchestra. First performance: Sheffield Festival, 2 October 1902, Agnes Nicholls, Muriel Foster, John Coates, David Ffrangcon-Davies, cond. by E.E. First London performance: 26 October 1902. cond. by E.E. Dedication: H.M. King Edward VII. Publisher: Boosey, 1902. See **1911** for substitute No. 2. *The Queen.*

Separate arrangement from the *Ode* – Song, *Land of Hope and Glory* (with different words by Benson from version in No. 7 of *Ode*). First performance: London, June 1902, Clara Butt (contralto).

Hymn, *O Mightiest of the Mighty*. First performance: Westminster Abbey, Coronation of Edward VII, 9 August 1902. Dedication: H.R.H. The Prince of Wales. Publisher: Novello, 1902.

Part-song (S.A.T.B.), *Weary Wind of the West* (T. E. Brown). Composed November 1902. First performance: Morecambe Festival, 2 May 1903. Dedication: Composed for Morecambe Musical Festival. Publisher: Novello, 1903.

---

[2] Adaption of trio section of *Pomp and Circumstance* March No 1 in D major.

Songs, *In the Dawn* and *Speak, Music* (A. C. Benson), op. 41, Nos 1 and 2. Dedication, No. 2: Mrs E. Speyer, Ridgehurst. Publisher: Boosey, 1902.

Song, *Speak, my heart* (A. C. Benson). Publisher: Boosey, 1903.

Five Part-songs from the Greek Anthology (T.T.B.B.), op. 45. Completed on 11 November 1902. 1. Yea, cast me from heights (Anon., tr. Alma Strettell); 2. Whether I find thee (Anon., tr. Andrew Lang); 3. After many a dusty mile (Anon., tr. Edmund Gosse); 4. It's oh! to be a wild wind (Anon., tr. W. M. Hardinge); 5. Feasting I watch (Marcus Argentarius, tr. Richard Garnett). First performance: London, Royal Albert Hall, London Choral Society, cond. by Arthur Fagge, 25 April 1904. Dedication: Sir Walter Parratt. Publisher: Novello, 1903.

Instrumental:

Skizze, pianoforte solo. Composed 1901–2. Dedication: Prof Julius Buths, Düsseldorf. Publisher: *Musik-Beilag zur Neuen Musik-Zeitung*, Stuttgart–Leipzig XXIV Jahrgang; Novello, 1976.

Offertoire (andante religioso) for violin and pianoforte. Dedication: Serge Derval, Antwerp. Publisher: Boosey, 1903.

1903 *Choral and vocal:*

The Apostles, an oratorio for soprano, contralto, tenor, and three bass soloists, chorus, and orchestra, op. 49. (Libretto compiled by Elgar from the Bible and other sources.) First performance: Birmingham Festival, 14 October 1903, Emma Albani, Muriel Foster, John Coates, Kennerley Rumford, Andrew Black, David Ffrangcon-Davies, cond. by E.E. First London performance: Royal Opera House, Covent Garden, 15 March 1904, Agnes Nicholls (soprano), Louise Kirkby-Lunn (contralto), John Coates (tenor), Kennerley Rumford (bass), Andrew Black (bass), David Ffrangcon-Davies (bass), the Hallé Orchestra and Choir, cond. by Hans Richter. Composed late December 1902 to June 1903. Dedication: A.M.D.G. Publisher: Novello, 1903.

1904 *Orchestral:*

Concert Overture, *In the South* (*Alassio*), op. 50. Composition begun 1903, finished 21 February 1904. First performance: London, Elgar Festival, Royal Opera House, Covent Garden, 16 March 1904, The Hallé Orchestra, cond. by E.E. Dedication: To my friend Leo F. Schuster. Publisher: Novello, 1904. Extract available separately: *In Moonlight* (*Canto popolare*) for small orchestra, for violin and pianoforte, viola and pianoforte, cello and pianoforte, clarinet and pianoforte, for organ, and as song for high or medium voice with pianoforte. First performance of version for small orchestra: Herefordshire Philharmonic Society, cond. by Dr G. R. Sinclair, 22 November 1904. Publisher: Novello.

Military March, *Pomp and Circumstance*, op. 39. No. 3 in C minor, completed 20 November 1904. First performance: London, Queen's Hall, 8 March 1905, cond. by E.E. Dedication: Ivor Atkins. Publisher: Boosey, 1905. (See also **1901**, **1907**, and **1930**.)

1905 *Orchestral:*

Introduction and Allegro for String Quartet and String Orchestra, op. 47. First sketches, 1901, completed 13 February 1905. First performance: London, Queen's Hall, 8 March 1905, London Symphony Orchestra, cond. by E.E. (Solo quartet, A. W. Payne, W. H. Eaynes, A. Hobday, B. P. Parker.) Dedication: Professor S. S. Sanford, Yale University, U.S.A. Publisher: Novello, 1905.

Instrumental:

In Smyrna, pianoforte solo. Composed October 1905. Publisher: Daily Mail, Queen's Christmas Carol Book, 1905; Novello, 1976.

Vocal:

Part-song (s.a.t.b.), *Evening Scene* (Coventry Patmore). Composed 21–24 August 1905. First performance: Morecambe Festival, 12 May 1906. Dedication: In memoriam R. G. H. Howson. Publisher: Novello, 1906.

1906 *Piece for Organ.* 'For Dot's nuns.' (His sister was in a convent.)

Choral and Vocal:

The Kingdom, an oratorio for soprano, contralto, tenor, and bass soloists, chorus and orchestra, op. 51. (Libretto compiled by Elgar from the Bible and other sources.) Composed between 1901 and August 1906. First performance: Birmingham Festival, 3 October 1906, Agnes Nicholls, Muriel Foster, John Coates, William Higley, cond. by E.E. First London performance: Alexandra Palace, 17 November 1906, Cicely Gleeson-White (soprano), Edna Thornton (contralto), John Coates (tenor), Dalton Baker (bass), Alexandra Palace Orchestra and Choir, cond. by Allen Gill. Dedication: A.M.D.G. Publisher: Novello, 1906.

1907 *Arrangement:*

Victor Bérard, *Berceuse – Petite Reine*, arr. for violin and pianoforte. Publisher: Ashdown, 1907. (Probably arranged *c.* 1880.)

Chamber music:

Andantino for violin, mandoline, and guitar. Unfinished. Sketched 15 January 1907 in Capri for a barber's shop where Elgar found the barber and customers making music while they waited.

Orchestral:

The Wand of Youth, Suite No. 1 for orchestra, op. 1A. Final revision of music Elgar wrote for a children's play (see **1867**) which he had revised at various earlier dates. 1. Overture; 2. Serenade; 3. Minuet; 4. Sun Dance; 5. Fairy Pipers; 6. Slumber Scene; 7. Fairies and Giants. First performance: London, Queen's Hall, 14 December 1907, cond. by Sir Henry J. Wood. Dedication: C. Lee Williams. Publisher: Novello, 1907. (See also **1915**, *The Starlight Express*.)

Military March, *Pomp and Circumstance*, op. 39, No. 4 in G major. (Completed 7 June 1907.) First performance: London, Queen's Hall, 24 August 1907, cond. by E.E. Dedication: G. R. Sinclair. Publisher: Boosey, 1907. (See also **1901**, **1904**, and **1930**.)

Vocal:

Two Single Chants for *Venite* in D and G. Composed May 1907. Publisher: New Cathedral Psalter, and Novello, 1909.

Two Double Chants in D for Psalms 68 and 75. Composed May 1907. Publisher: Novello, 1909.

A Christmas Greeting (C. A. Elgar), carol for two sopranos, male chorus *ad lib.*, two violins, and pianoforte, op. 52. First performance: Town Hall, Hereford, 1 January 1908. Dedication: Dr G. R. Sinclair and the choristers of Hereford Cathedral. Publisher: Novello, 1907.

Part-song (S.A.T.B.), *How calmly the evening* (T. Lynch). Publisher: Novello, 1907, in *Musical Times*.

Part-song (S.A.T.B.), *Love* (Arthur Maquarie) op. 18, No. 2. Composed 2 June 1907. Dedication: C.A.E. Publisher: Novello, 1907. For *O Happy Eyes*, op. 18, No. 1, see **1889**.

Four Part-Songs (S.A.T.B.), op. 53. Composed in Rome in February 1907. 1. There is sweet music (Tennyson), dedication: Canon Gorton; 2. Deep in my soul (Byron), dedication: Julia H. Worthington; 3. O Wild West Wind (Shelley), dedication: W. G. McNaught; 4. Owls (E.E.), dedication: Pietro d'Alba (Peter Rabbit).[3] Publisher: Novello, 1908.

The Reveille (T.T.B.B.), op. 54 (Bret Harte). Composed in Rome, 20–26 December 1907. First performance: Blackpool Music Festival,[4] 17 October 1908. Dedication: Henry C. Embleton. Publisher: Novello, 1908.

1908 *Orchestral:*

The Wand of Youth, Suite No. 2 for orchestra. op. 1B (see **1907**). 1. March; 2. The Little Bells; 3. Moths and Butterflies; 4. Fountain Dance; 5. The Tame Bear; 6. Wild Bears. First performance: Worcester Festival, 9 September 1908, cond. by E.E. First London performance: Queen's Hall Orchestra, cond. by E.E., 17 October 1908. Dedication: Hubert A. Leicester. Publisher: Novello, 1908. (See also **1915**, *The Starlight Express*.)

Symphony No. 1 in A flat major, op. 55. Composed between 13 June 1907 and 25 September 1908. First performance: Manchester, Free Trade Hall, 3 December 1908, The Hallé Orchestra, cond. by Dr Hans Richter; first London performance: Queen's Hall, 7 December 1908, L.S.O., cond. by Richter. Dedication: Hans Richter, Mus. Doc. True artist and true friend. Publisher: Novello, 1908.

Vocal:

Song for voice and pianoforte, *Pleading* (A. L. Salmon), op. 48. Orchestration added 13 November 1908. Dedication: Lady Maud Warrender. Publisher: Novello, 1908.

[3] A white rabbit belonging to his daughter Carice which lived from 1905 to May 1910.

[4] Elgar's association with the Blackpool Festival is commemorated by a kind of heraldic shield in the Tower Ballroom.

Song for s.a.t.b., *Marching Song* (Capt. de Courcy Stretton).
Composed 1907–8. First performance: London, Royal Albert
Hall, Empire Day Concert, 24 May 1908. Publisher: Novello,
1908. (See also **1914**, *Follow the Colours*.)

1909 *Orchestral:*

Elegy for string orchestra, op. 58. Completed 24 June 1909. First
performance: London, The Mansion House, 13 July 1909, at
memorial concert of Worshipful Company of Musicians. Dedication: In memoriam late Junior Warden of Musicians'
Company, Rev. R. H. Hadden, M.A. Publisher: Novello, 1910.

Vocal:

Part-song (s.a.t.b.), *Angelus (Tuscany)*, op. 56. (Words from
Tuscan dialect.) First performance: London, Royal Albert Hall, 8
December 1910. Dedication: Mrs Charles Stuart-Wortley.
Publisher: Novello, 1909.

Chorus (s.s.a.a.t.b.), *Go, Song of Mine*, op. 57 (Calvacanti, tr. D. G.
Rossetti). Composed at Careggi in May 1909. First performance:
Hereford Festival, 9 September 1909, cond. by G. R. Sinclair.
Dedication: Alfred H. Littleton. Publisher: Novello, 1909.

Carol (s.a.t.b.), *Lo! Christ the Lord is Born* (Shapcott Wensley).
Composed in 1897. Publisher: Novello, 1909. (See **1897**.)

Song, *The Kingsway* (C. A. Elgar). Composed 25–27 December
1909. First performance: London, Alexandra Palace, 15 January
1910. Publisher: Boosey, 1910.

Song, *A Child Asleep* (E. B. Browning). Composed December
1909. Dedication: Anthony Goetz (son of Muriel Foster) 'for his
mother's singing'. Publisher: Novello, 1910.

Elegy (s.a.t.b.), *They are at rest* (Cardinal Newman). First
performance: Royal Mausoleum, on anniversary of Queen
Victoria's death, 22 January 1910. Publisher: Novello, 1910.

Song-cycle with orchestra, op. 59, Nos. 3, 5, and 6. (1, 2, and 4
never composed) (words by Gilbert Parker). Composed December 1909–January 1910. 3. O, soft was the song; 5. Was it
some golden star?; 6. Twilight. First performance: London,
Queen's Hall, 24 January 1910. Jaeger Memorial Concert. Muriel
Foster (mezzo-soprano) and orchestra cond. by E.E. Publisher:
Novello, 1910.

Song with pianoforte, *The Torch*, op. 60, No. 1. (Words by E.E.
under pseudonym 'Pietro d'Alba'.) Composed 23 December 1909,
orchestrated 26 July 1912. First performance: Hereford Festival,
11 September 1912. Muriel Foster (contralto), cond. by Dr G. R.
Sinclair. Dedication: Yvonne. Publisher: Novello, 1910. (See also
1910.)

1910 *Orchestral:*

Concerto in B minor for violin and orchestra, op. 61. Composed
between April 1909 and August 1910. First performance:
London, Queen's Hall, Philharmonic Society concert, 10
November 1910, Fritz Kreisler and orchestra cond. by E.E.
Dedication: Fritz Kreisler. On the score is inscribed a quotation in

Spanish: 'Aquí está encerrada el alma de . . . . . (1910).' Publisher: Novello, 1910.

Romance for bassoon and orchestra, op. 62. Composed 1909–10. First performance: Herefordshire Orchestral Society, 16 February 1911. Edwin F. James (bassoon), cond. by E.E. Dedication: Edwin F. James. Publisher: Novello, 1910. (Also for bassoon and pianoforte and for cello and pianoforte, both arr. E.E.)

Vocal:
Song with pianoforte or orchestra, *The River*, op. 60, No. 2. (Words by E.E. under pseudonym 'Pietro d'Alba'.) Composed 18 February 1910, orchestrated July 1912. First performance: Hereford Festival, 11 September 1912. Muriel Foster (contralto), cond. by Dr G. R. Sinclair. Publisher: Novello, 1910. (See also **1909**.)

1911 *Arrangements:*
J. S. Bach, *St Matthew Passion*. Two chorales, arr. for three trumpets, four horns, three trombones, tuba. First performance: Worcester Cathedral (from the tower), Three Choirs Festival, 14 September 1911.
J. S. Bach, *St Matthew Passion*. Performing edition, with Ivor Atkins. Publisher: Novello, 1911.

Orchestral:
Symphony No. 2 in E flat major, op. 63. Composed between 1903 and February 1911. First performance: London Music Festival, Queen's Hall, 24 May 1911, Queen's Hall Orchestra, cond. by E.E. Dedication: to the memory of His Late Majesty King Edward VII. Publisher: Novello, 1911.
Coronation March, op. 65. Parts of *Rabelais* ballet (1903) incorporated. First performance: Westminster Abbey, Coronation of King George V, 22 June 1911. Publisher: Novello, 1911.

Vocal:
O *hearken thou*, offertory for chorus and orchestra, op. 64 (*Intende voci orationis meae*). First performance: Westminster Abbey, Coronation of King George V, 22 June 1911. Publisher: Novello, 1911.
The Queen, for chorus and orchestra. Substitute No. 2 of *Coronation Ode* (1902), when *Ode* was revived for Coronation of King George V. Publisher: Novello, 1911.

1912 *Dramatic:*
Masque, *The Crown of India* (Henry Hamilton), for contralto and bass soloists, chorus, and orchestra, op. 66. Sketches from 1902 to 1912 used in composition. 1. (*a*) Introduction, (*b*) Sacred Measure; 2. Dance of Nautch Girls; 3. Hail, Immemorial Ind; 4. March of Mogul Emperors; 5. Entrance of John Company; 6. Rule of England; 7. Interlude; 8. Warriors' Dance; 9. Cities of India; 10. Crown of India March; 11. Crowning of Delhi; 12. Ave Imperator. First performance: London Coliseum, 11 March 1912. Marion Bealey, Harry Dearth, cond. by E.E. *Suite* from *Crown of India* (comprising Nos. 1 (a), 2, 5, 8, Intermezzo, 4) first performed

Hereford Festival, 11 September 1912, L.S.O., cond. by E.E. Publisher: Enoch, 1912.

Choral and vocal:

Ode, *The Music Makers* (O'Shaughnessy), for contralto or mezzo-soprano, chorus, and orchestra, op. 69. Work in progress from 1902, completed 21 August 1912. First performance: Birmingham Festival, 1 October 1912, Muriel Foster, cond. by E.E. First London performance: Royal Albert Hall, 28 November 1912, Muriel Foster, Royal Choral Society and orchestra, conducted by Sir Frederick Bridge. Dedication: My friend Nicholas Kilburn. Publisher: Novello, 1912. (See p. 360)

Anthem (S.S.A.A.T.B. and organ), *Great is the Lord* (Psalm 48), op. 67. Composed between August 1910 and March 1912. First performance: Westminster Abbey, cond. by Sir Frederick Bridge, 16 July 1912. Dedication: Very Rev. J. Armitage Robinson, D.D., Dean of Wells. Publisher: Novello, 1912. Orchestral accompaniment 1913.

Cantique, op. 3, arranged for small orchestra. First performance of this version: London, Royal Albert Hall, 15 December 1912. Dedication: Hugh Blair. Publisher: Novello, 1913. (See **1879**, *Intermezzos.*

1913   *Orchestral:*

Carissima, for small orchestra. First performance: Gramophone Co. recording at Hayes, Middlesex, cond. by E.E., 21 January 1914. First public performance: London, Royal Albert Hall, 15 February 1914, cond. by Landon Ronald. Dedication: Winifred Stephens (sister of Muriel Foster). Publisher: Elkin, 1914.

Symphonic Study, *Falstaff*, in C minor, with two interludes, op. 68. Early sketches dated 1902, completed 5 August 1913. First performance: Leeds Festival, 1 October 1913, cond. by E.E. First London performance: Queen's Hall, 3 November 1913, cond. by Landon Ronald. Dedication: Landon Ronald. Publisher: Novello, 1913.

1914   *Orchestral:*

Sospiri for strings, harp, and organ, also for violin and pianoforte, op. 70. First performance: London, Queen's Hall, 15 August 1914, cond. by Sir Henry J. Wood. Dedication: W. H. Reed. Publisher: Breitkopf and Härtel, 1914.

Carillon, op. 75, recitation with orchestra (E. Cammaerts). Composed November 1914. First performance: London, Queen's Hall, 7 December 1914, Tita Brand (speaker), cond. by E.E. Publisher: Elkin, 1914.

Vocal:

Harvest anthem (S.A.T.B.), *Fear not, O Land* (Joel ii, vv. 21–24, 26). Publisher: Novello, 1914.

Anthem, *Give Unto the Lord* (Psalm 29), for S.A.T.B., organ, and orchestra, op. 74. First performance: London, St Paul's Cathedral, Festival of the Sons of Clergy, 30 April 1914. Dedication: Sir George Martin, M.V.O., Mus.D. Publisher: Novello, 1914.

Part-song (S.A.T.B.), *The Birthright* (G. A. Stocks), with bugles and drums *ad lib*. Publisher: Novello, 1914.

Follow the Colours, adapted for solo and optional male chorus from *Marching Song* (see **1908**). First performance: London, Royal Albert Hall, 10 October 1914. Publisher: Novello, 1914.

Song, *Arabian Serenade* (Margery Lawrence). Publisher: Boosey, 1914.

Song, *Chariots of the Lord* (John Brownlie). First performance: London, Royal Albert Hall, 28 June 1914. Publisher: Boosey, 1914.

Song, *The Merry-go-round* (Florence C. Fox). Composed *c*. 1914. Published in *The Progressive Music Series* (U.S.A.) between 1914 and 1920 by Silver Burdett Co., Morristown, New Jersey.[5]

Song, *The Brook* (Ellen Soule). Composed *c*. 1914. Published in *The Progressive Music Series* (U.S.A.) between 1914 and 1920.[5]

Choral Song (S.A.T.B.), *The Windlass* (William Allingham). Composed *c*. 1914. Published in *The Progressive Music Series* (U.S.A.) between 1914 and 1920.[5]

Two choral songs (S.A.T.B.), op. 71. No. 1, *The Shower* (Henry Vaughan), dedication: Miss Frances Smart, Malvern; No. 2, *The Fountain* (Henry Vaughan), dedication: W. Mann Dyson, Worcester, No. 1 'at Mill Hill', No. 2 'at Totteridge'. Both sketched in 1913. Publisher: Novello, 1914.

Choral song (S.A.T.B.), *Death on the Hills*, op. 72 (Maikov, tr. Rosa Newmarch). Composed January 1914. Dedication: Lady Colvin. Publisher: Novello, 1914.

Two choral songs (S.A.T.B.), op. 73. No. 1, *Love's Tempest* (Maikov, tr. Rosa Newmarch), dedication: C. Sanford Terry; No. 2, *Serenade* (Minski, tr. Rosa Newmarch), dedication: Percy C. Hull. Composed January 1914. Publisher: Novello, 1914.

1915 *Dramatic:*

Incidental Music for *The Starlight Express*, op. 78 (play by Violet Pearn based on story *A Prisoner in Fairyland* by Algernon Blackwood). Orchestral entr'actes and songs for soprano and baritone soloists: Baritone: 'To the Children', 'The Blue-Eyes Fairy', 'Curfew Song (Orion)', 'Night Winds', 'My Old Tunes', 'They're all soft-shiny now', and (duet) 'Hearts must be soft-shiny dressed'; Soprano: 'I'm everywhere', 'Oh stars, shine brightly', 'We shall meet the morning spiders', 'Dandelions, Daffodils', 'Laugh a little ev'ry day', 'Oh, think beauty', and (duet) 'Hearts must be soft-shiny dressed'. First performance: London, Kingsway Theatre, 29 December 1915, Clytie Hine (soprano), Charles Mott (bass), cond. by Julius Harrison. Publisher: 'To the Children', 'The Blue-Eyes Fairy' and 'My Old Tunes', Elkin, 1916. Items from *The Wand of Youth* Suites Nos. 1 and 2 (see **1907** and **1908**) were incorporated into this score.

---

[5] Copies of these 'lost' songs may be seen at Elgar's Birthplace.

Orchestral:

Symphonic Prelude *Polonia*, op. 76. First performance: London, Queen's Hall, Polish Victims' Relief Fund Concert, 6 July 1915, cond. by E.E. Dedication: I. J. Paderewski. Publisher: Elkin, 1915.

Une Voix dans le Désert, op. 77, recitation with orchestra, including song, *Quand nos bourgeons se rouvriront*, for solo soprano (E. Cammaerts). First performance: London, Shaftesbury Theatre, 29 January 1916, Carlo Liten (reciter), Olga Lynn (soprano), cond. by E.E. (Later performances by Beecham.) Publisher: Elkin, 1915.

Choral and vocal:

The Spirit of England, op. 80 – see **1916**.

1916   *Choral and vocal:*

The Spirit of England (Laurence Binyon) for tenor or soprano solo, chorus, and orchestra, op. 80. Nos. 2 and 3 composed 1915, performed separately 1916; No. 1 completed 1917. 1. The Fourth of August. First performance: Birmingham, 4 October 1917, Rosina Buckman (soprano), cond. by Appleby Matthews; 2. To Women. First performance: Leeds Choral Union, 3 May 1916, John Booth (tenor), cond. by E.E.; 3. For the Fallen. First performance: Leeds Choral Union, 3 May 1916, Agnes Nicholls (soprano), cond. by E.E. First London performances of 2 and 3, Queen's Hall, 8 May 1916, Agnes Nicholls (soprano). First performance of complete work: London, Royal Albert Hall, 24 November 1917, Agnes Nicholls (soprano), cond. by E.E. Dedication: To the memory of our glorious men, with a special thought for the Worcesters. Publisher: Novello, 1917.

Orchestral:

Le drapeau belge, op. 79, recitation with orchestra (E. Cammaerts). First performance: London, Queen's Hall, 14 April 1917, Carlo Liten (reciter), cond. by Hamilton Harty. Publisher: Elkin, 1916.

Song, *Fight for Right* (W. Morris). Dedication: Members of the Fight for Right Movement. First performance: London, Queen's Hall, March 1916, Gervase Elwes (tenor). Publisher: Elkin, 1916.

1917   *Dramatic:*

The Sanguine Fan, Ballet (based on a Fan by Charles Conder), op. 81. First performance: London, Chelsea Palace Theatre, 20 March 1917, as part of revue *Chelsea on Tiptoe*. Ballet arranged by Mrs Christopher Lowther, cond. by E.E.

Extract, *Echo's Dance*, for pianoforte, published by Elkin, 1917.

Vocal:

The Fringes of the Fleet (R. Kipling), four songs for four baritones and orchestra. 1. The Lowestoft Boat; 2. Fate's Discourtesy; 3. Submarines; 4. The Sweepers. First performance: London Coliseum, 11 June 1917, Charles Mott, Harry Barratt, Frederick Henry, Frederick Stewart, cond. by E.E. Dedication: Admiral Lord Beresford. Publisher: Enoch, 1917.

Inside the Bar (Gilbert Parker), song for four baritones unaccompanied. Added to *Fringes of the Fleet* and first performed London Coliseum, 25 June 1917, by above singers. Dedication: The 4 Singers. Publisher: Enoch, 1917.

1918 *Chamber music:*

Sonata in E minor for violin and pianoforte, op. 82. Finished 24 December 1918. First public performance: London, Aeolian Hall, 21 March 1919, W. H. Reed (violin) and Landon Ronald (pianoforte).[6] Dedication: Marie Joshua. Publisher: Novello, 1918.

String Quartet in E minor, op. 83. Finished 15 September 1918. First public performance: London, Wigmore Hall, 21 May 1919, Albert Sammons, W. H. Reed, Raymond Jeremy, Felix Salmond. Dedication: The Brodsky Quartet. Publisher: Novello, 1918.

Vocal:

Song, *Big Steamers* (Kipling). Publisher: *Teachers' World*, 19 June 1918.

1919 *Chamber music:*

Quintet in A minor for strings and pianoforte, op. 84. Composed between 15 September 1918 and January 1919. First public performance: London, Wigmore Hall, 21 May 1919, Albert Sammons, W. H. Reed, Raymond Jeremy, Felix Salmond, William Murdoch (pianoforte).[7] Dedication: Ernest Newman, Publisher: Novello, 1919.

Orchestral:

Concerto in E minor for violoncello and orchestra, op. 85. First performance: London, Queen's Hall, 27 October 1919, Felix Salmond, and L.S.O., cond. by E.E. Dedication: Sidney and Frances Colvin. Publisher: Novello, 1919.

Arrangement of above as *Viola Concerto* by Lionel Tertis. First performance: London, Queen's Hall, 21 March 1930. Lionel Tertis (viola), B.B.C. Symphony Orchestra, cond. by E.E.

1921 *Transcription:*

J. S. Bach, *Fugue in C minor* [Elgar op. 86]. Completed 24 April 1921. First performance: London, Queen's Hall, 27 October 1921, cond. by Eugène Goossens. Publisher: Novello, 1921. (See also **1922**.)

1922 *Transcription:*

J. S. Bach, *Fantasia in C minor*. Completed June 1922. First performance: Gloucester Festival, 7 September 1922, L.S.O., cond. by E.E. Publisher: Novello, 1922. (See also **1921**.)

Parry, *Jerusalem*, orchestration added. First performance: Leeds Festival, 1922.

1923 *Transcription:*

Handel, *Overture in D minor* (Chandos Anthem II), transcr. for

---

[6]First performance was by Reed and Elgar on 14 October 1918, at Severn House. It was played on 13 March 1919, by Reed and Anthony Bernard at a British Music Society Meeting.

[7]The Quartet was first performed privately by Reed, Albert Sammons, R. Jeremy, and F. Salmond at Severn House on 7 January 1919. The Quintet was first performed privately at Severn House on 7 March 1919 by Reed's quartet and E.E.

orchestra. Completed by 27 May 1923. First performance: Worcester Festival, 2 September 1923, L.S.O., cond. by E.E. Publisher: Novello, 1923.

Battishill, Motet, *O Lord, look down from heaven,* orchestral accompaniment. Completed May 1923. First performance: Worcester Festival, 6 September 1923.

S. S. Wesley, Motet, *Let us lift up our hearts,* orchestral accompaniment. Completed May 1923. First performance: Worcester Festival, 6 September 1923.

Dramatic:
Incidental music to *Arthur* (Laurence Binyon). First performance: London, Old Vic, 12 March 1923, cond. by E.E. (on first night only; afterwards by Charles Corri). Unpublished.

Instrumental:
Memorial Chimes for a Carillon. First performance: Opening of Loughborough War Memorial Carillon, 22 July 1923. Unpublished. Also arr. for organ by E.E.

Vocal:
Part-song (T.T.B.B.), *The Wanderer* (E.E., adapted from *Wit and Drollery,* 1661). First performance: London, Wigmore Hall, 13 November 1923, the De Reszke Singers. Publisher: Novello, 1923.

Part-song (T.T.B.B.) *Zut, zut, zut* (Richard Mardon, pseudonym of E.E.) First performance: London, Wigmore Hall, 13 November 1923, the De Reske Singers. Publisher: Novello, 1923.

1924 *Chamber music:*
March for violin, violoncello, and pianoforte. For the Grafton family. Unpublished. (It is a sketch for the *Empire March.*)

Orchestral:
Empire March. First performance: Wembley, British Empire Exhibition, 21 July 1924, cond. by Henry Jaxon. Publisher: Enoch, 1924.[8]

Vocal:
Pageant of Empire (Alfred Noyes), Eight songs for solo or S.A.T.B. 1. Shakespeare's Kingdom; 2. The Islands; 3. The Blue Mountains; 4. The Heart of Canada; 5. Sailing Westward; 6. Merchant Adventurers; 7. The Immortal Legions; 8. A Song of Union. Nos. 5, 7, and 8 arr. for S.A.T.B. First performance: Wembley Exhibition, 21 July 1924. Publisher: Enoch, 1924.

1925 *Vocal:*
Part-song (T.T.B.B.), *The Herald* (Alexander Smith). Publisher: Novello, 1925.

Part-song (S.A.T.B.), *The Prince of Sleep* (Walter de la Mare). Publisher: Elkin, 1925.

1927 *Instrumental:*
Civic Fanfare. Written for mayoral procession, opening of

[8] This march was not played at the opening ceremony on 23 April because of 'difficulties in the way of the Brigade Bands co-operating etc etc' (Elgar to Lady Stuart, 16 April 1924).

Hereford Festival, 4 September 1927. L.S.O., cond. by E.E. Dedication: Percy C. Hull. Unpublished.

Obbligato for carillon to go with tune of *Land of Hope and Glory*, composed for diamond jubilee of Canadian confederation. Played by bells of Ottawa Peace Carillon to accompany massed choir conducted by Cyril J. Rickwood, Ottawa, 1 July 1927.

1928 *Dramatic:*

Incidental music to *Beau Brummel* (B. P. Matthews). First performance: Birmingham, Theatre Royal, 5 November 1928, cond. by E.E. Unpublished, with exception of *Minuet*, Elkin, 1929.

Vocal:

Carol (S.A.T.B.), *I sing the birth* (B. Jonson). Completed 30 October 1928. First performance: London, Royal Albert Hall, Royal Choral Society, cond. by Dr Malcolm Sargent, 10 December 1928. Dedication: Rev. Harcourt B. S. Fowler, Elmley Castle, Worcs. Publisher: Novello, 1928.

1929 *Arrangement:*

Purcell, Motet, *Jehova, quam multi sunt hostes mei*, accompaniment for orchestra. First performance: Worcester, 10 September 1929.

Vocal:

Carol (S.A.T.B.), *Good Morrow* (George Gascoigne). 'A simple carol for His Majesty's happy recovery.' First performance: Windsor, St George's Chapel, 9 December 1929, cond. by E.E. Publisher: Novello, 1929.

1930 *Orchestral:*

Severn Suite, op. 87, for brass band (scored by Henry Geehl). Sketches of 1879 and 1903 were used in this work. 1. Introduction (Worcester Castle); 2. Toccata (Tournament); 3. Fugue (Cathedral); 4. Minuet (Commandery); 5. Coda. First performance: Crystal Palace Brass Band National Championship (test-piece), 27 September 1930. Dedication: G. Bernard Shaw. Publisher: R. Smith, 1930. (See also **1932** and **1933**.) Fugue composed 1923. Minuet adapted from Minuet of *Harmony Music No. 5* (**1879**) and No. 5 of *Six Promenades* (**1878**).

Military March, *Pomp and Circumstance*, op. 39, No. 5 in C major. First performance: London, Kingsway Hall (H.M.V. recording session), L.S.O., cond. by E.E., 18 September 1930. First public performance: London, Queen's Hall, 20 September 1930, cond. by Sir Henry J. Wood. Dedication: Percy C. Hull. Publisher: Boosey, 1930. (See also **1901, 1904,** and **1907.**)

Vocal:

Song, *It isnae me* (Sally Holmes). First performance: Dumfries, October 1930. Joan Elwes (soprano). Dedication: Joan Elwes. Publisher: Keith Prowse, 1931.

1931 *Orchestral:*

Nursery Suite. 1. Aubade (uses Hymn Tune in F of 1878); 2. The Serious Doll; 3. Busy-ness; 4. The Sad Doll; 5. The Wagon Passes; 6. The Merry Doll; 7. Dreaming – Envoy. First performance: London, Kingsway Hall, H.M.V. recording session, 23 May 1931, L.S.O., cond. by E.E.; first public performance: Queen's Hall Promenade Concert, 20 August 1931, cond. by E.E.; as a ballet arr. Ninette de Valois, Old Vic, 21 March 1932, cond. by Constant Lambert. Dedication: Their Royal Highnesses the Duchess of York, and the Princesses Elizabeth and Margaret Rose. Publisher: Keith Prowse, 1931.

1932 *Instrumental:*

Sonatina for pianoforte. Dedication: May Grafton. Publisher: Keith Prowse, 1932. Revision (1931) of work composed in 1889.

Adieu for pianoforte (also transcribed for violin by Josef Szigeti[9] and orchestrated by Henry Geehl). Publisher: Keith Prowse, 1932.

Serenade for pianoforte (also transcribed for violin by Josef Szigeti). Dedication: John Austin, friend and editor for many years. Publisher: Keith Prowse, 1932.

(These works were almost certainly written many years earlier.)

Orchestral:

Severn Suite, op. 87. Arranged for orchestra. First performance: London, E.M.I.. Abbey Road recording studio, 14 April 1932, L.S.O., cond. by E.E. First public performance: Worcester Festival, 7 September 1932, L.S.O., cond. by E.E. Publisher: Keith Prowse, 1932. (See also **1930** and **1933**.)

Vocal:

Unison Song, *The Woodland Stream* (Charles Mackay). Composed 1932. First performance: Worcester Schools Music Festival, 18 May 1933. Dedication: Stephen S. Moore, Worcester. Publisher: Keith Prowse, 1933.

Unison Song, *The Rapid Stream* (Charles Mackay). Publisher: Keith Prowse, 1932.

Unison Song, *When Swallows Fly* (Charles Mackay). Publisher: Keith Prowse, 1932.

Ode for chorus, *So many true princesses who have gone* (Masefield). First performance: London, Marlborough House, 9 June 1932, at unveiling of memorial to Queen Alexandra.

1933 *Transcription:*

Chopin, *Funeral March from Sonata in B flat minor*. First performance: London, E.M.I. Abbey Road recording studio, B.B.C. Symphony Orchestra, cond. by Adrian Boult, 30 May 1932. First public performance: London, Queen's Hall, 25 February 1934, Royal Philharmonic Society memorial concert to Elgar. Publisher: Keith Prowse, 1933.

Instrumental:

Organ Sonata No. 2, op. 87A (arr. by Ivor Atkins of *Severn Suite* with cadenza and coda composed by Atkins). First performance: London, Organ Music Society, 1933. Publisher: Keith Prowse, 1933.

[9] In his transcription of *Adieu,* Szigeti worked in a theme from the first movement of Elgar's Violin Concerto as a counterpoint.

Orchestral:
> *Mina*[10] for small orchestra. Sketched in 1932 for pianoforte. First performance: E.M.I. recording studio, New Light Symphony Orchestra,[11] 8 February 1934. Dedication: Fred Gaisberg. Publisher: Keith Prowse, 1934.

PROJECTED WORKS

The following are works which Elgar, in his maturity, contemplated writing. Some of the sketches remain in the British Library); others he used in other works. His plans for a Hardy opera and *King Lear* are not included because no sketches exist.

1892　*The High Tide*, cantata for soprano, possibly bass, chorus, and orchestra, based on 'The High Tide on the Coast of Lincolnshire (1571)' by Jean Ingelow. 'Toyed with' in 1893 and 1901 (for 1902 Norwich Festival).

1901　'Welsh Overture' (sketch used in *Introduction and Allegro*, **1905**).

1903　*Rabelais*, a ballet (*Gargantua and Pantagruel*).
Concert overture, *Cockaigne No. 2*.
Fantasia for Strings. Dedication: Hans (Richter).

1905　Scene, *Callicles* (M. Arnold). For Muriel Foster. Sketches also 1927.

1906　Oratorio: *The Last Judgement* (third part of trilogy).

1908　*In Memoriam* (2 June 1908), 'In memory of a seer.' (This may have been a work planned to commemorate Jaeger, whose death was by then inevitable.)

1909　*Tuscan Fantastico* in A flat.
Scherzo for pianoforte and orchestra.
Opera in Three Acts.
Choral Suite, some to words by W. S. Landor. Planned as 1. Introduction; 2. In a Vineyard; 3. Angelus; 4. Dance; 5. Vintage; 6. Envoi. No. 3 was completed and published as op. 56, No. 1.

1917　*Ozymandias* (Shelley).

1930　*Soliloquy* for oboe, for Léon Goossens. (Orchestrated 1967 by Gordon Jacob. First performance: B.B.C. Television, 11 June 1967, Léon Goossens, conducted by Neils Gron).

1932-3　Concerto for pianoforte and orchestra, op. 90. Sketches worked on in 1909, 1914, 1917, 1925, and 1932.
Tarantella (Belloc) for baritone and orchestra.
Opera in two Acts, *The Spanish Lady*, op. 89. (Libretto by Sir Barry Jackson from Ben Jonson's *The Devil is an Ass*.) Sketches incorporate material dating from 1878. For details see *Elgar O.M.* by Dr Percy Young (London, 1955), pp. 360–75. Two songs, *Modest and Fair* and *Still to be Neat*, edited by Percy Young, were published by Elkin in 1955, and a suite for strings, edited by Dr Young, in 1956.
Symphony No. 3, op. 88. Fragmentary sketches in British Library, some of which were reproduced in W. H. Reed's *Elgar As I Knew Him*.

---

10 Mina was Elgar's cairn terrier.
11 Elgar criticised this recording as being 'too fast' (letter from Carice Elgar Blake to F. Gaisberg, 15 February 1934) and a new record was made by the Light Symphony Orchestra, conducted by Haydn Wood, and was issued.

Following is a list of Elgar's self-quotations and quotations in *The Music Makers*. The page numbers refer to the vocal score:

PAGE

3–4   Prelude: 'Enigma' theme from *Variations*, op. 36.

5   At 'dreams': theme from *The Dream of Gerontius*, op. 38.

6   At 'sea breakers': theme from *Sea Pictures*, op. 37.
      At 'desolate streams': 'Enigma' theme.

8   At 'for ever it seems': 'Enigma' theme.

11   At 'empire's glory': *Rule Britannia* and *La Marseillaise*.

42   At 'on one man's soul': 'Nimrod' theme from *Variations*.

44   At 'and his look': theme from finale of Symphony No. 2, op. 63.

65   At 'the glorious futures we see': 'Enigma' theme.

66–67 At 'in our dreaming and our singing a little apart': theme from Violin Concerto, op. 61.

69   At 'out of the infinite morning': main theme of Symphony No. 1, op. 55.

84–85 At 'a singer who sings no more': 'Novissima hora est' from *Gerontius*.

APPENDIX III   Select Bibliography

A. WRITINGS BY ELGAR

Preface to *The Singing of the Future*, by David Ffrangcon-Davies, London, 1904.

Lectures delivered to Birmingham University, 1905–6, published as *A Future for English Music and other lectures by Edward Elgar*, ed. Percy M. Young, London, 1968.

Falstaff: analytical note, London, 1913.

My Friends Pictured Within (Enigma Variations), London, 1928.

Notation, London, 1920.

Foreword to *Forgotten Worcester* by H. A. Leicester, Worcester, 1930.

Programme Notes for Worcestershire Philharmonic Society, 1898–1902.

'The Quadruple Alliance', letter in *Times Literary Supplement*, 4 September 1919.

'Scott and Shakespeare', letter in *Times Literary Supplement*, 21 July 1921.

'A Visit to Delius', *The Daily Telegraph*, 1 July 1933.

B. BOOKS AND ARTICLES ABOUT ELGAR AND HIS TIME

Anderson, W. R. *Introduction to the Music of Elgar*, London, 1949.

Atkins, E. Wulstan. 'Music in the Provinces: the Elgar–Atkins Letters',

Proceedings of the Royal Musical Association, London 1958.
The Elgar-Atkins Friendship, London, 1984.
Barber, Cecil. 'Enigma Variations – The Original Finale', *Music and Letters*, April 1935.
Bax, Sir Arnold. *Farewell, My Youth*, London, 1943.
Bennett, Joseph. *King Olaf, Analytical Note*, London, 1896.
Bonavia, Ferruccio. 'Elgar' in *Lives of the Great Composers*, Vol. 3, London, 1935.
'Elgar' in *The Music Masters*, Vol. 3 – The Romantic Composers, London, 1952.
'Edward Elgar' in *The Symphony* (ed. Ralph Hill), London, 1949.
Boult, Sir Adrian. *My Own Trumpet*, London, 1973.
Buckley, R. J. *Sir Edward Elgar*, London, 1905.
Burley, Rosa and Carruthers, Frank C. *Edward Elgar : the record of a friendship*, London, 1972.
Byard, Herbert. 'Edward Elgar' in *The Concerto* (ed. Ralph Hill), London, 1952.
Cardus, Sir Neville. 'Elgar' in *A Composers' Eleven*, London, 1958. (Originally in *Ten Composers*, London, 1945).
Colles, H. C. Analytical notes of First Symphony, Quintet, and Violoncello Concerto in *Musical Times* of, respectively, December 1908, November 1919, February 1920.
Articles on Elgar in *Grove's Dictionary of Music and Musicians*, 3rd and 5th editions, London, 1927 and 1954.
Collett, Barry. *Elgar Country*, Kidderminster, 1978; (rev.) London, 1981.
Collett, Pauline. *Elgar lived here*, London, 1981.
An Elgar Travelogue, London, 1983.
Cox, David. 'Edward Elgar' in *The Symphony*, Vol. 2 (ed. Robert Simpson). London, 1967.
Cumberland, Gerald. 'Elgar' in *Set Down in Malice*, London, 1919.
Dann, Mary G. 'Elgar's use of the Sequence', *Music and Letters*, July 1938.
De-la-Noy, Michael. *Elgar the Man*, London, 1983.
Dunhill, Thomas F. *Sir Edward Elgar*, London, 1938.
Eickhoff, Louie. *Elgar : the Hampstead Scene*, Pamphlet, 1980.
Fanselau, R. *Die Orgel im Werk Edward Elgars*, Göttingen, 1974.
Fox Strangways, A. H. 'Elgar' in *Music and Letters*, April 1934.
Gaisberg, Fred. *Music on Record*, London, 1946.
Goossens, Eugène. *Overture and Beginners*, London, 1951.
Gorton, Canon. *Interpretation of the Librettos of the Oratorios :* 1. The Dream of Gerontius; 2. The Apostles; 3. The Kingdom. London, 1907.
Gray, Cecil. 'Edward Elgar' in *A Survey of Contemporary Music*, Oxford, 1924.
Greene, H. Plunket. *Charles Villiers Stanford*, London, 1935.
Grew, Sydney, 'Sir Edward Elgar, O. M.' in *Our Favourite Musicians,* London, 1924.
Hodgkins, Geoffrey. *Providence and Art*, Pamphlet, 1979.
Howes, Frank. 'Edward Elgar' in *The Heritage of Music*, Vol. III, Oxford, 1951. 'The Two Elgars' in *Music and Letters*, January, 1935. *The English Musical Renaissance*, London, 1966.

Hurd, Michael. *Elgar*, London, 1969.
Jackson, Sir Barry. 'Elgar's "Spanish Lady"', *Music and Letters*, January, 1943.
Jaeger, A. J. *Analytical Notes* of *The Dream of Gerontius*, *The Apostles*, *In the South* and *The Kingdom*, London, 1900, 1903, 1904, 1906 respectively.
Johnstone, Arthur. *Musical Criticisms*, Manchester, 1905.
Keeton, A. E. 'Elgar's Music for "The Starlight Express"' in *Music and Letters*, January, 1945.
Kennedy, Michael. *Elgar Orchestral Music*, (B.B.C. Music Guide), London, 1970. 'Elgar and the Festivals' in 'Two Hundred and Fifty Years of the Three Choirs Festival' (ed. B. Still), Gloucester, 1977.
Knowles, John. *Elgar's Interpreters on Record: an Elgar discography*, London, 1977, 2nd ed. 1986.
Lambert, Constant. *Music, Ho!*, London, 1934.
Langford, Samuel. *Musical Criticisms* (ed. N. Cardus), London, 1929.
McVeagh, Diana M. *Edward Elgar: His Life and Music*, London, 1955. 'Elgar's Birthplace' in *Musical Times*, June, 1957. 'Elgar', article in *The New Grove Dictionary of Music and Musicians*, Vol. 6, pp. 114–30, New York, 1980 and London, 1981.
Maine, Basil. *Elgar: His Life and Works*, Vols. I and II, London, 1933; 1973.
Mason, Daniel Gregory. *Contemporary Composers*, New York, 1918.
Monk, Raymond (ed.), *Elgar Studies*, Aldershot, 1990. (Contains contributions by Robert Anderson, Peter Dennison, Michael Kennedy, John Knowles, Diana McVeagh, Jerrold Northrop Moore, Ian Parrott, Michael Pope, K. E. L. Simmons, Ronald Taylor, Percy M. Young).
    Edward Elgar: Music and Literature, Aldershot, 1993. (Contains contributions by Robert Anderson, Christopher Grogan, Michael Kennedy, Christopher Kent, Ivor Keys, Diana McVeagh, Robert Meikle, Ronald Taylor, Brian Trowell, Percy M. Young).
Moore, Jerrold N. *An Elgar Discography*, London, 1963.
    Elgar: a Life in Pictures, London, 1972.
    Elgar on Record: the Composer and the Gramophone, London, 1974.
    Music & Friends: Seven decades of Letters to Adrian Boult (ed.), London, 1979.
    Spirit of England: Edward Elgar in his World, London, 1984.
    Edward Elgar: a Creative Life, Oxford, 1984.
    Elgar and his Publishers (ed.), Oxford, 1987.
    The Windflower Letters (ed.), Oxford, 1989.
    Edward Elgar: Letters of a Lifetime (ed.), Oxford, 1990.
Mundy, Simon. *Elgar, His Life and Times*, Tunbridge Wells, 1980.
Music and Letters. Elgar Memorial Issue, January, 1935.
Musical Times. Elgar Memorial Issue, April, 1934. (Contains list of articles on Elgar published in *Musical Times* in his lifetime.)
    Elgar Centenary Number, June 1957. (Contains contributions by Vaughan Williams, John Ireland, Julius Harrison, Sir Arthur Bliss, Herbert Howells, Gordon Jacob, Edmund Rubbra, Patrick Hadley, Sir Jack Westrup, Sir Steuart Wilson, H. W. Sumsion, Eric Blom, Frank Howes, Sir George Dyson, Sir Thomas Armstrong, Sir Ernest Bullock, W. Greenhouse Allt, Edric Cundell, R. J. F. Howgill, Maurice Johnstone, Eric Warr.)

Music Student, The. Elgar Issue, August 1916. (Contains contributions by Edward Bairstow, E. J. Bellerby, W. W. Cobbett, T. F. Dunhill, William Eller, Nicholas Kilburn, Percy A. Scholes, Rev. G. C. Surtees-Talbot, and W. Wells-Harrison)

Newman, Ernest, *Elgar*, London, 1906.
'Edward Elgar', No. 2 in *The New School of British Music* in *The Speaker*, 22 December, 1901.
'Elgar and his Enigma' in *Sunday Times*, 15, 23, 30 April, 7 May, 1939.
'Elgar and his "Stately Sorrow"' in *The Listener*, 11 March, 1954.
Analytical notes of Violin Concerto, Second Symphony and *Spirit of England* in *Musical Times* of, respectively, October 1910, May 1911 and May 1916.

Parrott, Ian. *Elgar*, London, 1971.
Philip, Robert. *The Recordings of Edward Elgar (1857–1934), Authenticity and Performance Practice* in *Early Music*, Vol. 12, No. 4, November 1984, pp. 481–9.
Pirie, Peter J. *The English Musical Renaissance*, London 1979.
Porte, John F. *Sir Edward Elgar*, London, 1921.
Elgar and his Music: an appreciative study, London, 1933.
Powell, Richard C. 'Elgar's "Enigma"' in *Music and Letters*, July 1934. (See reply by Fox Strangways in January 1935.)
Powell, Mrs. Richard C. ('Dorabella'). *Edward Elgar: Memories of a Variation*, London, 1937, 2nd ed. 1947, 3rd ed. 1979.
Redwood, Christopher (ed.), *An Elgar Companion*, Ashbourne, 1982. (Contains reviews of early cantatas and articles by, *inter alia*, C. Elgar Blake, N. Cardus, R. Fiske, F. Howes, H. Keller, G. H. Lewis, C. Mackenzie, D. Mitchell, E. Newman, C. W. Orr, D. Powell, M. Sargent, G. Sampson, P. Scholes, G. B. Shaw, R. Terry, and J. A. Westrup.)
Reed, W. H. *Elgar As I Knew Him*, London, 1936, 2nd ed. 1973.
Elgar, London, 1939.
'Elgar' in *Cobbett's Cyclopedic Survey of Chamber Music*, London, 1929, 2nd ed. 1963.
'Elgar's Violin Concerto' in *Music and Letters*, January, 1935.
'Elgar's Third Symphony' in *The Listener*, 28 August 1935.
Shaw, G. Bernard. 'Sir Edward Elgar' in *Music and Letters*, January 1920.
Sheldon, A. J. *Edward Elgar*, London, 1932.
Shera, F. H. *Elgar: Instrumental Works*, London, 1931.
Shore, Bernard. 'Elgar's Second Symphony' in *Sixteen Symphonies*, London, 1949.
Simmons, K. E. L. and Marion. *The Elgars of Worcester*, Elgar Society, 1984.
A Walk Round the Elgars' Worcester, Parts I, II, and III in *Elgar Society Journal*, May 1985, September 1985, January 1986.
Speyer, Edward. *My Life and Friends*, London, 1937.
Stockley, W. C. *Fifty Years of Music in Birmingham, 1850–1900*, Birmingham, 1913.
Strand Magazine. 'Dr. Elgar': an interview by Rupert de Cordova, May 1904.
Thompson, Herbert. *Analytical Note on Caractacus*, London, 1898.
Tovey, Sir Donald F. Analytical notes of Elgar's Symphony No. 2, *Falstaff*,

Enigma Variations, Cockaigne, In the South, Introduction and Allegro, Violin Concerto, Violoncello Concerto in *Essays in Musical Analysis,* Vols. II, III, IV, and VI, London, 1935-9, also in *Some English Symphonists,* London, 1941.

'Elgar, Master of Music' in *Music and Letters,* January 1935.

Van Houten, T. J. L. 'You of all People', in *Music Review,* May 1976. 'The Enigma – a solution from Holland', in Elgar Society *Newsletter,* January 1976.

Various Authors. *Edward Elgar: Centenary Sketches* (contributions by Sir John Barbirolli, Carice Elgar Blake, Sir Adrian Boult, H. A. Chambers, Bernard Herrmann, Alan J. Kirby, Yehudi Menuhin, Dora M. Powell, Stanford Robinson, David Willcocks, Percy M. Young), London, 1957.

Vaughan Williams, Ralph. 'What Have We Learnt from Elgar?' in *Music and Letters,* January 1935.

Vaughan Williams, Ursula. *R.V.W., a Biography of Ralph Vaughan Williams,* London, 1964.

Watkins Shaw, A. *The Three Choirs Festival,* Worcester, 1954.

Westrup, J. A. 'Elgar's Enigma'. *Proceedings of the Royal Musical Association,* London, 1960.

Wood, Sir Henry J. *My Life of Music,* London, 1938.

Young, Percy M. *Elgar, O.M.,* London, 1955; 2nd edn, 1973.

Letters of Edward Elgar and other writings (ed.), London, 1956.

Letters to Nimrod from Edward Elgar (ed.), London, 1965.

A Future for English Music: and other lectures by Edward Elgar (the Birmingham lectures) (ed.), London, 1968.

Alice Elgar: Enigma of a Victorian Lady, London, 1978.

APPENDIX IV   Recordings conducted by Elgar

Here is a list of gramophone records conducted by Elgar, who was the first great composer to take advantage of the opportunity presented by the invention of the gramophone for preserving his interpretations of his music. The dates and facts are taken from Jerrold N. Moore's comprehensive *Elgar on Record* (London, 1974), to which readers are recommended for fuller and fascinating detail. The list is in chronological order of recording sessions. All recordings were made for the Gramophone Company and appeared under the H.M.V. label. Only recordings which were later issued to the public on a commercial basis are included. For destroyed discs, please see Dr Moore's book.

1914 21 January:
   Carissima (D 176), reissued in Pearl GEM 111. The orchestra in

pre-electric recordings until 1921 is described as 'Symphony Orchestra'.

26 June:
Pomp and Circumstance Marches Nos 1 and 4 (D 179) and *Salut d' Amour* (D 180), reissued in Pearl GEM 110. *Bavarian Dances* Nos. 2 and 3 (D 175–6), reissued in Pearl GEM 113.

1915 29 January:
Carillon (Henry Ainley, reciter) (D 177), reissued in Pearl GEM 112.

1916 18 February:
The Starlight Express, Agnes Nicholls (soprano), Charles Mott (baritone): 'To the Children' and 'The Blue-Eyes Fairy' (D 455), 'Curfew Song' and 'My Old Tunes' (D 456), 'Tears and Laughter', 'Sunrise Song' and 'Come, Little Winds', Wind Dance (D 457), 'Hearts must be soft-shiny dressed' and 'The Laugher's Song' (D 458). Reissued in Pearl GEM 111.

16 December:
Violin Concerto (severely cut) Marie Hall (violin) (D 79–80). Reissued in Pearl GEM 112.

1917 28 February:
Bavarian Dance No. 1 (D 175), reissued in Pearl GEM 113; *Cockaigne* (abridged) (D 178), *The Dream of Gerontius*: Prelude and Angel's Farewell (abr.) (D 181), reissued in Pearl GEM 111; *The Wand of Youth Suite No. 2*: 'The Tame Bear', 'Wild Bears' (D 178), reissued in Pearl GEM 110.

4 July:
Fringes of the Fleet, Charles Mott, Frederick Henry, Frederick Stewart, Harry Barratt (baritones). 'Fate's Discourtesy' and 'The Lowestoft Boat' (D 453), 'Submarines' and 'The Sweepers' (D 454). Reissued in Pearl GEM 112.

1919 22 May:
Polonia (cut) (D 493), reissued in Pearl GEM 113; *Chanson de Nuit* (D 180); *Wand of Youth Suite No. 1*: 'Overture', 'Sun Dance', 'Serenade', 'Little Bells' (D 48), 'Fairy Pipers', 'Moths and Butterflies', 'March', 'Fairies and Giants' (D 468), reissued in Pearl GEM 110.

22 December:
Violoncello Concerto (1st and 4th movements abr.), Beatrice Harrison (cello) (D 541 and D 545), reissued in Pearl GEM 113.

1920 24 February:
Selection *The Sanguine Fan* (D 596), reissued in Pearl GEM 114. *Enigma Variations*, 'Nimrod' and 'Dorabella' (D 582) reissued in Pearl GEM 114.

16 November:
Enigma Variations (R.B.T., W.M.B., and R.P.A.) (D 578); (Ysobel, Troyte, and W.N.) (D 582), reissued in Pearl GEM 114. Re-recording of Adagio, *Violoncello Concerto* (D 545), reissued in Pearl GEM 113.

1921 11 May:
Enigma Variations (Theme, C.A.E. and H.D.S.-P.) (D 578);

(G.R.S., B.G.N., Romanza and E.D.U.) (D 602); (E.D.U. conclusion) (D 596), reissued in Pearl GEM 114.

7 December:
Fugue in C minor (Bach-Elgar) (D 614), reissued in Pearl GEM 115. *King Olaf:* 'A Little Bird in the Air' (arr. for orch. by E.E.) (D 614) reissued in Pearl GEM 114. Royal Albert Hall Orchestra.

30 December:
In the South (cue 17 to end, abr.) (D 785–6), reissued in Pearl GEM 115. Royal Albert Hall Orchestra.

1922 10 November:
Sea Pictures, 'In Haven', 'Where Corals Lie'. Leila Megane (contralto), R.A.H. Orchestra. (D 674), reissued in Pearl GEM 115.

1923 8 January:
Sea Pictures, 'Sea Slumber Song', (D 674), 'Sabbath Morning at Sea', 'The Swimmer' (D 675), Leila Megane (contralto), R.A.H. Orchestra. Reissued in Pearl GEM 115.

26 October:
Overture in D minor (Handel-Elgar), *Fantasia in C minor* (Bach-Elgar) (D 838); *In the South* (start to cue 17, abr.) R.A.H. Orchestra (D 785). Reissued in Pearl GEM 115.

1924 5 March:
Symphony No. 2 in E flat, 1st and much of 2nd movements (D 1012–14), R.A.H. Orchestra. Reissued in Pearl GEM 116.

20 March:
Symphony No. 2 in E flat, rest of 2nd and 3rd and 4th movements (D 1014–17), R.A.H. Orchestra. Reissued in Pearl GEM 116.

1925 16 April:
The Light of Life (Lux Christi) : Meditation (D 1017); *Symphony No. 2*, part of 1st movement (D 1012). R.A.H. Orchestra. Reissued in Pearl GEM 116.

All the above were acoustical recordings, made in H.M.V. Studio, Hayes, Middlesex. The remainder which follow were electrical. Recording venue is indicated.

1926 27 April:
Overture, *Cockaigne* (D 1110–11), reissued in RLS 713; *Pomp and Circumstance* Marches Nos. 1 and 2 (D 1102) reissued in RLS 713; *Chanson de Nuit* (D 1236) reissued in HLM 7005 and RLS 713. R.A.H. Orchestra. Recorded in Queen's Hall.

28 April:
Enigma Variations (D 1154–7), reissued in ALP 1464, RLS 708, and SH 162; *Fantasia and Fugue in C minor* (Bach-Elgar) (W 749), reissued in RLS 708 and HLM 7107. R.A.H. Orchestra. Recorded in Queen's Hall.

30 August:
The Light of Life: Meditation (D 1157), reissued in RLS 713. R.A.H. Orchestra. Recorded in Queen's Hall.

1927 26 February:
The Dream of Gerontius (recorded at a performance in the Royal

Albert Hall), Margaret Balfour (contralto), Steuart Wilson (tenor), Herbert Heyner (bass), Royal Choral Society, R.A.H. Orchestra. 'Praise to the Holiest' and 'And now the threshold' (D 1242), 'Go, in the name of angels and archangels' and 'Come back, O Lord' (D 1243). Some extracts unpublished and now destroyed. Reissued in RLS 713 ('Go, in the name of angels' also in HLM 7009); 'Kyrie eleison' and 'Rescue him', from E.E.'s test pressing, issued in RLS 713.

1 April:

Symphony No. 2 in E flat (D 1230–5), reissued in RLS 708 and SH 163. *Chanson de Matin* (D 1236), reissued in HLM 7005 and RLS 713. London Symphony Orchestra. Recorded in Queen's Hall.

15 July:

Pomp and Circumstance Marches Nos. 3 and 4 (D 1301), No. 3 reissued in HLM 7005 and RLS 713, No. 4 in RLS 713; *Bavarian Dances* Nos. 1 and 2 (D 1367), reissued in HLM 7005 and RLS 713; part of 3rd movement of *Symphony No. 2*, with Elgar's voice at rehearsal, issued in RLS 708 and SH 163. L.S.O. In Queen's Hall.

4 September:

Civic Fanfare (first performance, recorded at opening service of Three Choirs Festival, Hereford Cathedral, L.S.O.). Issued from E.E.'s test pressing in RLS 708 and SH 175.

6 September:

The Dream of Gerontius (recorded at Three Choirs Festival, Hereford Cathedral, Margaret Balfour (contralto), Tudor Davies (tenor), Horace Stevens (bass), Sir Herbert Brewer (organ), L.S.O., Festival Chorus). 'So pray for me, O Jesu, help' (D 1350), reissued in RLS 708 and SH 175; 'Jesu! By that shudd' ring dread' and 'Take me away' (D 1348), reissued in RLS 708 and SH 175, 'Jesu! By that shudd' ring dread' also in HLM 7009.

8 September:

The Music Makers (recorded at Three Choirs Festival, Hereford Cathedral, Festival Chorus, L.S.O., Sir H. Brewer (organ)). 'We are the music makers' and 'A breath of our inspiration' (D 1349), 'For we are afar with the dawning' (D 1347), reissued in RLS 708 and SH 175.

1928 3 February:

God Save the King and *O God Our Help in Ages Past* (Croft), Margaret Balfour (contralto), L.S.O., Philharmonic Choir (C 1467), reissued in RLS 713; *The Banner of St George*: 'It Comes from the Misty Ages' and *Land of Hope and Glory*, issued from E.E.'s test pressing in RLS 713. Recorded in Queen's Hall.

23 March:

Violoncello Concerto (Beatrice Harrison, New Symphony Orchestra) 1st and 4th movts. (D 1507, D 1509), reissued in RLS 708 and SH 175. Recorded in Kingsway Hall.

13 June:

Violoncello Concerto (Beatrice Harrison, New Symphony Orchestra) 2nd and 3rd movts. (D 1508), reissued in RLS 708 and SH 175. Recorded in Kingsway Hall.

19 December:

Wand of Youth, Suite No. 1, Overture, 'Serenade', 'Minuet', 'Sun Dance' (D 1636), 'Fairy Pipers', 'Slumber Scene' (D 1637), 'Fairies and Giants' (D 1638), reissued in RLS 713. L.S.O. Recorded in Kingsway Hall.

20 December:

Wand of Youth, Suite No. 2, 'March', 'Little Bells', 'Moths and Butterflies' (D 1649), 'Fountain Dance', 'The Tame Bear', 'Wild Bears' (D 1650), reissued in RLS 713.

Beau Brummel: Minuet (D 1638) reissued in RLS 713. L.S.O. Recorded in Kingsway Hall.

1929   6 November:

Improvisations Nos. 1–5, Elgar playing the pianoforte. Issued in RLS 713. Recorded in Small Queen's Hall.

7 November:

Sérénade Lyrique and *Rosemary* (D 1778), reissued in RLS 713.

May Song (D 1949), reissued in RLS 713.

Carissima (E 547). Issued in RLS 713.

New Symphony Orchestra. Recorded in Small Queen's Hall.

8 November:

Falstaff: Two Interludes (D 1863), reissued in RLS 713.

Minuet, op. 21. Issued in RLS 713.

Mazurka (Japanese Victor JF 38 only), reissued in HLM 7005 and RLS 713.

Salut d'Amour (E 547) Issued in HLM 7005 and RLS 713.

New Symphony Orchestra. Recorded in Small Queen's Hall.

1930   15 September:

Suite, Crown of India: 'Minuet', 'Warriors' Dance' (D 1899), *March of the Mogul Emperors* (D 1900), reissued in RLS 713.

In the South (up to cue 26) (DB 1665), reissued in RLS 713. L.S.O. Recorded in Kingsway Hall.

18 September:

Pomp and Circumstance March No. 5 (D 1900), reissued in HLM 7005 and RLS 713.

In the South (cue 26 to end) (D 1666–7), reissued in RLS 713. L.S.O. Recorded in Kingsway Hall.

20 November:

Symphony No. 1 in A flat (1st movt. to cue 40) (D 1944–5), reissued in RLS 708 and SH 139. L.S.O. Recorded in Kingsway Hall.

21 November:

Symphony No. 1 in A flat (1st movt. cue 40 to end of 3rd movt.) (D 1945–7), reissued in RLS 708 and SH 139. L.S.O. Recorded in Kingsway Hall.

22 November:

Symphony No. 1 in A flat (4th movt., retakes of parts of 2nd and 3rd movts.) (D 1948–9), reissued in RLS 708 and SH 139. L.S.O. Recorded in Kingsway Hall.

Suite, Crown of India: Introduction, Dance of the Nautch Girls (D 1899), reissued in RLS 713. L.S.O. Recorded in Kingsway Hall.

1931 23 May:

Nursery Suite: 'Aubade', 'The Serious Doll', 'Busy-ness' (D 1998), 'The Sad Doll', 'The Wagon Passes', 'The Merry Doll', (D 1999), reissued in RLS 713. L.S.O. Recorded in Kingsway Hall.

4 June:

Nursery Suite: 'Dreaming', 'Envoy' (D 1999), reissued in RLS 713. L.S.O. (W. H. Reed (violin), Gordon Walker (flute)). Recorded in Kingsway Hall.

11 November:

Falstaff (start to cue 76) (DB 1621–2), reissued in BLP 1090, RLS 708, and SH 162. L.S.O. Recorded in E.M.I. Studio No. 1, Abbey Road.

12 November:

Trio of *Pomp and Circumstance* March No. 1 ('Land of Hope and Glory') briefly introduced by E.E. and filmed by Pathé News. Soundtrack issued in RLS 713.

Falstaff (cue 76 to end) (DB 1623–4), reissued in BLP 1090, RLS 708, and SH 162. L.S.O. (W. H. Reed, solo violin). Recorded in E.M.I. Studio No. 1, Abbey Road.

1932 4 February:

Falstaff (cue 44 to 62) (DB 1622), reissued in BLP 1090, RLS 708, and SH 162.

Bavarian Dance No. 3 (DB 1667), reissued in HLM 7005 and RLS 713. L.S.O. Recorded in E.M.I. Studio No. 1, Abbey Road.

14 April:

Severn Suite: Introduction (Worcester Castle), Toccata (Tournament) (DB 1908), Fugue (Cathedral), Minuet (Commandery) Part 1 (DB 1909), Minuet Part 2, Coda (DB 1910), reissued in RLS 713. L.S.O. Recorded in E.M.I. Studio No. 1, Abbey Road.

14 July:

Violin Concerto (1st and 2nd movts.) (DB 1751–4), reissued in ALP 1456, RLS 708, and HLM 7107. L.S.O. Yehudi Menuhin (violin). Recorded in E.M.I. Studio No. 1, Abbey Road.

15 July:

Violin Concerto (3rd movt.) (DB 1754–6), reissued in ALP 1456, RLS 708, and HLM 710. L.S.O. Yehudi Menuhin (violin). Recorded in E.M.I. Studio No. 1, Abbey Road.

7 October:

Pomp and Circumstance Marches Nos. 1 and 2 (both cut) (DB 1801), reissued in HLM 7005 and RLS 713. B.B.C. Symphony Orchestra (Berkeley Mason, organ). Recorded in Kingsway Hall.

1933 21 February:

Overture, Froissart (DB 1938–9), reissued in RLS 713.

Contrasts: The Gavotte (DB 1910), reissued in RLS 713.

London Philharmonic Orchestra. Recorded in E.M.I. Studio No. 1, Abbey Road.

11 April:
Overture, Cockaigne (DB 1935–6), reissued in ALP 1464 and RLS 713.
Pomp and Circumstance March No. 4 (DB 1936), reissued in HLM 7005 and RLS 713.
The Kingdom: Prelude (DB 1934), reissued in RLS 708 and SH 139. B.B.C. Symphony Orchestra. Recorded in E.M.I. Studio No. 1, Abbey Road.
29 August:
Serenade for Strings (DB 2132–3), reissued in ALP 1464 and RLS 713.
Elegy for Strings (DB 1939), reissued in RLS 713.
London Philharmonic Orchestra. Recorded in E.M.I. Studio No. 1, Abbey Road.

All the recordings listed above have now been re-transferred to compact disc as The Elgar Edition. The acoustical recordings, 1914–1925, are available on Pearl GEMM CDS 9951–5. The electrical recordings, 1926–33, are on EMI in three volumes, Vol. I CDS 7 54560–2, Vol. II CDS 7 54564–2, Vol. III CDS 7 54568–2. Each contains three CDs. Vol. II contains hitherto unpublished 'Sérénade Mauresque', recorded with New Symphony Orchestra in Small Queen's Hall on 8 November 1929.

Because of their historical interest, the details are included here of the recordings Elgar supervised from his death-bed.

1934   22 January:
Caractacus: Woodland Interlude (DB 2147), Triumphal March (DB 2142), reissued in RLS 713. Reissued on CD in The Elgar Edition, Vol. III.
Dream Children Nos. 1 and 2 (DB 2147), reissued in RLS 713.
L.S.O., conducted by Lawrance Collingwood. Recorded in E.M.I. Studio No. 1, Abbey Road.

Another historically interesting record, issued by the Elgar Society in 1980, is 'Elgar's Interpreters on Record' (ELG 001). Among the items included are the *Crown of India March* (its only recording) by the Black Diamond Band in 1912, Edna Thornton singing 'Land of Hope and Glory' in 1908, Andrew Black singing the 'Sword Song' from *Caractacus* in 1906, Sir Henry Coward conducting the Sheffield Choir in 'The Dance' from *From the Bavarian Highlands* in 1920, John Coates singing 'In the Dawn' in 1915, Rosina Buckman singing 'Pleading' in 1920, Percy Pitt conducting the B.B.C. Wireless Symphony Orchestra in the *Empire March* in 1924, and Carlo Sabajno conducting the La Scala Symphony Orchestra in the conclusion (fig. 51 to the end) of *In the South* in 1909.

Classified Index of Works

Arrangements and Transcriptions of Music by other Composers

Chamber Music

Choral Works

(cantatas, oratorios, etc.)

Church Music
(including early unpublished items)

Dramatic Works
(ballet, incidental music, masque, recitations, etc.)

Juvenilia

(excluding unfinished works)

Miscellaneous

Orchestral

mas discussed, 84–6; connection
with *The Music Makers*, 85, 86, 253,
360; original ending in ballet, 88*n*;
discussed, 90–101; first German performance, 125; Shaw on, 210
Violin Concerto in B minor (op. 61), 35,
37, 49, 100, 145, 160, 161, 184, 248,
350–1, 357*n*; 'soul' enigma, 97,
160–1, 233–4; Alice Stuart-Wortley
as the 'soul', 160–1; first sketches,
229, 230–1; completed, 231–2; rows
over first performance, 232; discussed, 250–1; E.'s harp part for,
310; Menuhin and E. record, 320–1;
in Paris, 323
Violoncello Concerto in E minor (op.

85), 29, 35, 72, 184, 186, 280, 355;
first theme composed, 273; E. con-
tinues work on, 277–8; completed,
279; rehearsal and first performance,
279–80; discussed, 282–3; E. records, 310, 312; as Viola Concerto,
328, 355
Wand of Youth, The (op. 1A and 1B), 353
Suite No. 1 (op. 1A), 29, 186, 251,
312, 348; composed, 222–3; and
Starlight Express, 267–8
Suite No. 2 (op. 1B), 29, 186, 302,
312, 337, 349
Original music, 20–1
Woodland Interlude (*Caractacus*), 75,
113; on E.'s death-bed, 329–30; see
also *Caractacus* under Choral

Organ

Eleven Vesper Voluntaries (op. 14), 44,
45, 340
In Moonlight (Canto popolare from *In the
South)*, 347
Memorial Chimes for a Carillon (arr.), 356
Piece ('for Dot's nuns'), 348

Sonata in G major (op. 28), 62, 342;
discussed, 58
Sonata No. 2 (op. 87A) (arr. of *Severn
Suite* by Ivor Atkins), 358; see also
Severn Suite under Orchestral

Part-Songs, etc.

After Many a Dusty Mile (op. 45, No.
3), 221, 347
Angelus, The (op. 56), 228–9, 350, 358
As torrents in summer *(King Olaf)*, 343
Bavarian Highlands, From The (op. 27),
56, 99, 142, 342; first performed, 58
Birthright, The, 353
Death on the Hills (op. 72), 353
Deep in my Soul (op. 53, No. 2), 221,
349
Evening Scene, 200, 348
Feasting I Watch (op. 45, No. 5), 221,
347
Fly, Singing Bird (op. 26, No. 2), 56,
342
Fountain, The (op. 71, No. 2), 259, 353
Good Morrow, 315, 357
Go, Song of Mine (op. 57), 221, 229,
302, 350; composed, 228
*Greek Anthology, Five Part-Songs From
The* (op. 45), 221, 347

Grete Malverne on a Rock, 343; see also
Lo, Christ the Lord under Church
Music
Herald, The, 356
How calmly the Evening, 349
Immortal Legions, The, 356; see also
Pageant of Empire under Solo Songs
I sing the Birth, 357
It's oh! to be a wild Wind (op. 45, No.
4), 221, 347
Leap, Leap to the Light (Sword Song
from *Caractacus*), 344
Love (op. 18, No. 2), 222, 340, 349
Love's Tempest (op. 73, No. 1), 353
Marching Song, 349; see also *Follow the
Colours* under Solo Songs
My Love dwelt in a Northern Land, 45,
221, 340
O happy Eyes (op. 18, No. 1), 56, 71,
340
O wild west Wind (op. 53, No. 3), 349

Pianoforte Solos

Solo Songs and Song-Cycles

Unfinished and Projected Works

(including Lost Works)

General Index

126, 129, 172, 178, 192, 202, 210, 354, 357; E.'s university professorship, 154, 174, 178; E.'s university lectures, 154, 156, 174–6, 178, 184; E. unforgiving over *Gerontius*, 120; E. conducts C.B.S.O. inaugural concert, 292
Birmingham Festival, 30, 38, 53, 65, 82, 83, 107, 122, 144, 150, 153, 174, 203, 345, 347, 348, 352; commissions *Gerontius*, 105–6; *Gerontius* failure at, 115–19; commissions *The Apostles*, 189; *The Apostles* performed, 194; *The Kingdom* performed, 202; *The Music Makers* performed, 254
Bispham, David, 191
Black, Andrew, 67, 133, 191, 193, 194, 197, 343, 344, 345, 347, 370
Blackpool Festival, 224, 349 and *n*
Blackwood, Algernon, 276, 353; and *Starlight Express*, 267–8
Blair, Hugh, 54, 55, 56, 68, 230, 288, 341, 342, 352; plays Organ Sonata, 58
Blake, Carice Elgar, *see* Elgar Blake, Carice
Blake, Samuel, 296
Bliss, Sir Arthur, 64, 187; E.'s coolness to, 295–6, 300
Blom, Eric, 16
Bonavia, Ferruccio, 40, 118, 147*n*; on *The Apostles*, 194; on poor E. performances, 203
Boosey and Company, 89, 115, 168, 211
Boult, Sir Adrian, 158, 208, 227, 251, 270, 274, 288, 290, 294, 299, 320, 323, 358; E.'s coolness to, 120; first conducts 2nd Symphony, 285; on E.'s conducting, 304
Bowen, York, 265
Bradford, Yorkshire, 124, 178, 272
Brahms, Johannes, 33, 36, 75, 82, 103, 125, 128, 129, 130, 131, 150, 175, 227, 282, 319, 333
Brand, Tita, 266, 352
Brema, Marie, 132, 196, 266, 345; in first *Gerontius*, 118–19
Brewer, Sir Herbert, 155, 295, 301–2, 307, 346; E. scores his *Emmaus*, 126
Brian, Havergal, 228
Bridge, Frank, 265
Bridge, Sir Frederick, 62, 65–6, 352
Brinkwells (E.'s Sussex cottage), 277, 278, 279, 284, 291, 292; E.'s first visit, 273; E. describes life there, 274–5; chamber music written there, 275–6;

Cello Concerto written, 277–8, 279; E. unable to buy, 289; E. leaves, 294
British Broadcasting Corporation, *see* B.B.C.
British Medical Association, 27, 30
British Music Society, 278, 354*n*
Britten, Benjamin (Lord Britten of Aldeburgh), 39, 70, 71, 180, 209, 253; on 'For the Fallen', 181
Broadheath, Worcester, 17, 18, 19, 91, 140, 147*n*, 182, 236, 308, 335, 352*n*; E. born at cottage, 18; E.'s nostalgia for, 273
Broadwood, Lucy, 104
Brodsky, Adolph, 103, 130, 131, 240, 265, 270; on *Gerontius*, 133; offers E. professorship, 174; E. begins string quartet for, 223; plays Violin Concerto in Vienna, 265; plays Concerto when 75, 306
Brodsky Quartet, 224, 355
Browning, Elizabeth Barrett, 101, 345, 350
Browning, John, 67, 344
Bruch, Max, 100
Bruckner, Anton, 82
Buck, Dr Charles, 31, 33, 35, 36, 40, 42, 43, 65, 339; E. first meets, 30; E. letters to quoted, 31, 32, 33, 34, 35, 36, 39, 40, 41, 44, 51, 104, 320
Buckle, Sybil, 308
Buckman, Rosina, 354, 370
Bülow, Hans von, 153
Burley, Rosa, 52, 55, 58, 68–9, 82, 92, 146, 151, 176, 195, 212, 213, 286; on Elgar in 1891, 51–2; on *Caractacus* at Leeds, 67; on 'Romanza' variation, 96; on *Gerontius*, 107; on E.'s resentments, 139–40; on seeing Severn House, 242; friendship ends, 286, 320; E.'s letters to, 201–2, 255
Burne-Jones, Philip, 297
Busoni, Ferruccio, 90*n*, 130
Buths, Julius, 126, 130, 174, 179, 219, 270, 347; at first *Gerontius*, 124–5; conducts *Gerontius* at Düsseldorf, 127–9
Butt, Dame Clara, 101, 134, 169, 171, 196, 270, 291, 345, 346, 354; and *Gerontius*, 119
Butterworth, George, 70
Byrd, William, 16, 23

Caldicott, A. J., 27, 337

Cologne, 198; begins *The Kingdom*, 199–200; spiritual crisis, 200; second U.S.A. visit, 201; *The Kingdom* performed, 202; contemplates third oratorio, 203–4; at *Cockaigne* rehearsals, 211–12; planning symphony, 212, 214–15; composes *Grania* music, 215; *In the South* rehearsal, 216; composes *Introduction and Allegro*, 218–19; visit to Italy, 221–2; third U.S.A. visit, 222; fiftieth birthday, 222; begins 1st Symphony, 222; sees Italian riot 224; completes 1st Symphony, 225; success of 1st Symphony, 226–8; visit to Venice, 228–9; begins 2nd Symphony and Violin Concerto, 229; at Tintagel, 231; Concerto finished 231–2; first performances, 232–4; letter to Richter, 233; progress with 2nd Symphony, 234; conducts in Brussels, 234; finishes 2nd Symphony, 236; visit to U.S.A., 236–7; description of 2nd Symphony, 237–8; puzzled by cool reception of 2nd Symphony, 238–9; gloom over finance, 240; visit to Turin, 240; moves into Severn House, 240–2; writes *Crown of India*, 242; tours with L.S.O., 251; completes *The Music Makers*, 252–3; visits to Italy and Wales, composition of *Falstaff*, 255; opera projects, 255–6; *Falstaff* coolly received, 256; makes first recording, 259; walks out of R.A. banquet, holiday in Scotland, outbreak of war, 260; joins special constabulary, 265; success of *Carillon*, 266; composes *Starlight Express*, 267–8; stops work on 'For the Fallen', 268–9; composes *Sanguine Fan*, 270; tours music-halls with *Fringes of the Fleet*, 271; homesick for Worcester, 271–2; ear trouble and depression, 272; at Brinkwells, 273; throat operation, 273; life at Brinkwells, 274–5; writes chamber music, 275–6; begins Cello Concerto, 277–8; rejects peace ode, 277; burglary at Severn House, 278; completes Cello Concerto, 279; snubbed at rehearsal of Cello Concerto, 279–80; visits Belgium, 284; hears Boult conduct 2nd Symphony, 285; Alice Elgar dies, 285; his grief, 286–7; readjustment, 289–92; upsets choir at Hereford,

293; greets Strauss, 294; leaves Brinkwells and Severn House, 294; Bach transcription completed, 295; reaction against his music, 297–8; opinion of *Beggar's Opera*, 297; writes *Arthur* music, 298; poor royalty returns, 299; dispute over part-songs, 299; cruise to S. America, 300; at Wembley Exhibition, 300–1; has operation, 302; at Three Choirs Festivals, 302–5; revisits old haunts, 302, 319; seventieth birthday, 306–7; death of Schuster, 307–8; his dogs, 308; makes first recordings, 309–10; friendship with Shaw, 313–15; writes *Severn Suite*, 314; writes *Nursery Suite*, 315–16; Dent article controversy, 316–18; seventy-fifth birthday, 320; records Violin Concerto with Menuhin, 321; B.B.C. Elgar Festival, 323; flies to visit Delius, 323–4; dismayed by events in Germany, 324; 3rd Symphony commissioned, 324; begins opera, 324–5; progress of 3rd Symphony, 325–7; cancer diagnosed, 328; supervises last recording session, 329–30; death, 330; places he loved, 333–4

Characteristics: disillusion, 120, 128, 199, 202, 254, 277, 286, 289, 297–8; 'Edwardianism', 163–4, 183; generosity, 126, 158, 223; love of countryside, 18–20, 33, 69–70, 81, 113, 252, 272–3, 328, 333–4; patriotism, 66; political outlook, 34, 165, 167, 332; social inferiority, 51–2, 139–40, 331–2

Financial affairs: 62, 68, 77, 123, 124, 128, 224, 240, 241, 265, 289, 299, 307

Health: 39, 47, 51, 127, 177, 189, 190, 219, 221, 252, 272, 289, 302, 308, 328–30

Honours: 172–3, 182, 240, 318

Lectures and speeches: 154, 167, 174–6, 178

Literary tastes: 19, 257, 274, 284, 292, 317

Opinions on: being Master of King's Musick, 181; Cenotaph ceremony, 284; choral conductors, 57; Christmas, 291; contemporaries' music, 63–4, 295; copyright, 167, 309; English public, 64, 110, 140, 269, 297; folk-song, 104; modern singers, 300,